DUDLEY MOORE

The Melancholy Clown

DUDLEY MOORE

The Melancholy Clown

An Authorized Biography

by

BARBRA PASKIN

New Millennium Press
Beverly Hills

All photographs courtesy of Dudley Moore
unless otherwise stated.

First published 1997 by Sidgwick & Jackson,
an imprint of Macmillan Publishers Ltd.
First New Millennium edition 2000.

ISBN: 1-893224-17-1

Printed in the United States of America

New Millennium Press
a division of NM WorldMedia, Inc.
350 S. Beverly Drive
Suite 315
Beverly Hills, California 90212

www.newmillenniumpress.com

10 9 8 7 6 5 4 3 2 1

To my father,
Manny Paskin,
and in memory of
the greatest gift
he ever gave me—
his unconditional
love

And for Daphne,
my mother, who
continues to be my
support and
inspiration

CONTENTS

ACKNOWLEDGMENTS ix

PROLOGUE xiii

PART ONE

1. CHILDHOOD (1935-1946) 3
2. SCHOOL DAYS (1946-1954) .18
3. OXFORD (1954-1958) 33
4. BEFORE THE FRINGE (1958-1960) 45
5. *BEYOND THE FRINGE* AND ALL THAT JAZZ (1960-1962) . .54
6. NEW YORK (1962-1964) 70

PART TWO

7. . . . BUT ALSO PETER COOK (1964-1965) 85
8. SUZY (1965) 98
9. *CYNTHIA* AND OTHER FILMS (1967-1971) 106
10. *BEHIND THE FRIDGE* (1971-1973) 122
11. TUESDAY (1973-1976) 133
12. TURNING POINTS (1976-1977) 149

PART THREE

13. HOLLYWOOD (1977-1978) 159
14. A PERFECT *10* (1978-1979) .169

15. SUSAN'S SEX SYMBOL (1979-1980) 184

16. *ARTHUR* (1980) 197

17. MUSICAL RHAPSODIES (1981) 211

18. *SIX WEEKS* (1981-1982) 221

19. STARDOM AND DOUBTS (1983-1985) 241

PART FOUR

20. REFLECTIONS (1985) 261

21. BROGAN (1985-1986) 266

22. BACK TO WORK (1987-1988) .280

23. TROUBLE IN MUNCHKINLAND (1989-1990) 300

24. AN ORCHESTRAL TRIUMPH AND A CHICKEN
    CHASE (1990-1991) 311

25. NICOLE (1992) 325

26. THE MELANCHOLY CLOWN (1992-1993) 334

27. NOWHERE TO HIDE (1993-1994) 347

28. GOODBYEEE PETER COOK (1995) 362

29. INTO THE DARKNESS (1995-1996) 376

30. TRAGIC REVELATION (1996-1999) 400

31. FACING THE CHALLENGE (2000) 410

Epilogue 419

Afterword 422

Credits 426

Index 436

ACKNOWLEDGMENTS

This book would not have been possible without the enormous contribution and kindness of the vast number of people who talked with me.

First of all, however, I owe an eternal debt of gratitude to my friend and colleague Ian Brodie, first for encouraging me to embark on this mammoth undertaking, and then for remaining staunchly supportive throughout. His guidance and suggestions as this book progressed were invaluable, particularly when I felt almost buried beneath the thousands of pieces that made up this vast jigsaw puzzle.

Among the many people who gave me their time and generosity I would first like to thank Barbara Stevens, Dudley's sister, who was unfailingly generous and, luckily, blessed with a crystal-clear memory, unlike her brother! My thanks, too, to Teifion Griffiths, Jim Johnson, and Peter Cork, who filled in so much of the teenage years. And to Suzy Kendall and Brogan Lane, for their overwhelming candor about their ex-husband, who remains their friend to this day. And to Dudley's son, Patrick, whose reflections were, at times, very painful for him.

Among Dudley's friends of more than thirty-five years, I am indebted particularly to Peter Bellwood for his untiring and generous input, and to Francis Megahy, Ben Shaktman, Alys Kihl, and Gillian Lynne. Thanks also to Lou Pitt, Dudley's close friend and loyal agent; to Susan Anton for her refreshing insight; to Celia Hammond, Dudley's first girlfriend; and to Liza Minnelli for her long reminiscences of a special friendship.

Jonathan Miller, Alan Bennett, and John Bassett were invaluable in recalling the *Fringe* years, while John Dankworth, Vic Lewis, and Joseph McGrath filled in so much of Dudley's early working life.

Leslie Bricusse and Blake Edwards shed enormous insight on the inner angst, as did Dudley's secretaries Ruth Forman and Sam Veta, and Dr. Evelyn Silvers, his last psychotherapist. Else Blangsted in Switzerland and Thomas Leahy, Dudley's former majordomo, were unusually perceptive about the man they both greatly love.

An immeasurable gratitude belongs to Rena Fruchter and her husband, Brian Dallow, the most giving and solid influence in Dudley's life today, who became immensely supportive during the latter months of this book when events took a bizarre and personal twist. And a special thanks to Lin Cook who, while still mourning the death of her husband Peter Cook, talked openly and painfully with me about Peter's turbulent relationship with Dudley. This book suffers the loss of Peter immensely but is compensated by Lin's halting and moving comments.

There now follows a complete alphabetical list of those people who, in Britain, Hollywood, New York, Switzerland, Italy, Germany, and Australia, were kind enough to talk about Dudley for this book. To all of them, a deep gratitude, for without them this would have been a very different book:

Tony Adams, Julie Andrews, Ken Annakin, Susan Anton, John Bassett, Peter Bellwood, Alan Bennett, Marsha Berger, Tony Bill, Jacqueline Bisset, Else Blangsted, Paul Bloch, Marshall Brickman, Leslie Bricusse, Ray Brown, Tita Cahn, Charles Champlin, Chevy Chase, George Christy, Dick Clement, Alexander Cohen, Lin Cook, Peter Cork, Brian Dallow, Rod Daniel, John Dankworth, Amelia David (the Duplex), Bo Derek, Phyllis Diller, Stanley Donen, Carol Doumani, Susie Dullea, Blake Edwards, Ahmet Ertegun, James Evens, Bryan Forbes, Ruth Forman, Patricia Foy, Rena Fruchter, Kenny G, Patrick Garland, Sir John Gielgud, Dr. Martin Gizzi, David Green, Teifion Griffiths, Celia Hammond, Goldie Hawn, Peter Hemmings, Jonathan Hewes, Arthur Hiller, Jim Johnson, Chris Karan, Suzy Kendall, Alys Kihl, Dr. Louis Kwong, Cleo Laine, Brogan Lane, Thomas Leahy, Martin Lewis, Vic Lewis, John Lithgow, David Longman, Tony Luke (BBC), Peter Lydon (BBC), Gillian Lynne, Elizabeth McGovern, Joseph McGrath, Robert Mann, Francis Megahy, Jonathan Miller, Sir John Mills, Liza Minnelli, Barbara Moore, Nicole Moore, Patrick Moore, Roger Moore, Peter Morgan, Laraine Newman, Nanette Newman, Anthony Page, Jerry Pam, Itzhak Perlman, Oscar Petersen, Bronson Pinchot, Lou Pitt, Carl Reiner, Ann Reinking, Paul Reiser, Casey Robinson, Dr. Bernard Rose, George Schlatter, Ben Shaktman, Ned Sherrin, Dr. Evelyn Silvers, Sir Georg Solti, Mary Steenburgen, Barbara Stevens, Brenda Vaccaro, Sam Veta, Bruce Vilanch, Jan Wallman, Aileen (Jo) Weld, Robin Williams, Linda Yellen, Bud Yorkin, Howard Zieff, Pinchas Zukerman. And also the following: AFI, AMPAS, BFI, *Boston Globe*, Charles Kaye, Victor Lewis-Smith, London Records, Spotlight.

For their general assistance and tolerance I'd also like to thank Molly Shaw in Lou Pitt's office and Debbie Rose Andrews in ICM's New York office.

My appreciation to Barbra Streisand, who graciously allowed me to be present with Dudley throughout the early days of filming *The Mirror Has Two*

Faces. And especially to Jerry Pam, for his endless encouragement and support through the darker days of this book.

My thanks, too, to Tony Luke, my former BBC radio producer who raided the BBC and BFI archives in London, and to my brother, Simon, who elicited other research during the hours that Los Angeles sleeps while London remains wide awake.

And to Sheridan Morley who long ago lit the fire beneath me and proved an immeasurable guide.

But most of all, my greatest debt and thanks belong to Dudley, not only because after years of being pursued by my colleagues he allowed this to be the only biography he has ever authorized, but for opening up to me in the most extraordinary way. I had thought, after fifteen years of interviewing him for the BBC, that I knew him well but, like most people, it turned out I had known him very little.

I know him now and I have been greatly touched by his soul. The time he has given me, the endless hours he has suffered while my birds perched on his gentle shoulders and preened his eyelashes, have been incalculable. His candor, generosity, and grace under fire (not to mention various avian offerings) affirm my belief that he has the hugest heart on this planet. He is a very special man but a melancholy clown. My one wish for him is that one day he will find the peace and happiness that have eluded him for most of his life. And which he so very much deserves.

PROLOGUE

"How strange for Dudley to be without the ability to play the piano. Take away anything else he feels, but not that—it's so big, and so tragic. He is not a religious man but he knows there must be a reason—that he has actually been CHOSEN to make some impact with this role and he has a mission now to bring good to others from his struggle."

—RENA FRUCHTER

In June 1999, following more than two years of neurological testing and uncertain diagnoses, Dudley Moore was confirmed to be suffering from the rare neurological disorder, progressive supranuclear palsy (or PSP), a Parkinson's-related disease that relentlessly attacks the brain cells that control balance, eye movements, and some mental and motor functions. It is degenerative and incurable. For Dudley, it signaled an end to the world of comedy and music he had loved and embraced for more than forty years.

Over the last two years, Dudley had been promising to talk exclusively with me once the details of his illness had become known. Now he has kept that promise. He put no restrictions on our interview. Nothing was off limits. In October 1999, a few weeks after he released a terse statement announcing his illness, I was on a plane to New Jersey.

For the previous two years Dudley had been living in a small New Jersey town amid the family of his long-time classical musical partner and close friend, Rena Fruchter. Together with her composer husband, Brian Dallow, and their grown-up son and three daughters, they had given Dudley a life he had never really known before, a loving, intimate, all-supporting family cocoon, filled with more than the normal share of aunts, uncles, cousins, and grandchildren. To many in his new, extended family he was "Uncle

Dudley" (or "Duddy" to baby Dvorah) and he had come to rely on them for a peace and refuge he had seldom found in the past.

The Dallow-Fruchter home was on a tree-lined avenue reminiscent of an English suburb. A warm, unpretentious three-story house, part Victorian in design and British in ambiance, it could have jumped out of a Thomas Kinkade painting. Red and gold autumn leaves paved the front lawn. Chattering gray squirrels bounced along the pavement and scampered up the towering elm to join the cardinals and chickadees that hovered on a low bough, singing their own mellifluous serenade.

The face that greeted me eagerly at the door seemed little changed—the same pixie pucker of a smile, the usual tousled hair, the familiar expression of warmth. Later, the eyes would betray the inner anguish. But for that moment, no. It was not so much in Dudley's face that his ordeal was immediately expressed, but in his body.

His shuffling movements, his faltering speech, his awkward imbalance—there lay the grim reality of a horrendous illness, a disease so merciless that the medical prognosis is an average life expectancy of no more than eight years.

He hugged me tightly, happy to see a familiar face. He saw few people now, almost none of his old friends, though in truth he had retreated from them some years ago. But he and I had traveled much of this terrible journey together from its earlier stages, and only a few months earlier he had come to visit me in Los Angeles.

We perched on a couple of stools drinking coffee in Rena Fruchter's warm kitchen, the last light of a late autumn afternoon filtering through the window. Dudley's coffee soon sat forgotten and his eyes grew wistful as he reflected on this terrible time in his life.

In the hours and days that followed, he was remarkably forthcoming, sometimes gut-wrenchingly candid. As we talked about the terrible illness, which I had witnessed for so long without either of us knowing its true nature, I saw his tears and his laughter, his fleeting hope and agonizingly prevalent despair, and the pain of his soul when he told me he'd said goodbye to his most precious companion of life, the ability to play music. It was good to be around him again and at the same time unbearably sad to see the extent to which he had been affected by this devastating disease.

There is no cure for PSP, and drug therapies used in Parkinson's have been of only limited help for the movement disorders. Experimental procedures being tested in Parkinson's, such as the implantation of fetal brain tissue, have proved unavailing in PSP. Treatment therefore focuses on alleviating the symptoms. A wheelchair is often necessary after five years and ultimately some sufferers can become bedridden, with dementia a possibility.

This is the awful destiny that Dudley now faced.

Life was now drastically different for the man who was once Cuddly Dudley at the peak of a glorious career. It was a career he relished, from the early irreverence with Peter Cook to the American movies and his concerts with the world's leading symphony orchestras. He was a multitalented star adored the world over and he had reveled in the accouterments that fame brought him.

The contrast now was shocking. Dudley was walking away from a lifetime as a performer with infinite sadness. He had always believed that when his film career faded, he would continue to perform as a jazz or concert pianist. How could he ever have anticipated that a devastating diagnosis of an incurable brain disease would bring the curtain down on his glittering career?

The passive side of Dudley's nature had accepted his fate, finding it almost impossible to summon up the motivation to fight the battle that could buy him the precious time needed while doctors sought a cure. "I find it hopeless," he told me, "and I think what's the point? It's so hard to fight." He paused to assemble his thoughts. When they emerged, in typical contradiction, it was from the other side of his nature. "But I don't feel the outcome of this disease necessarily has to be tragic. I suppose it could be hopeful."

He spoke not hesitantly but in spurts, his speech often slurred. The words came slowly and took a noticeable physical effort. He sighed often and there were many pauses. I could feel with him the terrible frustration as he attempted to articulate his thoughts. But in the process of transferring them to speech, he kept losing the thread. It was, he said, slightly akin to having something on the tip of one's tongue but being unable to access the thought. "It's very hard to express myself fully, and to say those things that I want to. I give up. My thoughts are not always able to be amplified, sometimes I just lose contact with the thought or its original meaning. And I find it very exhausting to say the things that I want when I can't find them. They disappear into a blank space, it's a blank connection...oh Gawd!"

These last words tumbled out in a frustrated gesture after a long pause. He had wanted to say more but had lost the thought. He sighed wearily and stamped his foot as if to force the continuation of his thoughts to return. "It's like I know it's there and I'm trying to hold onto it and I'm trying to get it and drag it out.

"It's very difficult but one tries on occasions to leap that ravine and get the message out, but I don't know. I have a problem getting my act together to say things. My spastic voice should be an indication of the difficulty I'm having, the laborious voice is very difficult. My thoughts go somewhere else and I can't bring them back and...oh Gawd...it's very difficult."

His anguish at being unable to continue to express himself was immense; shifting body movements accompanied his painful attempts to access the thoughts. Sometimes he gave up trying to find them and get them out and his sentence would disappear under a big sigh that prefaced his weary "Oh, Gawd."

Despite his handicaps his doctors assured me his mental acuity was intact and certainly his memory was much better than I had known it to be for years. "He's very sharp," Rena told me. "More and more I find he knows things I wouldn't expect him to be aware of, simply because they don't seem important enough."

At New Jersey's Kessler Institute, where Christopher Reeve received treatment after his paralyzing 1995 accident, Dudley had earlier been devoting at least three half-day sessions a week in physical therapy, working on his speech and balance. But lately it had became more difficult to summon up the impetus. All too often he felt there was little point in going through the arduous therapy that to him seemed to bear little result. "It's just so hard to fight. To walk around the block every day, to work hard at therapy, to get on a treadmill. I think what's the point, the end is the same."

As for his musical prowess at the piano, "I feel it's all rather hopeless," he sighed. "My hands don't work in concert. The messages are still going out from my brain but it's impossible to get the hands together to play the right speed."

His face became contorted with a look of utmost despair. "It's dreadful because it's probably the one thing that I really regret saying good-bye to, the ability to play with two hands. It's agonizing. I just can't play the sounds I hear in my head. My fingers don't respond properly. I think what's the point. So I'm not practicing. That's something that I've given up. It doesn't seem worth the trouble. I think its fair enough to say that I have envisioned a life without being able to play music. It's a great emptiness."

It was heartrending to see this talented performer resign himself to never playing the piano again. Rena, a world-class pianist, used to push him every day to play at least a little. Now she had stopped. "I still think it would be better, but it seems to be depressing to him."

Yet every indication pointed to Dudley's left hand remaining reasonably unimpaired. Coordination between his left hand and brain still flowed in a direct line. I reminded him that Ravel, among others, had written a concerto for the left hand. "Yes, but it's not something I want to do," he replied. "It doesn't provide what I'm used to." But wouldn't some acceptable sound be better than no sound at all? "Not to me. It's different. It wouldn't be so good."

At the root of his acceptance of his inability to play lay a deep-rooted emotion. "Are you afraid to try?" I asked. "Yes I am," he admitted. "I'm afraid of failure. Failure to produce the sounds that I love."

I had heard this before. Fear of failure had dogged Dudley through life but he had often managed to combat the demon. "You can't give up now," I urged. "Well I can," he responded glumly with a shrug, "because it's hopeless."

Still, Dudley has always been a man of contradiction and barely an hour after this conversation, we returned to the subject. This time he shifted gears. "Maybe the ability to produce the sounds will come back," he allowed, "and maybe the right hand will straighten itself out."

By nature, Dudley had never been an optimist. His tendency had always been to shroud himself in passive acceptance that made the prospect that he would go down fighting seem sadly remote. But he believed it wasn't his natural instinct taking over this time. "I just feel this is a fairly ghastly disease so I don't have many optimistic feelings about it."

But in his own way, Dudley was fighting back.

PART ONE

CHAPTER 1

CHILDHOOD

1935-1946

*"Dudley's never made peace with his mother. The world is very hard on flaws
and mothers are no exceptions. Dudley wasn't tall, he did have a clubfoot,
and he was handsome and talented. His very existence is a dichotomy
no matter what his mother would have done with it."*

—ELSE BLANGSTED

Dudley's misfortune was to be born—in Charing Cross Hospital,
London—with a clubfoot and a withered, skinny, shorter left leg. Both his
feet had been turned in and were clubbed, although the right one would
naturally correct itself in time. But the left leg was particularly small and
misshapen. It was not, for thirty-four-year-old Ada Francis Moore, a very
Good Friday at all on that blustering nineteenth day of April, 1935. And
for the new arrival it hardly marked an auspicious start to this strangely
cold new world.

The young mother was devastated. Incapable of accepting the weeping
bundle as her own, she held the tiny baby above her head and yelled, "This
isn't my baby, this isn't my baby!" She clearly did not want this sickly,
underweight, shriveled baby boy. She loathed that he had been born with a
deformity and found it frightening and shameful.

And so began a childhood that left Dudley with a feeling of being
unwanted and unloved that would haunt him far into adulthood, laying the
foundation for a desperate quest for true love.

When husband John came to collect Ada from the hospital several
days later, it was with reluctance and a heavy heart that she took little
Dudley Stuart John back to their home.

The Moores lived on the Becontree Estate, a sprawling council housing estate in Dagenham, Essex, some ten miles east of London's cockney East End, entirely separate from London, despite its proximity. It was at Dagenham, four years earlier, that Ford had built the largest car plant in England, recruiting its huge workforce from the enormous surrounding population.

Home to some ninety thousand people since its construction in the twenties by the London County Council, the Becontree Estate occupied three thousand colorless acres, its spartan terrain and unremitting uniformity being only occasionally alleviated by a patch of green. More than twenty-six thousand council houses, each one more or less identical to the next, lined the streets in endless brick terraces. There was no town center, only sporadic rows of shops scattered in odd areas. Still, the wide streets made perfect playgrounds for the children, and there was in the air the feeling of a new town still in its birthing stage.

The Moores' house at 14 Monmouth Road was little different from any of its thousands of neighbors. It shared a porch with the house next door and downstairs it had a tiny front room, a small back parlor, and a kitchen—all leading off a narrow passageway. Upstairs were two bedrooms, a toilet, and a bathroom, which was usually the warmest room in the house.

It was to this ordinary-looking council house, furnished largely on credit, that Ada Moore brought her newborn son.

If Dudley's parents were ambivalent about his arrival, it was an emotion not shared by his 5½-year-old sister, Barbara. She was excited by her new brother and watched him with unceasing fascination as her mother sat in the front room with Dudley on her lap, bouncing him to stop him from crying, and massaging his left leg.

Ada had not wanted another baby, and much later she would tell Dudley that the only reason he'd been born was because her idolized brother Billy, a missionary in Africa, had died of a mysterious tropical disease, and she, grief-stricken, had conceived Dudley as a substitute.

"She had wanted to produce something perfect," says Dudley. "But, instead of producing the perfect brother, she produced this leg."

Having lost her much-loved sibling, Ada had hoped to transfer her affections to this child. Instead, his arrival turned out to be a bitter physical disappointment.

The guilt and humiliation Ada felt about her son's clubfoot were unrelenting, even though her own mother had suffered from the same condition. A few years later Dudley would overhear his parents talking about his grandmother having what they described as "a green leg." Eventually he deduced that this was their code for her clubfoot. It had skipped a generation and gone to him.

Doctors have never been sure why some babies are born with talipes, more commonly known as clubfoot, but this congenital abnormality, occasionally hereditary, afflicts the fetus during pregnancy. Three areas of the foot contribute to its deformity: the forefoot is pointed down, the heel is turned inward, and the ankle is turned sideways toward the other leg. The result is a hunched-up foot that resembles the shape of a club or—as Dudley would years later sketch in therapy—a horse's hoof.

Since the foot has in essence swiveled to one side, the leg also tends to turn inward from the knee down. In Dudley's case, the effect was similar to having two right legs, one of which was also very withered and half an inch shorter than the other, a not unusual outcome.

For the taliped, the condition is both discomforting and debilitating. Since the turned-in heel cannot lie flat on the ground, the affected foot is incapable of performing with normal freedom. A series of operations, each targeted toward one of the three affected areas, is the only way to alleviate the disability. Plaster and manipulative castings can help to straighten the leg, and raised shoes and splints or irons can help support the damaged limb.

This was the future that lay ahead for Ada Moore's new baby.

For a mother to learn on delivery that her baby has talipes is a shocking experience, accompanied by immense anxiety, depression, and (since the defect arose during pregnancy) overwhelming guilt. Nowadays counseling is recognized as essential for parents of such babies, but in the thirties such guidance was not available.

It is little wonder that Ada felt ashamed and frightened. And saddest of all, she would instill in her son the same deep shame she herself felt about his deformity.

As soon as he was old enough to understand, she would tell Dudley quite bluntly that she had wanted to kill him at birth because she felt so angry at herself and so badly about the pain that lay ahead for them both. "She said I would suffer unbearably," Dudley recalls, "but obviously it was the pain *she* was going to suffer, feeling as she did that she was on trial for producing a hunchback."

When he was only two weeks old, Dudley had the first of what seemed to him endless operations that would become a way of life in his childhood years. Ada was terrified about the thought of these operations, which exacerbated her unhealthy neurosis about his foot. His father, however, displayed equanimity, if not rigid silence, about his son's condition.

John (Jock) Moore was a taciturn, passive Scot who had been born out of wedlock and had grown up in harsh orphanages in Glasgow, where his feet had been beaten every night for no apparent reason.

Thin, sprightly, and short—both he and Ada were only five foot three—he had taken a mail-order course in electricity and eventually landed a job as an electrician for Stratford East Railway, earning five pounds a week. The hours he worked were long and arduous, and whatever time was left revolved around St. Peter's, the local church, where he looked after the financial records.

Ada Francis—her name had been misspelled the masculine way on her birth certificate and, being a stickler for accuracy, she always signed her name "Ada Francis (sic)"—was a shorthand-typist whose interests lay in Tibetan philosophy and the church. An attractive brunette, two years younger than her husband, she was a repressed and extremely anxious woman who had suffered a nervous breakdown as a teenager. Yet every so often a perky sense of humor rose to the surface. She was the strength of the family and she dominated it with a tight rein.

She was not a cold woman, but, like her husband, she was entirely undemonstrative when it came to showing love. Years later, Dudley would learn that she had wanted to leave Jock just a few weeks after getting married.

Ada was one of nine children, so there was no shortage of aunts and uncles to visit the Moore family on Monmouth Road, although there were no outward demonstrations of affection and Dudley's physical deformities were studiously never mentioned. Aunt Marjorie and Uncle Bernard (Ada's brother and sister) came round with an occasional gift for the children and, despite the lack of endearments, their visits were always greeted with delight by Barbara and Dudley.

Ada's mother, "Bammy," was a frequent visitor, coming over every Wednesday for dinner, and she always had presents for the children. Bammy walked with a cane and, perhaps because she also had a bad leg, was very protective of Dudley.

"She promised him a toy bus if he would stop biting his nails," his sister Barbara recalls. "And, when he got it, he played with it all the time. He loved that little bus." The gift appeased Dudley's jealousy of his cousin Stanley for owning a colorful train set with blinking lights.

Sometimes Ada's friend Olive, who worked at the docks, stopped by for tea and a chat, and every Monday afternoon, Mrs. Hooper, who lived opposite the Moores, came over to have tea with her friend Ada, whom she always called "Aida."

The early Christmases were spent at their grandparents' home in Hornchurch, where the whole family gathered. Ada's side of the family was very musical and they all played different instruments, particularly the piano, violin, and organ. Bammy's husband, William, had a good singing voice and led the family in carols around the piano, to the loud accompaniment of Ada's surviving brother, Bernard, who belonged to the choir.

Dudley has no memories of his grandmother, who died when he was very young, but he does remember his grandfather later, when he lived above a candy store with his daughter Eva. "I was very frightened by him once when he showed signs of violence and threatened me. I can't remember what I did, but he told me if I'd been his son he'd have thrashed me."

His grandfather, William Owen Hughes, was Welsh and wrote slim books on Christian Science, which Dudley's mother kept in the front room of their house. When he wasn't working in the City he practiced faith healing from the distance of his bed, and he would receive telegrams from clients thanking him for the work he'd done on their kidneys, only to receive another the following day asking him to please start work on their headaches.

He was a clownish man who laughed a lot and had a great sense of humor, but, like most of his family, he remains a mystery to Dudley. "I never got any straight answers out of my mother," he reflects, "because I don't think she got any straight answers out of her father."

Christmas in the Moore household was austere. There was no tree and there were no decorations save for paper chains that Barbara and Dudley would cut from colored pieces of paper and hang from wall to wall. Presents were restricted to one apiece, and even Christmas lunch was a simple affair consistingof a small chicken.

Though the Moores were poor, there was little difference between them and others nearby. Dudley did not recognize poverty. He only knew they weren't rich, since to him wealth meant owning a bike with three speeds rather than a fixed wheel.

His father always seemed to be working: even at night, when supper was over, he would pull out his huge drawing boards with electrical diagrams and pore over them for hours.

In many ways the Moores were a typical suburban working-class family. There were few outings, although occasionally Ada and Jock managed to take the children on a day trip to Bournemouth or Chalkwell Bay with a pile of sandwiches and a Thermos flask. Sometimes they played games; Dudley was particularly fond of playing chess with his mother.

Although there was little money, Ada was meticulous about saving whatever she could so that they would be able to take an annual vacation. To the envy of their neighbors, they became the only family on their road to go away for two weeks every August, to Southend or Clacton, where they stayed in a boarding house near the beach.

Back home, Dudley and his sister spent most of their time flicking through comic books, but were always ready to glue themselves to the radio at five o'clock for *Children's Hour*. Their next-door neighbor had the only television on Monmouth Road, and sometimes Barbara and Dudley would go over there to watch the black-and-white images flickering on the tiny screen.

Dudley's early years were lived in the shadows of a looming war, and when he turned four, in April 1939, the family was preparing to face the inevitable. They had already been kitted out for gas masks at the local library. Now there was a bomb shelter in their garden. It was to characterize their life for the next five years.

The Ford plant in Dagenham presented a potential target for bombers and on September 1, as a safety precaution, Ada and the children were evacuated from the house, as were so many families living in and around London. Jock remained behind.

Ada's diary records their evacuation: "We got up early at 3:30 A.M. and left with packs on our backs to walk to Dagenham Docks. I was lucky and got a lift with the children. We walked to the docks, four mothers with children under five, it was horrible."

They couldn't walk very fast because of Dudley's leg, which caused him to limp, and Ada had to keep telling Barbara to slow down. Once at the dock, a boat took them around the coast to Yarmouth, while they all sang "Over the Border," and they spent two days in a hotel room that they shared with their next-door neighbor and her two young children. It was a nightmare for Ada, who found the hotel very noisy, and for Barbara, "because we had to climb up a hundred steps to get to it."

Two days later, on September 3, 1939, war was declared with Germany. The next morning, coaches lined up to take the evacuees into the country and disperse them among various homes throughout Norfolk. Ada and the children ended up in Plumstead, with its tiny post office and church, and Barbara remembers the three of them sitting forlornly in the churchyard while the people of the village picked out whom they wanted to take back to their homes.

Fortunate to be selected by Captain and Mrs. Coltart, a kindly, affluent couple, the Moores settled into the maid's quarters, where they would remain for the next eight months. Jock managed to visit them at least once, but it took him the best part of a day and a night to reach Plumstead in the prevailing war conditions.

Dudley enjoyed his relocation. The Coltarts had a large holding, big enough to be called a small farm, from which they supplied eggs and fruit to the International Stores, and Dudley became very friendly with the gardener, Herbert Harmer, and hung around him, chasing rabbits, collecting eggs, and spending long hours with him in the greenhouse.

"My mother started getting very worried about Dudley," recalls Barbara, "because very often he wouldn't eat his dinner. And then we discovered that he was regularly having cheese on toast with Herbert in the greenhouse. No wonder he wasn't hungry later!"

The following April, Dudley turned five and began attending the local infants school. But barely a month later the family was allowed to return to its house in Dagenham. Life settled back into a routine on Monmouth Road, and Dudley enrolled in Fanshawe Infants School to resume his schooling, while Ada embarked on a new job as a bookkeeper.

There was a clinic in Dagenham attended by Miss Wells, a physiotherapist from Upminster, and Ada frequently trundled over there with both children in tow so that Dudley could have regular massage and plaster treatments. While he was being attended to, Barbara amused herself with magazines in the waiting room.

Despite all the attention that Dudley needed, Barbara never felt neglected. She was a bubbly girl with many school friends and always seemed happy. As for Dudley, who had to suffer the frequent and painful ministrations to his leg, Barbara says he never complained once.

At night there was homework. And The Piano.

A few months before Dudley was born, Jock Moore had bought the piano from John Watson, the second husband of his birth mother. Although this side of his family's history was never explained to Dudley, he knows that Jock was actually born John Havlin, but for some reason was given the name John Moore and put into an orphanage. Why he was given that name is a mystery. So is the reason for Jock's mother not keeping her son, although they later resumed contact. And where did the name "Havlin" come from?

Jock himself only learned his real name when he turned twenty-six. But whatever his mother told him then and what he later told Ada was never fully passed on to Barbara or Dudley, or to Jock's step-siblings.

Jock's diary, which recently came to light, has an entry in 1947 that makes reference to his illegitimacy without explaining it: "Was informed by Ada that the Taylors [neighborhood acquaintances] know my family at Southend. It happened when Ada showed Mrs. Taylor a paragraph in the *Daily Mirror* referring to one of my sister's daughters being married to a Chief Petty Officer. Through this incident, Barbara was told and shown my birth certificate with my real name but not used by me."

Barbara remembers nothing of that conversation. As for the birth certificate, which might have explained who Jock's father really was, it has long since disappeared.

Although she played infrequently, Ada loved the piano, and its sounds entranced Barbara. Ada taught her some basics and allowed her to begin piano lessons. She was an avid student and could play quite adeptly for a ten-year-old.

It was now, while bombs screeched overhead, that Dudley discovered what was to become a lifetime's passion for music.

He clambered up to the battered brown upright with its wooden inlay and Victorian candlesticks and tinkered with the keys. The piano had a reproduction Sheraton stool with a broken handle for adjusting the height, and Dudley had to keep banging it back into place so it didn't fall apart while he was sitting on it.

The Moores became inured to the sound of London being battered, under continuous blitz from above. Every night, after dinner and homework were over, the family went down to the shelter to sleep. Then one night in November 1940 they remained in the house. Maybe it was raining. Or maybe Ada was just fed up with the continual upheaval. Whatever the reason, she decided they would sleep that night on the floor in the front living room.

It was the night that a Nazi bomb had their address on it.

The children were sleeping together on the floor on a makeshift bed that had been tucked into an alcove in the wall. Dudley recalls having pushed his sister out of the way during the night and, when the bomb hit at three in the morning, he woke to find himself at the bottom of the blanket. He was more bemused to find his head sticking out of the bottom than by the fact that they'd been bombed.

The bomb had crashed down the front of the house and into the garden, where it settled in the large crater that it made. It was just four yards away from where Dudley and his sister had been sleeping. Miraculously, it hadn't exploded.

"There was this loud noise," Barbara remembers, "and things fell down everywhere. My father got up straight away and cut his toe on some glass that had smashed when a picture fell off the wall."

Satisfied that his family was safe, Jock Moore went to the kitchen to make some tea—the eternal British pacifier in times of crisis. At that moment, two firemen shouted from outside. "Don't light the gas!" they yelled. "The gas main has burst!"

To the 5½-year-old Dudley, this was a real adventure—"just like the air raids, when we'd go running down the path to the shelter."

The family was evacuated to a nearby council house on Baron Road that looked no different inside from the one they had been forced to vacate. Outside, however, it had the advantage of both a front and a back garden. It would remain Dudley's home for the next eighteen years, and his parents would live there for the rest of their lives.

Gradually life returned to normal. Unlike many families, the Moores had been lucky. They were able to make the transition to a new home relatively smoothly, having lost none of their furniture or property. What damage they had sustained was made good some months later under a war-damage claim that amounted to four pounds. Almost everything had remained intact. Even the piano.

Dudley loved that piano. His mother had now started teaching rudimentary music to pupils in her spare time, and she passed some of her knowledge on to Dudley. Graduating now from merely tinkering with the keys, he enjoyed the sound and thought it "made a nice noise." Ada must have thought so, too, and she enrolled him in music lessons when he turned six. It was clear that both Dudley and Barbara would carry on her family's musical tradition.

Life revolved around the house and the shelter in their garden. Barbara remembers a time, even while his leg was in yet another plaster cast, when Dudley trudged to the top of the air-raid shelter and whizzed down it on an old tricycle.

Jock and Ada Moore were religious people who went to church frequently—twice on Sundays—with their children. Dudley was fascinated by the clergy he saw there, and perhaps it was here that, unconsciously, the seeds were laid for his later desire to play-act. "At home," recalls Barbara, "he used to whip the white tablecloth off the dining-room table and drape it around him, then walk off down the garden path pretending to be a priest."

In those early years life was hard. There was a shortage of food and money; ration books were the norm, and coupons for food and clothes were carefully meted out.

With the war still raging, there were no visits to the carnival and the circus was a fantasy to be drooled over in books. Although Dudley himself is convinced there were no such outings at all, Jock's diary shows there was at least one trip to the zoo with both children when Dudley was six. Their main treat was the local cinema. On very occasional evenings Ada would pack a pile of sandwiches and take the children to meet their father at Chadwell Heath station as he came home from work. Then the four Moores would go to the nearby Gaumont cinema and settle in the stalls, eating their supper, while they watched the film.

Jock Moore worked long days, and the cinema was as much a treat for him as it was for the children. His job meant he had to leave the house before dawn every morning—often he worked weekends, too—and walk to the station to take a train to work. When he came back home in the early evening, he would sit in the kitchen on an upturned box that was used for cleaning shoes, making grumpy remarks while Ada stood preparing supper at the kitchen table. There was a mangle dangling under the table, and Dudley grew up believing it was the bottom half of his mother, and that "I came out of the mangle instead of her womb."

Dudley loved his father dearly and adored his sweetness. But at the same time he despised his lack of strength. "I was enormously angry at his passivity and his inability to show me answers."

Barbara remembers her father as a very quiet man. "He was very fond of both of us, but he wasn't a great talker. And he was never strict. My mother was. She didn't exactly lay down the law, but she certainly ran the family. And yet she was also very nervous."

In time, Dudley would inherit the passive side of his father, learning to live with an unquestioned acceptance of people and life. But he also inherited his mother's anxiety—an emotional state that has never left him.

By now, Dudley's education was being continually interrupted by operations on his bad leg and lengthy hospital incarcerations. He still remembers the sinking feeling of waking up depressed in the mornings with the awful thought that nurses were coming to his bed to give him an enema before wheeling him off to the operating room.

His stays in the hospital were lived out with the visions and sounds of war all around him. These were traumatic times, when he was the only boy in a ward full of badly wounded soldiers. He was surrounded by pain. "There was a soldier in a bed across from me," he recalls, "and when the doctors came to look at him they drew curtains around the bed, and I could hear him screaming, 'No! No! No!' I was very frightened."

There were lighter occasions, but at the time he was too young to recognize the humor in a dire situation. One of them occurred when he'd been wheeled into a darkened operating room and left alone for what seemed like hours. "Finally," Dudley recalls, "this doctor came in and said, 'It's the right leg to come off, isn't it?' And I squeaked, 'No, no. You've got to do something to the left leg.' It turned out he was trying to be funny, but I thought he meant it. I thought he was going to take off my leg."

Ironically, after one of these operations, his father brought him a present of a lead soldier on horseback with one of its legs missing. Jock repaired it by sticking a match in the leg socket, but it kept falling out.

Dudley grew up dreading the isolation of hospitals and the long recovery periods during which he felt utterly abandoned. Sometimes he was left alone for weeks at a time, and on one occasion the hospital had to send word to his mother that he was pining away because they hadn't been to visit him. But it couldn't have been easy for his family to get around in those days when London was being blitzed, and some of the convalescent homes were a long railway journey away. Nevertheless, the insecure and emotionally deprived six-year-old began to believe he'd done something wrong. "My family used to appear at the bottom of my bed every two weeks, it seemed, and sit around shiftily."

Dudley was becoming deeply traumatized by his childhood isolation, which kept him apart not only from his family but also from other children. His solitary confinement led to a terror of rejection and abandonment that would become a lifelong fear. Yet, ironically, in later years he would also find himself seeking increasing isolation and solitude.

Years later, one of Dudley's therapists would tell him of psychological studies that showed that children under five who are left on their own for more than two weeks generally freeze up and never quite crack out of it. The fear and guilt take a grip on the psyche that can never be entirely loosened.

His parents were both very repressed individuals, not given to expressing their emotions. "They created an aura of repression and suppression around themselves. They were two of a kind," says Dudley. "I don't know that either of them could express love very well, either to each other or to us." There was certainly nothing warm or affectionate from Ada. Barbara remembers, "We'd kiss her good-bye in the morning when we went off to school, but she wasn't one for putting her arms around us."

The emotional effect on Dudley cut deep. He desperately felt the emptiness of having no hugs and no kisses in his life. "My mother's excuse sometimes was that I shouldn't be touched because the plaster might break on my leg. So I often felt as if I were stuck on the mantel with a sign reading, 'Don't Touch Him.'"

Sometimes Ada had to massage his leg, and at those times Dudley felt a gratitude for the physical connection—"At least the awful thing was being touched and handled in a fairly sympathetic manner." But the first time he experienced any show of affection from a woman was when he was seven. And it came not from his mother but from a nurse.

It was Christmas, and Dudley was spending it in St. Winifred's convalescent home in Barnet, North London, recuperating from his sixth operation. On his first night, the lonely, frightened little boy was being looked after by Nurse Pat. When she tucked him in, she asked if he'd like her to kiss him goodnight. Dudley, who'd never had that from his mother, said no, but as she walked away he changed his mind.

She came back to his bedside, bent down, and kissed him lovingly and gently. And that kiss, which has been imprinted ever since on his emotional psyche, affected his whole life. It was at that moment, with a complete stranger, that he found the kind of loving attention his own mother had been incapable of giving him and for which he would continue to search for most of his life.

"Nurse Pat was one of the first people who was genuinely sweet to me," Dudley recalls, "and I was very touched by her. I've looked for that tenderness ever since. It haunts and sustains me. Which is why, I suppose, I live for touching and being touched."

So strong was the impact of Nurse Pat's tenderness toward Dudley that fifty years later he would try to find her. "She was truly an angel of mercy, and I can still feel that sweet kiss. It was probably the first taste of real, unqualified, uncomplicated affection I had ever had. It's always stayed with me. In many ways my entire life is based on recapturing that single moment of affection."

When he was discharged and sent home, he knew for the first time the feeling of being cared for in a gentle, warm way. And now he knew what he was missing.

The piano became his emotional refuge. Music was an outlet for the dwarfish boy to vent the increasing aggressions he was feeling about his clubfoot and the thin leg that was so often either strapped into irons or encased in plaster after yet another operation.

Though deeply attached to his mother, Dudley was also very angry with her. Years of therapy since have removed the anger, but back then he was just an innocent child seething with resentment. His mother's obsession with his foot made Dudley also become obsessed with it, and her guilt made him feel he had done something wrong. Ada swung from one end of the scale to the other in her attitude toward his leg. Either it wasn't there at all or it was a totally afflicting, paralyzing problem. And Dudley was angry at her for not being consistent in her attitude.

But it was also hard on Ada, who was always dragging him off to clinics or hospitals—especially since she was terrified at having to travel any distance. Visiting her son while he was in hospitals or convalescent homes must have been very harrowing for her, particularly in the tense wartime conditions.

Barbara remembers visiting Dudley with her mother some Sunday afternoons while he was in St. Winifred's in Barnet. Jock Moore was working, so they had to go alone, and it was a journey that took almost half a day across the sprawling railway network around London. Other visits including Jock are recorded in his diary, although Dudley's angst does not seem to have been noticed in any of them. "He was very pleased to see us and seemed very happy" was a frequent comment by his father.

While Dudley was recuperating from an operation in Old Church Hospital in Romford he had one amusing escapade that he later related to his sister. "Dudley was in a ward where there were a lot of wounded soldiers," recalls Barbara. "They wanted to smoke, but they weren't allowed to. So Dudley would keep lookout for the Sister and they would all light cigarettes and hide them under the bedclothes!" Whether he was found out or routinely transferred, he was soon moved to where he could do no further mischief.

Dudley was an intelligent boy and quick to learn. After a couple of weeks in the hospital he came home and, just two weeks later, achieved the distinction of top of the class in exams.

He had lived much of the first seven years of his life in casts, splints, wheelchairs, corrective devices, hospitals, and surgery. While other kids were learning to play soccer, Dudley was being shuffled in and out of the hospital.

One of his operations was described by his mother as slicing him "up the back of the leg and along the side to loosen something up." Such explanations, cloaked as they were in mysterious terms, were more frightening to Dudley than the reality of the operations.

It was a grim rearing for a child, and it is little wonder that the young Dudley, far from being comedic, was actually growing up very somberly, his sense of humor severely stunted.

When he wasn't in the hospital having an operation, he was at home recovering in splints. He spent so much time in the hospital, where the distance between him and another person in the next bed was six feet, that when he finally got out in the world and found himself only two feet away from another boy he became quite frightened.

There was one more operation he might have had to correct his deformed leg, but now Ada decided Dudley had been through enough and she called a halt. She felt he was becoming very upset by all the solitary confinement.

Ada now took Dudley to a Mr. Miller, a bootmaker at Spitalfields Market in London. He fitted the boy with a pair of boots, the left one specially built up to cater to his clubfoot and with a slight heel to compensate for the leg that was a half-inch shorter than the other. Jock Moore now had the additional task of nailing new soles on the boots whenever they wore down.

When he turned eight, Dudley graduated to Green Lane Junior School. He still recalls the trauma he felt when, on his first day, he had to face an entire classroom of faces staring at him. "My mother came with me into the classroom and was standing at the front, very protective and anxious. I was very frightened when the teacher told everybody there was a new boy in the class."

His mother was a strong, dominating woman, and she had put these qualities to good use when the headmaster of the school had not wanted to accept Dudley. "He wanted Dudley to go to a special school where they could cater to the needs of his leg," Barbara recalls. "He didn't want the worry of Dudley falling down in the playground and being responsible." But Ada was determined that her son would have a normal education. She fought and she won.

As most children do, Dudley soon settled down and began to feel comfortable in his new surroundings. And, unlike other kids, he didn't have a long walk to school—this one was at the bottom of their back garden, just beyond the fence.

By now Dudley was sharing Barbara's piano teacher, Miss Hoggard, a

kindly soul with a stutter who gave them weekly half-hour lessons for a
shilling each. Irene Hoggard was not an especially proficient teacher,
however, and failed to instill in Dudley the discipline to practice regularly.
Barbara has wry recollections of those days when she would practice assiduously all week long yet still get her knuckles wrapped, while Dudley never
practiced at all and sailed through his lessons.

Barbara was now playing the piano in the school dance band and had
to study a book on syncopation. She couldn't understand most of it and
gave it to Dudley, but was dumbfounded when he grasped it instantly.

Barbara was very protective of her younger brother and was happy to
share social outings with him. She was a mature thirteen-year-old and,
during school holidays, when both parents were working, it was she who
looked after Dudley. "We used to go to the cinema together on a Monday
afternoon, into the top row for a shilling. And then we'd get home just in
time to see our piano teacher kicking her heels on our doorstep waiting
for us."

Sometimes Barbara's friend Joan Baker joined them at the cinema,
and then both girls found themselves having to deal with Dudley's more
ebullient nature, which occasionally took over. "There used to be an
organist between films," Barbara recalls, "and, when the organ rose up,
Dudley would put his fingers in his mouth and whistle. Joan and I were
aghast, and we'd have to shut him up."

Dudley was very fond of his sister. He found her "nice and romantic," but felt there was something strange about her because she seemed so
much taller than anyone else in the family. She had green eyes, like her
mother, and an overbite—two qualities Dudley would always find attractive
in other women.

It was around now, when he was eight, that Dudley began choir
singing. He had been a boat boy, carrying the incense, in St. Peter's, his
father's church, but it had no choir, so he switched to nearby St. Thomas's,
which had a strong choral tradition. He loved church music, loved the
ethereal sound of angelic voices, and in time he would sing the entire range
from soprano and alto through to tenor and bass.

There was seldom much leisure time for Jock or Ada to spend with
Dudley or Barbara—Jock was working round-the-clock, and by now Ada
had taken on another job in her spare time. But one wet afternoon after
the war, Ada took Dudley to the cinema to see *Carry On London*, with
Kenneth More. They loved it so much that they sat through the second feature and watched it again—the only time they ever liked a film enough to
see it twice.

Ada and Jock unquestionably loved their children, but they were so
emotionally repressed that they were unable to express it. Dudley passion-

ately wanted more from them, and, from his vantage point as a young child, he could not understand why they did not seem to love him. Anguished beyond belief, he was convinced he had done something to prevent them from loving him.

"I remember the time when I was standing in a room with my mother, who was on the point of giving up the ghost. She said, 'If you don't behave yourself I will...' The threat was there—what was it she was going to do? What was it I was going to do?"

Dudley loved his family very much, but his parents' suppression of their feelings had made him very wary. "I was ludicrously passionate to the point where I just shrank from showing it, and so I didn't express what I should have to any of my family."

Although the operations on his foot had been relatively successful in straightening his left leg, he never grew another inch. Both his parents were short, and he often asked his mother if his height would ever change, but she always told him, "Don't worry, dear, you'll be as big as Uncle Bernard." That didn't encourage Dudley much, since Uncle Bernard was only five foot eight. In the end it was Barbara who grew to Uncle Bernard's height.

Nature turned off Dudley's growth clock when he reached 5 feet 2½ inches, although he had yet to realize it. As he grew older, he would spend many agonizing years perceiving his height and his clubfoot as a reflection of his inadequacies.

CHAPTER 2

SCHOOL DAYS

1946-1954

*"He was an indefatigable and dedicated clown, but at the same time
he was also very introspective—much more than most kids at that age."*

—TEIFION GRIFFITHS

When Dudley was eleven, he entered Dagenham County High School, just a few hundred yards down the road from his house.

The school was run by Miss Williams (whom the pupils nicknamed "Bill") and Mr. Grainger, the headmaster. When Grainger saw Dudley's name on the list of new entrants, he summoned Ada to the school to discuss any special attention that Dudley's foot might require. When they met, Ada told him she was very proud of her son, but it was clear to Grainger that she was both possessive and unsympathetic toward him. She appeared conscience-stricken and responsible for Dudley having a leg that sometimes needed to be in irons, but at the same time she insisted that he was to be treated as an ordinary boy.

The County High was a large, mixed school attended by several hundred children. It was the only grammar school in Dagenham and was, inexplicably, saddled with a charter that also provided for children outside of the borough. Consequently, because of the serious shortage of available places, thousands of local children who had passed their eleven-plus exam were unable to enter the County High and instead were allocated to nearby secondary-modern schools. In a sense, it became the luck of the draw whether a child landed a place or not. Dudley was one of the lucky ones.

It was a very musical school, with its own choir and orchestras, and should have been the perfect environment for a child with musical gifts. But Dudley soon discovered how cruel and hostile other children could be.

His lack of height, his wizened leg, and his clubfoot made him an easy target for bullies, who learned quickly how to make his life unbearable, and he was constantly being taunted by them.

His leg became an object of gleeful ridicule. Kids would shout "Hopalong!" behind him and mimic his limping gait. It didn't help that he had to wear short trousers, which made it harder to hide his defect. The only boy with a clubfoot in the County High School, he was desperately self-conscious and would express his rage by stamping on the floor, hoping it would collapse and he could disappear through the hole. "I projected on to my leg all my feelings of inadequacy and self-loathing."

Ada Moore did not want Dudley to feel there was anything wrong with him, but she sent out mixed messages from which he sometimes deduced that it didn't matter and at other times that it mattered more than anything. So acute were her anxieties that sometimes she found herself calling him a complete cripple. Yet at other times, pretending there was no problem at all, she would tell the confused child he was perfect. Her attitude presented a bewildering dichotomy to her son, in whom she soon planted the idea "that I was either a genius or a piece of crap."

He was a hardworking boy who loved studying and, in front of his classmates, he would often put up his hand and ask the teachers for more work, not realizing this would alienate him even further from his peers. But he'd led a very isolated life and was largely unversed in the ways of children of his age.

He soon became known as an overachiever, which gave the bullies even more cause to make his life unbearable. And this they did with unwavering enthusiasm, knocking his pencil box off his desk in class, pulling down his shorts in public, and generally imbuing the youngster with the belief that he had no right to exist.

There was, however, a marvelous respite from all this adversity. During midterm break, Dudley went to Norfolk to stay with Herbert Harmer, the Coltarts' gardener, and his wife, Jean.

He had a wonderful stay in their rural surroundings and made himself very useful. He fed the geese and chickens, collected the eggs every second day, and helped Jean to shell vast piles of beans. He loved to go rabbiting with Herbert, and the two of them were like little boys as they ran across the fields yelling at the rabbits. A sensitive boy, Dudley paid particular attention to wildlife and, when he woke each morning, he studiously checked on the swallows' nest that rested beneath the gutter outside his bedroom window.

He was fascinated by the broad Norfolk dialect—particularly Jean's, which was also partly Scottish. "Herbert says 'ar,'" he wrote to his parents, "and Jean says 'oi.' It's a queer mixture!"

His propensity for humor was now beginning to surface. "I certainly remember your letter about the bees," he wrote to his mother in rounded handwriting. "The thing was 'buzzing' with things about those bees!"

By now Barbara had left school and was a sophisticated sixteen-year-old. She had a job as a shorthand-typist and was contributing to the household funds. Meanwhile Jock Moore had been elevated to a better position on the railway—checking faults in axles—and the family became marginally more prosperous.

This allowed them to indulge in a rare treat—a Sunday visit to the cinema in a box seat, and the added luxury of a box of chocolates. They went to see *Red River* at the Regent Cinema, but the fog was so thick outside that "somehow it penetrated inside the cinema," recalls Dudley, "and we could barely see the screen."

His mother still kept up the family tradition of an annual vacation and, in the summer of 1947, she took them all to a boarding house in Thorpe Bay, near Southend. Each morning Dudley and Barbara would wander over to the beach with a bucket and collect cockles. "We brought them back to the landlady," Barbara remembers, "and she'd cook them for our supper. But one night, after eating them for tea, I became terribly ill in the night, and I've never eaten cockles again."

It was now, at the age of twelve, that Dudley began composing. Paralyzed by apprehension, his emotional unrest led to his first musical composition. It was titled "Anxiety," and exists today as a reminder of his early angst. Years later one of his wives would discover the score, across which in his neat schoolboy hand he had written "Allegretto moderato misterioso sostenuto," and have it blown up to poster size; it still hangs on the landing in his house.

As he began to develop an interest in girls, a new anxiety began to set in. While his schoolmates were shooting up all around him, Dudley was not growing any taller, and his height—or lack of it—was humiliating him further. He suffered from such low self-esteem that he was too shy even to summon up the courage to approach a girl. He believed that being small was a disadvantage and felt unworthy of anything—"a little runt with a twisted foot."

He vividly remembers learning about sex for the first time from Kenny Vare, the school bully. Kenny came running into the school playground as if he were bearing the news of the Vikings' landing. "Do you know what you have to do when you grow up?" he said to Dudley. "You have to put your winkie in a girl." Dudley was aghast. "By this time, having already masturbated myself into the ground, I thought, 'My God, I've ruined myself for this ghastly task.'"

Dudley's secret sexual indulgence had become quite an obsession.

Since the age of six, he had been performing his dastardly deed while ogling pictures from his father's hidden collection of magazines. "I remember coming six times in one evening when I was supposed to be doing my homework," he recalls. "I just sat there masturbating, with my parents next door. That always made things a little more titillating. I had a carpet by my bed, and I used to ejaculate all over it and then rub it in. The carpet became like sculpted grass. I'll never know why on earth it was never discovered, except that my mother would occasionally say, 'This carpet's got all funny. Very strange, isn't it?'"

Dudley's masturbation may have been a way of making himself feel more wanted than he thought he was. It was never mentioned by his parents, although his mother must have had an inkling of what was going on. But, being a very sexually repressed woman, it's unlikely that she would have known how to broach the subject with her son. Still, as Dudley recalled later, she did once catch him at his furtive pastime.

They could not afford a television and family entertainment centered around the radio. One night they were all sitting together in the lounge—"it was the only room in the house, besides the bathroom, where you wouldn't freeze to death in winter"—silently listening to a concert. His mother was sitting opposite Dudley, darning socks, while Dudley had his hand in his pocket, having a quiet grope.

"We were listening to Mado Robin, a coloratura soprano, who was singing an aria. Suddenly she hit an extremely high note, prompting my mother to say, without missing a beat, 'This woman is singing the highest note that's ever been sung don't do that dear.' The moment was frozen in my mind because my mother had discovered me."

For many years after that, Dudley remained fixated with coloratura singing and could be found in the early hours of the morning frantically turning the radio dial to find a coloratura aria by which to masturbate.

Although his foot was often an impediment, he adored sports and was extremely athletic. He loved football, but it was hard for him to kick the ball and he had to wear a slipper inside his shoe as a buffer. Cricket and tennis came easier and he played both with some skill. Swimming was another enjoyment, although exposing his leg and foot was always an embarrassment.

Academically, Dudley was often close to the top of his class. But his scholarly demeanor remained unpopular and the school bullies still kept him in sight as their prime target. Dudley's angst at their behavior was unabating. Years later he would meet one of his aggressors and remind him that he had "beaten the shit out of me. But he didn't remember. None of it. All that pain. And he didn't even remember!" He never told his mother about these episodes, which were growing in nastiness and frequency.

Sometime during his thirteenth year, a psychic switch flipped in Dudley's head. He had had enough. He was tired of the humiliation of it all, tired of feeling constantly surrounded by the enemy. One day in class he made a crass joke to his teacher. It was entirely out of character, and his classmates stared at him in astonishment—but not without an admiration that instantly conveyed itself to Dudley. Now he knew what he had to do. It was the turning point in his young life.

Forced to develop a classic defense, he had discovered that playing the fool could go a long way toward self-preservation. Once he started being funny and making fun of the teachers as the others did, he found himself accepted. He had tried to combat the bullying by being a clever dick. And it had worked. "It was my way of defending myself," he reflects. "How can someone take a punch at you when they're laughing?"

Like most comedians, Dudley had found that comedy deflected his peers' aggression. His humor was a strong weapon and he began to wield it with vengeance. Almost overnight he metamorphosed from class book-worm to class clown.

But there was a price to pay.

He had always been an excellent student and a voracious reader, absorbing two or three books a night. Becoming the school comic put a stop to that. He no longer worked so hard, and saw his academic brilliance begin to dissipate. He had become the class clown only to neutralize hostilities, but, as he became less interested in developing and learning, his grades began to suffer. "Academically it started slipping away," he says, "and that made me angry. It still does." His popularity was zooming, but his self-esteem was plummeting even further.

Many years later, in therapy, having realized the mechanics of what had happened to him, he stopped trying to be funny. He wanted to spend a year without cracking a smile, as penance for all those years of being "a sycophantic creep."

In spite of his anger and helped by an increasing love for music, his confidence was growing. He spent long hours after school practicing the piano and he began learning to play the violin.

The foot no longer affected his mobility, but it still embarrassed him greatly. One of his strongest early memories is the day he was at last allowed to wear long trousers. Finally he could cover up his thin leg. "It was a gorgeous moment. People couldn't understand why I was so excited to be wearing them!"

A month after his thirteenth birthday, Dudley had a violin audition at the Guildhall School of Music and won a scholarship to attend weekly lessons. He also won a scholarship to the Royal Academy of Music, but his mother, driven by her excessive anxiety, opted for the Guildhall because it was a few stations closer on the underground and meant he would not have to change trains.

Ada's anxiety is deeply imprinted on Dudley's memory. "I can still see her running alongside a 106 bus," he recalls, "with me standing on the bus platform because I hadn't got off in time with her and the driver had driven away. There she was running up the street after this bus. Another anxious moment for her."

At the Guildhall he studied musical theory and composition, while keeping up both piano and violin. His parents had scraped up the money to buy Dudley his first violin, an instrument he adored passionately, "but I was so desperate to play it really well that I wasn't any good at it." He had a different teacher almost every week, which frustrated and dismayed him and may have had something to do with his eternal belief that he could never master the instrument. But he was proficient enough to entertain family and friends in impromptu concerts at home. He stood in the garden playing the violin for neighbors, his sheet music held up by clothespins on the line. People came by to watch, while his mother nodded appreciatively, "Oh yes, dear, that's so lovely." She never praised Dudley much, but he lapped up whatever she gave him.

His talent was becoming recognized by outsiders. The Stratford Music Festival held a competition and Dudley entered. "He was in bed one day with the flu," Barbara remembers, "and this letter arrived. I took it up to him, and when he opened it, they told him he'd won first prize for composing a carol. He was very excited and felt better immediately."

By now, Dudley had developed a normal fourteen-year-old's interest in girls. It was, he would later admit, the beginning of a lifetime's dedicated interest in sex. "I would look at girls and suddenly all I wanted to do was to love them, have them kiss me. Sex really had me by the ears."

His first tentative sexual encounter appalled him. "The girl wasn't beautiful, but she was well-built. We hid behind her house, and I had to stand on a pile of bricks to reach her. Then she pulled my hand up to her breast. It was the first one I'd ever touched. I felt this 'thing' and thought I'd put my hand on a sheep's eye or something."

Afterward, he felt totally disgraced. It didn't hold him back, however, and he ventured forward, increasingly brave, perfecting his kissing technique and fondling the occasional breast.

But if his approach to the opposite sex was tentative, his embracing of music was not.

For some time he'd been "messing about" with the organ in church. Now, with the guidance of Leslie Taylor, the head of the Guildhall, he took it up seriously. As the church organist, he liked the feeling of sitting higher up than the congregation and looking down on them. "I enjoyed feeling sort of isolated, as well as very feted."

The pedals presented a problem, as his bad foot needed still more elevation, and he used to spend hours in the organ loft at St. Thomas's trying to get his foot to work more efficiently. His answer was to build an extra rubber heel on to one of his mother's old right court shoes—right, because it made up for his inability to turn the left foot outward—and cut a groove in the sole so he could strap on the shoe and wind the lace round the back of his leg. This had the effect of pulling his toes up to an angle that allowed him to match the agility of his right foot.

He found the organ a natural progression after the piano and soon he was playing at church services, earning a few shillings for official functions. But the cash never lasted. He dreamed of buying a bike but usually spent his money in coffee shops and ice-cream parlors.

Barbara had an office job in Moorgate, just a few stations away on the underground. Some Saturday mornings, she recalls, when she left her office, she would walk down to the Embankment to meet Dudley at the Guildhall. "Occasionally we'd go up to South Kensington to a concert at the Albert Hall. Other times we'd go home on the train, have our lunch, and then go off to the Gaumont cinema to see a film."

Dudley was now making up for his earlier isolation and was becoming very sociable. On Saturday afternoons, if Barbara wasn't free, he would swim in the local baths, topping this off with a row on Barking Lake. When the weather was fine, he and his friend Michael Austin would race each other over to the park for a game of cricket or tennis.

Michael was Dudley's best friend at school. Their favorite extracurricular activity was to go down to the local youth club every Thursday night. For Dudley, that was a treat akin to Saturday-morning cinema, which he could never attend because he was studying.

At the club, he and Michael played snooker and table tennis. But most of all Dudley loved dancing, and he jived away many an hour with Shirley Vare, sister of the school bully, to the sound of Frankie Laine records.

He may have been insecure and thought the girls did not want to be with him, but in truth he was becoming very popular with the opposite sex, who found him extremely attractive. "He certainly seemed to get on pretty well with the girls," recalls Barbara, "and he always used to have a fair number of girlfriends at school. I remember coming home one day and finding one of them there."

Dudley's biggest dream at this time was to own a bike. He was an avid collector of cigarette cards but would give away his precious tokens in exchange for bike rides. "I was *mad* about bikes. But my parents couldn't afford one. And then I bought one for ten bob off a schoolmate. I couldn't believe I'd got this bike. It had a fixed wheel, so I tended to fall off it at times, but I didn't care. It was wonderful."

Although the Moores survived fairly well, there was very little money for luxuries. After they'd paid the weekly rent of one pound, there was less than five pounds to take care of the family's necessities. Sometimes even those were hard to afford. "My parents never mentioned the fact," reflects Dudley, "but I guess they were poor, because they would stand in front of the butcher's shop and debate whether they could manage to buy three rashers of bacon or just two."

When he turned fifteen in April 1950, Dudley applied his concentration to studying in earnest for his O level exams. He had his hopes set on university, which in those Dagenham days was a very lofty ambition indeed.

A new teacher had just started at the County High, and it was he who would take Dudley through his last years of school. Peter Cork was only eight years older, but he was to strike up a friendship with the teenager that endures to this day.

Cork, in his first school teaching position, became Dudley's music master and was vividly struck by his pupil's musical prowess from the first moment of hearing him play. "He had incredible musicality, which was astounding in a boy of his age. It was an amazing ability and, aside from playing the piano, violin, and organ, he also composed and became my choir accompanist at school."

Although Dudley couldn't memorize very much, he astounded his teacher with his extraordinary talent for sight-reading. Cork once gave him a six-part Bach fugue and was dumbfounded when Dudley played it perfectly on sight. "He was very self-assured as far as his music was concerned. It always used to annoy me a little bit that he never seemed to work at anything and then he'd turn up with something quite brilliant, having worked on it at the last moment."

Cork lived in nearby lodgings run by Mrs. Knobbs, whose home was filled with Victorian treasures. "She had a wonderful old-fashioned piano with a candelabra," Cork remembers—"a real Victorian period piece, with a glorious book of Victorian piano duets. Dudley used to come round and we'd have enormous fun playing them. We loved these wonderful, sentimental things and got such a kick out of doing them."

It was around this time that a new family moved into 112 Baron Road, just up the street from the Moores. The Griffiths were a warm, outgoing Welsh family, the youngest of whom was thirteen-year-old Teifion.

Teifion, now headmaster of a school in Cardiff, still remembers watching Dudley every Saturday morning as he strode past the Griffiths' house, violin case under his arm, on his way to the station for his lessons at the Guildhall. They met eventually and after several chats, mostly about music, Dudley persuaded the newcomer to join the choir at St. Thomas's. By now Dudley had become the assistant organist and choirmaster, and the young Welsh boy was deeply impressed.

"He used to practice a lot," recalls Teifion, "and I would turn pages for him in the organ loft while he played pretty heavy stuff like Handel and Bach. He was also brilliant at extemporizing on modern tunes. He'd take a simple tune like 'Baa Baa Black Sheep' and play it in the style of Schubert or Beethoven. It was brilliant."

The two soon became inseparable friends, and Dudley was a regular visitor to the Griffiths' household, which was considerably freer and more relaxed than his own. Some Saturday afternoons, while Teifion's parents were working, they got together at the house with two other boys, Tony Lambert and Leonard Marchant, and would raid the kitchen and rustle up bangers (sausages) and mash, devouring them during intense debates about girls.

There was also a lot of serious discussion about the meaning of life and dissertations on poetry and music. And, even then, an unusual amount of introspection. "Dudley talked a lot about how he felt and why he felt that way," says Teifion—"much more than most teenagers do at that age. I think that's what led him later into analysis."

Invariably these serious ruminations would give way to musical jam sessions. They closed the curtains and larked around, with Dudley playing the piano, Lenny the flute, and Tony the violin, while Teifion played a tea-chest and broom like a bass. "It was hilarious," the Welshman recalls— "a bit like Tom and Jerry."

Dudley always regarded these visits as a treat and was particularly fond of Teifion's parents, whom he found unusually warm and tolerant.

His own parents, however, were less receptive to the outside world, and Teifion often found it quite difficult to get past Ada Moore when he went down the road to visit his friend. Sometimes when he called round, Ada would stand firmly in the doorway and put him off by saying Dudley was out or busy. "She lived a fairly strict routine," says Teifion, "which was a very ordered and structured existence. It was always extremely difficult to get into their house after a certain time of night, and if she was listening to the radio, she would put a cloth round the doorknocker so they wouldn't be disturbed."

Though Ada seemed not to relish some of the company her son was keeping, Teifion regarded her as a caring and protective mother. "Maybe she thought we would be deflecting Dudley from his studies," he considers. "It was silly really, because he was so very bright."

Still, there were many occasions on which Teifion did get past Ada Moore's commanding presence at the front door, and on those evenings he would delight in watching Dudley play the piano in the front lounge while Sparky the cat curled up in the armchair listening to the music.

"Dudley was very excited when he found something new and interesting," says Teifion. "He wanted to share it with people, and he'd say, 'Come and listen to this,' and then play some wonderful Bach piece that he'd latched on to. It was very good for my musical education."

Dudley's social life was becoming packed full. He was now one of the leading lights of his small community and, according to Peter Cork, one of the most popular boys in his school. "He had this amazing capacity to make everybody laugh. I would just get the choir to a serious moment, when Dudley, who was my piano accompanist, would twinkle with something and the whole thing would collapse. I used to get so angry about it, but it was typical of him."

Teifion Griffiths remembers Dudley being in great demand at parties, where he would sing silly songs at the piano in his highest squeaky soprano—the sort of things he would later do in his professional career.

For the last year, Dudley had been hanging out at Kingsley Hall, a Methodist community center run by Sidney Russell, a tall, thin, and deeply intense man. It was similar to a center that Gandhi had run in India; in fact, Gandhi had visited and stayed at Kingsley Hall in earlier years.

At Kingsley Hall Dudley often played the piano for the old people—to the delight of Sidney Russell—while Peter Cork organized concerts with the school choir and orchestras. On one occasion, Dame Sybil Thorndike came to the Hall, and two boys were invited to solo there. Dudley was one of them. "He played the violin," recalls Cork, "and Dame Sybil was very taken with him. He thinks he never mastered the violin, but he really was very good, and I remember writing something for him that he performed with the orchestra."

Russell was particularly fond of Dudley, and he felt sorry for the teenager who had so much talent but no money for little pleasures. He was very generous to him and helped him in small financial ways—buying him books that he needed, or occasionally giving him money to go to the theater. But Russell's sexual orientation was open to question, and Dudley remembers feeling distinctly uncomfortable every time Russell embraced him. "He would sort of hold me very tightly, and I got a sense of some mild 'stuff' going on. I didn't like that at all."

Teifion Griffiths found Russell "a rather creepy fellow" and never warmed to him at all. "I think he found Dudley an attractive person to have around, but Dudley was always wary of him."

Jim Johnson, another teenage habitué of Kingsley Hall, was aware of their misgivings. "Sidney Russell," he recalls, "had a popular phrase that was 'demonstrative affection,' and it was a euphemism for wanting physical contact.

"We knew that Sidney Russell was different from our own mates who liked to cuddle girls, and his 'demonstrative affection' sometimes made us feel uncomfortable. In those days you didn't even say the word 'homosexual.' But we respected him enormously, and he was very discreet. He would never have done anything to tip him over the edge or bring bad publicity to Kingsley Hall, which he loved very much."

Jim was a year younger than Dudley and the star piano player at Kingsley Hall, where he played regularly in religious services. The two had met when the County High School choir had gone to Kingsley Hall to sing Handel's *Messiah*. Dudley accompanied on the piano, and Jim Johnson, who was standing at the back of the hall, remembers being "absolutely gobsmacked by his playing. And I was a bit put out, too. It was a wonderful and definitive performance, and I was teased unmercifully about it afterwards."

As well as offering entertainment to old people, Kingsley Hall was like a further-education center for the youths of Dagenham. Sidney Russell was a caring, interested figurehead, and under his nurturing eye, the teenagers examined art and literature and learned about travel and subjects not generally available to them—especially to those who attended secondary-modern schools. It opened up a whole new world for their young, receptive minds, and they would never forget the man who influenced them. Years later, as adults, many would return to Kingsley Hall to socialize with old friends or lend a charitable hand, even though they had moved far away.

With Dudley now spending so much time out of the house with his friends, it must have been quite difficult for Ada and Jock fully to appreciate this side of their son's nature, given their own preference for privacy.

"Mrs. Moore used to get into a dressing gown very early in the evening and more or less switch off the house," remembers Teifion. "She and her husband were a bit reclusive, and I don't think they had a lot of visitors. It must have been very odd having this gregarious son, with people knocking on the door, always hanging around in the road, shouting and singing and generally behaving in a very extrovert way.

"Jock was a nice bloke—very quiet and timid, a gentle man. He was very shy and pleasant, quite warm. He'd always smile and say come in. His wife was the dominant partner. She was perfectly affable whenever I spoke to her, except that she didn't always invite me inside. She was a fairly brusque woman. Brusque and intense. A heady combination. I think Dudley found her both warm and cold."

Teifion's own parents were much more outgoing, and they loved having Dudley around to their house. Mrs. Griffiths adored him, which sometimes irritated Teifion. "I used to find it pretty annoying. Whenever we had run-ins, she'd say, 'Why can't you be a nice boy like Dudley?' He had extraordinary charm and that used to get up my nose a bit. Not only was I in his shadow as far as the fact that he was skillful, but also my parents thought he was a well-behaved, charming lad, while I was pictured as a naughty boy."

Dudley probably got a few giggles out of that, because he was very much the ringleader in their antics. Which led him into trouble on more than one occasion.

The two boys used to annoy the locals with their habit of running around shrieking, "It can't go on! It can't go on!" in high, squeaky tones. "Dudley was a big one for shouting out crazy things in funny voices," recalls Teifion. "I think he was practicing for later years.

"One night we were standing by a lamppost making our stupid noises and laughing as usual, and a couple of roughnecks came along. Dudley was looking right at one of them and they assumed that we were taking the piss out of them, so one of them turned round and thumped Dudley."

Peter Cork had cause to remember the incident. "He turned up in school the next day with a black eye. It wasn't great timing, because we had to take the school photograph that morning. I think he told his mother he'd walked into a door." Actually Dudley told her that he had fallen off a chair, and she never questioned his story.

Teifion had a girlfriend, Ruth Levine, and she was very excited to learn that Marie-José, a French exchange student, was coming to live with her family for a while. She invited Dudley and Teifion to go with her to meet the French girl when she arrived, and one Saturday afternoon the three of them trundled off to Ilford to greet her off the coach.

"When she emerged from the bus," Teifion recalls, "Dudley was immediately bowled over by her. She looked a bit like Leslie Caron. We took her back to Ruth's house, and Dudley hung around there for the rest of the day. He was terribly smitten with her."

Marie-José became Dudley's first real love.

She was a warm, gregarious girl with a radiant smile and a provocative overbite that Dudley adored. They became close friends very quickly, and their friendship soon advanced into vague sexual excursions that mainly consisted of passionate smooching and physical explorations of each other's intimate possessions.

"He went overboard about her," recalls Peter Cork. "We used to have exchange students at the school, so she joined us for a while. They were always together, and it was a pretty deep relationship."

After Marie-José returned to France, Dudley went to Paris on a school trip, feeling very elegant in his new prefect's blazer and hoping she would come to meet him. He was crushed when she didn't show up. Soon after, however, he returned to France—this time at the invitation of her parents. He stayed with the family in the French countryside of Noisy-le-Grand, just outside Paris, enchanting them with his piano playing, but finding it rough going since no one in the family except Marie-José spoke English.

The relationship progressed in the gazebo in her garden, but it never went further than "a certain dipping in of the toe," because, without knowing why, Dudley was scared to make love properly.

Undeterred, Marie-José stole some condoms from her stepfather and tried to persuade Dudley by dangling them in front of him. But he refused to use them and was obsessed that their absence would be noticed. "I was terrified that her stepfather would count them and find some missing, so I made her put them back."

Despite Dudley's interest in girls, it was music that dominated his passion. By now his organ accomplishments at St. Thomas's were earning him one guinea a performance at church weddings, which was a small fortune in those days. One Sunday he racked up five weddings and made over five pounds. To his parents, that equaled five weeks' rent.

Church music had become a central part of his existence, and Dudley eagerly looked forward to choir practice on Thursday nights and the serious choir singing on Sundays and holidays in a full church. He had never lost his pleasure in looking down on the congregation. Perhaps, given his sensitivity about his height, it made him feel taller. He was so enveloped by his zeal that, as adulthood loomed, he discarded his ideas of becoming a violinist and thought instead of becoming a church organist and choirmaster.

But Dudley's musical horizons were about to widen. Drastically. He heard a record of Erroll Garner playing "The Way You Look Tonight," and in it discovered a whole new arena—jazz.

He was fascinated by Garner's style—"the steady beat in the left hand and the way the melody sort of wriggled around inside that rhythm"—and he became a frequent visitor to the local music shop, where he would pick up whatever he could find by Garner.

There was a jazz record club in Dagenham, and Dudley began dropping in on the sessions. Gradually he learned to appreciate the virtuosity of Oscar Peterson and George Shearing (who would later become his friends), and Fats Waller and Stan Kenton. But Erroll Garner remained a massive influence. Dudley wallowed in his sound and began experimenting with it himself on the piano.

Occasionally he took acting roles in school; at Christmas he played the angel in the local pageant. However, he crossed swords now and then with Mr. Grainger, the headmaster, who thought Dudley was a bad influence because he was always clowning around. This ruined his chances of becoming head boy, which he had longed for, and, instead, he ended up as deputy head boy.

Barbara, now twenty-one, remained extremely fond of her brother and, during an end-of-term holiday, took him for a fortnight to Bournemouth, where at night they gorged themselves on concerts and the cinema. "We were quite close and got on very well together," she says, "but I'd still admonish him if necessary. I used to tell him off at breakfast that he hadn't washed his neck—things like that. He was at a Just William age then and wasn't worried about his appearance."

Dudley was working hard again and striving for good grades, knowing he'd need them if he was to have any chance of going to university. He had acquired eight O levels and was taking three A levels, in French, Latin, and Music. By now he'd also been attending the Guildhall for five years.

Peter Cork isn't sure whether it was he or the headmaster who came up with the idea, but one of them suggested that Dudley apply for an organ scholarship to university. "His musical talents overflowed in all directions, but his capability on the organ was incredible."

Dudley was happy to entertain the suggestion. He was anxious to please people, and it seemed a distinguished thing to do. Besides which, he was passionate to go to university.

He entered a competition for an organ scholarship at Cambridge, but was so desperately nervous that he botched the examination. When the opportunity arose to qualify for Oxford, he was convinced, after the Cambridge experience, that he didn't have a chance and determined at least to relax and enjoy himself.

His specially crafted playing shoe provoked some eyebrow-raising when he produced it. "There I was, going in for my organ scholarship at Oxford and saying, 'Will you excuse me? I just have to put on this contraption.' And out came this old brown shoe of my mother's with the boot lace tied around the back of my leg. I was still very self-conscious of my foot, so for me to do that showed just how much I wanted to get into university."

Returning home after the examination, Dudley told his parents he thought he had played quite well and had a fifty-fifty chance. According to Jock's diary, he spent the next two days in "restless and distracted anticipation." By the third day, when the letter arrived from Oxford to say whether or not he'd been accepted, he was a nervous wreck.

So was his mother. She took the letter into his bedroom and he opened it with quivering hands. "We are pleased to announce," it said, "that you have won a McKinnon Organ Scholarship to Magdalen College."

Dudley was beside himself with excitement. He couldn't believe his luck. As for his mother, "She snatched up that letter and went running out of the house, down the road, shouting, 'My son's going to university!' I was highly embarrassed and froze up there in the bedroom, hearing her screaming down the street like Archimedes!" Ada Moore had hoped

Dudley might become a professional organist and had prayed hard for his acceptance into Oxford, and now the dream she had cherished for her son had come true.

Dudley's parents weren't the only ones to be thrilled at the news. Over at the County High, there was absolute jubilation. "It was a tremendous boost to the school," recalls Peter Cork. "This was Dagenham, after all, and for somebody to get into university was a certain cachet. But to get into Oxford, and to get a scholarship to Oxford, was a wonderful achievement. The headmaster was so delighted that he gave the whole school a half-day holiday in honor of the occasion!"

Dudley was no slouch when it came to celebrating, and he and Teifion downed countless cider toasts in his honor. "Dudley used to carry a flagon of cider under his arm as he walked around," Teifion recalls. "We used to think he was very, very daring!"

Dudley's last school year was spent preparing for Oxford, although he remembers not applying himself particularly hard. "I was supposed to study, but I stayed away from music lessons a lot because I disagreed with Peter Cork on certain theoretical points."

Cork has no recollection of any discord, though he concedes they probably argued a lot. "There wasn't much to do during that last period except study composition. And with Dudley he could wait till the very last moment and produce something remarkable."

There was a lot of partying during that last year, and Dudley's talents were constantly in demand. "He did a Schubert parody, *Die Flabbergast*," Peter Cork recalls, "and the reaction was of tremendous amusement. Everybody loved it. I used to improvise around the tunes of the day, and Dudley once said, 'I wish I could play chords like you.' Which was a bit rich, really, when you consider what he went on to do!"

There was a slight hiccup when Dudley was mistakenly called up for national service. Somehow the news of his university place—which would have exempted him—had not been relayed by the school to the authorities, and that left him eligible for the draft. In a spirit of patriotism, he trundled off for a medical exam, which, not surprisingly because of his clubfoot, he failed. "I was very thankful," he admits, "because I was so anxious to go to Oxford. I couldn't wait to get there."

But his excitement was about to take a monstrous dive into disillusionment. Dudley was about to enter the real world.

CHAPTER 3

OXFORD

1954-1958

"The name 'Cuddly Dudley' began at Oxford, and it's stuck with him ever since. But he was called that with good reason. He had an unforced, unpretentious wit that was very appealing, and people genuinely admired and liked him very much."

—PATRICK GARLAND

Dudley was not prepared for Oxford. After years of dreaming of university, he was in for a major disappointment when he got there.

Desperately intimidated by the other students, he hated university life from the start. He felt ill-equipped to be in the presence of very superior beings who had enjoyed a classical education, were older, and had done national service. All the old anxieties began to resurface—along with a new one.

Dudley had vaulted over the class barrier by winning a scholarship to the university, but he now became acutely aware of his working-class background. Surrounded by upper-class accents in Magdalen College, he felt more inadequate than ever.

Class was a strong presence in England, and Dagenham-bred Dudley now became very conscious of it. The upper-class students around him had a smoothness and polish that he felt far beyond him. He sensed that money had given them a sense of security he had never had. And he was intimidated by their voices.

Oxford was then, as it remains today, one of the most beautiful universities in England. Its sweeping English lawns, shaded by age-old trees, provided the perfect pastoral setting for the cloisters of the colleges. It was dotted with chapels and bell towers, and so moved was Dudley by the beauty of the Magdalen Tower spire that decades later he would reprint it on Christmas cards.

His room lay at the top of a dark, narrow, twisting staircase in St. Swithin's Quad. There was an upright piano in one corner and a record player in another, and a table, chair, and bed filled the rest of the room. His scout—the porter who made Dudley's bed every morning and brought him hot water with which to wash—was called Haynes.

Magdalen was one of three Oxford colleges with the strongest choral tradition. It had its own choir, and organ scholars were also cathedral organists who played at daily services. The chapel at Magdalen was one of the most exquisite in Oxford, and Dudley found its beauty quite over-whelming. "There I was," he reflects, "this clubfooted wanker sitting on the organ seat, playing this beautiful organ in this stunning chapel. I felt I really didn't deserve to be there."

In his autobiography, *The Long-Distance Runner*, Tony Richardson wrote that "Freedom was the most vital release Oxford gave anyone. Achievement wasn't the aim—unless you wanted to achieve... Forget all other pressures... Find yourself by being without pressure. Spend the days drinking coffee in the cafes, lying in the grass, drinking late at night in your rooms. Find yourself with people doing the same as you..."

This, then, was the environment in which Dudley found himself in the autumn of 1954. But it was hard for him to experience the freedom and light-heartedness that Richardson had enjoyed six years earlier. All he could feel was that he did not fit in with the austere surroundings.

Peter Cork has strong recollections of Dudley's anxiety at that time. "He'd come from a very humble background, and going from that council home into the intellectual society of Magdalen College was quite a shock to him. He felt very much a fish out of water."

Theater director Anthony Page was an Oxford contemporary to whom Dudley often voiced his unhappiness. Frequent visitors to each other's rooms, they enjoyed deep, introspective discussions over countless pots of tea. And it was during these times that Page first sensed the early shades of the darkness that would plague Dudley intermittently throughout his life. "There was always a rather melancholy side to him," he reflects, "and that was fueled partly by his temperament and partly also by the fact that the dean was rather old-fashioned and class-conscious and conse-quently that was reflected a bit in the snobby social life of the college. I found it very refreshing that Dudley wasn't a stuffed shirt. There was always something very original and unique about him."

In spite of Dudley's anxiety, every now and then his penchant for humor would briefly arise. One of his music teachers had a stammer and, meeting his new students for the first time, he addressed Dudley. "What's your na...na...name?" he asked. Dudley looked at him innocently. "Mo...mo...Moore!" he replied, and a titter ran round the classroom.

Social occasions were agony to Dudley. He remembers going to one party with his heart in his mouth lest he put a foot out of place and being asked if he would like black or white coffee. Coffee, being expensive, was a rare treat for Dudley "and not knowing what was meant by 'black or white,' I selected very gratuitously the word 'black' and was given a cup of black coffee. I looked at it and said, 'Well, can't I have some milk then?'"

His young friend, Teifion Griffiths, visited Dudley and found him at odds with his surroundings. "Oxford was a fairly rarefied atmosphere, and it was confusing for Dudley to find himself around people with money and different social mores, coming as he did from a working-class estate. It was something of a culture shock for him."

Dudley's letters home to his parents reflected none of his insecurities. They talked of endless choir services and organ playing, and gave explicit diagrams of the campus and how to find his college when they came to visit.

But there were some light moments. At nineteen, Dudley got drunk for the first time and fell in the river. "It was a wonderful experience," he recalls. "Some people on the bank saw it and asked me to jump again, so they could take a photo. Which I did. And they sent me some prints."

Academically, he was working very hard, his days an organized jumble of tutorials and research. He sang in the choir and played violin and piano in the orchestra and the organ at chapel services. Formal education was confined to the academic theory of music.

Dudley's music tutor, Dr. Bernard Rose, found his young student very appealing. "He was a very cuddly sort of a chap with a great sense of humor. He used to come to tutorials with another student, Anthony Sharp, and between them they were extremely amusing and good fun. Our tutorials were never terribly serious affairs.

"Dudley was a very good violinist and extremely talented with the organ and piano. I knew of course about his clubfoot, but he had a special shoe that he wore for playing and it never seemed to restrict him."

Years later, Bernard Rose was cleaning out a cupboard in the organ loft and found a strange contraption. "After some mild curiosity about what it was, I remembered it was Dudley's old playing shoe."

Dudley's first two years were miserably insecure, although he made a few friends and felt particularly close to David Lloyd-Jones, then an expert on Borodin who would later become conductor of the Welsh Symphony.

On occasions, friends from Dagenham came to visit. Jim Johnson, who was now in the Royal Air Force, trekked from his base with a friend and was amazed to see in Dudley's room more books than he'd ever seen before in his life. "Dagenham wasn't like that. None of us had come from a literary background, so we weren't used to seeing lots of books." He persuaded Dudley to play the piano, and "My friend stood there with his mouth wide open, because he had never heard anything like it."

The toughest part of Dudley's first few years was "not knowing how to open my mouth without having it sound like an old saw, because, coming from Dagenham, I spoke in a very sloppy suburban accent." He tried imitating other students, but ended up with "a peculiar voice with vowels lurching in every direction and no idea where they were going to land."

Dudley welcomed his end-of-term visits home, although initially they were disorientating. Returning to Dagenham's working-class environment at first made him uncomfortable. Although he had not picked up an upper-class accent, his voice had nevertheless changed and he felt as if he were speaking a different language, which people viewed as strange. For the first time he felt trapped by the suburbia in which he'd grown up. Oxford had exposed him to wider thought and another view of life. He was realizing that there was a huge world outside of Dagenham, and it was one he wanted to discover.

After a few days, however, he resumed his social life at home with relish. He took long hikes with Teifion Griffiths, who reveled in Dudley's stories of the various snobbish characters he'd met at Oxford. Sometimes they cycled into the farming country just a few miles away, where they would listen to the wind and talk about unrequited love. Dudley had visited Marie-José in France one more time, but, to his dismay, their affair had petered out. His girlfriend now was Jean Priest, a secretary in Dagenham, but Dudley was still afraid of sex and theirs was more a platonic relationship, though he was very fond of her.

Dudley still sang with the choir at St. Thomas's when he was home, and played the piano for the old people at Kingsley Hall. He wanted in some way to repay Sidney Russell for his kindness. Russell had bought him books that he had needed for Oxford, and had paid for his specially made organ-playing boot, the cost of which had been beyond the resources of the Moores.

"Money was very tight for my parents then, because Barbara got married around the time I went to Oxford, so they had to cash in their life-insurance policies to take care of everything. Even though I'd won a scholarship, I still needed money for various odds and sods."

Dudley was living very frugally at Oxford on the few pounds that he had, and he saved carefully for extra clothes. In a letter to his parents in December 1955, he related how, after saving enough money, he had gone down to the local shop to buy the waistcoat for which he'd been yearning. "I went with my money, gazed at it outside the window for about a quarter of an hour, then decided I would buy some books instead. I can't lash out much on clothes and I think the waistcoat I have at present will suffice."

Dudley still had one habit that he had not shaken off.

He had discovered in a music shop in Oxford a record by Mado Robin, the French coloratura soprano who had years earlier been such a source of inspiration for his ineluctable sexual activities. On this record, Robin sang the highest note ever recorded, and, just like years before, Dudley's whole body trembled when he heard it. He didn't dare buy the record, because he knew it would keep him from studying; instead, he took to frequenting the music shop. There, wearing his father's raincoat, he would slip into a glass booth and play certain tracks to which he would masturbate. "The owners of the shop always wondered why I never bought the record," he says. But eventually he did. And he didn't leave his room for a week.

Through his traumatic childhood, Dudley had become accustomed, though hardly inured, to being treated with disdain. Suffering it again at Oxford, although this time it was because of his background rather than his physical appearance, he tried to shrug off his peers' insensitivity by keeping one colorful vision in mind as his incentive. "I was fascinated by the image of some luscious creature leaning across the piano while I played, whispering requests and making overtures."

Although no such fantasy was realized at that time—and, anyway, Dudley was still feeling fairly loyal to Jean Priest, who often came to visit him—it was a picture he kept vibrantly alive in his head. One day, he vowed, it would become real. But he could never imagine the extent to which it would happen.

Dudley's music was paramount in his life and, in addition to his musical studies, he now belonged to several musical societies. Anthony Page, who regarded Dudley as a considerable musical talent, spent many hours discussing music with him.

Dudley's sister had moved with her husband Bernard and their baby daughter Helen to Burford, about ten miles outside Oxford, and she visited Dudley on his twenty-first birthday, in 1956. By then he had settled down more, and he was proud to show her round the college he so admired. "He had a room that overlooked the deer park at the back," she recalls, "and he used to put a big load of salt on the windowsill because the deer loved licking salt. He was pretty involved by then as an organist, and I remember he had to leave early and dash to evensong because the main organist had become ill."

Dudley had become a prominent member of the Oxford University Orchestra and was constantly playing at their concerts. Now he turned toward acting.

Both Oxford and Cambridge universities were nationally recognized for their tradition of amateur theatricals. Their legendary rivalry, famously manifest in the annual Boat Race, also encompassed a continuous stream of theatrical productions, and these were a compelling attraction for the undergraduates of each university. Cambridge had its revered Footlights Club; Oxford the Dramatic Society (OUDS) and the Experimental Theatre Club (ETC).

Dudley joined the ETC, which tended to include lighter material than its more heavyweight sister, OUDS, and Anthony Page, who had now begun directing plays, decided to cast him in *Antony and Cleopatra*. Dudley vividly recalls one of the performances, which took place in a small Elizabethan theater in Abingdon. He played Enobarbus and, to disguise the thinness of his left leg, he wore a piece of fluttery cotton that hung down from the knee. "I remember a guy called Richard Selig laughing very audibly all the way through my death scene, which I thought was a bit unfair on me."

Dudley may not have been satisfied with his performance, but Anthony Page, who was particularly impressed with the music he wrote for the play, found him capable and responsive and cast him in many of his subsequent productions.

Despite the hardship of a lack of funds, Dudley was surviving well enough. He kept on hand a good stock of jam, marmalade, Marmite, and fish paste and tried to allay his mother's worries that he wasn't eating enough. Indeed, in a letter to his parents in October 1956, he proudly told them of a recent evening when he had chipped in with some other students. "We bought bread, butter, corned beef, tomatoes, and cheese for dinner. It was very cheap and, boy, was it filling! We could hardly move after such a banquet!"

One of his few luxuries was to allow himself the *Radio Times* every week, so that he could schedule concerts to listen to on his tiny radio. Occasionally there was a gift of a couple of pounds from someone in Dagenham, and this would carry him through the next several weeks. As meticulous as his mother in such matters, he would take his couple of banknotes and deposit them in the bank, carefully logging such entries in his diary.

Whenever she could, Ada Moore sent care packages to her son, and she even managed to do his washing through the mail. Dudley recalls sending her his dirty clothes, which within the week would return all neatly laundered and wrapped up with a bag of sherbet lemons.

It was around this time that Dudley met fellow student John Bassett and began a lifelong friendship.

Anthony Page was directing *The Changeling* and persuaded Bassett to play the trumpet while Dudley played the organ. "It was a nice bit of music that any trumpeter worthy of the name could have played with some ease," recalls Bassett, "but clearly I did not deserve the title. Dudley was very kind and didn't let on that I couldn't play a note, and whenever I let forth with my piercing notes he would play something that went with it rather than what he had already written."

Dudley also acted as a deaf mute in the production and had to play the violin while scampering up and down stairs at the same time. But, because he had one leg shorter than the other, the effect was unintentionally hilarious.

Dudley's work in *The Changeling* was, to Anthony Page, "very moving and very spontaneous. He wrote the most wonderful music, and was very resourceful. There was an incredible inventiveness and musicality about him. He was exceptionally talented and a pleasure to work with because he was also very amusing to be around."

With Page's appreciation of Dudley, John Bassett saw an increased confidence beginning to take hold of his new friend. It seemed to him that Dudley took great pleasure in his talent being wanted and needed. Although Bassett had not known him before then, he had the impression that these were first steps into a social world that Dudley would never have taken without Anthony Page's enlistment of his talent.

Though some of Dudley's insecurities were now subsiding, he still felt very much outside of the mainstream. Yet it's interesting to note that, while he considered himself largely unhappy and inferior to his peers, the perception of the people around him at that time was markedly different.

"He never gave me the impression he was unhappy," says his music tutor, Bernard Rose. "But, if he was, I was certainly never aware of it. He always seemed to be having a good time and making jokes."

Barbara, visiting Dudley one weekend, thought he looked particularly happy. And his parents also commented on his contented state—although Jock's diary entries talked mainly about his campus activities, which seemed pretty varied.

"I know Dudley was very nervous as a working-class lad coming to such a nobby place," reflects John Bassett, "but his music encircled him. It was the one thing he was superb at, so I got the impression that the social questions didn't come into play."

Perhaps the disparity is explained most succinctly by Teifion Griffiths. "Dudley was a chameleon. He could carry off most things using his funny accents and different voices, so unless he chose to talk about it one would not have known he was feeling at all anxious."

John Bassett had his own jazz band at Oxford, The Bassett Hounds, which played regularly in The Cellars, a campus night haunt. "Dudley loved jazz but didn't really know a thing about it. He wanted to know how jazz was made, and he cracked the code in five seconds flat. After that, he began playing with us on Saturdays, and he soon became very popular."

By day Dudley was studying classical music; by night he was playing jazz in the student nightclubs. The applause he heard boosted his self-esteem and his confidence now soared.

In the midst of a very crammed academic life, Dudley still looked forward to occasional visits from Teifion Griffiths, who had now joined the army. On his way to his army base for his initiative test, Teifion stopped at Oxford and found Dudley standing in that night as organist. The two went off together to evensong, and Dudley told his friend, "Listen carefully for the music and you'll hear 'Blowing Wild,' that pop song by Frankie Laine." "Sure enough," recalls Teifion, "there it was. He did that a lot. He'd slide in the pop songs of the day in the style of a perfectly straight Bach-style fugue. And he did it effortlessly."

To Teifion's eyes, Dudley seemed much happier than when he'd last seen him, and he was struck by the steady stream of people that flowed in and out of his room. The two stayed up talking and clowning around until four in the morning, when Teifion sneaked out of the window to hitch a lift to his base.

Now in his third year, Dudley's penchant for humor was making itself well-known. Through his attachment to The Bassett Hounds, he had begun writing sketches and performing outrageously comic and bold improvisations. And his musical parodies were like nothing heard before. He found himself increasingly being requested for cabarets. There were more acting stints and piano solos for the Film Society. And a growing number of parties. No longer did he feel out of place. He had rediscovered comedy. Dudley felt like the school clown all over again—"a guy who improvised and generally made a fool of himself."

Years later he would rationalize his early commitment to comedy: "The whole motivation comes from a fear of expressing rage, so you do it obliquely. Being funny renders you innocuous, but it also allows you to be hostile without its being felt as hostility by others."

Dudley was enjoying comedy more and more. It was becoming an obsession alongside his music. Eventually it would supersede even that. Once again, he had found the acceptance he craved by making people laugh. Dudley Moore had become Oxford University's Clown Prince.

He was now so much in demand that the diaries he kept while at Oxford, at first so sparse on the social side, became a jumble of engagements from organ practices and orchestral recitals to jazz concerts and cabaret. And there were innumerable dinners with fellow students.

Theater director Patrick Garland, two years younger than Dudley, was at Oxford and remembers being very struck by Dudley's performing capabilities and charm. "He had become one of the most prominent humorists in Oxford. He was unquestionably The Star and was gifted with immense spontaneity. Some people are natural clowns, and Dudley had that clown quality about him. Much of his later works were based very much on what he was doing in Oxford in the mid-fifties. What was particularly sweet was his tremendously affectionate nature, and it seems to me he's never really altered. Although I scarcely knew him, I admired him enormously from afar."

The admiration turned out to be mutual, because almost two decades later Dudley would name his son after Patrick Garland, although it would be many years more before Garland would learn of it.

By now, it was becoming clear that Dudley was a serious hit with the female sex. He was still racked with self-doubts, but, perhaps because of his humble view of himself, he discovered that women found him incredibly attractive.

"He had terrific success with the ladies," recalls Patrick Garland, "but not so much because he was good-looking, I think, but for the better reason that he was naturally funny, and girls like men that make them laugh.

"We all thought Dudley would go on to become one of the premier funny men, but the thought of him becoming a handsome sex symbol was something none of us would have ever believed possible, although he was always very attractive."

Dudley had now proven himself in several dramatic productions, many for Anthony Page, and he found that acting gave him a tremendous surge of self-esteem. Playing characters such as Autolycus and Offenbach's Orpheus, his performances won praise both from his fellow actors and from other students.

His natural and spontaneous comedic quality was apparent to everyone, but, as he told Patrick Garland, it became a slight embarrassment to him—though he didn't allow it to oppress him. There were many college parties and sometimes Dudley would arrive and see all the guests sitting in a semicircle waiting for him to turn on an act and let the show begin. "I think he got quite irritated by that," says Garland, "although it was a compliment to him."

In spite of his embarrassment, Dudley was greatly flattered by the attention he was receiving. He was so elated that in 1957, after taking his Bachelor of Arts degree in music, he opted to remain for another year to study for a Bachelor of Music degree in composition. Celebrity was a novel delight for Dudley and an experience he wanted to perpetuate. That it came in his third year was not the best of timing, since it was his finals year and he had to prepare for exams. But by now he'd become intoxicated by the reaction of audiences and the applause and the laughter.

Dudley did not collect his B.A. until years later, but, as a graduate, he could now wear a gown as a symbol of his achievement. In a letter to his parents in March 1958, he described his graduating gown. "It cost four guineas but my hood is a very splendid affair being much more impressive than most of the other types."

He went on to ask if they would object to his touring Europe with John Bassett's jazz band during the summer holidays, and then revealed an upcoming engagement. "I am playing at the Albert Hall, fee ten guineas, for a big meeting in connection with my tutor's brother-in-law (Lord Chesham) on April 25th. Should be good fun! Winston Churchill will most likely be there, he is the chairman of the committee."

Dudley Moore had come a long way from the day he had first walked so nervously through the portals of Magdalen College. No longer was he condemned as the runt of the litter, the child no one wanted, the boy everyone picked on because of his height and his foot. Now they picked on him for entirely different reasons. He may have been small, but his quick wit, cherubic features, and brilliance on the piano made him a romantic target for the girls at Oxford.

Yet for all his romantic entanglements, he had yet fully to consummate a relationship. At twenty-three, Dudley was still a virgin.

His last few months at Oxford were packed solid with university cabarets and concerts. So crammed now was his time that the diary note of his treatise deadline had to be squeezed in between masses of engagements and countless scribbled notes for sketch ideas.

Outside Oxford, he performed with Prunella Scales at the Royal Court cabaret—an occasion he looks back on with great fondness, for he found Prunella to be an enchanting, funny girl. And there was a college revue that the ETC group took to the Edinburgh Festival as a fringe performance.

It was in Edinburgh that Dudley would finally shed his sexual apprehensions.

One of the actresses who was attending the Festival was particularly attractive, and Dudley watched, fascinated, as the other men circled her like peacocks. He persuaded her to go out with him, and during their conversation the subject somehow arose that he had never yet made love to a woman. She, being slightly older than him and considerably more experienced, was intrigued by the revelation and convinced him to try out this unfamiliar activity.

They arranged to meet at midnight in Oxford, but she missed the last train from London and Dudley had to wait with fear and anticipation until five in the morning, when she arrived on the milk train. "We had to check into a hotel as a married couple," recalls Dudley, "and I was terribly embarrassed."

Afterward, he viewed the entire experience rather dispassionately. It had not been particularly earth-shattering, and really the anticipation had probably been more exciting than its fruition.

Though he saw her again a few times, it was only as a friend. For her, this had clearly been a one-night stand, but he was disappointed not to be able to pursue the brief intimacy they had established. He had felt, in a way, connected to her. She, in an entirely different way, felt connected to him, too, since shortly after their encounter, she discovered she was pregnant—a situation she resolved with great alacrity.

In June, Magdalen College held its traditional Commemorative May Ball, marking the end of Trinity Term. It was a grand and glittering occasion, and the John Dankworth Band were hired as the main attraction. Cleo Laine, not yet married to Dankworth, sang with the band, and when they ended at 3 A.M., they adjourned to another room for a buffet breakfast.

"As we were serving ourselves," recalls John Dankworth, "we became conscious of some wonderful jazz being played. We looked around to see if it was a record and realized it came from an upright piano that had its back to us. Someone was playing on the other side, and it was obviously someone very good who knew what they were doing.

"We listened for about fifteen minutes while we ate breakfast, and then decided to see who was creating this sound. We went around the piano and there was Dudley playing. We congratulated him and had a chat. He knew who we were and was pleased to be noticed, and I told him, 'If you're ever short of a job, let me know, because you'd make a good pianist for the band.'"

Dudley was thrilled at the chance encounter, then put it out of his mind to prepare in earnest for his looming Bachelor of Music degree. "Typically, he'd left it till the last moment," recalls Peter Cork. "He had to compose a piece, and he literally ended up writing a string quartet in the last fortnight before it was due."

Dudley wryly recalls his efforts. "Talk about doing stuff by candlelight! That's literally what I was doing into the early hours, trying to finish this quartet that I'd been committed to. When I heard it much later, I was amazed at how much feeling there was in it."

As his tutor, Bernard Rose, reflects, "If he'd done more work he would have got a first-class degree. In fact he got a second. But then he was doing so many things he couldn't possibly have done them all and done them brilliantly. The interesting thing was that I could never tell whether he'd go the classical music route or the jazz route. In the end, he did both."

There was no question that Dudley was an outstanding organist and, in a move that must have filled his mother with the greatest pride of her life, Bernard Rose offered him the post of organist to Queen's College, which meant also becoming a tutor and choirmaster. It was the culmination of the dream that Ada Moore had carried in her heart for many years.

Overwhelmed by the offer, Dudley thanked Dr. Rose for the wonderful opportunity and left his room. Five minutes later he returned and, in one of the most momentous decisions of his life, told his disappointed tutor, "I don't think this would be the life for me."

It was July 1958, and the world of entertainment had already beckoned. Dudley realized he wanted to be a performer more than anything, and there was no way he could accept this lofty university position while also performing a nightclub act.

And so it was that Dudley Moore at last blew out the flames of his long-smoldering desire to be an organist and choirmaster. Whatever it would take, he was heading for show business, determined to be a comedy and musical entertainer.

But not even he could have imagined the heights to which he would ascend in his newly chosen career.

CHAPTER 4

BEFORE
THE FRINGE

1958-1960

*"He always thought of himself as a funny musician. He never thought he could
be an actor; he never thought he could be acceptable on stage. But he
wanted very much to perform. It was hugely important to him."*

—BEN SHAKTMAN

The great privilege of youth," Patrick Garland would later assert, "is that
it can do things without much effort." Dudley was about to epitomize those
words.

Graduating from Oxford in the summer of 1958, he was passionate
to work, and it didn't matter to him where he did it. Through John
Bassett's mother, he rented a room in the block of flats where she lived in
Hampstead. It was only a bedsitting room, but the landlady, Jill Lobb,
found him enchanting and agreed to let him use the piano and telephone
in her own flat. The rent was ten shillings a week for the tiny room, on top
of which he had to feed money into the meter for the gas fire. He gave a
note to the milkman to leave him one pint a day. Dudley was elated. He was
on his way.

Charming his way into countless auditions, Dudley landed gigs up
and down England, working on sketch ideas every free moment. There
were dates in nightclubs and cabarets, often playing his now clearly defined
Erroll Garner style of jazz, or combining his comic sketches with parodies
of classical music.

One engagement took him to a working men's club in Manchester,
where he found himself sandwiched between a stripper and a comedian.

He played a couple of musical pastiches on the organ—a satire on Schubert's *lieder* and an obscure piece from Benjamin Britten—but his wit sailed over this particular audience's head. "It was desperately embarrassing because nobody took any notice." There was also an appearance on Scottish television, in which he played a sheik and, according to Jock's diary, "fooled all of Scotland."

London at this time was a thriving center of jazz, and Dudley flooded the clubs with pleas to play. One of his first Soho engagements was at Ronnie Scott's jazz club, where Teifion Griffiths went to hear him. "I was still in the army," recalls Teifion, "but I had a few days' leave and I went to see Dudley the first night he was in the club. He was brilliant, of course—no surprise to those of us who had grown up around his talent. He seemed in his element, and it was as much fun to watch him as it was for him to play."

These were exciting times for Dudley. His piano playing thrilled the club audiences, and his adrenaline was flowing. Even though he was living on cornflakes, he never felt deprived. He was having a great time and felt certain he could always earn his living playing in a bar or a club, earning ten shillings a night to pay the rent. He considered himself very lucky.

Dudley had felt greatly imprisoned within the orbit of his family and Dagenham. His music was like a huge jet carrying him off to another world. No wonder he felt lucky. He was free.

He still played occasionally with John Bassett's band, and The Bassett Hounds became a regular sight in London hotels, particularly the Dorchester and the Savoy. And he had now assembled a part-time trio with Hugo Boyd on bass and Derek Hogg on drums.

By now, Dudley's name was turning up as a pianist on lists everywhere, and one of them landed him in ITV's Holborn studio, which was where Barbara Moore, a young jazz singer, first met him.

"I was doing a demo session and had to sing 'I'm a Stranger in Paradise,'" she recalls. "In walked this little chap who said 'Good morning' and sat down, very po-faced. That was Dudley.

"We started running through the piece, and at first he played it straight—pure Borodin. And then we both began to change styles. He started playing it differently and I began to send it up, and in the end we were both wreathed in smiles. The producer wasn't pleased with us at all, but we left the studio just roaring with laughter."

Dudley and Barbara (whose same name as Dudley's sister led to obvious confusion) became firm friends from the start.

Barbara, a divorcée with a four-year-old daughter, was living in her mother's Victorian house at Ealing Common, and every Sunday Dudley went over there with Hugo Boyd, his bass-player friend, to rehearse on her mother's grand piano and enjoy a huge Sunday lunch.

They landed an engagement at the Café des Artistes on the King's Road, for which Dudley's trio was paid the regal sum of two pounds a night. "We were the stars," says Barbara, "but it was a right dump. There was a madman running it who we called Nick the Greek. He swindled everybody—including us—but we had a good time."

While still at Oxford, Anthony Page had arranged for Dudley to audition for George Devine, who ran the Royal Court Theatre. Devine had been unimpressed by his talent. "He told me I had a lot to learn," says Dudley, "which didn't please me, since I was so desperate to land anything I could. Anthony just laughed throughout the whole audition." By now, however, Anthony Page had himself graduated and was a director at the Royal Court, and, although neither he nor Dudley recalls how he got the job, Dudley landed the position there of resident composer writing incidental music for plays for five pounds a week. For the time being, at least, he was assured of being kept in a reasonable supply of cornflakes.

His first assignment came from director Lindsay Anderson, to score *Serjeant Musgrave's Dance*. As Anthony Page recalls, "Dudley tended to work at the last moment, and Lindsay Anderson gave me the task of getting the music out of him. Usually I'd get it by having to stand over him or sit there with him. But the music he came out with was brilliant, and Lindsay loved it."

Other productions followed at the Royal Court Theatre, among them Bill Gaskill's *One Way Pendulum*.

By day, Dudley worked in the theater. Come nighttime it was jazz that continued to engross him. He was convinced that as a jazz musician he would win not only the status he yearned for but also women. And, quite aside from the girls whom he believed he would attract, jazz also appealed to his emotional nature.

He had now become an accomplished jazz pianist, still with a style highly evocative of Erroll Garner. John Dankworth, remembering the young student who had so impressed him at the May Ball, recommended Dudley to noted bandleader Vic Lewis, who was looking for a new pianist.

"There was a knock on my door one morning," recalls Vic Lewis, "and there was this little chap standing on the front doorstep. 'Mr. Lewis, sir,' he said. 'I believe you are looking for a piano player, sir.' He kept on calling me 'sir'; everything was 'sir.' I said, 'Will you drop the "sir"?' 'Yes, sir!' he said. And it went on and on like that."

Lewis took Dudley down to the rehearsal hall and listened to him play. He was impressed. "You play very well," he told him—"a bit like Erroll Garner. But you don't play like that all the time, do you?" Dudley looked at him uncomprehendingly. "What do you mean?" he asked.

"Well," replied Lewis, "you can't be playing your own thing with the band playing their stuff, you know. You have to back them up. When it comes to your solo then you can play like that."

That sounded fine to Dudley and Lewis hired him.

There was just one problem: Dudley continued to play like Erroll Garner, even behind other solos, and the boys in the band didn't like that at all. As Vic Lewis remembers, "I had to pull him aside a few times and say, 'Look, Dud, the idea is when you're in the band you've got to just play the chords, and that gives a rhythm beat to the bass and drums. And you form the rhythm section.'"

To the chagrin of the other players, Dudley continued as before, and some of the band players "would get really pissed off, and tell me so to my face."

Garner had been his first jazz hero and, decades later, Dudley would try to film a documentary about his life. He did once get the chance to meet his idol, but the encounter was disastrous. Garner came to a club where he was working, but in his nervous eagerness to impress this legend, Dudley dropped a bottle of Coke on the keyboard. "Everything from middle C down to G was ruined. I looked at this mess and tried to play— then when I looked up he was gone!"

For the next several months Dudley played three or four dates a week with the Vic Lewis Orchestra, earning around forty pounds a week. Once he settled down, Vic gave him little spots to play with the bass and drums. "I really loved the boy," he says. "He was very kind, although he seemed to have some insecurity. My wife and I became very fond of him and kind of adopted him. He was a very nice young man with a great sense of humor and a huge love of music."

The band played all round England and then, to Dudley's intense excitement, they landed a booking for a six-week American tour of the northern army bases. "It wasn't the best way to see America," he later admitted. "Instead of working the jazz clubs, we played at military camps."

Although Dudley had settled down and was now playing with the band rather than against them, not every member had been won over by the zeal-ous youngster. Especially Roy East, who played alto saxophone, and "hated my guts." But, on the plane over to America, Dudley began to fool around with some comic improvisations and Roy laughed at him for the first time. Now they could be friends. It flashed through Dudley's mind that this was a repeat of what had happened at school. From that moment on he became the clown of the band.

In America, Dudley's enthusiasm could not be contained. Swinging GIs and medics applauded the brassy sounds of the band and, amid the rousing of saxophones and trombones, Dudley pounded the keys of his piano, still very much à la Garner.

At one of the band's last dinners, Dudley sampled oysters for the first time in his life. They didn't go down very well. "I thought it would be desperately exciting," he remembers, "but it was a terrible experience. I was really sick, and haven't said boo to an oyster ever since."

The last venue on the orchestra's tour was New York, and Dudley instantly fell in love with the city. "I was so excited to be there. I remember coming out into Times Square and seeing the steam pouring out of the middle of the road. And that smell of New York has always remained in my mind."

He was captivated by some of the jazz artists that he heard in New York. He went to Birdland and heard the blind pianist Lenny Tristano. And he heard other jazz greats like Dwike Mitchell and Willie Ruff. It was all so exciting for the youngster from Dagenham.

It was no surprise to Vic Lewis that, when it came time for the band to return to England, Dudley decided to remain.

"I was staying on for a bit myself," recalls Vic Lewis, "so I suggested sharing a room together. We stayed at the Forest Hotel and went to masses of clubs and saw a lot of shows. At the end of the two weeks I went back to England, but Dudley stayed on."

New York in the late fifties was a mecca for aspiring jazz musicians, and Dudley sought every opportunity to play. Amid sporadic unemployment and digs at the YMCA, "where I almost got punched up by some bloke who wanted to use the phone while I was on it," he landed odd gigs at some of the seedier clubs. He met Jeanne Gilbert, producer David Merrick's girlfriend, who took him in tow and looked after him. With her help he auditioned for every talk show on the air, from Steve Allen to Ed Sullivan and Jack Paar. But nobody seemed to want him.

John Bassett's mother had told Dudley about the Duplex, a popular nightclub in Greenwich Village, and he landed a brief engagement in its downstairs bar. It was there that Ahmet Ertegun, the president of Atlantic Records, encountered him the night before Dudley was due to return to England.

"This young fellow played fabulously, extremely well," recalls Ertegun—"a little bit in the style of Erroll Garner, though not entirely. He also had his own style about him. I was absolutely dumbstruck, and when he'd played a few numbers I told him, 'My God, you are terrific. Come to my office. I'm the head of Atlantic Records and I'd like to make an album with you.'"

But Dudley explained that he was returning the next day to England. Says Ertegun, "I thought he told me he was sailing back. So I assumed he must be a sailor!"

Although Dudley did not take up Ertegun's offer then, years later he would eventually record albums for the Atlantic label.

That Ahmet Ertegun had been so impressed by Dudley's talent as a pianist came as no surprise to Jan Wallman, who was about to take over the management of the Duplex. "He played marvelously," she recalls, "and that was particularly amazing to us all because it was such a terrible piano that they never bothered to tune. He was wonderful and loads of fun, and he brought something very refreshing and different to that place."

Dudley would have liked to have stayed in New York, but he had become unbearably homesick and yearned for the familiarity of England and his friends and family. And so, in early 1959 at the tender age of twenty-three, he passed up the opportunity he'd just been offered and flew back home.

As it turned out, his timing was perfect. John Dankworth's pianist was leaving, and Dankworth invited Dudley to join his band.

Dankworth ran one of the top bands of the period, and Dudley was thrilled to be given such a grand opportunity. But he was still on his Erroll Garner kick, playing in that style even behind the rest of the band, and there was a lot of disagreement between him and the others as to what chords he should be playing. He got many dirty looks from the saxophone section, who clearly didn't like this young man who'd just joined them.

Some of the band resented that Dudley had not worked his way up through the usual channels: They felt he'd leapfrogged into the job instead of paying his dues. Ironically, given Dudley's earlier encounters at Oxford, they also observed a class difference. This time it was in reverse. By now he had lost his Dagenham accent and the other band members viewed him suspiciously, not certain that he was one of their working-class kind.

Like Vic Lewis, John Dankworth soon discovered Dudley's individuality. "He was quite inexperienced at that kind of band work, which is a skill that's acquired over years. Dudley was a soloist from the start. He wasn't meant to be a rhythm-section pianist, so he didn't have the attributes that would have come if I'd picked an up-and-coming youngster who'd never played with a band in his life."

But ultimately, and talent aside, it was the very quality that had endeared Dudley to Vic Lewis's musicians that finally won over the band members.

"He could be very funny and very spontaneous," recalls Dankworth. "We once had to fly somewhere to play a date and we were all shepherded into the airport departure lounge. There was a picture of the Queen on the wall, and Dudley started doing Queen-like impersonations and really hilarious things. He had the band in stitches, and that's when he won them over."

The band kept Dudley busy at least four nights a week (for which Dankworth believes he was paid about ten pounds a gig, although Dudley thinks it was only five pounds), and he began making television appearances with the band, along with occasional spots of his own or with his trio on *Late Night Line-Up*. That led to their own concert at the Royal Festival Hall.

Dudley was becoming a permanent fixture in the London clubs. His tenure with Dankworth, and his growing renown, had imbued him with more confidence and self-esteem than ever before.

Dudley had always found it hard to accompany other musicians and know exactly what they wanted. The trio allowed him the freedom to play whatever he liked. And it was with his trio that he first met the man who would later become, and remains, one of his dearest friends.

Cambridge University's prestigious Footlights Club—of which Peter Bellwood was president and David Frost secretary—had just opened a club room and, in celebration of the event, they threw several huge parties. People came from all over England—some to party, others to offer their musical talents. Dudley, with Derek Hogg and Hugo Boyd, was among the latter. It was now that he met Peter Bellwood, who recalls the entire evening as "wildly entertaining and never-ending, with a jazz concert that continued through the early hours of the morning."

Dudley's earlier work at the Royal Court had given him a reputation ("deservedly or not") for writing incidental music for plays. Admiring his talent, in early 1960 Lindsay Anderson recommended him to Ben Shaktman, a young American playwright who was in England on a Fulbright Scholarship and had been offered his own production at the Royal Court by George Devine.

Lindsay Anderson and Tony Richardson had committed to Shaktman's idea for a show called *Song in the Theatre*, an evening of songs from stage shows, with scenes from various musicals. Devine assembled a company that included Albert Finney, Alan Dobie, and Zoe Caldwell. And he assigned Dudley as its music director.

"The linchpin of our show," recalls Shaktman, "was a classical Peking opera, *The Jade Princess*, and Dudley had to study this Chinese opera and train the actors to perform it. The challenge was enormous, because he had to help them merge this mercurial type of music with Western tradition.

"The rehearsal was hysterical, because we all had to learn from recordings how to make those sounds. We were monkeys imitating. Dudley had to convert it into something that the Western range could handle and he did it brilliantly. He was a wonderful coach and his musical direction made it delightful. They performed it yeomanly."

Song in the Theatre—for which Dudley also wrote an original song for *As You Like It*—was a huge success, and the *Times*'s critic opined that "Dudley Moore's musical direction made it delightful."

In addition to his theatrical endeavors, Dudley had also been writing jingles for ad agency director Francis Megahy. The two had met some time earlier at a party and had become good friends, and Megahy had persuaded him to write the music for commercials for Persil detergent and Pepsodent toothpaste among others. Megahy had recently begun directing in earnest, and Dudley was scoring Megahy's first film, *Just One More Time*, which would be seen at the London Film Festival.

Dudley and Hugo Boyd still dropped in at Barbara Moore's house some Sundays, and it was on one of these occasions that Barbara saw the comic brilliance of Dudley's improvisational skill.

"One Sunday it was pissing down with rain," she recalls, "and we were all having lunch at the table which looked out on to the garden. My daughter had left a large plastic doll out there. She'd flung it down and it had fallen towards the window with legs akimbo and its dress pulled up.

"Dudley saw that and suddenly his eyes began to glaze over and he let a bit of dribble trickle down his face and went into that awful old cockney man's voice. 'Thar she lies—naked, flagrant, *arsking* for it!' And on and on it went while he got pink and flushed and his fork shook in his hand as he played this frustrated old pedophile. It was extremely funny."

Though he was making good money, Dudley's lifestyle hadn't changed much—except for the acquisition of a Mini with a broken window that cost him forty pounds, after he'd had to abandon his 1935 Austin ("Evie") on the side of a road. He was still a very untidy character, according to Ben Shaktman. "He was incredibly messy. His place was always very cold, and he would work in his father's big, old coat and write on the back of shirt boards. You had to walk up endless stairs to get to the flat, and it was one of those rooms where you had to push stuff away to find a surface to work on. All I really remember is the piano. It was the only thing you could see. Everything else was scattered around it."

Around this time, the BBC's flagship arts program, *Monitor*, made a documentary showing the different lifestyles of two contemporary composers: Dudley and Peter Maxwell Davies. They were the same age, but they lived in a vastly different fashion.

Dudley's sister, Barbara, watched the program with her husband. "It showed Dudley and Peter, each working in their different flats. Peter's was tidy, but Dudley's was dreadful and incredibly messy. We were living on an army base at that time, and one of the wives who lived near us came over and offered to tidy Dudley's flat up for him."

After the favorable reception of *Song in the Theatre*, director Bill Gaskill asked him to write the incidental music for some Royal Shakespeare Company productions, but Dudley claims that Gaskill hated everything he ever wrote. "*Nothing* I did was of interest to him. He kept sending me back to rewrite everything."

Some time later they worked together on a version of *The Caucasian*

Chalk Circle, but again Gaskill was unhappy with Dudley's music and made him continually rewrite.

When Peter Hall took over the production, he remarked to Dudley, "It's not a very good musical score, is it?" To which Dudley wanted to respond, "That's because Bill Gaskill never approves of anything I write in the first place."

About this time, Vic Lewis offered to take Dudley under his wing. "We were very much at the end of the big-band era at that point," recalls Lewis, "and I decided to pack the band in and become an agent. Dudley wanted to go out on his own, and I said, 'Fine, you can sign with me.' So he did, and he became the first artist I ever signed."

Vic booked him into a number of clubs, among them the Cool Elephant and the Blue Angel, where he became a popular draw.

And he now made his first record. "Strictly for the Birds," for the future Beatles producer George Martin, was a jazz rendition of a lullaby that he'd performed at Oxford for a production of Aristophanes' *The Birds*. The flip side of the record was titled "Duddley Dell," intended to be the reverse of "Deadly Dull."

And then John Bassett came along with a proposition that was to change the entire direction of Dudley's life.

CHAPTER 5

BEYOND THE FRINGE AND ALL THAT JAZZ

1960-1962

"I don't know what my mother thought about Dudley going into show business. She'd always had dreams of him becoming an organist in a cathedral."

—BARBARA (MOORE) STEVENS

The Edinburgh Festival was, as it still is, an annual showcase for the arts. An unparalleled and internationally acclaimed potpourri of drama and music, since the mid-fifties it had been running under the aegis of Robert Ponsonby. In 1960 John Bassett was his new assistant.

There had always been fringe shows running alongside the Festival, in the form of unofficial performances given by small or experimental theater and revue groups. Now Ponsonby suggested adding an official late-night comedy revue as part of the main Festival, and Bassett proposed it be made up of two graduates from Oxford and two from Cambridge.

The first choice for his Oxbridge quartet was Dudley and, when John Bassett asked him to recommend someone else from Oxford, Dudley suggested Alan Bennett, whom he had used for one of his Oxford cabaret evenings and who had played in a fringe revue at Edinburgh the previous year.

Bassett also went to Jonathan Miller, then a junior doctor at University College Hospital, London, whose comic mimicry had made him famous in Cambridge's Footlights Club and who had earlier performed with the Footlights in two revues in London. Miller, in turn, suggested Peter Cook, who had already written two revues for West End clubs and was keen to bring to the London scene the satirical cabaret he had seen in Berlin and Paris.

The first meeting of the four took place in an Italian restaurant close to Jonathan's hospital. "Dudley," recalls Jonathan Miller, "had a reticent puckishness about him," but the overall feeling was of wariness between them all. According to Miller, "We instantly disliked one another and decided that it might be a profitable enterprise." They settled on the title *Beyond the Fringe*, recalls Dudley, "because we couldn't think of anything else and it had a lunatic ring to it."

John Bassett recalls everyone being rather careful and quiet. "Nobody said anything at first, because no one wanted to tell a joke that might not prove funny to the others. Alan was particularly quiet, because he was very shy. But I do remember Dudley doing a Groucho Marx and following an attractive waitress in through one swing door and out of another."

Still under contract to John Dankworth, Dudley asked for time off to prepare for Edinburgh. "He asked me for three weeks off," recalls Dankworth. "But everybody had heard a bit about what Dudley was doing around town and there was already something of a buzz about *Fringe*. So, when he came to me, I said, 'Sure, but don't feel bound to it. I think somehow you won't come back after three weeks, but you must do what you want to do.' I had a feeling that he wouldn't be back."

Dankworth was right. When *Beyond the Fringe* opened in August 1960 at Edinburgh's Lyceum Theatre, it became an immediate draw for the Festival. "I had absolutely no doubt we would be a success from that first night in Edinburgh," says John Bassett.

Dudley was now dating Jennifer Cuany, secretary to both Robert Ponsonby and John Bassett, and they were staying together in Edinburgh for the duration of the show.

Dudley's good friend Barbara Moore went along to keep house for them, and she recalls a very heady first night. "It was an amazing atmosphere. Absolutely electric. The ladies were leaping on to their seats and throwing their fur coats in the air. It was brilliant, and the next day there were about eight or nine offers from the West End."

They were sharing the Lyceum with Maggie Smith, Tom Courtenay, and Ralph Richardson, who were appearing in a Restoration comedy, and, being infinitely lower in status, the *Fringe* team found themselves allocated dressing rooms way up on the fourth floor. John Bassett recalls one night when all were on stage except Dudley, who was in the toilet, having no idea the curtain had already gone up. "We could hear the chain being pulled way up above us and we knew he had to come down four flights of stairs and that the other three men would have to fill in because he wasn't emerging. And then we heard this whistling as he descended slowly, because he thought he still had a good ten minutes before the start of the show. There was this *horrendous* gap, and only *we* knew who had pulled the lavatory chain, only *we* knew who was descending the steps slowly, only *we* knew who was whistling. It was very funny."

Critical reaction was excellent, although major public acclaim would not come until later. When it did, *Beyond the Fringe* would become one of the West End's greatest-ever attractions and go on to repeat its triumph on Broadway.

It was during the *Fringe* run in Edinburgh that Dudley met Robert Mann and established the basis for a lifelong friendship. Mann was—and still is—first violinist with the Juilliard String Quartet, who were also playing at the Festival. Isaac Stern, who had seen *Beyond the Fringe* and been very impressed with its wit, told Mann to see it, saying he had been "wowed by this guy who put on a wig like Myra Hess and sang like Aaron Copland."

Mann went to see the show and, struck deeply by Dudley's "sensational subtlety and quick qualities of music-making in his presentation," went backstage to meet him. "I discovered very quickly that he was a brilliant sight-reader of classical music, almost nonpareil. I'd very seldom met with a mind that could absorb music he really didn't know and perform it extemporaneously. And there began our long friendship."

While Dudley was in Edinburgh, the post of conductor of the Edinburgh Festival Ballet became vacant and he decided to audition for the job. He conducted a couple of modern works but, though he performed quite well, he didn't yet have the requisite ease and authority that he would later acquire. Surrounded by musicians who were looking to him for some sort of lead, Dudley felt very self-conscious and "had problems getting the instruments to come in together at one particular moment in the music."

Peter Cook's agent had convinced the Fringers that theatrical producer William Donaldson was the man to mount *Beyond the Fringe* in London, and after some persuasion, Donaldson agreed. It was some achievement, since he had not even seen it yet. The twenty-three-year-old producer had just gone bankrupt over the financial disaster of John Bird's revue *Here Is the News* and was convinced that nobody would want to charge him with another theatrical responsibility so soon. Eventually Donaldson brought in impresario Donald Albery, who gave them the Fortune Theatre for what was initially intended to be a six-week run.

Meanwhile, Dudley was still writing occasional music for theater productions and he embarked on the musical score for *Platanov*, which would star Rex Harrison and Rachel Roberts. He was now earning more money than ever and decided to move into a larger flat. As it happened, John Dankworth and Cleo Laine were moving out to the country and he took over the lease of their flat in Maida Vale.

When Dudley told his parents he was earning a hundred pounds a week, their jaws dropped in astonishment. "Do you know how long it took us to save a hundred pounds?" they told him. "Twenty years!" "But they didn't make me feel guilty in any way," says Dudley, "because they were so delighted and thrilled. Their attitude was wonderful." Still, it must have required a huge adjustment for them to accept that a son who had grown up with so many emotional and physical defects was about to become part of a West End show.

Before coming to London, the show played a week in Cambridge, where it was a huge success, and in Brighton, where audiences were far from enthusiastic. As Alan Bennett recalls, "We'd all come down after great success from Edinburgh with the sound of applause ringing in our ears. But in Brighton the loudest noise was the sound of seats tipping up as people left the theater. They didn't like it at all—it was a disaster. Donald Albery, the coproducer, looked at us all and then said of me, 'The blond one will have to go.'"

It was in Brighton, however, that legendary theatrical producer Alexander Cohen saw the show and instantly decided to take it to America. "Brighton was hardly the best place to see it," Cohen reflects, "because the performers almost outnumbered the audience and it was hard to get a feel of the show. But curiously my mind was made up from the top of the show, when Dudley walked on the stage, sat down, and played 'God Save the Queen,' and the few people there were so genuinely puzzled that they didn't know whether to stand or sit. So the confusion and fun began at the start."

Cohen was fascinated by the differences between the four young university graduates. "Jonathan had an intellectual wit, and Alan had a wry, detached sense of the world and its irony. When you came right down to it, the only two comics were Dudley and Peter. My feeling was that they were excited; the other two cared less, and their lives didn't depend on it. I got the feeling that Dudley and Peter's lives depended very much on the show working out."

The night before the London premiere, William Donaldson took the cast to see a blue film as a preopening treat. "We were all slightly nervous and giggly," says John Bassett, "because it was much more illegal than it is now and we were all very innocent. We went to this house in Bond Street, and an old tart took us to her bedroom and started showing us films which were terribly old black and white, very flickery, and had obviously been made in Egypt. We were hysterical with laughter. Jonathan and his girl-friend Rachel, both being doctors, started giving a medical commentary, Dudley and Peter were in stitches, and Alan was so embarrassed by the whole thing that he crawled under the bed to hide. It was mind-blowingly funny!"

With no ill effects from their brief sortie into the demimonde, they opened the next night, May 10, 1961, at the Fortune Theatre to a rousing reception.

Beyond the Fringe was an instant wild success and would eventually become a cult classic and the forerunner of an entirely new wave of comedy in Britain. Irreverent, daring, even offensive, it turned theater upside down. In Kenneth Tynan's estimation, this was when "English comedy took its first decisive step into the second half of the twentieth century." Bernard Levin, in the *Daily Express*, made the sweeping assertion that the theater had now "come of age." His reaction was "one of gratitude that there should be four men living among us today who can come together to provide, as long as memory holds, an eighth color to the rainbow."

Britain at that time was still largely smothered by a cloak of Victorian Puritanism. Revues until then had been lighthearted offerings that took great care not to give offense. *Beyond the Fringe* changed all that.

Underneath the national mood of apathetic acceptance of the status quo, there was an uneasy discontent. Particularly among the university generation, there was a feeling of disenchantment and a stirring of a more cynical social awareness.

Fringe was a cocktail of silly, funny sketches blended with others that were satirical and biting. They dealt topically with political and world issues and poked fun at the prevailing sexual hypocrisy. As Alan Bennett reflects, "We dealt with things that young people made jokes about in private but never publicly, like politics and the monarchy. It was very daring and wasn't like any other revue that had been seen before, so it was a breath of fresh air.

Jonathan Miller believes that audiences had been waiting for something like *Fringe* without being aware of it. And from the moment they opened, he says, all four men knew that something unusual was taking place. "There was," he recalls, "an intensity of laughter that made us feel that something strange and rather special had happened."

Everybody came to see it. When the Queen attended one night, Alan Bennett was asked to delete a sketch in which he said the word "erection," but he priggishly refused. "I'd never do it today, although, if I recall correctly, I didn't quite say the full word."

The night the Queen was due to attend, Dudley was playing before the show with his trio in the orchestra pit. "I knew the royal family was coming and I looked up and thought, 'Oh yes, that's probably where the Queen will sit,' and then found myself glazing off. And as I refocused I realized I was staring straight at the Queen. Not a very good idea. I was highly embarrassed."

John Dankworth and Cleo Laine, who had been such an integral part of Dudley's career up until then ("All we did was help to keep the wolf from the door," disclaims Dankworth), were among the *Fringe* audience. Which is where John met Dudley's mother. "She was an absolute darling and quite enchanting in her own way. A real cockney lady who was obviously very proud of her son. It was hard to believe that she'd produced this erudite tough-speaking Oxfordian. She sounded to me like an irrepressible cockney lady who would say just what she thought and wouldn't let herself be inhibited by anything. A great sense of humor."

Though Dudley himself only wrote three or four of the twenty-two sketches in *Beyond the Fringe*, his working-class irreverence inspired some of the others. But his most brilliant contributions were at the keyboard, where he exhibited a zany and innovative skill. As Jonathan Miller puts it, "He secreted music like sweat."

His parodies were wonderful. A Brechtian opera was sung in ersatz German; there was an amazing rendering of "Little Miss Muffett" as might have been arranged by Benjamin Britten and sung by Peter Pears; and a classic was his wildly witty arrangement of "Colonel Bogey" that couldn't seem to come to an end but went on and on.

They were parody at its cleverest, and probably the finest of their kind since Victor Borge. They required an intimate classical knowledge, and his clowning added to their strength.

Peter Bellwood, whom Dudley had met at Cambridge a few years earlier and who was now sharing a flat in Battersea with Peter Cook and his girlfriend Wendy, viewed Dudley's contribution as astonishing. "He was quite spectacular and helped to make the show unique. He was a great comedian and capable of causing helpless laughter. They all had that capacity, but in very markedly different ways."

Audiences were in hysterics over Dudley's comic antics and reveled in his playful musical pastiches. His career had reached new heights, and the *Times*'s critic described him as "something of a virtuoso on the piano." Dudley, however, felt he was not contributing much at all to the show, since he mainly was responsible only for the music. The verbiage came from Jonathan, Peter, and Alan.

He felt vastly inferior to the others. Some of that was the inner demons of the English class system at work. Cook and Miller were sons of the more privileged middle class; Dudley and Alan Bennett were scholarship boys from the sticks. But, far worse, Dudley felt intellectually and physically dominated by the others, whom he found "extraordinarily out of my reach. I didn't contribute a word to the writing, because I was so intimidated by them. Their thrust was every area I knew nothing about. Psychology, philosophy, and current events weren't up my alley, it seems, so how could I contribute in those areas. What did I know?"

Jonathan Miller, perhaps with hindsight, denies that Dudley had cause to feel inferior. "I was a dyed-in-the-wool intellectual from the moment I went to school. That's the way I was brought up. It's not better, it's just different. We all had our different interests, that's all. I felt very inferior to Dudley with respect to his music. I felt he had an astonishing, almost promiscuous skill at playing the piano that to me seemed very enviable.

"His presence in the show was indispensable," insists Miller. "He may not have written much, but it didn't matter. The whole character of the writing was determined by who was present. I know his height bothered him, and I do understand that short people can feel diminished in some way to people who are tall, but he more than made up for it."

John Bassett, conceding that Alan and Jonathan's intellects were "streaks ahead of the others," affirms that Dudley's musical talent "was easily up to anything that Jonathan and Alan could think up in the way of verbalizing."

Still, Peter Cook, detailing his memories in *Esquire* some years ago, wrote, "Apart from his musical contributions, Dudley's suggestions were treated with benign contempt by the rest of us. He rarely voiced an opinion during the years we performed in London. He was in awe of Jonathan Miller's spectacular ability to speak at length on everything under the sun. Alan Bennett also inhibited Dudley, mainly with his scholarly demeanor. And I wore a cloak of precocious urbanity, which did little to encourage friendships."

Cook claimed that Dudley's preference for clowning over political dialogue was not always appreciated by his colleagues, and Dudley, whom Jonathan Miller once described as "an endearing musical clown," admits that the political content of the show became quite painful for him. "I was always terrified that we'd get arrested for everything we did. I was very timid. And Jonathan, Alan, and Peter treated that fear with total scorn, thinly disguised. It hurt me."

There was a repressed anger in him now over the sense of inferiority he was harboring. Decades later, Dudley expressed that anger when he told me, "I'm a performer. And there is an intellectual exercise in that. I'm as intellectual as any of them in an area they know zip all about—music. To write music is in itself an intellectual activity."

Alexander Cohen saw some of the "benign contempt" to which Peter Cook referred. "It was true. I felt it. It was particularly shameful since without Dudley they were nowhere, and it took them quite some time to figure that out. They have come to appreciate his contribution, but they certainly didn't show it, didn't acknowledge it."

Years later Dudley would look back at some of the old film footage of *Fringe* and hold his breath. "To see the *pain* of the person I was—I can feel it palpitate. I'm amazed that I *lived*!"

In spite of those adverse feelings, Dudley was breaking out of his shell and treading the boards of life with new confidence. For once there was no worry about the future. With the present holding such high rewards, it seemed only likely that success would continue. "Once I knew the show was a hit and felt we would be there for a while, I began to feel secure in what I was doing."

It helped his fractured ego to be in continual demand as an entertainer in his own right. After *Fringe* ended at night he jazzed it up until the early hours, either alone or with Hugo Boyd and Derek Hogg who made up his trio, and every Sunday night they played opposite John Dankworth at the Marquee off Oxford Street.

The two had remained friends, and Dudley played piano on Dankworth's record "African Waltz," which became a big hit. He also appeared, very briefly, in a film with Cleo Laine, in which he accompanied her at the piano, playing "'Round Midnight" with his back to the camera the entire time.

John Dankworth recalls, "Dudley would come along after *Fringe* was over and play with Cleo [Laine] in different places. He was her accompanist at the Savoy in Brewer Street, and also at the Jack of Clubs, which was a less salubrious nightspot."

It was through his jazz that Dudley met the man who would become his closest friend through the early sixties.

Soon after the opening of *Fringe*, young photographer George Hastings had seen Dudley play the piano in a Soho nightclub, and impulsively had picked up the double bass in the club and accompanied him. They ran into each other later at a party, and ended up at George's flat, where they played music for the rest of the night. It was the start of their long friendship, and from then on Dudley spent most of his spare time in George's flat in Shepherd's Market, Mayfair, where there was a grand piano that George liked to pound with a dramatic flourish.

George Hastings was an elegant, worldly figure, two years older than Dudley. Amusing and urbane, he came from an upper-class background but, unlike those who had so intimidated Dudley in Oxford, he was also a sensitive and vulnerable man. He was extremely artistic and, although very much part of the upper-class social scene, he also had many artistic friends from lower down the scale.

He had a ribald sense of humor that appealed vastly to Dudley's own, and the two loved to indulge in endless hilarious conversations—usually centered around sex. George's abiding passions were jazz and classical music, and he and Dudley spent long hours playing together, Dudley on piano, George on double bass.

Music was an integral part of Dudley's life. Especially, these days, jazz, which he found deeply expressive. "I wanted love but wasn't able to ask for it. And jazz was a passive way of making my feelings available to whoever might pick up on it. It became nostalgia for the love I wanted as a kid."

Years later Dudley admitted that women were the sole reason he'd begun playing jazz professionally. He found it a visceral and unambiguously sexual form of music, with an excitement capable of manifesting itself in other areas. If one could improvise well on the keyboard, he surmised, one could also improvise well in bed.

Enjoying his new celebrity, Dudley was able to hide his sensitive, easily bruised psyche behind a smoke screen of scatological humor. The string of beautiful blondes that always seemed to flock around him helped to boost his self-esteem and revived the Oxford tag of "Cuddly Dudley."

Women found his warmth and humor immensely attractive, and responded accordingly. They wanted either to mother him or to love him. Often both at the same time. Coupled with his vulnerability, there was a potently engaging charm. It was a combination hard to resist. As Alan Bennett recalls, "He had a lot of sex appeal, and that gave him a very busy love life, which was highly enviable to all of us."

Girls seemed to pour out of the woodwork when he was around, and his three colleagues were perpetually amazed at the stream of females that always seemed to parade in and out of Dudley's dressing room. "I did rather make up for lost time," he confesses impishly. "But it was marvelous."

Among the plethora of females, a few became especially important to Dudley, particularly Anna Leroy, a gorgeous young singer and dancer who absolutely idolized him. She was in the chorus of *Oliver!*, and Dudley took Alan Bennett along to a matinee. Ever afterward, Alan referred to her as "sibilant Anna," because she had a sibilant "s" that came shining through the chorus.

Anna was devoted to Dudley and was always trying to make his messy apartment tidier and more appealing. It didn't seem to make much difference to Dudley's sloppy mode of living. Nor to his sense of freedom, which eventually he felt was being threatened by her adoration.

There were other girlfriends. He became deeply attached to Rosemary Bond, but that became rather complicated when he also fell for her sister Patsy, whom he "fancied like mad." One night, approaching Patsy's flat for a late assignation, he ran into his friend Francis Megahy, who happened to be Patsy's boyfriend and was also on his way to see her. Dudley told Megahy he was going to a party and must have ended up on the wrong road, but later that night, when he returned, he ran into Megahy again, as he was leaving Patsy's flat. Somehow he emerged from that incident with their friendship intact.

Dudley still went home to Dagenham most Sundays for lunch with his parents. And he stayed in touch with his old Dagenham friends.

Jim Johnson, his former pal from Kingsley Hall, persuaded him to visit the school where he was now a teacher and play for the pupils. Afterward they went over to a party at another teacher's house, where they congregated around the piano and nibbled saveloys. "One of the guys there was a bit grubby," recalls Johnson, "and Dudley was so worried about this that he wrote his own name on some raw saveloys, so that after they were cooked he knew which were the ones he had touched and not that other person."

In October 1961 Peter Cook realized his long-cherished dream and opened a nightclub (formerly a striptease club but redesigned by Sean Kenny) on Greek Street, in the heart of Soho. The Establishment was a perfect venue for the kind of scathing satire Peter wanted to see performed in England. Its advantage—one withheld from *Beyond the Fringe*—was that, as a private club, it was exempt from the Lord Chamberlain's censorship.

Kenneth Tynan, when he saw the Establishment's debut show, found it "more scurrilously outspoken than anything else of its kind in Europe." John Bird and Eleanor Bron were among the performers, and Peter Cook persuaded Dudley to play in the basement with his jazz trio "at slave labor rates." Peter was rightly sure Dudley would enjoy this, since it offered a further opportunity to meet gorgeous young women.

By this time Dudley was more than ever convinced that what he wanted to do with his life was perform on stage, make people laugh, and play jazz because it attracted women. So that's what he did. He played jazz. And he certainly attracted the women.

"I remember one night," says John Bassett, "when Dudley was playing in the basement of the Establishment, as he often did. There were three girls sitting on the edge of the stage under the main body of the piano, waiting to see at the end of the evening which one of the three he would take home."

There were, at this time, many girls in Dudley's life—Jennifer Cuany had now moved to New York and Anna Leroy had become history—but most of them passed steadily through rather than remaining around for long. "We had a competition once," recalls Bassett, "to see how many girls we could sleep with in twenty-four hours. And I remember that Dudley won the contest."

According to Jonathan Miller, "He was very playful, a bit like a cherub, with a Pan-like capacity to enchant ladies—who always seemed to be very tall, with long legs. I think he found them very fuckable. He liked that size girl. A lot of us do. You haven't got to be small to like girls that size. They're interesting, from the point of view of having a good time."

Jazz wasn't Dudley's only solo excursion away from *Fringe*. He was also appearing in a weekly Southern Television variety series, *Strictly for the Birds*, which had as its signature tune his own earlier recording of the same title.

Every Friday when the curtain came down on *Fringe* he would drive to Southampton in his Mini to record the show with his trio. And it almost landed him in trouble with the law.

Driving excessively fast late one Friday night—there was no speed limit then but reckless driving was punishable—he went hurtling past a side alley where a police car was half hidden.

"As soon as I saw them start to come after me," he recalled, "I slowed down immediately to a crawl and they almost crashed right into me. It could have been disastrous. I gave up driving Minis soon after that, because I thought I'd kill myself in one."

It was now that Dudley suffered the first tragedy of his life. And it was one for which he was entirely unprepared.

He had formed a close bond with Hugo Boyd, who'd been playing bass with him for the last few years. They had met at the Chelsea Arts Ball, where Dudley was playing the piano. Hugo had joined him in an impromptu performance, and Dudley was so astonished by what he heard that he stopped playing. "I couldn't believe this guy was so wonderful and so enthusiastic. He was a miraculous bass player."

From that moment on, Hugo was a regular fixture whenever Dudley assembled his trio. He couldn't read music, but it didn't seem to impede his talent. However, he wasn't keen on the idea of being a permanent member of the trio—at twenty-six his sights were set on becoming an architect.

Hugo was an avid driver and had spent months remodeling a Lancia that he had entered in a rally in Turin. He planned, on his way back from Italy, to meet up with Barbara Moore, who was vacationing in France with her daughter and another friend. But he never arrived.

As Barbara Moore recalls, "Hugo was coming to pick us up in Saint-Raphaël and drive us back to England with him. I waited for him for two days and then found another way to get home. When we got back that night, I turned on the television at my mother's house to watch the news. And that's when I heard that Hugo had been killed in an accident. The car had skidded off a bridge along the French coast and crashed on to a railway track below.

"I was in terrible tears and went rushing straight off to the Fortune Theatre. Poor Dudley had also seen the news and he was devastated, but he still went on and did the show. It was very sad."

Dudley broke down after the show that night. Hugo's death had a great impact on him, and it would take him a long time to recover from the loss of such a dear friend.

The shock would be compounded some years later when Pete McGurk, who subsequently took over from Hugo as Dudley's bass player and became another good friend, also died tragically when he committed suicide over an unhappy love affair.

Despite the success of *Fringe*, Dudley still lived in a state of perpetual chaos that bordered on squalor. Happy in mundane surroundings, he seemed oblivious to the mess, and visitors had to step over a floor that was littered with milk bottles, records, and lightbulbs.

John Bassett often visited Dudley at home and found him living in a shambles. "He was sleeping on a bed that was a terrible broken-down old sofa with springs sticking out, and he didn't have a blanket, so he used his daytime coat that had two buttons missing. There was a Marks & Spencer down the road, and when Dudley had dirty washing, he would buy fresh underwear and a shirt from Marks and then throw his dirty clothes into the room where Dankworth used to keep all his orchestrations. He never washed them; he never did anything except gradually fill up this room until it was well above waist high in dirty socks and pants and shirts and pajamas."

Dudley's friend Barbara Moore finally took things in hand. She made up bundles of washing to load into the Mini and drove back and forth to the launderette. Eight carloads later, the largest laundry chore in Maida Vale that week had been completed.

Dudley had been asked to score a ballet for Elizabeth West's Western Theatre Ballet, and it was now that he met a woman with whom he would form an enduring friendship. The young ballet dancer who'd been commissioned to choreograph the work was Gillian Lynne, now a renowned film and stage choreographer.

She came up with a jazz version of "The Owl and the Pussycat," which Dudley loved because it was so different from anything he'd done before. "I used to meet him backstage at the Fortune," recalls Gillian, "or hang out where he was playing at Ronnie Scott's or the Establishment, so I could grab him when he was finished. He was a brilliant composer but quite reluctant, and I'd have to sit him down and make him write.

"One time we were really up against a deadline and he sat on the piano stool, put his hands over the keyboard, then looked up with that adorable face and said, "Can't we just go to the pictures?" Most composers are like that. They'd rather not do it."

During the day, she worked with Dudley at the Maida Vale flat. But it was a wonder that any work ever got done there. As Gillian soon discovered, "Everybody wanted to get in his bed. He had a window where you could climb out onto the roof, and there were a few times when I'd be holding on to a girl who was about to come in through the front door while he smuggled somebody else out of the back window.

"He was always surrounding himself with these incredibly glamorous but, I thought, cold women. It was strange, because he was an incredibly friendly, funny, intuitive, lovely guy. But I felt there was a massive gap between the way he thought about himself and what he really was."

Occasionally Dudley's sexual escapades interfered with business. One night, in his dressing room, he was making love to one of his amours, when he heard his cue. He was supposed to be on stage, but at that moment the earth was exploding for him. "I jumped up, hair dripping wet, and fled down the stairs and ran onto the stage. The others just looked at me. They knew exactly what I'd been doing!"

In spite of his comic antics on stage every night, jazz still occupied his attentions. His trio now was completed by bassist Pete McGurk and drummer Chris Karan, a Greek-Australian who had so impressed Dudley when he heard him play one night at the Establishment that he fired Derek Hogg and hired Chris on the spot.

George Hastings was a regular at the Establishment, where he loved to watch Dudley play. And to introduce him to women. George was a glamorous figure who knew everyone from society people to models. He was dashing and sexy, and he used his attractive personality to bring Dudley together with these beautiful women. All Dudley had to do was spot a gorgeous face and say to George, "Cor, look at her!" and his friend would be off to bring her over.

John Bassett, who often hung out with these two randy males, was a fascinated observer of George's pandering ways. "He was like a faithful spaniel, and if Dudley was interested in someone, he would go over to the girl, tell her Dudley wanted to meet her, and then get her into the circle. It was amazing. It worked every time."

But women didn't take up all of Dudley's attention.

Lindsay Anderson had wanted for some time to work again with Dudley. He'd liked Dudley's previous work for the Royal Court and now asked him to write the incidental music for his new production, Max Frisch's *The Fire Raisers*. It would be the last time they would ever work together.

The play was a parable ostensibly about a man burning down a house, and Anderson felt it should be punctuated with a picture of the atom bomb exploding. Dudley, however, thought the idea was silly and told him so. "I said it would be like telling the audience, 'We don't think you're going to get this point so here's an extra explanation.' And Lindsay got very angry and wouldn't speak to me again. It was unfortunate, and it became our great parting."

Fortunately it did not hamper Dudley's reputation, and he was heartened to be asked to score a new musical revue, *England Our England*, and to learn that Gillian Lynne would be the choreographer.

He'd also just been named Britain's top jazz pianist, so it was no surprise that, at twenty-six, he was now being talked about as a brilliant success.

But writing the music for *England Our England* meant that Dudley had to work round the clock. As soon as the curtain went down on *Fringe* each night, he would drive to places like Wolverhampton and Hull where the company was rehearsing. "I'd write and rehearse all the next morning, then drive back to London for the next show. It was ridiculous."

It was a hectic schedule. According to Gillian Lynne, "There was a song we had to come up with that was giving us trouble. Finally Dudley said, 'We'll have to take a purple heart each, because we're going to have to work all night.' And that's what we did. We worked all night long, and just about got the thing done."

On opening night at the Arts Theatre, Cambridge, they were still working on the final touches. "Dudley had changed some of the score at the last moment," recalls Gillian. "He always did that—he was never satisfied with what he'd done. In the end, he played the piano with the orchestra and I had to sit on the piano stool with him in the pit, counting them through it. That was our first night!"

Even youth has its limits. After months of burning the candle at both ends, Dudley became ill with a mystery illness "which Jonathan Miller diagnosed for me as a liver complaint of some sort. We all went to him with our physical problems, since he was also a doctor. I felt dopey and weak from doing so much. It was a hell of a strain."

He was forced to take an absence from *Fringe*, and the press played it up, announcing that the pressure of show business was taking its toll on him. While Robin Ray stepped in to understudy for him, Dudley set off for a vacation in Italy.

Waiting for his flight at London Airport, he met John Gielgud. Gielgud had seen and greatly enjoyed *Beyond the Fringe*. He suggested to Dudley that he look up his friend Lilli Palmer, since Dudley was going to Portofino where she lived, and he wrote a letter of introduction. "Darling Lilli," he scribbled on a tiny piece of paper that Dudley has preserved, "This is to introduce Stanley Moon, the brilliant young pianist in *Beyond the Fringe*—I know he would love to call on you and you will find him most charming."

Dudley read the note on the plane, but he was so embarrassed by Gielgud's inadvertent misnomer, that he never did go to visit the actress. Despite rumors that he would never return to *Beyond the Fringe*, Dudley regained his strength and was back on stage within the month. Soon he was performing double chores again, on stage at night and working during the day on recording.

Beyond the Fringe was headed shortly for America, and new performers were being auditioned to replace the Fringers in London. According to Donaldson, David Frost was passionate to take over Peter Cook's role. Cook, however, was equally passionate that he should not. "Over my dead body!" he told Donaldson, and since the Fringers had the power of veto, Frost did not get the part.

The *Fringe* team had renegotiated their salary for the American run, and Alex Cohen agreed to pay them £750 a week each plus 6 percent of the gross box-office receipts. It was five times the figure they were earning in London.

Dudley was still playing jazz at the Establishment many nights a week, and now he recorded the first of more than a dozen jazz albums. *Theme From Beyond the Fringe and All That Jazz* included Dudley's theme tune for the stage show together with a collection of jazz favorites, all performed with Chris Karan and Pete McGurk.

It was during one of his nightly forays into the jazz world that Dudley saw the woman who would become the first serious love of his adult life.

Celia Hammond was a tall, blonde, and beautiful model whose face shone out of many of the leading magazines of the day. "I'd seen her in *Vogue*," he remembers, "but one night, while I was playing at the Establishment, I saw her dancing and became desperate to know her."

Discussing modes of approach with George Hastings, he was finally persuaded to send her a telegram. "I wrote something that said, 'Hi, I'm Dudley Moore, I would love to meet you, is there any way of doing it?' I spent the next two days sitting by the phone just waiting for her call. Finally she called."

Celia was already involved with photographer Terence Donovan, but she was captivated by Dudley's irrepressible charm. "He was very shy," she recalls, "and I found that deeply attractive. Most of the men I met were very forward, which I didn't find very appealing. Dudley had a vulnerability about him that to me was utterly endearing. I watched him play at the nightclub and I fell in love with his music. Because of his shyness, he communicated a lot through his music, and I felt he was talking to me when he played. He was irresistible."

To Celia, who'd mainly been exposed to more sophisticated men, Dudley was wonderfully down to earth, attractive, and very funny. "He had this mischievous face with mischievous eyes that were enchanting. And as I got to know him, I saw that sense of mischief come out in his behavior."

During their first heady days together, Dudley was in heaven. "She was the one girl I was absolutely mad for and who I never dreamed I'd be able to come to grips with. When I finally did, it was the most extraordinary experience. I was so turned on to her that I couldn't think of anything else."

But there wasn't much time for them to get to know each other. America was now looming fast for *Fringe*, with only a few weeks left before their departure. Determined to make the most of their time together, Celia and Dudley became inseparable.

Celia was shocked by the mess she found in Dudley's flat. "He was totally useless at looking after himself. He obviously just played the piano all day and didn't bother about his flat. I cleaned up some of the cupboards and found jars and tins of things that had what looked like mushrooms growing out of them and huge sprouting molds. It was unbelievably awful. Yet it made me feel very motherly and protective, which was something I hadn't experienced before."

Celia had recognized Dudley's vulnerability from the moment they met. But she was saddened to discover the extent of his self-consciousness about his clubfoot. "It used to hurt me that he kept his sock on when he was taking a bath," she recalls. "He didn't trust me enough for it not to make a difference." Dudley was afraid that if Celia saw the imperfection of his foot, she would care less about him. "He didn't understand," she reflects wistfully, "that if someone cares about a person, it doesn't matter if they've got three heads, and I kept telling him that. It couldn't have mattered less to me, but I don't think he ever accepted that."

With America now a few days away, Dudley was feeling overwhelming angst at the thought of being separated from Celia, and he begged her to go with him. But her career had taken off in Britain and she feared that, if she left, she would disrupt it. After much indecision, Celia decided to stay in London, but promised Dudley that she would join him later.

Beyond the Fringe had now been running in London for over a year. It had widened the scope of contemporary British humor, influencing a new breed of comic performer, and was the precursor for a satire boom that would include *That Was the Week That Was* (which made David Frost an overnight star) and *Monty Python*.

And it had launched what would become four of the most famous names in English entertainment.

Those four were now on their way to Broadway.

CHAPTER 6

N E W   Y O R K

1962-1964

"Here was this brilliant talent, wonderful-looking, absolutely cuddly, and deliciously wantable fellow but who had not been blessed with height and had been given a clubfoot, and I felt he was going after all the wrong people just to compensate for that. It was as if he was saying, 'I might be little and I might have a clubfoot, but look who I can get!'"

—GILLIAN LYNNE

The *Fringe* foursome were not thrilled to learn they would have to travel to New York by ship, but John Bassett had assumed—wrongly as it turned out—that they would want to use the voyage to rehearse some new material for the American opening. Jonathan and Peter, both now married and with their wives in tow, particularly resented the long trip on the SS *France*. Dudley, however, was somewhat cheered when he discovered a mass of flowers sent to his cabin by one of his adoring girlfriends, model Cindy Cassidy.

"It was nowhere near as glamorous as we expected," recalls Alan Bennett. "We weren't treated like celebrities. They couldn't fit us into the main dining room, so we had to eat in the nursery. I remember Peter having caviar for his breakfast, but other than that we weren't treated royally at all. We didn't play for the passengers—nobody asked us. There was even a talent contest, but we weren't asked to perform. We were just treated like ordinary passengers."

The show went to Toronto, then to Washington and Boston. And finally—New York.

When it opened on Broadway, in October 1962, *Beyond the Fringe* was greeted with tumultuous applause. Alistair Cooke, writing in the *Guardian*, noted that "the four irascibles of the nonestablishment have come to New York to present their clownish commentary of the world before Cuba."

It played to sellout crowds, which included many transatlantic *Fringe* fans who, according to Cooke, turned out in sufficient numbers to cue the Americans when the accents grew unintelligible. One of the theatergoers was President Kennedy. He'd already seen the show in London; now he came back for more.

Alexander Cohen had been asked for tickets to be set aside for the President and his party, but was not convinced he was really coming, until he stumbled across some Secret Service men in the theater the day before the Kennedys were supposed to attend.

"Wherever the President went," explains Cohen, "there was supposedly a red phone to launch any attack. I came into the theater and saw the security men installing this red phone in the box office, and the moment I saw that, I knew the President was definitely coming."

The night President Kennedy attended the show, he went backstage during the intermission and chatted with the four young men in their appallingly dirty dressing room on the first floor.

As Alexander Cohen recalls, "The President then asked if there was a lavatory backstage. We really had no facilities at all—just the most disgraceful-looking 'broom closet' on the first-floor landing. And Hildy Parks, my wife, was left to guard the door until the President was finished, and then she escorted him back to their seats. The next day, he sent Hildy a dozen red roses for looking after him while he was in the loo."

Alan Bennett made sure the incident would be recorded for posterity and scrawled across the washroom wall, JOHN F. KENNEDY PEE'D HERE and dated it.

Dudley was sharing an apartment with John Bassett on East 63rd Street, near the Queensborough Bridge. Owned by musical star Joan Diener, it was an expansive affair with two huge bedrooms and garish paintings-by-numbers throughout the flat. It soon became a popular gathering place and, despite the constant mess, there was always a welcome mix of music and laughter, "with a lot of quiet, deep talks about what we wanted to do in the future," recalls Alan Bennett. "And when we got hungry from our talking, Dudley cooked scrambled eggs, which he was very good at."

The apartment also became a refuge at one point. "When the Cuban Missile Crisis happened," recalls John Bassett, "Alan Bennett was *terrified* that the bomb was going to be dropped, so he came and stayed with us for two nights. He felt, if we were going to be blown up, it would be better to be blown up together."

It was a time of great concern for everyone, as Bennett recalls only too well. "It really was quite frightening. We all were very worried. The first thing we expected was riots, because everything was so tense and edgy. I don't think I really believed we would be blown up, but it was a terribly nervous time and we all wanted to keep together because we didn't know what might happen."

Dudley was now spending a lot of time with Bennett. A shy, soft-spoken Yorkshireman who took to chewing his tie when he was nervous, Alan hailed from similar working-class roots to Dudley's ("sunken middle class" he called it) and, despite his bespectacled scholarly demeanor, he had a warmth and humor that matched Dudley's own. He also had been at Oxford at the same time as Dudley, although they had only met once or twice when Bennett had appeared in one of Dudley's cabarets.

According to Alexander Cohen, "Jonathan and Peter were very aggressive and condescending. Dudley and Alan were the least pretentious of the four."

Reflects Alan Bennett, "Jonathan and Peter were both married, so Dudley and I tended to be together. Also, I didn't know anyone in New York and I was quite lonely. Sometimes I watched him play jazz, although I usually didn't like clubs. And we always dined together before the show at Barbetta's, an Italian restaurant on 46th Street, where we ate everything that was fattening and unhealthy."

Dudley dined on exactly the same meal there every night for about a year— gazpacho soup, fettucine, and chocolate mousse.

Barbetta's had the distinction of a maître d' who, Dudley recalls, "always greeted us with the words, 'Ah—Meester Cook, Meester Moore, *Be'ind the Fri'ge*.' He couldn't get any of the words right, and I said to Alan that it sounded like a good title for something."

Beyond the Fringe was now the toast of Broadway and the four performers were lionized in New York. Everybody wanted to know them.

The show's success allowed Dudley to play his music around Greenwich Village once the curtain came down after the night's performance, and he was a frequent attraction at the Blue Angel. At Michael's Pub, where he played for a week, he ran into Rex Harrison, who was also appearing on Broadway at the time. "Awfully good," said Harrison, who had stopped by to listen to Dudley's jazz, "but very loud!"

At the prestigious Village Vanguard, Dudley was persuaded to join Gerry Mulligan on stage. Mulligan, says John Bassett, "obviously respected Dudley as a musician, but fell about at the way he was accompanying him in an Erroll Garner style. Garner was a musician who rarely accompanied anyone, and Mulligan was collapsing with hysterics at the contradistinction of style."

Back in London, Dudley was being greatly missed by the remaining two-thirds of his trio. "I'm sitting in your old dressing room feeling very miserable," Peter McGurk wrote to him. "We just played the 8:25 P.M. set (after talking to you) and I found the old eyes full of tears. I miss you an awful lot, both playing and having a laugh, and the club doesn't seem the same."

The success of the Establishment in London had made it possible for Peter Cook to open another Establishment club in New York. Dudley was often to be found playing jazz in its back room (presided over by den mother Sybil Burton), to the delight of Peter Bellwood, Cook's ex-flatmate, who had come out from London to mount a revue at the club. Though he and Dudley had known each other casually ever since their first encounter at the Cambridge Footlights Club, it was here that a deep and lasting friendship began between them that would continue, even when the distance of different countries separated them.

Dudley was proving as popular with American women as with English girls, but he wasn't overly taken with them yet—although that didn't mean he was giving his active libido a rest. "There seemed to be an endless succession of girls," recalls Jonathan Miller, "and they all looked very much the same—tall, blonde, and gorgeous."

Meanwhile, letters poured in from Cindy Cassidy and Celia Hammond, both missing him wildly. Cindy favored cables and was becoming quite famous to the men at the post office in London for the touching words she transmitted to Dudley. Once, when she was particularly down and sending him yet another cable, they consoled her by saying how much they looked forward to her telegrams and please could she send one to them. Presumably they meant at the post office's expense.

Dudley, however, was desperately missing Celia, and there were endless phone calls and letters across the Atlantic. Ridden with insecurity, he worried that she might no longer want him—especially since she was torn anyway between him and Terence Donovan. He wavered between ecstasy after their reassuring words to each other and misery that her feelings would not sustain their physical separation. He was excited when she agreed to come out to New York for a few weeks—a fact he even mentioned in a letter to his parents.

"With Celia coming," John Bassett remembers, "Dudley wanted me to leave the flat, but then said I could stay, if we could soundproof and work out the sleeping arrangements. We'd both been sleeping in the double room until then, because he wanted to keep one room absolutely pristine for Celia.

"We had to test the question of the soundproofing, so I stayed in the double room and he went into the single room with the gargantuan bed that he intended to share with Celia. He shut the door and then started making the most extraordinary loud noises, like a woman having an orgasm, to see if I could hear them! It was so naive and sweet. He could just as easily have clapped his hands or shouted, but instead he made these amazing loud groaning noises!"

Dudley didn't like the apartment at all, and had been trying to find someone to take it over ever since he'd begun renting it. One of the prospective tenants who turned up to look at it was John Gielgud. As Dudley recalls, "I opened the door and the first thing he said was, 'I'm so sorry about that awful story that went round about the letter of introduction I wrote you for Lilli Palmer.'"

By now, Gielgud's earlier muddling of Dudley's name had become an in-joke and all of Dudley's friends were calling him "Stanley Moon," so it was hardly surprising that Gielgud himself had heard of his gaffe. Dudley found the whole thing rather amusing and he was far too taken with Sir John's gentle niceness to let it remotely bother him. The mileage he would continue to get out of it would be more than worth the embarrassment that had prevented him from meeting Lilli Palmer.

When Celia Hammond arrived in New York, Dudley was in bliss. He squired her delightedly around town, proud to have this beautiful woman by his side and cheering at his performances on stage.

"She was a rather aphrodisiac presence," recalls Jonathan Miller—"a long-legged blonde figure, very much out of that sixties world of miniskirts and ravishing legs." Alan Bennett recalls that, of all the women he'd seen around Dudley, she "was the only one who ever actually talked to the rest of us."

It was an exotic time for the lovebirds. With *Beyond the Fringe* the surprise hit of New York, there was an endless stream of high-profile events to which they were invited. "It was incredibly exciting," Celia remembers. "I was very young, and it was all so completely different that I was quite stunned by it all. There were loads of parties, and I think the shy side of Dudley found it hard to handle. But he knew he had to socialize because it was part of the show-business scene and you were expected to go to all these things."

Neither Dudley nor Celia was gregarious by choice, and the times they treasured were the ones they spent quietly alone with each other. During the day there were walks in Central Park and Manhattan, exploring New York. At night, when the curtain came down, they dined in a tiny restaurant in the heart of the theatre district and visited some of the jazz clubs. And there were endless hours at the piano back at the apartment, where Dudley would play for Celia and compose songs for her.

When she eventually returned to London, Dudley resumed his insecurities over their relationship. And Celia, who had more than a few of her own, resumed hers. George Hastings found himself playing the role of spy in the affairs of Celia and Cindy, who was also planning to visit Dudley in New York. ("I hear Cindy's back," he wrote in a coded letter to Dudley, "but I've carefully avoided mentioning the NY threat to C.") He became Celia's confidant, the man she went to for reassurance about Dudley's love.

"She is helplessly mad about you," George wrote to Dudley, "and never thinks of anything much but you. She worries dreadfully that you've gone off her, and the more she loves you the more lovable she seems. Sometimes she sort of snuggles and says, 'Tell me some Dudley stories.' Great God on a bicycle, what a girl!"

Celia spent endless hours with George at his flat ("He was my minder"), but if she ran into him while she was with Terence Donovan, she would cut him dead. "She always looks guilty or uncomfortable," wrote George, "if she sees me when she's with T, which is always."

By now Dudley had moved to a brownstone apartment "a bit like the Georgian houses behind Harrods" at Washington Square North. It was run by Jo Mullin White, who became deeply and maternally attached to Dudley, and they spent many hours in long discussions about the meaning of life. Jo sensed whenever Dudley was feeling depressed and tried to elevate his sagging psyche with little notes of inspiration.

Gillian Lynne, whose career was now booming, happened to be choreographing a new ballet for the Edinburgh Festival, and she asked Dudley to write the score—a challenge that appealed to him.

Collages was an innovative series of small ballets combining modern and classical dance. "We had to do it for nothing," Gillian recalls. "There was no money at all, and Dudley wrote the most wonderful opening ballet called *Symbol*.

"Neither of us was particularly happy, romantically speaking, at that time, and *Symbol* was the culmination of our thoughts about how difficult it is to find someone who's willing to love you as much as you love them and how often somebody wants to love you but you don't want them."

Another ballet they created was *Soccer*. Gillian was mad about football, and the ballet symbolized the hordes of people who went to the game as part of their lives every week. "Dudley's music was incredible," describes Gillian, "and anyone who heard it has never forgotten it. That music of his put me where I am."

In one of the earliest examples of Dudley's inordinate generosity toward his friends, Gillian found herself flying every Friday night to New York on tickets that Dudley sent her, and staying in a room that he rented for her in Washington Square. There they worked all weekend until she returned to London on the Monday.

Although Dudley was in a successful Broadway show, he was beginning to feel fairly clouded about life—a state hardly helped by his withdrawal symptoms over Celia's absence. He sensed she had retreated slightly, and he conveyed his fears to George Hastings.

As it happens, Celia was feeling deeply hurt by a thoughtless comment that Dudley had made to John Bassett. The two men had been thumbing through *Playboy* and, seeing a girl with huge breasts, Dudley tactlessly told Bassett that he wished Celia was built that way.

Celia was a sensitive girl and very critical of her body. Though she was now regarded as one of England's most desirable models, inwardly she did not share the admiration. It was inevitable that, to a woman as critical about herself as Celia was, Dudley's insensitive remarks would cut very deeply and serve to make her feel less attractive. But the fault was perhaps less Dudley's than his friend's. John Bassett had returned to London by now and, taking Celia to dinner one night, had repeated the story. He thought it amusing, but he had underestimated the depths of her vulnerability.

The entire romance between Celia and Dudley might have ended there but for the intervention of George Hastings, who, running into Celia a bit later, sensed a coolness in her manner and eventually extracted the entire story from her. George spent hours trying to reassure her that Dudley adored her the way she was and that his tactless remark was simply normal male nature.

When George explained the chain of events to Dudley, he was appalled that he could have hurt Celia in such a way. Didn't he of all people understand how a physical imperfection—real or imagined—could wreak such pain? He phoned Celia and, in an emotional outburst, apologized for his schoolboyish insensitivity. Now he understood why she had seemed so horribly distant to him on the phone recently.

And he wasn't convinced that the damage had been repaired.

Gillian Lynne—a gentle, sensitive woman—was very touched by Dudley's pain. "He was miserable so often, and I was very aware that on the one side was brilliance and on the other was a gaping hole.

"He really had such a hang-up about his foot, and one day I said, 'This dumb foot: take the boot off, let me look at it,' and I forced him to take the boot off. I was really cruel, but he didn't have much choice because there I was pulling it off. I looked at it and said, 'It's the most darling little foot,' and gave it a kiss or two. And that, I thought and hoped, got over that."

Some months later Celia flew out to New York one more time. Dudley was immensely excited and hired the largest Cadillac he could find to meet her at the airport. Back at the Washington Square apartment, they were soon deluged with phone calls from Terry Donovan, begging Celia to return to London.

Celia had felt torn between the two men almost from the start. And she hadn't quite forgiven Dudley for the awful gaffe he'd made a few months earlier. "Maybe," she reflects now, "that was the beginning of the end. When you're young, bodies are very important and remarks like that hurt you a lot and make you very insecure. It can be very damaging, and it made me feel I wasn't woman enough."

Eventually Celia decided to return to London and to Terry. She told Dudley the relationship was over, but she did it in a way that she regrets even now. "Looking back on it," she admits, "I think I behaved like a little bitch. I just walked out of his life without a backward glance, and I'm ashamed of that. I could have done it less hurtfully, broken it more gently, but I didn't really give him any notice and I think that was very cruel."

Dudley was desperately hurt. "I don't think I had the gumption to ask her to leave Terry," he recalls, "but I begged her to stay."

Celia, today a deeply caring woman who runs a home for abused and stray cats, reflects that Dudley's niceness may even have affected their breakup. "He'd always treated me like a princess, but women are perverse creatures. They want to be put on a pedestal and loved and admired, but when they get it they can't always handle it."

Dudley was devastated at losing Celia. According to Barbara Moore, who was staying in New York at the time, "His heart was broken. I'd never seen him so sad."

Celia's rejection stabbed Dudley to the core and left him deeply depressed. It reactivated all the old emotions of unworthiness that had surrounded him since childhood. All the frustrations and anxiety, once diminished if not dormant, now enveloped him entirely.

He was embedded with feelings of grayness and unable to express the enormity of his feelings. "I was in and out of love and lust, not able to get either, and I felt life was passing me by and I wasn't driving the train. I was very hidden then. Socially I was on a great deal, wanting to push myself forward, but I wasn't comfortable or able to relax. I was ashamed to talk about the worthlessness I felt."

In the midst of his agonizing pain over Celia, Dudley was also worrying about his parents back in Dagenham. Jock was about to retire and, although the rent on the house was minimal, his pension was unlikely to make life easy for himself and Ada. Dudley wrote to them with a check for two hundred pounds, and told them he was arranging for a standing order for fifteen pounds to be paid to them every week. "Thanks to you," Jock wrote back, "I shall look forward to happy times without worry."

Meanwhile, Dudley's work on *Collages* continued. It seemed the only respite from his grayness, as a scrawled note in his diary for a Sunday in June 1963 attests:

A good afternoon's work. 4½ hours on the *Symbol* ballet. It's funny. The only cure for my depression ... is activity. Once I get into my work, the pressure of "LIFE" itself is taken from me and I am able to think clearly and without obstruction. Work makes me able to cope with my reality and fight off the cloying fingers of fatalism and resignation. Not that I could ever let myself resign from my constant struggle to discipline myself. It has to be a victory for my soul—there is no alternative. Thus my true self—or at least a better self—must and will emerge. But the certainty that I will win through does not ease the problem as it stands. When it finally happens, I shall probably not be able to believe I existed in my other condition.

Gillian Lynne found herself facing major problems. With *Collages* just days away from the opening at the Edinburgh Festival, the lack of finances became acute. "We ran out of costumes and had no money to buy more," she recollects, "so Dudley went out and bought some in New York and put them on the plane.

"There was now a steady stream of people driving to Prestwick to receive money from Dudley and costumes from Dudley. He was incredible. Such a buddy. Such an inspiration. Some years later I tried to pay him back and kept sending him checks. Finally, he said, 'If you do this any more I shall wipe my bottom on the check, tear it up, put it in an envelope, and send it back to you!'"

Dudley continued writing to Celia. "For a long time," she recalls, "they were very beautiful letters—very loving and sad. But then they began to get chidingly angry. I think he was disappointed in me."

Celia had been Dudley's first adult love, and it would take him a long time to get over the blow of losing her.

After her departure, to appease his pain Dudley threw himself into a succession of meaningless romances and one-night stands with the most beautiful women who came his way. His philandering led to one particularly amusing episode, recalls Barbara Moore, who was staying with him at the time in Washington Square.

"I was in the lounge listening to records with my boyfriend, and Dudley was in his bedroom with a girl. He had a bed that was on castors, and he must have been overenergetic, because we heard this awful rumbling and suddenly there was a tremendous crash behind our settee. The bed had obviously gone flying and hit the adjoining wall. In my mind there was a panic rush of female, clad in nothing, dashing across the hall. And then Dudley ran out and just stood there in the hall looking terribly bewildered. It was the funniest thing I'd ever seen."

Amid the random female encounters—including one with a girl who, according to Alan Bennett, "had such big tits, she looked like her arm was in a sling"—Dudley resumed his relationship with Cindy Cassidy. Aware of his failed romance with Celia, she flew out to New York to console him, and the two whiled away long lunches with Peter Bellwood.

"Cindy was very sweet," Peter recalls, "but Dudley was still very unhappy. He was devastated by the breakdown with Celia. On the other hand, neither of us was keen to be between women for long. I was involved in some unhappy affairs myself, so we spent much of the time commiserating over the appalling cock-ups that we got ourselves into."

Dudley was an extremely sympathetic friend and often went beyond the call of duty to make amends with Peter's various girlfriends. He had about him a mollifying quality, and if Peter needed a message sent to a girl who wasn't talking to him, Dudley would call her for him.

Until now, Dudley had enjoyed a fairly close relationship with Alan Bennett. But that, as he vividly recalls, was about to come to an abrupt end. "We had a sketch that Peter Cook rather unkindly called the Boring Old Man sketch, where Alan was interviewed by all of us in turn, and one night I played it a little differently, to try and get something out of the audience. And it worked—or so I thought."

When he came off stage, Dudley told the others he thought they'd given a good performance that night. Alan turned to him and replied tersely, "I think it's the worst performance we've ever given." According to Dudley, they barely talked again to each other all the time they remained in New York. He was sad and baffled.

"It was strange to have been going out to dinner with a guy every night and then suddenly have it stop so completely. I never understood it; it was a total mystery. I guess he thought I'd tampered with his words, but I found it difficult to believe the way he reacted."

Years later, Dudley asked Alan about the incident and was astonished to discover that he had no memory of it. Dudley's highly sensitive psyche had internalized the hurt and kept it alive in his memory. As with the school bullies much earlier, once again he had taken deeply to heart something that had been long forgotten by the others concerned.

Ben Shaktman, now back in New York after his work for the London stage, resumed his friendship with Dudley and saw a different man from the one he'd known at the Royal Court.

"*Beyond the Fringe* had given Dudley the most breathtaking lease of life. He became recognized with as powerful a comic mind as the other three powerful minds, and that, coupled with the fact that he could be loved and seduced and chased after by beautiful women, was a very important gate-opening for him. But that wasn't enough when he didn't have those same beliefs about himself. And yet when he was depressed—and I saw him in deep funks—he worked right through it. You knew he was in a rotten mood, but he would write absolutely brilliant music. And if he said anything half-funny in one of those moods, it would be absolutely hysterical."

Dudley was now replaying all his old anxiety and angst from the past. He was continually reading books on philosophy and psychology, but nothing seemed to cure his state of grayness, for which Celia had been merely the catalyst. "I think my parents' attitude had caught up with me. I felt it was slightly tainted to say the least, and all their anxiety and guilt had been passed on to me and it was coming out again. It just all caught up with me at that point."

As he told Ben Shaktman, "If only I could use words the way you do I would be a very happy man. I'd really be able to explain myself to myself and other people." He was about to start learning the process.

At the urging of Peter Bellwood, Dudley now embarked on his long journey into therapy—a journey that would take decades to complete.

As Peter Bellwood recalls, "The relationship with Celia had been very intense and had left him deeply unhappy. I was very affected by the fact that Dudley was feeling so much pain. I suggested therapy to him more with my fingers crossed, hoping it might help, rather than with any wisdom or insight to its value. But Dudley had got to a point where he was hurting so much. And it did seem to help, because it gave him an opportunity after that to go somewhere regularly and talk about what was causing him this anguish."

By now the *Fringe* foursome were starting to get on each other's nerves—not surprisingly after so long together. Jonathan had a row with Alan Bennett one night and flipped over a table in his anger, and Peter Cook upset Jonathan by improvising a walk-on during his philosophy sketch. But they felt committed to staying out of England until April 1964 and the start of a new British tax year.

A few months earlier Alan had taken a vacation on the Isle of Man and in a long letter to Dudley (that reflected none of the animosity that Dudley was so sure now existed), he said he was very happy not to be working, and marveled that "I haven't been Recognized once, even though I'm wearing a great big tee shirt with Emily Nist, Beyond the Fringe on the front." It suited Alan's unassuming nature that nobody on the Isle of Man could care less about such matters. He told Dudley he'd be quite content to remain there, rather than return to America. He did not greatly relish the fast pace of New York, and was anxious to get on with other things.

The others felt pretty much the same way—particularly Jonathan, who wanted to get back home and raise a family in England.

Tax laws notwithstanding, one by one they left the show, to be replaced by other actors. Alan Bennett and Jonathan Miller went their separate ways, and Peter Cook returned to London to work on new revue material. By March 1964 Dudley was the sole survivor of the original cast.

Before the famous quartet disbanded, they had done for American comedy what they had done earlier in Britain: inspired a new generation of comedians. They had also won a prestigious Tony Award and put British comedy firmly on the Broadway map.

Despite their mild disagreements, Dudley missed them very much when they were gone. They'd been like family for almost four years. For the next few weeks, he assuaged his sorrows nightly when the curtain came down by playing with a trio at the Village Vanguard. And with Dizzy Gillespie he recorded a script and score—mostly improvised—for *The Hat*, a short cartoon in aid of world peace.

A letter from Alan Bennett cheered him up immensely. "I had my first driving lesson today," Alan informed him from the Isle of Man in his broad Yorkshire phraseology. "Bowling along I was like ninepence. And right enjoyed it I did." He had just seen *The VIPs*, which he strongly recommended to Dudley. "Burton is so good. It's the eyes that do it, scorch marks they are, or pissholes in the snow." He opined to Dudley that the success of *Fringe* had been because "it was true when we did it and some of it true always. So it could stand by itself and made for itself a place in which it could stand. Anyroads, Stanley Moon, take care of yourself."

In April 1964 Dudley left *Beyond the Fringe*.

For some time he had been working with Ben Shaktman on a musical version of Eugene O'Neill's *The Emperor Jones*. Both were greatly enthused over the project, and when James Earl Jones agreed to climb aboard as the star, the musical was commissioned to play at the Boston Arts Festival.

"Dudley had always had a tension between himself as a popular musician and entertainer and the classical, serious Oxfordian that he studied to be," explains Ben Shaktman. "I think that's why he jumped at *Emperor Jones*, even though he was occupied with therapy and heartbreak and performing. The score was a serious, modern, symphonic work, and it's something he'd been desperately wanting to accomplish."

While he worked on the score, Dudley rented a house on Cape Ann, near Boston, where Peter Bellwood joined him for a few weeks. The house was on a cliff, and its entrance faced a huge home owned by the man who headed the bottling concession for Coca-Cola in South America.

"The guy had this huge wrought-iron gate," recalls Peter Bellwood, "across the top of which was written in metal letters TRANQUILITY. So one day Dudley and I got a red-hot poker and burned into a piece of wood the word ANXIETY. We nailed this piece of wood on our gate, right opposite his gateway, so that every time the owner drove out of Tranquility he would always see these two guys staying in the house called Anxiety."

Back in New York, with only three weeks until the opening of *The Emperor Jones*, the serious preparations began. It was a grueling time, recalls

Ben Shaktman. "We worked days, weekends, every moment we could grab. Dudley flew to London and conducted his score with a pickup symphony orchestra, then recorded it, and flew back with the tape. Then we started rehearsing properly with James Earl Jones, Daniel Negrin, the choreographer, and fourteen dancers for the balletic sections."

Dudley's lot on *The Emperor Jones* was not the happiest. There was friction between him and Daniel Negrin because Negrin's steps did not always fit Dudley's music. "It was," says Shaktman, "the classic story where the choreographer said, 'The composer can't count beats,' and the composer said, 'The choreographer can't count.' But we could hardly go back and rerecord, so eventually Daniel had to back down."

They opened on a blisteringly hot August day in front of forty-five hundred people in the Boston Public Garden. The show ran a week but never made it beyond Boston. Carlotta O'Neill, the playwright's widow, refused to give Shaktman the rights to perform it elsewhere, and Dudley's magnificent score—for which he was paid £350—was never played again.

In the meantime Dudley had been asked by the BBC to take part in the filming of *Beyond the Fringe* for television. With no other work on offer and now feeling very homesick, he decided to return to London.

Ahead of him, though he didn't know it then, lay an extraordinary working relationship that would span more than a dozen years and produce one of the most famous comedy duos in English history.

PART TWO

CHAPTER 7

... B U T   A L S O
P E T E R   C O O K

1964-1965

"Peter and Dudley were two of the greatest comedy talents ever to hit British television. They were absolutely brilliant, and some of the funniest comedy originated from them. I felt very privileged to work with them. But they both had their own separate demons, and that was a tragedy."

—BRYAN FORBES

Now back in London, Dudley joined his former teammates to record, in front of a live audience, *Beyond the Fringe* for the BBC. It was August 1964, and the first time they had all seen each other for several months. Pleased to be reunited, they enjoyed working together again, but the original spark had now gone and they failed to capture quite the magic and innocence of earlier *Fringe* days.

Still, their success had given Dudley the confidence that he could make it as an entertainer and, determined to achieve this end, he landed a number of spots on the television arts programs *Tempo* and *Late Night Line-Up*, sometimes reunited in his jazz trio with Chris Karan and Pete McGurk.

He had, without being aware of it, unconsciously absorbed and was emulating the styles of some of the comedians he most admired, particularly Peter Sellers and Marcel Marceau, yet he managed to avoid becoming trapped within the mannerisms of any of them. What was emerging, consequently, was a style entirely of his own, with a vast and varied range as physically comic as it was verbal.

But his comedy was only a part of Dudley's considerable talent. In these early sixties jazz was still the dominant passion in his life, and his trio soon became a regular fixture in the main clubs around Soho.

Dudley had moved in with George Hastings, himself a great jazz lover, and the sounds of their combined music could often be heard in the alleys surrounding the Shepherd's Market flat. George now had a steady girlfriend in Alys (Lysie) Kihl, a music student who, like Dudley, was a graduate of the Guildhall School of Music, and she was vastly entertained by the endless jam sessions in the flat.

"I was a most delighted listener," she recalls, "and shared their enthusiasm. I didn't play much with them, because I'd been classically trained and wasn't a jazz player, so I felt rather intimidated. Occasionally I would play the flute when friends came round, and sometimes I played the odd classical duet with Dudley."

Dudley wrote dozens of jazz numbers during this period, one of which he named "Lysie Does It." Another, rather haunting, number was "Sad One for George."

They were very much a threesome in those days. When George and Lysie took a holiday in Porto Santo Stefano on the Italian coast, Dudley joined them and they had a wonderful carefree romp during which George shot a series of pictures with Dudley acting the clown around a topless Lysie. "They were a very entertaining couple," she recalls, "and it was a fabulous time for all of us because we seemed to share so much."

Though the reteaming of the *Fringe* players had been unexceptional, it was notable for having brought Dudley and Peter Cook together again. Dudley, who enormously admired Peter's comedy inventiveness, was keen to work with him again. The seeds had already been planted in New York, when, toward the end of *Fringe*, they began improvising together quite a lot. "I could see they had something," reflects Alan Bennett. "They sparked each other off, and they knew it, too, because even then they were talking about doing things together."

Peter Cook was also a majority shareholder (with Nick Luard, his partner in the Establishment club) of the satirical weekly *Private Eye*, and he decided to put out some satirical recordings. He asked Dudley to join Richard Ingrams, John Wells, and William Rushton, among others, in recording an EP entitled *Private Eye Sings*. This was followed almost immediately by a larger LP, *Private Eye's Blue Record*, and a flexidisc attached to a *Private Eye* front cover—featuring Prime Minister Alec Douglas-Home sitting on a toilet—that was presented at the October 1964 election. Although Dudley's was but one of the voices on these records, his legendary partnership with Peter Cook was on its way.

Joseph McGrath, a jolly Scotsman for whom Dudley had worked on *Tempo*, had been commissioned to direct a one-hour television variety special and he wanted Dudley to star in it. This, Dudley saw, could be the opportunity he'd been looking for to work with Peter Cook. Fortunately Joe McGrath had no objections when Dudley suggested it to him, and *The Dudley Moore Show* went into production with two stars instead of one.

"Peter and Dudley bounced off each other perfectly," McGrath fondly recalls, "and they were always coming up with new sketch ideas. One time, the three of us were going somewhere in a minicab and there was a terrible smell inside. We finally realized that it was human excrement. So we stopped the cab and Peter and Dudley did fifteen hilarious minutes with the minicab driver, who just denied the whole thing. Of course they ended up with a script about it."

The Dudley Moore Show worked so well that Tom Sloane, head of Light Entertainment for the BBC, commissioned Moore and Cook to team for a regular fortnightly series, with Joe McGrath holding the reins. And so was born *Not Only ... But Also*, a series that so far exceeded the expectations of the BBC hierarchy that, after its transmission on BBC-2 in January 1965, it was immediately repeated on BBC-1.

The first program went out under the title "The Dudley Moore Show Starring Not Only Dudley Moore but Also Peter Cook and John Lennon." In one sketch, filmed on Wimbledon Common, they did a takeoff on the sometimes mannered style of BBC's *Monitor*, during which John Lennon was seen in slow motion swinging on the children's swings. Dudley was pushing him, but eventually he pushed so hard that John's contact lenses fell out and were lost in the grass. McGrath had to stop filming while everyone searched frantically among the tall blades. "Luckily," he says, "John had another pair on him. Because we never found the first ones."

John Lennon was paid only fifteen pounds for his appearance on the program—not even enough to cover his lost contact lenses—but he relished every minute of working with Peter and Dudley. "At the end of the show," McGrath recalls, "we all went for a Chinese meal at the restaurant round the corner, and John, who was very somber by the end of dinner, suddenly got up and sat on top of the table and said quite seriously to the boys, 'I really dig what you're all doing.'"

Not Only ... But Also had a loose concept based on a series of sketches that were first improvised into a tape recorder and then knocked into script form. Not surprisingly, there was a lot of deviating from the script once they got into the studio to record in front of an audience. One sketch with two men in a pub talking about being harassed over the phone by Sophia Loren and Brigitte Bardot ran five minutes in rehearsal. When they did it with the audience, it lasted twelve minutes.

The sketches ran the comedy gamut from two idiots in cloth caps discussing imaginary adventures involving famous film stars to an upper-class twit whose life's work consisted of teaching ravens to fly under water.

Many lunatic characters emerged from this lopsided view of life, but the most famous of all were those cloth-capped idiots. "Pete" and "Dud" were two brainless, self-indulgent, bigoted men, who besides fantasizing wildly about women and sex, discussed universal issues of life and philosophy with breathtaking inanity. The characters were drawn from Dudley's own Dagenham background and, years later, these Pete and Dud sketches were issued on an LP as *The Dagenham Dialogues*. He based Dud on someone who went to his church. "I never knew his name but he was a strange sort of cloth-capped individual who was obviously very down on himself. He almost made me cry because he was so pathetic and didn't know anything about anything."

Dud and Pete became cult heroes to millions of viewers who perhaps recognized in them some echo of their own or neighbors' idiosyncrasies.

No program featuring Dudley would have been complete without a musical interlude, and he provided it with relish at the jazz piano, occasionally throwing in one of his incomparable parodies.

Nothing like this had ever been seen before. It was entertainment of a unique kind and became a milestone in British television, establishing Cook and Moore as a brilliant comedy team, whose names were beginning to be mentioned in the same breath as the historic Goons. Everyone wanted to be on the show. Long before *Monty Python* was devised, John Cleese found his way on to the program in a bit part as a waiter. And Joe McGrath recalls a passionate phone call from Peter Sellers. "He told me, 'I'm absolutely hysterical with laughter after watching the show. Please can I be on it, because those guys are what comedy's all about at this moment. I have to be part of it!'"

Dudley was thrilled to work with Sellers, who was his idol. But it wasn't the easiest of shows to pull together. "Sellers was always difficult to work with," explains McGrath, "because he was a great giggler and he laughed all the time. It was to hide the nervousness, but it reached the stage where they were all doing it and I had to say, 'You've got to stop the laughing and really get down to work, because this is live television.'"

One of Dudley's favorite sketches was actually inspired by the BBC. It was a confrontation between a scriptwriter and the head of the BBC, and was analogous to one experienced by the comedy scriptwriter Johnny Speight (who wrote the landmark television comedy series, *Till Death Us Do Part*) about the number of "bums," "tits," and "buggers" being uttered on a program. "You can't say 'bloody' this many times," he was cautioned— "you've already said 'bum' five times." Finally Speight said, "All right, I'll drop one 'bloody' if you'll let me have another 'bum.'"

Dudley and Peter, to their amazement, got away with words that had never been used before. "Peter loved it when we got away with things," recalls Dudley. "Like the time he talked about a bottle of wine, which instead of being called Chateauneuf-du-Pape was called Shat All Over the Carpet. We used 'bloody' and got away with it, but we were criticized for it. My mother must have had kittens—it was a word I was never allowed to use at home."

His mother may have missed that one. Now that he was earning decent money, and receiving a few hundred pounds a month in American *Fringe* royalties, Dudley had bought his parents a television so they could watch him. But the greatest compliment he got out of Ada was, "You put me right orf to sleep, dear. It was lovely." "That was her greatest compliment," he recalls wistfully. "It put her to sleep. Made her forget everything that was painful about the world, I suppose—which God knows she seemed to be aware of."

Occasionally, Pete and Dud's ribald ramblings provoked the ire of some people. But the BBC was fairly lenient in censoring the material. Most of it was left to the producer's discretion, although Joe McGrath recalls moments of dissent with Tom Sloane. "Tom said, 'If this is Light Entertainment, I'm in the wrong business,' and Frank Muir, who was dead keen on the show, told him, 'Then I think you are in the wrong business.'"

Terry Jones, one of the subsequent *Monty Python* troupe, who later substituted for Dudley in a couple of Amnesty International stage appearances, was vastly influenced by what he saw in *Not Only ... But Also*. "Those shows had a big effect on the way I thought about comedy. They had wonderful visual puns and visual jokes. One of the best was The Order of Leaping Nuns, where all these nuns were leaping around on a trampoline— to get closer to God I suppose—and I can remember seeing that and falling apart. It played around with images that you wouldn't expect, and Michael Palin and I later did a lot of jokes for *The Frost Report* that were very heavily based on leaping nuns!"

It would be remiss not to mention One-Legged Tarzan, which has gone down in the annals of comedy history. It was Peter Cook's first sketch, written at the age of eighteen, performed at Cambridge, and later acted out in *Beyond the Fringe* as One Leg Two Few. In it Dudley played Mr. Spiggott (a name they would use often in future work, and the name by which Peter later signed letters to Dudley), a one-legged actor auditioning for the role of Tarzan. Cook, as the producer, told him, "Your right leg I like. I have nothing against your right leg, but then neither do you. You are deficient in the leg division to the tune of one."

Considering Dudley's self-consciousness about his left leg, and that most sketches were drawn from the duo's own experiences, it was hardly surprising that journalists would claim Peter had written this sketch especially for Dudley. In fact it was Peter Bellwood who had inspired the sketch. One day Bellwood was standing on one leg in his Cambridge house scratching the sole of his foot, and the two of them had launched back and forth into some wild dialogue. "Years afterward," recalls Bellwood, "Peter told me I was the coauthor of the sketch—which pleased me a great deal, since he had got so much mileage out of it."

The Moore—Cook relationship was a disparate coupling, evolved out of an attraction of opposites. "We were diametrically opposed in everything," Dudley claims and, indeed, while Peter loved political debates, Dudley preferred to discuss the less intellectual pursuits of women and sex.

Peter Cook, two and a half years younger than Dudley, was a sophisticated, urbane, acerbic wit with a mocking, devilish mind and an austere ability to conjure a subject out of thin air, then spin around it an absurd web of the most lunatic logic. Dudley, on the other hand, was gentle, sensitive, and outgoing, and completely down to earth. He viewed Peter as the driving force behind their partnership. Whereas his own ideas were suburban and innocuous, Peter's became flights of fantasy, outnumbering Dudley's imaginative wanderings by "sixteen to one."

Dudley was a perfect foil for Cook, but much more reactive, and he frequently broke up in gales of laughter. Peter enjoyed making his partner "corpse" and, when he could see it about to happen, would indicate it to the audience, to their immense delight.

Unlike Peter, who was largely content to play a sketch and make his point, Dudley lived to give pleasure and hear approval from an audience. Alan Bennett had already observed that. "Dudley was very conscientious about not giving up, and he always plugged away, trying to pull the audience in if they weren't responding." Dudley wanted to feel the instant love and togetherness of the audience, says Peter Bellwood, by now a close friend to both Cook and Moore. "He needed that acclamation, so there was a tendency to play to the audience far more than Peter did. But the paradox of their two approaches actually worked very well together."

The phenomenal success of their partnership, Jonathan Miller believes, was unexpected, "because there was nothing to indicate it was going to happen. And yet when it did happen it seemed quite natural. Once you saw what they were doing together, it seemed inevitable."

The closing number of every show was "Goodbyeee," a silly song that ended in Dudley's trademark high falsetto, and this became their signature tune. When they recorded it some months later, it went straight into the top twenty on the record charts, where it remained for several weeks.

At last Dudley was receiving the acclamation he so desperately sought. He seemed on the surface to be happy and serene, but that was the mask of the clown. Only at home with George and Lysie, where he felt comfortable to be himself, did the reality emerge. As Lysie recalls, "He never stopped talking about how he felt, and we were totally aware of his appalling insecurities. One moment he'd be totally secure and jolly, and then all of a sudden he'd get serious and talk about his misgivings and anxieties."

In a way, George and Dudley were two of a kind. They were both attractive men, yet hugely screwed up and lacking in self-esteem. George presented an urbane, charming, and witty facade, but underneath he was a quivering wreck who began drinking at midday. A depressive and an alcoholic, he related entirely to Dudley's feelings of inadequacy.

As for Dudley, his affair with Celia Hammond had left him feeling morose for well over a year. Now he began to emerge from the cocoon of despondency that had engulfed him for so long, although he had seldom wanted for female company. Playing jazz in the London clubs, he was surrounded by girls who were drawn to him through his music. Having women constantly around helped to satiate his longing to feel loved, and they were happy to oblige. There was an endless succession of young, leggy, usually tall blondes jumping in and out of his bed.

A few affairs lasted longer than the usual flings, one of them being with Shirley Anne Field, who enjoyed Dudley's affections for several months. But there was never just one female in his life at a time, and the back of his diary had a crammed list of "Girls to See Again." One would not have been enough to feed his huge emotional void. Seldom would it ever be.

In April 1965, he turned thirty. And for Dudley the usual reflections at this milestone were made all the more intense by a restless urge to return to serious music. His classical side had given way in later school and Oxford years to jazz, but he was now feeling restive about its neglect. What he really wanted was to write an opera, but he was too undisciplined to get around to it. He had already vaguely mapped out an idea to write what was essentially a romantic piece of work that would blend the accessibility of *West Side Story* with the musicianship of *Peter Grimes*.

Yet he found it hard to apply himself, which depressed him greatly. He felt desperate and, more than anything else in the world, craved some sort of organization to his life. He had always believed that, by the time he reached thirty, he would be where he wanted to be. He had never clearly defined that place in his mind beyond knowing that it was somewhere close to the pinnacle of success. But where, he wondered now, was that?

Dudley's practical musical tuition had pretty much ended in school, and there lay the root of his frustration. Lacking a teacher to inspire him, Dudley had allowed impatience to overtake him far too early. Instead of slowly perfecting his playing, he had dived eagerly into new waters without mastering the previous wave.

The discipline of daily piano practice had ceased when he entered Oxford, where his studies were concentrated on the theory of music. It was that inability to focus on the technical side of playing and writing music that dogged him now and exacerbated his feelings of inadequacy. He knew in his heart that the potential for something good, if not great, was in him, and yet he was incapable of putting it down on paper.

In a brief respite from his increasingly haunting thoughts, less than a week after his thirtieth birthday, Dudley was best man at the country wedding of his dear friends George and Lysie. He brought a choir up from London and played a poignant wedding anthem which he had especially composed.

He was still playing jazz with the trio, alternating regularly with John Dankworth at the Cool Elephant on Margaret Street, a romantic nightclub in the West End. And it was here, in the early summer of 1965, that he met the girl who would become his first wife.

Blonde, beautiful, and on the seriously leggy side, twenty-one-year-old Suzy Kendall came from a middle-class family in Derbyshire, where she had spent ten years in a convent. Hoping for a career as an interior designer like her father, she had studied at Derby Art College and then gone to Positano in Italy to paint. There she met and married a jazz musician, but the marriage ended after just six months.

Returning to London, her good looks diverted her into modeling, but that did not last long. Her first assignment was a disaster when she had to model an ostrich-feather hat during a millinery show and, unable to see through the feathers, missed the end of the ramp and fell off the walkway. Director Christopher Miles, Sarah's brother, persuaded her into acting and signed her to play a model in his film *Up Jumped the Swagman*.

She was now receiving plenty of attention for her work, although her greatest acclaim would come later with her poignant performances as the poor little rich girl in *Up the Junction* and the schoolgirl with a crush on Sidney Poitier in *To Sir With Love*.

Dudley had already seen Suzy on Lance Percival's television variety show and had expressed a desire to meet her, but when he saw her at the Cool Elephant one night he decided to press harder.

As Suzy recalls, "He'd asked an old boyfriend of mine if he was still going out with me, and very naughtily my old boyfriend said yes, which wasn't true. So Dudley had left it at that. But when he saw me on this night he came over and had a drink with me at the bar. The person I was with had disappeared by then, and Dudley asked if I'd like a lift home. Which of course I did. He was lovely, and I found him very amusing and very sweet."

Unlike most of Britain, Suzy had not seen *Beyond the Fringe* or *Not Only ... But Also*. She had no idea, even, that Dudley was a comedian. "All I knew about him was his jazz that he played with his trio at the club. The music was incredible and it knocked me out. Of course within about a week I realized that he was also very much a comedian."

At five foot five, she was less than three inches taller than Dudley—which rather contradicted the constant assertions in the press that he only liked to date tall women.

"Dudley had always been a great crumpet man," recalls Vic Lewis, who was now a close friend and father figure to Dudley after briefly serving as his agent in the months before the *Fringe*, "but when Suzy came along he dropped a lot of that. There was a long bar in the Cool Elephant, and sometimes if he came in late he'd just sit there with Suzy. I often saw them nattering at the bar with his arm around her and thought it looked like something special."

Dudley's jazz, which had overwhelmed Suzy, was now traversing the country, not only via television but in public engagements that ran the gamut from nightclubs to universities. But soon Dudley's darker side was reasserting itself, and almost daily therapy seemed not to help much, although he was at least beginning to come to grips with the anger he had long harbored against his mother for her attitude toward his foot.

For the first time he was recognizing why he had been so drawn to comedy. Only now, through much introspection and psychotherapy, did he understand that he had become a comic to deflect the hostility directed toward him in his youth. The discovery filled him with resentment, and he was angry at the realization that he had allowed his intellectual potential to be wasted.

There was another cause for his dejection. It focused, as it had for long, on the lack of discipline in his life, which he seemed incapable of imposing, no matter how much he wished it. He believed that if he could only force himself to do four hours of composing and practicing every day then everything else in his life would fall into place. It seemed to him ludicrous to crave this so much and yet be unable to impose it upon himself.

His creative attempts succumbed to trivial distractions. "I put a pencil down," he would fret, "then I can't find it and the whole day is finished because I can't find the rotten pencil. So I go to the pictures. It doesn't matter that there are six more pencils in the bedroom. It's ridiculous."

Ridiculous maybe, but it was nagging away at him and causing him increasingly more anxiety. No matter how hard he wanted to establish a routine of musical practice, he just could not enforce it. "Practice, practice, practice!" composer Patrick Gowers had told him, after hearing and applauding his 1960 concert at the Royal Festival Hall, and Dudley knew how crucial that was if he were to attain the peak level of musicianship he wanted so much to reach.

In spite of his melancholy, 1965 was proving a highly fruitful year. As well as live jazz performances in the London nightclubs, there had been innumerable appearances on television (*Juke Box Jury*, *Late Night Line-Up*, *The Braden Beat*, *Sunday Night at the London Palladium*, *Billy Cotton's Band Show*, *The Wayne and Schuster Show*) and regular radio spots with the trio on *Jazz Club*, *The Lively Arts*, and *Late Night Extra*. There was also an expected leading role in *Love Story*, a terse television drama directed by Roman Polanski, and an astonishing and largely improvised mock opera, *Lady Chatterley's Lover*, with Peter Ustinov, in which Dudley took the guise of various composers. Most amazing of all was *Offbeat*, a classical music program in which he played seventeen assorted characters from the world of music.

And then there was Suzy.

There was still a plethora of women floating around his life, but Dudley reveled in Suzy's company. She was the perfect soul mate, with a huge and appealing sense of humor, and she understood his insecurities. Instead of laughing them off as unfounded, she tried to bolster his self-belief, all the while encouraging his talent with her gentle admiration.

Dudley still went to his parents in Dagenham most Sundays for lunch. Now he began taking Suzy with him.

"His mother was a very dear woman," Suzy reflects. "Not physically demonstrative, but she always gave me a hug. I loved her dearly. She was a smashing person, really sweet and jolly. A complete innocent. But very private. Both his parents were, and it was really difficult to get them to go anywhere. Jock was a bit diffident, never one to raise his voice. They seemed very sweet together."

Suzy was acutely aware that Dudley had felt deprived of love during his childhood, but as she got to know Ada better, she saw in her a quietly caring mother. "In her own way she was very loving and warm. I think she always felt guilty about his leg, yet, like a lot of people of her generation, she swept the issue under the carpet and that isn't necessarily the best thing for a child. It doesn't mean that she was unfeeling; she just didn't know how to deal with it."

Suzy found Ada very supportive of Dudley, "and immensely proud of him. I think she showed that to him. But then you could show it to Dudley and he wouldn't recognize it, so he wouldn't necessarily have felt it. He always thought he wasn't lovable, so he could never quite understand that somebody could love him."

It was now that Dudley's trio recorded *The Other Side of Dudley Moore*, the second jazz album with Chris Karan and Pete McGurk. He wrote five of the eight tracks, which included the earlier numbers he had written for George and Lysie, and a special one for Suzy, called "Sooz Blooz." It became Britain's biggest-selling jazz album of 1965. Despite inner yearnings to write serious music, he was still very much engulfed in jazz, and this album was soon followed by another, *Genuine Dud*.

The success of *Not Only ... But Also* had made Dudley and Peter Cook widely sought after for other show-business projects, and it was inevitable that films would follow.

Bryan Forbes had assembled an expensive, £750,000 black comedy, *The Wrong Box*, based on a novel by Robert Louis Stevenson and Lloyd Osbourne. In his opinion, Cook and Moore were two of the greatest comedy talents ever to be seen in British television and he asked them to play brief roles. "They were great exponents of black humor," says Forbes, "and I thought they'd be marvelous in the film." He was right, although holding their own against such a formidable cast (made up of Ralph Richardson, John Mills, Peter Sellers, Wilfrid Lawson, Tony Hancock, Michael Caine, and Forbes's wife, Nanette Newman) was not easy.

The comedy concerns a battle between the families of the last two survivors of a tontine, a financial arrangement in which the last surviving member inherits the fortune. While the surviving elderly brothers (John Mills and Ralph Richardson) scheme to kill each other off in order to gain the inheritance, Moore and Cook, as their two greedy, villainous nephews, also plot against them to grab the inheritance for themselves.

Their scenes were filmed over a two-week period in September 1965 on location in Bath.

It was not an easy introduction into film for Dudley who, for almost the first time in his career, found himself answerable to someone else rather than his own sense of comedy. He found Forbes, a former actor, reluctant to rely upon the comic instincts of his comedians during scripted scenes. Forbes was looking for exaggerated gags and heavy-handed slapstick and he showed his actors how he wanted something played, but Dudley was unhappy at having his comedic hands tied. He didn't like this style of direction and disapproved of Forbes's attitude toward comedy. "Bryan gave you very little room to do your own thing," he says, "and I felt I wasn't being allowed to do what I was being employed for. It wasn't much fun for me."

Bryan Forbes, who in spite of Dudley's discomfort became a lifetime friend, has somewhat different recollections of the experience and was astonished to hear that Dudley had felt unhappy during the filming. "I certainly didn't notice that at the time, although, if I'm honest, Peter was more at ease in front of the camera than Dudley. Possibly Dudley found it not that easy to take direction, because they'd been so used to working on their own.

"They weren't straight actors and they had to learn a new technique. They hadn't had to stick to scripted dialogue before, and Dudley didn't exactly take to it like a duck to water, whereas Peter adapted more easily.

"I think they were both somewhat in awe of acting with Ralph Richardson. Quite rightly. And it was a very distinguished cast, like a Who's Who of acting. It was a microcosm of the best of British talent. But they came into the film absolutely at the peak of their fame in television terms and were absolutely brilliant."

In spite of Dudley's own unease during the filming of *The Wrong Box*, the film seems to have been an intensely happy experience for everyone else concerned. "We were all together a great deal and we had hilarious times," recalls Nanette Newman. "There were a lot of laughs, and Dudley was always incredibly funny. Every night we'd go to look at the rushes and end up in fits of laughter."

John Mills had no scenes with Dudley but spent a lot of time on the set watching him at work. "I found it particularly enjoyable to be around him and Peter," he recalls. "They always seemed to be laughing, which made it a lot of fun for the rest of us. I can understand Dudley being nervous, but he had no reason to think he was bad, as I later heard he did, because he was nothing of the sort. He was very good."

Bryan Forbes's own memories are of a hilarious couple of weeks filled with perpetual laughter. "We gagged an awful lot, and I encouraged that because it fitted into the spirit of the piece. We used to have marvelous lunches sitting around in the trailer and we laughed ourselves sick. Dudley was always outrageous, with a bizarre, sometimes macabre, sense of humor. It was a very happy film to be on, and I thought Peter and Dudley were marvelous and contributed enormously."

When *The Wrong Box* was released, Forbes's direction emerged as astute and incisive and nowhere near as formulaic as Dudley had believed. But Dudley was so unhappy with the work he'd done—"I thought my perform-ance was hideous, and I was very embarrassed about it"—that he did not attend the premiere—a fact that could scarcely have escaped Bryan Forbes, since it had been arranged for Dudley to sit between Forbes and Nanette Newman.

"I was very disappointed he didn't come," says Forbes, "both for him and myself. Although I'm glad it didn't spoil our friendship. But Dudley has had his share of demons to contend with, and not turning up at the premiere was an example of his angst."

The film was received with mixed reception. The London critics were generally very unkind, although some called it British comedy at its best, largely due to Cook and Moore, "who graced the screen with their unique brand of unadulterated lunacy." Kenneth Tynan, in the *Observer*, though praising their "exemplary slickness," was disappointed that the script "leaves no room for the kind of improvised comedy on which their genius thrives." In America, by contrast, Cook and Moore won kudos in "a farce so fantastic and explosive that it virtually pops right out of the screen" said the *New York Times*, and *Newsweek* dubbed it "as funny, sunny, and urbane a movie as any audience could ask for."

Ultimately, the film was not a success at the box office, although years later, it would be regarded as a comedy classic. Dudley and Peter's first film together had not been the wild smash hit they both hoped. But they had hardly emerged as losers.

CHAPTER 8

S U Z Y

1965

"I couldn't understand how anybody who was so funny, so musically talented, and so attractive to women could possibly have any problems. But angst goes so deep that, if it's there, it's there. It has to do with self-esteem. Dudley just wasn't easy in his skin, and that was a mystery—probably as much to him as it was to anybody else."

—DICK CLEMENT

With his newly accumulated wealth, Dudley had taken a ten-year lease on a Cheyne Walk flat in Chelsea. He was there very seldom, and it was mostly a convenience from which to conduct an affair with wealthy socialite Diana Phipps, from whom he'd taken the flat. Diana, in her early twenties, was tall, leggy, and brunette, with a flair for interior design. She adored Dudley, and was always adding some expensive new decorating touch to the home.

These were difficult months for Suzy, who was head over heels in love with Dudley but found her happiness periodically interrupted by his various wanderings. Far from instilling confidence in his girlfriends, Dudley did the reverse, and Suzy must have suffered immense insecurities by his instinctive philandering.

But, in spite of other female distractions, Dudley was spending so much time with Suzy that eventually he decided to move in with her, and the two settled into the domesticated warmth of her own Chelsea flat. Public appetite being what it was, the couple soon became prime fodder for celebrity-hungry photographers. "We never did anything very much," says Suzy, "but somehow whenever we went out there was always a press photographer taking pictures."

The popularity of Dudley and Peter Cook had reached immense proportions. They were being courted everywhere, and even topped the bill at the Royal Command Performance, throwing in some good-natured, and probably not unexpected, jokes at the expense of the royal family.

The unprecedented response to *Not Only ... But Also* resulted now in a second series, produced by Dick Clement, who recalls a memorable first meeting with the comedy duo at the BBC's White City studio.

"Peter made me feel deeply stupid, because the speed of his brain was so fast that it overawed me. I felt better later when I heard that Alan Bennett had had the same reaction—he said it would take him a week to produce a joke that he'd nurtured like a rose and delicately produced, while Peter would come out with twenty jokes in sixty seconds."

The partnership was still in the blooming stage. They were having fun with their work and each other, although there were some mildly stormy moments. Dudley was irritated with Peter's lack of directness in dealing with people, while Peter became irritated with Dudley's logical mind, which was in such direct contrast to his own. But their occasional squabbling worked as a creative catalyst, and on the whole their relationship was a close and symbiotic one.

"There was a great confidence for Dudley in knowing that so many ideas were coming out of Peter's head," says Dick Clement. "Peter was incredibly prolific, and it gave Dudley an enormous security. They were very easy together and had no real ego problems. It was a very smooth team, and they fed each other extremely well."

Some of the most inventive and hilarious moments were caught in the filmed sequences, which did not always go as planned. One snowy winter's day provided an unexpected gem on film for Clement.

"We were filming an opening segment of Dud and Pete having an out-of-season holiday, and we went to the funfair and asked if we could get the Big Dipper going. This bloke said he could get it to the top, but with all the ice on the rails, he didn't know if it would make the next crest. We all looked at each other and said, 'Please let's hope it doesn't!' And as the light started to fade we got this amazing shot of Dud and Pete getting to the top loop of the Big Dipper—then it went down and up ... and then back and forward ... and back ... and then it finally got stuck and settled there. It was hysterical!"

Another memorable sketch was an opening sequence with Pete and Dud talking to camera while rising and separating from each other. As the camera pulled back, it showed them both standing on Tower Bridge, one on each side. The bridge had been raised while the two were standing on it.

Dudley's music was becoming as satirical as his dialogue, and his Bo Duddley sketch, Papa's Got a Brand New Bag, in particular, was notable for its ambiguous lyrics. Now and then their humor and language went beyond what was considered tasteful on television, resulting in heavy mail for the

BBC. Frank Muir, as head of Comedy, had a diplomatic standard response for irate viewers, assuring them that "We're always pushing the boundaries of taste because they are constantly changing, and it's letters like yours that help us know when and if we have overstepped the mark."

It was now, as the second series drew to a close, that they filmed a sketch that could have proved fatal for Dudley.

"The moment that nearly ended Dudley's career," recalls Dick Clement, "and probably mine as well, and which was terribly frightening, was when we were doing a sequence in the Thames. Peter and Dudley were sitting on a large board suspended by four cables that had to be lowered into the water, and as the board hit the Thames, the cables went slack and one wrapped itself across Dudley's shoulders and neck. I could see that when they lifted the strain and the cable became taut again, it might slice his head off. It was one of those moments when it was completely out of my control, because the cables were being operated by a crane-driver who was beyond shouting distance."

In the end the cable gave Dudley only a glancing blow, but it was the most terrifying moment of his career for Clement, who was convinced that Dudley was about to be decapitated.

It has been written that the couple finally went so far astray that the BBC pulled the show off the air. In fact they had an open brief to return with a new series. "The BBC had a laissez-faire attitude at that time," says Dudley, "and it was left to us whether we would do another or not, and we did eventually come back for a third series."

Sadly, and with a remarkable lack of foresight, the BBC erased almost all of the tapes. Today, nothing remains of this vintage show except some filmed sequences and a compilation tape salvaged from surviving video.

Earlier in the series, Cook and Moore had played a rather muddled sketch about a bumblebee. They now recorded this as a single. Sung in a Liverpudlian style, the duo's harmonizing led people to believe they were listening to a Beatles record. "People thought it was John Lennon singing," laughs Dudley, "but it was me, for crying out loud! It zoomed up the charts because everyone thought it was a Beatles record, and it did great at first, but when people found out it wasn't the Beatles, it sank without a trace."

For the past two years, since returning to England, Dudley had continued with his therapy. Unlike in America, where the examination of the mind was being recognized as valid as any other medical treatment, psychoanalysis was looked down on in England. Most people didn't understand it and were likely to assume someone was marginally mad if he was in therapy.

"In England people gravitate to a cup of tea and pretend everything is fine," reflects Dudley. "I hated that attitude. Any kind of psychotherapy was looked on with considerable scorn there. People preferred to tell you to pull yourself together, and I felt like throwing a phone at somebody when they said that. It's ignorance."

His close friends could see that therapy was clearly proving of some benefit to Dudley, and he spent many hours discussing his treatment with George and Lysie Hastings. Lysie believes "he desperately needed to open up about himself, and therapy helped him do that. In those days all us young, trendy people in the sixties were trying everything. Sex, drugs, and therapy. It was the older generation who wouldn't go near it."

Dudley should have been earning commission from the number of people he was passing on to his psychotherapist, Dr. Stephen Sebag-Montefiore. Says Lysie, "Dudley put me on to him, and I put someone else on to him, and in the end we were all going to see him! And we all talked with each other about our therapy. Nothing but. It was the most marvelous point of conversation. We never shut up about it."

But Dudley felt most people were still unaware of its value. "The wonderful thing about therapy," he told his friends, "is that it makes you realize you have every right to be anxious about being alive."

In that case, then, everything was fairly normal. Because he certainly was suffering inordinate anxieties about his existence. What Dudley really wanted was the security he believed he would achieve once he came to know and understand himself. He hated that he felt afraid of people and that he was wasting so much of his time and energy by being anxious. Only when he was working did he feel some relief from his haunting thoughts.

And yet even his work provoked anxiety. What was the point, he wondered, of knocking himself out, playing the piano, and being funny on television? Fame, success, acclaim—what did it all mean in the end? He felt he had little to offer, and that a successful career had little to do with a successful life.

On the surface, Dudley seemed to hold the world in his grasp but underneath he was unable to feel any sense of accomplishment. He was riddled with depression about his future and how he could fill and justify his life. He should have been reveling in a sense of tingling anticipation about his career and the fame that was pouring his way. Instead, in his almost relentlessly melancholic state, he felt himself hovering above a chasm of hopelessness.

For some time Dudley and Suzy had been looking for a home to buy, and now they found what they'd been searching for. Bentham House was a tall, two-hundred-year-old Georgian house on a Hampstead hill with seven rooms on four floors. It had an enchanting walled garden where squirrels mischievously romped, and part of the foundation had been built around a tree trunk. Underground springs ran through the basement. Although it was in the heart of Hampstead, it had the ambiance of a small country manor.

The couple established a cozy, familial lifestyle, and Suzy bought two Persian cats to make it even more domestic; one they named Charlie, the other Ada, after Dudley's mother.

"We were real homebodies," says Suzy, and they did, on the whole, prefer to stay home alone or entertain friends at little dinner parties. And play music. Dudley had a piano in the first-floor living room and a Hammond organ in the basement kitchen, so he was able to wander between instruments as the mood took him.

The huge kitchen, with its stripped pine that was all the fashion then, became the focus of informal gatherings. It was modern without being ostentatious, and was full of the antiques that Suzy and Dudley loved to collect.

Sometimes they took drives into the country in Dudley's black Maserati, a flashy number with its own fridge, in which he stashed lemon-flavored Popsicles and champagne, but which caused him immense irritation "because the ice was always melting when the engine was turned off." If he forgot to turn off the fridge, the battery would be dead the next morning. The windshield wipers didn't work too well, and once, when Dudley was doing a two-week tour of England, he had to keep stopping to use a potato to wipe off the rain.

Or they would take off in Suzy's car, her second yellow E-type Jaguar. Dudley had bought her the first as a present, but the day he gave it to her, he parked it overnight in the street and it was promptly stolen. Immediately, and before even notifying the insurance company of the loss, he replaced it with an identical model.

His relationship with Suzy had not impinged on his friendship with Peter Cook, and he and Suzy took a long vacation on the island of Grenada with Peter, his wife Wendy, and their baby. Actually, it wasn't supposed to be a vacation at all. Peter had persuaded Dudley to join him so they could work on a film idea without the constant interruptions of telephone and friends. But he had told Dudley one thing and Wendy another. After they arrived in Grenada, it became abundantly clear that Peter was unwilling to work and, on one of the few occasions on which Dudley really lost his temper with Peter, he stood on the beach and screamed at his partner that he'd dragged them all the way out there under false pretenses.

Stanley Donen, the eminent director of such classic films as *Singin' in the Rain* and *Funny Face*, was a passionate Anglophile and now lived in London. He adored English comedy and became a devotee of *Not Only ... But Also*. "Peter and Dudley were the most brilliant artists I'd ever seen," he recalls. "They bowled me over. So I got in touch with them and said I'd love to do a movie and could we all think of an idea. It was the first time I'd called any performer to say I liked them so much that I wanted to work with them. Nor can I think of another instance since."

As it happened, Peter and Dudley had already written a rough script (if Peter had applied himself in Grenada it would now have been a polished script) that was a comedy version of the Faust story, with Peter as the Devil and Dudley as the man who sells his soul. Donen loved the concept and worked with Peter Cook on shaping the screenplay. The result was *Bedazzled*, and, in order to make it on a small budget (six hundred thousand dollars), Cook, Moore, and Donen took not a single penny in salary.

It was, Peter Cook would later claim, the only film with which he was ever remotely satisfied. Dudley enjoyed making it and found Donen, though "very opinionated," to be very nice. "He wanted things done his way, but there was an understanding between us that they might be done differently."

The film costarred Raquel Welch and Eleanor Bron and was a blithe, bizarre number that turned logic upside down, as Peter was so fond of doing.

The story revolves around George Spiggott, played by Peter, and Stanley Moon, played by Dudley. Just as Peter Cook had always assumed Spiggott's name wherever possible (from his One-Legged Tarzan sketch), so had Dudley often used Moon's name after John Gielgud had inadvertently identified him as Stanley Moon in his introductory letter to Lilli Palmer. It appealed to his sense of humor now to use this name for his character in *Bedazzled*.

Stanley Moon is a cook in a Wimpy hamburger restaurant. Infatuated with a waitress (Eleanor Bron), he is too timid to speak to her. Befriended by George Spiggott (who turns out to be the Devil), after failing in an attempt to kill himself, he is offered seven wishes in exchange for eternal damnation. In the hope of winning his waitress, Moon accepts and in the process encounters the Seven Deadly Sins.

The most memorable of these, for a variety of reasons, is Raquel Welch as Lillian Lust. For the bed scene in which she was supposed to seduce him, Dudley wore three pairs of underpants, "thinking, if I got an erection, maybe three pairs would help! I was even thinking of tying down my genitals with a plaster. I thought it was going to be very embarrassing. Ultimately it turned out to be unerotic, because I was caught up in thinking of the script."

As Stanley Donen laughingly attests, "I think Dudley was quite aroused by her. But that's what she was supposed to do. That's why she was in the movie—and, God knows, she was about the sexiest-looking creature that ever walked at that moment. That's the disease of being a male—that constant randiness that we can't deny Dudley always had. He would see a girl and become very aroused."

It was the first movie that Cook and Moore had carried on their own but, according to Donen, there were no nerves about being the stars.

Donen admired them enormously, and believes that helped to allay any trepidation they might have felt. "The whole point is to have somebody in charge who really appreciates what you're doing, and I adored them both and admired their talents. So there was no question about their being terrified. We all seemed very much of a group."

With most of the filming fairly close to London, Suzy was often able to join Dudley on location and Stanley Donen was a little nervous at first, thinking he should have put her in the film. "I was a bit ill at ease about that, but once everything was cast, it was out of my hands. She seemed delighted and happy to be there when she came down to the set, and the three of us often ate together."

In many ways, Dudley was the antithesis of the character he now found himself playing. Moon's ineptitude when approaching the opposite sex was hardly a trait of Dudley's; nor did Dudley suffer constant rejection though he always feared it.

"Stanley Moon," says Donen, "was a terrified creature who never had the courage to try anything. That's not Dudley Moore. Stanley was terrified to approach a woman, and that's certainly not Dudley. He may be afraid of rejection, but he still proposes himself. That's the measure of courage—to do things you're afraid to do.

"Dudley was remarkably insecure, and I was very aware of that, but I think that's one of the reasons he's so intelligent and gifted. He drives himself harder and harder to be wiser and funnier, more self-deprecating, more gifted, more understanding, and wiser. I understood that, and I understood the insecurities he'd carried from childhood."

One of the most bizarre scenes from the film had Raquel Welch gyrating on a bar counter above Dudley, who was dressed in a nun's habit. "To see this gorgeous creature barely clothed and bumping and grinding away just above a nun who is sitting smoking and drinking was an outrageous image," Donen laughs. "Another hilarious scene has Dudley being shown around the nunnery by Peter and letting off endless raspberries."

That scene happens also to be Dudley's favorite, though it was not the easiest to achieve. "It was murder when we came to loop the sound," he remembers wryly, "because I had to match all these raspberries, and I was really straining my cheeks to come out with the sounds. At the end of the looping my cheeks ached like mad with all the blowing."

There was so much laughter on this film that Dudley sometimes lost control. In one scene, he and Peter were whizzing around in bumper cars at the fair. Peter sat next to Avarice (Daniele Noel), while Dudley sat next to Gluttony (Parnell McGarry), who was stuffing herself with cream buns and looking remarkably bored. "I wasn't supposed to be laughing, but suddenly I got the giggles and I just couldn't stop."

Donen was also in fits of laughter half the time and found it hard to control himself. "I always say making movies is anything but fun," he reflects, "yet there is one exception and that is *Bedazzled*, because it was just so funny. My main problem was keeping quiet during the takes—I could barely restrain myself from laughing. There was never any tension and we had a lot of fun, but they were both also very serious artists. They didn't take filmmaking at all lightly."

If there had been any tension, Dudley would have taken his usual escape route out of it. There was always a piano on the set, and while new camera positions were being set up Dudley would lose himself in music. "Whenever I looked up," says Donen, "there he was playing. It was delightful. He's a very dedicated musician with a remarkable taste and ear. And out of it came the most marvelous score."

Dudley's music for *Bedazzled*, which he also performed with his trio and singer Barbara Moore, had Donen in ecstasy. "It was agreed from the start that he would do it, and it was wonderful. I loved what he wrote. I expected it to be good, but it turned out to be better even than that. It was full of variety, of all kinds of music."

Dudley would always consider *Bedazzled* one of his favorite films, but the public obviously did not agree. When it was released the following year, it received a tepid reception that Dudley believed was because it was so different from anything he and Cook had done since their television series. Significantly, the film would fare much better in those countries where the series had never been aired.

For three years, Peter and Dudley had shared a remarkably successful comedy partnership. Now they decided to move in separate directions for a while and see where it would take them.

While making *Bedazzled*, Peter had been told by Stanley Donen that he could become the new Cary Grant. Now he decided to go off in search of that far from inglorious possibility.

And so Dudley, for virtually the first time since *Beyond the Fringe* began in 1960, was entirely on his own.

CHAPTER 9

CYNTHIA AND OTHER FILMS

1967-1971

"He felt he was wasting his life. He really felt, and I think still does, that music was very important and he hadn't fulfilled himself, he hadn't written the thing that he wanted to write. He didn't know what it was, but time, as he said, was just passing and he still hadn't got down to doing it."

—JOSEPH MCGRATH

Joe McGrath had long wanted to work again with Dudley, and in the spring of 1967 he had the opportunity. Producer Walter Shenson, for whom Joe had worked on the Beatles' film *Help!*, offered to finance a film if McGrath could come up with a story. Dudley was eager to work with the Scotsman again. He liked McGrath's cheeky sense of humor and his directing style, which allowed his actors considerable freedom.

Together, they conceived *30 Is a Dangerous Age, Cynthia*, about an obscure musician, Rupert Street, trying to carve his niche in life by composing a successful musical before his thirtieth birthday, six weeks away. It bore more than a passing resemblance to Dudley's own life, although Dudley, now almost thirty-two, had already seen his landmark birthday come and go without the dream being fulfilled.

Shenson agreed to finance the film for five hundred thousand pounds, but was insistent that the hero also be searching for a wife by the age of thirty, and he brought in John Wells to split the screenwriting chores three ways. Dudley objected to Rupert's pursuit of a wife, but was overruled. "I really wanted it to be a simple story about a man who wants to compose music. It seemed to me irrelevant that he get married."

Joe McGrath agrees that Shenson had a lot to do with altering the shape of *Cynthia* just before they began shooting. "In a way, it was changing direction as we were doing it. And perhaps we compromised on some things that we shouldn't have compromised on."

Oddly, the casting of the girlfriend was one that defeated Shenson and McGrath for quite a while, even though the answer was staring them in the face. As written in the script, the girlfriend was an artist born in Belper, Derbyshire. Just as Suzy Kendall had been.

"Dudley had actually written the story around us," Suzy relates, "but he didn't try to get me cast for it. He never even mentioned me. It was Joe McGrath who finally said, 'Why can't we use Suzy?' I was very happy that he wanted me to do it, because he was a wonderful and funny man to work for and an old friend of Dudley, which made Dudley feel particularly comfortable."

The title itself (contrary to belief) meant absolutely nothing and was one that Dudley had simply picked out of thin air, but there were many autobiographical touches throughout the film, few of which were recognizable. The name of Rupert's girlfriend, Louise Hammond, was a composite drawn from Celia Hammond and Louise McDermott, a girl Dudley had known at school. As for Rupert Street, Dudley fondly named him after Rupert Bear, tagging him with a surname that amused him, as Rupert Street is close to London's Tin Pan Alley.

One autobiographical incident in the film was directly attributable to Dudley's mother, who had always done his laundry through the mail during his Oxford days and, like Rupert's mother in the film, had usually included a bag of lemon candy and some bread pudding in the return package.

There was, however, one scene that had nothing to do with Dudley's reality and was a particularly unpleasant experience for him. He had to ride a horse, which he'd never done before in his life. "He was terrified," says Suzy. "He hated horses, and was extremely frightened. But Dudley trying to get on the horse was one of the funniest things I've ever seen. In the end he had to be lifted on, and there are some funny shots of him looking incredibly uncomfortable. He was not happy at all."

Dudley had always used his irrepressible humor and a multitude of different voices to relieve tension. On *Cynthia* he went one step further. "He got into a habit of farting before each take," relates Joe McGrath, "and it was hysterical. The boy would run across and slate it, and then Dudley would go 'Pppff!' I'd see his face turn bright red and I'd say, 'OK, calm down now, calm down and...action'—and then he'd blow it. He did that on every take, and in *Cynthia* there were something like six hundred takes. Even if he wasn't in the scene but was on the set, he'd run across and fart before we slated."

"But it didn't stop him from being professional. He was absolutely marvelous. There was a great feeling on the set around him, and everybody respected him."

It was inevitable that his sense of humor would rub off on the others, and sometimes it felt more like being in a graduation school for pranks than on a film set.

Joe McGrath had to go to Dublin for a few days' location work, and he took Dudley and art director Brian Eatwell with him. On their second night, Brian arranged dinner for them with three Irish girls, which progressed to a disco and a very late night. The following morning over breakfast they met and compared notes, each having paired off and gone separate ways around midnight. "We all were rather strangely quiet," laughs McGrath, "and a bit downcast. And then it transpired that, as far as romance was concerned, the night had been a washout for every one of us. We couldn't work out why this was, and then Brian burst into giggles and said, 'Maybe the fact that the three women were nervous nuns had something to do with it.' He'd set the whole thing up!"

Despite Dudley's misgivings about the restructuring of the story, the role was tailor-made to display his myriad talents. As actor, comedian, and musician it was a remarkable show of skill. A high point was his ballad to Suzy à la Noel Coward, which managed within it to mimic Bach, Beethoven, Mozart, and Handel. He did it all in *Cynthia*, from playing the piano, violin, and mandolin, to singing rock 'n' roll. He even managed a tenor duet with himself, and a bit of soft-shoe shuffle. As one American critic later commented, "That guy's a British Sammy Davis. There's nothing he can't do."

The film was a happy one to make for all concerned—particularly for Dudley in working with Suzy. "He seemed to be very happy at that time and very relaxed," recalls McGrath. "He was wonderful to work with, because he gave it 100 percent attention and thought about what he was doing. What was marvelous was that he so obviously enjoyed it."

McGrath knew that Dudley had experienced a difficult time with Bryan Forbes, since Dudley had often called him during the filming of *The Wrong Box*. "The worst thing you can do with some comedy actors," explains McGrath, "is show them what to do, because then you destroy their vision and their instinctive way of doing it. So I just let Dudley get on with it, and it worked out brilliantly."

As well as starring in the film, Dudley was also writing the score. But he was being painstakingly slow about it. Eventually Walter Shenson admonished him for taking too long and told him they had run out of money and he would have to stop. "Dudley was very upset about that," recalls Joe McGrath. "He came in and said, 'I'll pay for the rest of it.

Whatever the difference is, I'll make it up.' He felt very strongly about it, but they managed to sort it out."

Dudley was anxious to capture the right music for the mood of the film but, following his usual creative pattern, he didn't produce it until the very last moment. He was still scribbling away when Suzy drove him to the studio where a full symphony orchestra was waiting to record the score. "He finished it in the car," she recalls, "literally minutes before they were due to start recording. But he was always like that, doing everything at the last second. Always brilliant at the last minute. Because he would do so much and reject it. It was never good enough, until finally time ran out and he had to go with whatever he'd done."

Dudley conducted the orchestra himself. It was the greatest thrill of his life, and he was deeply moved by the experience. He was so overwhelmed by the occasion that, even when they had the score in the can, he asked if they could do it just one more time, so he could savor the experience again. Much later, an American critic would describe the score as "a respectful homage to composers like Elgar and Delius and inventive in its orchestration, creating a sensual feel for mood and atmosphere."

Clive Donner had hoped Dudley would score *What's New, Pussycat?* and Dudley already agreed, but when it came to the crunch, he was still in the midst of composing *Cynthia*. In the end, Donner brought in Burt Bacharach, who, years later, would score Dudley's Hollywood hit movie *Arthur*.

Dudley's reputation as a film composer was gathering momentum, and as soon as he had completed *Cynthia*, Anthony Page asked him to write the score for his film version of John Osborne's *Inadmissible Evidence*, in which Nicol Williamson hauntingly played a middle-aged solicitor on the verge of a nervous breakdown.

The score—including a theme tune which Dudley sang himself—was not much appreciated by Osborne, who to Dudley's chagrin deemed it merely "adequate," although that was sweetened considerably by Anthony Page's vociferous approval.

"I felt he wrote a very effective score," says Page. "It was very spare, with some sixties pop music—just what was needed for this film. His ability as a composer was brilliant, and I'd always admired that, ever since the first things he'd done for me in Oxford. He had an incredible love of music, and I could see he was still deeply immersed in that passion.

"There was one occasion when he came to work with me at the studio and I saw him arrive. But he stayed in his car for half an hour and I thought he must be ill, so I went down to him. I found him just sitting there, engrossed in a Beethoven symphony on the radio. He couldn't bring himself to leave the car until it was over."

There was one tiny upheaval these days in Dudley's settled home life at Bentham House. Ada, the Persian cat, was pregnant, and Suzy, who was in Belgrade filming a new movie, had left Dudley in charge of the preparations for feline motherhood.

"While I was gone," she recalls, "Ada gave birth to three kittens. I had a friend who wanted two, so I told Dudley to give them to her. But when I got back, three months later, there were all the cats. He couldn't bear to part with any of them. So we ended up with a total of five cats, which I wasn't terribly pleased about."

Dudley was very conscientious about raising the kittens, Sadie, Rupert, and Stanley, and his diary faithfully registered their weekly needs—when to start them lapping milk and when to begin them on soft foods. There was even a late entry that gleefully recorded they were "now off Ada." As Lysie Hastings observed, "He loved his cats so much and was utterly faithful to them. They were very important, and meant a lot to him."

Dudley missed Suzy a great deal during this time and flew often to Belgrade to see her (leaving elaborate notes to the maid about looking after the kittens). Coincidentally, during the time she was away, there had been more therapy sessions than in previous months. In a touching note in his diary, he wrote, "I miss Suzy (miss as in want)."

Shortly before Christmas 1967 he flew to New York for the premiere of *Bedazzled* and caught up with several old friends, including Peter Bellwood, who conveniently was getting married during Dudley's visit. It was the high point of his trip. When *Bedazzled* was released there, it was to poor reviews.

Time asserted that Cook and Moore "have failed to grasp the basic difference between a four-minute skit and a 107-minute movie." Charles Champlin, in the *Los Angeles Times*, called it "the most infuriating picture seen all year—because the best of it is so deliciously inventively good and the worst of it so appallingly, distastefully awful."

Dudley shrugged off the bad reviews and ten days later proudly sent a car to Dagenham to drive his parents to London for the British premiere. But the British reviews turned out to be just as scathing as their American counterparts. The general consensus was that Cook and Moore had failed to make the transition from the small screen.

Once again, Dudley was facing another rejection. His career so far had been a mystifying roller coaster of ups and downs, a pendulum constantly swinging between success and failure. In many ways, this would become a pattern from which he would never break free.

In March 1968 Dudley and Suzy flew to New York for the opening of *Cynthia*. The American critics raved about it, some of them describing it as the best thing they'd ever seen. *Esquire* acclaimed it as "genius ... one of the best films ever made with a major talent," while *Variety* and the *Hollywood*

Reporter called it "an important film." In Britain, however, the film would not be released until much later in the year, and then the reviews were infinitely less pleasing.

While they were in New York, Dudley and Suzy took in a few plays on Broadway and went to see Neil Simon's *Plaza Suite* on the same night as Jackie Kennedy. They were shocked at the way people were reacting to her presence—some left their seats to walk to the front of the theater and ogle her—and when some women shouted "Who's she with?" Dudley, disgusted, yelled back in a squeaky falsetto, "Donald Duck!"

Back in London he reteamed with Peter Cook in a new movie, Richard Lester's black comedy *The Bed-Sitting Room*, based on a bizarre antiwar play by Spike Milligan and John Antrobus. Set just after the end of the shortest nuclear war in history (two and a half minutes), the film satirizes the horror and devastation of nuclear war to emphasize its pacifist message.

The film depicts a handful of survivors attempting to overcome the physical-mutation effects of radiation. Among them are Ralph Richardson (Lord Fortnum), about to turn his home into a bed-sitting room, pregnant Rita Tushingham (Penelope), and her overzealous parents (Mona Washbourne and Arthur Lowe), who slowly mutate—one into a cupboard and the other into a parrot, which is eventually cooked and eaten. Dudley himself eventually mutates into a dog.

Peter and Dudley played two moronic policemen whose main contribution to the scene of disaster consisted of a warning to "Watch out, move along!" which they hurled down through megaphones as they hovered in a broken-down Volkswagen suspended beneath a helium balloon.

Dudley, who had come to believe that directors, on the whole, were power mad, found in Dick Lester a man who disliked everything that he or Peter did. "He wasn't prepared to let us be ourselves. I ad-libbed a bit, but, since he was directing the invention of that, too, I still wasn't allowed to do my thing."

Lester, whose previous films included the Beatles' *A Hard Day's Night*, seemed not at all sure of his intentions with *The Bed-Sitting Room*. Dudley remembers him continually asking for different opinions but rejecting them all, "which was very disconcerting, so the film lacked any thematic direction. He gave peculiar instructions that were hard to follow, and I couldn't understand what he wanted."

The most unsettling event took place when Cook and Moore had to go up in the balloon on a particularly windy day. A balloon expert, who went with them, admitted that he would not normally go up on such a day because they were at the mercy of the winds. The moment he spoke, the balloon fell violently to the ground and Peter, who had been kneeling

down, suffered a severely damaged cartilage. He had been planning a
month's vacation, and he got it—all spent in the hospital after surgeons
removed the cartilage.

Apart from his conflicts with Dick Lester, Dudley found it a jolly film
to work on. He liked Arthur Lowe and Mona Washbourne, and found Rita
Tushingham funny and pleasant—and very short. "We were all billed in
order of height. It went from Peter, then down to me, and finally Rita, who
was even shorter than me."

Dudley was fairly absorbed whenever he was working. It was when he
wasn't working that he became riddled with anxieties. He was now utterly
immersed in psychotherapy and, aside from regular therapy sessions, was
reading everything he could lay his hands on, devouring Freud and R. D.
Laing in a desperate attempt to understand and exorcise the ghosts that
haunted him: an obsession with his physical deformities and a persistent and
morbid feeling that time was moving on without his achieving certain ends.

Suzy saw the torment and understood his pain but was helpless to pull
him out of it. "Dudley was always searching for better creativity, especially
in his music. He could have been a great classical pianist if he'd gone that
route, but then we'd have missed a lot of wonderful humor.

"He was never satisfied," she reflects. "He always questioned whether
he was really successful or really happy, and I think he simply tended not to
see the reality. Maybe he was happy and successful anyway but simply didn't
know it."

Suzy was the constant factor in Dudley's life. The question of marriage had occasionally been raised between them, but they had never got
around to it—and Dudley had often publicly proclaimed his abhorrence of
the prospect of marriage. But in June 1968 at last it happened.

"He put a colander on his head," recalls Suzy, "went down on his
knees, and said, 'Will you marry me?' It was so funny. I said yes, and we
arranged the day and place. I asked two of my friends to come up, but I
didn't tell them we were getting married because I thought, if we don't do
it, then it won't matter and they'll just have a nice day in London. I wasn't
terribly sure even then that we were going to do it.

"The morning we were supposed to get married, he got out of bed
early and went into town. So I thought, 'OK, he's forgotten. Never mind.'
But in fact he'd gone to buy a ring, which hadn't occurred to me, and he
came back with it and of course I wasn't dressed, thinking he'd forgotten.
It was all quite amusing. We'd almost done it so many times or thought
about it and then not done it, because we were really happy not married."

They married very quietly at the Hampstead register office. Nobody
knew about it except Suzy's two friends. Dudley's secretary, Diana, only
learned about it when Suzy phoned her afterward.

There were no doubts the marriage would last. "They looked perfect together," observed Gillian Lynne, and indeed they were a wonderful couple—happy and in love. "Suzy was very good for Dudley," says Joe McGrath, "although it came as a surprise when they got married."

There was one sad note for Dudley. Just a few days after he and Suzy were married, Pete McGurk, the trio's bass player, committed suicide over an unhappy love affair with a Belgian girl. He was the second of Dudley's bass players to die, after Hugo Boyd's tragic accident seven years earlier. For quite some time after that, Dudley had nightmares that he might truly be jinxing anyone who took over the bass seat in his trio. When he eventually found a permanent replacement, it was Welshman Peter Morgan, who today remains alive and well.

Ken Annakin had asked Dudley and Peter Cook to unite in *Monte Carlo or Bust!*—which in America was titled *Those Daring Young Men in Their Jaunty Jalopies*, an attempt (much resisted by Annakin) by Paramount chief Robert Evans to cash in on the success of Annakin's earlier *Those Magnificent Men in Their Flying Machines.* It was a big-budget action comedy set in the 1920s, with a large cast that included Terry-Thomas, Tony Curtis, Susan Hampshire, Gert Frobe, Walter Chiari, Jack Hawkins, and Eric Sykes. Dudley and Peter played two competitors in the Monte Carlo Rally who battle obstacles that include snowstorms and precipices as well as escaped German convicts being chased by lunatic Italian police.

The film was shot in Sweden and Italy and, with perfect honeymoon timing, Dudley took Suzy with him on location.

Despite the logistical problems of filming abroad and with such a large cast, Dudley found Ken Annakin to be receptive and easygoing. Like Joe McGrath, Annakin was a director who did not believe in putting actors into straitjackets, which suited Dudley perfectly.

"Some actors really need you to guide you to what you want," says Annakin, "but with Dudley it was very much a joint affair and I didn't feel I was forcing anything.

"He worked very closely with Peter, and they were very happy to be together on the movie. They saw it as a good chance to continue the comedy they were doing so well, although I always felt that Dudley was a more obviously brilliant talent than Peter."

In one of the trickiest scenes, they had to drive down a toboggan ride, speaking their lines at the same time. It was a hairy ride and took a very long two minutes to wind down the run with all its turns and zigzags. Laughs Annakin, "It was probably the only time they did a scene in one take, because they desperately didn't want to have to do that ride again."

Dudley, as he had been on *Bedazzled* despite its small budget, was acutely anxious about the cost of *Monte Carlo or Bust!*, although he did not transmit those concerns to Annakin. He was worried lest too much film was turning over in the camera, even though he wasn't paying for it, and "I couldn't believe what was being spent just on my wardrobe. My overcoat and pith helmet alone cost a fortune."

Despite the upheaval of being on location for so long, it seemed a happy atmosphere around the film—except for Tony Curtis's bad temper when he had to dangle from a cliff by one arm.

As Ken Annakin recalls, "Everyone appeared to be very happy, but I'd heard stories that off the set Dudley and Suzy weren't getting on too well. Dudley had a piano in his trailer, and he played whenever he had the opportunity. I always thought that if things weren't going too well, it didn't make so much difference to him, because he would just slip away into his own world at the piano. I was very envious that he could just sit there and do it. Sometimes he parodied stuff, but very often he just slipped away into vague compositions that seemed to develop a tune, things he never seemed to repeat."

If there were any problems between Suzy and Dudley, not a hint of them leaked out in the steady stream of postcards and letters sent back to parents from their Italian locations. Nor were any apparent once they returned home to Hampstead, where life resumed a chaotic normality at Bentham House. They were real homebodies, and Suzy loved to cook for Dudley—especially his favorite roast lamb and leeks with Brussels sprouts and roast potatoes, followed by jelly. And Suzy always ensured there was plenty of salt on hand. "He loved his salt," she laughs. "He used to carry a horn around with him that was loaded with it, and he'd buy tomatoes and pour salt on them and eat them all the time. In the street, anywhere."

Friends were always dropping by. George and Lysie Hastings were frequent visitors. So was a teenage Tina Brown, whose parents were good friends of Dudley and Suzy. And, of course, there was Peter Cook. "He was much more prickly then—more competitive than in later years," says Suzy. "He and Dudley were very close, but not like brothers. They never had that kind of closeness."

Francis Megahy, another frequent guest, glimpsed a sense of competition in Peter that was absent whenever he saw the duo work on the taping of *Not Only ... But Also*. "Most of the time," he reflects, "what I saw between them was each reveling in the other person being so funny. But the dinners at Bentham House were a bit different. After dinner, Dudley would sometimes play the organ, and he was brilliant and very amusing. And then Peter would get into a competitive frenzy and stand up and do his Elvis Presley imitation, which was embarrassing because it was so terrible. He was a very amusing man, but this was something he could not do."

Robert Mann, Dudley's friend from New York since those first heady days of *Beyond the Fringe* at the Edinburgh Festival, sometimes stayed at Bentham House with his wife, Lucy, whenever he came to Britain to perform with the Juilliard Quartet. "I remember turning up at the house one time," recalls Mann, "and walking up the narrow staircase just as Peter Cook, who'd also been staying there, was coming down with his luggage. One of us had to back up because there wasn't room to pass.

"We loved staying there. Lucy and I were very fond of Suzy, who was adorable, and Dudley was very affectionate with her. They were very fond of each other."

Dudley and Suzy were, as Dick Clement puts it, "the quintessential sixties couple." Their life was a gregarious one, filled with fun and friends.

Every Saturday they pottered along the King's Road, browsing through the boutiques and always ending up in the antiques market. They lunched at the 235—invariably on cottage pie with Brussels sprouts—and in the evening went dancing at the popular nightclub the Aretusa. On Sundays they went over to Dagenham for lunch with Dudley's parents.

"We went there every single Sunday for lunch," recalls Suzy, "and it was always exactly the same wonderful meal: roast lamb and gravy that his mother cooked with two Oxo cubes, and a jelly that she had made the night before. There was one time when Dudley decided to go on a diet, and when we went down to lunch, everything was exactly the same except the gravy looked like thin water. And Dudley said, 'Mum, what have you done with the gravy?' And she said, 'Well, you're slimming dear, so I only put one Oxo cube in instead of two.'"

In August 1968, clearly believing that the BBC was not entitled to have Peter and Dudley all to itself, ITV contracted them to three hour-long programs called *Goodbye Again*, intended for American broadcast. But they failed to capture the spirit of *Not Only ... But Also*. Unhappy with the hour-long format, they also had some personality clashes with the director, who wanted to slow down the pace. Peter thought their scripts fell short of their usual standard, and Dudley felt their work was very stilted.

Stanley Donen had been enchanted with Dudley's earlier score for *Bedazzled*, and now asked him to score his newest movie, *Staircase*, which starred Rex Harrison and Richard Burton as two gay hairdressers.

"In my opinion," says Donen, "Dudley was a great composer, and I knew he would do a wonderful job. And, sure enough, he wrote the most fabulous score, which was a perfect fit for the film.

"I can't stand scores that try to evoke an emotion from the audience that is lacking in the scene. Dudley is able to write a score that doesn't plead for an emotional reaction but that at the same time supports and complements the sequence. The score for *Staircase* is remarkable and fabulous in its musicality. I asked him many times after that to score for me again, but by then he was a movie star."

Dudley's classical side was still very much in the closet. Some of his closest friends, who believed he could have become a classical performer, felt that he gravitated toward jazz because he was running away from the greater challenge of classical music. Lysie Hastings remembers Dudley once telling her and George that he felt safer in jazz, because, unlike in classical music, mistakes could be amended.

Robert Mann disagrees. "What he did in jazz was a very positive commitment. It wasn't to escape. It was purely because he loved it. Certainly he questioned the idea of playing classical music in performance, but only because he knew that he had not put in the physical preparation that was needed. And it wasn't because he was lazy. It was a lack of motivation to really commit himself to a public stance with classical music. He didn't have that motivation. The closest he got was in the kidding around in the parodies."

In the living room of Bentham House, Dudley was at his happiest playing piano to Mann's violin. It was evident to Mann "that he was a facile instrumentalist on the piano, but he hadn't spent the hours that were necessary to give him the physical strength in his fingers, so he was much more at home playing in a way that would satisfy a Bach rather than a Brahms. We almost never got together without playing at least one Bach sonata for violin and piano."

When *30 Is a Dangerous Age, Cynthia* was at last released in October 1968, Suzy was still on location in Belgrade. Dudley sent a limo to pick up his parents and he escorted them to the London premiere, along with a life-size cutout of Suzy, which he snuggled close to throughout the whole movie.

In spite of Dudley's versatility, the film received only mixed reviews. Although the American critics had loved it, the British critics were quite scathing—probably having expected a film more in line with Dudley's previous slapstick. John Russell Taylor wrote in the *Times* that the film gave the impression of "being made up as they go along" and that to a considerable extent "this vehicle for Dudley Moore stands or falls on how far you go for him. I quite like his music but fail to find him very funny."

Joe McGrath blames the response on the critics' perception of Dudley. "Here was Cuddly Dudley making his own movie and doing the whole show—writing the music, the script, the acting. And the feeling was, Who does he think he is? We had the worst press in the world. Leslie Halliwell wrote, 'Dudley Moore, a small star on a small screen who will never make the big one.' When Dudley heard that, he got hysterical with laughter."

But Dudley wasn't laughing about the critical reaction to the film. He was now suffering grave doubts about the likelihood of any successful film career. Nothing on celluloid had worked so far, neither with Peter Cook nor without him.

It was obvious that his career was terribly inconsistent. No matter how hard he tried to pick projects that would be winners, half the time they seemed doomed. He began to doubt his instincts—a doubt that would intermittently plague him throughout later years. Riddled as he was with insecurities, this did nothing for his self-esteem, although Peter Cook often claimed Dudley "was prone to worry unrelentingly and to question himself when he had no need."

With *Cynthia* not faring well critically, Dudley became increasingly introspective and more despondent. As 1968 gave way to a new year, he felt turbulent inside. He was trying so hard to break new ground, only to be frustrated every time he tried something different. Worse, whenever he achieved some success, he seemed incapable of enjoying it. Instead, he hovered on a melancholic plateau, worrying endlessly about what he had not achieved. Devoid of any enthusiasm, all he could feel was that he was wasting time hoping something worthwhile would come along.

A random diary note, written just before his thirty-fourth birthday in April 1969, highlights the acute despondency he was feeling about his life:

> There is the predictable confusion, depression, the indecision, the paralysis of mind, the lack of purpose, lack of faith, lack of enthusiasm—in short, the feelings of life rushing by like an express train while one stands powerless on a windy platform, dazzled by its power, its ruthlessness, its unstoppability. I am thirty-four very soon. You would think that at that age one has some reasonable way of life that affords one a smidge of satisfaction. You would think that it would have been possible at least to enjoy oneself. But no. Greyness abounds and clots the system. The futility of my life and of every sort of activity is overwhelming. The knowledge that the way out of this impasse is hidden from me is intolerable. The mechanics of my mind have been set and it is difficult to negate the past, break one's personality down into workable components and reassemble them.
>
> How does one replace one's mother with the person she should have been and get one's feelings to recognize this new face and ignore the old?

It didn't help Dudley's emotionally fractured state to see that he and Suzy were now having severe problems. But it could not have been the most relaxed atmosphere for a marriage, with Dudley drooping and hanging around the house in a perpetual state of dismal anxiety.

Francis Megahy witnessed Dudley's melancholia during those days. "One evening," he recalls, "Suzy and Dudley came to dinner in my flat in Primrose Hill, and Dudley was so morose that Anthea Disney, my wife at that time, closed the door behind him when they left and said, 'That man is never going to set foot in this apartment ever again!'"

If *Cynthia* had failed to live up to Dudley's hopes, *Monte Carlo or Bust!*, released in July 1969, surpassed them. Showing Cook and Moore in one of the best performances together, it won them at last the critical accolades that had been so lacking for their previous film encounters.

Dudley was ebullient and, revitalized, went back into the music studios to record a new jazz album, *The Dudley Moore Trio*, with Chris Karan on drums and Jeff Clyne on bass.

The healthy box-office returns of *Monte Carlo or Bust!* gave Cook and Moore a much needed ego boost, but that was promptly deflated when *The Bed-Sitting Room* opened. The critics had no idea what to make of this social farce, though they certainly made enough of it to know they did not like it. Dudley had been right when he had feared the story and characters would take a backseat to Richard Lester's indecisive direction. "One laughs from time to time," wrote the *New Yorker*, "but as in so much modern English far-out satire, there's no spirit, no rage, nothing left but ghastly, incessant, sinking island humor." *Variety* decried it as "a film of nonsense where the characters' humor remains alien to laughter."

The previous year, Dudley had seen Woody Allen in *Play It Again, Sam* on Broadway and thought it the funniest play he'd ever seen, but, daunted by Allen's brilliance, he turned down producer David Merrick's offer to perform it himself in London. In the summer of 1969, after spending months worrying about what he hadn't achieved in his life, and with Suzy by now growing irritated with his moods, he changed his mind and agreed to stage an English adaptation, though he only changed odd phrases such as "TV dinners," which became "fish fingers."

Play It Again, Sam focuses on the trials and tribulations of a young film critic struggling to revive his self-respect and sex life after a demoralizing divorce. His confidence shattered, he conjures up the spirit of Humphrey Bogart as a sexual role model. But his vain attempts to emulate Bogie's dashing lovemaking techniques are doomed, and his search for self-identity leads him to the realization that he is more acceptable to women as himself.

The play opened in London at the Globe Theatre in September 1969. The reviews were mixed. Irving Wardle, in the *Times*, wrote "the show may scrape home simply on the appeal of Dudley Moore minus piano and eight appetizing girls, otherwise it supplies yet another instance of the folly of trying to anglicize American comedy," and Sheridan Morley noted in *Tatler* that Dudley "makes the best of a rather uninspired comedy. We are lucky to have Mr. Moore who has wisely turned the play into an evening with Dud." Some critics complained that Dudley had not captured Woody Allen's personification of neurotic, failure-haunted, urban Jewish-American manhood gone to seed. Dudley was undeterred by such remarks, since he was more interested in the play's comic intention of contrasting the reality and fantasy of sex. As for the Jewish comic gloom so peculiar to Allen, he dismissed it as being "only a matter of cultural background."

Dudley, who had always loathed one-dimensional characters, liked the role immensely. He identified with the hero's deep anxieties, which to some extent resembled his own. In many ways, performing this play was yet another form of therapy.

It was ironic that Dudley was playing a man suffering from the pain of a broken marriage at a time when he was experiencing such acute marital problems himself. Certainly they had influenced his preparation for the part and given his performance a deeper sense of pathos.

The troubles that afflicted Dudley and Suzy seemed insurmountable. Suzy desperately wanted a child, but Dudley was dead against it. His belief that he and Barbara had not originally been wanted by their parents, coupled with the trauma of his painful childhood and the fear of passing his deformity on to a baby, made the whole idea of fatherhood quite abhorrent. Although Suzy understood his reasons, accepting them was another thing altogether, and it made her feel infinitely less loved to know that her husband did not want her to bear their child.

Compounding their tension was Dudley's sense of being trapped—not by Suzy, but by the whole idea of marriage. He felt closed in, cut off from others, and the demands of being answerable to another person made him feel less in control of his life. The result was that Dudley was becoming moody and difficult, and Suzy was feeling hurt and unloved.

He was sad to see this happen. He was genuinely fond of Suzy and had been very much in love with her, but he just could not give her what she wanted.

Two months after *Play It Again, Sam* had opened, Dudley and Peter embarked on a third (and ultimately final) season of *Not Only ... But Also*. It began broadcasting in the spring of 1970, and their teaming was as fresh and funny as it had ever been, their creative relationship as effective as always. Theirs was a mutual admiration that allowed each to benefit from the other and draw inspiration. "He makes me laugh a lot," Dudley explained to one critic, "and I make him laugh a lot. We're greatly amused by each other, and there's an enjoyment and enthusiasm about being together."

But underneath the admiration lurked a more invidious emotion. Envy. Dudley was envious of Peter's prolific wit and the speed of his intellectual brilliance, while Peter was envious of Dudley's acute musicality and his extraordinary popularity. It was subtle yet—still mere envy—but in time it would alter to jealousy and almost rot the bond that held them together.

It was very wearing on Dudley to work on the show by day and at night perform in the theater. But he had always felt creatively on top while working under pressure, as he had during the early days of *Fringe*, and he thrived on having his energies stretched. The intense effort seemed to generate even more energy in him, so that, far from being overtired when he reached the theater in the evening, he often felt quite vigorous.

He was curiously flat when the series ended in the summer of 1970, though he was still performing the play, and he seemed more tired than when he'd been working at full stretch—perhaps because there was more time to reflect on what was happening in his personal life.

Only a few close friends were aware that Dudley and Suzy had now been living apart for some months. Dudley had moved out of Bentham House and into Lysie and George Hastings' Camden Town home, taking with him his beloved Hammond organ.

He and Suzy still met regularly for dinner or to visit friends, and they continued to visit his parents as a couple. They were too embroiled in each other and too close as genuine friends to suffer the normally ignominious results of a breakup, although it was no less painful. They still cared deeply for each other. It wasn't surprising that, during the latter months of 1970, Dudley was seeing Dr. Sebag-Montefiore, his psychotherapist, as often as three times a week.

Lysie remembers Dudley being very sad and "in quite a muddle. He had a little room with its own kitchen where he liked to close himself up. Then he'd emerge and be the old Dudley and we'd have lots of laughs and play music, but then he'd suddenly disappear again into his little cubbyhole."

Dudley's misery was temporarily eased by the arrival in London of Robert Mann for a series of concerts. Mann was saddened to see the breakup of two of his favorite people. "They were very fond of each other, and even through all the breakups, Dudley was very concerned and anxious about Suzy. He was always on the outer edge of an anxiety eruption. He handled himself marvelously, but inside were all these bubbling anxieties that in a sense were directing his traffic.

"It wasn't so much that he was unhappy that it was ending, but more because it was causing pain to everyone concerned. Dudley had a strong will to love and live. Even during a breakup, that's where he was at. His one positive strength during this romantic unhappiness was the solace he found in his jazz."

Not Only ... But Also had been such a major success outside Britain that Peter and Dudley were now being courted by other English-speaking territories. In January 1971 they flew to Sydney to film two television specials for the Australian Broadcasting Commission, which were later broadcast in Britain under the title *Pete and Dud Down Under*. At the same time, Dudley also arranged a three-week tour of Australia for his jazz trio, taking himself, Chris Karan, and Peter Morgan, who had now become the permanent bass player, to Sydney, Melbourne, Brisbane, Adelaide, and Canberra. The tour was hugely successful, and while they were in Australia, the new trio recorded an album entitled *Today*.

Although he did not find a psychotherapist in Australia, Dudley was still intent on working out his emotional problems and had brought along several books to read. Concentrating as hard as he was on his psyche, he recalls a particular dream that he had at this time. "I was looking at my finger, and out of it came this gelatinous mass that formed itself into a strange turtle-like creature and sort of crawled behind a corner. And I knew it was going to meet people, and I thought, 'That's OK it's all right to be that angry amongst people.' It was very significant to me, to learn that I could be angry in front of people."

Somehow, whenever Peter and Dudley came together, creative ideas poured out of them. The spring of 1971 in Sydney was no exception, and out of it flowed their next collaboration.

CHAPTER 10

BEHIND
THE FRIDGE

1971-1973

*"Dudley always had angst. He couldn't exist without it. His main problem
was that he didn't realize how talented and loving and giving he was.
Even when the proof of his validity was in front of him, he found it
difficult to recognize. You can have all the proof in the world, but if
you don't feel it in your heart and soul, then it doesn't count."*

—Suzy Kendall

The ideas that Peter and Dudley nurtured led to a new revue that would
combine some old sketches from the past with a series of new ones.
Recalling the maître d' at his nightly dinners at Barbetta's with Alan
Bennett during *Beyond the Fringe*'s run in New York, Dudley named this new
show *Behind the Fridge*. It was an in-joke, and it had a faintly self-mocking
ring that appealed to Dudley and Peter.

They decided to premiere the revue in Australia, and it was rapidly
booked by noted Australian producer Colin McClennan across the entire
country and New Zealand in a five-month tour that would begin in late
summer.

While he was in Sydney, Dudley had met Australian journalist Lyndall
Hobbs. She was in charge of an event at which he'd made a guest appearance, and he "fell madly in love with her from that moment." Lyndall was
tall, blonde, and gorgeous, and she was the first woman Dudley had felt any
passion for since the disintegration of his marriage to Suzy. He pursued
her wholeheartedly, and eventually wore down her initial ambivalence.

Back in London, their relationship continued via long phone calls that lasted into the early hours. Dudley found himself so desperately missing Lindy that after barely a week at home he flew back to Sydney to see her. Knowing that she would be waiting at the airport to meet him, he cabled a friend and asked him also to be there, "in case press are hovering." If they were, he somehow managed to escape their observation and the romance went unreported.

But a few weeks later, in an attempt to give his marriage another chance, he invited Suzy to fly out and join him on a trip to Fiji—a vacation that both enjoyed relatively free of any disagreements.

When they left, they flew briefly to Hong Kong and they were on their way to Bangkok, when a message arrived from Diana, their secretary. Bernard, Dudley's brother-in-law, was trying to reach them to let them know that Jock, Dudley's father, was seriously ill.

They caught the next flight back to England, and Dudley went straight to Dagenham to see his father. The news was not good: Jock Moore had cancer of the colon.

It was clear that his father did not have long to live, and Dudley remained at the Dagenham house to be nearby. It was a chilling experience for him to see his father in the hospital, and there were many sleepless nights. "I remember waking up one morning, horrified that there would be this terrible hole where my father had been."

Within a few weeks, Jock had deteriorated to the point where the hospital warned Ada and Dudley that he could go at any moment. "When the call came that he was about to go," Dudley remembers, "my mother said, 'Don't let's hurry. Please don't let's hurry. I don't want to see him die. I don't want to see him struggle.' Neither did I—I couldn't bear to see him that way."

By the time they reached the hospital, Dudley's father was dead.

Jock had said little during his lifetime, but as he lay dying, the last thing he told his son was, "Dudley, my boy, don't let it pass you by." He had seen the sadness in him after all.

At the funeral, in St. Peter's church, Dagenham, Dudley, who was accompanied supportingly by Suzy, went to pieces. He'd taken over all the arrangements himself and played on the organ all of his father's favorite music—everything he could think of. "I was dreadfully upset and I just couldn't stop sobbing," he recalls. "The tears were pouring down my face while I played all these pieces. Maybe it was the music, but I don't think so. It was very difficult when I lost my first parent and I was very unnerved by it."

As his sister, Barbara Stevens, recalls, "Dudley felt a lot of regrets when my father died. He would have liked to have taken him out more often, and done more for and with him. He was very saddened."

Dudley had always loved the sweet-natured man with the quiet, hidden disposition, but he had never really known him, never really done anything alone with him, never had one of those son-to-father conversations that his friends enjoyed. Even his father's diary, which would only come to light years later, revealed nothing. To Dudley, Jock would always remain largely a mystery. "I wish we'd talked more," he frets. "I wish I could have found out who he was."

He kept his father's watch and ring—which he still has to this day—and returned to Australia.

His attempt to work things out with Suzy had not succeeded—"I think I was afraid of the continuity"—although they would remain deeply close in heart and in constant touch forever.

Back in Sydney he resumed his romance with Lindy Hobbs, but by now his emotions were swinging up and down. "Feelings come and go," he wrote to Suzy. "I don't feel a great deal for Lindy nor she for me. It's when one tries to force feelings to stay put that trouble starts."

Work seemed the only salve, and he plunged into shaping the new show with Peter Cook.

Though now twelve years older than in their *Fringe* days, if anything Peter and Dudley were even more impish and irreverent. The interim years of their partnership had honed their talent and they were now more polished and self-assured than ever before, with an even greater gift, it seemed, for sending audiences into paroxysms of laughter.

There were fifteen scenes in *Behind the Fridge*, three of them being Dudley's piano pieces. A couple of their earlier trademark sketches included One-Legged Tarzan, and as usual they poked fun at the vicissitudes of life. But not everyone was open-minded enough to appreciate their lopsided perspectives.

Gospel Truth was one of the funniest and cleverest sketches they'd ever written. In it, Matthew, a reporter researching an in-depth profile of Jesus for the *Bethlehem Star*, interviews Arthur Shepherd, who claims to have witnessed the birth of Christ. It was inevitable that the sketch would outrage some people, and the theater was inundated with protests of sacrilege from religious groups.

The Bible Belt notwithstanding, the entire show was an uproarious success when it opened in October 1971. "A supremely well-worked evening," said the *Melbourne Herald*, and the *Melbourne Sun* acclaimed it as "a brilliant night."

The duo played nightly to sold-out audiences. "There were some nights," recalls Dudley, "when I couldn't think of anything being more enjoyable. After each show I'd be absolutely ecstatic. It was marvelous."

Dudley adored Australia. He particularly liked Sydney, which combined the best of his favorite worlds—the modernity of America and the quaintness of colonial Europe—with an inordinate amount of sunshine, and he was captivated by the open, down-to-earth people, whom he found warmly receptive. He would come away with many new friends.

But the relationship between Dudley and Peter was not so enchanting. It was now becoming seriously threatened. By Peter.

Cook had been a social drinker ever since his Cambridge days, but now his drinking was growing seriously out of hand—to such an extent that he was often bombed by the time he walked onstage.

Dudley believes Peter's excessive drinking began on their opening night in Melbourne, when he received his divorce papers from Wendy. "He felt terrible about it, and I remember him diving into the pool in a fit of agony. To my mind, he became an alcoholic from that moment on."

One night, when the effects of imbibing were still upon him, Peter slurred his lines to the point where he completely threw Dudley, unnerving him for the rest of the performance. They had a tremendous row after the curtain went down. "You're bloody drunk all the time," Dudley accused him. "I can't stand it." The situation was intensely volatile and threatened to cause a permanent rift between them.

As Dudley later told lyricist Leslie Bricusse, a friend since the sixties, "He comes on so hopelessly drunk and starts ad-libbing on something that's got nothing to do with anything you've ever performed. Imagine being in front of fifteen hundred people and trying to get through it, never knowing what you're going to get."

Though Dudley and Suzy had split, it was an unusual separation, since they continued to write to each other and to make plans for a reunion. Dudley's diary during his entire Australian tour was littered with notes about Suzy's filming movements, where she could be reached, and things to tell her, and he suffered immense frustration if he tried to phone her and could not contact her.

He wrote from the President Motor Inn in Melbourne to tell her:

Getting the show into shape has been something of a headache, especially when Peter was consistently throwing wine, spirits, champagne, and valium down his throat at a rate that showed up on stage. I had a large and pretty extended argument with him about this and told him I didn't think I could face this tour with the real possibility of him being bombed out of his head every time we went on stage.

He refuses to believe that drink plus valium is a pretty irritating combination and makes people doubly pissed. We have a curious relationship, he and I. We're still very nervous together when things aren't discussed openly.

Peter seemed to be drunk every night, and in an effort to teach him a lesson, Dudley himself got mildly drunk one evening before the show. Afterward, he told Peter he thought they'd given a great performance, but Peter denounced it as their worst. "Well," Dudley retorted, "now you know what it's like to play opposite someone who's inebriated." After that, Peter's drinking calmed down, and with the first week of the show under their belt, his anxiety seemed to subside.

They had marvelous reviews, but also managed to find themselves banned from the airwaves after using "filthy" language on Dave Allen's talk show. "Peter said 'pissed,' 'bum,' 'tits,' all our familiars," Dudley wrote to Suzy, "but I guess Australia is further behind the times. I switched the microphone off, but nobody seemed to pick up on that—a case of visual euphemism."

It hadn't helped matters that Allen himself told some Jewish jokes that were all taken as anti-Semitic. It seemed, to Dudley, to be an unduly sensitive reaction. "Mind you," he opined to Suzy, "quite possibly some people feel rather guilty about the Jewish population here, since Jews are banned from most golf clubs, so people don't want to be reminded of their prejudice by hearing Jewish jokes."

Telling Peter about his drinking problem had taken a load off Dudley's mind. Besides which Peter seemed, at least for now, to have it under control and was being reliable again.

In spite of the separation, Suzy remained close to Dudley's mother. One Sunday she sent a car to bring her over to Bentham House for lunch, and now she saw a different side to Ada, who oscillated between sadness and relief that Jock was no longer around. "Mr. Moore didn't like me talking too much," she told an astonished Suzy. "Now I can do just as I please." And she admitted there had been times when Jock didn't speak to her for days at a time.

Suzy missed Dudley desperately. She wanted to talk to him, but was reluctant to phone in case he was involved with someone. So she sat at home, lonely and thinking of him.

He, in turn, was thinking a great deal about her. "We'll see each other soon," he wrote to her. "I miss you, so seeing you is something I relish and look forward to. Life is odd but one has to accept that, I think, to find happiness. I wish I knew how one banishes depression for good. It's a slow process. I wish life were simple. Rather I think life *is* simple but I, for one, haven't quite found the formula."

In mid-December Dudley flew home for ten days, just behind Suzy, who'd flown in from Rome, where she was making a film. They spent much of the next several days together, including Christmas, until she left for Switzerland to resume filming and he returned to Sydney.

Early in February 1972, after a tremendously successful five months

(*Above*) John (Jock) Moore, Dudley's father.

(*Above right*) Ada Francis Moore, Dudley's mother.

(*Right*) A rueful expression on the cherubic face.

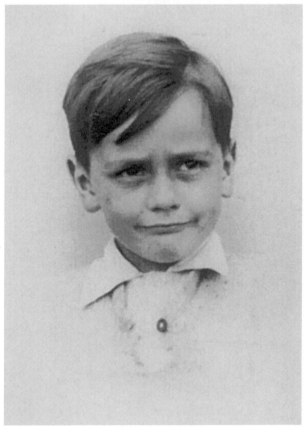

(Left) Enjoying a game of cricket.

(Below) Dudley's favorite shot of himself with his parents, looking out the window of their Baron Road house.

(Left) In Paris with Marie-José, Dudley's first love.

(Opposite top) An Oxford University production.

(Opposite bottom) Not only Dudley Moore but also Peter Cook.

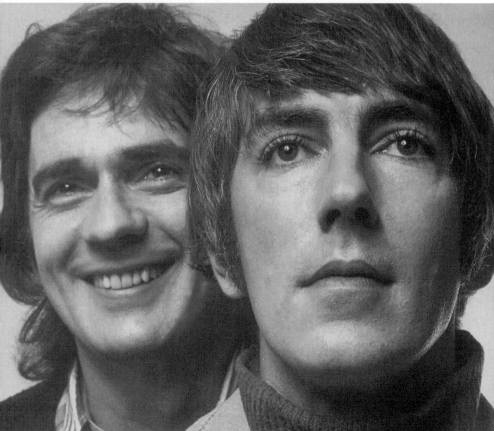

Alan Bennett and Dudley backstage in New York with Anthony Newley and Joan Collins.

Peter Sellers hands an *Evening Standard* award to the Fringers.

One of the few existing photos of Dudley
with Tuesday Weld and baby Patrick.

The only time Dudley grew a
beard until another brief
recent attempt.

With Susan Anton at Carnegie Hall.

Young Patrick gets an early piano
lesson from his father.

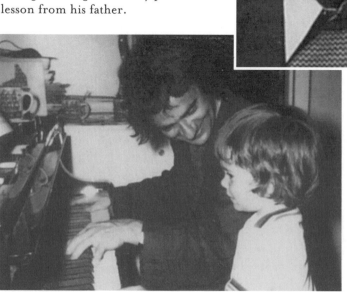

With Elton John.   With Julie Andrews.

With Lou Pitt.

With Peter Bellwood, a
close friend since *Beyond the Fringe* days.

of touring Australia and New Zealand, Dudley and Peter returned to Britain, where the show was to be mounted later in the year by Bernard Delfont under Joe McGrath's direction.

But there was no protracted rest for Dudley. He appeared as a guest on several variety shows, from Val Doonican to Sheila Hancock, and played dozens of gigs with his trio. Patrick Garland organized a poetry reading with Diana Rigg, Michael Hordern, and Malcolm Muggeridge at which Dudley played the piano, and his rendering of a Scott Joplin rag elicited a subsequent letter of praise from a normally curmudgeonly Muggeridge.

There was also a BBC television series with Lulu, and he had immense fun working with the perky singer in *Not Only Lulu But Also Dudley Moore*, although he recalls having to write a sketch and deriving no pleasure whatsoever from the process. "I hated it, and I didn't do it very well. I'd always coasted in before on the tails of Peter."

It was now, after a three-year absence, that Dudley returned to films, in Will Sterling's ambitious version of *Alice's Adventures in Wonderland*. Fifteen-year-old newcomer Fiona Fullerton played Alice, and Michael Crawford the White Rabbit. Ralph Richardson played the Caterpillar, Flora Robson the Queen of Hearts, Peter Sellers the March Hare, Robert Helpmann the Mad Hatter, and Spike Milligan and Michael Jayston rounded out the stellar cast.

Dudley, in an endearing performance perfectly suited to his childlike demeanor, played the Dormouse. He had to wear a heavy disguise and, during the Mad Hatter's tea party, his two false front teeth accidentally fell into the teapot. Ultimately, Dudley felt that "most of us were too covered by facial hair and teeth and our eyebrows didn't show. That was fatal, because then we became expressionless and nobody could relate to us."

The public must have agreed, because the film, when it was eventually released, turned out to be a major box-office disappointment in which the vast talents and special effects were largely wasted. Neither Dudley's delightful performance nor John Barry's marvelous score was able to save the production.

With his marriage in irretrievable disarray, Dudley picked up the threads of his social life. Lindy Hobbs, who had moved to London to work, had now met impresario Michael White and faded into Dudley's background. Years later she would end up in America, where she became Al Pacino's live-in girlfriend.

At a party, Dudley met twenty-two-year-old Lynsey de Paul, who'd just had a big hit as a songwriter, and for a brief time they enjoyed a surreptitious affair. It almost—literally—didn't get off the ground, since the first time he went to her flat, he sat on her couch, as antiquated as the deceased great-aunt from whom she'd inherited it, and fell straight through to the floor.

It wasn't the only slapstick moment of their affair. When he took Lynsey with him to a recording session one night, he arrived in a Beetle—the Maserati was in the garage being repaired—with a shattered windshield through which he'd punched a tiny hole so he could see to drive. When he got inside the car he slammed the door, and two seconds later the entire windshield fell out on top of him.

Their relationship didn't last long, primarily because Dudley had now started a new affair—with Lysie, George Hastings's wife.

As Robert Mann points out, "Dudley was a person who found himself—a little bit like Beethoven—falling in love with people even if they were married to somebody else. He was very impressionable that way."

George had always encouraged flirtations between his wife and other men, but, as Lysie reflects, "He didn't like it if I fell in love with them, and when Dudley and I really had a proper affair he didn't like that."

Since for so long George, Lysie, and Dudley had been a threesome, life not surprisingly now became rather strained and difficult between them all. Lysie had been unhappy in her marriage for a long time and had pretty much made up her mind to leave George, but she was still with him when the affair with Dudley began. "It was all a bit messy actually," she recalls, "and terribly awkward. But Dudley always used to get himself into those situations, pinching his best friends' women. Another man might have said, 'No, I can't do this.' But he did it. And not just once. Dudley had no compunction about taking women off people, even if they were really close to him. His sense of conscience was rather unevolved, not very strong."

Lysie could hardly be called blameless herself, but she says that Dudley "was very persuasive and very hard to resist. He knew what he was doing, and if you've got that power maybe you can't resist using it."

After much painful deliberation, Lysie decided she could not live with George anymore and arranged to move out with their two children. The night before she left, rather bizarrely, they had one more of their musical evenings. Dudley played the piano, George the double bass, and Lysie sat there, listening, just as in the early days, when it was all beginning for them. "It was," she says, "like nothing had happened. But of course everything had happened."

After Lysie moved out, her relationship with Dudley grew stronger. Though optimistic about the future, which hovered "like a new era in my life," she was also feeling deeply vulnerable. Dudley, too, was immensely sad about the breakup with Suzy.

In a sense they were natural for each other at that moment. They had known one another for so long and were such close friends that they felt at their most comfortable when they were together. They had a lot of fun, and made each other laugh until they cried. They were together constantly, and for a while it was a wonderful romance.

But Dudley's philandering made it hard for the woman in his life. "He was always womanizing," says Lysie, "even when he was in love. It was like a habit. And then it would be fine again. He's very difficult. One moment you think he really loves you, and the next you're left totally insecure. He's so unpredictable."

In September, Dudley and Suzy's marriage came to an official end, on the grounds of incompatibility. After the divorce hearing, which Suzy attended alone after Dudley had dropped her off round the corner, Dudley arrived in a chauffeur-driven Rolls-Royce—funereal black, naturally—to collect her from the court. It was a charming if futile gesture that didn't begin to assuage the extreme pain that the divorce caused them both.

The night before, at George and Lysie's house, Dudley had closeted himself for hours with his beloved piano and improvised emotional music that revolved around Suzy and himself. They were both unhappy that their lives had not managed to converge successfully, for they still bore the fondest affection for each other. "In hindsight," Suzy says now, "we should never have got married. We were just so happy the way we were before."

At least their friendship, unlike the marriage, would never die.

When *Behind the Fridge* opened in London at the Cambridge Theatre toward the end of November 1972, it was with great expectations. The previews had been tremendous, and the show was booked out for a solid six months. But the opening night was a near catastrophe and portended hugely troubled times ahead.

A backstage snafu caused a delay in the curtain going up and, while the audience gave a slow hand clap, behind the curtain Joe McGrath and Dudley were slowly going nuts. Dudley covered his anxiety with his classic lunacy—dancing with Joe, making funny faces in the direction of the audience whom he couldn't see, and pretending to flash his bum. All the while he was putting on funny voices and making rude noises and, as he had done since his school days, covering up his feelings with outrageous humor.

"It was funny," Joe McGrath recalls only too vividly, "but it wasn't funny. He was trying to calm himself down, and he started singing, 'It doesn't re-ally *matter*, it's not re-ally im*portant*.' But it was. It was terribly important to him."

But it was not a technical hitch that was causing Dudley's angst and preventing the show from opening on time. It was his partner. Peter Cook was completely and hopelessly drunk.

Joe McGrath had to dress Peter and walk him around in circles in his dressing room to try to sober him up. And that, McGrath is convinced, was the night that everything changed between Peter Cook and Dudley Moore. Until then, Peter had been very much the leader of the two, the man who usually had the last word in the writing and what they would do. That night the balance shifted completely. "Dudley was very angry," recalls McGrath. "He told me, 'I've had it. I'm getting out of this. It's driving me up the fucking wall. I can't be dealing with it. It's totally out of control, and I've got to make my own future.' And that's when he began to take over and become very strong."

Whatever the reason for Peter's drinking—and, despite their closeness, Peter did not discuss his feelings with Dudley—by the time they opened in *Behind the Fridge*, it was making Dudley so anxious that he was very close to a breakdown himself.

"When the curtain went up it was nearly half an hour late," McGrath remembers—that night etched in his memory ever since. "Peter was a zombie on stage, and Dudley had to carry him through the entire first ten minutes of it. There wasn't even an understudy. How do you understudy a two-man show?

"Both Dudley and I felt at the end of that first night that we were so lucky to get through it. The next day, in a review, George Melly said, 'Magisterial Peter Cook was brilliant last night.' It broke us up."

Dudley took his mother to the opening night and to the big party afterward, which was attended by dozens of celebrities in a club in the City. "He was very good with her," says McGrath, "and she just sat there having a drink and enjoying it all."

Many of Dudley's sketches came out of his own experiences, but they sailed over his mother's head without her realizing he was talking about his parents—although he believes she was well aware that much of his material came out of an angst that she never quite understood.

One of the sketches Dudley wrote was about a film star (Cook) being interviewed by his father (Moore), who asks how his film is going. The son replies, "Fine, I'm sorry I couldn't get back," and the discussion surrounds his inability to return home to bury his mother because he was working abroad in Yugoslavia:

SON:
I couldn't get back because if I'd come
back we might have lost the snow.

FATHER:
What do you mean, son?

SON:

Well, you see, Dad, if I'd gone to Mum's funeral, by
the time I got back to the location, maybe the snow
would have melted and the continuity would not have
worked out and the film would be messed up.

FATHER:

Of course. I understand, son.

Explains Joe McGrath, "It was a very funny sketch but very bitter, and
there was a terrible amount of truth in it. It was something we all worried
about, being away from our families while we were on location. Dudley said
it had a lot to do with how he felt about his parents, even though it was his
father who had died and he had gone home in time."

Dudley and Peter were critically selective of the sketches they included
in the show. One that made it—though they would not later use it in the
American run—had Dudley made up as a black man singing "Ol' Man
River" in a shower. The more he sang, the more his makeup began washing off, and the more his voice started to become English, until in the end
he was completely white and sounded like Noel Coward.

The London critics weren't as wild about *Behind the Fridge* as their
counterparts had been in Australia. Although the *Times* called it "original
and intelligent fun and fans will need no encouragement to see the pair in
action," Sheridan Morley noted in *Punch* that "a few of the sketches are not
exactly in mint condition and there is a terrible dearth of punchlines. In
search of them, sketches are prolonged far beyond their natural life, occasionally bolstered by irritating fits of giggling."

Peter Cook later claimed that he and Dudley performed "rather la-
zily in the West End and didn't work hard enough at it," whereas in
America they had better direction. But director Joe McGrath views it
rather more significantly.

"What really got me," he says, "was that Peter went on television saying,
'We need a stronger director,' which upset me, but Dudley, who's a very
amiable, easygoing man, just said, 'Forget about it.'

"I think in a way Peter wanted to start all over with someone else in
America because it might have been awkward otherwise. I don't know if he
was embarrassed over what had happened that first night, because he never
said anything about it, although after Dudley had a big row with him that
night, he did seem to become more reliable and was fairly OK for the rest
of the run. But I know the truth of what happened that first night, Dudley
knows what happened, and so did Peter."

There was a slightly odd moment one night for Dudley. He was in his dressing room getting ready to go onstage, when he dropped his cuff links on the floor. "I shouted, 'These bloody cuff links—they've rolled behind the fridge.' And then I realized what I'd said. I couldn't believe I'd said the title of the show in another context. I thought maybe it was a portent. God knows of what."

American producer Alexander Cohen, who had known the two men since *Beyond the Fringe*, had seen the show in its first week and decided immediately to take it to Broadway. "The boys were thrilled," recalls McGrath. "That's what made me laugh when Peter said we didn't really take it seriously, because they took it so seriously."

Says Alex Cohen, "I loved the show when I saw it, but as I left the theater, I ran into Clive Barnes, the *New York Times* critic. He said, 'You're not thinking about bringing that to New York, are you?' And I said I was. 'You've lost your feathers!' he told me. He hated it."

Dudley, however, was extremely nervous about the thought of touring and had serious reservations now about going on to America with the show. Peter's drinking was growing worse, and Dudley felt he could not face much more. He was deeply concerned that things were likely to deteriorate rather than improve and would affect them professionally. Convinced it would be "hell on wheels," he decided not to go.

Thus, New York was put off for a long time. But eventually Dudley capitulated to Peter's pleas and Alex Cohen's offer to pay them around seven thousand dollars a week each, plus a percentage of the box office, and in the late summer of 1973—after a three-week vacation with Lysie sailing a yacht around the Greek Islands—Dudley found himself headed for America's East Coast.

On the plane going over, he expressed his anxiety to Peter. They had to make the show work, he told him. They'd won a Tony for *Fringe*, and they owed it to themselves to equal that success. But by the time they landed in New York, Peter was already drunk again, and Dudley had to fill in both their entry forms at immigration while Peter sat crying silently in a corner.

"He used to cry quite a lot," recalls Dudley. "I don't know why he was crying this time. He was not a very happy character. He had a lot of angst but he didn't talk about it. Just like I didn't talk about mine to him. I think we both gravitated toward being isolated. His was an anxiety that was inexpressible."

Normally the more dominant of the two, Peter may have been upset over his own incapability at that moment and that Dudley appeared to be taking over. Whatever the case, the tears continued in the bustling customs hall.

It did not bode well for the American months that lay ahead. Nor for the future of their partnership.

CHAPTER 11

TUESDAY

1973-1976

*"All great clowns who can translate the humor and humanness of frivolity
and human vulnerability and error, whether it's a Chaplin or a
W. C. Fields, have fairly brooding insides. Dudley's no exception."*

—ROBERT MANN

Behind the Fridge needed to be reworked for American audiences—not least
its name. On the plane, Peter Cook had suggested to Dudley the new title
of *Good Evening*, and Alexander Cohen, who found the former title silly and
meaningless, adopted Peter's suggestion.

They launched into rehearsals, and it was now that Cohen caught a
whiff of bumpy times ahead. "We worked intensively," he recalls, "and
Dudley was always good at that. But Peter was constantly either changing
rehearsals or turning up late for them."

Good Evening premiered in October 1973 in Boston—where Peter fell
off the stage into the orchestra pit during a blackout—and opened in New
York two weeks later. Dudley was full of trepidation, but needlessly. When
the curtain came down on the first performance, critics proclaimed the
show "the surprise hit of the year."

Lysie Hastings had flown out to be with Dudley for the Broadway
opening, but she soon realized that he had reverted to his old ways. "It was
very tricky, because in the middle of the night some female would telephone and I soon realized he'd been acquiring more women since he'd
been in America. It was ridiculous and absolutely hopeless." At the end of
a week, they reached a mutual agreement that the relationship should end.
A sad Lysie flew back to London, resigned to the knowledge that Dudley
wanted to be free.

By now, Peter's erratic behavior had resurfaced, causing considerable concern—particularly to Alexander Cohen. "He'd lost his ability to control himself and he was pretty bad," Cohen recalls. "There was one day when he didn't show up at all for the matinee. It was 1:30, and we were due to go on at 2 P.M. The half hour is sacred in the theater, and Jerry Adler, the stage manager, got very worried.

"Finally we went to his apartment, broke in, and found Peter passed out on the bed. We did everything to him—threw water over him by the glass, revived him, and literally slapped him awake—and dragged him in the car to the theater."

In the meantime, the theater announced that Peter had been delayed in a traffic accident, and Dudley went on stage and entertained the audience for forty-five minutes. The show finally went on at a quarter to three—almost an hour late. "It was unheard of in the theater," says Cohen. "It was irresponsible and unprofessional—which is about the worst thing I can say about a human being.

"After the performance, Dudley remonstrated with Peter and it was a very ugly moment. It was horrible and terrible, and you could tell that this was going to be a tough go. But I think part of what held them together was financial, because they had hit a stride and I was paying them a great deal of money. So they kept going."

Some time earlier, Dudley and Peter had created two characters who reveled in obscene conversation, and their underground act went down riotously when they performed some of it in the New York clubs. For a lark, they decided now to hire a recording studio and make some private tapes of their improvised chatter. The results were the infamous Derek and Clive, who would become in time as notorious as their renowned idiots, Dud and Pete. In fact Derek and Clive were punk versions of Dud and Pete who loved to talk dirty. Real dirty.

They recorded their conversations with wild abandon and strictly for their own fun, going beyond the boundaries of their usual work, in which they felt they weren't allowed total freedom in what they performed. They had intended to record just one item, but what they ended up with was a mass of material that dealt with the unspeakable.

The sketches relied entirely on the use of vulgar language, and the choice of subject matter made them utterly unsuitable for general distribution. Cancer, sex, masturbation—nothing escaped their lewd attentions. One track (The Worst Job I Ever Had) had Peter describing in graphic terms how he'd had to remove lobsters from Jayne Mansfield's rectum.

Dudley justified the tapes by pointing out that entire classes of people in Britain talked like Derek and Clive, whose sole means of communication was in language many people considered obscene. He had always had a very ribald sense of humor and claimed to have been "talking dirty" since the age of thirteen. He found it fun, and was always baffled when this more outrageous side of his humor was greeted with puritanical shock.

Some years earlier, while in New York with *Beyond the Fringe*, Dudley had enjoyed a brief but passionate fling with Tuesday Weld, an American sex kitten who looked not unlike Brigitte Bardot. A former child star, with a pouting, pubescent sex appeal, she had once been described as a younger version of Marilyn Monroe.

Born Susan Weld, she had legally changed her name at fifteen. ("She was always 'too too' much in her moods," says her mother, Aileen ("Jo") Weld, "so we called her by the nickname of Too or Too Too, which somehow became Tuesday.")

Her acting career had begun as a thirteen-year-old nymphet in a low-budget 1956 film, *Rock, Rock, Rock*, that contained thirty musical numbers for which Connie Francis dubbed her voice. A year later she played the teenage baby-sitter opposite Paul Newman and Joanne Woodward in *Rally Round the Flag Boys!* A Hollywood talent scout saw her in New York and beckoned her to the West Coast and, after her portrayal as Danny Kaye's crippled daughter in *The Five Pennies*, she was put under contract to Twentieth Century Fox. Her education suffered—"I studied for ten minutes at a time on studio sets between the ages of fourteen and seventeen"—but she was a smart girl who read Nietzsche for pleasure. Her most highly praised film was *Pretty Poison* with Anthony Perkins, but it was her least favorite, during which "not a day went by without a fight."

Before she was twenty, the provocative green-eyed blonde had been linked romantically with a multitude of Hollywood stars, and was Elvis Presley's first major love affair after he left the army and returned to civilian life. She was considered a fine actress, but made few films of merit; among the films she turned down were *Lolita*, *Bonnie and Clyde*, *Cactus Flower*, and *True Grit*.

One of the most talked-about personalities in Hollywood, in earlier days she had been the archetypal show-business brat, which led to her being dubbed Tuesday Wild. She did little to eradicate the reputation, which was epitomized by her appearing on a national television talk show barefoot, unkempt, and clad in an old nightgown. She claimed scarcely to know who she really was and that her behavior was in rebellion for the intrusion on her privacy. Her bohemian ways were intended to shock people, and they soon became a part of her persona.

But this was 1973, and that side of Tuesday had calmed down. A little.

One December evening, alone and miserable in her New York flat, she called Dudley. He could hear the pain in her voice and asked if she wanted him to come over. She did. So he went. And he stayed.

Dudley had always found himself drawn to people in need. Tuesday

was no exception. Married once before—to Roddy McDowall's secretary
Claude Harz, now a screenwriter—and with a six-year-old daughter,
Natasha, she came from an emotionally disturbed background and, like
Dudley, had suffered a traumatic childhood.

Her father, Lothrop, had been a banker and the black sheep of his
family. An unpredictable man given to wildly changeable moods, he had
never wanted children but ended up with three, and resented their
presence. Jealous and possessive, he allowed his wife no friends, while he,
unemployed, spent his days in the local saloon. Forced on to the poverty
line and into a New York tenement flat, he died when Tuesday was three,
and his widow had pushed the youngest of her two daughters into modeling
to help make ends meet.

Tuesday later claimed that she suffered a nervous breakdown at the age
of nine, was a heavy drinker and pot smoker by the age of ten, had her first
serious love affair at eleven, and at twelve tried to commit suicide by
swallowing a combination of sleeping pills and alcohol.

Dudley found himself attracted by Tuesday's independence. "I
thought she was a scoundrel, a scamp," he says, "but I couldn't control
anything from her, and that was the fascination—because, as I told her,
rather cruelly, she wasn't my type."

Actually, Tuesday had already found her type in Peter Cook. Some
time earlier, having called Dudley at the hotel one day and found him out,
she talked instead to Peter. Before long, the two became embroiled in an
affair. Peter, however, had now become engaged to actress Judy Huxtable,
and when Judy flew from London to be with him a few weeks later, the brief
romance, such as it had been, was over.

Leslie Bricusse had known Tuesday Weld since moving to California
in the mid-sixties and had always been struck by how remarkably bright and
intelligent she was. "Normally you'd see a pretty blonde and think she was
dumb," he reflects, "but with Tuesday, not a bit. She was far ahead of most
people. She was very funny, with a mind like a razor—as sharp as can be.
She was very bright, very witty, and a real killer. She was a real heartbreaker,
and left a trail of broken hearts behind her. I thought she was going to go
on to a spectacular career, and a lot of people thought she was the most
wonderful thing in the world."

Dudley says he never knew what Tuesday saw in him. What she may
have seen was someone who was infinitely more reliable than herself. And
she needed that in her life. Because Tuesday, despite having calmed down
considerably, was still very erratic.

Robert Mann, who lived in New York, recalls his first encounter with
Tuesday. "My wife and I had visited Dudley backstage, and he said he wanted
us to meet someone. He took us outside the theater, and we found our-

selves swept into a limousine, inside which sat Tuesday. She said 'Hello' and nothing more."

The foursome went to a party in a huge house where everyone seemed to be moving around without relating to each other. Eventually Dudley suggested that they go to eat, but by then Tuesday had disappeared. They found her at last in a room on the top floor, watching television. "We can't go yet," she told them, slightly tipsy. "I'm on the Johnny Carson show and I want to see myself."

Eventually they all ended up in a restaurant, seated around a tiny table. By then, Tuesday was fairly loaded. "Dudley felt a little uncomfortable," recalls Mann, "and tried to make conversation—mainly with me. He was ignoring Tuesday quite overtly. All of a sudden she turned her head around to us and said to Dudley, 'Who the fuck are these people?' He was very embarrassed."

It was not to be a brief romance for Dudley and Tuesday, but it would be far from a smooth ride—turning in time into a stormy relationship that would plague all their later dealings with each other.

This was early days, however. In a letter to his mother in January 1974 Dudley told her about his new girlfriend. "She is a lovely girl, warm and straightforward and honest ... we have good happy times together and it is nice to feel love for someone again. It is a calm, warm, cosy love and not the overblown romantic sort that can only spell disaster eventually. Of course I can't predict how long we will feel good together."

Dudley was playing jazz whenever and wherever he could. Taking advantage of the success of *Good Evening*, he found himself in demand by the Manhattan clubs, including Michael's Pub, where Woody Allen often played clarinet, and he was persuaded to give impromptu performances after the curtain came down at night on his show.

In February 1974 Suzy stopped in New York for a few days on her way back from Los Angeles, and she and Dudley spent a lot of time talking and lunching together. Since their divorce, they had come to settle into a close friendship. "It was lovely to see her," he wrote to his mother. "She's now back in London and we phone each other occasionally. We had a good time together and get on so much more easily now we are apart."

Dudley's emotional problems were far from resolved and he was still heavily committed to therapy, yet he was unable to discuss it with Peter Cook, who had no sympathy for the process. "I don't know why Dudley keeps on trying to find himself," Peter would tell anyone who listened. "I found him years ago."

Peter despised psychotherapists, though he had once seen one himself. "He didn't like them," says Dudley. "He didn't respect them, and he told them lies."

In a rather illuminating observation that hints at a darker depth, Peter once stated that the reason he didn't go into therapy was because he didn't think he would like what he found and he didn't think anybody else would either.

But if he couldn't discuss his therapy with Peter, Dudley was able to hold forth with other close friends. Gillian Lynne, now an established choreographer, was working in New York and became aware for the first time that Dudley was caught up in psychotherapy.

"I didn't think he was wonderfully well when I saw him," she reflects. "I asked him, 'What's the matter?' And he said, 'I've just had an aggression session with my shrink today. I've been shouting a lot and I'm worn out.' I said, 'But, darling, I could have given you a ballet class and got the same results for nothing.' I didn't agree with all of that. I thought he was the most wonderful person, who didn't need any of that stuff. I still don't think he did."

Bryan Forbes, who was in New York with his wife, Nanette Newman, evidently agreed with Gillian Lynne. "How much is it costing you to go to analysis every morning?" he asked Dudley. "A hundred and fifty dollars an hour" was the answer. "Why don't you pay me instead?" Forbes suggested. "Nanette and I would be happy to talk to you, and we'll even cut the price."

Bryan was casting *The Stepford Wives* and was convinced that Tuesday would be perfect for the leading role. He signed her to star in the film and arranged costume fittings. But she had yet to have the necessary medical examination to satisfy the insurance company—a formality on every film— and it was then that Forbes ran into a problem.

Tuesday confided to the doctor that she suffered from terrible migraines and often had to lie down in a darkened room for two days. Hearing that, the insurance company refused to insure her—not unnaturally, since it would have to pay for any lost filming time due to illness. "I had to break the news to her that she was out of the picture," recalls Bryan, "and she was very angry with me. I told her 'Darling, when I go for a medical and they ask me how I am, I say I'm great, I'm terrific. I'm awfully sorry, but I have to recast you.' It was a tragedy for me. I thought she was a marvelous actress."

Meanwhile, *Good Evening* was proving to be the smash hit of the season. It won a Grammy for "Best Spoken Word," and in April the wildly impudent revue won Dudley and Peter a special Tony Award for their "unique contribution to the theater of comedy."

Dudley sent his mother a photograph taken at the Tonys and indicated his growing contentment with Tuesday. "Apart from our odd crisis—which incidentally is always to our eventual advantage in terms of mutual understanding and closeness—we have a lovely time together. She is full of mischief so we have a lot of funny times. She is a very special girl, alarmingly honest—a trait that she requires from me, which is sometimes difficult."

He was, he added, enjoying a quiet, uneventful, domestic life—between his hotel and Tuesday's apartment—which satisfied him. "My life with Tuesday is full and complete. Whether it lasts or not is not important. The fact that it is good now is all that counts." It was the second time within five months that he'd mentioned the unimportance of how long their relationship would last. In retrospect, it was perhaps a significant comment. For what he omitted to tell his mother was that Tuesday was also a very unusual and unconventional young woman.

Robert Mann recollects the night that Dudley turned up at his flat near Central Park with Tuesday in tow. "She came in, said 'Hi,' and walked straight into our kitchen without saying another word. Then she opened the fridge and found a rather exotic jar of chutney, which she took out, found herself a spoon, and then sat down on the sofa eating the entire jar of chutney.

At least she closed the fridge door that time. She had a propensity for leaving them open, as she did with all doors, claiming that she liked to be able to see everything—"If I don't see it, it doesn't exist."

Mann was fascinated by Tuesday and became quite fond of her. He found her amusing and bright and even enjoyed her argumentative debates, which seemed to encompass everything under the sun. Nevertheless he was always aware "of daggers. She could be very disparaging, but it would never be peremptory behavior. It was more of a twist in conversation, where you felt that your point of view was beneath serious consideration and she'd be a bit contemptuous about it. It was very subtle."

Good Evening had been such a hit that it was now booked for a national tour, starting in February the following year. But Peter's problem with alcohol was frequently spiraling out of control, making Dudley very anxious about touring. Lysie Hastings, who was visiting New York and staying with Peter and Judy, also observed that Peter's drinking was "beyond excess."

According to Peter Bellwood, who knew Cook well and had shared a flat with him in London, "When he was sober Peter was a very sweet and gentle man underneath his acerbic character, but when he was drunk he could be quite vicious." Alexander Cohen concurs. "There was a good Peter Cook and a bad Peter Cook. When he was sober, he was a very good, intellectual, and wildly witty man who was vastly entertaining. When he was drunk, he was a vicious anti-Semite, violent about minorities. Not a nice guy to be around at all when he was drinking."

That was all too evident one night at a Christmas party in the New York home of Jerry Adler, who was now directing *Good Evening*. It was then that Peter's increasingly caustic attitude toward Dudley surfaced in a publicly vitriolic manner.

Alexander Cohen was one of the guests and was appalled when Peter made "a vicious remark" about Tuesday, offending Dudley violently. "Peter suddenly said to Tuesday, in front of everyone, 'How does it feel to be the only woman in town who fucked the entire company of *Good Evening*?' It was horrible. And from that moment on I mistrusted him totally."

Dudley, who has always downplayed the darker side of Peter's nature, admits the vitriol was there, but "you sort of accepted it in him."

Dudley's passive acceptance of human nature is a thread that has run through his life. "You expect your best friend to shit on you," he expostulates, "and you have to be prepared for that. I thought it was a bit ludicrous that he would be vitriolic, but I shrugged it off. I was resigned to it and just licked my wounds in a corner, like a cat."

Nevertheless, Peter's relentless and perverse cynicism was taking its toll on Dudley. "If I'd been a clubfooted dwarf from Dagenham," Peter was fond of telling people, "then I'd be that ambitious, too." His slashing comments hurt Dudley deeply. Publicly he dismissed them as opportunistic attempts to get a laugh, but privately he was finding them far from amusing.

"I think there was quite a jealousy between them by this time," says Lysie Hastings. "For one thing, Peter always came up with the ideas, and he was terribly respected by other comics in the business, who thought he was the most brilliant comic ever. Peter knew he was clever. He was almost too bright for his own good, and I think Dudley was probably jealous of that, because he didn't have the same intellect and quickness. And Peter was probably jealous of Dudley's ability as a musician, because everybody loved it. And he also recognized that women seemed to prefer Dudley."

Though Dudley was reluctant to go on tour, once again Peter cajoled him into agreement. After a brief break, during which Dudley made a quick trip home to see his family and organize the decorating of a house he'd bought in Islington (he'd given Bentham House to Suzy after the divorce), the show opened in Washington in February 1975.

For a while, he, Tuesday, Natasha, and her tutor seemed to be one big happy family. Dudley was growing very attached to Natasha. She was a sweet girl, and he enjoyed her immensely. But, by April, Tuesday was fed up with being on the road and phoned her mother to say she was flying back to Los Angeles to escape the boredom. "If you want to go, I can't stop you," Dudley told her, handling her with a loose rein. Typically, by the following day she had changed her mind.

What Tuesday really wanted was to be settled in a home where she could look after Dudley and her daughter. With the tour due to end in Los

Angeles in July, she planned to fly there ahead of him and search for a house where they could put down roots. But a week later she was again expressing her restlessness to her mother and said she was thinking of leaving Dudley.

Dudley saw his fortieth birthday come and go without the trauma that had been attached to his thirtieth—although he was feeling plenty of anxiety now about Peter's alcoholism and Tuesday's erratic moods. He was also becoming restless, and was ready to move on to some greater challenge than *Good Evening*. "Frankly," he wrote to his mother from Philadelphia, "I wish the show were over. I have performed it enough times now to satisfy my wildest enthusiasm."

Dudley was not an extravagant man and had always been very careful with his money, investing it wisely. His income now put him into Britain's highest, 90 percent, tax bracket, but performing outside England for eleven months of a tax year meant his considerable American earnings would be exempt. "If things turn out as expected," he wrote to his mother, "the money I will have from the show will, on being invested, yield me enough interest that I really needn't have to work again if I don't want to." For Ada, who still worried about her son, that must have been a pleasant and deeply reassuring piece of information.

Meanwhile, Peter's drinking was pulling them further and further apart. "I was conscious that he really wasn't with me," Dudley recalls. "He really didn't have any interest in what I was doing, and therefore quite understandably he was pissed on stage. And there was nothing I could do."

While Dudley was in Philadelphia, Tuesday flew back to Los Angeles and checked into Cedars of Lebanon, a Beverly Hills Hospital. She phoned her mother and told her she'd flown in to have what her mother's diary describes as a "baby operation."

A concerned Jo Weld, on her way to see Tuesday, stopped at her local market to buy flowers and was "sick and humiliated" to be told that Tuesday had actually arrived the day before and had been shopping there the previous night. Embarrassed and upset to learn that her daughter had arrived earlier and not called her, Jo returned home instead of going to the hospital.

Tuesday never told Dudley she'd been pregnant. Nor did Jo ever mention it. It would be twenty years later, as this book was being written, before Dudley would learn about the abortion—to his astonishment.

The relationship between Jo Weld and her daughter had been a volatile one ever since Tuesday's teenage years. At fourteen Tuesday had flown into a screaming tantrum when her mother told her they were moving back to the East Coast, where Jo had a job waiting. "I'll never be able to be an actress if we move from here!" Tuesday yelled. Her frenzied anger lasted three days, after which her mother capitulated and they remained in

Los Angeles, where Jo steered her daughter's career. By the age of sixteen Tuesday had moved out of their home and bought her own house.

These days, anything was likely to drive her into a fit of abusive rage or, almost worse, freezing silence, and Jo found herself walking on verbal eggshells around her "hard-boiled and cold" daughter.

"I'm sick inside at Tuesday's uncontrolled violence," her mother said a few weeks after the abortion. In an appalling fight, Tuesday had flown at her mother "screaming the most foul words I ever heard," and Jo's older daughter, Sally, had to intervene and stop her.

By now, *Good Evening/Behind the Fridge* had run for four years across three continents—a record for a two-man show, and especially remarkable given the deteriorating relationship between the pair. It was, perhaps, something of a wonder that they'd managed to complete the run at all.

Dudley, according to Alex Cohen, "kept performing with Peter in spite of the fact that he truly didn't want to, and you can't be more generous than that. The hardest thing for most people is living with another person, and the only thing harder than that is living with another person on stage."

Dudley was having his own problems off stage with Tuesday—she was unpredictable and argumentative, and there were endless rows that always left her the victor—but he could not turn to his work for relief, because he was having even larger problems there.

In July the show ended up in Los Angeles for a six-week run. Tuesday wanted to stay there and resume her film career, and had already found them a house to rent. She was angry when Dudley arrived late, having first spent time with Suzy, who was on her way back to London. Furious, Tuesday felt he should have come straight home to her instead.

Meeting Dudley for the first time, Jo Weld was enraptured by him. "He was such a charming man and very funny, and he and Tuesday were very amusing and playful with each other."

Peter Bellwood, who had now settled in California, came to visit the couple in their rented house, and found Tuesday quite enchanting. "I always had a wonderful time, because I thought that Tuesday was very funny. She always made me laugh. She had a kind of partly Judy Holliday quality, but there was another side to her that was not ditsy. She seemed to be on another level someplace—some very strange, crazy place. They certainly had a volatile relationship."

Dudley's life, already far from placid, was now loudly disrupted in late July by Tuesday's announcement that she was pregnant. By now they had already run into such turbulent weather that their ship was in danger of capsizing altogether. The news of her pregnancy changed everything.

With Dudley unaware of the earlier abortion three months before, the pregnancy came to him as a bombshell. It was news that he found hard to take. For one thing he simply was not parental material, and he recognized that fact. As when Suzy had wanted a child, he also feared that his physical deformities, which had been partly hereditary, would be passed on to any child he fathered, and the thought was horrifying. He also still did not want children because the belief still preyed on him that he and Barbara had not been wanted as babies. And he was immensely concerned about his future with Tuesday.

"I was appalled when she was pregnant," he admits, "and I ran amok. I didn't know what to do. I wanted her to abort it, and she refused—rightly. And I was afraid at the thought of being tied to anyone for twenty-odd years."

After the end of his marriage to Suzy, he had vowed never to embark on such a journey again. He needed to retain a sense of freedom, and the commitment of marriage impinged too much on that need. Besides which, he did not exactly have a propensity for monogamy.

Nevertheless, his sense of honor ran deep, and he asked Tuesday to marry him. Begged her, in fact, since she alternated constantly for and against it. After her first marriage ended in divorce, she had told American critic Rex Reed that she was soured on the idea and if she ever married again it would have to be for money—"and I mean a lot of money." But now she was pregnant with Dudley's baby. "I think she believed having a baby would be the greatest gift to me," he reflects. But she kept changing her mind. "I may have the baby," she told him, "and I may not." He was almost delirious with anxiety. He insisted on knowing, and the uncertainty drove him nuts. "I used to go backwards and forwards, backwards and forwards, until I made myself dizzy."

In some ways, Dudley was bewitched by Tuesday. And who wouldn't be? She was a genuinely funny woman, extremely intelligent, and gorgeous. At thirty, she was very much a child-woman, capable of being both endearingly childlike and sexily sophisticated. And, despite all their fights, there was some perverse challenge in constantly trying to win their verbal disagreements, even though Dudley always lost. It was that other side of her that he wanted to try to change—the erratic behavior that manifested itself in awful tantrums and the aggressive humor that could be so nasty and destructive.

Once Tuesday had been given something, she didn't want it. And no sooner had Dudley asked her to marry him and she had agreed, than she changed her mind altogether. In September she told her mother that Dudley had moved out of their rented Bel Air house and she needed to find a new, cheaper, place to live for herself and Natasha. But the pendulum of her life with Dudley was constantly on the move, and within a few days she called her mother back to say that Dudley had returned and they were going to marry. "If we don't get married this time," Tuesday told her mother tremulously, "I'm afraid we never will."

Two days later, there was a knock on Jo Weld's door. Tuesday, Dudley, and Natasha were standing there. "We're married!" Tuesday announced, and she hugged her mother. They had tied the knot in a Las Vegas chapel. They all stood, arms around each other and crying. "Now," Natasha beamed brightly, "I'm Natasha Harz Tuesday Ker Weld Moore."

They were living at this time in Bel Air's Roscomare Road, in a house that had been owned by the late comedian Wally Cox, whose close friend Marlon Brando had used to visit him and spend the night on the sofa. Cox's ashes had been scattered all over the ground, and Jo Weld always felt very uncomfortable walking around the garden. "I didn't want to tread on Wally," she fretted.

While Tuesday prepared for the baby's birth, Dudley contemplated his pending fatherhood with considerable angst. All the old fears about his foot were resurfacing. In those early days of Tuesday's pregnancy he felt the way his mother had when she knew she had given birth to a baby with defects. Dudley could not bear the potential burden of giving life to a maimed child.

In mid-October he and Tuesday flew briefly to London, where they met Barbara and Dudley's delighted mother. They also went to dinner with Lysie Hastings, who had now reverted to her maiden name of Alys Kihl. She observed that the couple "seemed very sweet together, happy and holding hands."

It was almost one big family. For, in an extraordinary coincidence, Lysie was now living with Tuesday's ex-husband, Claude Harz. They had met in New York when Lysie was staying with Peter and Judy Cook. Yet Dudley never reestablished contact with George Hastings—once his closest friend. They had grown distant after Dudley's affair with Lysie, and, to George's eternal sadness, Dudley allowed the friendship to dissolve entirely.

By Christmas, Dudley's fears about the baby had subsided. After all, he reasoned, his own genetic defects had skipped a generation. If the pattern recurred, his own baby would be normal.

Jo Weld, who was living on welfare and food stamps, had a welcome Christmas surprise when the American Legion delivered her two boxes of fruit, vegetables, and ham. "There really are good people in the world," she thanked them tearfully. There was more than enough for her own needs, and she passed most of the food on to Dudley and Tuesday, who were throwing a big party. She went out to their house on Christmas Day, but left after ten minutes when Tuesday became angry with her and shut herself in the bedroom.

Apart from marital rumpuses, which were many, life for Dudley was fairly uneventful. The spacious garage made a perfect studio, and he was content to play his piano there. Friends visited the house, and Peter Bellwood was always vastly entertained whenever he went for dinner.

"I always thought Tuesday was a remarkable actress, but I don't think she was a homebody," he reflects. "There was one time when she'd made a nice dinner and she gathered up the plates, continuing to talk, and without so much as batting an eyelid she put all the dirty plates with the forks and knives on them in the fridge. We didn't quite know why she had done this, but it was all so completely unconscious that it was delightfully loony. Then she took out a tub of ice cream from the freezer, which had been turned up so high that there wasn't any chance of it melting before the following week. This sort of stuff was going on all the time. It was a great giggle."

Most of Dudley's days were spent at the piano, but whenever he felt itchy he would go off and meet various producers, none of whom seemed to know quite what to do with this short, middle-aged man from Dagenham. "I suppose I was waiting for them to say, 'My God, you're the fellow we've been looking for!'" he reflects, "but of course it never happened."

In January 1976 he flew to New York for a week of meetings. A few days after his return, Jo Weld received a frantic call from Tuesday saying Natasha was hysterical and asking her to come up to the house. She had just thrown Dudley out after discovering he'd been with another woman while he was in New York. Dudley later confessed to Jo his ambivalence about marriage. He knew he should not have admitted his indiscretion to Tuesday, but had felt unable to lie to her since she always saw through him anyway. The hotels around town were getting quite used to Dudley by now. This time when he moved out it was to check into the Bel Air Sands. But, as usual, the tiff did not last for long, and less than a week later he was back home and behaving as a concerned father-to-be—making hospital arrangements, shopping for a baby carriage, and even attending Lamaze labor classes with Tuesday.

A few weeks after that last snafu, Tuesday's mother received an excited lunchtime phone call from her daughter. The baby was on its way. "She sounded so happy, and I packed a case and went over to the house while Dudley went to the hospital."

Dudley had hoped to witness the birth of his first child. But it was not to be. Complications suddenly set in, and he was abruptly ejected when the medical team had to perform an emergency cesarean. The umbilical cord had wrapped itself four times around the baby's neck and twice around its body, so the child was unable to descend through the birth canal. Every contraction brought it closer to strangulation.

For a while, Dudley suffered more than the usual prenatal fears. But the doctors excelled themselves, and, at 10:30 that February night, Patrick

Havlin Moore was born. He was in perfect health. Dudley was jubilant.

"When Dudley came back, about 1:30 in the morning," recalls Jo Weld, "he was ecstatic. I had a chocolate cake and champagne ready, and we drank a toast and he ate most of the icing off the top of the cake. Then he went into the garage and played the piano for over an hour. It was the most triumphant and glorious music I have ever heard."

Dudley named his son after director Patrick Garland, his Oxford contemporary, whose niceness Dudley had never forgotten. Garland himself never learned of the connection until many years later, and when he did, he was at the same time flattered, bemused, and embarrassed. "I'm amazed that I had such an effect on anyone," he says. "It's a very noble and touching tribute, but I don't know that I deserve it. It makes me blush." Patrick's middle name came from Dudley's father, who had been born John Havlin.

Dudley was exultant about his new son, and for the next few weeks his life revolved around Patrick, Tuesday, and Natasha, who was developing a motherly instinct toward the new baby. But he was also seeing Dr. Milton Wexler, his new psychotherapist, with increasing regularity.

Life in the Moore household soon became far from smooth again, as Jo Weld discovered when Tuesday called her late in March to say that Dudley was insisting on being able to go off with other women. He was, according to Tuesday, even receiving love letters at the house, which she pounced upon and read with increasing despondency.

"Some men—most men—are like that," says Jo Weld. "But Tuesday couldn't handle it. She was very possessive, and she couldn't bear that Dudley was seeing other women. You can't own people. You can only have a little at a time out of their lives. But Tuesday wanted more. She was very demanding and very jealous."

It was true that Tuesday was by nature a demanding woman. But at that moment in her life, having just given birth to her husband's baby, it must have been especially devastating to learn that he preferred to be with other women. Her anger, which masked a deep hurt, fueled the fire, and there were endless rows.

By the end of April, Dudley was looking particularly drawn and unhappy. He tried to put a good face on things, for the last thing he wanted to do was leave Tuesday and Patrick. At least he could lose his troubles in music, alone with his piano in the garage.

Among all the bad times, however, there were occasional moments of sweetness. Jo Weld arrived at their house one morning to take Dudley to the airport for a flight to London and witnessed a touching farewell scene. Tuesday and Dudley were holding hands, and Natasha was wrapped around his leg, begging him not to go.

A few weeks earlier, humorist Martin Lewis had assembled more than a dozen of Britain's greatest comedians for a three-night charity benefit at Her Majesty's Theatre in London in aid of Amnesty International. It was a summit meeting of British comedy, and among the notables on stage were the *Monty Python* gang, John Bird, Barry Humphries, Eleanor Bron, Bill Oddie, and Tim Brooke-Taylor. And the ex-Fringers, Alan Bennett, Peter Cook, and Jonathan Miller.

The only person missing from this comedy extravaganza—which was also filmed for video release as *A Poke in the Eye*—was Dudley himself, who had been unable to fly over in time. Terry Jones substituted for him and, when he reached London at the end of April, Dudley recorded a narration for the video version as his contribution.

By now the private Derek and Clive tapes that he and Peter had recorded a few years earlier had somehow multiplied like rabbits and burrowed their way through the showbiz world with wild abandon. They had become so wildly popular underground that Island Records now offered to issue them on an album. Originally tagged as *Derek and Clive (Dead)*, some new material was added to the original, and the first of a trio of albums was released under the title *Derek and Clive (Live)*. They were, says Dudley, "the most obscene things you've ever heard in your life."

It was a wonder that the albums ever made it past the rigid censorship controls of the time. *Derek and Clive (Live)* comprised such vulgar and sexually oriented jokes, that the cover had to carry a warning: "This record contains language of an explicit nature that may be offensive and should not be played in the presence of minors." Considering the comic reputation of the duo, everyone probably thought the warning was some sort of joke. Until they played the record.

People were particularly amazed that Dudley, who wrote such emotional music for his jazz albums, could have such a ribald outlook. But, as he points out wryly, without implying any other comparison between them, "Mozart had a very scatalogical sense of humor, too. He was always talking about farting and cunts and asses. He had a very basic sense of humor. I don't find anything wrong with that."

The album was an amazing success, and over fifty thousand copies were sold within a few weeks of its release. Four thousand copies immediately were exported to America, and the record ultimately became the duo's biggest-selling album. It would be followed by two more—*Derek and Clive Come Again* and *Derek and Clive Ad Nauseam*—and they remain three of the most notoriously raunchy comedy albums ever released. "We went just about as far as we could go with pure filth," Dudley admits gleefully.

But while Dudley was holding forth on the unspeakables, his marriage was failing. "I just couldn't find a way to get hold of Tuesday. I think it was a fairly perverse situation where I didn't like the way she was and I needed to change her. It was a futile gesture. She was a real brat—the one person I could never lord it over verbally."

Returning to Los Angeles, Dudley rekindled an old friendship with Anthony Page, who was making *F. Scott Fitzgerald in Hollywood*, a television movie in which he had cast Tuesday as Zelda, the other half of another famously erratic marriage. "I could see they were having a very difficult time," says Page, who witnessed the tension between Tuesday and Dudley. "It was very stormy. She turned up on location with lots of suitcases, and then Dudley followed and they were together again. And then he left and they weren't."

On Mother's Day, in May, Tuesday turned up at her mother's with a bottle of champagne and the news that the marriage was over. Later that day, Dudley admitted to Jo that he was tired of being Tuesday's "whipping boy." She was too demanding, and he wouldn't take it any longer. Jo ruefully told him, "I was just about to bow out of her life myself as her whipping boy and let you take my position!"

A weary Dudley moved out of the house—for the last time, he vowed—and into the Chateau Marmont, a hotel in Hollywood on Sunset Boulevard. Less than a fortnight later, however, he and Tuesday had become reconciled and he moved back home.

Dudley had always been attracted to women with vulnerability and needs, and Tuesday certainly had both. But so, too, had Dudley, and his self-esteem was being chipped away by Tuesday's constant battering. Yet it could hardly have helped Tuesday's own fragile sense of security to know that Dudley was pursuing other women and seemed to prefer being away from their home more often than he was in it.

In many ways, Dudley simply wasn't marital material. He still found marriage altogether too confining. There had always been in him a fear of not being in control, and he again felt trapped by having to be answerable to someone else at all times.

But it wasn't just marriage that was the problem: there was also an increasing need to be on his own.

The seeds for solitude had been sown way back during his early hospital years, in those long incarcerations when he'd been left unvisited by his parents. The roots had taken a strong hold, and they were now beginning to produce shoots. In a sense, he had been bred for a life of isolation.

Dudley was aware of the reasons for the conflicts within him, and he tried to quell his desire to leave home. He had responsibilities that he had never known before. He had a son now, and he was determined to try to keep the marriage afloat.

But the continual discord between him and Tuesday was pulling them both down. It was proving immensely destructive, not only for them, but also for Patrick. Just how much longer could it go on?

CHAPTER 12

TURNING POINTS

1976-1977

*"He doesn't strike me as very happy, poor old thing. He's always seemed
to be searching for something in a rather peculiar way, and that's where
California didn't help him very much. Because he was surrounded
by all that ghastly West Coast new-age nonsense."*

—JONATHAN MILLER

I n June 1976 Dudley flew to London, accompanied by Tuesday and
Patrick, to begin work on a new film with Peter Cook, *The Hound of the
Baskervilles*. It was a comic version of the classic Sherlock Holmes tale, and
"something that Peter very much wanted to do. The ideas were his, and we
both thought it could be the funniest film ever."

They also recorded *Derek and Clive Come Again*, a racy album that was
loaded with inane tales of masturbation. Nothing and no one was sacred.
In one sketch, Derek (Dudley) tells Clive (Peter) that he had ejaculated
over a picture of his father's face; in another he recalls the time when he
shoved a Jaffa cake into his mother's mouth and her right breast fell off.
And Picasso was accused of having painted his penis several different colors.

Tuesday seemed content in London for a few weeks, although she
complained to her mother that Dudley had "reverted to his old wishy-
washy self." Ironically, since she had been accusing Dudley of being an
uninterested father, she noted, "He loves Patrick almost to a fault, he car-
ries on so."

It was a busy time for Dudley, crammed with recording sessions and
discussions about future projects, and he also squeezed in musical appearances on radio and television. There were meetings with Chris Karan and
Peter Morgan to set up engagements for the trio, a party for Nanette

Newman, a speech at the Royal College of Music as a favor to his old Oxford tutor, Bernard Rose, and the wedding of his sister's daughter, Helen, in Upminster.

Maybe a wedding in the family was just what was needed to restore good spirits and thoughts of a hopeful future. Certainly Barbara, his sister, saw nothing to indicate that Dudley was despondent over his own marriage. "He seemed fine and happy. They both did. We hadn't seen them since Tuesday was pregnant, so it was a marvelous reunion and a particular thrill for my mother to see Patrick."

A Guinness commercial took Dudley to Amsterdam for a few days, and several engagements at Burke's club with his trio kept him musically busy. At Ronnie Scott's jazz club he joined Dizzy Gillespie for an improvised interlude.

He also spent a good deal of time with Peter Cork, his early music master. Now fifty, Cork was anxious to change the direction of his work and become a professional composer, and Dudley was giving him invaluable guidance. The student had become the teacher.

Over the years, Dudley had always been concerned about his weight. Being short, any slight weight gain tended to show up on his face and stomach, and he was constantly on and off diets. Fasts were frequent. The last few weeks of heavy socializing in London had taken their toll, so, leaving Patrick with a nanny in London, he and Tuesday flew off to a fat farm in Marbella, where Dudley managed to fast for fifteen days, outfasting Tuesday by five days, after she sneaked out of the window to visit a local restaurant.

After their divorce, Dudley had given Bentham House to Suzy. Although he still had the lease of the Cheyne Walk flat, which was soon to expire, he now took Tuesday to inspect the house he had bought some years earlier in Islington. BBC producer Jonathan Powell was renting it at the time. As he later related to John Bassett, Tuesday took one look at the house, wailed "Dudley, it's so dirty," and immediately walked away. In fact, as Powell told John Bassett, they never even put a foot over the threshold.

Tuesday eventually flew back to Los Angeles, but leaving Dudley alone in London caused her considerable anxiety. "He's being a lover boy again," she told her mother unhappily. "I know his voice when he's hiding something."

Dudley had been in and out of England for much of 1976. The out part was largely due to his being allowed to stay for only sixty-three consecutive days before becoming subject to Britain's extortionate tax laws. His latest exit now took him back to Los Angeles for a week, during which he made up for lost time and socialized madly at parties with friends. He was beginning to get the hang of Hollywood's modus operandi. Then it was back to London to see Robert Mann performing with the Juilliard String

Quartet at the Queen Elizabeth Hall before returning to spend a relatively quiet Christmas at home with Tuesday and Patrick.

For the first few months of 1977 he stayed at home in Los Angeles, working on the script of *The Hound of the Baskervilles*. Writing had never come easily to Dudley and, although he was making considerable headway with Peter Cook via the telephone, it was a tortuous process. Still, there was time for a full social calendar, and there were countless dinner parties, all mingled with Dr. Wexler's psychoanalysis.

Life had settled down to an uncomfortable truce with Tuesday, although it was an uneasy existence. By now the Moore family was ensconced in a newly rented house on Doheny Drive in the foothills of Beverly Hills. But not for long.

"It seems a long time since I visited Dagenham," Dudley wrote to his mother at the end of March, "but I'll be in London in May when we start filming *Hound*." His mother was always eager for news of Patrick, and Dudley told her of his son's latest developments. "He is a real little boy now and is starting to walk, God help us. He seems outrageously delighted that he is a biped and laughs insanely as he totters toward you and then collapses on your safety with a giggle." Tuesday, he told her, was about to start a new film called *Dog Soldiers* and "is characteristically nervous and irritable."

Dudley's belief in himself was at a fairly low ebb these days. Unsure of himself and his emotions, he found himself spending too much time pondering the advancing years, and this led now to the development of a film treatment called *The Joy of Sex*. It was, says Peter Bellwood, who worked with Dudley in turning it into a screenplay, "based on Dudley's experiences with Tuesday" and centered on a hero who was filled with anxiety, grief, and rage.

On the surface, it was about a man in his early forties going through a midlife crisis and pursuing gorgeous women in the hope of recovering his former youth. Underneath, it dealt with deeper issues: a man's fear of approaching old age and death, of going through a whole life without realizing who he is, and of coming to the end of it without having done what he really wanted to do. If this sounds familiar, that's because it was inherently the theme of *10*—the movie that would turn Dudley into an American star—although *The Joy of Sex* preceded *10* by a couple of years.

Robert Mann, who had flown into town for a series of concerts that Dudley attended, now saw a fairly distracted and confused man. "There was a lot of disharmony. Dudley was not a shouter, not a physical abuser, and what I mostly observed was extreme discomfort. Verbally, Tuesday was very good at putting anyone down. She did it very well with me, too. She just had that kind of personality. It wasn't evil or anything, and it probably came from a lack of confidence. She'd learned that the best form of defense was attack."

Like most of the women Dudley became involved with, Tuesday was a strong presence; Francis Megahy, who considered her one of the funniest people he'd ever met, says she was "an extremely formidable character. Tuesday was very opinionated, and so was Dudley. That may not be apparent, because he's not aggressive or confrontational, but he knows what he thinks and he doesn't have much doubt about it, and he wants to do things his way like he's always done. When you have two people like that, life can be difficult."

Dudley had been searching for a new agent and asked Sue Mengers, who was Tuesday's agent, if she could recommend someone. He was hoping she would take him on herself, but she was already swamped with a huge client list. The man she recommended was ICM agent Lou Pitt.

Lou was a rather solemn young man who had risen through the ranks from mailroom to agent. He was particularly thrilled to meet Dudley and to be asked to represent him, and needed no introduction to his work. From *Beyond the Fringe*, one of the first plays he saw on Broadway, to *Good Evening*, he had long been an admirer of Dudley's talents.

Pitt did not share Dudley's beliefs that Hollywood was not ready for "a clubfooted dwarf with a Dagenham accent." To him, the measure for all success was talent, and Dudley had a surfeit of that. He was infected by his new client's fierce determination to become a success in America. "He was absolutely ready to explode," recalls Pitt of their first meeting. "He'd made a commitment to settle down and to advance his career here, and he had a solid desire to work in American films. He was very frustrated. He'd come from such a rich performing background but had yet to translate it to an American film audience."

Meanwhile, Tuesday was away on location in Mexico filming *Dog Soldiers* with Nick Nolte. This was probably fortuitous timing for her and Dudley, since, although they talked often on the phone, it afforded them some breathing space apart. An interesting entry in Dudley's diary in April 1977 showed some unusual thoughts during this time:

Feeling of ludicrousness of people and situations and lack of feeling therein. Disinclined to phone anyone as not positive about wishing to see anyone when sex is to be fulfilled. Feeling of emptiness in merely contacting someone with a view to sexuality only. In most cases it seems friendship not present in these proposed encounters so no one gets a call from me! And I am left vaguely annoyed that my motivation is changing and "depriving" me of sex!

He flew to San Francisco to see Tuesday on location, but their reunion was brief and he returned the next morning, although by the following week she herself was back in Los Angeles for studio filming.

Tuesday was deeply possessive of Dudley and jealous of the time he was away from her. She used his various absences to accuse him that he was not a good father. She could be acutely scathing and demeaning, and her constant attacks made Dudley feel there was something wrong with him. "There may," he surmises, "have been some poisonous thing between us that just pecked at us both when we were together. I found the situation very difficult and impossible."

Once, when Tuesday had been particularly nice, Dudley told her, "My God, that's the person I've been looking for!" But Tuesday replied, "Well, that's the last you'll ever see of her." "And it was," he says. "I never saw that sweet, nice person again. Tuesday said that wasn't really her. And I guess it wasn't. She'd just been hurt too much in the past, I suppose."

Ben Shaktman, his longtime friend, was moved by Dudley's difficulties with Tuesday and recalls endless conversations about his internal turbulence. "He felt that she was going through a lot of pain and was clearly unstable. And there was a fear of being with someone who he genuinely felt was out of control. But she was an actress, a very complete performer and a very smart lady, and she could pull out all the stops when she wanted to.

"Dudley just didn't know what to do, because now there was also Patrick to worry about and that was a factor. He felt helpless to be able to leave or to help Tuesday, because he was seriously concerned about her psychological and physical stability. He kept putting his hands over his head and saying, 'Why did I do this? How do I get out of this? Do I want to get out of it or don't I?'"

A genuine desire to make things right with Tuesday made Dudley fly to Mexico for a few days to join her on location in Durango. After he returned, he sent her a cable: "Hello dog soldier," he wrote, "I love you, miss you. I know Durango is irresistible but don't stay too long. I don't like it without you."

There was one more trip to Mexico, and then he returned to London. During rehearsals for *The Hound of the Baskervilles* he set up some cabaret engagements at Burke's with the trio and visited his mother for Sunday lunch. Old friends, who hoped to hang out with him during his Dagenham excursions, found it frustratingly difficult to get close. "Mrs. Moore was quite possessive," recalls Teifion Griffiths, Dudley's friend since his teenage years, "and if I arranged to go and see Dudley, I felt I was intruding, because she only had so many hours with him herself. He was the center of her interest, and she missed him a lot."

One Sunday, Dudley asked his mother why she was so reluctant to have Teifion come to the house. She broke down and said it was because she wanted him all to herself. "It was sweet," says Dudley, "but at the same time I found it immensely suffocating."

By now the anger he had carried for so long toward his mother had subsided. Years of therapy had brought him to understand that, despite all the pain he'd suffered during childhood, for which he'd always blamed his mother, she had only done what she had thought best for him. He felt a strong allegiance to her now and enjoyed his Sunday visits. Life had become fairly hectic, and the house in Baron Road was one of the few places he was able to relax and feel cosseted. He looked forward to his Sunday lunches, and the cup of tea that followed on the back porch.

Late in June 1977 filming began on *The Hound of the Baskervilles*, under the direction of Andy Warhol protégé Paul Morrissey. Peter Cook later described it as "a mess with some funny moments. Asking Paul Morrissey to direct English comedy is like asking me to direct an improvised movie about junkies in L.A. Not compatible at all."

Dudley agrees that the film was a debacle and attributes the failure to its director. "Paul Morrissey frustrated us at every turn, and we should have dumped the entire idea."

Since he and Peter had chosen Morrissey, they were also partly responsible for the result. Based on his previous films, they had expected that Morrissey would be easy to work with. He turned out to be the reverse.

Dudley disagreed entirely with Morrissey on the subject of comedy. "I couldn't believe how strangely anal he was about everything," he says. "Basically he wanted something comedic to happen whenever we did anything. It was an obsession with him, and it took all the fun out of doing it. It could have been the funniest thing, but it didn't work because he was somewhere else. I had no idea what he wanted."

The film presented Peter Cook as a comic version of Sherlock Holmes, complete with hair net and dressing gown. Dudley was cast in multiple roles, first as a moronic Dr. Watson (for which he adopted a Welsh accent that he based on Teifion Griffith's father), then as Mr. Spiggott, a hopping one-legged lunatic, and finally as Sherlock Holmes's mother. On paper it seemed funny enough, but on celluloid it fell flat. There was no real plot, just a series of crime-solving episodes.

By now Tuesday and Patrick had joined him in London. Tuesday had at last found a house in Los Angeles that she was madly in love with and begged Dudley to buy it. They didn't know it then, but it once had been Rudy Vallee's old beach cottage, though it was now highly dilapidated. Dudley could not yet get away to see the house, but he sent for paperwork on the property.

Dudley had now decided to make Los Angeles his permanent home.

He was, after all, married to an American woman who wanted to remain there, and he himself liked California a great deal. As for his career, that— he hoped—was portable and he could continue it anywhere.

For the last year he had been sorting out the details of applying for American residency, and now he made arrangements to dispose of all his financial holdings in Britain. He also reminded himself in a diary note to make a new will in California and to buy a burial plot there. Later jokes for the benefit of the Inland Revenue ("I'll live and die in Los Angeles") may not have been made entirely in jest.

When filming on *The Hound of the Baskervilles* ended in July, Dudley and Tuesday flew to Los Angeles so that he could view the house she was so passionate about—a three-bedroomed pied-à-terre overlooking a stretch of deserted beach at Marina del Rey, near Santa Monica. The day after they returned, she saw her mother, who later observed in her diary, "Tuesday will put her enormous pressure on Dudley—buy the house for me or I'll leave you."

Dudley stayed four days in Los Angeles—long enough to initiate plans to buy the house and to see his psychoanalyst. But he wanted Tuesday to retain the Doheny Drive house. Perhaps by now he was com- ing to accept his need for isolation. "He always had that reclusive side to him," says Lysie Kihl, "and constantly needed a bolt-hole to re- treat into."

From this time on, Dudley would always ensure that the woman in his life had another home to go to whenever he had that urge for solitude. If she didn't own one, he would buy one for her.

Back in London a few days later Dudley told the British press that his seesaw marriage to Tuesday was now definitely stable. "I've made a big effort and so has Tuesday, and we're perfectly happy together now," he assured them, in one of his more blatant attempts to deceive journalists.

With Dudley in London, Tuesday began work on a new movie in Los Angeles, *A Question of Guilt*. She asked Jo Weld to accompany her on the set one day. "She was lonely and drained from her work," remarks Jo, "and said she needed her mother. So of course I went." A few nights later, Jo cooked some of her legendary chili and took it up to the house on Doheny Drive, but Tuesday "had just come in and was obviously expecting a man, so I put down the chili and left."

In London, Dudley and Peter Cook made a hilarious appearance in an ABC documentary "To the Queen! A Salute To Elizabeth II," perform- ing some skits on the lifestyle of the royal family.

Paul Morrissey had now edited *The Hound of the Baskervilles*, which Dudley also scored on a shoestring budget, but both Dudley and Peter thought it was so awful that they edited another version of their own—the one that would ultimately be released. Their version, said Peter, was "marginally better, but there's still no making it any good."

The film flopped miserably when it came out in England. *Variety* noted "Cook and Moore have deteriorated into almost complete reliance on lavatory humor to get laughs," but in America the film would not be released for a couple of years.

Which, as it happened, was lucky for Dudley, who was on the threshold of taking his first major steps in Hollywood.

PART THREE

CHAPTER 13

HOLLYWOOD

1977-1978

*"Acting is a way of hiding oneself. It's a form of denial of who we really are.
Extroversion in comedians like Dudley is really a symptom of introversion.
We're basically very shy, have a very low self-esteem, and we're like
children who need a quick fix, or else we wouldn't be performing."*

—CHEVY CHASE

The latter part of 1977 was a busy time for Dudley.

In England there were jazz bookings at the Cambridge Arts Festival
and discussions for a new Australian tour for the coming spring. He and
Peter were offered twenty-five thousand pounds to film half a dozen commercials for the London Electricity Board, and they began negotiating for
a third Derek and Clive album.

The extraordinary success of Derek and Clive had now reached
American ears, and they were becoming cult figures across the Atlantic.
Their notoriety led to an appearance on American television, where they
hosted a segment of NBC's irreverent late-night comedy show *Saturday Night
Live* with Chevy Chase.

Lou Pitt, Dudley's new agent, was now seeing a lot of interest in his
client. "He had a tremendous cultish following and I kept getting calls
from people who had the Derek and Clive recordings. It was only a
question of someone being in a position to take advantage of that."

Somebody was. That someone was Chevy Chase.

Lou Pitt recalls, "He was a huge fan of Dudley and Peter and he was
about to make *Foul Play*, his first movie. He called me and said, 'This is my
first film and I may be shooting myself in the foot, but I just have to have
Dudley play a part.'"

Dudley was flattered and pleased when Pitt relayed the conversation, but after reading the script, he passed on the offer. To Dudley, the role in *Foul Play* was that of another sex-starved twit and the kind of caricature part he was anxious now to move away from. He was tired of playing undersized, oversexed idiots.

Colin Higgins, who had scripted *Harold and Maude* and *Silver Streak*, was making his directorial debut with *Foul Play*. Swayed by Chevy's urgings, he refused to take no for an answer and begged Dudley to reconsider. But Dudley turned it down again.

Higgins, now keener than ever to secure Dudley for his film, suggested threading two roles together into one. Faced with Higgins's relentless pursuit and a greater character opportunity than had first been presented, Dudley reluctantly gave in. In November 1977 he flew to San Francisco for ten days of filming. His fee was $27,500. There had been many turning points in his career up till now, but this film would be the one to set him firmly on the road to stardom in America.

Foul Play is a comedy thriller in which wisecracking, affable police lieutenant Chevy Chase falls for librarian Goldie Hawn, who becomes unwittingly involved in a plot to assassinate the Pope and is chased by various nefarious creatures of the underworld.

Enter Dudley as a chubby, sex-obsessed, and sex-starved maniacal orchestra conductor who rescues Goldie from her pursuers in a singles bar and offers her safe refuge in his apartment—a haunt so crammed with sex-aid devices it would put any sex shop to shame. His subsequent romantic failures with Goldie become the film's running gag.

The film climaxes with Dudley conducting a glitzy performance of *The Mikado* in the presence of the Pope. Chase arrives in time to foil the dastardly assassination attempt and is romantically reunited backstage with Goldie, while our hapless conductor, anxious to avoid another unlucky encounter with her, disguises himself in sunglasses to finish the concert.

It was a small part, but it was just the kind of role that Dudley had always carried off with comic brilliance.

He worked well with Colin Higgins, who would later make the comedy hits *Nine to Five* and *The Best Little Whorehouse in Texas* before his death from AIDS at the age of forty-seven.

Dudley was hilarious in the film. He had only three scenes, but he milked them for all he was worth. "There was one take in the police station," recalls Chevy Chase, "where we must have done it forty times because I just kept laughing my guts out every time Dudley walked by. I remember looking at the rushes and saying, 'God, is he funny!' But I'd already known how funny he was. Goldie was in hysterics all the time."

Goldie Hawn, a bubbly girl with an Academy Award already behind her, was making her tenth movie. She found Dudley immensely entertaining. "He was one the funniest people I've ever worked with," she giggles. "We did one scene that became a tour de force for him. We must have shot it twenty-five different times, and he was just as funny every time. I remember howling with laughter and thinking, 'How can he make it seem so fresh every time?' Maybe the first or even the second time, but twenty-five? He was hilarious."

Dudley admired Chevy Chase, a creative young comedian who was a regular part of the innovative *Saturday Night Live* team. Most of Chevy's work on that show was entirely improvised, whereas Dudley's improvising had usually taken place within the framework of a scripted outline.

Chevy, who had admired Dudley's work for several years, was such a fan of his early English films that he could almost quote scenes verbatim. "Probably one of the funniest movies I had ever seen," says Chase, "was *Bedazzled*. I loved it. It's a classic. It was absolutely brilliant. And, much as I admired Peter Cook, the talent that Dudley had was so extraordinary, it went even beyond that."

Chevy, whose own humor, like Dudley's, came from tremendous rage as a child, was glad to have Dudley's support during his first film. At that time, Chevy admits, he was "full of crap and full of myself," yet he was almost reverential of Dudley and learned a great deal from the seasoned comedian.

"Comedy's about making people laugh," says Chevy, "and at the end of the day, it's all about getting the laugh without going so far over the top as to be unbelievable. It took me a long time to reach that point. Dudley combined both and helped to show me how to do it. He was so good in *Foul Play*, so wildly weird and funny, that it affected me for years. My problem then was that I simply didn't know how to act. I'd done *Saturday Night Live*, sure, but I didn't do what Dudley did. By watching his performance, I learned so much. I learned more from him than he'll ever know."

Dudley enjoyed the film, but he was unhappy with his performance. He considered it over the top and very predictable—just as he had expected it to be when he read the script. *Evening Standard* critic Milton Shulman later called it one of Dudley's poorer parts—an opinion with which Dudley agreed. The public and other critics, however, did not.

With its release, Dudley's performance as the sexually exasperated swinger almost upstaged both Chevy Chase and Goldie Hawn. As Bryan Forbes observes, "It was Dudley at his best. He was incredibly funny and absolutely brilliant." Critics were generous with their praise, and *Newsweek*'s David Ansen declared, "Comic laurels go to the pint-sized Dudley Moore as a closet swinger eternally caught in kinkiness interruptus by endangered Goldie; it's a crude running gag which Moore milks for more than it's worth."

Dudley was still absorbed in psychotherapy, and by now he'd tried almost every form of it. The grayness and depression had subsided, but he still felt he wasn't in total command of his life, nor did he know precisely what he wanted from it.

At Dr. Wexler's suggestion, his treatment had evolved into group therapy, and he found this more enlightening and helpful than any other form of analysis he had tried before. He sat in a circle with a couple of film actresses, an architect, a director, a script supervisor, and a rather wealthy nonachiever, and chatted endlessly about his inner problems. When Dudley felt too weighed down by the gravity of the situation he threw out the odd joke and filled the room with laughter.

As the therapy sessions continued, Christmas came and Dudley communed closer with Hollywood friends including Leslie and Evie Bricusse and comedian Phil Silvers and his therapist wife, Evelyn.

Evelyn had known Dudley ever since Tuesday, a few years earlier, had called Evelyn, her longtime friend, and told her about "this wonderful fellow you've got to meet." The Moores had become regular visitors to the Silvers' household, and Dudley particularly looked forward to Evelyn's annual Christmas-tree-trimming party, a tradition he would enjoy for many years.

Evelyn was immensely helpful to Dudley, who was able to discuss areas of psychoanalysis with her that took him far beyond his regular sessions with Dr. Wexler.

In February 1978, when the Academy Award nominations were announced, Tuesday found herself nominated as Best Supporting Actress for her work in *Looking for Mr. Goodbar*. Two months later she nervously arrived at the awards on Dudley's arm, but lost to Vanessa Redgrave's brilliant performance in *Julia*.

Immediately after the Oscars, Dudley took his jazz trio—Chris Karan and Peter Morgan—to Australia and New Zealand for a tour. In Sydney they recorded a new album—*The Dudley Moore Trio Live*—during a concert at Sydney Town Hall. It included "Song for Suzy," and Dudley threw in a jazzed-up version of "Scheherazade" and a Chopin pastiche. "It was a bit like performing in an aircraft hangar," recalls Chris Karan, "but we had a lot of fun. We had a terrific momentum going, because we were playing every night, and I think being together for all that time came out in the music."

Chris had been with Dudley since 1961 and the formative days of the Establishment in London. Now he sensed time was running out for the trio. "Dudley was getting more and more involved in Hollywood, and I could tell that's where he wanted to be and that his career was going to be there. I had a feeling we weren't going to do very much after the tour was over."

He was right. It would be another fourteen years before the trio would perform together again.

In May 1978 Dudley and Tuesday flew to Cannes, where *Who'll Stop the Rain?* (as *Dog Soldiers*, the film she had made with Nick Nolte was called in America) had been awarded special honors. All the Hollywood studio executives were there, and Dudley was summoned to the Hotel du Cap by Michael Eisner and Barry Diller, who headed Paramount Studios, for whom Dudley and Peter Bellwood were writing *The Joy of Sex*. Eisner and Diller were impressed with Dudley's performance in *Foul Play* and wanted to discuss future moves in his career.

When he arrived, Dudley found himself squeezed into the middle of a production meeting and, once there, felt utterly ignored. Eisner and Diller seemed hardly to know he was there. "What do you want to do next?" they asked Dudley, then turned away without listening to his answer. "I couldn't believe it," he recalls now. "Not to give me even the courtesy of seeming interested! I couldn't understand why."

While Dudley squirmed during this peculiar encounter with Hollywood's new moguls, Tuesday was holding court with show business reporters from around the world. She showed off photographs of Dudley with Natasha and Patrick, extolled his comic genius, and described future projects they would embark on together. Maybe she was trying to deflect the increasing rumors that were swirling around the tumultuous marriage.

Ultimately their brief sojourn in Cannes did little to heal their wounded relationship, and a couple of weeks after they returned to L.A., Tuesday told her mother that she and Dudley had split up and she was moving back to New York. A few days later Dudley also told Jo Weld he felt their marriage was beyond repair.

In July 1978 *Foul Play* premiered in San Francisco. It became a major box-office hit and would go on to gross more than $70 million. The critics loved director-screenwriter Colin Higgins's borrowed car-chase scene from *Bullitt* and his reworked segments from various Hitchcock thrillers.

Although Dudley only had three scenes, his performance gained major attention and netted him a Golden Globe nomination. Americans had not seen anyone quite like him before. There would be no going back. The role may have been relatively small, but it established him as a firm presence in Hollywood.

Despite the kudos of a newfound popularity far away from home, Dudley still felt acute impatience about his life and was more anxious than ever to reach a full understanding about himself. He was, just then, more interested in getting his head together than his career. He had always felt relatively optimistic about his career, had always held a conviction that work would be continually available to him, in some form or other. As

Francis Megahy had observed since the sixties, "There was always a contradiction about him, which was the confidence about getting work on the one hand, and the depression about his life on the other."

Dudley's therapy group was at this time the priority in his life. It was in this group that he had encountered the Paramount executive who ultimately commissioned him to write *The Joy of Sex*. It was here, too, that he met director Blake Edwards.

Blake was a Hollywood legend. He had directed the classics *Breakfast at Tiffany's*, *Days of Wine and Roses*, and *A Shot in the Dark*. There had also been some box-office failures, notably *The Great Race*, *The Party*, *Darling Lili* (starring his wife, Julie Andrews), and *The Carey Treatment*, which was so butchered when MGM recut his final version that Edwards refused to work in Hollywood again. He took himself off to Europe for six years, and it was there that he resurrected Peter Sellers's career—floundering after his near-fatal heart attack—with three hugely successful Pink Panther films.

Blake and Dudley had met briefly once before, though neither remembered where, but it was in therapy that Blake came to know him. He was astonished by Dudley's openness. "He seemed to be truly unafraid of talking about the most intimate details," recalls Blake. "He was courageous enough to say anything, whereas most of us avoided or flirted around what we wanted to say. He allowed himself to be very vulnerable, and gave us all a real perception of himself. We were all stunned whenever he shot his mouth off, but it was very emancipating."

Dudley admired Blake's films—particularly his work with Sellers—but he was concerned that Blake might regard his therapeutic emoting as an audition and explained his anxiety to the director. Once that was off his chest, he was free to continue with his self-discovery without feeling intimidated by Blake's presence.

Meanwhile, Tuesday was back and forth between New York and Los Angeles, seemingly uncertain as to where to put down roots. During this time, Patrick stayed with Dudley in the Marina beach house. Now a robust two-year-old, he was becoming confused by his two fathers—the one he knew as a living man and the one who seemed to be trapped inside a television. When Dudley made an appearance on the early-morning show *Today*, Patrick pointed at the screen in bewilderment. "Dada!" he shouted, confused and bemused, then burst into tears and ran out of the room.

Back in Dagenham, Ada Moore followed Dudley's career with interest and pride. She still lived in the tiny council house on Baron Road, and seemed content to tend her roses and take short walks up to the shops. She missed her son greatly, although with Barbara in constant contact, she did not feel alone. "I often look at the snaps I have kept," she wrote to Dudley late in August. "Old photos of you and all of us. They occupy a whole evening sometimes."

For most of Dudley's years in psychotherapy he had only had to bare his soul to one person, his therapist. Now, in group therapy, he found himself revealing his innermost angst and insecurities before a roomful of people and having to deal with their judgment. To his surprise, instead of criticism, there was admiration and acceptance. Dudley was at last beginning to learn that he could be himself in front of people and still be accepted for who he was, warts and all.

It was after one of these group sessions that Blake Edwards drew Dudley aside and asked how he'd feel about making a movie with him. Dudley was surprised but elated. "I guess my posturing during therapy had seemed like auditioning after all."

Actually it hadn't. Like Chevy Chase, Blake had long been an admirer of Dudley's work. Years earlier, after seeing him in *Bedazzled*, Blake had tried to obtain from Stanley Donen the rights to turn it into a musical with Dudley. He particularly loved the sequence with the nuns on the trampoline and thought it would be hysterical to catch that on stage. It never happened.

The role he offered Dudley now was in *The Ferret*, which Blake hoped would spawn an entire series, as *The Pink Panther* had done. Dudley's character was the son of a famous Second World War superspy, code name the Ferret, called upon by the American President in times of international crises. Brought in to resolve one such crisis, the Ferret decides instead to hand it over to the inept son he's never seen. Entirely out of his depth, his son, a double bassist in a symphony orchestra, assumes the Ferret code name with hilarious results.

Blake knew comparisons with Inspector Clouseau from his Pink Panthers would be inevitable, but he saw *The Ferret* more as a suspense comedy rather than burlesque slapstick like the Panthers.

Dudley fell in love with the concept and signed a contract with Blake to make five Ferret films, the first of which he would also write. He was excited about the fun and silliness that he knew he would experience with Blake, and couldn't wait to get started.

Early in September, he flew to New York to stay with Tuesday and the children.

While he was out one evening, Tuesday suffered a seizure. Summoned by Natasha, Jo Weld rushed into the living room and found her daughter lying on the floor after rolling off the couch. Jo recalls that when Dudley returned to the apartment he was flummoxed by her explanations—especially since Tuesday had recovered and seemed normal. But soon after that she had another attack in front of him. He was petrified. Jo Weld remembers that when Tuesday woke up, she smiled up at a dazed Dudley and asked him what happened. He told her she'd had a fit and gone out like a light.

A few days later Dudley left for London and Jo took Tuesday to the doctor for a brain scan. When he produced a tray of needles, Tuesday threatened to leave and she was given a less severe form of examination. Dudley, in London, was now very anxious about not only his wife but also Natasha and Patrick. "He was hysterical," observed Jo Weld. "He telephoned and said he would take the two children into his care if there was any chance they would be jeopardized." Only when Jo assured him she would remain with her daughter and grandchildren did he calm down.

The doctors determined that Tuesday had suffered some epileptic fits. She would need a constant companion for a month and would have to take antiseizure medication for a year—which meant no alcohol. Tuesday, who liked to drink, was not thrilled with that news. The night before beginning the course of treatment, she ordered her mother out of her room. It was her last night for drinking, and she intended to make it a good one.

She spent most of the next few days in bed, getting up only to eat and leaving total chaos in her wake. Her anxious mother watched nervously. She was terrified her daughter might suffer a seizure in the bath and drown. Also, against doctor's orders, when she did get up, Tuesday was taking Patrick out, and Jo was deeply worried that she might have a fit while alone with her son. What if she had a seizure while crossing the road with Patrick? Her fears may have been excessive, but the responsibility was too much for Jo. As soon as a nurse could be hired, she planned to return to Los Angeles. She felt she could do nothing more for her daughter, who anyway resented her presence.

Tuesday eventually made a full recovery and never again had a recurrence of the fits.

Meanwhile, in London, Dudley reunited with Peter Cook to record a new album, *Derek and Clive Ad Nauseam*, which would later be distributed with a vomit-bag for those who might find its contents too extreme. They also taped a video version of the session, which would eventually be released as *Derek and Clive Get the Horn*.

The album, which Dudley never felt to be as good as the others, was even more vulgar than the earlier ones and contained more than a hundred uses of the word *fuck*. One of the sketches has Clive telling Derek that he had masturbated over a picture of the Pope; in another he expresses the wish to be a murderer like Myra Hindley, so he can have visits from Lord Longford, who turns him on.

It was their third and last album. And, although they continued to see each other and discuss potential ideas, it would be virtually the last time the two would work together.

In spite of its humorous aim, Dudley saw the album as full of the kind of anger displayed when two people are on the verge of breaking up. The filmed version was, he believes, a documentary about two people who were tired of working together and wanted to see the back of each other.

They were, Dudley admits, very aggressive with each other during the recording. "Everyone thought we'd taken something, but we hadn't—we just got very belligerent with each other. Peter's rage was quite bitter and seemed directed at me a bit. He always appeared to be trying to get a rise out of me. I don't know why, and I didn't confront him. I just let it pass."

The long collaboration was essentially over. Dudley had already struck out on his own, and now that he was living in America, he felt committed to a different professional life. Peter must have sensed that their working relationship was coming to an end and was letting out his inner unhappiness. He knew Dudley was about to return to Los Angeles, and knew, too, that he had now made it his home.

Peter had perhaps first sensed the breakup during the run of Behind the Fridge, seven years earlier, in Australia. There, after one of his drunken soliloquies on stage, he had turned to Dudley and said, "I suppose you won't want to go on working with me now." Dudley didn't, but he remained with him nevertheless.

According to Alex Cohen, their Broadway producer, Peter felt abandoned, but Cohen insists it was not Dudley's fault. "He gave and gave and gave until there was nothing left to give. You could hardly call that abandonment, but I think that's how Peter viewed it."

As Joe McGrath recalls, for a long time Peter had been saying things Dudley found disparaging and hurtful. "He used to say in front of people, 'I wish I'd been forced to play an instrument when I was a child; then I'd always be able to make money playing in a bar.' He said it as a joke, but it wasn't a joke. He was jealous."

Peter Bellwood had known Peter closely for many years, and understood him better than most. "Dudley deciding to go and seek his fortune in Hollywood was exactly the kind of thing about which Peter could be his most caustic," he explains. "He was very affected by Dudley leaving, and had the capacity to feel deeply rejected and abandoned."

Peter Cook said many times that the relationship he shared with Dudley was the best of his career. "It had been a collaboration where you just looked up to heaven and hoped it would last," says Bellwood. "That's how brilliant it was. When that best collaborator decided to leave, it became hard to deal with on a rational level. Peter's way of expressing his pain was through self-destructive behavior that became fueled by his drinking.

"A breakup can be as intense as any bitter divorce. There's rampant paranoia and envy and a belief that lives have been destroyed. It got very intense and vitriolic."

Many years later, Alexander Cohen arranged a meeting between Dudley and Peter in London, hoping to bring them back together professionally in a new stage revue. "Peter was violently jealous of Dudley's enormous success by then," remembers Cohen, "yet he wanted nothing more than to work with Dudley again, and his attitude was if we could effect a reconciliation it would be great. But Dudley was sick and tired of the abuse. He told me, 'I can't do it and I won't do it,' although he'd been gentlemanly enough at least to meet with Peter as I had asked."

Meanwhile, Dudley and Peter Bellwood had now finished *The Joy of Sex*, and had handed the completed script to Paramount.

What Michael Eisner had wanted was a series of sketches in the sex-manual style of the book by Alex Comfort. What he got was a story, based around Dudley and Tuesday, about a middle-aged man who leaves his family to pursue all the fantastic girls of his dreams. Eventually he returns, after realizing his fantasy females are as real as everyone else in his life.

Paramount liked the script but balked at the idea of Dudley taking the role. Lou Pitt recalls, "They said they wanted Ryan O'Neal or Burt Reynolds for the role. But Dudley wanted to do it himself. He saw it as a potential vehicle for him, and perhaps subconsciously had written it in that direction."

Paramount tried reworking the script but didn't know how to handle it. Eventually they gave up on the project but allowed Dudley and Peter to go elsewhere with it. Lou Pitt took it to Warners, and was very close to a deal, when something happened to put the entire project into suspension. That something was a phone call from Blake Edwards.

A few days away from the start of filming his new movie, *10*, Blake's star, George Segal, angry that his editor wife was not being made associate producer, had walked off the film. Blake immediately sent the script over to Lou Pitt. He was offering the part to Dudley.

Pitt read it and thought it was sensational. It was provocative, with a lot of different levels to it, and he could see it was a great opportunity. He called Dudley late at night in London, where he was visiting his mother, and told him he loved the script and thought he should do it.

Lou's call was followed by another from Blake. Surprised and rather tickled by Blake's obvious interest in him, Dudley read the script as he flew back to Los Angeles a few days later while Lou Pitt sweated for his decision. Pitt was convinced this would be a breakthrough movie for Dudley and was anxious for his response.

He need not have worried—Dudley loved the script. "I'll do it!" he told Lou when he landed in Los Angeles, and he jumped as high as his short frame would take him.

Which, as it would turn out, was nowhere near as high as the stardom that was waiting for him just around the corner.

CHAPTER 14

A PERFECT *10*

1978-1979

*"There's nothing about Dudley that I don't like, and I can't say that about many
people—particularly people I've worked with. He's just an amazing human being."*

—BLAKE EDWARDS

In those heady last days of 1978, Dudley had the same feeling that he'd
enjoyed twenty years earlier when he had just left Oxford and was plunging
forward to make a career for himself. There was an excitement in the air,
a sense of starting over again in a new world.

Word of this exciting import was now getting around town. The
Hollywood Women's Press Club presented him with their Golden Apple
award for Male Discovery of the Year, given to the most exciting new male
personality on the Hollywood scene. It was obvious he was no newcomer,
but the audience present at the awards gave him a standing ovation when
Bette Davis announced him the winner over another new arrival whose
time was yet to come—Richard Gere.

The filming of *10* coincided with another date on Dudley's calendar:
he had agreed to perform at the London Palladium for a week with Cleo
Laine, and now had to call John Dankworth to be released from their
engagement. It was the second time he'd had to ask Dankworth to excuse
him—the first had been nineteen years earlier, when he was offered *Beyond
the Fringe* at the Edinburgh Festival.

Dankworth, assuming Dudley had only a small role, was not pleased.
He didn't see why the film company could not work around Dudley, who,
in his typically modest manner, had neglected to explain to John that it was
actually the starring role that he'd been given. When Dankworth realized
what the job involved, he immediately wrote to Dudley expressing his

support. "I didn't realize it was the leading part you'd been offered," he said. "Had I done so, I wouldn't have considered even for one moment keeping you from doing the film. But I hope sometime you can return the favor by doing some other project with us."

Dudley would return the favor, but not for another three years.

It was ironic that he had won the role through George Segal's last-minute departure from *10*, for this paralleled what had happened when Blake made his first Pink Panther film. Peter Ustinov had been set to play Inspector Clouseau but backed out suddenly, leaving Blake to recast the movie. His choice was Peter Sellers, and the result was a successful chain of Pink Panther movies and the renaissance of Sellers's career.

His role in *10*, that of a forty-two-year-old man suffering from a midlife crisis, was perfect casting for Dudley and was changed only slightly to allow him to step into the shoes vacated by George Segal. Instead of a Beverly Hills dentist, Blake made the role of George Webber into that of an award-winning songwriter, allowing Dudley to display his prowess at the piano.

A victim of middle-age restlessness, George Webber becomes smitten by a gorgeous blonde (Bo Derek) whom he spots in a car en route to her wedding. Pursuing her to the church, he later returns to discover her identity, then leaves his girlfriend Samantha (Julie Andrews) to follow this goddess to Mexico, where she is honeymooning with her new husband. George believes that if he can acquire this fantasy girl—a perfect ten on his rating scale and therefore, to him, the perfect woman—he will also find total happiness. Ultimately he discovers he has confused beauty with perfection and returns to his girlfriend.

Dudley related perfectly to George Webber and his struggle to come to terms with the reality of life and people, rather than the fantasy of how he wanted them to be. Like Dudley, George was a man who looked outside himself for happiness rather than inside, where his problems were most painful.

It was another ironic coincidence that *The Joy of Sex*, which Dudley had written with Peter Bellwood, had dealt with the same subject. The only difference between *The Joy of Sex* and *10* was that in Dudley's script the man chased several fantasy women instead of one, and he went back to a wife and family instead of a girlfriend.

Dudley gave *The Joy of Sex* to an astonished Blake Edwards, but to this day he has no idea whether Blake ever read it. Certainly it was never mentioned again.

Dudley was thrilled about embarking on *10*. It was his first starring role in an American-based, American-financed film, and it came at a time when he really wanted to play that kind of part. His fee was one hundred thousand dollars, which seemed a fortune. In terms of what the film went on to make it was a pittance.

Filming began in November 1978 in Los Angeles, before moving to
locations in Mexico and Hawaii, where they were rained out twice in the
worst storms the islands had known in a hundred years.

There had been one mild hiccup beforehand. When Blake told Julie
Andrews, his wife, that he was signing Dudley, she expressed some concern
about the disparity in their height. Julie, a tall woman, was worried about
the sight of the two of them together. "I thought it would be very unflattering to Dudley," she recalls. "And then Blake reminded me that Dudley
always went out with giant ladies without thinking anything about it—and
nor, presumably, did they. That was before I met Dudley. Then once we
met, there was no problem at all, because he's so damned attractive anyway
that I completely forgot all about the height difference."

Nevertheless, in an effort to minimize the gap, Blake asked Dudley to
wear boots with 5½-inch heels. Dudley warned him they'd look like
medieval torture boots, but he had them made anyway. Blake fell down
laughing when Dudley wore them. "It was hysterical when he put them on.
He looked like Boris Karloff—an absolute monster. Eventually we had the
boots gold-plated on a platform and settled for something smaller."

In *10*, Dudley was able to play a role that took him far away from the
caricature parts of his past. Previously he had always played characters with
funny accents or different faces. He had clung to these as protective covers,
afraid to discard them and be stripped bare. Now he felt ready to project
his own qualities into a part. George Webber was basically a straight role,
made funny by the situations he got into. Dudley's portrayal was sensitive
and vulnerable, of a man trying desperately hard to be sophisticated but
constantly tripped up by his distracted clumsiness.

Blake Edwards knew he'd made a good choice. In Dudley, he saw some
of the same attributes that had attracted him to Peter Sellers—an extraordinary physical comedy coupled with an uncanny instinct for comic timing. Yet Dudley had something more, if it could only be captured—a deep
sensitivity that not only was endearing but would also bring a touching
realism to the role. "I kept sitting in those therapy groups listening to
Dudley," Blake remembers, "and there were so many things in his personality that coincided with the character in *10*. It was amazing."

Not surprisingly, Blake dropped out of the group therapy sessions
during the filming. Dudley muses, "He didn't feel he could handle us
spilling out what had happened the week before, then going back to the set
the next morning. He was right about that."

Julie Andrews, who with her husband became close friends with
Dudley, has the fondest memories of working with him. "At first he was a
little shy," she recalls, "but eventually we got to be great chums. We had our
Englishness in common, and certain kinds of vaudeville jokes and shtick.

He was adorable. We laughed a *great* deal and had an enormous amount of fun. I adored his irreverence. The delight of working with him was tremendous, and it was lovely to watch his instincts at work."

Not widely known about Julie is that she possesses an exceedingly ribald sense of humor, and it gelled extremely well with Dudley's own. "He was far worse than me," twinkles Julie, "quite wicked and naughty. But it was impossible for anyone to take offense. It's just cheeky."

The opening scene of *10* was a surprise birthday party, and several celebrities turned up as extras in the kind of scene that Robert Altman would later adopt as a trademark in his movies. Among them were Dyan Cannon, Jon Voight, Henry Mancini, and Peter Sellers.

In the first of the many films he would produce with Blake Edwards, Tony Adams helped organize the party sequence, which was catered in true Hollywood style by the eminent restaurant, Chasens. "It was very cinema verité," recalls Adams. "The problem was that everyone had had a few drinks and they were incapable of staying in character. Sellers kept calling Dudley 'Dudley' instead of 'George.' When Blake saw the rushes, he realized it wouldn't work and he decided to reshoot it with regular actors."

No one knows what happened to that excised scene but it contains one of the rare occasions on which Peter Sellers played the drums on film since his early years as a variety performer.

Dudley had been astonished to see so many stars on hand, but they were equally taken aback by his new appearance. His fine hair had been permed, and he wore one-inch lifts in his shoes that made him appear taller. He had also gone on a crash diet, which he kept up throughout filming, and had lost over fourteen pounds.

Dudley had tried a multitude of diets throughout his life. This one was a breakfast diet and meant that as soon as he awoke he ate a plate of trout (usually two) surrounded by brussels sprouts, broccoli, green beans, snow peas, and cabbage, liberally sprinkled with powdered seaweed concentrate, which he followed with papayas, figs, and nuts. With that lot inside him he didn't eat again for the rest of the day. Nor did he think of eating until he was in bed at night, when he would fall asleep dreaming of the following morning's meal.

His crash diet had been prompted by not wanting to look like a pumpkin when he appeared seminude in the film's orgy scene. But it would be more than his new slimness that would be revealed.

Over the last two years, group therapy had brought Dudley to the point where he now felt a certain ease with himself. After years of feeling inadequate because of his height and his clubfoot, he had come to realize that he was acceptable as he was. He had spent almost twenty years trying to change, but his greatest realization now was that he did not need to change at all. His height, his foot, his leg—these still made him uncomfortable, but now he was able to live with his discomfort without feeling inferior because of them.

He used all of his feelings now in the role, and in so doing he allowed his vulnerability to expose itself. He had spent so many years trying to hide it that now he felt a kind of relief and a calmness in allowing his real self to come forward for the first time and to meld with the characterization.

Nevertheless, not all of his vulnerability was on show. Julie Andrews caught fleeting glimpses of another man beneath the surface of the happy-go-lucky imp. "With all the humor, all the fun, all the roaring with laughter and rolling around the floor," she says, "I felt that somewhere under all of that there was a darker Dudley that he didn't let us see. It was more my woman's fancy instincts, but I felt he kept a certain part of himself constantly in reserve. I sensed shades of a melancholy man underneath, but I never found out where it came from."

When Blake came to shoot the orgy scene in *10*, he realized he needed to make it clear that everyone was naked yet without presenting total frontal nudity. He decided to place Dudley between two nude girls and have the three of them walk past the camera so that their rear ends would be in shot from the thighs up. He was deeply concerned, however, that in order to do this Dudley would have to strip. Blake had spent enough time in Dudley's presence during therapy to recognize the extent to which he was unhappy about his thin, misshapen leg and his clubfoot, and he wrestled with a way to film the scene without showing Dudley's leg.

"I agonized about it for a long time," he remembers, "and finally I decided to ask him what he felt about it. Without hesitation he just dropped his pants—in front of everybody—and we got the shot. It was a terribly courageous thing, and it took an awful lots of guts to do that.

"We didn't talk about it afterward, and I was so overwhelmed with his gesture that I would have found it hard to say anything myself. The great thing was that everyone saw it and it was really of little consequence to them. Because Dudley is Dudley. So he's got a gammy leg—so what?"

Back home that night, Dudley suffered a delayed reaction. He was horrified to think he'd really done that, and seventeen years later the memory still makes him cringe.

The role of the perfect ten was played by twenty-two-year-old Bo Derek, a stunningly beautiful actress married to film actor John Derek, who had been a leading man during the fifties. She had made only two previous films, *And Once Upon a Time* and *Orca—Killer Whale*, but she was remarkably self-assured in spite of her lack of experience.

10 was a huge step for her, made less intimidating by the atmosphere on the set and her costar's relaxing attitude. "He was marvelous to work with and wonderfully talented," she reflects. "He had the quality of being lovably funny and sexy at the same time. I think he was a little self-conscious, but he was very sweet and made it very easy. He knew this was all pretty extraordinary for me and was very sensitive to that."

Dudley liked Bo. He found her untemperamental and charming, though somewhat reserved, and he was impressed that a girl of her age could act so naturally and without embarrassment.

Bo and Dudley were, in Blake Edwards's opinion, a perfect couple. "We couldn't have done any better. She was such an unusually beautiful-looking woman, and when you put that together with the qualities that comprise Dudley, it was a magic pairing."

Even more magic was the combination of star and director. They were a brilliant team, Dudley and the director who had steered Jack Lemmon to an Oscar nomination for *The Days of Wine and Roses*.

Dudley relished the time he spent with Blake, whom he felt was the best director he'd ever worked with. Blake seldom discussed scenes with him and allowed him to do his own thing, even to colloquializing the script a little, and he felt a freedom he had never felt before. If this was what it was like to make Hollywood movies, then Dudley wanted more.

For Julie Andrews, the making of 10 was one of the best experiences she had ever known on a film set. Not only was she being directed by her husband, but she was working with someone who was immense fun and who wanted nothing more than to have a wonderful time while he worked.

"Blake and Dudley were terrific together," she laughs. "They were two naughty boys—deliciously funny and outrageously ribald. Whenever Dudley did something particularly funny, Blake would break up and practically be on his knees. It was just a marvelous experience and lucky all round. Dudley was one of those rare, wonderful choices, and Blake has that phenomenal instinct that sees the possibility."

While they were filming in Mexico, Dudley spent a couple of weeks at the Acapulco home of his lyricist friend Leslie Bricusse and his wife, Evie. As it happens, George Hamilton was also a houseguest and was in the throes of separating from his wife, Alana. The two actors took great solace in each other, as they discussed how such a major investment in their lives had come to a bad ending. "That's when Dudley's more solitary and isolated state became apparent to me," says Bricusse, "although he always masked what he felt. He always said things in a funny way, but they went against the grain of what he was really feeling inside."

Bricusse had known Tuesday and Dudley since long before their marriage, and had always felt their complex personalities boded ill for a future together. "I'd always thought they were a pretty combustible possibility. I hoped for the best, but I didn't really believe, deep down, that it would work."

In the middle of filming, Christmas arrived—and with it a holiday break. Tuesday sent Patrick and Natasha to stay with Dudley over the holidays at the Marina beach house, and they were happy to bask in the California sunshine far from the wintry cold of New York, where Tuesday had now settled.

Dudley was writing to his mother regularly, keeping her in touch with his latest endeavors. Ada adored receiving his letters, and treasured them greatly. "It was so nice to get your letter," she wrote to him just after Christmas. "I can read it over and over again."

She wished she could see her son more often. Separated by six thousand miles, she missed him terribly and followed his movements avidly. But she was far too nervous a woman to dare to set foot on a plane, and had to be content with Dudley's periodic letters, visits, and phone calls. Although she had been blessed with granddaughters through Barbara's marriage, she pined for news and photographs of Dudley's son. "I have Patrick's photo in a frame," she wrote, "and I look very often at my snaps. It makes me very happy to see them."

Dudley's attempts to understand his childhood angst and his mother's early apparent lack of love were growing more overt. His probing questions were usually evaded by Ada but had nevertheless caused her to reflect often about his psychological wanderings, although she always told him he had seemed a happy boy.

Until that Christmas, Ada had always signed herself "Mother." Now, as she signed off in one of her longest-ever letters to her son—four pages— she wrote, "I see you prefer 'Mum' so here goes. My New Year resolution— away with the more formal title of Mother. All my love, Mum."

Ada Moore wasn't the only person back home who was missing Dudley. Peter Cook was also feeling quite bereft, and would call Dudley's mother and Suzy Kendall as a way of feeling closer in touch. Although he knew their partnership was really over, he still harbored hopes of future projects together—especially another series of *Not Only ... But Also*.

"I do think that when we manage to do another series," he wrote to Dudley teasingly, "your mother should become a regular along with Dud and Pete. I don't want to press you when things are obviously going so well for you in the States. I like to think that when you become 'hot' and 'enormous,' it will make it easier for us to do a decent movie together with our choice of director."

Peter was, he wrote, feeling especially happy just then. "I think it's probably to do with seven months' sobriety (with four major lapses) that has brought about this change. For the last month I have no longer resented not drinking, something I never thought would happen." Peter believed *Derek and Clive Ad Nauseam* to be their best album so far and loved what he had seen of the film they had shot at the same time. "It works really well visually," he told Dudley. "Some of the stuff in the control room is hilarious. Never have two comedians slagged each other off so comprehensively."

Cook noted that with Julie Andrews in *10* "at last you're working with someone your own age and with a similar sense of humor," and, knowing that Dudley's hair had been curled for the movie, pointed out that Dudley always seemed to be following in his footsteps. "I had my hair permed before you did; I worry, you worry; I move to Hampstead, you move to Hampstead; I get divorced, you get divorced. Does this mean I'll be moving to the Marina?"

In the first week of January 1979, filming on *10* resumed in Hawaii. By now the word had spread that Dudley's performance was turning out to be exceptional. Tony Adams, Blake's producer, called Lou Pitt and told him that Dudley would become a sex symbol out of the film. "Are you crazy?" replied Lou, and decided Tony was nuts.

Tony Adams wasn't the only person to be raving about Dudley's work. Orion, which was financing the film, had seen some of the rushes, and Mike Medavoy, one of the executives, called Lou Pitt to tell him of his excitement about Dudley. "That internal enthusiasm is always a trigger," says Pitt, "and I knew something big was going to happen for Dudley from *10*."

In the latter part of filming, where George Webber follows Jenny, his perfect ten ("actually an eleven" he tells his analyst), on her honeymoon, Dudley had to film some of his more intimate scenes. One of them had him running across the hot sand in a baggy sweatsuit that covered up his gammy leg. The result was astonishingly Chaplinesque.

Bo found Dudley's antics hilarious—to his occasional irritation. He especially objected to her giggling while they were rolling around in the surf together. "You can't giggle," he admonished her. "You're supposed to be serious." She still couldn't stop.

Apart from the giggling, he found Bo easy and comfortable to work with. He was particularly charmed by her husband, John Derek, who almost daily left photographs outside Dudley's hotel room that he had shot on the set, some of which he had first elegantly framed.

There were, however, some moments where Dudley felt very ill at ease. They came when he and Bo were naked in bed as they romanced to a recording of Ravel's *Bolero*. It was an embarrassing interlude for Hollywood's newest British import.

"I think he was rather shy," says Bo Derek, "and a little nervous, although he really didn't show it. I purposely tried to make it as casual as possible, so as not to make him more nervous than I think he was. I felt we were both kind of nervous, and whenever we finished something we would look at Blake for reassurance."

Dudley was relieved when the scene had been shot, but his relief was short-lived. The next day Blake Edwards decided to reshoot it in dimmer light.

For all his rapport with the role, Dudley had some reservations about the way in which George Webber behaved. He especially disliked George's moralistic and chauvinistic attitudes. As with many of Blake Edwards's films, *10* is littered with social comments. One in particular implies a promiscuity in people who have sex without also wanting a relationship. Dudley vehemently disagreed with that point of view. He felt that people who slept with others more freely than most were simply having a good time. It was, he said, the way he would like his own life to be.

There was a piano on the set, and Dudley was able to play in between takes. Bo Derek was very moved when she first encountered the musical side of her costar. "Hank Mancini had already written a lovely theme tune for the film," she recalls. "It was gorgeous, and everyone loved it. Then one day, while the crew was setting up lights, the place started getting quieter and quieter, and then I heard Dudley playing this theme tune. And all of a sudden it took on a whole new magic that it hadn't had before. To watch him play was just incredible, and it was another side of him that I don't think anyone had ever seen."

Playing the piano in between filming gave Dudley immense personal enjoyment. He played for himself, and it didn't matter if there was one person around or fifty hammering away—as long as he could play, he was happy. "It was a sheer delight to watch him," says Julie Andrews, who cherished those moments as a bonus to her day. Before filming was over, he went into a studio and recorded cassettes of some of his music, which he gave away as parting gifts.

As filming neared its end, Dudley was presented with an inflatable adult doll. He got a lot of mileage out of that doll, putting on shows in the doorway of his trailer dressing room. Tony Adams remembers watching Dudley appear and disappear in the doorway, pretending to make love to the doll, "and sometimes having the doll make love to him. It was totally filthy and hysterically funny."

The doll caused Dudley some embarrassment when filming wrapped and he was returning to Los Angeles. He had stacked the doll at the top of his bag and covered it up, but as he walked through the airport, he heard that all bags would have to be examined. He was in a panic. "I thought, 'My God, I've got this flaming inflatable rubber doll right on the top,' and I didn't know what to do with it."

Somehow he came up with one of his inane stories and the doll was smuggled undetected onto the plane.

Dudley came away from *10* having enjoyed the best film experience of his career. He was becoming tuned in to his feelings and starting to express what he really felt inside. For the first time he had felt comfortable to let those inner feelings emerge on screen, thanks partly to the security Blake had imbued in him and partly also to the results of his accumulated therapy. He had projected his real personality onto the character he played, and it had worked.

He was now feeling the happiest he'd ever felt about himself. Previously he had not been saying, doing, or being what he wanted. Now he felt himself creeping toward that objective. He had to some extent come to terms with the inner demons that had been battling away inside him for forty-odd years, and he was able genuinely to like the person he saw himself to be. "The discovery of myself," he told Blake Edwards, "was the single most important development that had ever occurred in my life."

Back in Los Angeles, a letter from his mother praised his appearance in Jonathan Miller's documentary "The Body in Question," which had just been broadcast on the BBC. "It was really wonderful to see you," she told him, "and you played the piano beautifully."

By now *Foul Play* had been released in England, and although Ada had not seen it, she was basking in the praise her son was receiving. "A boy at the post office said you were very good," she wrote to him, "he is the post-mistress's son, quite a charmer ... and in the *Sunday Mirror*, a paper I do not usually buy, the comment was very favorable. 'Riotously funny scenes,' they said, 'and well worth a visit.'"

Dudley was now being written about in the British newspapers as an emergent Hollywood star who was receiving invitations to the most exclusive parties and being lauded in the gossip columns. But, they asked, whatever had happened to the once stinging satirist who wasn't afraid to knock the system or ridicule the holiest of establishment figures? Had he gone stereotypically Hollywood?

Dudley hadn't gone anything. He had never been a satirist. The label had stuck from *Beyond the Fringe*, but the satire had come from the other three performers. Dudley himself had always been too afraid of reprisal to knock or ridicule the system. As for going Hollywood, all he was doing was enjoying the fruits of his labor. If, by English standards, relishing the sunshine, living on the beach, and mixing in celebrity circles meant that he had "gone Hollywood," that was tough luck.

His lifestyle was fairly modest and certainly no more luxurious than it had been in Britain. He had never been materialistic, had never felt a need to surround himself with possessions, aside from an impressive wine collection and occasional antiques that gave him aesthetic pleasure. True, he had his 1963 Bentley, but he had exported that from England mainly as an asset to sell, if he ran out of money.

Meanwhile, his stormy four-year marriage to Tuesday Weld was all but over and they were now discussing a divorce settlement. Later, Dudley would term the divorce "amicable," but Tuesday was less kind—"He's a major asshole," she told reporters. During their time together they had had over twenty breakups, culminating in this last, yearlong separation. Constant arguing and fighting had made life stimulating, but their character differences could not be resolved.

One of those differences was Tuesday's penchant for telling peculiar stories. After meeting one of Tuesday's girlfriends, Dudley called Jo Weld with a disturbing tale. The girlfriend had told Dudley how sorry she had been to learn about their "non-normal baby." Tuesday had told her there was something drastically wrong with the baby and it had been put into care and was living elsewhere. "Dudley was unnerved by this total fabrication," says Jo Weld. "So was I."

Tuesday could not resist telling lies, but they were not always so harsh. Occasionally they were a source of great amusement—especially when she told everyone her mother was dead, sometimes with her mother sitting in front of her. "It would be great to catch her eccentricity on film," Dudley said once. "She's still one of the funniest women I ever met, which is probably how we got tangled up together."

In April 1979 Dudley flew to New York to visit his son. He was cheered to find him in good shape. "I have no worries about Patrick surviving the divorce!" he wrote to his mother. "As long as Tuesday and I don't feed him the idea that there is anything tragic about our split, everything will be all right and I don't think he will have too many problems dealing with the fact that we live separately."

His mother's reply surprised Dudley. "It is so very lovely to have a child," she wrote. "My happiest moments were when you and Barbara were children. Trials were many but they are now memories. You always get plenty of anxiety with children but it is surprising how you can get by." Perhaps this was Ada's way of expressing to Dudley that she had loved him as a child, even though he had felt otherwise.

All his life Dudley had longed for the easy love of a parent. Although he never received that, through therapy he had come to accept that somewhere deep down his parents had loved him and had tried to do the best for him in the only way they knew how. "It's clear that Dudley's mother loved him completely," says his psychotherapist friend Evelyn Silvers. "She was no more ill-equipped to raise her son than any of the rest of us. But she was a frightened lady."

With filming on *The Ferret* scheduled to start in late summer in Europe and Brazil, Dudley flew to London briefly in June. He saw his family and made a guest appearance on *The Muppet Show*, in which he played the piano and had a row with Animal. Afterward he was given a silver Kermit that registered him as guest No. 79.

While he was there, he saw *Derek and Clive Get the Horn*, the film he and Peter Cook had made of their last Derek and Clive record. He liked it a lot—and much more than the record—but before any sort of release could be contemplated it would need to be viewed by the British Board of Film Censors for a rating. It was highly unlikely that they would find in it much to approve.

Some time earlier, a prankster had somehow substituted the covers on several hundred copies of the first album with ones that announced the recording as a reading of Black Beauty. That was particularly unfortunate for one seven-year-old girl, who found herself introduced at an early age to the scatological smut of Derek and Clive. It was unfortunate, too, for the distributors, who were royally sued by the child's father.

In late June, back in Los Angeles, Dudley felt more settled than ever—a sense that was reinforced by the arrival from England of more than seventy pieces of luggage, which included paintings, furniture, his electric piano, and his Hammond organ. The rest of his books and records were also crossing the Atlantic, and with their arrival, Dudley's move from England would become permanent.

By Hollywood standards, his airy beach house was modest. It had three floors, and the front door opened onto a beige and white living room that was dominated by a black Yamaha grand piano. One end of the living room was a dining area with a French table that seated twelve people. The other end had sofas looking out onto the beach.

Dudley was glad that he had chosen to put down roots in America. He found himself more at ease around Americans, more in tune with their line of thinking and their openness. Americans were comfortable being ambitious and derived pleasure from being successful, and he felt his own career would flourish in the midst of that attitude.

As *10*'s release date grew closer, there was a mild sense of anticipation. Publicist Paul Bloch, vice president of Rogers and Cowan, a heavyweight publicity firm, had been assigned to shape Dudley into an international movie star. "The word of mouth is incredible," he wrote to Dudley. "A lot of very important people are very excited about your role in it!"

Dudley was remarkably cool about the excitement. After all, he'd been performing for twenty-one years now, and the vacillations in his success over the years had made him fairly inured to the potential of great acclaim. While recognizing that he was on the brink of a new career direction, he was feeling less anxious about his future—although anxiety was still very much a dominant factor in his life—and more relaxed about what life might bring. He had an almost childlike assumption that everything would work out well.

There were still career setbacks, however. Just a few weeks before the
start of shooting, Blake had first postponed and then canceled *The Ferret*.
There had been acute problems with the script, and he had not been able to
come up with the budget he felt the film warranted. Dudley was deeply
disappointed, because he'd really wanted to make the film. However, he
remained philosophical about it all. "Anxiety," he told the *Los Angeles Times*,
"comes from the desire to control both yourself and other people and then
finding you can't. It's been both an anxious and a frustrating time, but one
has a way of getting less fraught about things as time goes on."

Dudley had now, somewhat belatedly, come to the conclusion that he
and marriage were not exactly a combination made in heaven. Easily
discouraged by a lack of self-esteem, he had an emotional fragility that easily became exacerbated when he was living with another person. He was a
man who needed to be mainly on his own.

Although his marriage to Tuesday had ended in all but name, Dudley
was anxious to spend as much time as possible with his son, and he often
flew to New York to be with him. He was shedding his earlier fears of
fatherhood and beginning to take a great pleasure in the boy. In New York
to promote *10*, he took Tuesday to a film screening. He was adamant that
Patrick should see his parents getting on well together, even if they were no
longer cohabiting. "Dudley loved his son," recalls Julie Andrews. "He
made enormous efforts to fly to New York to be with him. I saw that, and
I thought at the time that was pretty nice. I'm always admiring of a parent
who tries like he did to keep their relationship together." But it was not
easy for Patrick. Nearly twenty years later he would reflect back and tell me,
"I remember feeling sad because my parents weren't together, and I wanted
them to be together so very much. My sister told me they fought a lot and
there was a lot of screaming, but I was so young I don't remember any of
that."

By now Dudley had acquired a secretary. Ruth Forman had known
him since January. They had met at a Malibu party and had dated sporadically during the filming of *10*. "He was a genuine and generous man," she
recalls, "with tremendous humility and a lot of tenderness in the way he
spoke and treated me."

Ruth recalls Sunday-afternoon parties at Blake Edwards's house where
the *10* gang gathered for dinner and watched a movie and other friends—
Michael and Pat York and Michael and Shakira Caine—stopped by.

One evening, while dining with friends, they met "a shy artist
wearing crazy tennis shoes." His name was David Hockney. Another afternoon they went to brunch at Jane Seymour's house. Ruth remembers that
day, "because Jane was so exquisitely beautiful and hospitable. She was
absolutely charming."

Soon after, by the time Ruth had replaced her romantic role with a secretarial one, Dudley began dating Jane and would often tell Ruth that he was "just popping round to Jane's house" and would see her later.

Though their little romance had ceased, the relationship between Dudley and Ruth had developed into a deep friendship. Always generous to his friends, on her birthday he gave her the down payment for the black Jeep she had not, until then, been able to afford.

In October 1979, 10 was released with a huge publicity campaign.

Orion may have been hoping for a reasonable success with the film, but no one was prepared for the overwhelming, runaway hit that it became. Dudley had been very depressed when he first saw the rough cut. He told Blake it was terrible and far too long, and he wanted to shoot himself. And Bo Derek recalls, "I had heard things that were not very positive about it, so it was shocking when it came out and was such a success."

Critics were mesmerized by the fantasy of 10 and by Dudley's magical performance. "Mr. Moore is superbly comic," declared the *New York Times.* "With this film he at last becomes an American film star." *Newsweek* observed, "He turns this libidinally crazed fool into a hilarious and wholly sympathetic figure," and *Time* magazine noted, "This film could provide him the chance, finally, to find the large audience he deserves."

It did. The public embraced it instantly. Lou Pitt was amazed. He had thought the film good, but had not envisaged such a great success. The night it opened he visited several cinemas and was astonished by the masses of people he saw lined up all around the block. Audiences loved 10. They flocked to see it not once but several times, and became so involved in the story that they talked back to the screen. One man became so angry with Dudley for not consummating his relationship with Bo Derek that he jumped out of his third-row seat and shouted to the screen, "Are you fucking crazy, George? Do it, for Chrissakes!"

10 became the surprise hit of the season and signaled megastardom for Bo and Dudley. Bo's serene face smiled from magazine covers on every newsstand. Her cornrow hairstyle from 10 was soon in demand in hair salons across the nation, and John Derek enhanced his wife's appeal by merchandising a million-selling poster of his blonde goddess. At twenty-three, Bo had become Hollywood's new sex princess.

Blake Edwards was ecstatic with the reaction. In order to make the film with Dudley, he had been forced to accept a substantially lesser fee for himself than when George Segal was his star. "Orion said my deal was too rich to allow for Dudley, because he was an unknown factor," chuckles Blake. "So I agreed to take a percentage of the gross instead. Thanks to Dudley, I got very rich indeed!"

As well as having a flair for physical comedy that evoked memories of

Chaplin, Dudley had proved also to be a convincing romantic leading man. Hollywood now found itself with a new male sex symbol. Tony Adams had been right after all when he'd made that early prediction to Lou Pitt.

Julie Andrews had always agreed with Tony. "I wasn't surprised about the reaction to Dudley, because I knew he was very sexy," she says. "I was thrilled at the success of the film and for what it did for him, and I think it gave him great confidence."

Dudley himself was astonished at the reaction. He thought the film was funny and warm, but he was astounded at the gigantic hit it became and that people were returning to see it three or four times.

Overnight, it seemed, Dudley had become a massive success. *10* would catapult him into an American heaven that was far more adulatory and would offer richer rewards than he had ever experienced in Britain.

CHAPTER 15

SUSAN'S SEX SYMBOL

1979-1980

*"I thought it was all rather a lark. When someone you know very well
becomes a sex symbol, it's a bit of a joke. But I wasn't surprised.
My only surprise was that they hadn't got on to him sooner."*

—ALAN BENNETT

At forty-four, Dudley had suddenly become America's newest, and most unlikely, sex symbol. Billboards along Sunset Boulevard showed a cutout Dudley hanging on to a chain between Bo Derek's ample cleavage, and he was happy to be suspended so prominently above the streets of Los Angeles. Feminists were extremely angry, but Dudley just chuckled with amusement over the political debates raised by the ads and settled into a cozy acceptance of his new image.

There was, he thought, something rather droll about becoming a sex symbol at his age. With a divorce from Tuesday on the horizon, he was virtually a single man again, and if this meant women were going to be chasing him—although when hadn't they been?—he was hardly likely to fight them off.

His new image came as no surprise to Dudley's friends. "He'd always seemed much of a sex symbol to me," says Peter Bellwood. "I never thought of him leading a monastic existence. After all, he was always surrounded by birds." As for Blake Edwards, he had already witnessed Dudley's sex appeal in countless group-therapy meetings. "We had some terribly attractive ladies there, and I saw how they went after Dudley and how they felt about him."

10 had opened the portals of Hollywood for Dudley when he had been wondering about his future. Now he was basking in glory and trying to catch his breath. The hardest part for someone coming fresh to such a reception would be to keep everything in perspective, but Dudley took it in his stride. He had, after all, lived with some form of success ever since his *Beyond the Fringe* days in 1960. What was new now was the scale of it, so much greater than anything he had experienced in Britain. And this time he wasn't lurking in the shadow of Peter Cook—the acclaim was for him alone.

"I think," Dudley told me at the time, "you get to a point in your life where you say, not in a blasé way, 'There's no reason why I shouldn't be successful at what I do.' If you assume you're going to be successful, then you generally are."

His confidence now was rooted in his discovery that he was his own man and that what he felt and thought were all right. "The fact that I've accepted myself for who and what I am is the greatest change in me. I think I always knew who I was, but the difference is I now allow myself to be who I am. I own up to it. There's still pain and sadness in my life, but that's unavoidable."

Few artists had come to America as a virtual unknown and scored as heavily as Dudley. Most of the British actors working in Hollywood had been known previously to audiences through their English films, but not Dudley.

Although it was *10* that projected him finally to film stardom in his own right, Dudley believed that he would have made it one day even if he hadn't met Blake Edwards at that fortuitous moment in therapy.

As his old friend Francis Megahy points out, "The great thing about *10* was that Dudley learned to do what all really big stars do, which was to play himself. That's the real trick."

With *10*, Dudley had begun to show his emotions for the first time. Since childhood he had believed that if he revealed his inner self he would be rejected for it. After being conditioned to repress his emotions, he had now learned not to hide his vulnerability and, to his amazement, had discovered people found that endearing. Hollywood started to pay attention and to consider Dudley bankable—the one thing that really counts in the film industry.

Orion's Mike Medavoy, who had seen Dudley's potential long before *10* was completed, had already told Lou Pitt about a script that Orion had taken over from Paramount. Its title was *Arthur*.

Medavoy wanted to cast Dudley in the title role, but the film's producer, Charles Joffe, who since 1969 had been almost exclusively associated with Woody Allen, wanted Martin Mull, a well-known American television actor. By coincidence, Mull was about to start *Serial* with Tuesday Weld, and their work together would lead to an intense affair. Medavoy sent the script to Lou Pitt but asked him not to show it to Dudley; he did not want to disappoint him if he couldn't have the part. In the meantime he worked on Charles Joffe to bring him around to the idea.

Ultimately Medavoy's persistence paid off. Orion decided not to make the film with Mull, and Charles Joffe finally agreed to let Dudley take the role. Production on *Arthur* would start the following May.

In the winter of 1979, *Variety* announced that Lou Pitt had negotiated colossal earnings for Dudley's next two movies. For *Wholly Moses*, a biblical spoof, it was claimed he would earn ten times the salary of *10* and more than thirty times the salary he'd been paid for *Foul Play*, so crashing through the million-dollar barrier. For the second movie, *Arthur*, it was claimed he would be paid substantially more than $2 million. Actually it wasn't until after the release of *Arthur* (for which his fee was four hundred thousand dollars) that Dudley moved into the millionaire-earning bracket.

In November, Dudley began filming *Wholly Moses* for *Saturday Night Live* director Gary Weis, who was making his feature debut. It was an incomprehensible choice for Dudley, who had committed to it before knowing what a success *10* would be.

Wholly Moses cast Dudley and Laraine Newman in dual roles, with Dom DeLuise, James Coco, Madeline Kahn, John Houseman, and Richard Pryor lending support. The story was not dissimilar to the previous year's *Life of Brian* from the Monty Python team, about a man whose life parallels that of Jesus.

Harvey (Dudley) is a language professor, vacationing in the Holy Land to forget his latest unlucky sexual misadventure. Inadvertently, he and another traveler (Laraine Newman) discover some ancient scrolls bearing the legend of Herschel, an overlooked hero whose life parallels that of Moses.

The scrolls reveal that Herschel had been floating down the Nile in a cradle on that same fateful morning as Moses, but with a helpful shove from the latter he had sailed on past the bulrushes, leaving Moses to be found and groomed for greatness.

Years later, Herschel (Dudley), now a shepherd, is standing on a mountain and hears God talking to him. What he doesn't realize is that Moses, whom he can't see, is standing on the *other* side of the mountain. Herschel believes he is the one being addressed, and that it is he who has been ordained to set free his people from captivity in Egypt. With the help of his wife, Zrelda (Laraine Newman), he sets about achieving this end, always one step behind Moses.

Dudley had the same misgivings about doing *Wholly Moses* that he had felt over *Foul Play*. In the latter he had ignored his instincts and allowed himself to be talked into the role, and ultimately it had led to great acclaim.

With *Wholly Moses*, his instincts again told him not to make the film, but this time it would have been better if he had followed them. But he found producers Freddie Fields and David Begelman so friendly and admiring that, although he thought they were nuts to be interested in the project, which he considered absurd, he agreed to make the movie. Once again he allowed himself to be flattered and "wet-noodled to death."

As filming proceeded, Dudley's fears were confirmed. He knew beyond question that he'd made a wrong choice, but there was no way to extricate himself. Maybe, he tried to convince himself, they could make the film better than it seemed. Maybe they could make it work after all. He was wrong. They couldn't.

Laraine Newman, his costar, believes *Wholly Moses* never had a chance, although the script was not that bad and the initial premise had potential. "Ultimately it was very formulaic, with no attempt at anything special," she says. "We both suggested various changes, but, apart from improvising in a few places, they didn't happen."

Wholly Moses was the first film David Begelman had produced since the scandal that unseated him as president of Columbia for forging a check in the name of actor Cliff Robertson. He was, Laraine Newman recalls, a charming man and a great raconteur. "You could go to him, tell him what you wanted, and he wouldn't give it to you. But still you'd leave thinking you'd got it."

Laraine was particularly uncomfortable with her part, and thought she was terribly miscast. "I felt I had no business being the love interest. It was very embarrassing for me, because I realized my only function was to be a babe, and I don't qualify for that."

Filming took place in Death Valley, the arid desert beyond Los Angeles. Director Gary Weis liked Dudley enormously and got on well with him. Dudley liked Weis's good humor and thought he was very funny, but he considered him not critical enough and indiscriminate in printing too many takes. It gave him little hope for the outcome.

Ruth Forman, Dudley's secretary, saw a change in Dudley while he was working on the film. "During *10* he had been alive and vibrant and having a wonderful time, but he wasn't like that with *Wholly Moses*. He was much more subdued—almost morose."

The fault lay partly in Weis's inexperience. Also, at a time when Weis needed to be at his sharpest, he was suffering from intense personal problems that impinged on his work.

Despite the reigning chaos, there were, inevitably, moments of jollity. Dudley and Laraine shared a similar humor and background. Both had been among the first of a new breed of performers who wrote their own comedy material. Laraine had been a founding member of the improvisational comedy group the Groundlings. She also had been one of the original cast members on *Saturday Night Live*, and had met Dudley briefly when he and Peter Cook had appeared on the show two years earlier.

She found him adorable and sexy. "I was very attracted to him, and we dated for about a second. We had a common language, and we laughed our guts out. Dudley and Jimmy Coco were very funny together, and, when Jimmy wasn't around, Dudley and I often went off and played stupid word games that kept us in stitches. We spent a lot of time waiting and laughing."

She remembers Dudley keeping her vastly amused with tales of his childhood. "He often described himself as a horny kid when he was growing up, and told me how he had masturbated so much as a child that there was crust on his bedsheets. They were funny stories!"

Ultimately, everything bad that could happen to a film happened to *Wholly Moses*. It was a creative disaster. Even when filming was over and the actors went back into the sound studio to loop dialogue, the filmmakers continued to try various tricks to enhance the film. They considered interjecting it with narration, but couldn't make up their minds which character should be the one to narrate. "In the end," says Newman, "we didn't do it because we were expected to write it there on the spot. It was a catastrophe. I'm just sorry an opportunity to be with somebody of Dudley's caliber was lost on something like that."

When the film was released the following June, it was to abysmal reviews, although Dudley emerged reasonably unscathed. "Its only redeeming feature," wrote Gene Siskel in the *Chicago Tribune*, "is the comic pacing of Dudley Moore, who manages to undersell his droll sense of humor." *Variety* claimed "a couple of okay slapstick moments remind us how funny Moore can be, but in the long run, there's nothing he can do with the material," and the *Hollywood Reporter* noted, "the film unfolds smoothly but is ultimately rather dull due to Weis's undistinctive direction."

The film was bound to upset the Jewish world with its irreverence, and Orthodox groups condemned it as "the most vicious attack on the Jewish religion in the history of the American movie industry."

To the amazement of critics, the film reaped massive figures at the box office during its opening week, eclipsing movies with John Travolta and Clint Eastwood. Just as quickly, however, the grosses began to spiral downward.

Dudley was not happy with the film, nor was he pleased with himself for having ignored his original misgivings. The experience taught him to be more guided by his instincts, although it was a lesson he would not always remember. In spite of the disappointment of *Wholly Moses* and the cancellation of *The Ferret*, 1979 had been an excellent year for Dudley.

He had spent so many of his early years dreaming of fame, fortune, and beautiful women. Now he had them all. And he was finding that

American fame brought with it a different reaction from the public. In Britain, people treated celebrities with dignity: They looked, but tended not to stare, and seldom approached. Now people were stopping him wherever he went, though it was not invasive. His supermarket trips, in the past fairly swift, became longer as people congregated around him while he pushed his shopping cart down the aisles; he seldom escaped from the dry cleaners now without signing a few autographs; and in restaurants dinner was constantly interrupted by visits from other diners wanting to shake his hand.

The pint-sized comedian was up there with the Hollywood elite. He was invited to Hollywood A-list parties and exclusive screenings. Cary Grant was his neighbor at one of these gatherings, Gene Kelly at another. He found it all very exhilarating, and this was reflected in his letters home.

His old music master and friend, Peter Cork, recalls that he and Dudley years earlier had seen a film starring Leslie Caron. "When he got to Hollywood, he had a date with her, and he wrote and told me about it. It was extraordinary. He also said in his letter how Alice Faye had come up and spoken with him. I think he was very astonished by everything that was happening."

By December 1979 Dudley and Tuesday were hammering out the last details of their imminent divorce petition. She, after a brief but passionate romance with Martin Mull, who had left his wife for her, was now seeing Al Pacino. Several years earlier they had enjoyed an intense love affair, and now it flared back into life.

The acting profession is a relatively small world, and inevitably relationships become intertwined almost to the point of incest. Dudley would have a brief romance with Marthe Keller, who previously had a long relationship with Pacino, who in turn ended up living with Lyndall Hobbs, with whom Dudley had had an affair during the dying days of his marriage to Suzy Kendall. And Tuesday's ex-husband, Claude Harz, was now living with Alys Kihl, with whom Dudley had enjoyed an affair during and after her marriage to his best friend, George Hastings.

On Christmas Eve 1979 Dudley arrived in New York and stayed at the apartment of Freddie Fields, one of *Wholly Moses*'s producers. He had flown out to be with Patrick over Christmas, and his son was ecstatic to see his father. They spent Christmas Day together, some of it in the park while Tuesday went to see Pacino, and Patrick reveled in Dudley's company.

Patrick was not an easy child to parent, as Tuesday's mother discovered when she was in New York looking after her daughter's household. After taking care of Patrick one day, Jo Weld—a professional baby-sitter in Hollywood—concluded that he was entirely lacking in any sense of discipline. He showed only animosity and obstreperousness.

It was hardly surprising, considering the example of Tuesday's ways at the time, that Patrick was growing up both undisciplined and willful.

Early in January 1980 Dudley flew to Australia for a few days, and then on to Europe to promote *10* to the European press. It was a whirlwind tour that took him to Paris, Sweden (where he ate the only mooseburger of his life), Brussels, and finally London. There he was put up royally in Claridges, and once he'd finished with the British, Italian, and German press, he spent the next few days distributing presents to his mother and his sister Barbara and her family, and catching up with Suzy Kendall and old friends Francis Megahy, Lysie Kihl, and Claude Harz. There were dinners with Lyndall Hobbs and Peter Cook, and meetings with Peter Morgan and Chris Karan.

Five days later he flew back to Los Angeles, and less than three hours after the plane touched down, he was sitting among a gaggle of Hollywood stars at the Golden Globe Awards, far from the Dagenham home he had just visited. His jet lag did not for a moment spoil his pleasure at being considered one of the Hollywood in crowd. Nor was he too disappointed when his Golden Globe nomination for *10* failed to convert into a win— the nomination itself was enough to thrill him.

By this time, *10* had already made $50 million in America on a $5 million budget. Dudley had been paid a flat hundred thousand dollars, but from now on he would always receive a percentage of the profits from all his films.

Socially he was everywhere. There were parties a couple of nights a week, and premieres, screenings, and interviews with journalists who were clamoring at publicist Paul Bloch's door. Dudley was still flying back and forth to New York and Patrick, and his diary was so crammed that, in the middle of February when one day appeared empty of engagements, he wrote across the page with an exhilarated scrawl, "FREE!"

Simultaneously Dudley found himself in wild demand as a single man. Women were pouring out of the woodwork as they had during the sixties in London. He had become, in his mid-forties, God's gift to women. He was surrounded by them, and had no qualms about enjoying this. In a pre-AIDS era, he believed adamantly in having as many female friends as possible and earnestly proclaimed his belief in the "meaningful one-night stand." Dudley was convinced one could experience the same emotion and closeness in a series of one-night stands as in a long relationship, and he couldn't understand why many people took a pejorative view of such behavior. He was, he admitted gleefully, girl crazy. The only difference between him and the sex maniac he had played in *Foul Play* was that no one could remotely describe Dudley as sex starved. The women who appealed to him were romantic, passionate, and huggable, with a sense of humor. He didn't go for the huge intellect: if he wanted to be stirred intellectually he had his books.

Not surprisingly, his comment about "meaningful one-night stands" found its way into the British and American press, with the inevitable distortions. Irritated with the way his remarks were being so publicly misinterpreted, he wrote to one magazine:

> Please don't perpetuate a misquotation that makes it seem as if I am suddenly running riot with heartless callous encounters with women. Firstly you make it sound as if I'm making up for lost time after years of deprivation.
>
> Secondly, don't perpetuate a quote that trivializes a notion that was meant affectionately. I said, "I am all in favor of meaningful one-night stands or one-week stands or one-year stands." You give a callous tone to a remark that was affectionate and humorous.

But, like many that Dudley wrote in response to criticism around this time, this letter was never sent.

He was now becoming a household name. Women found him sexy and attractive, and producers began offering him leading roles in their films. Nothing could have dented his appeal at this time.

Dudley had an intense desire for a close relationship, but he was also scared of commitment. He preferred to live alone, recognizing that he functioned better that way. "Anyone hidden like me is difficult to live with," he explained. It was an interesting statement, since for the last year he had been telling everyone how open he had become.

In reality, very few people would ever come to really know the man beneath the surface. Dudley let out only as much as he was able to reveal at the time, and there would always a part of himself that he would keep inside. This was one reason why he was so in favor of one-night stands. In these he felt safe. He could be enigmatic and to some degree anonymous. These weren't relationships that were predicated on who he really was inside, and in them he could find enjoyment without fear of being judged.

But all that was about to change, thanks to a leggy blonde named Susan Anton.

During the second week of February 1980 Dudley performed at the televised National Association of Theater Owners awards show in Los Angeles. It was there that he met the tall twenty-nine-year-old Anton, who sang a nominated song.

Susan, a detective's daughter from California, had gained fame in American advertisements as the Muriel Cigar girl. Briefly married once, to her manager, she was a singer of increasing popularity and had appeared in a number of television variety shows as well as her own. When she met Dudley, she was very sad at the breakup of an affair with Sylvester Stallone, who had returned to his wife.

Watching Dudley run through his performance in rehearsal, Susan recalls her powerful reaction. "I found myself laughing from a place I'd long forgotten about. This wonderful laughter came out of me, and it felt so great and I thought, 'I've got to know this man.' So I went over and introduced myself."

Dudley liked her immediately. It wasn't only her stunning looks: She also had a great sense of humor—something he found irresistible in women. They ran into each other again that evening at the postshow party at Chasen's, shared a few giggles, and went on their way. "The next day," says Susan, "I called my agent and asked how I could find Dudley. I just needed to know him. And apparently Dudley had done the same thing with his agent."

Susan was performing at the Sands Hotel in Las Vegas when Dudley called her. There were endless funny phone conversations, and ten days after they had met, Dudley flew up to Las Vegas.

When they saw each other, they both thought they'd made a big mistake. Susan was five foot eleven and towered over him. He'd forgotten how tall she was, and she'd forgotten how small he was. Awkwardly, they walked through the casino to get a bowl of soup, with Dudley's left shoe squeaking uncontrollably. "Here we were," Susan recalls, "this tall woman and this short man and this squeaky shoe going into the coffee shop for a bowl of wonton soup in the middle of the night in Las Vegas. What chance did this relationship have?"

But the more they talked, the more they began to feel comfortable and open with each other. Their discussion moved to Susan's room, where they talked for hours over a bottle of wine. Susan found Dudley's receptiveness refreshing. He had a gift for understanding people and accepting them for the way they were, and she felt a rare sense of being truly understood. "I told him I wanted to go to his room, go to bed with him, and have him hold me. Just hold me."

Their first night together was not without amusement, as Susan remembers. "He was very adamant about having the lights turned off. He kept talking about this clubfoot, and I had no idea what that was and couldn't have cared less. But he was so funny, because he went round turning off all the lights before we went to bed.

"In the morning I tried to sneak a peek at his foot, to see what he'd been talking about. Even when I saw it, I still couldn't figure out what the fuss was about. It was like, "Oh, that's what you're talking about!' I remember holding it and kissing it and stroking it and saying, 'What a sweet little foot.' It was obviously a tremendous source of pain for him, but also a part of him that you really loved, because it was an aspect of his being that made him who he was."

They ordered room service and lay in bed surrounded by enough platters of food to feed an army while watching *Wuthering Heights* on television. Then, Susan recalls, they both began to cry. "It was so cathartic. He was crying about all of his relationships, I was crying about all of my stuff, and I think that was the moment we fell into each other's arms and began our relationship."

Dudley had to fly to New York that day. He had promised to be there for Patrick's birthday. But he told Susan he would return to Las Vegas at the end of the week. And he did. They then spent the next three days together, and when at last he flew back to Los Angeles, it was with great reluctance. He did not want to leave Susan.

He'd grown to like American women. He admired their ability to capitalize on their assets and play down their bad points. There was an energy about them that seemed lacking in British women. And Susan was a gorgeous California blonde with, as it happened, an overbite like Suzy Kendall and Tuesday Weld. But, more than her looks, it was her jolliness that attracted Dudley. She was very outgoing with her emotions—the reverse of Dudley, who for all his talk, was still learning to shed his English reserve.

"Dudley," says Susan, "was the first man in my life who really taught me that I was complete and wonderful all by myself and that my value wasn't predicated on any partnership—be it daughter, sister, or girlfriend. That understanding he gave me was one of the most tremendous gifts of my entire life."

He was at first embarrassed by the disparity in their height—she was nine inches taller than he—and thought they looked a bit funny together. Indeed they did, but it was a congenial kind of funny, and he only really noticed it when he caught sight of them both in mirrors or shop windows. It inspired him to come up with a song for them—"I've Got You Under My Chin."

Actually, it was Susan's very tallness that brought about some of the empathy that she and Dudley shared. She had always had to deal with her height and had felt something of the same pain and anguish that Dudley had suffered over being small. "I always felt different from everyone else," she says. "While other girls were petite and cute, I towered over everyone, and it was awkward."

The man who'd been enjoying his widespread popularity with the opposite sex now found himself wanting only to be with this one woman. Suddenly the need for one-night stands was being replaced with a desire for monogamy. While Susan performed in Las Vegas, Dudley flew back and forth every few days to see her. He made plans for them to go on vacation together and, wanting to buy her a present, noted her ring size in his diary.

Less than a month after their first date they flew to Acapulco, where Dudley had rented a villa with a pool. They were only there for ten days, but Susan brought enough clothes for a month. "I'll never forget Dudley trying to lug those suitcases into the villa," she laughs, "because it looked like he was dragging dead bodies."

Dudley's clothes, on the other hand, could have fitted into a tiny flight bag. "He had a tendency to dress in a uniform, and at that time it was a striped T-shirt and white duck pants. He wore it the day we arrived until the day we left. He didn't like to be bothered with clothes, and he wore them till they fell apart."

Dudley had brought his present for Susan. Opening it, she found a little ring with a half-crescent abalone moon. Years later for one of her birthdays he had it remade from a diamond, adding a star to signify her universe was expanding.

The Acapulco vacation was idyllic and punctuated with constant laughter, as Susan remembers. "I would throw Dudley into the deep end of the swimming pool and he would sort of sink, which I thought was the funniest thing I'd ever seen. It was hysterical. Then he'd yell in a little-boy voice, 'Sev me, sev me,' and I'd have to jump in and save him. We spent two weeks of laughing and eating. And listening to music. That's when I heard his music for the first time."

During the vacation, Dudley read a script that kept him cackling with laughter as he turned the pages. Susan implored him to read parts to her, and she too found herself bursting into laughter. The script was *Arthur*.

In mid-April, Dudley took Susan to her first Academy Award ceremony, where he played the music for one of the nominated songs. They didn't stay long. Impatient to be alone with each other, they left after Dudley had finished performing.

A few days later they arrived for dinner at Lou Pitt's house and Dudley was astonished to discover he had walked into a surprise dinner for his own forty-fifth birthday. Among the guests were Jessica Lange and Mikhail Baryshnikov, and Susan was dazed by the new people she was meeting.

It was, as Dudley wrote to Suzy Kendall, a delightful evening. "They had some blow-ups of very early photographs of me, which was great fun to look at. I also had a 'gorillagram,' which meant somebody in a gorilla costume sang me happy birthday, and 'bellygram,' which is more my style, where a belly-dancer gave her all in a performance in front of my nose."

He told her he might go to Cannes before *Arthur* started shooting in June, in which case he would also pop over to England. "One of the problems," he confessed, "is that Susan is stuck in Los Angeles at the moment and I want to see as much of her as I can before I go to New York, which really means I should stay here."

Ruth Forman, Dudley's secretary, could see that Dudley was deeply in love. "He had a tremendous amount of love to give, and I think he started putting some of his life on hold to spend time with Susan," she says. "They were obsessed with each other. I saw desperation and passion for together-ness from both of them. They were inseparable, unable to be apart. Who knows who loved more?"

At that particular time it was Dudley who loved the most. Susan recalls he even expressed interest in getting married—which said a lot after all his talk in the press about how marriage was not for him and he'd never do it again. He did not actually propose to Susan, yet the topic was raised and he seemed very keen on the idea. By now, Tuesday had filed for divorce.

Susan, however, was still getting over her affair with Stallone and was less ready to commit. "When Dudley first falls in love," she reflects, "he completely falls that way. I think his addiction is that wonderful falling, and he loves to completely surrender himself to the fall. So he was much more committed and ready for marriage, whereas I wasn't because I was still getting over my previous relationship."

Still, she took him to meet her parents at their home near Los Angeles. Her father was not a happy man at that time. Bad eyesight had forced him to retire from the detective work he had loved, and he tended to take out his anger on his two daughters' boyfriends. Susan recalls that her father did not speak to Dudley once that afternoon. "As we were leav-ing, Dudley shook Daddy's hand and said, 'Well, it was nice meeting you, and next time we mustn't hog the conversation.' I saw my dad lose it a lit-tle there, because it was pretty damn funny. It took the heat off everything."

At the end of April 1980 Ada Moore was delighted to receive a letter from Dudley. He regaled her with a description of his surprise birthday dinner, omitting the belly dancer, and told her he expected to start *Arthur* a few weeks later in New York. He was, he told her, searching for an apartment there, large enough for Patrick and his nanny to stay with him during the filming. "Patrick can come and visit me on the set and see me at work, and I'm looking forward to really getting to know him during that period."

He told her *Arthur* was the funniest script he'd ever read, and he couldn't wait to start filming. "John Gielgud has been cast and I'm very pleased about that," he added, "but we're still looking for a lead girl. They've looked already at about two hundred and nobody seems to fit the bill completely."

As it happened, Liza Minnelli had originally been offered the role, but had twice turned it down because she felt she wouldn't spark with the other two actors who had been touted for the lead. Now the producers approached her again, without much hope that she would change her mind. But she did change it, and instantly. There was no way she could resist working with Dudley, whose humor she had long appreciated.

Before the cameras began rolling on *Arthur*, Dudley flew to Cannes for a brief visit and was royally feted by the press. Then it was on to London and his roast lamb lunch in Dagenham the following day with his mother. She was thrilled to see him but, as was her wont, managed to contain her emotions, so all Dudley got was a brief hug.

Dudley had always been very careful, if not frugal, with his money—a trait he had inherited from his mother. He had invested wisely, was not a big spender, and was now fairly wealthy. He worried about Ada Moore's living alone, and liked to think of her as enjoying some luxuries in life.

For some time he had been making her a weekly payment of a couple of hundred pounds, but she refused to spend it, saying she didn't need luxuries and, besides, if she had any, someone would probably try to steal them. He tried to persuade her to buy a new fur coat, but she was convinced somebody would think she had money and hit her over the head.

She may have been anxious that his success would not last, that one day she might again have to provide for her son. "No, I'm not spending that, dear—you might need that for a rainy day," she told Dudley every time he suggested she buy something. Much later, Dudley would discover she had religiously saved over eight thousand pounds for Patrick.

Ada had never visited Dudley in America. She was terrified to travel long distances. It was hard enough for her to leave the door on Baron Road and walk up the road to get fish for the cat. "The thought of flying would have petrified her," says Barbara, Dudley's sister. "There was no way we could have put her on a plane."

From London, Dudley flew to New York to settle in his temporary apartment and begin rehearsing *Arthur*. He had not managed to see Suzy during his brief trip to London, and she was particularly sad since he had grown the one and only beard of his life and she'd missed seeing it. "I'm so happy you're now getting the best work and that you're enjoying it," she told him in a letter. "Now if you would only record that song …"

Dudley had always promised her he would record "Before Love Went Out of Style," but somehow he had never got around to it. "Maybe I will one of these days," he wrote back. "I was planning to do some music in the last three or four months but a fit of laziness overtook me as usual and nothing happened." As for his beard, "I've shaved it off; it was getting very scratchy and I wasn't very comfortable with it."

In the first week of June 1980 filming began on *Arthur*.

CHAPTER 16

A R T H U R

1980

"Here's this incredible genius of a man who doesn't really know he's attractive but who knows what's funny. He understands Arthur's innocence and what a good person he is. Because that's Dudley, too."

—LIZA MINNELLI

Some actors spend a lifetime playing different roles yet remain associated with only one. For Dudley, that role would be Arthur.

A fabulously spoiled and rich drunk, Arthur Bach is a happy, fun-loving millionaire with a cackling laugh that will not rest, even in his sleep. He is a man with no desire to grow up, who likes to play with toy trains and surround himself with childish amusements. His wastrel activities are aided by his grudging butler Hobson (John Gielgud), whose affection is tempered with caustic contempt.

Arthur is faced with an awful dilemma that his wealth produces: of either marrying the local dreary deb down the road (Jill Eikenberry) or having his $750 million fortune cut off. He agrees to do the right thing (marry), but then falls in love with shoplifter Linda Marolla (Liza Minnelli). Every Peter Pan has integrity, and Arthur reluctantly returns to his fiancée, but he has not counted on the intervention of Hobson, who—unknown to Arthur—is dying and wants to see his employer happy in love before he departs from this world.

Ultimately, Arthur renounces his inheritance and prepares to march off, penniless, into the sunset with Liza, but, as befits any perfect fairy tale, the matriarch of the Bach family finally relents and grants him his inheritance.

Dudley was in raptures over the role. Lou Pitt recalls, "When Dudley was reading the script, he called me when he reached page 7 and said, 'This is fantastic,' he called me on page 14 and said, 'I love it,' and he called around page 60 and said, 'I've just got to do this. Who do I have to sleep with?'"

Steve Gordon, Arthur's writer-director, was, however, very worried about Dudley's accent. He had not written the role for an Englishman. "Can't you do it with an American voice?" he implored Dudley, who was adamant in his refusal. Even as filming began, a nervous Gordon kept asking, "Are you sure you can't do an American accent?" Dudley was sure. He knew he couldn't sustain an accent, nor could he concentrate on the role if he was worrying about his voice.

Dudley was drawn to Arthur's desire to enjoy himself to the fullest. And to laugh constantly. "Sometimes I just think funny things," Arthur tells a bewildered hooker after bursting into laughter for no apparent reason. To Dudley, Arthur was a nice, rather lonely, man—even though he was outrageously smashed a lot of the time. Dudley played him for real. He did not really think of Arthur as an alcoholic, but more as a person with a tremendous penchant for enjoying life, who did things to excess and wanted everyone else to have a good time too.

Dudley had always been fascinated by stage drunks. Once, during a performance with Vic Lewis's orchestra in 1959, he had staggered onstage pretending to be drunk and managed to maintain the act the entire time he was playing. Lyricist Leslie Bricusse, who had known Dudley since the early sixties in London, recalls a night early in their friendship when he first saw Dudley's alcoholic emerge. Bricusse had been dining with Laurence Harvey at the Guinea restaurant, off Berkeley Square, while across the room Bryan and Nanette Forbes were dining with Princess Margaret. "Dudley came in and joined us, and as we were leaving we stopped at the Forbes table. Dudley could do a marvelous drunk, and he turned to Princess Margaret and said, 'Goo' eve'ing, Yer Royal Highnessh. I shu'pose a blow job is out of the queshtion?' It was hysterical!"

Steve Gordon was a tall, lanky, wiry-haired New York Jew with a tremendous sense of humor that matched Dudley's own. He was also insecure and inordinately anxious. A year after the film was released he died of a sudden heart attack. Gordon had definite ideas about how he wanted Arthur to be played. This form of directing had never gone down well with Dudley, who made that clear soon after the first takes of the $7 million movie had been shot. He told the director that any indication of how he should play Arthur would result in his doing a terrible impersonation of a tall, lanky, wiry-haired New York Jew rather than what he felt to be right. Gordon respected Dudley's feelings. He trusted his instincts about the role and mostly left him alone.

Dudley was delighted at the prospect of working with Liza Minnelli, whom he considered a wonderful comedienne, and he was convinced they would sparkle together. They had known each other casually since the sixties, even before Liza was engaged to Peter Sellers, and Dudley vaguely recalls a night in London when he followed the couple's taxi in his Mini halfway across town to Peter's Mayfair home.

Liza had grown up around great American comics from Oscar Levant to Milton Berle, and had learned comic timing from her parents, Judy Garland and Vincente Minnelli. She had always been funny, but nobody had really known it. Certainly not Steve Gordon. At the first run-through for *Arthur*, Gordon turned to her in surprise. "You're really funny!" he told her. "No shit?" retorted Dudley, who had always loved Liza's humor.

Liza adored Dudley. Seldom had she met anyone who made her feel so understood. "He had, and still has," she says, "this incredible gift for making one feel important as a person—important for what's inside. He responded to the person I was underneath in a way that no one else had done. He made me feel very special, and I loved him for that."

They were an excellent team. Dudley was at his comic peak and, with him, Liza was funny, too. "We went together so well," she reflects. "We had the same kind of humoristic vision and traveled the same way in our heads. We'd almost feel guilty about it, because all someone had to do was say 'Nice morning, eh?' and we'd look at each other and for some reason we'd get hysterical.

"We could barely get through anything. One scene was ludicrous because we did about twenty-seven takes. Everybody kept breaking up laughing. First I went. Then he went. Then the director and the gaffer and the crew, and we had to keep stopping. What was wonderful on *Arthur* was that we always had an audience, and that was the crew. Finally one day they all came in with pieces of tape which they threatened to put over their mouths—they were breaking up so much and couldn't stand it."

Since Dudley's *Beyond the Fringe* days when Sir John Gielgud had inadvertently referred to Dudley as Stanley Moon (an appellation that had stuck ever since as his nickname among Dudley's friends), he had carried a deep fondness for the great actor. The opportunity to work with him now gave Dudley particular pleasure. There was a great deal of respect and humor between the two, and Liza could see they adored each other and derived enormous enjoyment from being together in spite of their different personalities. Whereas Gielgud was quite reserved and very introverted, Dudley was all over the place, playing the piano and enjoying what he was doing.

"I tried to be Rabelaisian with him as much as possible," Dudley remembers, "trying to gee him up and get him going. I knew he didn't want to be called Sir John. He wanted to be called Johnny. But nobody could bring themselves to call him Johnny, because he sounded so swish. So there I was trying to be hearty as hell with him."

Liza Minnelli also grew very attached to Gielgud. "John hates to be called Sir John by anyone he likes or has known a long time. So I called him Uncle Johnny all the time, and he got a great laugh out of that. He was very funny," she remembers, "and had a huge sense of humor, but he was never quite sure he was being funny. His lines were very raunchy, and to hear them spoken in that brilliant accent was magic. I just cracked up when he said to Arthur, 'Do you want me to come in there and wash your dick for you, you little shit?' It was wonderful, but he kept turning to me and Dudley and asking, 'Was that funny?' He was never sure.

A shy, quiet, self-effacing man, Gielgud enjoyed one of the best film experiences of his entire career. It was particularly ironic since he, like Liza, had initially turned down the script twice. "I thought it was rather smutty and a vulgar little film," he recalls, "so I refused it. But each time they asked me, they put up my salary twice, and in the end I decided to do it."

Although their acting backgrounds were entirely different, the veteran actor responded ebulliently to Dudley's energy and humor and was highly impressed with Dudley's spontaneity. "He was awfully clever because he improvised quite a lot," recalls Gielgud. "We used to rehearse all the time, but each time we did it, Dudley would throw in other little jokes and gags. I loved his humor and his sense of invention, of being able to go into a scene and decorate it with little touches of his own. He kept very correctly to the script most of the time, but one always thought he might suddenly come out with something unexpected. He was wonderful and very funny as Arthur, but I wasn't surprised by that, because I'd always admired him ever since *Beyond the Fringe*."

Working on *Arthur* was like being part of a close, happy family for five months. Sometimes, when filming ended early, Dudley and Liza went off for supper together. They spent hours talking and laughing, and formed a tight bond that has endured.

Throughout the filming, Dudley was back and forth to Los Angeles to see Susan Anton. Most weekends he would fly over on Saturday morning and return to New York either that same night or the following day. He and Susan might have but hours together, usually in the Marina house, but at least they saw each other.

Occasionally Susan was able to join him in New York, and John Gielgud was always amused to see them together on the set. "She was a very nice girl," he recalls, "and very, very tall—which used to make me laugh. I remember watching them walk off the set together. He'd have his arm around her waist while she towered way above him, and they'd stroll off into the moonlight. It was charming and funny."

Some of Susan's favorite moments were those spent around Dudley and Liza. "The first time I met Liza, who is bigger than life with a legendary image, she acted like an instant girlfriend," recalls Susan. "They were great pals. She and Dudley were always cracking up together. It was a lot of fun to be around that set, because Steve Gordon set the tone."

Steve Gordon was a very funny man. "He was so Jewish, as he kept telling us," recalls Liza Minnelli. "He'd often say, 'Oy ve, this isn't going to work! What am I doing?' and he always said he was having a heart attack. Always. At any given time you could turn around and he'd be taking his pulse. And unfortunately, as it turned out later, he was right. It was a horrendous loss. He was a hell of a man.

"But even when he was worrying he was *funny*, and hilarious things would happen. There was one time when it was dreadfully hot on the set and there was a fan next to Steve, who was sitting in his high director's chair. He was worried about a scene and he said, 'No, that's not quite right,' and started shaking his head, and he leaned back and his hair got caught in the fan."

Steve's excessive anxiety would undoubtedly have been fueled by one particular bungle, as John Gielgud recalls. "They had spent a fortune building a little car, which Dudley and I had to drive together on a race-track on a very, very hot day. But, when we went to shoot the scene, the car was too small for both of us. We tried to get into it and couldn't. It was quite funny to see us both try to squeeze inside. Eventually we had to redo the scene another way."

Dudley was now flying somewhere every weekend—either back and forth to L.A. or to some other city to see Susan perform. "I couldn't get rid of him," she remembers. "It was like wherever I was, he was. I'd never had anybody pursue me in such a fashion. He was on planes all over the place." He took in Chicago, Detroit, and Grand Rapids, and was relieved when Susan said she had a few days off. "Susan NY till Aug 5!!XXX" he scrawled exuberantly in his diary.

During the hot New York summer, Dudley spent a lot of time with his friend Robert Mann, who lived just off Central Park with his wife, Lucy. Mann was renowned for his musical evenings, when the cream of the classical music world congregated in his living room to give impromptu concerts. Dudley loved being part of these occasions, although he was nervous at playing the piano in such elite company.

One evening Mann was playing chamber music with violinist Itzhak Perlman and members of a string quartet. He suggested to Perlman that he and Dudley play together. "What can he play? He just plays jokes on the piano," answered Perlman. Mann thought about it for a second then suggested the Chausson Concerto in D major for violin, piano, and string quartet.

The piece is a particularly long and tricky one, and pianists have been known to omit some of the notes even when recording it. Dudley, who had never seen the music before, studied it for five minutes then said he'd try it. "I could see Perlman smirking like mad," recalls Mann, "while the others looked on very skeptically."

What Robert Mann knew, but the others did not, was that Dudley had an extraordinary ability to sight-read. To the immense delight of Mann, who had always been astounded by this exceptional facet of his friend's talent, Dudley read and played almost every note in that piece. "I had a wonderful time enjoying the open mouths of all the musicians," laughs Mann. "Itzhak was dumbfounded—he couldn't believe anyone could read like that. They all burst into applause when he'd finished."

Meanwhile Liza Minnelli was beginning to sense an edge to Dudley. "I could see the artistic melancholy of the musician in his eyes. It's a horrendous strain to be funny for eight hours every day and then wait for the next scene and then come back and be funny again. In between takes there was nothing to do, and I could see the musician in him was suffering."

Liza arranged for a piano to be installed in Dudley's dressing room at the Astoria studio. "It was wonderful to hear his music," she recalls. "I would hear these beautiful, melancholy, and incredibly tender interpretations of songs coming through the walls. Sometimes he'd play pieces he'd written, and other times I'd hear him play something absolutely silly. In a funny way I could judge when to go in and out of his dressing room by what he was playing."

Susan was opening in a new show at the MGM Grand in Las Vegas, and Dudley sent her flowers and a cable that read, "These are what Arthur gives to Linda so you know what that means. Have a good opening night with your new show. I love you Susan."

During a break from filming, Dudley flew to Vegas to see Susan's show and took with him Liza and her husband, Mark Gero. As Susan recalls, "I had rented a house and we all shared it for a couple of days, which was exhausting and fun, because Liza's energy level was amazing. I could hardly keep up with her."

Liza liked Susan and thought she and Dudley made an ideal couple. "They were very funny together," she remembers, "but they were also smart and gave each other room. They had a great relationship, and I loved their sense of humor. We had a lot of laughs, and I enjoyed being around them. It was easy and comfortable, and I could be myself instead of the cardboard cutout that people expect you to be."

As *Arthur* continued filming in a hot and very muggy New York, Liza and Dudley grew even closer. Often he played the piano in his dressing room while Liza sat beside him belting out song after song in her unmistakable voice. "There's a point in any film," she says, "where you can't remember the beginning and you can't see the end. We were just at that point, and Dudley's music helped get us through those frustrating times."

In the film Arthur has Hobson to rely on for his food. In real life Dudley relied on himself. "He had a stove in his dressing room," laughs John Gielgud, "and he used to cook lunch for himself every day. I don't know if that was because he didn't trust the studio catering!"

It was more probably because it was the only way he could be sure of getting his favorite fish every day, and cooked the way he liked it. It was not unusual to see Dudley walking around with a couple of frozen trout that he would place on a radiator to thaw.

"Fish—it was always fish!" Liza recalls of Dudley's invitations to join him for lunch. "It was frightfully English. He kept asking me if I wanted some trout, and I always said no. And then I'd bring in my peanut butter and jelly sandwich and he'd laugh his head off."

The most poignant moments in the film are those when Hobson is dying in hospital, and these were the ones that most appealed to Gielgud. "I loved those scenes," he reflects. "There was a certain pathos in my character of the butler and the fact that he knew he was going to die. That attracted me a great deal."

It was as Gielgud filmed his death scene that Susan, during one of her New York visits, witnessed his ability to ignore the unexpected.

As Hobson, Gielgud was lying in bed with a cowboy hat on his head and a miniature train that Arthur had brought to cheer him up. As he was emoting his death scene, a fly landed on the end of his nose, but he, being a consummate actor, carried on with his lines while the fly sat there calmly, unperturbed by the drama of the moment. "It was hilarious," recalls Susan. "We were almost peeing ourselves with laughter and trying not to let him see."

Gielgud was sorry when the filming of *Arthur* came to an end. "I loved working with Dudley enormously. Both he and Liza were very sweet to me, and enormously professional and proficient. They were both so charming to me, because they must have seen what a good part I had and it was really their film. They were a delightful pair, and I felt very much at ease with them."

His only disappointment was that he hadn't spent more time with Dudley. "It was a great pity we didn't do anything together off the set," he says wistfully, "but then we were all working so hard. I can't say how much I loved being around him, and I'd jump at the chance to work with him again."

When the movie was finished, the production team presented Dudley with a silver Tiffany flask. On it was an engraving that made no sense until read phonetically, and then it sounded like one of Arthur's slurred lines from the film. In fact Dudley's performance in *Arthur* was so authentic that for a long time he had to thwart rumors about his own drinking. He had always enjoyed a fine wine, but he seldom drank to excess and he was definitely not an alcoholic.

For several years Robert Mann had been urging Dudley to perform classical music in public, but Dudley had always refused the challenge, convinced he was not of the caliber for concert performance. Mann did not agree. He believed Dudley had the artistry. All he needed was more practice. "He always improvised for fun," says Mann, "but he never worked on passages."

One afternoon Mann was at the Marina beach house during one of his Los Angeles visits. He and Dudley had spent the day playing sonatas, and Ruth Forman, who was working in Dudley's office at the house, listened to them play. "I thought that I had died and gone to heaven," she remembers of that day. "It was so exquisite."

It was now that Mann again pursued the question of performing in public. He knew the manager of the Metropolitan Museum of Art in New York, he said. If she was willing, would Dudley commit to a concert? Mann's persistence paid off. At last, Dudley agreed.

Meanwhile, Blake Edwards, who had remained friendly with Dudley since their brilliant collaboration on *10*, came to him with a suggestion that he take over the role of Inspector Clouseau in *The Romance of the Pink Panther*. After a parting of their ways, Blake had given the rights to Peter Sellers to make the film on his own, but when Sellers died of a heart attack, Blake decided to go ahead with the movie himself. Although Dudley was very keen to work again with Blake, he had strong reservations about stepping into Sellers's shoes. He had decided by now that he didn't want to go on playing the kind of bumbling characters with which he'd been identified earlier, and Clouseau epitomized those roles. Accents, apart from regional British ones, had never been his forte, although in all likelihood Blake would have tailored the role to suit Dudley. More than that, though, was the greater concern that he would be criticized for taking over from Sellers, and he was sure the inevitable comparisons would not work in his favor. His decision to turn down the role was also influenced by the fact that he was being asked to commit to a series of five films, and he did not want to be tied down now.

At the end of September, Dudley flew to New York for the wedding of Robert and Lucy Mann's daughter, Lisa. The wedding took place in the Manns' large apartment, and Robert Mann fondly remembers Dudley playing a sarabande from a Bach suite as Robert walked Lucy down the living room aisle toward the bridegroom. "What was so delicious," Mann recalls, "was that as we were walking, Dudley began jazzing it up in a very tasteful way until it took on a whole new dimension. It was delightful."

By now Dudley and Susan Anton had been together for five months, and they were enjoying a deep and satisfying relationship. Not only were they soul mates, but Susan made the best chocolate-chip cookies Dudley had ever tasted. Occasionally Susan became frustrated by his even-temperedness. Dudley called it his "passive" streak, but, as one of his ex-therapists explains, "There's nothing remotely passive about Dudley. His feelings are so passionate that he holds himself in check." Sometimes Susan, who described him as "passive-aggressive," would see that passion pour out of him. "Dudley had this saying, 'It's in the silence,'" she remembers, "and I think his life was in his silence as a child, where he wasn't given permission to express a lot of things." Susan saw in him an immense amount of rage. "He was like a kettle with a lid on it, only letting out those emotions he'd been given permission to let out ever since he was a child."

That repressive side of Dudley drove Susan crazy. She was a very open girl, able to express her feelings, and sometimes she felt herself deliberately provoking Dudley just to try to get something out of him. "And then," she recalls, "he would erupt, and you could see all this suppression of rage and anger and unexpressed emotions bursting out, and it would be the most thrilling thing when it happened."

The press had a field day with the couple, and Dudley was happy to help them along. "People say never the twain shall meet ... but we do," he joked, while the tabloids debated his apparent fixation on tall blondes. It was a subject that had been raised ever since Dudley's early days of fame in England with *Beyond the Fringe*. But, given his height, it was a moot point, since just about all the women he met were taller than him.

It wasn't only the press who were amused by the couple's disparity in height. Tony Adams, Blake Edwards's coproducer, remembers Susan and Dudley arriving at a Malibu beach party Blake threw for his wife, Julie Andrews. "Watching Dudley and Susan walk down the sand dunes together was hilarious," laughs Tony. "First all we could see was Susan, and then a few minutes late Dudley came into view with his arm around her waist. Blake and I were standing together just shaking our heads. It was the funniest sight we'd ever seen."

Dudley was caught up in Susan's passion and enjoyment of life. Hollywood was full of beautiful women, but Susan was fun, too. They shared a mutual need for companionship, and the passion and feeling between them ran very high. He enjoyed her up-front attitude and her curiosity and willingness to learn. She was a nurturing, loving woman, and Dudley responded to that. He was still a man desperately searching for the love he felt he had never received as a child.

For her part, Susan felt Dudley was one of the sexiest men she'd ever known. She did not believe that a man had to be tall and muscular to be sexy. To her, Dudley was sexy because he was sensitive. He understood her problems and feelings. He listened to her, and he cared.

Before meeting Susan, Dudley had been the very opposite of monogamous. Now he wanted to be only with her. Even when she was on tour, he'd follow her if he could. Even to Tokyo, where the Japanese, he recalls, were "totally swept away by this long blonde thing."

Wholly Moses, which had opened to such unfavorable reviews in America just a few weeks after Dudley began filming *Arthur*, was about to be released in Britain, and in October 1980 Dudley flew to London to promote the film. He took Susan with him.

She was fascinated to see the council house where he'd grown up, and where Ada Moore still kept his bedroom the way it had been during his youth, with his football shirt and cricket balls piled in one corner. "You could almost see the *Playboy* magazines under the bed and imagine the repressed, secret life that went on in this little room," recalls Susan.

Dudley had described his mother to Susan as a timid, gray little sparrow. Now she understood why. "Hellos and good-byes were awkward moments for them. I think he wanted to run and grab her but didn't feel he ever could. He was too afraid of the reaction—who knows, she might have grabbed him back. They were both afraid to fully let themselves be seen, so they were always on the edge. It was very sad."

Susan fell in love with England. Like many Americans of her generation, she had grown up with an image of quaintly pretty villages, lush countryside, and Shakespeare. On this, her first visit to Britain, she was not disappointed. Dudley hired a car and they traveled across the counties, staying in country inns noted for their cuisine. They both loved good food, and they single-mindedly ate their way across England. Dudley had become something of a wine connoisseur by now—he had a huge collection of wine at home—and Susan's knowledge of reds and whites increased dramatically during their trip.

Dudley could not have passed up the opportunity to return to Oxford, and he proudly took Susan with him to Magdalen College one day. His former music tutor, Dr. Bernard Rose, was conducting the choir in the chapel. "I couldn't understand why all the men in the choir were looking up into the gallery behind me," recalls Dr. Rose. "In the end I turned round to have a look, and there was Dudley with this beautiful girl, about six foot tall, wearing a silver-lamé pajama suit. My choir was paying more attention to her than to me."

After the service, Rose persuaded Dudley to go into the organ loft, where he played some of Bach's most intricate organ music. "Even though he hadn't played [those pieces] for about twenty years," he recalls, "Dudley played them awfully well. And having done that, he then went down to the antechapel, where there was a grand piano, and played the fool. It was amazing. He extemporized brilliantly."

While he was in England, Dudley reunited with Peter Cook. They filmed three television commercials for Barclays Bank, as Pete and Dud. Fifteen years on, the memorable characters they had introduced in *Not Only ... But Also* were still much beloved in the British public's minds.

After a week in London, Dudley and Susan returned to Los Angeles in time to attend the wedding of Susan's sister, Peggy, in her parents' home. Susan's father was still trying to deal with the trauma of his failing eyesight and, not surprisingly, was feeling pretty bad-tempered toward life and everyone in it. He was a tall man—all the Antons were tall—and as he talked to Dudley, he made great fun of his height. Dudley was deeply offended and, upset by the remarks, took himself off to the bathroom, where he remained for an unusually long time. It didn't help that he had earlier been playing the piano while suffering from the worst hemorrhoids of his life. He was in such appalling pain he could hardly sit down.

The film that Dudley and Peter Cook had made of their last Derek and Clive session, titled *Derek and Clive Get the Horn*, had now been presented to the British Board of Film Censors. In November 1980 censor James Ferman wrote to the film company, and informed them of the difficulty facing the Board. As he observed:

> The point of this comic exercise is to be as offensive as possible and to break every taboo the performers can think of, however outrageous the results. Cutting would be pointless although we believe that the sequence about Jesus Christ and the sexuality of the lower half of his body is probably blasphemous in the legal sense of the term. If this is so, then this brief scene would have to be cut. The offensive references to the Pope and the Holocaust are not, in our view, illegal, though they will certainly prove deeply offensive to some people.

The Board believed the film could only be approved for private distribution, the cinema equivalent being either club showing or the "18R" category that they anticipated effecting within a year or more. "But until this is introduced," Ferman concluded, "there is no member of the Board who feels this particular film should be granted a certificate for general distribution and we do not think that many local authorities would be happy to see this sort of thing playing in their own public cinemas."

It was, really, no less than anyone had expected, and, although versions of the film were on sale in video stores, it would be another eleven years before *Derek and Clive Get the Horn* finally would become widely available to the public.

Meanwhile, some copies of the film were already floating around Los Angeles, and Dudley was happy to screen it for any of his friends who asked to see it. The first screening was by Peter Cook's close friend, Brenda Vaccaro, and she threw one of her famous huge parties to mark the occasion. "It was a triumphant success," she recalls. "Everyone came out for it—even members of the Monty Python troupe who were in town. Peter was staying with me then, and he was extremely proud of the film because it was an example of their exquisite brilliance at doing comedy together."

At the end of November there was a poignant letter from Suzy Kendall. Suzy, who was now happily married to Sandy Harper, an ex-boyfriend of Princess Anne, with an adorable daughter, Elodie, missed Dudley enormously and was acutely aware of his recent long silences. "You are my family," she told him. "You were my brother, my mother, everything. I grew up with you, you shaped my life, and you are so much a part of everything I am that I miss having you near. I miss your notes ... and I fear there is a part of my past that is going."

Now that Dudley was with Susan, who was often jealous of other people in his life, he felt guilty about the closeness he maintained with his ex-wife. In part this had been exacerbated by Tuesday Weld, who had been jealous of his continued friendship with Suzy. During their marriage, Dudley had found himself sneaking down to the basement and secretly phoning Suzy from there, only to be terribly berated by Tuesday when she later discovered they had talked. It had instilled in him a guilt about staying in touch with previous women who had been important to him, and so he had lately become less communicative with Suzy.

Early in December, Dudley flew with Susan to Hawaii and then to London, where he enjoyed carols in the Savoy Hotel courtyard and reunions with Cleo Laine and Peter Bellwood, who was in London for Christmas. Dudley was loaded down with gifts for his friends and masses of presents for Barbara and his mother. "I wish," he wrote wistfully in his Christmas card to Ada Moore, "I could tell you more easily how I love you but an awkward gesture will have to do. I know you can understand."

He never knew what to call her—Mum, Mother, or Mater—and in this card, which he kept until her death, he called her the lot.

Christmas was spent not in London but in Los Angeles, where Patrick and Natasha, Tuesday's daughter from her previous marriage, flew in to stay with Dudley at the Marina. Together, they all went Christmas shopping—"Engrave watch D loves S," Dudley reminded himself in his diary—and joined Evelyn Silvers's traditional tree-trimming party.

When Dudley was with his son, he was, observed Susan Anton, a loving, typical father. "He was always a little lost—he didn't know what to do, and discipline was difficult for him—but I always felt he was a good dad. He read to Patrick, played with him, bought him toys. And he always had a nanny around to make sure he was well cared for."

But Dudley found it hard to be a father, and was unsure of how to play that role. Emotionally he was very confused—torn between the need for his own freedom and his guilt at not being there more for Patrick. Susan Anton saw the huge conflict going on in his head. "I think the notion of loving anyone that much was just horrific for Dudley. I remember him saying that sometimes he wished Patrick and I were dead, because it was just too much for us to be here to love. It was so painful for him to care about anything so much and to be with someone he loved so desperately."

Dudley was still in therapy. Despite his public assertions that he had found himself and was happy about it, in fact he was still working intently to achieve a greater understanding of his inner self. Susan witnessed his struggle clearly. "He was desperately trying to claim who he was and understand himself. I've never seen anyone work so hard at trying to come to this understanding of why he was the way he was. He was trying desperately to be free of what other people wanted or needed him to be."

Dudley had now left Dr. Wexler and joined Evelyn Silvers's group for what would be his last foray into psychotherapy. He spoke so openly there that other group members began turning to him for guidance. Evelyn saw how much he was helping the others and asked if he'd like to colead a group studying substance abuse. Dudley agreed.

Evelyn Silvers believes Dudley missed his true calling. "He came to the therapeutic world with an inherent ability to be a therapist. It was natural for him to want to reach out and help other people. The insight he had—and still has—into humanity, his perception and sensitivity about people, and the understanding that he had for the entire psychotherapeutic process were highly unusual."

Dudley's greatest asset, says Dr. Silvers, was a lack of guile that allowed him to approach people with total openness, in turn making them feel unjudged. "He gave them the freedom to be themselves without imposing on them what he thought they should be. Not only did he help people to open up and look at what was really going on in their lives, but he gave them the ability to laugh at it and enjoy it as part of the process of living and learning.

"Dudley is a highly complex man, and it may be that complexity which makes it possible for him to be the talent that he is. It's also what gives him such an understanding of other human beings and their own complexities."

Early in January 1981 Peter Cook came to Los Angeles and stayed with Brenda Vaccaro. Peter had often said that, no matter what he did, Dudley always followed soon after him. This time the situation was reversed. Dudley had gone to Hollywood first, and now it was Peter who followed. He had just landed the role of the butler in an NBC comedy series, *The Two of Us*.

Peter was excited about his foray into a Hollywood sitcom, recalls Brenda Vaccaro—his elation being compounded by the fact that he had been off alcohol for twenty-two months.

"Peter had been a bit sad that his career wasn't taking off, and he felt a strong competitive strain with Dudley. He very much wanted to work here and be successful, even though he always said he didn't, and now he was getting his shot at it.

"He was in the best shape ever," Brenda recalls, "and Dudley was so happy and proud to see him in such great condition, ready to go to work and prospering. He was there with him all the way, and he couldn't have been a more supportive friend. They were like brothers. There was a tremendous kindness between them—though more from Dudley I think."

Meanwhile, having finally capitulated to Robert Mann's "wet-noodling me to death," Dudley was practicing in earnest with the violinist for an upcoming concert. Nevertheless, he remembers going "backwards into the whole thing kicking and screaming."

He still didn't feel comfortable, and told his friend it wasn't right that he should play in public. But Mann kept up the pressure. Finally Dudley broke down and cried, "I'm just not good enough, can't you understand!"

Robert Mann disagreed. He believed that, with practice, Dudley could be good, and he pushed him mercilessly until suddenly it really did feel right after all.

Dudley had been in America for five years but had never performed at a public concert. His music meant so much to him that he was afraid to expose it to judgment. True, he had ventured tentatively forward by playing jazz piano during talk-show appearances, but that was as far as it had gone.

Now he was ready to meet the challenge.

CHAPTER 17

MUSICAL RHAPSODIES

1981

"What is incredible is how he does brilliantly with one career and then opens up in another. But in the end it always comes back to the one thing that was always the most overwhelming—his music."

—PETER CORK

Dudley had for a long time been keen to resume his music-making on a professional basis, but had lacked the confidence to try. While he was well known in Britain for his virtuosity at the piano, in America they were oblivious to this side of his talent.

Cellist Lynn Harrell had met Dudley at one of Mann's musical evenings during the early seventies, when *Good Evening* was running on Broadway. Like Mann, he had been encouraging him to perform in public. Now Harrell was in Los Angeles, performing for the Los Angeles Philharmonic's chamber music society, and he persuaded Dudley to join him in one of their concerts at a local synagogue.

It was Dudley's unannounced classical debut in the United States, and his mastery at the piano as he accompanied Harrell and flautist James Walker in Weber's Flute Trio took the audience of nine hundred by complete surprise. Harrell was very pleased, and periodically twirled his cello—his personal sign of pleasure.

Susan Anton watched nervously from her front-row seat. She had brought with her a tiny tape recorder, and when Dudley began playing, she slid it out of her bag and hid it in her lap to record his performance. Later they would listen to the recording together, and from then on she would always sneak the tape recorder into Dudley's concerts.

His playing was "competent and earnest," announced the *Los Angeles Herald Examiner*, while expressing muted astonishment at the performance of the "British satirist turned Hollywood actor." Dudley also threw in one of his parodies—"The Green Green Grass of Delilah," his Tom Jones meets Beethoven number that had been so popular with earlier British audiences.

Dudley anticipated some snotty remarks and he got them from one local critic, who rated him "a 6," but he was pleased with his first public American effort. And so was Ernest Fleischman, the South African director of the Los Angeles Philharmonic.

Fleischman offered him the chance to make his orchestral debut in the Philharmonic's sixtieth-anniversary summer season in July. He suggested a Gershwin evening, a tradition popular with local audiences. The fee would be six thousand dollars for each of two concerts—far less than Dudley could earn as an actor, but more rewarding in personal terms. Nervous but thrilled, Dudley accepted and embarked on a feverish daily practice regime on the Yamaha grand in his living room.

His passion for jazz, however, remained very high. He still owed his longtime friends Cleo Laine and John Dankworth a favor after he'd had to bow out of appearing with them at the London Palladium during the filming of *10*. In February he reunited with the couple in a Hollywood studio to record a new jazz album, *Smilin' Through*. Dankworth produced, while Cleo sang, and Dudley played with a trio completed by Ray Brown on bass and Nick Ceroli on drums.

One of the tracks, dating from his Oxford days, was "Strictly for the Birds," on which Dudley also sang. His early Erroll Garner style reemerged on this album, and it is interesting to note that Garner, like Dudley, had also been a small man, and sat on telephone books while he played.

Dudley had fun with Laine and Dankworth. They were good-hearted, patient, and encouraging, and in between the playing there was a great deal of clowning around. Although Dudley's musical taste was shifting back toward his classical roots, he still felt a tremendous jazz influence at work, especially now as he played alongside Cleo and Ray Brown, who was one of the great jazz bass players and a former member of Oscar Peterson's trio.

It was a successful reunion and a triumphant return to jazz. As Leonard Feather wrote in the *Los Angeles Times*, "That Mr. Moore has kept up his piano chops is engagingly illustrated here."

Even though Susan encouraged his music, occasionally she became jealous of the time he was spending away from her. As Cleo Laine recalls, "She was quite volatile, and when we were doing the record together, it was quite frightening. She would phone up and say, 'When the fucking hell are you coming home?' He used to hold the telephone away from his ear, she was shouting so loudly!"

That possessiveness, a quality from which Dudley had always recoiled, was a portent of what lay ahead. Though Dudley was very attached to Susan, haunted by a childhood fear of abandonment and rejection, he, too, was also deeply jealous and possessive. He had always been this way with the women in his life, but, ironically, the moment they exhibited reciprocal feelings, he tended to retreat.

Until then, only two of Dudley's numbers had ever been given lyrics. Now Susan began writing words for more of them in an attempt to encourage his writing. Her favorite was "Patrick," a haunting melody he had composed years earlier for his son.

Susan had been another strong influence on Dudley's decision to perform in public. She had been pushing him almost since they had met, believing strongly that it was what he needed to do to feel more creatively fulfilled.

While Susan performed in Las Vegas and other cities across the country and Dudley flew to be with her, he was seeing more of the United States than ever before. Ruth Forman often drove him to the airport in her black Jeep. Many times she suggested arranging a limo, but, as she recalls, "he was just as happy having me take him in my Jeep or in his BMW. At the airport he'd go scurrying off carrying his own bag, and I often watched him and thought, 'Doesn't he realize how rich and famous he is?' He could easily have hired a limo and had someone carry his bag for him." While he was away, Ruth tended the house and looked after the tiny Pekingese, Kong, whom Dudley had inherited from Tuesday.

Meanwhile, *Arthur* was now roughly assembled and a private screening was held for the cast. Dudley didn't like the film. "Who wants to see this drunken idiot for an hour and a half?" he asked when the lights went up.

Steve Gordon had several different endings and couldn't make up his mind which one he wanted, but there was a consensus that the present one definitely needed to be changed. In Dudley's opinion, that was not all that needed to be altered.

As Liza Minnelli recalls, "Steve had cut the film so that it was now mostly about the friendship between Arthur and Hobson. There was no dramatic tension between the prince and princess. The Cinderella story wasn't there any more. Dudley went to Steve and said, 'Unless you put her back in the film, we're fucked. We don't have a story, we just have a lot of gags, and it doesn't work. You're not trusting your own instincts.' He went in there and really fought for me. He went to bat not only for Linda but for me. And Steve listened."

Shortly after that, they returned to New York to reshoot scenes. Dudley took Susan with him, and they stayed in the Waldorf Astoria. During one lunch break the two of them went back to the hotel. Dudley had just shot the scene where he had told everyone in the church to go home, there would be no wedding. The ensuing brawl with his jilted fiancée's father had left him with blood all over his face and a torn tuxedo. As Susan and Dudley were in the elevator to go up to their room, with Dudley still in full makeup and tattered clothes, a group of people stepped inside and joined them. "Dudley turned to me," recalls Susan, "and said in this forlorn voice, 'Susan, I told you I'd be home. Why wouldn't you believe me?' The implication was that I had beaten him up. I'll never forget the looks on those people's faces! It was very, very funny."

Early in March, Dudley flew to London for a week to see his mother and Barbara. He also caught up with his old trio mates, Peter Morgan and Chris Karan, who tried desperately to persuade him into another jazz tour. Their urgings were in vain: Dudley now had too many commitments in America.

In April, Dudley began preparing for his upcoming concert at the Hollywood Bowl, and as a promotional boost, he appeared at the press luncheon that traditionally kicked off the summer season. In front of local TV cameras, he cut the Los Angeles Philharmonic's sixtieth-anniversary cake with Ernest Fleischman and, ever the musician-cum-clown, mugged for the cameras, pretending to slit Fleischman's throat.

A few weeks later Dudley wrote to Suzy. "I wish I was living a little nearer," he told her, "so that I could say hello more often and tell you how much I think about you and hope for your happiness and safety. You are always going to be of enormous importance in my life, and I know that Susan realizes this, too," he reassured her.

Dudley's feelings toward other people in his life was still something of a bone of contention between him and Susan. She was as possessive as he was, and sometimes Dudley liked that. But now he was beginning to feel overwhelmed. There had been a mild confrontation about this, but Susan had now accepted that he was not prepared to sacrifice his past friendships and relationships. Dudley never took such understanding for granted. He knew the work that went into resolving these inner issues, and he was impressed by her efforts to overcome her jealousy, admiring her for clearing what he knew was a difficult psychological hurdle.

With the release of *Arthur* only a short time away, Dudley and Susan grabbed two weeks' vacation on Bora Bora. They were looking forward to total privacy but discovered, passing through Tahiti, that *10* had just opened there. The paparazzi followed them from Papeete to Bora Bora, where Susan "freaked out" when a press gang turned up outside their hotel room. It was hardly the most isolated of vacations after all, although after Dudley organized an impromptu photo session and posed for pictures, they were mostly left alone.

They had arranged to rent what they had been told was Marlon Brando's house and were looking forward to an exotic paradise. Instead they were confronted by a tiny shack, with nothing else in sight but three other similar shacks on stilts and the local airport with planes constantly landing and taking off. After a few days they gave up and moved to the Hotel Bora Bora on the other side of the island. The Brando house turned out to be simply a place where the actor had once stayed, which some enterprising travel agent now rented to any unsuspecting fool who fell for this sales pitch.

They discovered Bloody Mary's, a restaurant where they went every day to eat barbecued lobster or the best seviche they'd ever tasted. It was run by a crazy islander with an artificial eye who regaled them with outrageous stories about his deep-sea adventures and who seemed, to them, very Hemingwayesque.

Dudley and Susan adored Bora Bora and spent most of their time swimming and sunbathing. Dudley had brought with him his small portable keyboard and he assiduously practiced *Rhapsody in Blue* for the upcoming Gershwin concert. After two blissful weeks they returned to the real world, refreshed by their vacation and feeling closer than ever.

In New York there was a screening of *Arthur* just before its release. Leslie Bricusse recalls, "I was sitting between Dudley and Liza, and they were nervous as kittens. They didn't know for one second whether it was at all funny, and I sat there pissing myself for two hours. I told them it was one of the funniest movies I'd ever seen, but they just didn't know. Comedy is a very difficult thing to define, and neither of them thought it worked."

Francis Megahy also recalls attending a private screening just before the opening. "Nobody laughed," he recalls, "and they didn't seem to care for it at all. When it was over there was a gloomy atmosphere in the theater. Later, there was a party at an agent's house and everybody wanted to talk about everything but the film."

In June, Dudley embarked on a major publicity tour for *Arthur*—during which his publicist, Paul Bloch, made sure there was a piano in every one of the hotel rooms in which he stayed across America. In July the film had its Los Angeles premiere. Despite the extraordinary success it went on to enjoy, it opened to very mixed reviews.

In the opinion of the *New Yorker*, "Gordon's pacing is ragged, he has a pretty feeble sense of structure but it squeaks by. Considering that Arthur is a very thin comic construct, Moore does an amazing amount with the role...[but] Minnelli is an idea that doesn't work."

The *Village Voice* called it "an impeccably witty, consummately acted movie as long as Moore and Gielgud are on screen...[Their] timing has never seemed so right, so breathtaking... [But] the film is a gaudy, semi-precious setting with two crown jewels at its center."

However, the *Hollywood Reporter* declared, "One of the things that makes it all work so well is Moore. His great sense of comedy, including impeccable timing on delivery and reaction, gives the picture its momentum and style. His Arthur is probably the most lovable eccentric since Jimmy Stewart's Elwood Dowd in *Harvey*."

Vincent Canby, writing in the *New York Times*, also praised Dudley, considering him "if possible, more uninhibitedly comic than he was in *10*. His Arthur is an overage waif and a consistently endearing showoff. His timing is magical."

The public reception seemed unprecedented. From the moment *Arthur* hit the screens, it became a runaway success. Audiences had been starved of this kind of updated screwball comedy, and it became the surprise hit of the summer of 1981. In time it would join that exclusive club of movies to gross more than $100 million.

A week after the opening of *Arthur*, Dudley stepped on stage at the Hollywood Bowl to make his American orchestral debut. With Michael Tilson Thomas conducting, Dudley played *Rhapsody in Blue*, and was greeted with tumultuous applause, and some surprise, by the almost twenty thousand people present, most of whom had no idea that Dudley was a musician. He liked it that way. He liked to come from behind as an actor who also played the piano. At the end of the concert, he gave them a taste of jazz in a set of Gershwin tunes Moore-style.

Lou Pitt recalls that Dudley's concerts were sellouts for both nights. "It was amazing. I watched this little guy in this huge amphitheater, and the sound that came out of him seemed so much larger than life. I think he felt more comfortable in a smaller, more intimate, setting but the audience was very responsive."

To Susan, the night was "a total triumph—especially what he did with Ray Brown and Nick Ceroli. That's when he really comes to life, in the jazz."

But there were mixed reactions to his *Rhapsody* from the critics.

The *Los Angeles Herald Examiner* proclaimed his playing "as stiff and self-conscious as if he were practicing Czerny exercises and the orchestral work nearly always overwhelmed him." Another critic "soon felt Moore's musical limits" and considered that his sense of phrasing "became oppressively predictable." In the opinion of the *Herald Examiner* critic, he was an inspired satirist and a man of many talents, "but he is not a pianist of the caliber who should perform professionally with the L.A. Philharmonic."

Dudley's dismay at the critics' lukewarm reception was overshadowed by his pleasure at the enthusiastic audience response. He said he was too old to care what critics thought. But of course he did care very much, and was disheartened that he had failed to impress the reviewers. But his disappointment was soon to be tempered by the extraordinary success of *Arthur*.

He wrote to his mother a few days later, having already telephoned her with an account of the concert. She was proud of his success as an actor, but it was his classical music achievements that gave her the greatest pride and pleasure.

Regardless of the critics—or perhaps because of them—Dudley's performing fervor had now taken a hold. He was, at last, taking heed of Artur Schnabel's reference to "playing with love and patience." Dudley had always had the love but only now the patience to break things down slowly and go over each piece, practicing in a way he had never done before.

In the middle of July he flew with Susan to Japan, where she was to film a series of commercials. It was their second trip there together. While they were there they visited a fountain shrine in which water spouted out of a carved statue in the center. They watched the Japanese visitors reach for a copper ladle, take a scoop of water, sip it, and then throw the remaining water gently on the statue as a form of respect. Susan took a sip from her ladle and threw the water toward the statue, but somehow she missed it completely and instead sprayed a group of people standing opposite. "The two of us cracked up," she laughs, "and we ran out of there in a real hurry, because we'd clearly lost face."

Early in August, Dudley wrote again to his mother. *Arthur*, he told her, was doing well "and we're keeping our fingers crossed that it will sustain through the summer and be what they call in the industry 'a hit.' And as I have a small percentage of the film I hope to reap some reward from this financial success!" He told her he would be in London the following month with Susan, and asked her to expect them both for tea.

As Dudley had a percentage of the profits of *Arthur*, it was not surprising that his diary records weekly box-office takings during those opening months of the movie. He had inherited something of his mother's meticulous logging of every penny she spent or expected to receive, and kept very close tabs on how the film was faring financially.

He now had total approval over script, director, and cast for his future films—something he found slightly alarming, because he seldom trusted his instincts and felt incapable of making good judgments. This also meant that he frequently sat in on casting sessions for his upcoming movies—which was another way of meeting people and making friends. During one of these sessions he met Olivia Newton-John, and when she opened her Australian import boutique, Koala Blues, on Melrose Avenue, he turned up to wish her luck.

Despite his romance with Susan Anton, his eye was still sometimes caught by an attractive girl—especially one with an overbite—and there were quite a few dinners around this time with many new friends, among them Margot Kidder, who had played Superman's love interest, Lois Lane, in the 1978 movie.

Brenda Vaccaro recalls talking with Dudley at one of her parties when Anjelica Huston suddenly walked past. "He went nuts. This was long before she was a star, at a time when no one had taken note of her beauty. But he saw how sexy and beautiful she was. He was so cute as he looked at her, and he went running after her as if he could just take a bite out of her. He was crazy about her."

The transformation of Dudley was complete. He was now a fully fledged international movie star who, as the tabloids were fond of saying, had the unlikely distinction of being worth almost more per inch than any other star in Hollywood. It wasn't bad for a kid from Dagenham whose greatest wish as a youth was to have enough money to buy a bike. Now he could have the most expensive bike in the world if he wanted. But he didn't. He didn't particularly yearn for material things. What he yearned for was love.

His relationship with Susan Anton was deeply rooted, but, though he may have wavered early on in their romance, Dudley was feeling very marriage-shy. He'd already been married twice, although he considered neither marriage to have been a failure—"They were just relationships which stopped. Why should things last forever?" They were, however, expensive relationships when they came to an end. His divorce settlement with Tuesday had not come cheaply. When Tuesday divorced her first husband, Claude Harz, an aspiring screenwriter, she had not asked him for money. "I don't see any reason for Claude to have the obligation of alimony hanging over his head," she had said at that time.

She was not as munificent when it came to a divorce from Dudley. Convinced by her lawyers that Dudley was worth over £2 million, Tuesday had embarked on an exhaustive investigation into his business affairs—at Dudley's expense. The financial wranglings lasted quite a while until ultimately they settled on a figure of $345,700, with a monthly allowance of $2000 for Patrick's support.

Although Dudley and Susan weren't living together, most of the time they were in each other's house. Their life was based on a need to be with each other, and yet it depended also on each being able to remain independent. But their very intimacy led to some brooding. Dudley was afraid that the more intimate they became, the greater would be the fear of being abandoned. They were both, he said, black holes of need, trying to come to terms with their possessiveness.

Although therapy no longer played as crucial a role in his life as it had in the past, he was still deeply introspective as he pondered his emotional makeup and scribbled random thoughts in his diaries. "I look for her weak spots, crawl in, and rock myself to sleep," he wrote across a blank page. "I need either a feather or a knife, depending on how I feel."

In September Dudley flew to London for press interviews for *Arthur*, and in the midst of a whirlwind series of receptions he dined with Roger Moore at Langan's and had lunch with Barbara and his mother.

Ada, now eighty-one, was feeling particularly nostalgic just then. Perhaps she had a premonition about what was to come. She pulled out photos of herself as a young girl, and studied old photo albums with Dudley. "I don't know why you say you were unhappy as a child," she told him. "Look at this picture of you." And she showed him one where he was smiling.

Dudley had never given up trying to pry details of his childhood out of Ada. "What *happened?*" he would ask her, but she always changed the subject. "Look at that bird out there," she would say, fixing her gaze beyond him out of the window, and that would be the end of that.

For years Dudley had been talking openly about his childhood and describing his mother as an undemonstrative woman. In so many media stories across the world she was described as cold and unloving, although this may have stemmed from journalistic interpretations of Dudley's struggling explanations. Ada had never once mentioned these allusions, never expressed to Dudley that she might have been hurt by these public remonstrations. "She was just like I am really," muses Dudley wistfully, "a gray little sparrow."

As he left her this time, Ada looked at him in a peculiar and obsessive way. It was as if she had to put everything into that look because it was the only way to express what she felt. They looked at each other, and she nodded as if to say, "I know what we feel for each other and there's no way of unraveling it or making good the bad parts. This is the best I can do."

In that brief look, Dudley felt that everything had been straightened out. "She sort of touched me, and I thought, 'That's it, folks. That's all I'm going to get and as far as I want to go.' I felt that was all I could expect from her, and actually all that I wanted, all that I'd been trained to expect from her."

It was almost the last time he would see her.

He flew to New York to see Patrick briefly, then returned to Los Angeles to begin preproduction on his next film, *Six Weeks*.

Soon after his return, a strange incident occurred in England when confidential medical files from a London clinic were discovered on a council garbage dump in Leicester by journalist Eddie Hudson and his fourteen-year-old son. Dudley's was among them.

The files should have been incinerated but had mistakenly been simply discarded. They contained laboratory test results on thousands of important people, including the Duchesses of Kent and Gloucester, the Prime Minister's husband, Denis Thatcher, John Cleese, Rudolph Nureyev, David Frost, former prime minister Edward Heath, and model Jean Shrimpton.

Dr. Jean Shanks, head of the clinic, insisted the discovery would not embarrass anybody, since all the notes were in chemical abbreviations and could only be read by medical people. Eddie Hudson, however, was able to decipher more than enough to realize the files contained intimate and embarrassing details, none of which he ever revealed, that included test results for drug addiction and alcoholism, pregnancy tests, and venereal disease.

Amid all the furor, Dudley joked to the London papers that his medical records would make fascinating reading and he hoped people would find something in them of interest. Apparently they didn't. Dr. Shanks apologized publicly and the whole affair died a quiet death.

In mid-October, on Susan Anton's birthday, Ada Moore went into the hospital for blood tests. Dudley kept in close touch with the hospital and his sister Barbara while rehearsing scenes for *Six Weeks* at MGM Studios. When Ada took a turn for the worse the next day, Dudley flew quickly to London to see her in the hospital. The doctors told him she had suffered a series of small strokes years before without ever realizing it. Now the consequent damage was taking its toll.

Ada's father had been a faith healer, and Dudley decided to try that skill, hoping it might suddenly make her better. He put his hand on her head and pressed down. She knew what he was doing but indicated that it wasn't helping. "She was very nervous," he remembers, "like she knew she was dying." He stayed overnight in London, then returned to Los Angeles to begin filming.

He was now a major Hollywood movie star and had all the acclamation he had longed for during his entire life, but he was about to lose the woman who had done more than any other to shape his life, with all its ambition, fears, and years of inner loneliness.

Three days later, Ada Francis Moore died.

CHAPTER 18

S I X   W E E K S

1981-1982

"I always believed if he had let himself fully go he would have come through the other side. But he always said he was afraid that if he really let go and started crying, he wouldn't be able to stop and he would end up disappearing in his own puddle of tears."

—SUSAN ANTON

Dudley flew home for the funeral with Susan by his side.

His mother had been the most important influence in his life, but his reaction to her death was confusion. As Dudley gazed down at her body lying peacefully in the Dagenham funeral home, he didn't know what to feel or think.

Later that day he and Susan drove over to the house to pick up his sister, Barbara, and her husband, Bernard, before going on to the church. The sight that confronted them was like a scene from a Fellini movie. The street was lined with people, all there presumably to see Dudley, the celebrity, come home. Dudley and Susan were so astonished that, as they sat in their rental car at the end of the road watching the solemn line of neighbors, they began giggling hysterically. It took them so long to regain their composure that when they finally entered the house, Bernard berated them for their lateness.

At the funeral service in St. Peter's church, Dudley, who had cried like a baby at his father's funeral, remained dry-eyed throughout. His reaction puzzled him. He couldn't understand it. Nor did he play the organ as he had for his father. It was almost as if he'd been prompted by his mother to play at his father's service, and then when she had gone, there was no one left to prompt him to play for her.

As the minister was extolling Ada Moore to the mourners, a bemused Dudley whispered to Susan, "I don't know this person he's talking about!" and suddenly he burst into giggles, made all the more difficult to contain by the need to hide them from the rest of the congregation. The next day the newspapers noted that Dudley was so saddened during the ceremony that his shoulders heaved with uncontrollable sobs. Sometimes, as Susan Anton often observed, when Dudley was in a lot of pain, he expressed it through laughter. In a sense, that has been the story of his life. Still, his reaction at his mother's funeral was a bizarre coincidence. Ten years earlier, as Dudley, his mother, and Suzy Kendall arrived outside the church for his father's funeral service, the three of them burst into hysterical laughter for no reason at all, giggling uncontrollably until the sound of the choir burst from the church and froze their blood.

The inheritance that Ada Moore bequeathed to her son came not with her death but during her lifetime. Unintentionally she had left him with a multitude of emotions from which he would never be entirely free. His need for isolation, his fear of rejection and abandonment, his perpetual need for love—all stemmed from the anguish of his childhood.

Susan Anton believes that "Dudley had learned to put out a specific character as his way of existing in the world. But he really was two people. One was the comical, jolly, friendly fellow who had permission to travel anywhere in the world. The other, and the message Ada gave him, was this little damaged boy with a clubfoot who'd better stay home because he was not accepted."

Yet, with all the negatives, Dudley had inherited two positive traits from his mother without which his life would be very different today—the gifts of music and of humor. Ada was never conscious that she was being funny, but Dudley picked up on her innocent wit and honed it into a craft. Once, when he called her from Hollywood and said, "Hello, Mum," she asked who was speaking. "There are only two people in the world who can say 'Hello, Mum' to you," he told her, "and only one of them has a baritone voice." "Sorry," she replied, "I can't hear you too well. Hold on while I get my other glasses."

After Ada's funeral Dudley remained in London for a few days during which he worked a little and recorded a variety show, "An Audience with Dudley Moore," for ITV, with guests Lulu, Shirley Bassey, and Tom Conti. Then it was back to Los Angeles for *Six Weeks*, the first dramatic film of his twenty-two-year career as a performer.

Six Weeks was a moving story about the last weeks in the life of a dying girl, and Dudley had been looking forward to it for a long time, but a six-month Hollywood strike, coupled with a long search for the right director, had delayed production. It was the only time, other than with *Arthur*, that

Dudley, after reading the script, had called his agent and told him he absolutely had to make this movie. Other people had been keen to do the film, too. Nick Nolte and Audrey Hepburn were to have starred in it at one point, and, just before the script came to Dudley, Sylvester Stallone had been set to play the lead.

Tony Bill, a hot young director who had won considerable acclaim with his first feature, *My Bodyguard*, and who had coproduced *The Sting* and *Taxi Driver*, was hired to direct the $9 million film. He was delighted by Dudley's passion for the project and excited at the idea of showing a serious side of the actor that audiences hadn't seen before.

In *Six Weeks*, Dudley plays a married Congressional candidate, Patrick Dalton, who befriends thirteen-year-old ballet student, Nicky Dreyfus (Katherine Healy), and subsequently her rich cosmetics-tycoon mother, Charlotte (Mary Tyler Moore). When Dalton learns Nicky is dying of leukemia yet is bent on helping to get him elected, he allows her to work on his campaign. Gradually they all fall in love.

Dalton leaves his own family and Nicky "marries" him to her mother. When Patrick discovers that she has sacrificed her greatest hope—to dance Clara in *The Nutcracker* at the Lincoln Center—in order to campaign for him, he arranges for it to happen after all. That night, after achieving her dream, Nicky dies. Her life has been short, but very full, and the message is clear: There need be no boundaries to the realization of dreams.

It was a heart-wrenching and sweet story, written by David Seltzer and produced by Peter Guber and Jon Peters, who were on their way to becoming one of Hollywood's most powerful producing teams. Despite its tragic conclusion, it was uplifting and filled with joy and humor (although audiences ultimately would disagree). Dudley adored the story, and it would elicit some of his best and most natural work as an actor. He was drawn to its theme about the urgency of living, and saw in its enthusiasm for life a message of optimism.

Mary Tyler Moore was America's sweetheart. She had risen through television sitcoms, first with Dick Van Dyke and then with her own shows. Since her highly praised dramatic performance in Robert Redford's *Ordinary People*, she had read mediocre scripts for two years before being offered *Six Weeks*.

The first day of filming was a party scene, and she turned up wearing high heels that nobody liked. "I didn't want to wear flats," she said defensively, "in case anybody thought I was trying to accommodate Dudley's size."

Mary adored her costar with the same surname. "He was hysterically funny," she recalls. "Off camera he was wondrously entertaining and bright. On camera he was a wonderfully talented dramatic actor. I wasn't surprised, but I was very impressed."

Dudley found Mary creative and electric. He had always felt the best thing that could be said of any performer was that they were able to reciprocate thought and emotion. He felt that way about Mary.

Tony Bill was enthused by his two Moores. He knew he was in for a good time, and he wasn't wrong. With Mary playing a fairly somber role, it helped that Dudley kept her laughing and relaxed much of the time. They had a lot of fun together, and that grew throughout the picture until they became practically a comic team.

Tony Bill was just the kind of director with whom Dudley liked to work. Bill believed in allowing his actors to get on with their job without interference, and yet he encouraged a collaborative effort and Dudley enjoyed the team spirit that existed on the film. Sometimes he suggested dialogue changes for his character, and found Bill and writer David Seltzer receptive to his input.

Though he was deeply moved by the relationship between the characters, Tony Bill was also very concerned about the way it would be received. He was continually afraid that the film would be either too sentimental or too much of a downer, and he took immense pains to avoid oversentimentality.

Dudley had never before had a script that dealt with life as honestly as this. In a curious way, he considered the theme similar to that of *Arthur*. Arthur had wanted to have a tremendous amount of fun every second, and *Six Weeks* also was about grabbing hold of life and enjoying the moment.

Ballet dancer Katherine Healy, as young Nicky, made the most of her opportunity, bringing to the role a maturity, humor, and perception unusual for a girl of her age. She adored working with the two Moores, neither of whom she had heard of before this film, but was rather baffled by a tiny device that Dudley kept hidden in his hand.

Any film set that Dudley worked on was guaranteed to be full of fun and laughter. But one thing he tended not to do was perform practical jokes. He felt it took massive advantage of people, and it reminded him of things that had been done to him. The exception was HandiGas. Dudley had recently discovered this small rubber-accordion fart machine, and he unleashed the new toy on his unsuspecting colleagues with irrepressible glee. Tony Bill collected so many takes of Dudley at play that he assembled an outtake reel in which the fart machine was the main star.

The tiny gadget was so popular that Dudley had the manufacturers ship them to him by the carton, and he passed out dozens to the entire company. Mary Tyler Moore had some made in silver that she gave as farewell gifts to the cast and crew.

Susan Anton first encountered Dudley's new toy while they were staying in a hotel. They had ordered room service, and the waiter was uncovering the platters, when Susan suddenly heard "all these amazing farts. Dudley just kept on with the waiter—'Thank you, I'll sign for it.' Pff ... fkk! 'This looks lovely.' Erg ... fik! I couldn't believe it. I thought, 'My God, he's farting all over the place in front of this person! What is going on here? Even Dudley can't fart that much.' It was hilarious! Finally the guy left and Dudley showed me the toy."

From then on, Susan, Dudley, and HandiGas were inseparable. One night they went to the movies to watch *Ordinary People* and sat in front of two old ladies who clearly had been expecting to see the Mary Tyler Moore of her TV sitcoms. "She's not at all like Mary Richards!" one of the women yelled at the screen, whereupon, Susan recalls, "Dudley let out the biggest fart you've ever heard. Those poor little women were so disgusted they got out of their seats and left the cinema."

Throughout the filming of *Six Weeks* Dudley kept an electric piano in his trailer dressing room, and during breaks he used it to practice for his next concert, in New York in January. He was filming continuously now and was having to get up at three in the morning in order to practice his music.

Christmas was spent in a frenzy of filming, practicing, and sending gifts to friends he was too busy to see, but he found the time to give two very special presents. One was a $135,000 full-length sable coat for Susan. The other was a particularly memorable gift to his agent of six years, Lou Pitt.

Arthur had resulted in every other agent trying to lure Dudley away from Pitt and ICM. Dudley decided to publicize his feelings to the industry and, enlisting publicist Paul Bloch's help in the wording, he took a full page in the trade papers thanking Lou in poignant terms for his support, friendship, and efforts.

Lou Pitt had seen many things during his years as a Hollywood agent and little surprised him anymore. But Dudley's ad shook him to the core. Nobody had ever done anything like that before. Pitt was a private man who kept his personal feelings very much to himself. This was something everyone in the world could see, and when he read it he was frozen in shock. "I read it about ten times," he remembers, "and then I called Dudley. I was a gibbering idiot. I didn't know what to say to this man who meant so much to me and who was obviously saying I meant something to him and in so public a way. It was the most moving moment in our professional life."

Their relationship took on an added dimension after that. Ruth Forman, now about to bow out of Dudley's life as his secretary, was impressed by the depth of their friendship. "They were like brothers. Dudley loved Lou and trusted him, and Lou was as fine a human being as you could ever meet and he was devoted to Dudley. He really loved him, and there was nothing he wouldn't have done for him."

Ruth now had more work than she could handle. Dudley was receiving masses of fan mail, which she found impossible to keep up with because he insisted on answering every letter individually. She brought in her cousin, Sam Veta, to assist, and eventually Sam took over, remaining with Dudley for the next fourteen years.

Peter Cook's American television series, *The Two Of Us*, in which he played an upper-crust butler, had now debuted on American television. Dudley had made sure he would not miss it by jotting a reminder in his diary and underlining it twice, but when he watched the show, he was disappointed that it failed to make full use of Cook's talents. It seemed to him that Peter also had trouble speaking some of the lines, but then he had never been particularly good at remembering words that he had not written himself. The series was greeted with a less-than-rave reaction, which gave the British critics cause once more to examine Cook's career since his breakup with Dudley.

Peter did not view Hollywood as a good place to live unless one was driven by ambition to be successful. He was not, he claimed. "Dudley's ambition is much stronger," he said then. In truth, Peter's passion for success was immense, and exceeded only by his passion for alcohol, to which he'd now returned. While Dudley, Peter noted, had always been on the verge of enormous happiness, he, Cook, considered happiness to be one of the great delusions of living. It was an interesting observation from a man whose own demons would never be fully exposed nor even discussed by himself except in the most sardonic and cursory manner.

Late on New Year's Eve, Dudley flew with Susan to New York. They stayed at the Waldorf Towers while he prepared for his New York classical debut two days away, practicing with Robert Mann on New Year's Day at his apartment. It was reminiscent of all the times they had played there over the years. Those evenings, according to Dudley, had been "glorious battle-fields strewn with dismembered notes," although Mann's recollection is of many remarkable musical achievements. Then it had been for fun. Now it was for real.

If Dudley was nervous, he showed no sign of it the next night when he walked on to the stage of the Metropolitan Museum's Grace Rainey Rogers Auditorium. His New York debut was in front of one of the toughest musical audiences in America, but he was determined not to feel intimidated. This was, after all, what he most enjoyed doing—playing music. "Just remember you enjoy it," he reassured himself as he took his seat at the huge Bosendorfer grand piano. With him were Robert Mann on violin, Stanley Drucker on clarinet, and Joel Krosnick on cello.

They played Bach, Mozart, Bartok, and Delius, and at the end of the evening the audience let Dudley know he had not embarrassed himself. Their long applause acclaimed a highly proficient pianist. The *New York Times* wrote the next day, "He neither advanced the cause of music nor caused himself one moment of disgrace," and the *Washington Post* conceded, "He played well if not exuberantly."

Susan Anton was thrilled and proud. Her man had proven to New York what she had known all along, and she saw in him a certain elation that he had taken on the task and accomplished it. "There's always unfinished business when you're an artist at the level he is," she reflects, and you never reach a place where you say it was perfect. But Dudley always lived in fear of other people's opinions, and I think unfortunately that always dictated too much to him. He didn't allow himself to fully enjoy anything, because he was always waiting for the arrows through the heart. Especially with his music."

Dudley had now achieved a goal that he had never believed he could reach. Early in his twenties he had thought he would always be too nervous and technically inadequate ever to become a concert musician. Now he knew he'd been wrong.

Music these days was uppermost in his mind, and back in Los Angeles the following night he began writing the music for *Six Weeks*, which would take him through much of the summer of 1982. Lou Pitt had, to the producers' excitement, suggested that Dudley score the film, but he had taken some persuading. Not counting *The Hound of the Baskervilles*, which he had mainly improvised in 1977, he had not scored a film since *30 Is a Dangerous Age, Cynthia*, thirteen years earlier.

Writing the *Six Weeks* score did not come easily, and evoked emotional memories of his own childhood and the mother he had so recently lost. Also, as Susan Anton recalls, "a lot of his confusion and heartache over Patrick was engulfed in that score. He always drove himself crazy worrying if he could be a good father or give Patrick enough love."

Dudley cried a lot while he was composing *Six Weeks*. He was deeply moved by what he was writing, and felt for one of the rare times in his life that he was doing a good job. Getting it out was a mixture of "absolute bliss and absolute hell." Sometimes it became so emotional for him that he would go upstairs to Susan, tears still wet on his cheek, and tell her in his little-boy voice, "I's scared Susan." "I know you're scared," she answered, "but it's all right." A particularly sensitive eight-bar refrain that recurs throughout the score expressed, to him, his entire life.

The music he wrote could never be a complete release for his emotions, Dudley said; it could never fully illuminate his huge darkroom of memories. But it must have helped. The score he ultimately produced was haunting and exquisite and quite simply the best musical work he ever created.

Tony Bill believes Dudley rose to real heights and excelled himself. "But I think he burned himself out on it. He hasn't done a score since. He put so much into it that he never tried it again, and I don't think he ever felt that passionately again about anything else."

Sadly, the poignant score was overlooked when the film was later released and, like the movie, was virtually dismissed by audiences and critics alike. It would be one of the greatest disappointments of Dudley's career.

Six Weeks was not only memorable for Dudley's exquisite score; it was also where a young extra called Brogan Lane met him for the first time. Although they scarcely talked, it registered with Dudley that she was "incredibly beautiful." They would meet again four years later.

In February 1982, when the Academy Award nominations were announced, his work in *Arthur* found Dudley up for a Best Actor Oscar alongside Henry Fonda, Warren Beatty, Burt Lancaster, and Paul Newman. Sir John Gielgud was nominated for Best Supporting Actor, and Burt Bacharach's music for *Arthur* was also shortlisted. Liza Minnelli was not.

Dudley, who was stunned and excited by the accolade, was disappointed that Liza had been overlooked. For her part, she felt much as Michael York had felt when he'd been ignored for his work in *Cabaret* while Liza and Joel Grey both won nominations, and subsequently the Oscars. "I felt I'd done a good job," she muses, "I *knew* I did a good job—and in a funny kind of way that was enough. I also knew it was Dudley's time. It hurt my feelings, but it was fine because I knew I'd done such good work. And I was so proud of Dudley and John."

Before the Oscars were awarded, *Arthur* also received other accolades. Dudley won the Golden Globe as Best Actor for his performance (it was third time lucky for him, after losing for *Foul Play* and *10*), and he was presented with the award by Susan Anton. "That was fun," she recalls, "because we were all sure he would win. *Arthur* won a lot of awards that night, and afterwards we all went to a big party at Chasen's with Steve Gordon."

Dudley always found himself responding to specific emotions in a film script, as he did with his music. He was attracted to joy, tenderness, compassion, and humor, and saw sadness and humor as interlaced. He had learned that comedy was simply another side of drama, and whenever he had been faced with great pain, his tendency had usually been to laugh—as at his mother's funeral. He was drawn very much toward characters who wanted to enjoy themselves no matter what the circumstances against them, and to those who seemed to be breaking out of their mold—perhaps because he himself had spent a lifetime trying to break free of the restraints and expectations that society had put on him through class and physical appearance. His next movie encompassed all that he found most appealing.

In February 1982 Dudley began work in New York on *Lovesick*, another film that had taken a vastly long time to bring in front of the cameras. Dudley had contracted to make it two years earlier, just before leaving on his European tour to promote *10*. It had originally been titled *Valium*, but it ran into legal difficulties over the use of the drug's name.

Lovesick was written and directed by Marshall Brickman, who had been Woody Allen's collaborator on *Sleeper, Annie Hall,* and *Manhattan.* Some years earlier Peter Sellers had agreed to star in *Lovesick,* and Brickman still has a cassette recording of Sellers practicing some scenes as a Viennese psychiatrist educated in England. But Sellers died, and along came Dudley.

Paired with him was young Elizabeth McGovern, who had won immense acclaim—and an Oscar nomination—in Milos Forman's *Ragtime* the previous year. Brickman had wanted her from the start. She was an original and gifted actress with a wonderfully expressive voice, and she and Dudley melded delightfully on screen.

In *Lovesick* Dudley plays a married and very successful Manhattan psychoanalyst who inherits a new patient, an earnest young playwright (McGovern), when her own therapist dies. Falling in love with this nubile patient, he becomes a victim of his obsession and experiences ghostly visits by Freud (Alec Guinness), who feeds him mostly useless advice. In desperation he seeks the help of his eminent teacher (John Huston). Threatened with expulsion from the exclusive group of psychoanalytic bigwigs, he ultimately renounces them in favor of his love for McGovern.

It was a charming story, and one that the critics largely enjoyed. Audiences, however, were not too amused by a comedy about an affair between a psychoanalyst and his patient, and the film bombed.

Dudley was not an actor who immersed himself in endless research before starting a new role. Had he been, this was one film that would hardly have necessitated a visit to the local library. Dudley's entire life provided more than enough background for any film about psychoanalysis.

Marshall Brickman, who saw Dudley as a romantic leading man in the vein of Marcello Mastroianni, Jean-Paul Belmondo, and Cary Grant, found him eager to please. "He's a performing animal who loves to give people pleasure," says Brickman, "whether it's through laughter or music or just listening. Very different from Woody Allen, who always anguished when he had to perform."

A nervous and fairly inexperienced Elizabeth McGovern was acutely aware that she was working opposite one of the hottest actors in America, but Dudley put her at ease from the start. "He was a very warm person who liked people to like him," she recalls, "and they certainly did. He was very easy to be around, and had a way of making everyone feel good. He was very generous in that regard, and there was a sweetness and kindness about him that was very special.

"He had this manner of convincing you he didn't take it all that seriously, and that was really good for me, because I was so intense about everything. It taught me to lighten up."

John Huston at this time was seriously ill with emphysema and was constantly hooked up to a portable oxygen machine, which was disconnected for filming his scenes. Everyone found this extremely alarming, although it seemed not to impinge on the work.

Dudley had been particularly excited at the prospect of working with Sir Alec Guinness. Ever since he'd seen his classic first film, *Great Expectations*, he had admired the actor. He had even fantasized about him "as the brother I had never had." But Guinness spent most of his time in between scenes on *Lovesick* alone in his trailer.

"Guinness was a legend," says Marshall Brickman, "and nobody knew what to call him. Should it be 'Sir Alec,' 'Mr. Guinness,' or what? Finally it deteriorated to 'Alec.' He was wonderful to work with and meticulous about being Freud. He even asked me for a photograph he could study."

Dudley and Sir Alec, coming from such disparate acting traditions, never really connected, although they respected each other a great deal. When they had to retake shots, Dudley always did something different, whereas Guinness redid the same take every time. Muses Elizabeth McGovern, "Dudley was more spontaneous, but Alec worked at his performance very carefully and did not like a lot of improvisation, so it was difficult for them to find common ground."

Lovesick was a typical Dudley Moore set, full of humor and music. Brickman, who likens directing a movie to a bad baseball game—"with a lot of waiting around and then a bit of action and then more waiting"—admired Dudley's attitude. "He understood how everybody's best work occurs in an atmosphere of ease and fun, and he always went about creating that mood on the set."

It was his humor—sometimes very scatological—that took young Elizabeth McGovern by surprise. "His HandiGas gadget was impossible, and people on the set loved it that here was this hottest movie star in America who could be so crude. It just warmed us all up."

Brickman, whose job it was to ensure order in the chaos, was just as amused by Dudley's running gag. "In the middle of intense emotional love scenes there'd be this sound of breaking wind and we'd have to stop the camera. He'd apologize profusely, then do it again. And each time he said, 'I'm sorry, I promise I won't do it this time.' And it just got funnier and funnier. It was his way of being an irrepressible imp and loosening everybody. He couldn't help himself. He was five years old."

Nevertheless, in the midst of the humor, there were moments of tension. For one shot, Brickman described to Dudley how Spencer Tracy and Katharine Hepburn had played a scene and said that was what he wanted to capture here. "For God's sake," retorted Dudley, "I'm not Spencer Tracy, and if you wanted him you should have got someone who was." The spat was brief. Both men liked and respected each other enormously, and almost immediately they were apologizing profusely.

If Dudley was occasionally feeling tense during the filming of *Lovesick*, it was understandable. He was still working on the *Six Weeks* score, and it was draining his emotional energy. Yet the best moments for Elizabeth McGovern were those times when Dudley played the keyboard in his trailer. "It was so nice to sit and listen to him. He was very serious about his music in a way that he didn't seem to be about the movie business, and he worked very hard at it, which I didn't feel he did with acting." As Marshall Brickman fondly asserts, "It was the perfect way of earning a living—to have Dudley, the classical pianist, play music while we were setting up a new shot. It was wonderful."

Sometimes Dudley's son, Patrick, who was living with Tuesday Weld in New York, came to visit the set. He was a serious and intense little boy. He was also very musical, and listened to music with an attention that was unusual for a six-year-old child.

It was on *Lovesick* that Dudley learned the one and only magic trick of his life. In one of the final scenes, during a dinner party, he had to whip off the tablecloth leaving behind all the dishes crammed with food. After a few lessons from a magician, to everyone's amazement he performed it successfully on the first take. Brickman, however, decided to do another for luck, and wryly remembers they were then there for the rest of the day. "Finally, on the thirty-second take, he did it again, and after all that I ended up using the first take."

Throughout the filming, rumors swirled around Dudley and Elizabeth, especially when they spent most of the wrap party reportedly smooching behind a pillar. The tabloids were convinced they were having an affair, but Dudley denied this. For all his openness, he could be extremely secretive and enigmatic when he chose. In fact they did have a brief romance during the making of the film, but it never strayed much beyond the confines of the set or the hotel where they stayed.

Although it was mostly Dudley's humorous side that Elizabeth witnessed, she had a hint of a darker emotion at work. "I felt he carried lots of pain with him but, like most comics, always worked very hard to be the life of the room and keep everybody laughing. I sensed a melancholia of a man a bit on the run, but I had no idea where it came from, because I never got to know him on that level."

Marshall Brickman was also aware of a deeper emotion, although it was never overt. "Dudley," he ponders, "was always so available, interested, eager, funny, and on that you had to stop and think, 'Hey, wait a moment, isn't this guy ever depressed?' I recognized in him a kind of rage that expressed itself in a comic way. Anyone with that range and that emotional palette has got to be vulnerable to melancholy and depression, because the best, as the poet said, are full of doubt."

He remembers walking into Dudley's trailer one day and finding his star furiously typing letters. "Some critics had written something nasty about him, and he was writing these angry, funny, crazy letters in response. I thought it was a great form of therapy."

Dudley often wrote such letters, but he never sent them. Certainly he became a prolific letter-writer during the filming of *Lovesick*. *Arthur* had recently opened in London, and some of the English critics not only were scathing toward the film but used the opportunity to attack Dudley personally.

Dudley repudiated one critic's assumption that he regarded his club-foot and shortness as "facets of distinction." "That is vacuous, sarcastic speculation," he wrote, "and if you have really ignorant remarks like that to make, do it to my face and not in your magazine where you can lurk without any real fear of retribution."

He attacked one critic's assertion that he had cornered the market in "screwed-up vulnerability during a lull in the Woody Allen industry," asking anyway what lull had occurred in Allen's career to accommodate his own rise.

And he was driven nuts by sarcastic references to his therapy. "You are," he responded, "trying to make me out to be some sort of deteriorating mental case, intoxicated by what plasticity California has to offer, as if there is absolutely nothing there apart from palm trees and mixed drinks, a trendy generality about California that seems to pervade the lowest common denominators in journalism."

Not unnaturally he resented "the constant insinuation that my mind is turning into oatmeal. Your remarks about 'mental regression accelerated by a promotion machine' are insulting and untrue. It's hard to believe the degree of personal insult flapping around your article and I'm quite appalled at this manic rejection. Your journalism twitches with contempt, venom, ignorance, snobbery, and patronization.

"I hope you will stew in this peculiar acid of yours," he concluded. "It would give me great pleasure to think of you wasting away in your own vitriol. You are an ignorant, supercilious prick."

The *Observer* critic declared of *Arthur* that, "a laugh-starved American public will clutch desperately at any comic straw they're offered," but Dudley questioned the implication that the American public was more laugh-starved than any other. "Your contempt and sarcasm really stink," he wrote, "and waft above every paragraph. When I feel this sort of disdain then I must return it to the sour owner. I reject your review as much as you reject this film."

As for that humorless critic's opinion that there was "no comic momentum and scarcely a single amusing line," Dudley was incensed. "Have some breakfast next time you review a film," he suggested and in an oblique conclusion warned him, "Never eat pie in my presence."

In April 1982 Dudley attended the Academy Awards as a Best Actor nominee for *Arthur* and performed onstage with Liza Minnelli. He had been somewhat embarrassed to be nominated with such distinguished veterans as Fonda, Lancaster, Beatty, and Newman, all of whom had been previously nominated, and was relieved to lose to Henry Fonda, who had given a poignant performance with his daughter Jane in *On Golden Pond.* Amazingly, Fonda had never won an Oscar before, and by then he was seriously ill. He died four months later.

Dudley did take an Oscar home that night, but it wasn't his own. John Gielgud had asked him, in the event of his winning Best Supporting Actor, to accept on his behalf, and carrying out this task gave Dudley as much pleasure as if he had won himself. He was thrilled that Gielgud's performance had been recognized.

Dudley was now one of the most popular Englishmen in the world. If in his heart he was short, in Hollywood he stood tall.

The earlier wave of British expatriates known as the Hollywood Raj generation of actors such as Ronald Colman, Douglas Fairbanks, and Basil Rathbone had now been replaced with a newer, younger British colony that included Michael Caine, Joan and Jackie Collins, Jacqueline Bisset, Leslie Bricusse, Jane Seymour, Malcolm McDowell, and Michael York. Dudley was friendly with them all, and yet he never quite became an intimate member of the clique.

Most Sundays Leslie Bricusse and Michael Caine would alternate in throwing open-house lunch for any Brits in town. Dudley was a welcome visitor, and the women, Bricusse recalls, absolutely adored him. "He was a phenomenal personality with a blasting humor and totally adorable and irresistible. He always played the piano, of course—usually jazz—and everyone loved that. It's what made Dudley tall." Bricusse captured these occasions on tape, and somewhere is a recording of Dudley playing piano duets with André Previn, each improvising his impressions of various jazz players, Dudley as Erroll Garner and Previn as Oscar Peterson.

Dudley did not miss England—a fact for which he felt slightly guilty whenever he saw other expats waving the Union Jack and showing off their royal wedding memorabilia. He sometimes felt compelled to compensate for this by wistfully longing for Cox's Orange Pippins and choral voices— as if expecting an attack from people who thought he had deserted his homeland. But his connection to any place tended to be the work he was able to do and the friends that he made. They were his motivations for wherever he went in the world.

Dudley's romance with Susan Anton was now hitting storm clouds.

He was beginning to feel restless again. They were, the Hollywood tabloids were eager to announce, now granting each other total freedom to be with other people. Dudley insisted he did not want to know if she went with someone else, nor would he tell her if he should be the one to stray. Faithfulness, he avowed, was something that should drop in on you, not something to be worked at. Even so, they seemed seldom to be out of each other's sight and could still make each other feel possessive. When Susan flew back from New York with Christopher Reeve, then at the height of his Superman fame, the two arrived in Los Angeles smiling and clearly enjoying each other's company. The papers made a good deal of this, interpreting Dudley's reaction when he met Susan at the airport as one of jealousy.

In July, Dudley began filming *Romantic Comedy* in New York and Los Angeles. The film was an adaptation by Bernard Slade of his 1979 Broadway play and tells of a successful and often boorish playwright who doesn't realize he's in love with his writing partner (Mary Steenburgen), nor that she loves him. Their timing is a mess: when he's married, she's not, and when he's not married, she is. Dudley described this as a story of unsynchronized passion—a Hemingway quote that alluded to the writer's love for Marlene Dietrich. Every time Hemingway was married, she wasn't, and whenever he wasn't married, Dietrich was.

Director Arthur Hiller brought with him considerable acclaim for his earlier films *Love Story*, *The Out of Towners*, and *Silver Streak* (written by Colin Higgins, who later directed *Foul Play*). As it happened, he had previously turned down *Romantic Comedy*, but he changed his mind when Dudley and Mary were signed to the film. He believed they would be a brilliant cinematic partnership, and he was not wrong.

They were an impressive trio of talent, and among them had amassed three Oscar nominations—Dudley for *Arthur*, Mary Steenburgen for *Melvin and Howard*, and Arthur Hiller for *Love Story*. Like Elizabeth McGovern, Dudley's costar in *Lovesick*, Steenburgen had also won critical acclaim for her role in *Ragtime*.

The location filming in hot, muggy New York meant that Dudley was again able to have Patrick with him on the set. Arthur and Mary were both struck by how warm and playful Dudley was with his son.

Hiller, who liked Dudley immediately, describes him as the man with two Ws—warmth and wit. He found him to be a very skilled actor, whose talent flowed out with ease. "He had considerable charm," says Hiller, "which is what made him so different and why audiences wouldn't and still won't let go of him. Some people are 'on' all the time, and you enjoy that to a point, but Dudley is on with such warmth and wit and charm that you just don't want him to stop."

Dudley enjoyed filming the comedy, which, in true Bernard Slade style, was more verbally than visually witty—something that had always appealed to Dudley. Off camera, however, his own humor extended toward pratfalls and slapstick. In one shot he had to make his exit walking up a staircase, and as soon as Hiller called "cut" he immediately reemerged and slid playfully down the banisters.

Dudley and Mary established an instant rapport that evolved into a deep friendship. Mary's problem on *Romantic Comedy* was not the role but her propensity for collapsing into uncontrollable giggles. She found her costar riotously funny, and admits unabashedly, "It was like unleashed hysteria to be around him."

Dudley—who later said of Mary, "give her a thimbleful of jocularity and she's like a drunk with a bottle"—was drawn instantly to her abundant love of laughter. He discovered very quickly how to make her break up and ruin a take, and one day he decided to set a target for the number of times he would do this.

"He decided he was going to make me ruin seventeen takes that day," recalls Mary, "but he had this incredibly innocent way of doing it, so nobody ever suspected him of anything and instead they thought I had lost my mind and was unprofessional because I couldn't stop laughing. It was total sabotage."

For one close-up she had to look romantically at Dudley, who was standing behind the camera. "He stared downwards, and stupidly I looked down to see what he was staring at, and he had unzipped his pants and had one of those erasers with a brush on the end poking out erect from his trousers. Of course I completely collapsed!"

In spite of all the ruined takes, Arthur Hiller considered the couple first-rate together. Sometimes he, too, found himself the butt of their humor. "They would tease me with the way I said, 'Ready, action!'" he recalls, "and after a while I dropped the 'Ready' part."

Actually, the word he should have dropped was *action*. As Mary ruefully remembers, "Dudley came to me and said, 'Have you ever noticed the way Arthur Hiller says "action"? It sounds like a sneeze.' I hadn't, of course, but the next minute Arthur said, 'Okay, let's see this shot. Ready, acshun!' And of course it did sound exactly like a sneeze, and there was silence for a second while I managed to hold it, and then I just dissolved into laughter."

Although Mary Steenburgen seemed carefree and responsive to Dudley's hilarity, she was privately going through a deeply painful time. Few people were aware that her marriage to Malcolm McDowell was falling apart, yet Dudley felt her deep unhappiness. "He was incredibly sensitive and understanding," Mary remembers, "and picked up on things that nobody else guessed at. That was a *really* sad period in my life, and I think part of my laughter with him was because it was a place I could go and have a wonderful time. He was an amazing and dear friend, and I'll always be grateful to him for that."

Romantic Comedy returned to Hollywood, where Dudley prepared to record the *Six Weeks* score. As soon as he finished a scene, he would dash outside the soundstage, where a car would be waiting to take him across to a dubbing theater on the other side of the MGM studio. There he mixed the score and tried new musical variations until Arthur Hiller called him back to the set.

As usual, Dudley was still working up to the last minute, and shortly before recording the score for *Six Weeks*, he was frantically rewriting a crucial transition for the strings. At the recording, he played the piano and shared conducting chores with Richard Hazard. He even managed to insert new bars of music into the score and write the instrumental parts on the spot.

Music editor Else Blangsted, who would become a lifelong friend, recalls the orchestra being so moved by his score that, in an unprecedented act, they presented Dudley with four dozen red roses on the final day.

During their months together on *Romantic Comedy*, Mary Steenburgen had glimpses beneath Dudley's humor and music. "I saw a hint of melancholia in him," she reflects, "and I always thought of him as one of those beautiful French clowns that are laughing and crying at the same time. One of the things that makes him so magical is that he shows you a certain amount of that. You see the part of him that's dark, as well as the part that's hilarious. Most people spend their entire lives masking the darkness, but Dudley was much more open about it and much more available. He's certainly one of the most complicated people I know, but definitely one of the most appealing."

Dudley and Mary were both wonderful in the film, but in the end it didn't entirely work—partly because the pace was uneven and sometimes irritatingly slow, and partly because many scenes never lost the feel of a stage play.

Dudley was tired now. He'd made four films in a row, and the novelty of starring in Hollywood movies had begun to wear off. The passion to work had abated.

In September, Scottish astrologer Darlinda predicted that Dudley's friendship with Peter Cook would find itself under a lot of strain because of a published remark made by Peter. It was hardly the most improbable of predictions, since Peter had been making such remarks almost since they'd known each other. Cook's series *The Two of Us* had not been a success, and Peter had recently felt obliged publicly to deny charges of failure in his own career in the wake of Dudley's superstardom. "My career is not a flop," he told reporters, "and I'm not jealous of Dudley. I never wanted to be a big star.

Perhaps if I had been born with a clubfoot and a height problem, I might have been as desperate as Dudley to become a star in order to prove myself. That's all he ever wanted. I don't have the same need to prove myself."

The following month Dudley threw Susan Anton a surprise thirty-second birthday party. He blindfolded her and drove them to an unknown destination, and when he unmasked her, Susan found herself in a huge recording studio surrounded by dozens of friends in black tie and evening gowns. Dudley had hired two cameramen to videotape the evening, and the members of his trio were on hand in the form of Nick Ceroli and Ray Brown. One of the guests organized a male stripper, to everyone's mirth, and Sam Veta, Dudley's secretary, had arranged an enormous birthday cake on which Susan's face had been reproduced in icing. All night long Dudley played music, and he was still playing in the early hours of the morning when everyone had gone home save for Susan, Lou Pitt, and the cleaners. It was a charming evening for Susan's scrapbook of memories.

This birthday present was topped only by one other. Dudley had bound the score for *Six Weeks* in leather and dedicated it to her. Inside he wrote that she and the score belonged together.

In November Dudley was voted Male Star of the Year at the National Association of Theater Owners' annual celebration in Miami, sharing the honors with Goldie Hawn, fresh from *Private Benjamin*, who took the Top Female Star award. He'd come a long way since appearing with her and Chevy Chase in *Foul Play* four years earlier.

Lou Pitt flew to Miami with him and spent most of the flight in helpless laughter. Dudley had got hold of a "shit" cassette in which the entire six minutes consisted of the sounds of a man entering a toilet and his strenuous, puffing efforts to defecate. Pitt laughed so hard he had to get out of his seat and walk the length of the plane to catch his breath. By the time they landed, the entire first-class section had heard the tape and was in fits of laughter.

The summer of 1982 had seen the arrival of Steven Spielberg's endearing blockbuster *E. T.* Dudley and Susan loved the movie about the extraterrestrial creature, and it gave rise to a secret message between them. In the film, when E. T. leaves earth and says good-bye to Henry Thomas, they touch fingers and say, "Ouch!" After that, as Susan recalls, "Whenever anything became too emotional for us, we'd just look at each other and say, 'Ouch!' And we knew what it meant. It was like a magic word to make everything better again." That Christmas Dudley gave Susan a ring that spelled the word *Ouch* in diamonds, with a little ruby in the middle of the O, signifying the blood that was shed when they were hurt.

It was that Christmas that *Six Weeks* was released. And it resulted in the most painful setback that Dudley had suffered since moving to America.

During public previews earlier in the year, the film had received an amazing reaction, notching up the second highest audience response since *Jaws*. Universal were so excited about the reaction that they decided to make the film their Christmas movie. It was an appalling mistake.

Paul Bloch, Dudley's publicist, concedes the release was ill-timed. "You can't bring out a film at Christmas about a young girl dying. People want to rejoice during that season, not cry, and they rejected the film entirely—which was sad, because it was a very poignant movie and Dudley's music was phenomenal."

Dudley had poured his soul into the movie. He had put more of himself into this role than in any previous film. It was the richest acting experience he had ever achieved, and he gave some of his best work as an actor. When the film failed to ignite the box office, the outcome was correspondingly traumatic. It left him feeling angry and confused.

He was devastated by the reaction to *Six Weeks*. It wasn't just that the reviews were bad: some of them were downright vehement and scornful. *Time*'s review was headlined "Ghoul's Delight," and its opening sentence warned, "Before we go on, a swig of Maalox is indicated." The *New York Times* called the film "strained, farfetched, incredible, and unconvincing."

Dudley was bewildered. To him the film was sensitive and tender. It made him feel joyful, not ghoulish. The reaction was beyond his comprehension, and he was deeply hurt.

Susan Anton knew how much he loved the film, and was sad to see the depth of his disappointment. "It had taken a tremendous amount for Dudley to bring himself to face the greatest risk of all, which was to reveal his pain and on top of that to share his music. He really protected his music as his safe place to retreat, and through his music you really see and feel Dudley's soul. It comes right out of his fingertips onto the keyboard. It always destroyed me. So when that film and the music were received in such an unkind fashion, I think it did damage beyond anybody's knowing. Even beyond Dudley's knowing."

The impact was huge. Dudley had thrived and bloomed with public acclaim, and it had been a long time since he had faced rejection in so public a fashion—and never on such a scale. In some ways, Susan sees the debacle as having been the beginning of the end for them. "It was such a profound disappointment for him, and it's at those times that you shore yourself up and turn to whatever your addiction is—be it women or work— in order to validate yourself, or just to try to fill up the gap. I think that was part of what led to the end of our relationship."

Ironically, when his emotional confidence was so low, it was now that his male image was further boosted by an extraordinary interview for *Playboy*, in which almost an entire eight pages were devoted to explicit discussion of Dudley's sex life. Given this opportunity to discuss the subject, he embarked on it with prolonged relish, although he claimed there was nothing new to his ramblings. He'd been talking about these things for years, but previously nobody had given him a forum for his opinions. Friends called him to laugh about the story, thinking it had all been a huge joke, but were astonished when Dudley told them the article accurately reflected his feelings.

The interview was mainly devoted to his lifelong interest in sex and women, and he admitted that women were the obsession of his life. "What else is there to live for?" he asked. "Chinese food and women. There *is* nothing else. And one's desire for another person is the most flattering thing you can take from that person. Sex is the most important part of anybody's life. The ability to enjoy your sex life is central. I don't give a shit about anything else."

He revealed he had, just once, been to bed with two women. "I also tried it once with a male friend and a woman, but we just ended up laughing. I mean, it was like choosing ends: 'Which end do you want?' It was so exhilarating we couldn't do anything!"

It was interesting that, for someone as guarded as Dudley was capable of being, when it came to his sexual activities he was remarkably open, particularly with his male friends. He loved to talk about sex, and the intimate details of his various sexual interludes were always imparted with great enthusiasm.

Early in 1983 *Lovesick* opened, and, although the critics were infinitely kinder than they had been with *Six Weeks*, it was another film that would end up taking a nosedive at the box office.

"Forget *Six Weeks*," urged the *New York Times*. "Dudley Moore, incomparable in *10* and *Arthur*, is back doing what he does best." He really was. He was funny and sensitive simultaneously. *Time* magazine, while noting that some of the script wandered into contrived predictability, declared, "Moore gives a subtle, warm, finely tuned performance and Elizabeth McGovern shows enormous promise. The two of them form an odd combination but it works." This review gave pleasure to Dudley at a time when he was desperate for reaffirmation—so much so that he scribbled in his diary, "*Time* liked *Lovesick!*" One critic, however, claimed he had been looking forward to seeing a psychoanalyst on screen but what he got instead was Donald Duck. Elizabeth McGovern believes that "People took it seriously in a way it was never intended. They were quite offended by the idea of a comedy about a psychiatrist who has an affair with a patient, and a lot of people were very angry about it."

Although Dudley's score for *Six Weeks* was ignored by the Academy when the Oscar nominations were announced in February, it had not been entirely overlooked by Hollywood and he was heartened to receive a Golden Globe nomination, even though he did not win the category.

In spite of a lack of widespread appeal for *Six Weeks* and *Lovesick*, Dudley now emerged third in a national popularity poll of actors, behind Burt Reynolds and Clint Eastwood. Whereas those two men were seen as strong and macho, in Dudley people saw a certain vulnerability and sensitivity that was immensely endearing. Just as he had redefined the term "sex symbol," so he had established new parameters for the role of the traditional hero.

Dudley was forty-seven now, yet age had not tarnished his endearingly boyish looks, and the press continued to compare him to lovable, huggable animals like teddy bears and puppies.

Success had not changed his unassuming manner. He still drove himself to work in his orange BMW or the white Bentley with its baby-blue leather seats. At home he answered his own phone, made many of his own appointments, and cooked his own meals. And wore the same clothes. "He always had his little uniforms," says Susan. "For a while he was into wearing black pants, a yellow sweater, and a white shirt, and, once I realized that, I bought him three pairs of black pants, three yellow sweaters, and three white shirts."

Several months earlier, while Dudley was still riding high on the success of *Arthur*, Lou Pitt had secured for Dudley a hefty fee of $2.5 million for the remake of Preston Sturges's 1948 classic thriller *Unfaithfully Yours*.

It was a hundred times more than he had received for *Foul Play*, his first American film, and was solid validation that, despite the failure of *Six Weeks*, he was regarded as a fully fledged, multimillion-dollar Hollywood star.

CHAPTER 19

STARDOM
AND DOUBTS

1983-1985

"So many people feel good about Dudley, but it will probably never be enough. The hunger was never satisfied when it should have been taken care of, and that's Dudley's lot in life."

—ANN REINKING

In January 1983 Dudley began filming *Unfaithfully Yours*, now transformed into a comedy in which an obsessed orchestra conductor mistakenly believes his young wife is having an affair with his violinist friend and plots to kill her.

Howard Zieff, director of the hugely successful *Private Benjamin*, had several years earlier persuaded Twentieth Century Fox, who owned the original rights, to let him make this new version. He did not like to think of it as a remake, since it spiraled off in different directions from Sturges's film, and at one point he considered changing the title. He had originally wanted Peter Sellers to assume the role of the jealous conductor and had planned to utilize Sellers's talent for disguise by making him Italian. When Sellers died, Zieff looked elsewhere.

Who else to consider, but the actor who so often seemed to be following in Sellers's footsteps?

It was interesting that Dudley should be considered for so many roles that Sellers had either declined or been unable to accept, especially since he lacked two of Sellers's main attributes—he was not particularly good at accents, unless they were British, and nor were disguises a particular forte. What he did have in common with Sellers, though, was an extraordinary talent for physical humor. Few contemporary comedy actors were able to use their entire body as effectively as Dudley.

Zieff brought with him to *Unfaithfully Yours* two alumni from *Private Benjamin*: Armand Assante (as the young wife's supposed lover) and Albert Brooks (as Moore's manager). And for the role of the young wife he chose Nastassja Kinski—much against the wishes of the studio, who, after her darker roles in *Tess* and *Cat People*, believed that she was not light enough for the part and would bring the film down. "I never saw anyone else in that role," insists Zieff. "When I met her, she was a young twenty-year-old filled with vitality and humor, and I knew immediately that this was the girl that Dudley's character would fall in love with. She was so appealing and vivacious, so opposite to his conservative Everyman."

Dudley was very struck by Nastassja Kinski's likeness to the young Ingrid Bergman. She was a beautiful girl with a vulnerable, doe-like quality. *Tess* had made her a hot young star, but she was very self-critical, with a huge lack of confidence that brought out Dudley's nurturing, almost paternal, side.

Kinski felt deeply intimidated at playing comedy for the first time, but Dudley helped her to relax and enjoy what she was doing. "He was like the sun coming up," says Kinski. "From the very first day, which was very hard for me, he taught me to breathe in the situation and feed from him. He was so helpful and generous. He filled me as a partner and had so much respect. His support was wonderful.

"I'd never seen anybody so flexible and light in what they did. The great art is to float above the work, and Dudley could do that. He could change in an instant. He'd walk off and play the most wonderful piece of music, and then we'd do a take and he'd be back and ready. And he could do ten different things in a scene while most actors needed to prepare for one."

Not since *30 Is a Dangerous Age, Cynthia* had Dudley been able to incorporate so many of his musical talents within one movie. He played the piano and violin, and he conducted movements from Beethoven's Fifth Symphony and Tchaikovsky's violin concerto.

"Dudley is a consummate musician, which made him perfect for the part," says Zieff. "On every stage where we shot, we had a baby grand piano just for him, and he always played while we set up the next shot.

"One of the reasons I loved him for the part," he recalls, "was because he has fine English hair which flopped around, and I was looking forward to shooting the close-up with the hair flying in his face as he conducted the orchestra. But, without telling me, the hairdresser decided to give it more body and she fizzed up the hair with a perm so it was stuck up like an Afro. There went my shot. I was very disappointed."

Dudley liked Howard Zieff, whom he described as a teddy bear. He was a director who told his actors what he wanted and then left them to come up with it, although there were occasional arguments over what that might be. There was one brief moment when tempers flared and Dudley lost his cool. During one scene, Zieff asked Dudley for more. "What do you mean *more!*" shouted Dudley. "What *more* do you want? If you wanted more, why didn't you get someone else!"

Their differences were resolved pretty swiftly, but in the meantime Zieff had other problems and was battling internal politics at the studio. He was told to pull the plug on scenes that were already set up, lit, and ready to shoot. "There was this crazy power struggle going on," he recalls, "and it made the filming much more difficult for no other reason than they were flexing their muscles." Fox went through four producers on that picture, and the standing joke on the film was the question, "Who's our producer this week?"

One executive turned up on the set, uninvited, and sat down to watch the action. Dudley turned to him and said, "I'm sorry, you're in my eyeline. Please would you move?" The second time he moved, Dudley told him, "You're still in my eyeline." As Zieff recalls, "He moved that executive all the way around the stage until finally he left and everyone broke into laughter."

Dudley and Nastassja Kinski were a marvelous team. Dudley knew how to make Nastassja laugh and lose control any time he wanted her to.

Some of the filming took place in New York, and during lunch breaks Howard took his actors over to the Russian Tea Room. Howard had already seen how easily Dudley could reduce Nastassja to a giggling bundle. One lunchtime he discovered how it affected her physically. "Dudley was making his jokes and using the fart machine," he remembers, "and he was so funny on this day that she laughed so hard she wet her pants. Literally! She was wearing this crushed-velvet dress, and when she got up, the back of the dress was soaking wet."

In spite of all the hilarity and high jinks, Dudley's gray moods were reemerging, as Howard Zieff observed. "I think most people who deal in comedy are working out a pain. I was very surprised when I first saw it in Dudley, because the Dudley Moore you first meet is funny and jovial, with that silly giggle. And then after you've spent a month with him, you start to learn other things. He is quite melancholy at times. It's a very strong part of his makeup."

Dudley enjoyed making *Unfaithfully Yours* and he liked the movie when it was completed. The critics later agreed with him, but audiences were ambivalent.

A week after *Unfaithfully Yours* finished filming, Dudley cohosted the Academy Awards. He was so funny that even ultimate funnyman Walter Matthau collapsed in laughter as he watched the ceremony in his dressing room. Howard Koch, who produced the telecast, was prompted to write and tell Dudley that "90 million people fell in love with you that night," and director Marty Pasetta wrote, "Who else could have ad-libbed so brilliantly; your wit provided the show with some of its best laughs." As Marshall Brickman recalls, Dudley managed to compress into one dazzlingly psychotic monologue "a reference to both masturbation and pears—an accomplishment worthy of James Joyce."

Dudley had now been working continuously for eighteen months since October 1981. During that time he had experienced the death of his mother and witnessed the downfall of *Six Weeks*, a project very dear to his heart. He had worked so hard for so long; now it was time to have some fun for a while. He was, after all, a Hollywood star and in huge demand socially. There were parties and dinners with Glenn and Cynthia Ford, Peter Bogdanovich, Wayne Rogers, and Leslie Bricusse; a dinner for John Huston; an auction by Jane Fonda; a reception for David Hockney; dinner for visiting Vice President George Bush; birthday parties for Mary Steenburgen, Tina Sinatra, and Susan George; more dinners with Peter Bellwood, Francis Megahy, Parker Stevenson and Kirstie Alley, and Michael and Pat York; and a visit to Liza Minnelli's concert at Universal's new amphitheater.

Dudley needed to recharge his batteries, and for that he turned to his music. He appeared on a TV tribute to Bob Hope and, as the *New York Daily News* wrote, his appearance as concert pianist was "the one class act in the whole three hours."

With an engagement set for Carnegie Hall early in June, Dudley applied himself assiduously to six hours of daily practice at home. Despite his love for acting and comedy, it was to music that Dudley turned for greatest fulfillment. It was, for him, the more visceral art, the one through which he became emotionally charged. He worked from nostalgia in his music, and from a longing for the love that he had missed as a child. Given a choice, emotionally he would choose music; financially he would choose acting, although within a decade it would be his music to which he would turn to fill both needs.

For Carnegie Hall, he chose to perform the Beethoven Triple Concerto with violinist Robert Mann and cellist Nathaniel Rosen. Pinchas Zukerman would conduct the St. Paul's Chamber Orchestra.

"There was a lot of expectation," recalls Lou Pitt, "because the prestige of Carnegie Hall and the name made it seem more important than perhaps it was. But he was fabulous, and I felt very, very good for him, because the audience was with him all the way. One of the fascinating things about Dudley is that people watch him perform not with a critical eye but with an endearing eye. They want to like him."

Though the piano part sounds intricate, the most difficult part of the

Triple Concerto is that of the cello, not the piano, and Dudley felt comfortable and played with ease.

"He did himself and the music proud," said the *New York Post* the next day, adding that he played "with a large, clear, bell-like tone and an arresting style." *Time* magazine considered his performance was "sensitive and well paced," and the *New York Times* critic declared that Dudley "came away with considerable honor," adding, "clearly he is no amateur fumbler at the keyboard. His technique could not be called pristine but it served him quite well."

An appearance by Dudley would not have been complete without at least a hint of his irrepressible humor, and he provided that during the curtain calls. Mugging for the sold-out audience, he impishly flipped up his tails and threw a wicked, backward glance at the audience as he made his final exit.

Susan, who was performing in China, had flown in from Beijing to be with him, and was thrilled by the way he was received. "The idea of being at Carnegie Hall was immensely exciting, and it was wonderful to see all those people surrounding Dudley. There was an electric atmosphere."

Carnegie Hall was also where Tuesday Weld met the man who would become her new husband. Dudley had persuaded Tuesday to bring Patrick and Natasha to the concert and, at the reception afterward, Pinchas Zukerman, who was in the process of being divorced, met Tuesday for the first time. For the rest of the evening they scarcely took their eyes off each other, and eventually they left together, leaving Patrick and Natasha with Dudley. The romance that began that night soon evolved into a marriage that continues to this day.

Later Pinchas wrote to Dudley expressing his delight at the evening and suggesting another concert somewhere out of town and unnoticed by the press. "What about a jazz album with me and the orchestra?" he proposed. "If you'd like to do anything with me playing or conducting, I'd be happy to collaborate." It was quite a compliment from the virtuoso violinist/violist/conductor, who describes Dudley's musical acuity as "very talented but diffused because he hasn't found his complete niche in music."

Three days later Dudley played the Triple Concerto again, this time with the Los Angeles Chamber Orchestra. He completed the evening with some jazz, and received a rousing reception.

Susan was out of town and, although Dudley missed her, his wandering eye—an extension of his insatiable libido—was unable to restrain itself for long. "What do I want?" he wrote frustratedly in his diary. "What am I afraid of? What is she doing? What am I doing? I hurt Susan no matter what I do." Strangely, underneath Susan's name he wrote "My mother."

There was one nasty moment in the midst of Dudley's musical glory.

Susan, dressed in pajamas, was arrested in Los Angeles for drunk driving over a holiday weekend in June after crashing Dudley's second car, an orange BMW. Detained by the police, she was bailed out by Dudley, but neither of them would explain the details that led up to the accident. Had there been a fight between them? Had she found out about his increasingly roving eye?

As it happens, it was fortuitous that the BMW was out of commission, because soon after that Dudley himself was involved in a fatal accident on the freeway. "Thank God he was driving my Mercedes," recalls Susan, "because it was low to the ground and took the impact."

Dudley was driving home from Spago, the restaurant that had become a favorite for celebrities and where literary agent Swifty Lazar held his annual Oscar party, when a young drunk driver, careering along the freeway at over 100 mph, smashed into him from behind. Struggling desperately to retain control of the car, Dudley skidded to a halt against the center divider. He was lucky; he survived. The two men in the other car were both thrown out, and one of them was killed.

Phone messages poured in from his friends. "Are you dead or alive?" asked Else Blangsted, his music editor on *Six Weeks*, from Switzerland. An anxious Suzy called from London, as did Peter Cook and sister Barbara. Dudley was horrified that a man had been killed but he, himself, had not been hurt. He was just badly shaken up.

He flew to Denver and performed once more the Beethoven Triple Concerto at the annual Aspen Music Festival. He was, Paul Bloch recalls, "brilliant, exciting, and humorous." The night was wildly triumphant. Never before had Dudley received so many standing ovations. "I don't think this can possibly be duplicated in the years ahead," Paul told Lou Pitt as they drove back from the concert. "There'll be more concerts, but nothing can possibly be as successful as this."

Patrick was staying with Dudley for the summer, and the time he and his father spent together was bringing them closer. Now that Patrick had turned seven, Dudley was able to converse more with his son and he enjoyed the youngster's blossoming personality.

Patrick was an artistic boy who loved to paint, and Dudley's most cherished gifts were the paintings his son gave him. The walls of Patrick's room at the Marina beach house were (and continue to be) covered with his colorful efforts. Patrick had also inherited his father's musicality. Just as Dudley had done around the age of six, Patrick was now clambering on to his father's piano stool and tinkering with the keyboard, fascinated with the black and white keys and the sounds that emanated from them, and Dudley was looking forward to the time when they would be able to play duets together.

By August 1983 Susan, who realized that she and Dudley were unlikely ever to be married, publicly announced that she wanted a baby and would be happy to be a single parent. Dudley was so adamant about not wanting more children, however, that finally she dropped the idea.

Dudley was now once again feeling ambivalent about life, questioning his feelings about love and his seemingly relentless quest for it. He had come to believe that love was wrong for him, and was wary of allowing it to happen again. He had always feared losing control, and to him falling in love meant reverting to an infantile dependency.

It was ironic that he particularly believed actors should never marry actresses. He considered actresses to be hidden people who kept things inside, as his mother had done. Yet he had married two actresses and had dated others by the score. Was it in a childlike hope of mastering the mother/son situation he had never conquered as a boy? Were the lines so indistinct that he was imposing his mother's persona on these often-guarded women and yet was drawn to them out of his need still to reach toward his mother and pull out what she had never shown him?

Love, he had decided, was a false emotion based on unrealistic hopes and desires. In the women who attracted him he continued to search for the love he had never felt from his mother, always hoping it might be around the next corner. He could not abandon that desperate attempt to replace his deprivation, but the female boundaries were confused for him. He would never be able to get that love from his mother, for she was no longer there to give it to him. And even if she had been there, she had never known how to give that love—at least not in a way that could satisfy Dudley. And the love he received from his women was a different kind of love. It meant what it meant, but it could never mean the other. And so he went around in circles, constantly engaged in a futile search for something he could never hope to find.

In October, *Romantic Comedy* was released. The critics dismissed it as a filmed play, and one that did not work at that. Audiences were inclined to agree, and the film dived.

After a six-month break from filming, Dudley now went back to work and teamed with Eddie Murphy in *Best Defense*. In fact they shared screen credits but not the screen, for the two are never seen together during the film. Murphy had previously turned down the movie, but capitulated in the face of a million-dollar offer from Paramount for just a few weeks' work.

Kate Capshaw, as his wife, was Dudley's more visible partner, and with *Best Defense* he would be one of the few actors to work with both of Steven Spielberg's wives, though Kate, coming straight from *Indiana Jones and the Temple of Doom*, had only just become a glimmer on Spielberg's horizon at this time, and Dudley had yet to make *Micki and Maude*, which would team

him with Spielberg's first wife, Amy Irving. Helen Shaver costarred as
Dudley's illicit love interest, and the film was directed, produced, and
written by Willard Huyck and Gloria Katz, fresh from their writing of
Indiana Jones and the Temple of Doom.

The film opens in the Kuwaiti desert, where Eddie Murphy is an
American tank commander demonstrating a new tank, at the heart of
which is a sophisticated navigational gyroscope. When the navigation
system goes awry, the tank goes berserk and ends up in the heart of the Iraqi
war zone after demolishing an Arab village. Flashback two years earlier to
Dudley as the inept designer of the gyroscope who appropriates another
designer's plans when he is killed by an industrial spy.

The entertaining story would have worked better had Dudley's part of
it been shown in one single flashback, but instead the film cut back and
forth every few scenes between Murphy in Kuwait (actually Israel) and
Dudley, two years earlier, attempting to perfect this intricate equipment.

Dudley enjoyed working with Kate Capshaw and Helen Shaver, and
they found him hugely entertaining. He made going to work every day fun
in a way they had seldom known before. As for Eddie Murphy, who had met
Dudley some time earlier at a screening for *Derek and Clive Get the Horn*, he was
already an admirer. He loved Derek and Clive, whose scatological humor
was right up his street. Although he and Dudley never appeared together in
Best Defense, they did shoot one scene where they crossed paths, but it was
eventually cut from the final version.

Dudley thought the film was funny, and was amazed when it didn't
turn out the way he hoped. He took Helen Shaver to a screening and, after
the first hilarious minutes, turned to her and warned jokingly, "It's all
downhill from now on!" And it was—much to his surprise. Ultimately,
audiences and critics were irritated by the continual jump-cutting between
times and locales, and the film failed miserably. In Britain it was never
even released.

In November the Bricusses celebrated their silver wedding anniversary. All the Hollywood Brits were there, among them Rod Stewart, the
Collins sisters, and Michael Caine. Dudley played the piano, and at some
point during the evening ended up helpless with laughter on the floor with
Jacqueline Bisset. It was one of the rare moments they shared together.

"He was very shy," recalls Jacqueline, "and I never knew quite what to
say to him. Like many funny people, he was 'on' quite a lot, and I often
wished he would be less 'on' and more himself when I saw him. I thought
he was adorable, and fascinating, too."

Dudley had never quite got over the disappointment of *Six Weeks*, and
it was hard to ignore an inner despair that was growing with the release of
each subsequent movie.

Susan Anton tried to boost his morale during these moments of despondency. "I could see his personal pain and disappointment when things were met with less than raves, and I tried to heal him, make it feel better for him, because I hated to see him in pain."

By now, Dudley's romance with Susan had drifted into a seriously on-and-off position—mostly off—although he still cared enough about her to help finance her new house in Beverly Hills' Noel Place. His straying eye had returned with a vengeance. Monogamy had never been his strong suit, but it had prevailed for a while during Susan's reign. Now he was playing the field again.

For Susan, who had been with Dudley for over three and a half years and now sensed he had resumed his errant ways, it was a difficult time. Deep down she knew he was being unfaithful, but she chose to believe otherwise. Sometimes she asked him if he had been with another woman, but he always denied it and, because she wanted so much to believe him, she accepted the lie.

"The worst part," she recalls, "was that all the wonderful honesty we'd shared in the beginning of the relationship started to shut down bit by bit, and once you start keeping secrets, a relationship can't survive. We had a really great time for a couple of years, but the last ones were very painful on a lot of levels."

Christmas 1983 came and went amid a whirlwind of social engagements. One of them took him to an apartment in Westwood where he had an assignation with a young college student who had left a message on his answering machine. They had met while each was driving down Sunset Boulevard one morning. Ever since seeing *Arthur*, eighteen-year-old Nicole Rothschild had been a devout Dudley Moore fan, and when she saw him at the wheel of his distinctive white Bentley, she waved madly and shouted across, "Please, I *must* have your autograph!" Dudley, who was always touched by public appreciation and went out of his way to oblige his fans, pulled over into a parking lot beside Nicole. He found her instantly appealing. She was a bubbly, five-foot-five, green-eyed brunette with a laugh that put Goldie Hawn to shame. Instantly smitten, they exchanged phone numbers and soon began seeing each other.

Nicole's parents had divorced when she was young, and her mother, Gloria, then married Peter Rothschild, a descendant of the vast financial empire, but that marriage also ended in divorce.

Nicole soon became a regular visitor to Dudley's house, and he arranged limousines to take her to and from school and on shopping trips with her friends or sisters, although after a while that became so expensive that he stopped the practice.

Early in 1984 Dudley joined other Hollywood Brits to raise money for the British Olympic Team at the upcoming Olympic Games in Los Angeles. While Julie Andrews, Tom Jones, and Anthony Newley sang, Dudley performed at the piano with Cleo Laine and John Dankworth.

Leslie Bricusse, who organized the gala with Michael Caine and Sir Gordon White, the British millionaire entrepreneur who flew the British flag from his home near the Caine mansion, was in fits of laughter over the old "Dying Swan" routine that Dudley resurrected now with Dankworth. "As he played the piece, Dudley kept changing keys and playing lower and lower and moving his body at the same time until he came off the piano stool on to the floor. He ended up lying on the floor under the piano with his hands above his head still playing. It was brilliant."

Dudley's last few films had not done very well at the box office, nor with critics or audiences, but when *Unfaithfully Yours* opened in February, it was met with a more enthusiastic response than either of its two predecessors. Richard Schickel in *Time* magazine declared the film better than the original and "the range and control of [Dudley's] facial expressions a joyous astonishment." The film, he decided, was "smart, well-paced, nice-looking and reminds you of Hollywood's good old days without making you mourn for them."

Dudley's romance with Susan Anton, so powerful and obsessive in its early days, had now entered its final stages. Their relationship continued to linger on pleasantly, as Dudley put it, but he was now once again publicly avowing his disbelief in monogamy "unless it happens to fall on one like a Russian satellite out of the sky," and Susan must have realized their romance was almost at an end.

John Bassett, Dudley's former Oxford friend who had brought together the four members of *Beyond the Fringe* in 1960, came to Los Angeles and was touched by the poignancy of Susan's continued love. "She took a photograph of us," he recalls, "and Dudley told her it was probably the last photo she would ever take of him. You could see she adored him, and it was hard not to cry."

Despite his public statements to the contrary, says Susan, Dudley loved the process of falling in love. Sustaining the feeling after the initial adrenaline had calmed down was another matter altogether. "He was addicted to the thrill," she reflects, "because when you're falling in love, all you see is the newness and the excitement. But then you get into the nitty-gritty of really knowing somebody, and when they know you that well, it's like they're holding a mirror in front of you and you see yourself through them. You can't run away from it, and you can't ignore it. In Dudley's case, you leave because it's too much to look at."

Susan accepted and loved Dudley for the man she knew him to be. But he couldn't be happy with that, because it meant he had to take a deeper look at himself. "Whenever you have upset in a relationship," she says, "it's because you're confronting something within yourself that you've either got to address or not go there. And I think Dudley just couldn't go to certain places."

There was a great deal that Dudley would not face up to, says the woman who knew him intimately for more than four years. The hardest thing for him to accept was that anybody could possibly see him with all of his faults and still love him.

Dudley did not understand unconditional love, because he had never received it himself. From an early age he had been taught that there was a whole aspect of himself that he should be ashamed of, and it was a dilemma he faced in later life because it was at odds with the other part of him. "He could let a lot out," says Susan, "but he could not show it all, because he felt if it were all seen, then he would not be accepted."

In April 1984 Dudley returned to filming and was reunited at last, five years after *10*, with Blake Edwards. *Micki and Maude* was a comedy about a married television presenter whose cellist mistress, Maude (Amy Irving), becomes pregnant at the same time as his lawyer wife, Micki (Ann Reinking). Feeling bound to both, Dudley marries his mistress and gets away with bigamy until Micki and Maude meet in the hospital as each is about to enter the delivery room. Banned from seeing either of his babies, the end of the film sees him continuing a secret relationship with each woman, unknown to the other. Somehow it didn't seem inappropriate for Dudley to end up with two women by his side. He was, after all, now perceived as one of the screen's most romantic lovers.

"Dudley made each of us feel like the most special person, the most beautiful woman, in the world," said Amy Irving at that time. And Ann Reinking attests, "Dudley is tender and genuine, and because he's funny, he makes you laugh. Laughter makes you feel good, and a man who makes women feel good is going to be very popular with them. I think Amy and I just sat and laughed for three months. It loosened us up so much that we did things I don't think we thought we could do."

Still, Ann was aware of Dudley's sadder side. "Every really good clown has a tear in his eye. They illustrate both sides of human nature, the despair as well as the joy, and that's what makes them so good. They make you laugh, and that takes fear out of our lives momentarily. Loneliness and vulnerability are inherent in all of us, and I think the reason we connect to him is because he illustrates what we all feel. He touches us."

With *Micki and Maude*, Dudley was back in top form. "I loved Dudley in the role," says Blake Edwards, "and the combination with Ann and Amy was just terrific. It worked so well, and we all got along wonderfully. We had the best time on that film."

It was Dudley who had suggested Amy Irving for the role of Maude. He was a staunch admirer of the beautiful actress with the renaissance face, and had she not been married at the time to Steven Spielberg, one of the industry's most powerful directors, he would have pursued her into a romance.

Tony Adams, who was producing the film with Blake, recalls they struck up a close rapport from the start. "Amy was very enamored both with her role and with Dudley, and they hit it off immediately and spent a lot of time together. Amy was a very warm and funny girl. So was Ann. She had a wonderfully wicked sense of humor and a deep, gutsy, throaty kind of laugh that Dudley loved."

Dudley flourished in Blake's free and vivacious presence. Their sense of humor was compatible, and Blake also brought laughter to the set. In a scene where Dudley had to open a closet to take out a coat, out jumped a man in a gorilla costume and wrestled him to the bed as if trying to make love to him. "It was hilarious," recalls Tony Adams. "Blake had set the whole thing up and had the prop man assume this guise. Dudley was absolutely shocked. He thought someone was trying to rape him! The whole film was a constant state of Blake doing something to poor Dudley. And of course they both had their little fart machines with them."

The fart machine led Dudley to an utter Freudian slip with his lines. In one scene, the doctor told him one of his wives would have to be hooked up to "a fetal heart monitor." Dudley earnestly corrected him. "No, no, it's a heatal fart monitor!" he instructed, then burst into a high-pitched cackle when he realized what he'd said.

It was a comedy very much in the style of a French farce, with lots of doors slamming, people running in and out of rooms, and Dudley constantly trying to escape discovery by his other wife. But ultimately this film didn't work. The fault, Blake Edwards believes, lay with the ending. "We struggled a lot with how to do that," he remembers. "Dudley wanted to end up openly with both women, and as I look back now, I think he was probably right, although the timing for that may have been wrong.

"The film was funny, but I think middle America resented the fact that this guy was a bigamist. That right-wing Bible Belt is very powerful in the States, and I was certainly worried about that—as was the studio. I still thought it was a charming movie, and I'd have bet anything that it would have done very well. But it didn't."

Although audiences would be generally unreceptive toward *Micki and Maude*, the critics regarded the film favorably. When it was released in England, Iain Johnstone, reviewing for the *Times*, declared it "very funny thanks to a splendid comic performance by Dudley Moore. The film belongs to Dudley, [who] surmounts the random inconsistencies of the plot ... blending emotion and humour with the touch of a Cary Grant."

It was around this time that Dudley's longtime friend, the jazz singer Barbara Moore, came to visit Los Angeles for two weeks. She stayed in the elite Hollywood hotel, the Chateau Marmont, and Dudley sent a limo to pick her up one morning and bring her out to his house in the Marina.

"I spent a lovely day with my little treasure," she recalls. "We sat at the piano and had a giggle and talked and sang and played music. Later that day we took a delightful walk along the beach by the Marina, and every elderly person and child we passed along that stretch stopped to greet him, they were so pleased to see him. I found it very moving to see my old friend so beloved like that."

Barbara didn't see him again before she left. When she checked out of the hotel, she went to the reception desk to pay her bill. "There's no need for that," the manager told her. "It's already been taken care of by A Friend." He refused to tell her the name, but Barbara knew "damn well who it was. That's the only time in my long life that a man ever gave me anything. It was precious. He had no need to do something like that, but that's who Dudley is. I love the largesse and warmth of his heart. You can toast your hands on him."

With the money she had not spent, Barbara flew to the East Coast and spent two glorious weeks in New York.

Dudley had now launched a new partnership with his *Six Weeks* director, Tony Bill, who lived close to him in neighboring Venice. He had often told Tony how much he enjoyed playing the piano in places where he didn't feel "on stage"—places where he could see his friends, dine well, and play the piano when the mood took him.

A year earlier Tony had suggested opening a restaurant across the road from his office/studio/apartment building, and Dudley agreed to join him as a partner. Fifteen other investors climbed aboard, including Liza Minnelli and Tina Sinatra, and 72 Market St. opened in August 1984 amid the Hollywood fanfare that accompanies a special occasion. The oyster bar and grill became an instant attraction for the local showbiz crowd. The celebrity circle flocked to the restaurant, partly in search of good cuisine and partly in the hope of seeing Dudley play the gleaming black grand piano in the main dining room. They weren't disappointed.

In November 1984 Dudley flew to London to begin filming his next movie, *Santa Claus—The Movie*. It was his first production in England since *The Hound of the Baskervilles* in 1977, and with it he would earn $4 million, the highest fee he had ever been paid for a film. *Superman* producers Ilya and Alex Salkind had lured Dudley into this $50 million extravaganza, which was directed by Jeannot Szwarc, who had made *Jaws 2*. Filming took place at Pinewood Studios, much of it on a colossal stage where a vast grotto had been built, complete with towering floors, rows of workbenches, and a workshop for 250 elves.

Dudley played Patch (his son Patrick's nickname), who becomes chief assistant to Santa Claus (David Huddleston) but is then manipulated into joining an unscrupulous toy baron (John Lithgow) in a plot to overthrow Mr. Claus. The role had been written especially for Dudley and its child-like elements of eagerness and innocence greatly appealed to him. He had wanted for some time to make a special-effects movie, and loved the idea of speeding through the sky in a flying car.

On the first day of filming, Dudley walked into the studio and found a Selfridges bag hanging inside a wardrobe door. The S had been covered up and the bag now read "Elfridges." From then on, he seemed surrounded by a smaller world, with a new language that encompassed words from "elfishness" to "elf-efficiency."

With his 62½ inches clothed in an elfin garb of brown corduroy knee-breeches, flapping jacket, silk scarf, and woolly nightcap, Dudley looked the complete pixie.

He had long wanted to make a fantasy film, and one that his son would enjoy, but he found it immensely uncomfortable to be cast in the midst of hundreds of other men of his own size, although many were smaller. The first time Dudley saw them all together, he broke out in a cold sweat ("I thought it was fucking ridiculous!"), and after every take, he reverted to Derek and Clive–like obscenities in rebellion against the inno-cent niceness he had just portrayed as Elf Patch. It was incongruous, and John Lithgow was as amused by Dudley's bawdiness as he was to see his costar matched against so many other small people. "It looked very pecu-liar to me to see a cast of little men with Dudley looking bigger than any of them. I think it must have been a pleasure for him to be taller."

Surrounded by all the elves, Dudley remembers a moment of hilarity when David Huddleston, dressed as Santa Claus, got into a massive argu-ment with one of the elf actors. "It was the funniest thing in the world to see Santa Claus and this dwarf verbally sparring with each other, effing and blinding like mad!"

The Salkinds had advertised the film in the trade papers as the most expensive movie ever made, and were hoping to launch a series of Santa Claus movies, just as they had with *Superman*. It was a huge extravaganza to pull together, but it seemed to go so far over the top that it lost its vision and very early on the actors began to have misgivings about the film.

Over Christmas, in the coldest and bleakest three weeks of Dudley's life, the flying sequences were filmed on the gigantic stage built of pine. With the studio virtually empty and the Santa Claus team having dwindled to just a few actors, it was for Dudley one of the most boring experiences he ever had. That boredom was, however, alleviated by a particu-larly harmonious relationship with John Lithgow, the man who was once dubbed the film character actor of his generation after his Oscar-nominated performances in *The World According to Garp* and *Terms of Endearment*. Dudley found him particularly charming and liked the shy actor enormously.

Lithgow, who had grown up around the theater and had won a Tony for his first Broadway play, had long been a dedicated fan of Dudley. "As a teenager," he recalls, "Dudley was one of my great heroes, because I'd seen *Beyond the Fringe* on Broadway. I knew every single sketch and we discussed them endlessly."

It was through their *Fringe* debates that John saw the depth of Dudley's angst over his floundering relationship with Peter Cook. "He had such a complex relationship with Peter, and they were at that sad moment where Peter was so jealous and bitter about Dudley's success that the friendship was basically evaporating. I think Dudley was hurt and confused.

"It sounded as if he had done an awful lot to try to help Peter, but to no avail. Dudley felt very guilty about his own success—and how could he not? Peter's life was such a shambles, and at that point Dudley's life was still wonderful. He was basking in the glory of being a movie star, although I did slightly feel he was beginning to worry because *10* and *Arthur* were behind him. It's a curse having a big success like *Arthur*, because everybody measures everything against it."

One night Dudley took John to Langan's Brasserie, where he was instantly pronounced DOA by Peter Langan. Some time earlier Langan had invited Dudley to invest in his new restaurant venture in Los Angeles, but Dudley had turned down the offer. "Why did you turn me down?" Langan asked now, and Dudley explained that his accountants had advised him against it. "Then I don't need your custom here, thank you very much indeed," replied Langan, and walked away, instructing the waiter en route to "Give him a bottle of champagne and get him out of here."

John Lithgow was astonished at this lack of English dignity. "I'd never been to Langan's and I hadn't heard of Peter's reputation at that time," he recalls, "but it was one of those famous Peter Langan scenes. He was unbelievably drunk and abusive and incredibly insulting to Dudley. I couldn't believe my eyes. It was one of those very liberating moments for a character actor where you realize that whatever you do is no match for real life. It was just outrageous. Dudley had to field this incredible torrent of abuse, and he tried to shrug it off. He was magnificent the way he handled it."

They stayed in Langan's long enough to eat dinner and there was a brief argument afterward when Peter refused to let Dudley pay for the meal. Dudley insisted on paying, but Peter refused to take his check, which bounced back and forth between the two of them for some time. John Lithgow had never seen anything like it. "It was unbelievable. Dudley and

I laughed in amazement afterward, but it was extraordinary and I've never forgotten it."

Dudley himself was both embarrassed and shocked at Langan's tirade, even though after twenty-odd years of knowing him—he'd even played with his trio at Langan's first restaurant during the sixties—he had become fairly resigned to his erratic behavior, usually stimulated by alcohol.

"I want to let you know," Dudley complained later to Michael Caine, Langan's partner, "that another person was just thrown out of your restaurant. "Oh God!" replied Caine. "You wouldn't believe what great business Mirabelle round the corner is doing because of all the people Peter's throwing out of our place!"

Dudley did virtually no interviews while he was in England, which was unusual for the man who had accommodated the press for most of his career. This was in part because his gray mood had resurfaced at the imminent prospect of his impending fiftieth birthday, and also because he was trying to deal with a whirlwind of emotions over something entirely different.

An amazing thing had recently happened to him. Despite his intentions, Dudley had fallen in love again. Truly, madly, and very deeply indeed. But there was to be no happy ending to this romance, for the beautiful woman to whom he had lost his heart—and who also had given him hers—was married.

Dudley will never reveal the name of this woman, but it is clear she was one of the few great loves of his life. They were not only lovers but soul mates, too, and in letters and poetry they poured out their hearts to each other with a rare and blinding intensity. Moments apart were cruel and tearful; together, they rode the crest of blissful ecstasy.

Their affair was passionate and complete. And very short. Though she loved Dudley, she would not leave her husband, and Dudley, who had fallen so completely in love, was left to heal his shattered heart alone.

He wrote a multitude of thoughts on scraps of paper, giving vent to the angst inside him. A letter he never sent was tucked into a drawer, forgotten for years, a testimony to that love:

I feel that low ache of emptiness, that horrible need to hear your voice, that mortal need for your touch. I wrote your name in the sand and looked at those words. Tears come to me, tears that console unconsolingly. I drew lines across those words so that only the sand and I would remember that moment.

All the hurt he had suffered over his clubfoot and withered leg resurfaced in a poem he wrote to her:

Tormenting void, relentless still air of silence.
You have gone, sucked into the ether like a wisp.
I remain—I have lost my limbs—unable to thrash them even in
    the stupid fevered impotence of a Rumpelstiltskin.
Don't tell me it's better to have loved than not at all.
Not to have loved would have left me some remnant of sinew.
Now I am helpless. A fly plucked legless by those cruel children
    again.
Their taunts are flourishing, bold, hot, loud.
I cannot be sadder, my gut grows into a sanctuary for weeds.
Strong weeds that resist a knife.
I know I will survive. But for what—for whom?
Yes it is true. I hate being alive now. Who would have thought I
    could ever think it—I don't see any point in living any more.
But I will.
Busy, busy, busy. Keep the rats away.
Forget the dearest love of my life—the soft sweet love of my life.
    Oh, stronger pain I have never known. How can I live
    without you? How can you live without me? How can you
    live without him.

Dudley felt as if he was drowning in sadness. He thought constantly of this woman he loved so much, no matter where he went. Across an airline menu, he scribbled, "It took me twenty years of therapy to get to the point where I realized life wasn't worth living any more." Typically, for the man who had always believed humor to be another facet of sadness, he added as an afterthought at the bottom of the page, "Why is this funny? You can't get a worse situation than the last thought."

Back in Los Angeles in February, having completed *Santa Claus—The Movie*, Dudley found himself reflecting gloomily on his film career. He had embarked on *Santa Claus* thinking it would be enormous fun to make a fantasy film, but he was already fairly sure that it was more than mildly doomed. (The critics would later concur when it was released the following Christmas.) Meanwhile, with the release of *Micki and Maude*, Dudley once again was facing a disappointing response from his fans. He had enjoyed working again with Blake Edwards and liked the film they had made. Though nobody could ever predict what audiences wanted, he had believed the film would have considerable appeal at the box office. He was wrong.

John Lithgow had seen Dudley's expectations for *Micki and Maude* during the filming of *Santa Claus*. "He had great hopes for it. He thought it was a delightful film, and knowing that was on its way made him much more confident during the filming of *Santa Claus*. I never spoke to him after *Micki and Maude* came out, but it must have been a terrible disappointment to him when it didn't work." Hollywood liked it, however, and presented Dudley with a Golden Globe Award for his performance. Dudley, in self-deprecatory acceptance, suggested, "Steve Martin, Eddie Murphy, and Bill Murray must have been off form this year!'

Since *10*, Dudley had come to believe he was at his best when projecting facets of himself in a role. He wanted, more than anything, to show the tender side of his personality rather than the more manic, farcical side. Yet the films in which he did this had not done so well. It was ironic, since with *Six Weeks* and *Lovesick* he had done some of his best work as an actor. In those he had moved away from the physical humor that identified him so closely with Peter Sellers and toward a realm of charm more reminiscent of Cary Grant. Even *Unfaithfully Yours* and *Micki and Maude*, in which he had reverted to elements of his former caricature behavior, had not fared too well.

The overwhelming success he had found with *10* and *Arthur* had not been sustained, and the earlier roller-coaster pattern of success and failure was repeating itself. During the mid-eighties everything Dudley touched had turned to gold. He had reached a peak he had never known before, both as actor and musician. Now the tide was turning.

He felt hurt by the critics' vituperative attacks on his more serious films, and was disappointed that his fans, whom he adored, would not allow him to be someone other than an amiable drunk or a crazed sex maniac. Disillusioned, he told Lou Pitt he was taking a year off from making films. The thought of being in front of the cameras was suddenly quite appalling to him. Aside from his mental fatigue, he was, after eleven films in eight years, physically exhausted. He needed a break.

By now Dudley's relationship with Susan Anton was over, though they would continue to be friends. His romance with Nicole Rothschild had also ended. For the first time in years, he was alone.

He continued to brood about his approaching fiftieth birthday, just a few weeks away. It was a difficult milestone for the man who looked so much younger than his age and who still retained an inherent boyishness about his nature. Forty hadn't been bad at all, but fifty sounded serious— just as thirty had done—and he felt alarmed at the prospect. He found himself reflecting on his various accomplishments and what might now lie ahead. In some ways, he felt as he had just before he turned thirty, although at least that earlier feeling of futility was absent.

In April 1985, Dudley turned fifty.

PART
FOUR

CHAPTER 20

REFLECTIONS

1985

"Dudley is larger than life and larger than his height."

—ROGER MOORE

W hen the day of his fiftieth birthday dawned, in April 1985, it seemed somehow less fearsome than the awful anticipation that had led up to it. Dudley had half-jokingly contemplated spending it in some dingy motel, lying sobbing on a moth-eaten bed. In the end he spent a busy day with friends on both coasts of the United States.

In New York he lunched at a Japanese sushi restaurant with Susan Anton; then he flew back to Los Angeles for an intimate dinner celebration at his restaurant, 72 Market St., with a few close friends, among them Peter and Sarah Bellwood, Evelyn Silvers, Lou and Berta Pitt, Else Blangsted, and next-door neighbors Carol and Roy Doumani. Carol had arranged for fifty cheerleaders from UCLA to sing "Happy Birthday." Dressed in scanty outfits, they circled the long dining table, each holding a lighted candle and serenading Dudley. He was so touched that he kissed every one of them after blowing out each of the fifty candles.

The months leading up to his fiftieth birthday had not been easy for him. It was a time for reassessment. He considered spending more time with his music. Maybe he would do some concerts, maybe not. He felt a strong urge to reevaluate and perhaps to reorganize his life. He knew that anxiety about middle age was normal—after all, he had written the treatment for *The Joy of Sex*, which had dealt with male menopause. But now that it was upon him, fifty didn't seem such a depressing age after all.

Dudley's earlier feelings toward his physical deformities had never been entirely resolved. They tended to subside during periods of public acclamation—he had never felt so good about himself as during the *10* and *Arthur* eras—but, as he told me during this period of reflection, he was still very angry about his leg. His resentment would never entirely disappear and every now and then it would resurface, usually when his self-esteem had received a new blow.

"A gentle man in a rage," is how one of his former therapists described him, and indeed it was hard for Dudley to find peace within himself, conscious as he always was of his clubfoot and thin leg, which governed his entire attitude toward his physical appearance.

It is revealing that, while he claimed to need or want for nothing, he joked that he would like to be able to walk around in shorts and tennis shoes. Only he wasn't joking. On hot California days, while everyone else was running around in scanty attire as the temperature climbed to 100 degrees, Dudley suffered in long trousers, too self-conscious to wear shorts. Others could potter naked around their homes, but he had to be covered in a long dressing gown. He had everything, seemingly, except the ease to be himself.

He envied violinist Itzhak Perlman, a polio victim at the age of four, whose parents had made him feel so emotionally secure that he never suffered any negative feelings from being handicapped. "When you have a disability at a young age, depending on the attitude towards it," Perlman affirms, "you get used to it very quickly and it becomes a way of life. My parents accepted my polio as a fact and they didn't think of it as a hindrance. They never said, 'You poor baby, you're disabled, you don't have to try so hard.' They never made me feel deformed or that I was less than I was, so I didn't feel emotionally rejected."

For Dudley, reminders of his deformity were always with him. There were regular visits to the orthopedic doctor to be fitted for new boots—a complicated procedure that necessitated precise measuring and a plaster cast to make sure the size of the lift compensated for the shorter left leg. He was also noticing that his left hip was dropping slightly and his foot once again had a tendency to flick inward as he walked. His limp was becoming more pronounced. His doctor told him there was an operation in which the knee could be broken and moved around, but Dudley had suffered enough of those operations during childhood. He would put up with what was happening. And the anger, too.

Appearing on a talk show, Dudley was asked by host David Steinberg if success had not obviated his feelings toward his clubfoot. "With all of your talents and gifts," Steinberg told him, "no one notices such a small thing as that." Dudley looked at him and quietly replied, "Maybe—but that will never be enough for me."

Dudley's association with pain was so intimate that when happiness came his way he could only enjoy it for a while before he would have to return to the pain that he'd always known. "It was a familiar coat for him," reflects Susan Anton, "like the way he wore the same clothes all the time. He needed something constant around him to feel safe, and to give up the pain would have probably been too terrifying."

His last few films had hardly set the box office on fire and, though the potential success of a film had never been his reason for working, it was hugely disappointing to him that they had not been met with more enjoyment. In Britain there was an increasing belief that Dudley had "sold out," and he was criticized for making mediocre films that had the sole merit of swelling his personal fortune. Dudley dismissed the accusations and defended his choice of work. None of the scripts had been vacuous or meaningless. Some had been highly intelligent, and most had been very funny. Money had never been his motivation for work: He judged a film by the script, and if he liked it and believed he would have fun making it, then he chose to do it. It was easy for Dudley's friends to say, as they all did, that he had picked the wrong ones, but he had no regrets about those he had chosen (except for *Wholly Moses*). He had felt them to be good at the time, and still felt that way.

It was apparent that the public mainly wanted to see Dudley in his more extreme characterizations. In *10* and *Arthur* he had given them a persona that they loved, and they wanted more of that vulnerable lovability wrapped inside an outrageous exterior. But since *Arthur* he had moved away from slapstick and was now finding himself trapped by two of his greatest assets—his sensitivity and his charm.

Audiences hoping for another *Arthur* found it hard to accept him in such different roles. "The trouble is, when you do something so convincingly as *Arthur*, it's hard then to go off and do something else," says publicist Paul Bloch. "The public still loved him, but they wanted the other side of him. And for someone as sensitive as Dudley, who needed the applause, it was much more difficult when it wasn't there."

Leslie Bricusse believes that only two directors had been able to bring out the best in Dudley—Blake Edwards and Steve Gordon. "They really found something together. They were the two whose own mad humors matched Dudley's. I wish Dudley had gone on with Blake, because Blake knew how to use him, but I think Dudley tried to fulfill other fantasies of his own. He tended to go towards Gary Grant–type roles. His two great gifts are music and comedy, but he tried to move on to his third gift, which is charm, whereas what I think people wanted from him was a combination of the first two assets."

The Hollywood that Dudley had so eagerly embraced in the late seventies was changing. He had arrived at a time when the big-budget movie still meant a cost of substantially less than $10 million. *Arthur*, for example, had cost $7 million to shoot.

By the mid-eighties, movies had become more expensive to make. Budgets had soared, and consequently films needed to take more money at the box office to break even. To go into profit, a movie had to make 2.5 times its budget, and a film like *Six Weeks*—which had cost $9 million in 1981 and needed $22 million to recoup its cost—had a better chance of doing that than a *Santa Claus*, which, with a budget of $50 million, had to earn $125 million before seeing production costs returned.

With so much more money at stake the studios could no longer afford to take chances with the actors they hired. Hollywood was now a more aggressive industry, and more bankable certainties like superstars Bruce Willis and Sylvester Stallone were squeezing out the smaller stars.

As he had always done when he needed emotional solace, Dudley turned to the place where he felt most at home—his music. By day he practiced classical works; by night he played jazz at his restaurant. People turned up just to hear him play. Even the bar was jammed. The only disadvantage was that people remained at their tables after dinner to continue listening, which meant less turnover for the restaurant.

Ray Brown, Dudley's occasional bass player, joined him there once. He found the clatter of cutlery too noisy for his taste, "but I learned later that's the way Dudley liked it. He didn't want to feel everybody was listening to him."

Dudley's jazz was a particular favorite with veteran pianist Oscar Peterson. Dudley considered him an extraordinary pianist, but it frustrated him that he was unable to emulate Peterson's velocity and the ease with which he attacked the piano.

"Dudley was a very warm player," says Peterson, who first met him in 1973 when paying homage to his talents in *This Is Your Life*. "He's a very honest player and gives it the full range of emotions. Jazz is instant composition, so you have to really speak your mind musically at a given moment. And, unlike many jazz pianists, Dudley becomes very involved in what he does."

One of Dudley's improvised jazz sessions caught the attention of the *Los Angeles Times*'s eminent jazz critic Leonard Feather, who noted, "His hands have never lost their touch." Nor their concentration—despite the stream of women who joined him on the piano bench.

In spite of his occasionally melancholy, he was immensely popular with women, and they gravitated toward him just as they had during the sixties and his jazz-playing days in London clubs. It made no difference that he was short, had a clubfoot, and walked with a limp: to women the world over he was adorable, and it was no surprise when an American poll voted him one of the world's most eligible bachelors.

"He knew beauty better than anybody, and went for goddesses," says

Brenda Vaccaro, who watched Dudley become the center of attention at her parties. "He ran around after everything that was beautiful, and you couldn't hold him by the seat of his pants."

Certainly he was never lacking for the company of beautiful women, as his friend Francis Megahy experienced many times. "We often went out to dinner alone—usually discussing whether it would be better to be miserable or lonely. (I thought it was better to be miserable; he thought it was better to be lonely.) And it always fascinated me how girls found some excuse to stop by our table. Women have been hitting on Dudley all his life, and even if he was not interested in them. he was always as sweet and charming and nice to the pushy people. It sometimes got very tiresome, but he had amazing patience."

Dudley's aversion to monogamy had not changed. He was popular, he had no desire for an exclusive romance, and he continued to take full advantage of his immense sex appeal. He felt as youthful as ever and, though age might have etched his laugh lines a little deeper and given his face an extra maturity, he didn't look much different from when he had arrived in America ten years earlier with Peter Cook.

Now his life was about to take another turn, for he had already met the woman who would eventually become his third wife. Her name was Brogan Lane.

CHAPTER 21

BROGAN

1985-1986

*"Dudley is drawn to needy women because it fills the void of his own
neediness. It's as if that's the only way he knows love."*

—BROGAN LANE

Dudley had met Brogan four years earlier, when she was an extra, during
the filming of *Six Weeks*. He had been attracted to her then, but had taken it
no further than a couple of drinks.

A month after his fiftieth birthday, Dudley was lunching alone in the
Beverly Hills restaurant Ma Maison, when he caught sight of her sitting at
a nearby table with a group of friends. She looked over and quietly
mouthed, "Do you remember me?"

Did he remember! In seconds he was across the restaurant and at her
table. He thought she was the most beautiful person he'd ever seen, and he
couldn't keep his eyes off her. Nor his hands. It was love and lust at first
sight, and they were soon kissing and carrying on like two besotted
teenagers. Later she recalled, "For the first time I was unable to keep my
hands off a man. It was instant. I just wanted to be close to him, and he
wanted to be close to me."

Brogan was a tall, leggy, and extremely attractive twenty-nine-year-old.
A five foot eight, green-eyed brunette, she was a former model and aspiring
actress who had been married once, while very young, and had a twelve-year-
old son, John.

Brogan's exuberance for life was magnetic, and she was a balm to
Dudley's wounded soul, recovering as he was from his recent broken love
affairs. She was warm and gregarious, and he was drawn to her openness.

He had always been extremely passionate—something he had considered in his youth to be rather ridiculous for such a short man—and he fell fast and hard.

He threw a party to introduce her, and his friends liked her instantly. "Brogan was a breath of fresh air," says Peter Bellwood. "Dudley always had very glamorous girlfriends, and Brogan was no exception. But she didn't live the glamorous life like some of them, and she was completely down to earth, which is a lovely quality in a person. She had quite a tough background and was a very courageous woman, overcoming lots of Sturm und Drang of the past. We all have our crosses to bear, but there was something very gutsy about her."

Brogan's father had left his family while she was very young, and she had felt the loss keenly. Leaving home and marrying at seventeen, she had struggled to bring up her son alone after her marriage failed. Now he was away at boarding school while she was pursuing a career in Hollywood. The progress was slow. Brogan was dyslexic, which impeded her ability to learn and read scripts.

Dudley had always been drawn to women with emotional need and Brogan had plenty of that. As did he. Almost like children, each came to this romance looking for the parental figure that neither of them felt they had known in childhood.

"I was very needy," says Brogan. "I used to think all men were my father, and he thought all women were his mother, so we probably didn't have a very adult relationship going on. We were very codependent on each other, and we put a lot of expectations on each other."

Although it often seemed that women wanted to mother Dudley, Dr. Evelyn Silvers, his psychotherapist at that time, believes the opposite to be more true. "Dudley doesn't choose women who want to mother him; he chooses women whom he can mother. He chooses the wounded, so that he can take care of them, because then he's taking care of that wounded part of himself."

Dudley had arranged for the Marina beach house to have a complete overhaul, and moved out while it was being refurbished. He moved into Brogan's rented house in Burbank, where they adopted a life of easy comfort, with barbecues and picnics in the back garden. In this relatively new atmosphere of calm and peace, encouraged by Brogan, he spent more time at the piano. His impatient, rushing nature had slowed down, and he was anxious to master music in a way he had not done in the past. Instead of dashing through a piece and allowing his impatience to limit his achievement, he spent hours breaking down sections of a concerto, practicing vigorously until having mastered one piece he could continue to the next. At last he was taking the time to do what he should have done thirty years earlier.

While he was striving to achieve some intimacy with the music he played, he was trying also to achieve the same in his personal life, and during that summer of 1985 he flew to New York to spend time with Patrick, now a robust but reticent nine-year-old. Growing up was a frustrating process, made all the more confusing for a child whose parents lived three thousand miles apart.

Dudley had always agonized about his role as a parent, and violinist Robert Mann witnessed the endless conflicts over his son. "He took great pride in Patrick. But Tuesday kept putting him down as a father, and Dudley was vulnerable to that. So he had enormous guilt feelings. And because a lot of it was unfair, he was also resentful, and all those things were warring away inside him."

Tuesday objected to Dudley spending time with Patrick in her house in East Hampton, outside New York, and insisted he stay in a nearby hotel. He understood her feelings but was disappointed because he'd always enjoyed hearing her husband, Israeli violinist Pinchas Zukerman, practicing, and was riveted by the thought that the world-famous musician was playing just a few feet away. Once they had played some Handel sonatas together in Tuesday's Manhattan apartment. "They're really rather dull," Dudley told Pinchas. "Yes they are," replied Zukerman, and put away the music and his violin. They never played together again.

It was while Dudley was in East Hampton with Patrick that he contracted vitiligo. When they went indoors after swimming, he was horrified at the sight of his face in a mirror. It looked as if someone had taken a paintbrush and painted a narrow white streak from eyebrow to chin. When Cary Grant saw him later, he was astonished. "How did you get like that?" he asked. "It's vitiligo," Dudley replied, but Grant was skeptical and lifted up his ears, searching for a telltale surgical scar. He was convinced Dudley had undergone a face-lift.

Vitiligo can be severely disfiguring, especially for a black person—singer Michael Jackson suffers from the disease—because it removes pigment from the skin. Dudley was lucky: He had a fairly mild case that was visible only when the rest of his skin darkened and the afflicted part of his face remained white. But from now on he had to keep out of the sun entirely or wear a strong sunblock, and if he forgot, he became violently sick and fatigued.

In November Dudley made his first public appearance in months, playing the piano at a Los Angeles gala for the Princess Grace Foundation. He was warmly applauded for his virtuosity at the piano, and it was, as Prince Albert wrote to him after returning to Monaco, "a wonderful musical moment."

That same month Dudley flew to London, accompanied by Brogan,

Lou Pitt and his wife, Berta, for the royal charity premiere of *Santa Claus*, in the presence of the Prince and Princess of Wales.

Inadvertently, Brogan upstaged Dudley through her unawareness of British royal protocol. While Dudley went to the men's room, she took their tickets and sat in the front of the circle next to Diana, where Dudley should have sat. "I'm sure we're in the wrong seats," Prince Charles told her, not wanting actually to say that protocol required a man to sit between two women. "No we're not," Brogan assured him, blithely unaware of any faux pas, and pulled out the tickets. "Look, here are our seat numbers." Still Charles insisted. "I'm sure we're in the wrong seats." Brogan looked at him closely, then suggested brightly, "Well, let's see your tickets then!" Charles gave up and sat down.

While they were in England, Dudley took the Pitts and Brogan to Oxford University and proudly showed them around Magdalen College. Attending Sunday vespers, they joined a long line to enter the college chapel. When people saw Dudley, Lou Pitt recalls, "they told us to go to the front of the line. But he wouldn't do that. He never wanted to use his celebrity to get him anywhere." They sat through the service, and Pitt felt shivers run down his spine as he imagined Dudley playing the organ in that very chapel thirty years earlier.

The night before *Santa Claus* opened in Los Angeles, Brogan threw a huge party for all Dudley's friends. Most of them who had seen the film, including Ben Shaktman, knew it was not very good, "so Brogan wanted to create a lovely party for him as a cushion for the shit he would have to face in the press reviews the next day. It was a beautiful and protective gesture."

Brogan believed firmly in friendship, and was always surrounded by her own close-knit group. "Dudley didn't have any friends," she reflects. "He had acquaintances. He never seemed to be able to bond with his friends for some reason, and it was peculiar to me. He never made an effort to call anybody. He always waited for them to call him, and I didn't understand that. So I re-created his friendships and always encouraged his friends to come to every party and made sure we all had dinners together."

Though Dudley was unable to reciprocate friendship in the same way as those around him, his friends knew that whenever they called, he would respond immediately and they were touched that Brogan respected and encouraged their long-standing relationships.

"A man should keep his friendship in constant repair," wrote Dr. Samuel Johnson, and they were words with which Brogan wholeheartedly agreed. "What I loved about Brogan," reflects Peter Bellwood, "was that she was always pushing him to stay in touch with his friends and his past. She cared so much about him and was always setting up social things where he would get together with his friends. It's really due to Brogan that I saw

more of Dudley during that period than any other time. And less of him
after they split up."

American comedienne Joan Rivers had taken her unique brand of
acerbic humor to Britain, where the BBC had given her a talk show with
Peter Cook as her sardonic sidekick. She asked Dudley if he would appear
on the show, and in January 1986 he was reunited publicly with Peter, to
the delight of British fans.

The pair's relationship was now a shadow of what it had been, with
only rare rendezvous and nostalgic memories, which sometimes took place
in public. As partners, they were immortalized in the annals of British
comedy; as friends, Peter's drinking and overt jealousy toward Dudley had
distanced them in an irreparable way.

Even before *Beyond the Fringe*, it was Peter Cook who had been the handsome and brilliant golden boy, the one who felt he would end up as the
movie star. And, believes Leslie Bricusse, "Logically he should have been,
and that's what went wrong with Peter. He didn't care what he said about
anything. By then, his frustration with himself had also grown into frustration that Dudley had done it, and it underlined and reinforced his own
feelings and made him wonder what the hell he had done wrong or what he
hadn't done to make it happen for him."

Cook, however, denied having any such aspirations. "I'm not trying
to copy Dud," he insisted, "because I don't have the same need to prove
myself. I don't crave international stardom. As long as I have known
Dudley, he has wanted nothing else."

But that wasn't true. "I never wanted to be a 'star,'" says Dudley, who
at the time seldom bothered to refute Peter's egregious analyses. "I always
thought that I would be a character actor my entire life."

By all accounts, Cook was the one who craved the stardom—at least for
a while. "Peter always longed for that type of show-business success," avows
Jonathan Miller. "He wanted to be a movie star, and envied Dudley that
particular success. God knows why—it seems to me to be a deplorable condition. He was very envious of someone he knew very well who was no
longer working with him and who had made it in the terms that he felt
'making it' should occur. Alan Bennett and I were always rather puzzled by
both of them in that respect."

Peter once observed that satirists "are always devouring each other."
Certainly he had borne this out as far as Dudley was concerned over the
years—spurred on periodically by the British press, whose scorn had been
aroused by Dudley's twenty years in therapy and an inability to stabilize his
personal life. Sighting a photograph of Brogan and Dudley together at a
disco, Cook caustically observed to one English newspaper that she looked
like Mick Jagger.

It was such comments that had prompted Dudley for some time to stop calling Peter whenever he came to London. He was unwilling to place himself any longer in the line of Peter's seemingly relentless caustic fire. The continual bombardment had hurt him, and he was anxious to avoid any further heartache Peter might cause him.

Peter's girlfriend, Lin Chong, who later became his wife, could see how it hurt Peter when Dudley came into town without calling him. He was a proud man and never spoke of it, but she sensed it and was sad for him. "Peter didn't realize how much he could hurt a person," Lin insists. "It was just his sarcastic manner of speaking, and he assumed Dudley would know that he loved him and would forgive anything he said. But he misjudged Dudley's sensitivity. Sometimes I would tell him, 'Darling, don't say that, even if you're only teasing,' and he would reply, 'You don't understand our relationship,' which I didn't, but in a way I did.

"It didn't cross Peter's mind that he could hurt Dudley. Just as it didn't occur to him that he could hurt me. We had a very difficult relationship before it became good. And then he mellowed considerably over the years and became less cutting about the things he said."

After the brief reunion on the Joan Rivers show, Lin went to see Dudley and explained to him how Peter had changed and softened. "It was a good meeting," she recalls affectionately, "and up to the time Peter died, he never knew I'd gone to see Dudley. I think that was a turning point. Their friendship seemed to grow again between them, and Peter was a lot happier after that. But Dudley had to get used to a new Peter who wasn't saying hurtful things anymore—a Peter who was capable of sending him a fax to say 'I love you' instead of teasing him about his height and his foot. I think they grew closer after that, and maybe my little intervention acted as a catalyst."

Dudley was moved that Lin cared so much for Peter and that she had wanted so much to revive their friendship. Never again would Dudley be out of touch, though he would continue to feel a certain wariness about Peter's tongue. They talked constantly on the phone, and Peter was always leaving messages on Dudley's answering machine just to let him know what was going on in his own life, even telling him if he was going away for a few days.

Over the years, Dudley had acquired a considerable knowledge of wines, though he never regarded himself as a connoisseur. He was perfectly happy to imbibe ordinary plonk, but it was the great wines that interested him, and he was willing to invest a fair amount of money to procure the best and rarest vintages—sometimes spending hundreds of pounds on a bottle. He still had a large collection of several dozen cases back in Britain that were being stored by wine-broker Richard Kihl, Lysie's brother, and Dudley wrote to him expressing interest in building a collection of outstanding red Bordeaux. "By the way," he added, "my girlfriend and I had a superb 1899 Lafite in New York recently and we will always remember it." No wonder! It had cost over one thousand dollars—a great deal of money to pay for a red wine, Dudley conceded, but he had had the most wonderful time drinking it.

Brogan loved exploring those red wines with him. "We had one bottle that was dated 1891, and we were both wide-eyed, imagining what people looked like back then, what they wore, and how they behaved. We had the best time with wine, and when Richard eventually sent over the hundreds of bottles that Dudley had stored in England, we had a wonderful time demolishing that lot."

His friends were aware of Dudley's appreciation of wine and enjoyed sharing fine bottles with him, albeit sometimes unknowingly. Francis Megahy took Dudley and Brogan to dinner one night and insisted on paying the bill—a ritual too often won by Dudley. "At least let me pay for the wine," pleaded Dudley, looking embarrassed. Megahy refused, but when the bill arrived, he was astonished to discover that it came to eight hundred dollars. They had been drinking two-hundred-dollar bottles of wine. "The only thing that upset me about that," Megahy laughs, "was that I hadn't noticed! To me, the wine didn't taste any different from a twenty-dollar bottle." Dudley was acutely uncomfortable, "but I didn't care. It was a mere fraction of the dinners I'd had off him over the years."

Life settled into a domestic pattern for Dudley during the early months of 1986, and with Brogan by his side he enjoyed mixing with the Hollywood elite. They joined Jackie Collins and her husband, Oscar, at their nightclub, Tramp's, had dinner with Bob Dylan at Chasen's, and dropped in on a birthday party for Blake Edwards's daughter, Jennifer. Joan Rivers invited them to a dinner party at her Bel Air mansion, and Brogan was fascinated by the regality with which the comedienne conducted the proceedings—particularly the beeper that Joan kept by her side to summon the butlers for each new course.

Rowan Atkinson wrote to ask Dudley to take part in a Comic Relief benefit concert to help the famine crisis in Africa. Every top British comedian was set to participate, and Atkinson was anxious to secure Dudley, whom he described as "a sodding great star in the U.S. as well as in the U.K." Dudley was amused by Rowan's words, especially since he had just learned from friends in Britain that film critic Barry Norman had publicly declared he seemed desperate for new scripts. "Well pooh to him!" Dudley wrote back to one pal. "I'm not, and I'm not really keen to get back to work. I'm enjoying a period of relative tranquillity."

This sounded particularly good to an overworked John Cleese, who promptly confessed in a letter to Dudley, "I feel rather envious that you have had an absence from work. I'm finally writing a movie and look forward to two years' reclusive reading thereafter. Or," he added as an after-thought, "I may become a librarian."

The lease on Brogan's rented house had now expired, and with Dudley's Marina home still under reconstruction they moved into a Beverly Hills residence for a few months—the same house that David Puttnam would rent after them during his brief tenure in Hollywood as head of Columbia. It had once been the home of dietitian/author Gayelord Hauser and, whenever she was in Los Angeles, his close friend Greta Garbo.

It was here that Dudley inherited Thomas Leahy, formerly Hauser's capable young Irish houseman. He became a valued friend, and when Dudley and Brogan eventually moved, they would take Tom with them, leaving David Puttnam having to search for a new majordomo.

Meanwhile, back in Britain, Jonathan Miller had long since added a new talent to his versatile repertoire and had become an opera director of considerable distinction. His version of Gilbert and Sullivan's The Mikado at the English National Opera had recently been a huge success with Eric Idle as Ko-Ko, the Lord High Executioner. Peter Hemmings, director of the Los Angeles Civic Opera and an old friend and fellow Cambridge scholar, asked him to direct it as part of the next U.K./L.A. Arts Festival two years ahead.

Hemmings suggested casting Dudley in the role of Ko-Ko—a propos-al, he recalls, that was received with some ambivalence. "Dudley was an obvious choice to me. I'd always felt Ko-Ko must be the archetypal sexy little man, and that's what Dudley had always been in his films. But Jonathan was somewhat doubtful at the time, and so was Dudley. I think he'd got to the point where he was a bit afraid of public stage performance. So I took Jonathan down to Dudley's restaurant and we all sat together and talked. Gradually, as the place filled up, the two of them started playing to an audience, with bits of old Fringe skits creeping in. I knew by then I had them hooked."

Jonathan's Mikado was not a traditional one; he had updated the set-ting by fifty years and abandoned the usual japonaiserie, the fad that had inspired Gilbert's libretto. Instead of Japan in the late 1800s, the action now centered on the 1930s art-deco lobby of the Anglo-American hotel in Florence. The result was somewhat reminiscent of Noel Coward.

Dudley was intrigued by the idea of turning The Mikado into a kind of English romp, and he also liked the prospect of "singing in a mildly serious way." It would give him the chance to pretend he was a choirboy again, reliving one of the few periods of his youth he passionately missed. During his Oxford days he had often played in the orchestra pit during Gilbert and Sullivan operas, but he had never performed in one on stage. He relished the prospect of spending several weeks in the company of

Jonathan Miller, whom he considered one of the most extraordinary men he had ever known. He couldn't wait to get started, and a date was set for March 1988.

While Brogan encouraged Dudley to play more music in public, he in turn was nurturing her acting aspirations, and under his tutorial eye she was now taking singing and speech lessons. She was grateful for his help, and expressed it with thoughtful little gestures. At least once a week she would give him a romantic card, or scribble endearing words in his appointments book. Anticipating an entry for his birthday, he had already written across the page for that date, "Hi Brogan! Snooping again??? I love you." On his birthday, he opened his diary and saw she had drawn a huge heart around his words and added, "You caught me! Help! Love you forever." Dudley cherished that playfulness between them. Sometimes he could forget he was an adult and revel in being childlike with someone who shared that same taste.

Brogan organized a surprise birthday party, invited dozens of Dudley's friends, and chartered a large yacht complete with orchestra and caterers to take them on a cruise down the coast. Everyone was aboard and dressed in white when Brogan arrived at the Marina jetty with a blindfolded Dudley in tow. Leslie Bricusse recalls him screaming with astonishment at the sight of so many friends. "It was a smashing day for him, with all the people he was most fond of. Brogan loved doing things like that."

A few weeks later, to mark the anniversary of their meeting, Dudley gave Brogan an eighteen-thousand-dollar pair of earrings. She decided to wear them at the racetrack with Cary Grant and his English bride, Barbara, but, in a rush to leave, she stuffed them in her pocket to put on later. At lunch she went to pull them out, but they were gone. "It was the first time Dudley hadn't insured a piece of jewelry. Cary thought it was funny and joked about it. Poor Dudley tried so hard to keep his cool, but he was almost beside himself!"

Dudley liked Cary Grant, an expatriate like himself. Cary was elegant and amusing to be around, and Dudley and Brogan saw quite a bit of him— often in the company of Cary's close friend the television producer George Schlatter, for whom Dudley had hosted some variety specials.

They should all have been present one night at the Grants' Beverly Hills house, and Barbara cooked bangers (sausages) and mashed potatoes in the kitchen while everyone drank vodka cocktails and waited for Dudley and Brogan to show up. In the meantime Cary played with a home-movie camera, and Schlatter turned it on the veteran actor. "Relax," he told a self-conscious Grant—"you're mugging, that's terrible. You don't even sound like Cary Grant! Try again. Say 'Judy, Judy, Judy.'"

Thousands of frames and many cocktails later, Dudley telephoned. Hugely apologetic, he admitted he had thought their dinner date was for the next night. "He screwed up our dinner,' laughs Schlatter, "but somewhere there exists an 8mm screen test of Cary Grant doing Cary Grant, which was only made possible by Dudley's failing memory."

Dudley's life with Brogan was opening him up to the outdoor world for the first time in his adult years. She was constantly persuading him to venture into activities previously unexplored—even skiing, though that necessitated having boots specially made for his clubfoot. "It devastated him to have his foot exposed, but he did it, and we went on the bunny slopes. He was so proud of himself."

Under Brogan's adventurous thumb, Dudley even tried camping in the California mountains. When she told him they were going to sleep in tents, he was astounded. "He thought I was nuts. My mistake was I hadn't done it in so long that I forgot to bring pads for the ground, so it was pretty hard. But we slept in the tent and giggled and had great fun. We did that a few times, but I found him a little bed-and-breakfast place after a while, so he had a choice where to sleep. I always gave him choices."

One of their more adventurous excursions was into whitewater rafting. Dudley was reluctant at first, but Brogan begged him to try it. If he didn't like it, she would never ask him again.

Dudley planned the trip with his usual methodical care and invited a few friends to join them. He sent limousines to pick everyone up, and, one weekend in July, Peter and Sarah Bellwood, Lou and Berta Pitt, and Kirstie Alley and Parker Stevenson found themselves screaming down a river in northern California. It was hair-raising, even though they were rafting down the easiest part of the river.

Despite Dudley's initial reluctance and extreme nervousness, he soon became the captain of the group and sat in the front of the boat, wearing a huge grin and screaming bloody murder. People on other rafts recognized him—"Hey, Arthur!" they shouted. At one point his raft became embroiled in a water fight with another one, and they were soon hurling buckets of water at each other.

Peter Bellwood was amused to see his old chum having so much fun. "Dudley got into this with bells on, and in his overenthusiasm to saturate the other boat, he not only threw the entire bucket of water over them— including the bucket—but also managed to fling himself into their raft. Whereupon they took him captive and rode away. So we lost Dudley and our bailing bucket, and we had to enter into negotiations with this other raft in order to get him back—which took quite some time."

The relationship between Brogan and Dudley was expanding both their worlds. In a sense, Brogan was the little girl Dudley could take care of, the daughter he could help and protect. He showed her the finer things in life and she introduced him to the fun side of living.

Frank Sinatra invited Dudley and Brogan to spend a weekend at his Palm Springs estate, along with Gregory Peck, George Schlatter, Roger Moore, Michael Caine, and their wives, and he showed them proudly around the sprawling compound, saving the best for last. He had set aside one cavernous room for an enormous collection of trains and planes, and here he had built a miniature train station that was his pride and joy.

They spent the first night eating, drinking, and laughing until very late. Dudley, naturally, clowned around with the other guests and played the piano (although Sinatra refused urgings to sing). After that he seemed to go missing for a while.

The next morning he and Brogan did not come out of their guest cottage for breakfast. Nor did they emerge for lunch. Their curiosity piqued, the other guests crept under the bedroom window, where they heard muffled moans and groans of ecstasy emanating from the room. They tried to send in a lunch tray laden with vitamins and fruit juice, and when that was ignored, they placed a fire extinguisher outside the bedroom door.

"Dudley and Brogan spent the entire day 'shtooping,'" George Schlatter recalls. "He even missed cocktail time, which was extremely rare for him. We were all a bit in awe of this. We'd heard of his sexual prowess, but hadn't witnessed it."

Not for nothing had Brogan dubbed Dudley her "sex thimble!"

"He should tie a knot in that thing!" laughs Schlatter. "When he goes, UCLA will vie with the Mayo clinic for Dudley's vital organs so they can analyze them."

Early that evening, accompanied by a glowing Brogan, an exhausted-looking Dudley finally stumbled out of his bungalow, in time for dinner.

"Brogan was a large, lusty lady," says Schlatter, "and for Dudley to have survived was a feat in itself. He was certainly in a weakened condition, having stayed up most of the night with Frank—which is a fun experience in itself—and then all of the day with Brogan. I believe drinking with Frank that weekend was the only rest he got!"

Sinatra wanted Dudley to perform with him on stage in the gay musical *La Cage aux Folles*. Dudley thought the chemistry between them could be interesting, but his instinct told him he wasn't right for the role of Albin. He didn't like the show, nor did he consider himself ancient enough to play the aging drag queen. Flattered by Sinatra's request, he was tempted to ignore his instinct and do it anyway, but finally he declined the offer.

He had also been asked to do a musical version of *Arthur* on Broadway. He turned that down, too. He couldn't imagine *Arthur* as a musical.

Drunken songs, he wondered—how on earth could that work? Besides, he didn't like musicals and didn't want to be in one.

That was unfortunate for Blake Edwards, who some years later harbored hopes of Dudley playing the lead opposite Julie Andrews in the Broadway version of his film *Victor/Victoria*. "He's so musical and I thought he would have been brilliant, but he just didn't want to do it," recalls Blake. "I think it was a mistake on his part, but when you think about Broadway, you have to think of a year and a half out of your life. Dudley's music and concerts were important and it would have meant giving that up, but I always thought it was too bad, because it would have been really extraordinary."

During this long sabbatical from films, Dudley returned to writing. Not music, but words. *Musical Bumps* was a book full of musical anecdotes, interlaced with Dudley's own often humorous nostalgia. "I received my first musical bump at a very tender age when I was summarily informed that I was too small to carry the cross at the head of the church choir," he wrote. "Ricocheting about the musical world has enabled me to have a taste of everything from choral singing to cabaret, from madrigals to movie compositions, and from locations as varied as a bar in Greenwich Village and Carnegie Hall."

He had also written a postscript for a new book *The Complete Beyond the Fringe*, which incorporated all the scripts from the stage show. Strangely, of the four Fringers, only Dudley and Peter Cook seemed able to express delight about their endeavors of twenty-five years earlier. Jonathan Miller and Alan Bennett appeared almost embarrassed about the whole period.

"I don't think I ever had such grand excitement," Dudley wrote. "It was everything I had ever wanted, to be on stage in a revue." Still, he recalled, "To my fairly disguised humiliation I was not able to participate in any way that could be hailed as helpful. Therefore I was a mildly mute person on stage while the others flourished their wares shamelessly. I think my musical efforts were viewed somewhat patronizingly—certainly with little comprehension."

Dudley had been feeling very fatigued lately, and a battery of medical tests revealed an abnormally low white blood cell count. The doctors wondered if he might be suffering from the chronic fatigue illness Epstein-Barr Syndrome. He exhibited its various symptoms—anxiety, lack of concentration, sore throat, and a chronic fatigue that he told doctors he had experienced for the last eight years. None of the tests yielded normal results—except for his cholesterol level, which had dropped from the previous year's excessive high to an acceptable level—but nothing was ever pinned down. Maybe it was just a product of age, and eventually Dudley recovered his lost energy.

He may have taken time off from work but he was still much in demand. All the talk shows wanted him as their guest, from Johnny Carson and Larry King to David Frost and Terry Wogan. He flew to New York for a guest lunch appearance with the New York Philharmonic, catching up while he was there with his *Lovesick* director Marshall Brickman and *Saturday Night Live* producer Lorne Michaels. He took with him the usual handful of Nintendo games for Patrick, along with his portable Yamaha so they could play duets.

December 1986 was a whirl of moving back into the Marina house. Dudley threw a party to celebrate his return home. He had been away over a year. He arranged for Christmas trees and lights to be installed inside and out, and ordered dozens of Christmas puddings and Christmas crackers from Paddingtons, the English teashop in Hollywood.

His next-door neighbors were particularly glad to see him back in the beach house, for they had missed his music. Carol Doumani's first pleasure of the day was to wake up to the strains of Bach wafting over from next door, and she would open all her windows so she could hear better.

Dudley's Mediterranean-style terra-cotta house had been decorated in pale beach tones with curving white walls and pine floors, and Brogan's influence showed throughout its country interior. An antique Coca-Cola dispenser stood near a rocking horse, and teddy bears filled the master bedroom, with its tall French windows overlooking Venice Beach, the local bird sanctuary, and a public lavatory. On the landing Brogan had hung a poster-size blowup of Dudley's first composition, "Anxiety," written when he was twelve.

In the living room stood the grandfather clock that reminded Dudley of England, though he had bought it in California. Nearby was his favorite painting—a bleak English winter scene with children playing in the snow, bought one year down the King's Road with Suzy Kendall. Two grand pianos stood back to back, their lids covered with dozens of framed photographs and miniature glass animals. A set of encyclopedias rested on a shelf above the log fire. In the basement Dudley had installed a cold-storage vault for his wines, capable of holding a couple of hundred bottles.

Brogan wanted more than to just live with Dudley, but he wavered constantly in his feelings. First he wanted to get married, then he didn't. He had bought her a ring that she wore on her engagement finger, but a little later he asked her to put it on the other hand.

After one of their endless discussions about marriage, Brogan decided to be alone for a few days. "I have to give myself private time to work out what I want to do with my life," she wrote in a note for Dudley. "I guess it's easier for you to cope with this situation and your feelings. I have no idea how I'm going to work out my hurt." Still, she missed Dudley so much that she soon returned, although the marriage issue still simmered within her.

In February 1987 Dudley was playing jazz at his restaurant when, to his surprise, Bo Derek walked in and joined him on the piano stool. At that moment Eamonn Andrews appeared from a side door and announced to Dudley the familiar words "This is your life." It was déjà vu to Dudley, who had already heard those words once before, in 1973. He was now one of a small elite group to be handed their life twice.

Ushered over to ABC's television studios in Hollywood by *Arthur* chauffeur Ted Ross, he was reunited in front of a live audience with his sister Barbara, who had flown in from England, and Peter Cork, his former music tutor. Brogan was there, of course, and so were Joan Rivers, Jackie Collins, Tony Bill, and Robin Williams. While Cleo Laine, John Dankworth, Sammy Cahn, and Henry Mancini paid tribute to Dudley's jazz ability, Robert Mann, Itzhak Perlman, and members of the Los Angeles Philharmonic appeared as testimonial to his classical talents, and Peter Cook turned up via satellite.

Dudley took over the piano, with Ray Brown on bass and John Dankworth on sax, and Chevy Chase joined him for a few jazzy moments.

The show culminated with Bob Hope dubbing him "Sir Dudley of Dagenham," for which Hope commanded him to kneel, then observed with a wry laugh worthy of Peter Cook, "It doesn't make a hell of a lot of difference, does it!" Shown in Britain the following month, the program was transmitted as a rare two-parter.

The televised review of Dudley's life coincided with the end of his own ruminations. He had embarked on his two-year-long sabbatical with the intentions of reassessing his life and revitalizing his creativity, but nothing much had emerged beyond a long rest, a great deal of piano practice, and a heavily depleted bank account.

He was hardly broke. Years of wise spending and smart investments had protected his assets, and ever since *Arthur* he had negotiated a profit percentage of every one of his movies, but the refurbishing of the house had cost a small fortune. He still had the Bentley that he'd brought over in the seventies—its London license plates now replaced by the Californian proclamation "TENDRLY"—but its value had dropped, and it was almost constantly in the garage being repaired. The good life did not come cheap, and he decided he had better go back to work.

It really wasn't money Dudley needed, though. It was work. His earlier feelings of burnout had been replaced by a new vitality. He felt creative, and the desire—the need—to perform had returned.

For the last few months he had been making mild noises about returning to films. The scripts had continued to pour in during his sabbatical but none had appealed to him. Now one did.

CHAPTER 22

BACK TO WORK

1987-1988

"It sounds sappy, but working with Dudley is the most pleasant way there is of spending a day. Beyond the fact that he is one of the great physical comedians, working with a guy like that is the very reason you do movies."

—ROD DANIEL

In March 1987 Dudley came out of his self-imposed retreat and returned to work on his first film in two years.

Like Father, Like Son saw Dudley play an ambitious surgeon and strict father to sixteen-year-old Kirk Cameron. Accidentally they drink a brain-transference potion and their minds become trapped in each other's body, with hilarious results. By the time they return to normal, they have gained new respect for each other, and fresh understanding of the intense pressures they face in their individual lives.

Dudley struck up an instant rapport with director Rod Daniel and was enchanted by his exuberance. Daniel, who had made only one previous feature, *Teen Wolf* with Michael J. Fox, had a hearty sense of humor and laughed constantly, which made him a perfect match for Dudley.

He soon witnessed Dudley's ability to handle the unexpected. In one scene, after setting the living-room sofa on fire, Dudley had to push a burning sofa out of the French windows into the swimming pool and walk away as it sank to the bottom of the pool. But, as Rod Daniel recalls, the sofa didn't sink. "It stayed up there and burned and burned! It looked like a flaming battleship in that pool, but I kept the camera rolling because Dudley was still working and giving me one of those incredibly funny W. C. Fields reactions.

"People always said Brando was a pure improvisational actor, that it didn't matter what was scripted, he would always keep going. To me, Dudley was the same. If you didn't say 'Cut,' the guy would still be going. He's the purest form of comic, in the sense that it's never over for him."

In spite of the humor they shared, Rod Daniel saw the melancholia beneath the face of the clown. "You can't be 'on' that much, and he was painfully so. He's a great clown, but he has those two Shakespearean masks, the tragedy and the comedy. It's the thing that endears him to me, because you sense that. When the black comes to him, it must be overwhelming, and you want to grab the little son of a bitch and just hold him."

Brogan had been studying makeup so she would have something to fall back on while pursuing an acting career. With this film she landed her first assignment, and from now on she would always do the makeup for Dudley's film and television appearances.

Dudley had a lot riding on this film—not least the resurrection of his wilting film career. He had been criticized for doing less than the best material, and he needed this movie to restore his credibility.

In July he performed two nights of concerts at the Hollywood Bowl, playing part of Beethoven's Triple Concerto and excerpts from his own film scores, followed by jazz with Ray Brown on bass and Jeff Hamilton on drums.

Susan Anton, who had remained friendly with Dudley and was as much an admirer of his music as ever, had hoped to attend the concert but was caught in her own show in Las Vegas. "I know you're going to be wonderful," she cabled him. "Just remember if they can't take a joke, ... em. Now go and have fun."

He did have fun—especially with his jazz. Long after the orchestra had been sent home, Dudley was still playing. The audience loved it, and so did the critics. "He held forth respectably in both Beethoven and jazz," claimed the *Hollywood Reporter*, "and in general displayed the incredible talent that is Dudley Moore."

Dudley had recently bought another house—in Toluca Lake, an affluent retreat near North Hollywood, just a few streets away from the estate where Bob Hope had lived for decades. It was a French cottage on two floors with a swimming pool and a small garden. Brogan decorated it with a warm, nostalgic touch, hanging dried flowers from the kitchen ceiling and old pictures on the walls, which gave it a quaint charm. They liked to spend weekends there, when the beach at Marina del Rey became too populated, and then Brogan would fill the new house with friends and the strains of Dudley's piano playing could be heard throughout the neighborhood.

A few weeks after his concert at the Hollywood Bowl, Dudley flew to New Jersey to perform Beethoven's Triple Concerto again, this time in the distinguished company of Itzhak Perlman and Yo-Yo Ma. He more than held his own with the two world-famous musicians. Of the three soloists, the *New York Post* noted that "Moore seemed to have taken his job the most seriously." "The audience loved him," agrees Perlman. "He gave a really good performance, and we all enjoyed ourselves tremendously—especially in that delightful outdoors environment."

Dudley loved the Triple Concerto. He found it sweet and touching, especially the deeply stirring middle movement. It had merriment and joy, and he had always been moved most by a sense of wit in a musical work. He had never considered a sense of comedy to be incompatible with music and once ventured that, given a few differences, Itzhak Perlman might have made a fine stand-up ("or, in his case, sit-down") comic.

"I've always seen humor in life," admits Perlman, "and I enjoy and appreciate it and use it in my work. But one has to know when to apply it. In certain pieces of music a sense of humor and fun seems to fit, but obviously it depends on what you're playing. That's why it's particularly enjoyable to play with Dudley, who has so much humor himself and sees it in a piece of music."

The next day, Dudley flew to the Caribbean island of St. Barthélemy (known as St. Barth) with Brogan and Patrick, and they were joined in their beachfront villa a few days later by Tom Leahy; Brogan's son, John; with whom Dudley had already established an affection; and three of their Los Angeles friends.

Patrick, now eleven, had not easily accepted Brogan into his life, afraid as he was of losing his father, on whom he doted. It seemed to him that, whenever he came to visit, Dudley ignored him and played the piano all day. "I'd want to practice with him and he'd get pissed off, so I'd go back to my room and stare at the ceiling. And then in the evening he'd go out with Brogan.'" This had once gone on for a week, until an angry Patrick ventilated his hurt feelings. "My mother has remarried to Pinchas Zukerman and now Brogan has moved in with my father," he wrote in a poignant letter to Dudley. "I'm confused. I feel like a foster child."

Relations improved after that cry from the heart. Brogan, who understood Patrick's fears, tried to include him in everything that she and Dudley did, but it would be a long time before his antipathy subsided. He was an angry and unhappy boy who had not felt much security in his family relationship in New York. When Pinchas Zukerman came into Tuesday Weld's life, he felt his mother receding, and she now seemed to have little time for him.

Patrick used to follow her everywhere. One night, recalls his grandmother, Jo Weld, Tuesday and Pinchas went into the bedroom and shut the door in his face. "I don't think they even thought about it. They didn't do it on purpose, but Patrick walked back down the passage and threw himself on the couch. He was so angry and hurt, and it broke my heart."

In St. Barth, however, Patrick spent a lot of time with his father, and felt more reassured about their relationship. Sometimes, he recalls, they went in the ocean together at night, "and it reminded me of the times my dad used to take me to the beach and play volleyball or chase me along the sand. But I don't remember him doing that much after I was about five years old."

During the vacation, Dudley experienced a brief sense of relief over his physical abnormalities. Brogan remembers how he used to tell her wistfully that he yearned to run barefoot on the beach and feel normal without being so scared about his foot. In St. Barth he got his wish, and walked barefoot on the beach at sunset in front of their friends.

Long before his divorce from Tuesday Weld had become final in 1981, Dudley had publicly vowed he would never remarry. Marriage had never added anything to his life; indeed, it had taken away from it. Being married implied a respectability that he was incapable of acknowledging, a commitment to the future that he felt was impossible to make.

Marriage was too ensnaring for Dudley. It left him feeling starved of the rest of the world, filled with anxiety and a dreadful feeling of being unable to move. He once tried to explain these emotions and ventured, confusedly, that "being on such a monogamous level with my mother gave me the belief that I did not want to be married to her (my mother)—and therefore not to anybody else either." Even if this didn't make sense, somehow everything always went back to his mother.

Dudley also could not shake off his need for other women. He was addicted to them in much the way that Peter Cook was addicted to alcohol. He loved them and wanted them, but couldn't conceive of being tied down to just one woman. He needed to know there were many women who thought him desirable, and he craved their love and attention. In many ways it compensated for his shortness. Even in therapy he had never resolved this obsessive and compulsive side of his psychological makeup. Sex was paramount to him. He reveled in it, and when he was alone he loved to watch X-rated movies, which he ordered by the caseload, spending hours editing the best bits together. Sometimes his girlfriends would watch the films with him.

This was years before Michael Douglas publicly admitted to his addiction to sex and checked himself into a clinic to overcome his compelling need and to salvage his badly damaged marriage.

It was difficult for Brogan, who recognized Dudley's compulsion. Whenever they were out, women seemed to flock to his side. At home, the phone constantly rang with women wanting to see him. Dudley did nothing to discourage them. The rows were inevitable.

He was still seeing psychotherapist Dr. Evelyn Silvers, often twice a week. With her he believes he experienced the most valuable therapeutic exploration of his life. After one of their sessions that left him in a reflective mood, he wrote in his diary:

"Paradox"
I have stopped pretending to be God.
I have become God.
I have opened myself to criticism. The criticism will fade.
There is beauty in my heart.

Dudley's last foray into therapy was the only time he had worked with a woman therapist, and he came to depend enormously on Silvers, regarding her in some ways as the mother figure for which he had always envied others. He held her in great esteem, and once gave her a diamond ring as an expression of his affection.

He was now often to be found playing jazz at his restaurant in Venice, but he made a surprise appearance one night at The Loa, Ray Brown's jazz club in Santa Monica. "It was amazing," Brown remembers. "The women were lined up for two blocks down the street. We'd never seen so many people in that joint before."

Frank Sinatra and George Schlatter were among those who clamored for a seat. "Frank was a huge fan of Dudley," says Schlatter, "and he thought his musicianship was astounding. He adored watching him play, and at the end of every number that night he stood up to give Dudley an ovation."

Another of Dudley's followers was Chevy Chase, who had grown up around many jazz greats, hanging out during his formative years in New York jazz clubs. "Even more than his comedy, I like to listen or watch Dudley at the piano," Chase reflects. "There's an absorption in the art, a total peace. And the face gives it away. The face says his heart is working."

In September *Like Father, Like Son* had its Los Angeles premiere, at the Chinese Theater on Hollywood Boulevard.

Dudley had hoped his newest film would restore his ailing career, but though it came close to being a shrewd satire, it failed to live up to its full potential. The critics were almost unanimously, and rather unfairly, scathing. *Variety* dismissed it as "98 minutes of benign drivel," the *New York Post* deemed it "dismally, painfully not funny and one of the most desperate comedies ever seen," while the *Daily News* said, "The sallow photography makes him look as if he was in need of a doctor instead of just a new agent." The *New York Times*, at least, differed, declaring that "Dudley and Kirk Cameron are so clever and charming that they turn a potential dud into a sweetly engaging film." It was not the most auspicious return to film-making, although the movie would become a financial success, which compensated a little, since Dudley had a percentage of the profits.

A few days later Dudley was accorded the honor of his star being unveiled in the Hollywood Walk of Fame, just across the road from where his new movie was playing. He was now immortalized beneath millions of feet on Hollywood Boulevard, next to Louis Armstrong's star. It was, he told Johnny Carson that night, "pretty amazing!"

In November, Dudley was reunited on stage with Peter Cook for America's Comic Relief television special, hosted by Robin Williams, Whoopi Goldberg, and Billy Crystal. It was the first time they had performed together since the last Derek and Clive album in 1976.

They resurrected the immortal sketch One-Legged Tarzan, and it was clear to those present that there was still an enormous chemistry between them. Dudley cracked up the whole way through, and Peter seemed to take perverse pleasure in causing this. They were harmonious and relaxed, and the audience found them wildly funny.

Robin Williams, a cohost of Comic Relief since its inception, was a lifelong fan of Peter and Dudley, yet he had never seen them perform live until that night. "It was wonderful to see them together," he recalls ecstatically. "It's one thing to hear them on the albums and see their videos but quite something else to watch them together on stage and see how they played back and forth. I'd always appreciated them so much, especially in films like *Bedazzled* and *The Wrong Box*, which were really funny movies, like the next step up from the Ealing comedies.

"Peter and Dudley were obviously descended from the Goons, but they were great comics of their own who played off each other brilliantly. It was amazing for me to see them live and watch the two different energies at work—Peter's dryness and Dudley bouncing off of that on one leg. There was a real feeling of euphoria in the air that night, and they obviously enjoyed being back together again."

Despite their triumphant reunion, there was no sense that the couple might reunite permanently. The gulf between their two lifestyles was too wide. Peter, every inch of his tall frame an Englishman, loathed leaving London for any length of time and felt the deepest homesickness whenever he was away for more than a few weeks. As for Dudley, he was firmly entrenched in his California nest.

Age and Brogan were weaving a relaxed environment around Dudley, and it helped that financially he was secure enough not to feel pressured into accepting the next "bad" script that came across Lou Pitt's desk. More than ever before, he sought peace in his life these days, understanding that his best music would come when he played in an atmosphere of relative tranquillity. He spent hours every day at one of his two grand pianos, usually playing Bach, who had replaced in his heart the God in whom he had long ago ceased to believe.

Violinist Robert Mann was a frequent visitor whenever he was on the West Coast, and their times together were the best in Tom Leahy's memory. "One night they put on this concert for us, and they were fabulous together. Robert was very good for Dudley. He made him laugh, and it was rare to hear Dudley laugh like that—just really alive."

Director Stanley Donen was another familiar face at the Marina house. One evening Dudley jokingly revealed that he had never been paid for the extra work he had done on his *Bedazzled* score, and then was profoundly embarrassed when Donen made out a check on the spot for three thousand dollars. Dudley returned it a few days later with a note. "I guess having embarrassed you," Dudley wrote, "you did a wonderful job of making me feel more than small (!) by writing the cheque. I'm really sorry that I brought this up. I was only trying to be funny."

Brogan's Sunday lunches became a popular tradition with their friends, who enjoyed her food as much as hearing Dudley play the piano while she was cooking. Like Suzy Kendall before her, she usually served Dudley's favorite rack of lamb with pureed cream carrots and roast potatoes with mint, followed by jelly. That's when the grand bottles of wines in the vault were gleefully uncorked. "Dudley loved those festive gatherings," says Brogan, "and that's when that house came alive and had a different feeling to it."

Although Brogan brought a warmth and brightness to the beach house, she did not feel comfortable there. "It had Dudley's air about it—an air of being closed in—and it felt confined and sad."

Dudley liked pleasing Brogan with little acts of appreciation, and he particularly enjoyed buying her presents. Although frugal toward himself, he was wildly generous to others and spent thousands of dollars on antique jewelry for Brogan. He asked her to make out a wish list, and since what she wanted more than anything was to be Dudley's wife it was hardly surprising that this crept on to it:

A front porch for Toluca Lake. A white fence. A trip alone with you. A hat like the one from St. Barth's. Old European paintings. Bicycle. A HUSBAND!! Pillows. Ring. A big hug. Car. Compassion. You. Unusual plates. Tea cup poodle. Portable telephone. Write me a song, perhaps play with a saxophone. You to be happy. Grandfather clock. Your makeup artist as long as you can stand it.

Brogan's wishes were granted. All of them.

In spite of his earlier contrary feelings, Dudley decided he would marry Brogan, and in the back of his diary he scribbled out some prenuptial notes that included giving her the Toluca Lake house after their marriage.

Brogan had influenced and taught Dudley a lot—a fact that surprised him, since she was so much younger—and she had an intuitive directness that he found quite startling. He felt settled with her, too, which was unusual for him. In the past he had always become itchy and insecure when around a woman for very long, but now he felt taken care of in a way that he enjoyed, even though from time to time he still needed his own space and the attention of other women.

Nevertheless, there were arguments—many centered around the one issue Dudley had never been able to resolve in his life: his mother.

For many years he had felt guilty about playing the piano better than his mother, and he was convinced that sometimes this guilt took over and prevented him from playing—a belief that had been exacerbated, if not originally implanted, through therapy.

When his hand hurt one day and he had difficulty playing, he called Evelyn Silvers, who explained it was connected to his mother and suggested he come in for a session. Brogan did not share his therapist's belief that physical ailments could be triggered by past emotional upset. "Your hand doesn't have anything to do with your mother!" she shouted at him. "It has to do with you don't exercise or you may be getting older, but it has nothing to do with your mother!"

Another patient of Dr. Silvers was Susie Dullea, a longtime friend of Dudley's since the sixties when, as an unknown performer, he had filled in as piano accompanist to her father, singer Frederick Fuller, who was appearing in his own late-night show at the Edinburgh Festival at the same time as *Beyond the Fringe* was making its debut there. Formerly married to British theatrical director, Peter Coe, Susie and her husband, actor Keir Dullea, had been persuaded by Dudley some years earlier to join group therapy with "Rev. Ev." She recalls that Dr. Silvers had long been researching the theory that physical ailments could be provoked by emotional troubles. "She believed in the concept that things like arthritis are directly tied in with our emotional condition, and to me that made complete sense."

Everything seemed to revert to Dudley's mother; he never blamed his father for any failings, even though he too had been emotionally unavailable. Jock Moore had been passive and seldom spoke, and was never the male role model that Dudley had needed in his life. When Dudley had a postnasal drip one time, he attributed that entirely to his mother, because she had smoked. Yet so had his father. "He's never made peace with his mother," ventures his friend, the music editor Else Blangsted. "There were great conflicts because she was erratic in her love, and he always felt this inconsistency."

Ever since the overwhelming success of *Arthur* in 1981 there had been discussions about making a sequel, but nothing had ever matched the standards set by Steve Gordon, who had died tragically the year after *Arthur*'s release. Until *Arthur 2: On the Rocks*.

Andy Breckman, a comedy writer for *Saturday Night Live* and a devout Steve Gordon fan who claimed to know every line of the original script, had been working on a new script for two years, and Dudley grew convinced that this was the one that would do justice to the original. He was paid $3 million to star in the film and also to be executive producer. Veteran comedy director Bud Yorkin, former partner of respected television producer Norman Lear, was hired to direct.

In December 1987 Dudley, Liza Minnelli, and Sir John Gielgud—Hobson having been resurrected from the dead in a single, all too brief, flashback—were reunited in New York, with Brogan playing a small role as a waitress.

Arthur 2: On the Rocks sees Arthur and Linda now married and attempting to adopt a baby. But the father of Arthur's ex-fiancée has never forgiven him for jilting his daughter, Susan, at the altar. Bent on revenge, he buys out the controlling interest of the Bach family firm and manipulates the family into cutting off Arthur's finances. Convinced that Arthur can only be happy with money, Linda leaves him so he can marry Susan and have his fortune restored. Drunk, penniless, and down and out, Arthur is on the verge of capitulating to escape vagrancy, when he is visited by his beloved Hobson.

"You're a spoiled little shit," admonishes Hobson. "I've told you before, you can do anything with your life that you want. Stop your drinking." Refortified, Arthur sobers up and confronts Susan's father, who is ultimately forced to have the inheritance reinstated, leaving Arthur and Linda to be blissfully reunited.

Liza Minnelli, who would do an outstanding job of running Dudley's fan club if she ever chose to, was ecstatic about working with him again. "Here's this incredible genius of a man who doesn't really know he's attractive but who knows what's funny. He understands Arthur's innocence and what a good person he is. Because that's Dudley, too.

"It's an extraordinary thing," she ponders. "It's like we're less than lovers but more than friends. Sometimes we don't have to talk. We can just look at each other and know what the other is thinking. We went together so well."

The success of the original film had been an immense surprise to Sir John Gielgud. It had brought the unassuming eighty-three-year-old actor an entirely new audience who had never known him through his stage work. And it elevated his earnings to a level he had never known before. When he arrived in New York to shoot his one scene, he was astonished by the reaction of the cast and crew. "I turned up on this huge set under one of the bridges, and when everyone saw me, they all started clapping. I was very touched by that. I hadn't acted in New York for some years, and it was awfully nice to know that they still remembered me.

"I loved that butler, Hobson," he reminisces, "and I was so very glad they found a way to bring him back from the grave to advise Arthur on his new troubles. It felt very good to be working with Liza and Dudley again, even for only a few days."

Bud Yorkin, who had directed some of America's finest comedians—among them Dick Van Dyke—was fascinated by Dudley's originality. "The first take is usually the most spontaneous, yet if I said, 'Try it again,' Dudley would have us all in hysterics. 'Fuck it!' he would say, and then he'd say it again in nineteen different languages, from Pakistani to Japanese. He was very funny.

"Dudley and Liza together were a perfect combination. They're both very moist human beings who tear up easily. Whatever turmoil Dudley hides inside himself, you never know it from the surface. He was always so funny you figure the man never has a problem."

Although everyone worked well with Bud Yarkin, they felt the absence of Steve Gordon. "Everyone gave it their best shot," says Liza ruefully, "but we didn't have our *auteur*, and in a funny way we spent the whole time trying to do him justice. I think that shows, and that's not funny."

On Valentine's Day 1988 Dudley formalized his decision about marriage and proposed to Brogan, presenting her with an engagement ring of two heart-shaped diamonds separated by an emerald-cut blue sapphire.

One week later, as soon as filming had ended on *Arthur 2*, they flew to Las Vegas in the Warner Bros. jet, accompanied by the Bellwoods and the Pitts.

The Little Church of the West, which Liza Minnelli had recommended, was a tiny, homely chapel, unlike some more garish offerings of Las Vegas. Dudley nervously sat down at the church organ and played classical music while he waited for Brogan to appear.

When she entered the chapel, she took everyone's breath away. She was exquisite in a flowing low-cut wedding gown and a veil of tiny flowers. She held a bouquet of tulips and baby's breath, and was flanked by four bridesmaids in lavender gowns. Dudley looked unusually elegant in a gray, cutaway morning coat with tails and top hat. They made an exceptionally handsome couple.

When the short service was over, they left the chapel walking on a path of paper hearts. Dudley, wearing a wedding ring for the first time in his life, shouted, "This time this is the one!"

After a small reception they flew back to Los Angeles. An exhausted Brogan, still in her wedding gown, slept through the forty-five-minute flight. In the Marina house that night they held another wedding reception, this one for friends, who gathered around the long pine dining table and toasted the beaming newlyweds.

To Leslie Bricusse, they seemed compatible and happy, "and I wasn't surprised that they got married, even though Dudley had kept saying he wouldn't do it again."

They were soon deluged with telegrams. "Congratulations!" wrote Joan Rivers. "I hope you know in the Jewish religion an elopement means no gift!"

Dudley would say that with Brogan he married his mother, but he had married his daughter, too, for, as Brogan points out, they were over twenty years apart and she needed a father as much as he needed a mother.

There was one odd occurrence that first night. Someone called the house and asked for Dudley, and when Brogan said he wasn't around, the voice told her, "He's gotten married and broken Nicole's heart. I hope this woman is worth it." "I am!" replied Brogan, and the person on the other end hung up.

Dudley had told Brogan of young Nicole Rothschild, with whom he had earlier had an affair, but she did not know they had continued to stay in touch, even though Nicole was now married with two children.

A few minutes after that first call the phone rang again, and a new voice told Brogan, "It's Nicole." She sounded upset, and Brogan asked her what was wrong. "I just can't believe he got married!" she replied. Brogan, true to her belief in maintaining old friendships, told her she'd be welcome any time to come over and visit them.

On the Monday morning after their weekend wedding, Dudley reported to work for first rehearsals of *The Mikado*, with opening night barely two weeks away. Jonathan Miller remembers Dudley turning up with his new bride in tow, and it struck him that "she looked like Karen Black in *Five Easy Pieces*, as if she'd just tottered out of a trailer in rhinestone-encrusted high-heel shoes."

Appearance notwithstanding, Miller got on well with Brogan, who enjoyed watching the two men bat around every topic in the world.

Dudley had been looking forward to *The Mikado*, not so much because he had never appeared on stage in Gilbert and Sullivan before—although he had played the violin in *H.M.S. Pinafore* at Oxford and conducted segments from *The Mikado* in *Foul Play*—but more for the opportunity to work again with Miller, whom he regarded as a remarkable talent. However, he had not realized the amount of work the role entailed and was not as prepared as he should have been.

"He was rather ill-focused at the beginning," Miller recalls, "and hadn't bothered to learn it properly. It took some days for him to buckle down and really give it the same attention he gives to the piano. He thought he could wing it, and he often maddened his colleagues in the early rehearsals by not knowing the words or the music. We had to be very firm with him and tell him it wasn't something he could wing his way through. He suddenly realized it was a serious business and pulled his finger out, and once he learned it he did very well. He's a real actor, besides being a marvelously accomplished clown, and he did a wonderful job."

Dudley enjoyed the challenge, and found the stage surprisingly seductive now that he was treading the boards once more.

"Knock 'em out!" cabled his friend, the *Hollywood Reporter* columnist George Christy on opening night. And Dudley did. "A comedian of the first order," announced *Variety*. "His grab-bag of physical gags is still immensely entertaining and he is not at all out of his element while singing."

Dudley more than exceeded the hopes of Los Angeles Opera director Peter Hemmings, who had been so insistent about securing him for the role. "His sense of timing was excellent, and his bits of dancing were really effective. I think Dudley himself would say some of the dialogue didn't get itself entirely fixed into his head, so odd things came out from time to time, but it was a wonderful series of performances which I would love to do again."

However, Martin Bernheimer, the *Los Angeles Times*'s music critic, found little to commend in the production and, like other purists, bemoaned in Miller's 1930s production the loss of all that Gilbert and Sullivan fans held dear. As for Dudley, he claimed, "He flirts shamelessly with the audience, speaking his lines with relish, when he can remember them, and with a mercurial variety of inflections."

But most critics applauded Miller's *Mikado* for what it was—not another version of the traditional operetta but an innovative staging. "A gloriously antic night of opera," exulted the *Los Angeles Herald Examiner*, "a masterpiece of merry-making that preserves the work itself in all its romping, giddy glory. This is the triumph of Jonathan Miller's stagecraft and there is something akin to genius at work here. Moore is, in a word, wonderful and his Ko-Ko is first-rate stage invention."

Any trepidation Miller might earlier have felt about Dudley was replaced by unequivocal admiration. "I can't tell you what a pleasure it's been working with you again after all these years!" he wrote in a card to Dudley after the opening. "It's a brilliant performance and there are moments when it takes my breath away."

On Dudley's fifty-third birthday, in April 1988, Brogan threw a dinner party for fifty people, combining it with a celebration for Lou Pitt, whose birthday was the day before. Wolfgang Puck, Spago's celebrity chef, catered the dinner, and Brogan filled the room with candles and four hundred balloons.

She was always trying to think of special touches Dudley would appreciate, remembers Carol Doumani, their friend and next-door neighbor. "Brogan was devoted to making his life special and gathering his friends around him. We chuckled, because she always had a surprise party for him on his birthday and we figured that after a while he wasn't going to be too surprised. But he always acted like he was."

Arnold Schwarzenegger was a late arrival, turning up in the middle of dinner and puffing on a cigar. Brogan, who always spoke her mind, was not pleased and chastised him for his lateness.

For director Rod Daniel it was one of the most sparkling dinner parties he'd ever attended. "I got to talk to every icon I'd ever wanted to meet. I sat next to Mary Steenburgen and Malcolm McDowell, and, when I turned around, Jack Lemmon and Arnold Schwarzenegger were at the next table. What was really impressive for me—and maybe it shouldn't have been—was the level of star-power in that room to salute Dudley. It said a lot about him."

Brogan was creative and enterprising when it came to giving Dudley presents, and for this birthday she had Walt Disney's animation department make an electronically controlled bird that she perched in an antique birdcage near the front door of the beach house. Whenever the door opened, the bird sang "Tit willow, tit willow," Dudley's favorite song from *The Mikado*. "Brogan is bursting with wifeliness and the sense of belonging to you and consequently to us all," Else Blangsted wrote later to Dudley. "Anybody who can dream up that singing bird is a good match for you." But after a few weeks it drove Dudley nuts to walk into the house and hear the bird sing that song every time. He finally decided he'd had enough of "Tit willow" and dismantled the whole apparatus.

Brogan had deep feelings of nostalgia. She believed in celebrating the past, and was always seeking to provide Dudley with pleasant reminders of his earlier days. One of his favorite presents from her was a handwoven carpet depicting Oxford University. Dudley had always loved one particular picture of Magdalen College, and Brogan had sent it to weavers in New York who then handwove the carpet with its picture of graduates walking in the university grounds. "When I unrolled it," she remembers, "he just fell all over it in sheer amazement. He loved it."

One such surprise had taken all her resources to effect. With the help of Dudley's sister, she tracked down and exported from England the old upright piano that had been in the Baron Road house since Dudley was a child, together with the rickety piano stool onto which he had first tentatively clambered at the age of five.

When Dudley saw the piano he was curiously unimpressed. He explains why: "In a sense I thought it had always been there. I'd never thought of it as being in Baron Road but in my Marina house, because it was always with me in my mind."

The piano was placed in the living room, where it still sits today, in front of the grandfather clock and his favorite English winter painting. Everybody has one most treasured possession in their life. For Dudley, it would always be that piano. Now it would no longer be only a memory he had carried in his head, but also a physical reminder.

Early that summer, the Duke and Duchess of York—better known as Prince Andrew and Fergie—visited Los Angeles for the arts festival and attended a celebrity lunch for the British contingent in Hollywood, which included Roger Moore and Michael Caine. By the time Fergie and Andy arrived, over an hour late, the audience was well stoked on a continuous flow of cocktails.

Dudley went to sit between Brogan and Fergie, and was feeling so relaxed by then that he committed a breach of etiquette. "Hey, wake up, Dudley!" teased Prince Andrew, admonishing him for not pulling out the women's chairs. Dudley jumped up with an apologetic grin and did the honors.

Comedy writer Chris Langham and humorist Martin Lewis had written a speech for Dudley, but, as Lewis recalls, "He got about three inches into it and then took off on his own. He just went with the mood of the room and I couldn't understand why he'd asked us to write something for him, because he certainly didn't need it. He was outrageously funny."

It was the royals who laughed the loudest when Dudley—who declined Prince Andrew's suggestion that he stand on a box to address everyone—told the room full of guests that "Britain is a brilliant nation, brimming with attractive and talented people ... it's surprising really that no one wants to live there!"

Hollywood's forced jollity around Britain's minor royals made many observers cringe, but on that day Fergie responded to the celebrities in playfully boisterous form. This was the royal visit on which someone in a crowd yelled, "Fergie, I love you!" to which she shouted back, "I'll see you later!"

Earlier in the year, Dudley had planned the charter of a six-bedroom yacht to sail around the Greek islands in July with Patrick and Brogan's son, John, during their school holidays. He decided to take along the Bellwoods and the Pitts as well. He had already put down a twenty-thousand-dollar deposit, when a terrorist attack on a cruise ship in Piraeus made him change his plans. With Greece now too volatile for tourists, he decided instead to take everyone to Bora Bora.

The dates had to be brought forward by one day, and Tuesday, claiming this would not allow her enough time with Patrick, abruptly refused to let their son go, even though plans for the vacation had been agreed months before. Dudley was angry. Her decision seemed irrational and unfair, and it led to explosive phone rows between them that invariably ended with Tuesday hanging up on him. Their communications disintegrated completely, and Tuesday threatened Dudley with having to go to court if he wanted to see his son.

Patrick, who was caught in the middle of this ugly episode, wryly recalls, "I heard later that Bora Bora was boring, so in a way I was glad I didn't go."

Lou Pitt who had taken along two scripts, believing he'd have little time in which to peruse them, soon found himself without work. "I figured I'd read one script during the eight days we were there. By the end of the third day I'd read everything. And dived, seen the sharks, driven around the island, and seen where Marlon Brando lived. By the fourth day I'd done all there was to do."

The remaining time on Bora Bora was spent idly sunbathing and swimming, although after the first few days Dudley didn't seem terribly happy.

When they returned to Los Angeles, Dudley found a letter from a man who had been an apprentice coachbuilder at Stratford railway works, working alongside Dudley's father, Jock. Writing from his home in Essex, and perhaps inspired by one of the many interviews in which Dudley had been quoted as having known little about his taciturn father, Brian Beard threw some unexpected light on Jock's true feelings toward his son's early success.

"There are many instances that we are all unaware of in respect of how our parents feel and react to the success of their offspring," Beard wrote:

> My word, your dad was certainly proud of his son! Many times on our way home on the train your father would be reading the *Melody Maker*, an unusual thing even today for a man in his sixties.
>
> One evening we were both standing on the train on our way home and out came the *Melody Maker*. My curiosity got the better of me this particular night and I asked what it was he was interested in. He immediately replied, "I like to follow Dudley, my son's progress in the USA, he's touring there with an orchestra." He went on to talk of your talents and what a

brilliant musician you were. He was very proud of you and
from then on we always discussed where you were and what you
would be doing next.

It was a revelation for Dudley to discover that the quiet, hidden man
who was his father had been so proud of his achievements that he had not
only bought the trendy music weekly but had also discussed his son's
progress with his fellow workers.

Arthur 2 had its premiere now, but, despite everyone's hopes and
expectations, the film received catastrophic reviews. The dialogue was
nowhere near as funny as its predecessor's, nor did it contain the haunting
poignancy that had been so evident in the relationship between Arthur and
Hobson. Dudley, who considered the sequel to be better than the original
and had been anticipating his first film success in years, was surprised and
disappointed.

The *New York Times* deemed it "a lame sequel in which Arthur has
become a clamorous bore," and *USA Today*, who called for a moratorium on
any more *Arthur*s, declared it as funny as a hangover.

Time magazine called Breckman's script "so poverty-stricken that he
repeats all his worst jokes twice in an idea as unappealing as it is implausible,"
and denounced the film as a graceless sequel that made Arthur "so consistently irritating that you may wonder why you found him funny in the first
place. If you want to preserve your fond memories of *Arthur*," it urged, "stay
away from *Arthur 2*."

When the film had been privately screened, Warner Bros. received the
third most enthusiastic audience response in its history. Convinced they
had another huge hit on their hands, the studio had put their efforts into
a massive and expensive publicity campaign. But times had changed in the
seven years since the first *Arthur*. Alcoholism had now become an immense
social issue, and audiences were no longer able to laugh unashamedly at a
happy drunk. "Being drunk was not popular when *Arthur 2* came out,"
reflects Minnelli. "Nobody was drinking—it was the time of nonalcoholic
beer—and it was very, very unpopular to play a drunk. I remember one
critic saying to me, 'How can you be a member of Alcoholics Anonymous
and pretend you're in love with a drunk?' And I said, 'Excuse me—I'm an
actress!' Arthur's drinking wasn't the point of the film—just like it hadn't
been with the first one—but that's how it was perceived, because of the
times. It went against the social grain."

The original *Arthur* had become a huge box-office success, surpassing
the $100 million mark. Its sequel, however, failed dismally to emulate
that record.

In the meantime, spurred on by Brogan, Dudley was feeling an increasing urgency about mastering music, aware that the advancing years would limit his piano-playing ability. He wondered when he would start to get old, when would it really hit him? When would he get arthritis in his fingers or find his memory fading? He felt physically fine now, but he estimated he had about five years left in which to do youthful things.

He found himself needing less in his life these days than ever before. As long as he had his piano and the forty-eight Preludes and Fugues of Bach, which he hoped to record one day, he was content. More and more his life was becoming centered around the piano, with a bit of acting thrown in.

The atmosphere of his environment was important to Dudley. In his home overlooking Venice Beach in Marina del Rey he had created a sanctuary, a safe nest for himself. He was not particularly fond of the area itself. It wasn't greatly attractive and there wasn't much to look at—an often bleak beach, a public lavatory, and bird sanctuary on one side and a narrow alley on the other—but once inside the house he felt comfortable in his world.

Surrounded by Brogan's warmth, he felt relaxed and well cared for—a state that was enhanced by the solicitous presence of Tom Leahy, whom Dudley had installed in a nearby apartment. Tom came to the house two or three times a day to prepare breakfast for the couple, take the dogs to be shampooed, and look after Patrick or John whenever they came to visit. He was deeply fond of Dudley and, though he never overstepped the boundaries of their employer/employee relationship, was encouraged by Dudley to join in family and social events.

The household had grown now to a small staff. In addition to Tom and Sam, Dudley's secretary, he also had Dennis Koch, who walked the dogs twice a day, and a part-time housekeeper and maid.

Late in 1988 Glenys Roberts, an English writer who had known Dudley back in the sixties, wrote a story in *Vanity Fair* about the lifestyle Dudley was enjoying with Brogan. It portrayed him as a Peter Pan figure who refused to grow up, with Brogan playing the role of his bossy nanny-cum-baby-doll in their kiddy estate in Munchkinland—a picture filled in with observations from Peter Cook at his most acerbic. Cook had not intended to put down Dudley when talking to the journalist, but that was how it turned out. His remarks, he insisted later, had been off the record, but they had been used anyway.

Peter, the story asserted, was reacting to Dudley's absence like a jilted lover, with America as the "other woman." While he claimed to be happily living in Hampstead with his goldfish, his smoking, and his drinking to excess, his disparagement of his former partner never seemed far away. He ridiculed Dudley's lifestyle as vacuous and mocked Brogan's efforts to get him to enjoy the great outdoors, depicting her as a manipulating, controlling wife who had him under her thumb. "She has had a special boot made for his foot," he scoffed, "and marches him up and down the side of the Grand Canyon before breakfast."

Dudley expected Peter to have fun with Brogan, and anything to do with his life for that matter, and he publicly avowed that Peter could do nothing to offend him. What they had together had been valuable, and he accepted whatever Peter said about him these days. "He may despise me mightily," he said then, "but I know he loves me mightily, too." Privately, however, he never failed to be hurt by Peter's caustic comments. Peter apologized to Brogan—"I really didn't mean to say it in that vicious way," he told her—and was much kinder after that. But Dudley knew he had meant what he said.

Seven years later, Lin Cook would tell me with immense feeling that Peter had never intended to hurt Dudley. "Peter was amazingly quick with words and was always very sarcastic—not just about Dudley but about everyone in the world. It was just his clever way of talking and making people laugh. Some things sound funny when you say them but when you put them in print, the tone is lost in the translation. But I can honestly say with my hand on my heart that, in my thirteen years with him, Peter was never ever bitter or jealous of Dudley's success. He truly, deeply loved him."

Still, the entire *Vanity Fair* article left Dudley very angry. "I'm getting fucking tired of this," he told Los Angeles–based journalist Ivor Davis, who interviewed him for the *Illustrated London News*. "It's fuck Dudley time."

He could have added "again," for the British press seized upon the article as a fresh excuse to attack the Hollywoodization of Dudley. It irked him that people considered him to be shallow and lightweight, but he was not about to change his lifestyle to suit them. He had spent half a lifetime trying to break away from what he thought other people expected him to be, and he was not about to sacrifice his emotional gains now.

Quentin Crisp once told psychologist Dorothy Rowe that the difference between England and America is that "Americans want you to succeed because they feel you may drag them forward with you, but the British want you to fail because they fear you may leave them behind." Certainly the British press now fixated on Dudley's box-office failures and were almost gleeful to point out that his last big success had been *Arthur*, seven years earlier.

Eager to say he had sold out and become plasticized, journalists suggested Dudley's brains had been baked by the California sun, assisted in no small measure by an army of psychotherapists. What serious man, they questioned, would live in a "pink" house on the beach with personalized license plates on the cars in his garage? Had he not committed intellectual suicide by living in California?

In the opinion of Ivor Davis, Dudley had fallen victim to the great

American Dream cycle—build them up fast and knock them down even faster. That attitude had now crossed the Atlantic and pervaded Britain.

"I think the British were cross with him for leaving England," reflects Lysie Kihl. "He and Peter Cook were such a brilliant act that nothing ever was quite as wonderful again. In a way he was the bad guy for leaving. He spoilt our fun. This marvelous couple that we loved to watch wasn't there any more, and the British public was not happy about that. Also, the Brits aren't particularly enthralled by anyone who goes to Hollywood."

It was all right for David Niven to have lived in a pink house in the Hollywood Hills during his Hollywood heyday, but it was somehow ridiculous for Dudley to live in his terra-cotta home on the beach. The guest bathroom had a tiled mural that showed a cat labeled "Brogan" surrounded by half-eaten fish; above them smiled a king fish labeled "Dudley," who wore a crown. All very primitive psychological stuff, Dudley acknowledged.

It was exactly the psychobabble that irked Jonathan Miller, who held a scathing opinion of the city that Dudley had chosen to call home. "Los Angeles encourages people to indulge their wilder and more promiscuous forms of introspection," Miller scoffs, "and then provides them with a terrible vocabulary with which to conduct the introspection. It's hard to distinguish Hollywood parties from group psychotherapy. It's the most stunningly vulgar town in the world. There's a free gas escape of nonsense that prevails, and people, if they go on breathing it, become brain-damaged."

Dudley's home was depicted in print as a playhouse for adults, a house with no past, a sunlit house without shadows. But in fact it was saturated with Dudley's past, and the shadows were absent only from when Tom raised the electronic shutters until Dudley came along to close them again. Wary of people looking in through the living-room windows that overlooked the beach, he would shut out the natural sunlight and instead use artificial illumination that emanated from an elaborate system recessed into the ceiling. Still, an unnatural semidarkness seemed to pervade the house.

There were some who suggested that Dudley was living out a second childhood. The truth was that he'd never outgrown the first one. He dragged it around with him like a ball and chain. It was his anchor, and it weighed him down all the time. His past had settled around him, as much a part of his present as it would be of his future, and he was incapable of leaving it behind him.

"He was never able to take a step out of that darkness," Brogan recalls wistfully, "except temporarily. Maybe it was from childhood—learned behavior—but he was never able to shake off this kind of sadness he had about him. And he had a great deal of sadness."

In November, Dudley narrated for David Puttnam *The Adventures of Milo and Otis*, a charming film about a puppy and kitten who grow up together on a farm and become embroiled in various exploits. The film was a reworked version of Japan's *The Adventures of Chatran*, a story about a stray cat, which had evolved from six years of documentaries for Fuji TV to become the third largest-grossing film in Japanese history. For the English-speaking market it had been interspliced with another Fuji TV production, *Puski's Story*, about a stray dog.

Clearly, any film shot over such a long period had necessitated using many different animals as doubles, and their welfare led to some later concern. Milo and Otis were adventurous devils who found themselves in dangerous situations. In one shot a cat leaped off a high cliff into the sea, causing Dudley to wonder how it could possibly have survived. The American Humane Society contacted him and asked if he was aware that twenty-five animals had been killed on the film. He wasn't, of course, but as an animal lover he was greatly disturbed to think it might have happened.

Toward the end of 1988 a new album of Erroll Garner recordings was released. It was compiled from previously unreleased music, and Dudley was proud to be asked to write the liner notes, which he did at unusual length and with unmitigated admiration. "Nothing in the arts," he wrote, "has affected me quite as much, before or since I first heard Garner's music. He is not only a genius but a phenomenon with a uniqueness that is almost unbearably strong. He's probably the most important pianist I've ever heard."

For their first married Christmas, Brogan decorated the Marina beach house extravagantly, like a winter wonderland, and her family flew in to join them. The house radiated warmth, enhanced by log fires and the tiny colored lights of two Christmas trees.

One of Brogan's many creative presents to Dudley that Christmas was a diary she designed with a photograph from his life on every page. She gave him a duplicate for every year up to 2018. "Why did you only give me thirty?" Dudley laughed, when he counted them. "Does that mean I'm going to die after that?"

Inside the front page she had reproduced some words that Dudley had once flung at Lou Pitt in a moment of playfulness. "The trouble with you is that you don't live in the here and now. You live in the there and then— I live in the here and there, now and then."

"Now and then" was right.

CHAPTER 23

TROUBLE IN MUNCHKINLAND

1989-1990

"I experience relationships eventually as a form of death. I am attracted by someone who is sweetly and thoroughly focused on me, and then I run like a fool who feels that he will die from a sort of strangulation."

—DUDLEY MOORE

The earlier blitz of filmmaking had subsided and the film scripts and offers that still poured in to Lou Pitt's office tended to be remakes of *10* and *Arthur*, from which Dudley shied away.

There were many people around Dudley who attributed his ailing career to what they saw as the lackluster efforts of his agent to obtain good scripts. Lou Pitt was now one of Hollywood's top agents and represented Arnold Schwarzenegger among others. With his interests divided, people believed that Pitt had become less active in hustling for Dudley than in the past, a suggestion the *New York Daily News* had put forth two years earlier when reviewing *Like Father, Like Son*.

It was easy for his friends to say that he had the wrong agent, but Dudley was intensely loyal and would not have contemplated going to someone else. Besides, Pitt was more than his agent: He was one of his biggest fans. Indeed, he was like a brother to him.

In fact Pitt was constantly suggesting Dudley for various projects, and if the choice of films he ended up making turned out not to be the best, it was nevertheless Dudley himself who ultimately decided whether he wanted to make them.

For the last two years Dudley had been trying to get one particular film off the ground, and in the early months of 1989 he renewed his efforts.

Sketch Life was a poignant story of a man who falls in love with a mentally retarded younger woman. It had been around for a long time, but Hollywood was reluctant to tackle such a subject. From the moment Dudley read the script he had passionately wanted to make it with Brogan, but no studio seemed keen to have her untried talent in the leading role.

Dudley was convinced she could play the part and bring to it a humanity and warmth. In twenty years he had never before wanted to work with anyone close to him. He insisted that nepotism was not rearing its head—he was too fond of his work to allow that to influence him—yet his life with Brogan resonated so strongly with *Sketch Life* that he simply could not contemplate making it with anyone else. His confidence in her was absolute. "I know I can do it with Brogan without a doubt," he told one potential producer. "If not, then I have to say good-bye to the best script I have read in years."

In an effort to convince others of her talent, he asked his friend Francis Megahy to shoot a screen test. Megahy was impressed with Brogan's acting ability. "She did a few scenes and a monologue, and she was exceptionally good. It was very touching, and that should have assured everybody she could do it. Together, Dudley and Brogan could have made it work. You could see that. And it would have been brilliant."

Dudley did find a producer, but there was too much difference of creative opinion and eventually the deal fell through. He was back to square one. Believing that she was holding back the project, Brogan dropped out.

"We'd worked on it for two years and fought so long for it," she remembers sadly, "but I realized it was going to fold if I didn't back out. And that caused us a lot of grief, because I had needed him to be committed to his word of putting me in it, and he then felt I'd let him down by dropping out of it."

Maybe Dudley would have been able to get the project going if he still had the same pulling power of the days after *Arthur*, but he was no longer the bankable asset he had been in the early eighties.

If his career was on the skids, at least his popularity with others in Hollywood remained unimpaired. Joan Collins invited him to dinner with Liza Minnelli and the Bricusses, and there were parties with Charles Bronson and Frank Sinatra, and lunches with Gary Grant, Sidney Poitier, and Carol Burnett. Carol had not seen Derek and Clive and she pressed Dudley for a copy of the videotape. After he sent it to her, she wrote to him, "I had a cold and then I saw Derek and Clive. They are better than Johnson and Johnson!"

Dudley was still playing jazz, although not as much as he had in the past. When Vic Lewis, his first employer, flew to Los Angeles to record a jazz album with an all-star band, he rang Dudley and asked if he would like to play one number on it. Dudley agreed immediately. As generous with his time as he was with his money, he never forgot those who had helped his career.

In March 1989 he played once more at Ray Brown's club. It would be the last time. Director Rod Daniel, who never missed an opportunity to enjoy Dudley at the keyboard, was on hand to cheer him. "The guy was euphoric when he played the piano. That was his bliss. It was the place he went to be happy, and that's really when he came alive." Many among the audience—*Los Angeles Times* jazz critic Leonard Feather included—might have been forgiven for thinking Erroll Garner had been reincarnated. "There were many moments when it was possible to believe that he returned to us in the form of Dudley Moore," said Feather. "He's a pianist for whom the art of swinging is clearly a triumphant modus vivendi."

Oscar Peterson agreed, but wanted to hear more of Dudley's own style. "I admired his own personality in his playing," he says, "and I told him I was intrigued more by that than when he saluted Erroll Garner. I think perhaps he didn't have the opportunity he was looking for really to develop his own style, and that was a pity."

Among Dudley's offerings that night was one number he had played before. Titled "Brogan" and dedicated to his wife, it was two haunting tunes linked as one. Dudley had actually written it for Susan Anton some years before, but when Brogan heard it she loved it and asked Dudley to rename it for her, and she was always urging him to record it.

In fact she had been nagging him for a long time to record some of his compositions, but he kept saying he wasn't ready to do it. Finally, exasperated, she told him, "Fine! Just make sure it's all signed over to me when you die!"

In May 1989, having given up trying to get *Sketch Life* off the ground, Dudley began his next film, *Crazy People*, written by Robin Williams's award-winning *Good Morning Vietnam* writer Mitch Markowitz. It was an interesting coincidence that for his first film in eighteen months, Dudley had elected to make one with elements similar to the aborted *Sketch Life*.

He played a harassed, burned-out advertising executive who ends up in a sanitarium with mentally ill patients and enlists their assistance in writing "no-nonsense" ads that grab the public's imagination and, in the process, turn the world of advertising upside down. One advertisement for an airline declares that "Crashes are a fact of life and people die like crazy. But fly United," it urged. "More people arrive at their destination alive on our flights than others."

Daryl Hannah played the inmate with whom Dudley becomes romantically involved, Mercedes Ruehl their sympathetic doctor, and Paul Reiser was Dudley's advertising partner. Dudley liked the script and thought it funny and tender in its portrayal of people who had difficulty in knowing how to handle their lives.

As it happens, it was a role—as 10 had been—that came to him as a result of another actor vacating the part.

The production had been plagued with problems from the start. With John Malkovich as the male lead, filming had begun under the direction of screenwriter Markowitz, but he was yanked off it a few weeks later. Tony Bill was brought in as a replacement, but at the end of his first day as director, Malkovich walked out of the film. There had been rumors that Daryl Hannah would also leave and be replaced by Michelle Pfeiffer—who had been having an affair with Malkovich, who had left his wife for her—but in the end Hannah remained. It took little thought for Tony Bill, who'd drawn such a fine performance from him in *Six Weeks*, to suggest that Dudley take over the role.

"Everyone was very relieved that we were finally able to get back on track once Dudley took over," recalls Bill, "even though we had to reshoot all the work that had been shot with Malkovich. Dudley, as always, was very easy, and cracking up the cast and crew on a daily basis became par for the course."

Soon after he began work on *Crazy People*, Dudley struck up a close friendship with Paul Reiser. "I'd been a fan of his for years," says Reiser, "so it was a real kick for me to work with him. We were filming on location in Virginia, and Dudley was friendly to everyone. I remember being impressed at how unfailingly gracious he always was to everyone in this small Virginian town who wanted to chat to him or get his autograph."

The two men occasionally went off to dinner in a nearby restaurant club, and when Dudley took over the piano, Reiser marveled at his ability to sight-read. "He would just pick up a manuscript and play Beethoven right there on the spot, and it would blow me away. I'm a pianist, too, but not at all at his level. A few times we sat and played together, and that was a real bit of heaven for me—although it wasn't easy to keep up with him, because he's quite brilliant."

Reiser enjoyed these evenings—and not only for the opportunity to duet at the piano. "Some of my fondest memories," he laughs, "were going out to dinner with Dudley and discovering what eight-hundred-dollar bottles of wine tasted like!"

When *Crazy People* was released, it met with mixed reactions, although it had done marvelously in test screenings. People seemed to miss the theme and thought the film made fun of people in sanitariums. In fact it had tried to question the grounds on which people are incarcerated and where in fact the sanity in the world really lies. But its point was too subtle and, obscured by what humor there was, failed to communicate itself to audiences.

Dudley's marriage had now run into seriously bumpy ground. The continual stream of phone calls that poured into the Marina house from other women had led to huge arguments. Frequently when Brogan picked up the phone, the person at the other end would hang up, and Dudley was too often evasive about the callers. Her suspicions left her deeply insecure and feeling as if Dudley always had one foot out of the door. It made their relationship off balance and, as with Susan Anton, created dishonesty and fear.

Brogan decided she could not cope with the situation any longer and instructed Tom to pack up her possessions. She was moving out of the Marina house and into the Toluca Lake home. Just sixteen months after their marriage, Brogan was separating from Dudley.

Ironically, it was as her marriage was breaking up that the relationship between Brogan and Patrick began to flower. Patrick had joined them on the location of *Crazy People* and spent a lot of time with Brogan. "You don't really like me, do you?" she asked him one day. Then added, "That's OK—I don't really like you either." For some reason this struck them both as being immensely funny and they burst into laughter, the ice between them broken for ever.

Brogan wanted to serve separation papers on Dudley, and he drew up a divorce settlement, but after countless discussions they canceled the action. Brogan, however, would remain permanently in the Toluca Lake house, and, although Dudley often stayed there with her, their relationship would never again have the bloom and excitement of its earlier days.

The fragile, wounded girl that he had married was growing up. In the four years they had been together, Brogan had reached an understanding about herself. Her unceasing attempts to resolve her childhood problems through therapy had brought her to recognize behavior patterns that had been learned in childhood, and she no longer felt quite the same need to be driven by them. She had stopped searching for her father in Dudley, and he, therefore, could not now play the earlier role of filling her neediness—a role he sought in order to fill a neediness of his own.

But if Brogan had resolved some of her emotional fragility, Dudley had not. "Dudley is one who doesn't resolve," says Brogan, who believes one of his problems was that he never had the right therapist, "and when you don't resolve you become depressed."

In the summer, Dudley flew to Europe to surprise his sister on her sixtieth birthday, first staying overnight with Else Blangsted in Geneva. Barbara had no idea that her brother was in town and was flabbergasted when she came home from shopping and Dudley suddenly stepped out of a room with a grin on his face and a huge laugh at the sight of hers.

While he was in London, he reunited with Peter Cook for *The Secret Policeman's 10th Anniversary Ball*, a charity benefit for Amnesty International. Although another duo—French and Saunders—almost stole the show, Peter and Dudley's reprise in late middle age of the One-Legged Tarzan sketch from *Beyond the Fringe* seemed even funnier than the original. "Good comedy never dies," declared the *Times*, "it simply gets recycled for the next generation."

For a while Dudley and Peter would be partners again. The BBC was planning to assemble six half-hour programs, each with a new introduction, to be broadcast under the title of *The Best of What's Left of Not Only ... But Also*. They would also be released on a video. The content wasn't necessarily the best of the original series: It was simply all that could be salvaged, since remarkably the BBC had erased most of the programs and what remained had deteriorated badly. Of the three series that had been made—each comprising seven shows—only four episodes remained of the first series, three of the second, and none at all of the third, although the film sequences remained intact.

Once Dudley was back in Los Angeles, Brogan persuaded him to see a therapist with her in an effort to resolve their differences. She had always tried to open him up to his emotions, but to little avail. "He would listen to me, but he would fight what I said. He wouldn't talk things out—not with anyone."

Dudley had certainly become more open and vocal over the years, but he still had the same tendency to retreat into the long silences that had led to the breakdown of his first marriage, to Suzy Kendall. Therapy had helped in many ways, but the most important issues of all—those surrounding his childhood, his mother, and his lack of self-appreciation—had never been fully resolved.

He was reflecting a great deal about his childhood angst these days, and an entry in his diary read, "I died because of my love for my mother."

Brogan, like Susan Anton, believes that Dudley felt he belonged in his pain. "That's his skin and it's where he's comfortable, and somehow he feels he can't have better. I don't think he even knows that he's in it. If he was forced to see what he's been going through and acknowledge how much pain he's really in, he'd fall apart, because he'd be incapable of believing that he'd allowed it."

Dudley had always been attracted to strong-willed women, and Brogan was no exception. Though initially he sought his mother in his women, ultimately he ran away from any similarities—especially a controlling quality that he had resented in his mother. Brogan fought with him endlessly about his mother. "Leave her alone and get on with your life," she kept telling him. "Create the present. Live now, and start loving yourself and know how to receive love." But he couldn't. "He's not able to really love," she reflects sadly. "He does the best he can, but he's so afraid of his own shadow."

In November 1989 Peter Cook married his longtime girlfriend, Lin Chong, and called Dudley with the news. They talked often on the phone these days, and Dudley enjoyed their conversations immensely. Peter had a dry English wit that Dudley missed. The self-deprecating humor so characteristic of the British was in sharp contrast to the tendency of Americans to take themselves far too seriously. Dudley—who often referred to himself as a clubfooted dwarf, which he found both entertaining and philosophical—felt at home with the British attitude, and his long phone chats with Peter invariably left him in shrieks of laughter.

When Kingsley Hall, in Dagenham, had its fiftieth anniversary, Dudley recorded a videotape for the old people in which he played the piano and made some jokes. He had always felt grateful to Sidney Russell, the Hall's former administrator, who had been such a mentor to him in his youth. Now he could do something to show his appreciation, though he felt it was hardly enough.

He had always had an acute social conscience and felt guilty not to be doing more. He had always tried. From the days of *Beyond the Fringe* in New York he had begun making a monthly payment to his parents for their well-being—a payment that was increased substantially over the years and continued until his mother's death in 1981—and he made financial gifts to family members and loans to friends, as well as taking part in charity concerts and fund-raisers.

Back in the seventies, when Dudley had bought his house in Islington, it was still occupied by an old woman who had rented the house from the former owner. Rather than evict her, Dudley bought her a flat where she could comfortably live out her days. She was a complete stranger to him, yet his conscience could not ignore her.

Dudley had finally succumbed to Brogan's relentless urgings to record some of the music he had written over the years. His house was now equipped with a recording studio on the top floor, complete with piano, organ, and synthesizer, and he had installed state-of-the-art music computers so that he could mix his own recordings.

Brogan persuaded Dudley to invite saxophonist Kenny G to the house to check out his music and play a few tunes with him. Kenny loved what he heard and was amazed by Dudley's sense of melody, which he considers the most important part of any piece of music. "Song after song, each one of them had such a uniquely captivating melody. I don't know how he kept coming up with them like he did. He was, and still is, a great musician."

They played several pieces together that day, and recorded them on tape. "We were like two guys who could play anything together," says Kenny, "even though it was Dudley's music I was playing. I can remember the melodies even now, and I haven't heard them for years. That's how you can tell if a song is good—you don't forget the melody."

Dudley shut himself up in his studio and spent hours working on pieces that Patrick called his "hypnosis tapes." The result, months later, was *Songs Without Words*, an exquisite album of ballads that also included haunting themes from his *Six Weeks* score. It was his first album since the one he recorded in Sydney in 1978.

Kenny G had to obtain permission from his record company to allow Dudley to use some of the items they had recorded together. "They told me he could use one, but I said, 'Look, this is my friend and I really want to be on four songs at least.'" In the end he appeared on two of the tracks. The rest were Dudley at the piano.

The album, which Brogan coproduced, included an old track called "Patrick," which, as Dudley wrote to his son, "I dedicated to you and which I seem to remember writing mainly at a Playboy [Mansion] pajama party!"

Dudley had always been aware that he was living in highly unstable earthquake territory. Prophets of doom, even geologists, were predicting The Big One sometime soon, but Dudley would never have contemplated moving from the nest he had built. He would rather sit in the front line and be washed out to sea. Still, there were frequent tremors and, disturbed by the constant earth movement, Dudley ordered a geological survey so he would know what he might be facing if there was a major earthquake. Tom Leahy prepared several survival kits filled with canned food, torches, batteries, and radios, and scattered them around the house so there would always be one within reach. At least Dudley didn't sleep in a sweat suit like Jackie Collins, ready to spring into action if The Big One struck in the middle of the night.

Earthquakes weren't all he had to fear from living in Los Angeles, where the crime rate was frighteningly high. The violence was creeping closer. There had already been one murder just outside his house, and another on the boardwalk nearby—Tom Leahy had been appalled to see the blood-spattered jetty when he turned up for work one morning. Another time, a hand was washed up on the beach outside Dudley's living-room window, then sacrificed goats were discovered floating in the nearby canal. Venice was notorious for its crime, and gang violence was a particular fear of the residents. Dudley, however, felt relatively untouched by it all. Once inside his house, the outside world seemed a long way away.

Christmas was spent in the Toluca Lake house, which Brogan decorated with tradition and old-world nostalgia. Christmas stockings hung from the mantelpiece, and scented candles mingled their aroma with the fresh pine from the Christmas tree that was decorated with velvet bows and colored lights.

Dudley loved Christmas, and if he went slightly overboard in its celebration—the Marina house had two Christmas trees: one in the living room, one in the bedroom—it was his way of compensating for the bleak Christmases of his childhood home on Baron Road. The only decorations in that house had been paper chains that he and Barbara had made from colored paper and hung from wall to wall. There had been no Christmas tree, no turkey, no mistletoe, candles, or stockings, and they celebrated simply with a small chicken and Green Goddess liqueur—the only time Dudley ever recalls seeing alcohol in the home. Yet it was at that time that he had felt closest to his parents, even though they did little but sit around the radio listening to *The Goon Show*.

Brogan's Christmas present to him this year was a celebratory encapsulation of his life, a small acrylic globe inside which were miniature symbols of everything he held dear: a cutout Dudley sat at a grand piano, surrounded by a TV, music sheets, album covers—even trout and vegetables and his favorite champagne.

In the spring of 1990 Dudley appeared with Bo Derek on the Academy Awards show, to an appreciative audience. Their earlier partnership in Blake Edwards's movie *10* had been one of Hollywood's favorite couplings. "They presented the costume award," recalled Bruce Vilanch, who wrote some of the comedy material for that year's Oscars, "and Dudley told Bo, 'It's funny that we're presenting for costumes, because what I remember most about you in *10* was that you didn't wear one at all!'"

Soon after that, Dudley was lured back to Britain and into commercials by the English supermarket chain Tesco, which spent £3 million promoting itself. A sizable chunk of that went to Dudley—but not the £1 million that the newspapers claimed, although over the next few years it would amount to well over half that figure.

In a role perfectly suited to his physical comedy, Dudley played a Tesco buyer ineffectually chasing free-range chickens. There seemed little other work around and this suited him. He liked the farcical approach to the ads and, besides, commercials took only a couple of days to make, rather than the couple of months for a film.

The first ads were filmed in Oxfordshire and in Bordeaux—where he tracked down Camembert and wine but no chickens. Dudley relished being in the heart of wine country, but to his disappointment, as he later wrote to Peter Cork, "I didn't find any great wine there, although I was sitting on the hub of the industry. Instead, I was getting up at all hours and driving into deserted fields to chase chickens."

The series of ads showed him crashing through a vineyard, falling into a vat, and haring after a hot-air balloon that had taken off without him—always in a futile search for chickens. The commercials gave him a new lease on his acting life. They were an immediate and sensational hit in England, and popularized Dudley among a new generation of young kids.

Meanwhile the BBC was dragging its heels over the video compilation of *Not Only … But Also*. Peter Cook decided it was time to take matters in hand, and he sent a letter to Marmaduke Hussey, the BBC's chairman. Addressing him as "Dear Sir Marmaduke," he explained that they had been negotiating for what seemed like years, though the broadcastable material had been agreed the previous year. "Whilst spending the weekend with my mother in Hampshire," he wrote, "she inquired about the state of the negotiations. When I told her that there seems to be no particular progress, she suggested that I write to you, as at the age of eighty-one she feels that time is running out for her to see these programmes."

Peter sent a copy of his letter to his mother and another to Dudley, adding the scribbled wry comment, "I thought I'd try guilt!"

Hussey's reply to Peter assured him the programs were being pushed ahead. "The main thing," Hussey wrote back, "is that your mother must see them and when the video is completed, I hope she will accept one from me. PS: Not Sir Marmaduke and, sadly, not Sir Peter!"

While Dudley was in England, he and Brogan joined Peter and his new wife, Lin, for dinner. Ever since Lin had surreptitiously brought them closer together a few years earlier, they had always seen each other whenever Dudley was in London. Sometimes they would meet at Villa Bianca, Peter's local Italian restaurant in Hampstead; at other times they would gather at Peter's home, where he commandeered his own kitchen and served up Dudley's favorite roast lamb. Yet it seemed to Brogan that getting together was something of an effort. When she was around them, she felt an awkwardness between the two, and they seemed uncomfortable with each other.

Lin Cook, however, sensed no unease between them. On the contrary: "It used to fill my heart with joy when I listened to the two of them, because they always said just the right thing to each other and it would be so funny. They were both incredibly clever with words. I've never met two people who were quite like that, the way they talked to each other. They came out with the funniest things, and it sounded so natural even though it was so crazy."

Back in Los Angeles, Dudley was now living alone in the Marina house, although he was often to be found with Brogan in Toluca Lake. "He loved being in the Toluca house," she recalls, "and he felt comfortable and happy. We had the best times there. We cooked, we danced, we played, and he loved it—he thrived on that. And then he would be this loner and have to go back to the Marina house and be the recluse. He needed that other side of himself that he was never able to shake off."

Marriage was not a comfortable institution for Dudley, no matter how loving the woman nor how much he wanted to make it work. It simply was too much at odds with the darker side of him that needed to be alone and closed up. He found prolonged intimate situations difficult and he felt comfortable being alone—a state of mind that had developed from his early isolation periods in hospital.

Los Angeles, by nature and architecture, is a city that breeds isolation. Sprawling, with no real nucleus, it is a linear network of suburbs interconnected by freeways. Unlike most major cities, it is built entirely around the automobile, which makes every destination a chore to reach. Seldom can one simply walk down the road to the local market or go to a cinema or even hang out at a nearby cafe without getting into a car first and driving there.

Dudley was aware of the trap this created. "It's not like old Beethoven doing his work and then walking down the road and having a drink at the local bar," he told me then, "and I have to be very careful not to disappear up my own arsehole. It's all very well to ride my aerobic bike in the morning, but I used to ride a real bike and talk to real people. More and more one's life can be sustained in four walls."

Certainly the isolation was creeping up on him again. He seldom went to his restaurant any more, and those diners who hoped to see him play were constantly disappointed.

Carol Doumani had observed his increasingly reclusive behavior. During his time with Susan Anton she had frequently bumped into him while walking their dogs, and they had strolled together. "He liked that," she recalls, "and then gradually he stopped liking to be out. I think he was tired of people staring at him, yet he was always so gracious to anyone who stopped him. He used to sit on the balcony with Susan and they'd sunbathe, and then eventually he stopped that, too. Then, later, all the windows would be closed. And after that he just would never be out. I haven't seen him outside of his house for a long time, except driving in and out of his garage."

For a while at least, Dudley would be leaving the oppressive security of his Marina home. He was on his way to Europe to embark on a great musical challenge.

CHAPTER 24

AN ORCHESTRAL
TRIUMPH AND
A CHICKEN CHASE

1990-1991

"I think Dudley is only really alive when he's at the piano. There's an intensity and caring about his music that doesn't exist anywhere else in his life. Only through music is he able to show real emotion and achieve genuine happiness. And when he's involved in it, there's nothing else that's really important."

—RENA FRUCHTER

In May 1990, accompanied by Brogan, Dudley returned to Oxford University to accept his M.A., which he had never collected after graduating in 1958. This time he stayed in the President's lodgings, which had seemed so far away when he first arrived at Oxford. The night of his degree ceremony he gave a small organ recital in the Magdalen chapel and then transferred to the piano to delight the graduates with some of his parodies.

Dr. Bernard Rose, his old Oxford tutor, had always been struck by Dudley's contrasting musical talents. Many musicians had passed through Rose's hands since the days when he began teaching in 1933, but Dudley, he privately believed, was the only genius he'd ever encountered. "The extraordinary thing is he has different talents both as a classical musician and a jazz pianist. He's very clever. But I think he hasn't really known which way to go, and that's been the great sadness."

A few days later Dudley flew to Hamburg to host the television series *Orchestra!* for Channel 4. A definitive introduction to classical music, the series explained the role played by the various instruments and traced the

history of the orchestra, showing its evolution from a small group of players huddled around a keyboard into today's modern symphony orchestra
of over one hundred musicians. Producer Jonathan Hewes wanted to present the six-part series in a way that would reach beyond the normal classical musical audience, and he was convinced that Dudley's warmth and
humor would broaden the programs' appeal.

He planned to include Sir Georg Solti, one of the great conductors
of this century, as the focus of the program about conducting. "But when
we met him," says Hewes, "he was so charismatic and such a wonderful old
maestro with enormous energy that exhausted us all, we realized it would
be daft just to have him in one program, so we asked him to join with
Dudley for the whole series." The combination was electric. Dudley had
admired Solti since he was a youngster, and he was ecstatic, if somewhat
intimidated, at the prospect of working with the veteran conductor.

Solti recalls with amusement that when they met for the first time,
Dudley was very nervous around him. "I think he thought I would eat him.
And I, too, was very shy, because I had seen him many times in films and
had enormous respect for him."

For a man of seventy-seven Solti had an extraordinary vitality, and his
abundant energy inspired Dudley. They filmed with the Schleswig-
Holstein Festival Orchestra, an international group of young musicians,
and Dudley, who had never before attempted such massive works, played
sweeping pieces with Solti that included the first movement of Schumann's
piano concerto.

It would have been daunting for any concert pianist to play with Solti,
and Dudley was understandably nervous. But he performed with a mastery
that surprised even the conductor. "He's a splendid musician and played
the piano extremely well. He was quite frightened by it, but in a nice way,
and he was never afraid to say so. I liked that about him."

Dudley found the experience very grand. "Solti was always a source of
encouragement to me," he wrote to Peter Cork, his former music tutor,
"and has twice the energy that I have. He is very limber and a wonderful
person to be with, probably because he didn't insist on cramming what he
felt on to me."

The programs were immensely entertaining. Dudley's humor permeated the series without ever becoming irreverent, and he enjoyed a bantering
camaraderie with Solti, who is himself a humorous man. "We both love
laughing," says Solti, "and I tell jokes as much as him, so that was a strong
common bond that brought us quickly together. I didn't know when we
started that there would be as much humor as there turned out to be, but
I think humor is necessary sometimes in music, and it worked very well in
this instance."

Dudley's absorption in and devotion to the music were apparent, and he proved acutely knowledgeable about its history. Those who were formerly convinced he had sold out to Hollywood had now to admit they'd been wrong. No artist with baked brains could have tackled such a formidable task as this.

Dudley even enjoyed some free conducting lessons from Solti, and led the orchestra under the maestro's vigilant and critical eye. "I was afraid he would be mortified," recalls Solti, "but he wasn't and he did very well. He was not afraid, and he never lost his sense of humor in the remarks he made about conducting."

What Solti didn't know was that Dudley had already conducted full orchestras for some of his earlier film scores. "I thought this was the first time!" says the astonished maestro now. "It confirms anyway what impressed me the most about Dudley—his modesty. He has no star ideas. I, too, am not a megalomaniac, and he understood that immediately. I'm aware of my problems in music-making and my failures, and I never forget that. And he was the same."

Dudley loved working on *Orchestra!*, which would later win awards at festivals across the world, in Russia, Montreux, and the United States. The whole experience had been extraordinary for them all. "I had a tremendous time," Dudley wrote to Solti after returning to Los Angeles. "Your passion and intensity, your resilience and determination were there for everyone to enjoy—me above all others. Thank you so much for a lovely time and for an inspiration that will never leave me. I send you my undying allegiance."

With the series over, Dudley again felt himself to be at a crossroads in his life. Should he pursue his music or concentrate solely on acting?

His physical agility had been stretched to the limit with *Orchestra!* Working with Solti had reminded him of the strenuousness of classical performance and of just how demanding an instrument the piano was. It took not only a great deal of concentration and technique but also practice, and he noticed if he did not play for a day, his fingers became a bit stiff.

"I think there are a lot of things that one leaves until late in life," he wrote to Peter Cork, "and I'm not sure that I'm not leaving my piano-playing too late. I'm doing a lot on my own, mainly trying to learn the [Bach] 48 Preludes and Fugues, which is quite a task. I don't know quite why I'm doing it or who I'm doing it for, except for myself. It does give one a slightly futile feeling perhaps if this is the situation."

Dudley was confused. He wanted to play the piano, but felt it was not enough for him. What he really wanted was a good movie, and he still hoped for one, although without any great expectations.

There had always been a conflict between his musical and acting talents, as there had between the audiences for each. As television critic Victor Lewis-Smith would later declare in the London *Evening Standard*, "The multitalented are greeted with scepticism as though diversity inevitably equates with superficiality." Dudley had always been used to such scepticism, though sometimes he erroneously took it as a sign of his inferiority. His versatility was a rare talent in itself, and, far from being superficial, Dudley acted and reacted from a remarkable depth that brought with it tremendous anguish.

"It aggravates me," says Suzy Kendall, "when people say they love his music so much and he should do more of it, or they love his comedy so why doesn't he stick to that? The man is blessed with being multitalented, and I find it offensive when they talk as if he should do only one of those things."

Dudley's tempestuous marriage had now led to a new decision of divorce. Dudley sent John, Brogan's son, a comforting letter assuring him that he would always remain a friend and in touch for life. Divorce papers were drawn up. But once again they were never served.

"We had a strange relationship," reflects Brogan. "He wanted to divorce, I wanted it, then we didn't want it—it was that kind of codependency. Sometimes he stayed with me even though we weren't living together properly. We still traveled together and went out a lot, although by then we weren't having sex, but we couldn't let go of each other."

In August 1990 Dudley returned to London to film a new series of Tesco ads. Arriving at London Airport, he was recognized by a couple of boys and was amused to overhear them debating to each other, "Ere, shall we ask 'im if 'e's found them bleedin' chickens yet?"

He hadn't. Filming beside the River Tay now, he found salmon—but still no chickens. By now the ads had become so popular that, after the airing of each commercial, Tesco found its shelves stripped of chickens and whatever else it was that Dudley had managed to find instead of them, prompting Tesco chairman Sir Ian MacLaurin to announce his public pleasure in the daily growth of the Tesco brand. Dudley should have deferred his fee and accepted shares in the company—the profits were going through the roof.

So was his popularity in Britain. Ironically, the Tesco chickens—or absence of them—had brought him a new kind of fame and more success than anything he had done since *Arthur*, almost ten years earlier. His appeal now spanned the generations. The older generations knew and loved him for the work he had done with Peter Cook, while a younger generation knew him only through his Hollywood movies. Now an even younger generation had come to know him through the commercials.

His reborn popularity coincided with the thirtieth anniversary of *Beyond the Fringe*.

In those thirty years since first coming together on the Edinburgh stage, each of the four *Fringe* performers had achieved great things. Jonathan Miller, an incisive intellectual, had directed films, television, and operas; written books; and lectured all over the world. Alan Bennett had become one of the foremost social playwrights of his time. As for Peter Cook, he was one of Britain's greatest wits, dubbed by Peter Ustinov "the funniest man in the world."

Once patronized by his fellow Fringers for being the least intellectual, it had been little Dudley, the one who carried the largest chip on his shoulder, who, with all of his supposed defects, had become the cynosure of international attention and a sex symbol for women throughout the globe.

Of the four, Peter had been the one most likely to become the most successful. Yet now, in the summer of 1990, he was battling with alcohol and drugs and seemed content to shuffle around in daily indolence, drinking, golfing, and reading the newspapers. The *Daily Express* had epitomized his existence in a headline that said, "The star who was left behind when little Dud grew up into a giant." As Alan Bennett remarks, "Peter was the only one of us who really wanted the fame." When that fame went Dudley's way instead of his own, his friends believe it caused him tremendous jealousy. But Peter never shared the publicly expressed belief of Nick Luard, his former partner in the Establishment club and *Private Eye*, that Dudley was Cook's creation.

Still, the press asked now, had Dudley traveled too far beyond the fringe? Well, if he had, he was content to have done so, and had no regrets about the road he had taken. Certainly he could not think of anywhere else he would prefer to live, even though critics still liked to mock his emigration to Los Angeles.

"The British are very insular," says director Anthony Page, who had known Dudley since his Oxford days. "That's their nature. If you go away from England and work elsewhere, people don't like it. And when you come back, it's very hard to make them feel part of you. It's an age-old habit of the English, and that's the way of all small nations.

"I remember doing a London Weekend TV show which was an interview with Dudley. A lot of English people were asking him bitchy questions about Los Angeles and shrinks. They were very biting and destructive and putting him down for being in America."

Dudley may have been living in America, but he was still intrinsically English and surrounded by British nostalgia. His treasured Victorian upright piano from childhood sat near the English-style grandfather clock, a set of English wooden trains rested above the fireplace, and pictures of

English scenes were scattered throughout his entire house, from the painting of children playing in the snow to photographs of his beloved Magdalen chapel. He felt proud of his Englishness, a pride that stemmed from the richness of Britain's heritage.

Some of his letters to friends back home were now taking on a deeply nostalgic perspective, and he shared several pages of reminiscences with Peter Cork. "He had this tremendous urge to get back into his roots and remember the formative years," recalls Cork. "But we never got into anything personal."

Peter wanted to locate some Deanna Durbin movies and had enlisted Dudley's help in what had now become a minor obsession. This led Dudley to remember movies from his youth that he had long forgotten. "I think I was most influenced by Korda's *1001 Nights*," he wrote to Cork. "I was rather haunted by the mythological sequences of flying horses and goddesses with many arms. (Actually, as Peter pointed out, he had garbled his films and was thinking of *The Thief of Baghdad* and *Arabian Nights*.) As for Durbin, Dudley recalled his sister Barbara "bashing through her songs" on the very piano that now sat in his house. "I think she felt as if she was a sort of miniature Deanna Durbin. I remember her chortling away with all these Durbin songs, but I liked the tunes very much!"

Peter offered to send Dudley a heap of clippings that he had collected over recent years, but Dudley passed up the offer. "I don't read papers that print personal stuff about me," he said. "It's generally inaccurate and hurtful." Yet he did see some reviews of *Crazy People*, which had just opened in Britain, and noted a few scathing comments in his diary—"Moore meaning less" and "This film still turns out a dud," both from the *Daily Mail*.

Early in October, Dudley took Brogan to a birthday dinner at 72 Market St. To the friends who were with them, they seemed happily reunited, holding hands in a public display of affection. Brogan's naïveté often surfaced innocently at unexpected moments, as it did that night. For dinner, Dudley ordered abalone, usually a tough shellfish, and was surprised at its tenderness. "My God," he remarked to everyone at the table, "they must have beaten it to death in the kitchen!" Brogan looked across at him and pondered seriously, "I would have thought the heat from the cooking would have killed it."

They were together again a few nights later when Dudley performed at a tribute to Michael Caine in the presence of Princess Alexandra for the U.K. Festival of Britain. Roger Moore hosted the evening, and Dudley turned some traditional English pub music into a "Suite for Michael Caine," which he later titled "Fantasie-Impromptu," in the style of Chopin. While Dudley played to royalty, Brogan sat at his feet on the piano dais.

In November they returned to London for a promotional blitz to herald the BBC video release and television transmissions of *The Best of What's Left of Not Only ... But Also*. Dudley and Peter Cook appeared on every major talk show in Britain, and the newspapers were full of stories about the couple and their long partnership. The launch party attracted every leading alternative comic in Britain. Young or old, to them Cook and Moore represented two gods who had paved the way for the kind of comedy that now prevailed.

Before leaving London, Dudley had dinner with Peter Cook at the Villa Bianca in Hampstead, where they were joined by Francis Megahy, who also happened to be in town. "I'd forgotten how funny Peter could be," recalls Megahy. "He had us rolling on the floor that night. Those two had a real romance going. It had its ups and downs, but it was a romance all the same."

Peter Cook himself described his partnership with Dudley as a marriage—a very long-standing battered marriage, but a marriage nonetheless.

Then it was on to Italy to film two more Tesco ads. This time Dudley found tiramisu instead of those elusive chickens. Some time later he was having lunch in Upminster with his sister, Barbara, and she served him a delicious dessert. "What's this?" he asked her. "Tiramisu," she replied. "I love it!" he raptured. "Where did you get it?" She grinned back at him. "Tesco's, of course!"

He spent a quiet Christmas with Brogan in Toluca Lake, and on New Year's Eve they flew to Aspen for a week in which Brogan skied and Dudley played a rented piano for most of the time.

In January 1991 *Orchestra!* was transmitted on Channel 4, to resounding applause. "I enjoyed it enormously," says Itzhak Perlman, "and I thought it was great that Dudley could be so easy with this great maestro and with such humor."

As *Daily Telegraph* critic Max Davidson later declared of Dudley, "The man is congenitally incapable of solemnity, which paradoxically makes him the ideal person to front a program about classical music." Although a few purists disagreed and found the jocularity between Dudley and Sir Georg Solti inappropriate, most critics felt it was a brilliant approach.

"I so much enjoyed the programmes," Sir John Gielgud was moved to write to Dudley. "I worked with Solti years ago in Berlioz' *The Trojans* and found him extremely friendly and helpful as I am sure you must have done too."

In February, as Dudley and Brogan celebrated their third wedding anniversary, Dudley was honored at a gala tribute by the Venice Family Clinic for the unceasing support he had given to their work in providing health care to the uninsured, unemployed, and homeless. Paul Reiser hosted the evening, and Dudley provided some musical entertainment, accompanied by Kenny G on saxophone.

Dudley had always felt it necessary to contribute somehow in assisting people with no resources of their own. A firm believer in community activity, he had frequently helped the Venice Family Clinic by donating his time and money, hosting cocktail receptions at his house and restaurant, and playing piano at benefit concerts to raise money for the organization, which in the previous year had served over fifty thousand patients.

His contribution as a humanitarian was an aspect of his life that Dudley never discussed. He was reticent about his efforts and was embarrassed when they were acknowledged. A few years later it would come to light that Peter Cook had behaved in a similar manner. Charitable on a private scale, he helped a variety of individuals and not even his wife had known. Only after his death, when those people wrote to Lin Cook, would his private generosity be revealed.

Paul Reiser was on roasting form at the gala. He had written some bogus reviews of Dudley's work that he read out to the guests. "The *New York Times* said his music was much like Shostakovich but without any of the good stuff," said one mock review. "Dudley was an awfully good sport about it," recalls Reiser. "He adores being made fun of and being the butt of a joke. He does it himself—probably much more than he needs to."

A few nights later at Sammy Cahn's house Dudley took over the piano and also sang "The Nearness of You" without realizing Cahn had written it. Suzy Kendall had always liked Dudley's singing voice and had urged him, without success, to record it on an album. Sammy Cahn obviously shared the same opinion. Faxing his appreciation to Dudley the next day, he said, "I've heard my songs sung again and again but you were a joy to listen to last night. We were all wiped out by your singing. I know I've tried to get you to do a piano album but now you must allow me to try and bring about a piano and 'singing' album."

The time between films was now growing longer. Between 1981 and 1983 Dudley had made five films. That rate of activity had not been equaled since. Now he was averaging one film every two years. This could not fail to depress him, despite the success of his Tesco commercials. The fame and adulation were receding, and Dudley, whose self-esteem had in many ways been founded on public appreciation, was saddened at the collapse of what essentially was the only identity he had known since his school days.

"It was as if he'd done it all and was at this dead end," reflects Brogan wistfully. "I told him that the light in his eyes had gone and he needed to rejuvenate, but he wouldn't take charge of his life." In fact Dudley had never really pushed his career, except in its earliest days. Instead, he waited for things to proffer themselves. He had always allowed life to unfold, rather than pursuing it for himself. Although he had achieved so much, little of it had been instigated by him. Opportunities had simply hap-

With Brogan Lane, a few months into their romance, Patrick, and Brogan's son John.

Lying on the rug Brogan had woven for him from his favorite picture of Magdalen College, Oxford.

Rehearsing for his classical debut at the Metropolitan
with close friend Robert Mann.

With musical partner
Rena Fruchter.
(*Courtesy of Rena
Fruchter*)

With Suzy Kendall
and her daughter
Elodie, both sporting
"Dudley Moore"
sweatshirts.

With sister Barbara.

Dudley with
a new friend.

Blake Edwards was delighted to see Dudley at a performance of his Broadway show, *Victor/Victoria*. *(Courtesy of Barbra Paskin)*

With his jazz trio in Sydney.

(Right) A jazzy moment in London.

(Below) On the beach.

(Opposite) With Liza Minnelli after the final performance on their tribute to *Arthur* tour. *(Courtesy of Barbra Paskin)*

With Nicole
Rothschild.
*(Courtesy of
Barbra Paskin)*

Dudley with
the author's
bird.
*(Courtesy of
Barbra Paskin)*

pened, and he had gone with the flow. It was a strange paradox for a man who needed so much to feel in control.

In April 1991 he at last returned to the film cameras with a zany comedy for Disney, *Blame It on the Bellboy*. It was an ensemble story of triple mistaken identity, directed in London and Venice by Mark Herman, and among the cast were Bryan Brown, Bronson Pinchot, and Patsy Kensit.

Bronson Pinchot played an Italian bellboy whose mastery of the English language would have benefited from a visit to Berlitz. Given three envelopes to distribute to three guests with similar-sounding names in a Rome hotel, he inadvertently turns the world upside down for Messrs. Orton (a clumsy real-estate scout—Dudley), Horton (a small-town mayor turned Lothario—Richard Griffiths), and Lawton (a Mafia hit man—Bryan Brown). The hit man gets directions to a romantic rendezvous with a young woman whom he assumes to be his target, the amorous mayor is summoned to meet a lovely young estate agent whom he thinks is his dating escort, and the timid property scout turns up on the Mafia's doorstep believing their house is for sale and finds himself having to convince them that he is not their hit man.

While on location in Venice, Dudley arranged for his sister to fly out and join them, and when he wasn't filming they soaked up the Italian ambiance, drinking espressos in the piazza or checking out the best fish restaurants.

"Venice was wonderful," Brogan recalls, "but Dudley was not doing very well mentally. He was unhappy. He'd gained a lot of weight and he wasn't himself. I don't think he really liked doing the movie, and he hid a lot in the hotel and was very closed off to the cast."

In spite of his inner feelings, outwardly Dudley behaved as riotously as ever. Bronson Pinchot, who had his own television sitcom, claimed Dudley as his new idol. "He had a genius for making everyone feel unbelievably at ease, and when he walked on the set each day, his first order of business was to do something droll with the first person he saw—whether it was the man pushing the tea cart around or the gaffer. I told everyone at the time I wanted to be just like him."

The two shared a private joke that nobody else ever understood. Bronson had told Dudley a story that tickled his ribald fancy: his mother had seen a production of *The Sound of Music* with a thickly accented German woman playing the Mother Superior. When she asked Maria, "What is it you can't face?" the last two words came out sounding acutely reminiscent of Derek and Clive. "Dudley thought this was the funniest thing he'd ever heard," laughs Pinchot, "and after that he would always come on the set to wherever I was and say to me, 'What is it you cuntface?' and dissolve into laughter. Of course no one knew what to make of it, and to Dudley that was even funnier. Perhaps they thought he was being mean to this little American actor, or maybe they thought it was an affectionate term that he was calling me a cuntface!"

Back in London, as filming resumed at Shepperton Studios, Dudley and Brogan stayed at Suzy Kendall's house in Hampstead, which had been Dudley's old home during their marriage, while Suzy went off to the country for a vacation, leaving Brogan and Dudley to look after her cats and rabbits.

It was while he was in England that Dudley tried to catch up with another important fragment of his past. He was fifty-five now, but he had never forgotten the person who had shown him the first real affection he had ever experienced in his life. Now he tried to find her.

He visited Winifred House in Barnet, now a home for children with learning disabilities. In 1942 it had been the convalescent home where, as one of forty children, he had spent so many lonely anguished days and nights that had inexorably shaped his psyche. It was here, at the age of seven, that he had received his first kiss from a woman, and he wanted desperately to find Nurse Pat, the source of that early love. But the home's records did not go back that far and she was untraceable.

Disheartened at being unable to locate Nurse Pat, Dudley instead made a sizable donation to the home in gratitude for the kindness he had remembered from all those years ago.

In the meantime Brogan, who was always trying to find new ways of celebrating Dudley's past, attempted to reunite the *Beyond the Fringe* team. Three-quarters of her plan worked.

Alan Bennett recalls, "Brogan arranged for all of us to meet somewhere. So Jonathan, Dudley, and I turned up, and then Peter rang up from Islington—which was at least five miles away—and said he couldn't make it. I think it may have been a joke."

Dudley faintly remembers it as being slightly different. "We were all meeting at Villa Bianca in Hampstead and we were waiting for Peter and he called from Shepperton Studios to say he'd been held up there with filming and couldn't make it. So we all sort of dissipated into the night air."

Either way, the foursome never reunited. Which was a pity, because Dudley wanted to pursue his idea for them to get together to do a new *Beyond the Fringe* when they turned sixty. Peter was the only one of the four not to object to the idea; he found it rather intriguing. Dudley later reflected that it would probably have been only a one-minute joke when they all walked out onstage, and would not have survived beyond that.

After two months in Europe, he and Brogan filled up four cases with goodies that included homeopathic medicines from Switzerland, ten thousand dollars worth of jewelry from Italy, and a reproduction painting and triptych from England, and shipped them back to L.A. They themselves flew the Concorde to New York and then home, joined a few days later by Patrick.

Since the time when Tuesday Weld had refused to allow Patrick to join his father on the Bora Bora trip, she and Dudley had reached an uneasy truce, but their antipathy had never been resolved and they seldom talked now except to discuss Patrick's travel arrangements. Even then, wary of fights and having Tuesday hang up on him as was her wont, Dudley usually left it to Brogan to communicate with his ex-wife.

Patrick doted on his father and yearned to spend more time with him. In New York, he felt acutely uncomfortable living with Tuesday and Pinchas Zukerman. It seemed to the youngster that his mother expected too much of him and wanted him to be perfect. "I remember my dad saying he couldn't understand her ways, her kind of rules and expectations on a child. It took me a long time to get to the point of understanding what she felt and that she wanted me to be perfect to cover her own feelings of inferiority."

To celebrate their return home, Dudley and Brogan threw a large dinner party at the Toluca Lake house. Among the guests were Kenny G, English actress Nicollette Sheridan, who had become a close friend of Brogan's, the Pitts, and the Bellwoods.

"We used to love going up to that house," recalls Peter Bellwood, "because it was a very warm and intimate place and Brogan was always fun to be around. I remember that a food fight started that night at this beautifully laid table. The last thing you expect is that people are going to start throwing grapes at each other, but they did, and it escalated until grapes and anything else at hand were being thrown at everyone sitting there. I seem to recall getting into the spirit of that and enjoying it immensely."

Europe had been good for Dudley and Brogan. It had recharged Dudley's batteries, and they had enjoyed themselves in the months they had been away. "Dudley was a different person when he was out of the beach house," says Brogan. "When we went away we had the best time. He was more involved, more attentive, and more loving. But when he got back in the beach house it was like he became another person. It was weird. The energy was bad in that house."

Brogan had never really cared for the house in the Marina. She found it too dark and stifling and it gave her a bad feeling. "I didn't like being there with all the windows closed, and the shutters down, and the heat on. I always liked everything open, so the world could come inside. My form of freedom is having a window open during the night, but Dud would always say someone was going to break in. He was very, very security-conscious. He'd want me to come out in the garden or by the pool with an alarm button.

Toluca Lake was like Fort Knox, but the Marina house was even worse."

Dudley had been asked to write an introduction to a booklet for STEPS, an organization with which he'd long been connected that dealt with lower-limb deficiencies in children. "As one who has a clubfoot," he wrote in the brochure, "I feel enormous empathy with the families of children with congenital abnormalities of the lower limbs and hope that this association will be instrumental in eliminating some of the guilts and fears associated with such happenstances. They are no fault of parents and their mysteries should be dispelled by helpful information."

In August 1991 Dudley received a disturbing phone call from Bernard Stevens, his brother-in-law. Barbara had been taken to the hospital after collapsing and becoming unconscious. Doctors thought a blood vessel had burst in her head, and tests determined that she had suffered an aneurysm in the right side of her head. For the next forty-eight hours Dudley was in constant touch with Bernard. He faxed his sister in Old Church Hospital, the scene of so much of his own earlier pain. Barbara had suffered a stroke. In time she would regain her faculties, but would have to learn to write with her other hand and to take life more slowly.

Alistair Cooke, the eminent English broadcaster, had announced his retirement as host of the prestigious PBS drama series *Masterpiece Theatre*, and to his astonishment and amusement Dudley heard he was being considered as his replacement. It would have been an unusual choice, since he possessed none of Cooke's journalistic acuity, nor was his background synonymous with the kind of British productions that PBS transmitted under their umbrella title. But the job was never formally offered to him and he was saved the embarrassment of turning it down.

Meanwhile, Dudley had gone on a strict liquid diet after putting on weight in Italy from an excess of pasta. Noting his weight religiously in his diary—sometimes twice a day—he was elated when he saw several weeks later that he had lost over fourteen pounds and now weighed in at exactly one hundred and forty pounds.

His former partner had something to celebrate, too. Peter Cook called Dudley to exult that he was into his fifth week on the wagon. He was, he told him, looking to open a restaurant and bar, maybe a club along the lines of the Establishment, and he wanted to enlist some Hollywood members. Maybe, he ventured, Dudley could suggest some people in his new capacity as Overseas Secretary. Dudley was amused at the idea, but the club never materialized.

By now Dudley had agreed to tread the boards once more, in a new stage play, *The Lay of the Land*, at the Los Angeles Theater Complex. Mel Shapiro's play was about a married teacher who falls in love with one of his students, and had the features Dudley liked—comedy sprinkled with minor tragedy. Excited at the prospect, he threw himself eagerly into rehearsals, directed by Lee Grant. He was paid only a scale wage, $480 a week, but that didn't perturb him. He liked the play, and that was what counted.

The Lay of the Land opened to excellent previews, but Dudley's pleasure was short-lived. The play would never go further. The LATC ran out of money and the entire complex had to close down. The play never even made it to the official opening night.

With the Bentley constantly in and out of the garage, Dudley decided it was time for a new car and he splurged on a fifty-thousand-dollar Lexus. "I'm getting some personalized plates for my new car, which will read DUDLEX," he wrote to Else Blangsted in Switzerland. "Lexus should pay me not to have such plates! I think I shall bathe in a few laughs as I journey along life's highway!"

Professionally, it seemed to be a fallow time. Ideas were floated but came to nothing. He was asked to appear with his trio at the upcoming International Jazz Festival in Australia. He declined. Also in Australia, Colin McClennan, who had mounted the original *Behind the Fridge* twenty years earlier, wanted him to do a one-man show. Dudley found the idea appealing but was loath to commit to a long stage run. He did agree to play Badger in a British version of *The Wind in the Willows*, opposite Michael Caine's Toad, but the film was never made.

As the end of the year approached, Peter Cook called to wish him happy Christmas and told him his agent had liked *Blame It on the Bellboy*, which he'd seen at an advance screening. He didn't say whether he'd seen it himself, and Dudley didn't ask. He never asked whether people had seen him, or what they had thought. He believed that was asking for trouble. Either they would be obliged to lie or he would be embarrassed by the truth. Although the papers claimed that Peter never saw Dudley's films but waited for them to come on television, in fact Peter had attended a preview of *Bellboy*, taking with him Lin, Suzy Kendall, her daughter, Elodie, and John Cleese's wife. And he had liked it.

For the last two years, except for prolonged visits to the house in Toluca Lake, Dudley had essentially been living alone at the Marina. Although he spent a lot of time with Brogan, and liked to take her with him when he traveled abroad, mostly it was for companionship. Their relations improved when they were away but, as Brogan had already perceived, when Dudley returned home to the Marina beach house, he retreated into himself. His marriage had drifted into far-from-gentle waters, and he and Brogan were constantly attacking each other now.

Brogan's dyslexia led her sometimes to confuse words when she spoke, and these mistakes would be greeted with laughter or gentle correction by her friends. As her marriage to Dudley disintegrated further, her speech became a target. How could they communicate properly, she recalls him telling her, when she couldn't even speak properly? To which she would retort that he was the one incapable of communicating.

Brogan had always felt he suffered from a lack of clarity about himself and that he preferred to hide rather than search for the truth about himself. Like Susan Anton before her, she found herself provoking him to open up and explore his inner angst. But the more she tried, the angrier he became at her persistence. Opening up was a form of confrontation, and Dudley would only take that so far. Then he would retreat.

In a last bid to salvage their marriage, they tried joint therapy again. This time they found themselves resolving issues they had never previously been able to deal with, and after the sessions they went to dinner together and held hands, feeling a sense of relief that they had got rid of so much. But it was too little too late.

"We resolved such enormous things," Brogan reflects sadly, "but what had happened in our marriage was so deep that it had become irreparable. If we'd got to it sooner, I think we might have had a chance at having a really decent life together."

Dudley felt there was nothing more to be done. He cared for Brogan a great deal and had no desire to cut himself completely adrift from her, but he felt himself going around in circles and he really did not want to be married any more. He missed her closeness, but he felt that comparative isolation was the only answer—though he was not happy. "It is very lonely and isolating leading this sort of life," he scribbled in his diary.

At Christmas, Brogan took her son to Aspen, where she and Dudley had planned to spend the holiday together, while Dudley headed disconsolately to New York on Christmas Eve to be with Patrick. On the plane, he drafted a letter to Brogan: "I know to be together would make me the insufferable, intolerant, and anxious dick that I am. I need to be, at times, entirely alone, not beholden to anyone as to my comings and goings. You need someone to be a husband—to be there all the time."

It was his first Christmas away from her in the six years they had been together.

But what Brogan and none of his friends knew was that for a long while he had been secretly seeing the girl he had met several years earlier. Nicole Rothschild had come back into his life. And this time she would remain.

CHAPTER 25

NICOLE

1992

"Ever since I knew who Dudley Moore was, I wanted to be with him, as if it was my mission in life. I'm the luckiest girl in the world, and I know it."

—NICOLE ROTHSCHILD

Nicole was an attractive, bubbly, twenty-seven-year-old Californian with a huge laugh and, at five foot five, she was one of his few girlfriends not to tower over Dudley. She was natural and unsophisticated and exuded a perpetual warmth with an appealing childlike craziness that Dudley adored. "They were like two munchkins," describes Dudley's son, Patrick, and indeed they often behaved like children, laughing continuously and talking in the funny squeaky voices Dudley had used in his years with Peter Cook.

Nicole claimed to have been adopted at a tender age by Peter Rothschild, from the American side of the large Rothschild family, when he married Nicole's mother, Gloria. She was one of five sisters, and all were extremely close to each other. In 1984, after her earlier romance with Dudley, she had married Motown musician Charles Cleveland, a dark-skinned Creole and self-confessed drug addict who resembled tennis player Yannick Noah, and had borne two children, Lauren and Christopher. Though their turbulent on–off marriage had broken up—Charles would later claim that he had divorced Nicole after learning of the resumption of her affair with Dudley, just a year after he had married Brogan—they were emotionally intertwined, and had remained close friends and were often together. Nicole's world revolved around her family, and her sole ambitions in life were to be a wonderful mother and a devoted lover to Dudley. She adored him. Nothing else was significant to her.

Since their affair in the mid-eighties, Nicole and Dudley had stayed sporadically in touch. A few times Dudley had helped Nicole and her husband Charles financially. After Brogan had moved permanently out of the Marina house in 1989, Nicole had begun turning up unexpectedly on Dudley's Marina doorstep in the middle of the night, and if he was alone, he always let her in.

Although he and Brogan still spent a lot of time together, they were essentially now living an on–off marriage and, with its deterioration, Dudley had been seeing Nicole regularly. Still, their affair had been conducted with much secrecy. Often Dudley sent limousines to pick up Nicole from her home in Riverside, fifty miles east of Los Angeles, and bring her to a hotel near his house. Sometimes she stayed for a few days, sometimes a week or more, leaving her children in the care of Charles or one of her sisters.

In some ways Nicole bore an uncanny resemblance to Brogan. She, too, was dyslexic and had experienced a strained relationship with her natural father. Unlike Brogan, she had a hyperactive personality and also suffered from what Dudley believed to be attention deficit disorder.

To Dudley, she was the most naive woman he had ever known, and it was this absolute innocence that appealed so much to him.

Like so many of Dudley's women, Nicole suffered from an exceptionally low self-esteem and a huge emotional need that brought out the carer in him. It has often been said that opposites attract, and Dudley, himself a meticulous, structured, and rational man, was indeed attracted to entirely the opposite qualities in Nicole. But it was these very differences between them—her inexplicable irrationality and failure to see reason—that would trigger endless fights between them.

Possessing as she did such great insecurities, Nicole was acutely uncomfortable in social situations and she never ventured out publicly with Dudley. For all her laughter and sense of fun, Nicole was remarkably unself-confident and was happiest when she and Dudley were simply alone together.

An intensely private girl, she wanted to remain his secret—a desire he was happy to oblige—and there was almost never a trace of Nicole in the Marina house. One morning, however, Tom Leahy arrived to make breakfast and found a pair of high-heel shoes in the living room. Assuming they belonged to Brogan, he prepared an extra breakfast. "Where's Brogan?" he asked Dudley when he came downstairs. "I thought these were her shoes." "They're mine!' Dudley responded.

"Movies are fun, music is work," Dudley had often told Lou Pitt, "and when I feel like working then I'll play the piano."

As 1992 unfolded, music beckoned more strongly than ever.

For a long time Dudley had been reflecting on the future of his film career. He felt certain now that he would never have another success like *10* or *Arthur*, and it was obvious that he was no longer an immediate choice for Hollywood's biggest film producers. Convinced that his film career was beyond resuscitation—at least to the heights of the past—he turned back to the one constant love of his life, and scheduled a series of classical concerts across America and Canada.

Those who had always believed that his heart, soul, and greatest talent belonged in music were glad to see this. "I think he finds great happiness in his music," reflects Lysie Kihl. "He's very lucky to have it, because he would be a very, very desperate man without it." Choreographer Gillian Lynne also had always felt music was where Dudley channeled his greatest passion and where he felt most complete. "When he's performing it, he's a totally rounded person, completely in command of his brilliance and his mind and his feelings ... with no self-doubts."

Now that he was to be performing in public, Dudley put himself on a new diet and splurged two thousand dollars on yet another exercise machine that would soon accumulate dust. His perpetual dieting may often have made a physical difference but emotionally it did not always make him feel better about himself. "Lost Day," he wrote sadly during the first week of January. "No food. No sleep. Nothingness."

His marriage to Brogan had now disintegrated entirely. They had split up and reunited a few times, but, although they would continue to remain friends and spend much time together, the marriage was over.

Else Blangsted had been fond of Brogan and was saddened to see the breakup of their marriage. Yet she was not surprised. "The Brogan years were hard," she reflects, "and I kept feeling sorry for Brogan, who is like a milkmaid. She was so good and kind, and her whole soul and being went into what she could do for Dudley, but it didn't matter. All he felt was guilt about not loving her back enough. I think he gets married to please the ladies. He becomes their savior, and then he says, 'What am I doing here?'"

Dudley was always the pursuer in a romance and possessive about his women, but when they turned around and became possessive in turn, he was overtaken by an urgent need to retreat and recover his freedom. Subconsciously he searched for that bonding, yet he ran away when the women wanted to control him.

The need to be in control had been a recurrent factor throughout his life, probably in retaliation for his childhood, when he had felt helpless about his physical deformities, trapped in a life that was being controlled by both his mother and the situation. The fear of relinquishing control had been his motivation for forming his trio back in the late fifties, when he had despaired of being able to play as he wanted within the confines of John Dankworth's big band.

He poured out his angst over Brogan in endless conversation with Ben Shaktman. "She became too possessive," says Shaktman. "He told me she wanted to run his life. And I said, 'So what? Why not?' But he had a fear of possessiveness.

"I saw Dudley in tremendous pain about Brogan, because once again he'd found a woman who had a condition he had no control over. He could not control her dyslexia, and that was a seriously important part of their relationship. Brogan was smart with her fingertips and her nose and her sensitivity. She was not an intellect."

But Dudley wasn't interested in intellectual women. He never had been. In an odd way they made him feel uncomfortable. Peter Cook had often told friends that Dudley believed himself to be stupid, and certainly it was true that he had little faith in his own intellect and felt safer among women who would not make him feel inferior.

"Maybe I'm just no good at maintaining relationships," he sighed to Paul Reiser one night. "I felt very sad for him," recalls his friend, "and I really saw his melancholia come out during that time of the breakup with Brogan."

In spite of his relationship with Nicole, who tried to console him, Dudley felt frustrated and sad that he had been unable to make his third marriage work. He hadn't wanted to get married in the first place, and it was pretty clear that he wasn't cut out to play the role of husband, though he had tried.

In January, Dudley flew alone to London for a major publicity blitz for *Blame It on the Bellboy*. It paid off in Britain, but in America the film did not fare well. "The story is that it was not sold the right way," he wrote to his old friend Susie Dullea, now living in Connecticut. "I have a feeling that it was a fairly bland film and not really anything that caught anyone's attention."

Actually, a lot of people liked it, including former Monty Python member Terry Jones. "I thought it was a really nice film, and Dudley was great in it. The problem was it suffered from a terrible title. Certainly some of the films he chose to make did not do him justice, but I thought this one was vastly underrated."

While in London Dudley learned that Nicole, just a month short of her twenty-eighth birthday, had suffered a stroke. The cause remains unclear, and a deeply concerned Dudley felt helpless. He was relieved when he returned to Los Angeles and found that she was reasonably unimpaired by the trauma, though it would take a while for her to recover her ability to write, and her memory, always bad, had become worse, although that too would improve in time.

In February, Dudley performed with the Baltimore Symphony Orchestra, then flew to Connecticut for a benefit concert to raise funds for Susie and Keir Dullea, who were partners in the fledgling Stamford Theater Works. "He was very generous, and I can only ascribe it to an act of true friendship," says Susie Dullea. "It really put our theater on the map. We sold every seat immediately, and people talked about that concert for months after."

A few days later Dudley flew to London to join the BBC Concert Orchestra and his former trio mates for his first British concert tour. He was sad that Brogan wasn't with him, but was heartened when she sent him flowers to wish him luck. He played classical music and jazz in Brighton, Manchester, and Birmingham, and the highlight was three electric nights at the Royal Albert Hall.

The tour reunited him with drummer Chris Karan and bassist Peter Morgan for the first time in fourteen years. "I was so surprised to hear from him to ask if we'd be available," Chris Karan recalls, "and of course I said we'd love to do it. I'd more or less given up by then, because so many years had gone by. It was a little rusty, but the magic was still there and he still had an incredible feel."

When Dudley opened at the Royal Albert Hall, a huge contingent of friends turned out to see him play, among them his sister and her husband; Suzy Kendall and her daughter; Else Blangsted, who had flown in from her home in Switzerland; and Alex Cohen and his wife, legendary actress Hildy Parks, who had followed him to London after seeing him perform at Stamford. Lin and Peter Cook were also there, and Peter, recalls Lin, "was terribly proud of him and so happy to hear the applause for him that night in that magnificent place. It was really quite moving."

Although their marriage was over, Dudley and Brogan still spent a good deal of time together, both finding it difficult to sever their connection. When Dudley returned home after the BBC tour, Brogan threw him a birthday party with his closest friends around. Kenny G as usual brought his saxophone and ended up playing jazz with Dudley.

They had remained friends ever since their first meeting, when Kenny played with Dudley at the studio in his house, and Dudley had subsequently appeared in two of Kenny's music videos. "With certain people," says Kenny, "you know you can be a child and check all your adult inhibitions at the coat-stand. That's what I did around Dudley, and it's a tremendous ability he has that allows you to be that way."

The American television networks had long been considering Dudley for a program of his own, and now CBS gave him his first attempt at a sitcom. In *Dudley*, he played a twice-divorced father whose kids and ex-wives lived with him under the same roof. But the network must have felt that the

idea of a man living with two women was too risqué for its audience, and
after filming the pilot, it canceled plans for the entire show. Not even the
pilot was aired.

The year before, pianist Rena Fruchter had formed the nonprofit
organization Music For All Seasons (MFAS) with her husband Brian
Dallow, a British pianist and former schoolmate of former British prime
minister John Major, who had over the years administered several
American orchestras. Fruchter, forty-five, had been a child virtuoso, who
made her debut as a piano soloist with the Philadelphia Orchestra at the
age of only six. By the time she was eleven, she was already performing with
other notable orchestras, such as the Boston Symphony, and had achieved
national recognition. After turning professional, she had made a name for
herself as a soloist, performing in America and across Europe, had
released several recordings of her work, and for a few years had written a
music column for the *New York Times*.

With MFAS she aimed to provide live classical music performances
for people confined in hospitals, prisons, nursing homes, and schools for
special children. Already they had staged almost four hundred concerts
across the nation, and among the board members were Sir Georg Solti,
Maxim Shostakovich, Gian Carlo Menotti, Andre Watts, and Roberta
Peters.

Dudley had met Rena during his 1987 concert with the New Jersey
Symphony, and they had struck up a deep musical alliance and a close
friendship. She was good for him, and in the same way that Robert Mann
had been such an inspiration in earlier years, pushing him to perform at
public concerts, Rena was now doing the same. She asked him to lend his
name as honorary chairman of MFAS, but Dudley refused. "He felt if he
was going to do anything for us the he wanted it to be an active involvement," recalls Rena, who instead made him the organization's president.
"He didn't only want to play concerts, he wanted to help every step of the
way with the development and philosophy of the organization." And he
did. They were offered the option to become a branch of Yehudi
Menuhin's similar Live Music Now organization in the U.K., but Dudley
decided that MFAS should remain independent.

Dudley was now turning down more musical requests than he could
accept. Former First Lady Betty Ford asked him to appear at a charity
celebration with Liza Minnelli for the tenth anniversary of the Betty Ford
Center and was disappointed when he told her he had a previous commitment. "Liza will be so disappointed you can't make it," she wrote to him.
"You and she would make for a dynamic evening so I hope you won't mind
if I keep my fingers crossed and pray for a schedule change."

Dudley always acknowledged every invitation, even if he was unable to accept. Roger Moore had been after him for a long time to play at a UNICEF benefit, and Dudley apologetically explained in a long fax why he could not be there. "To Sonny Moore from Roger Ditto," Roger promptly faxed back. "By taking the time to write you have confirmed that of which I was always certain and that is that you are a straight shooter and an all around nice guy and you REMEMBER which is more than can be said for most of the pricks in our business ... your name came up last night at dinner with the Sinatras, they spoke very highly of you and admire your talent and all that shit ... 'I know him,' I bragged."

The two Moores had shared a running gag for years. "I always treated Dudley as my son," explains Roger, "and introduced him as 'My youngest son, Dudley—all the rest of them grew tall!'" They had been friends since the sixties, but Roger had actually known of Dudley long before they ever met. "I kept getting his fan mail," he recalls laughingly, "and I couldn't think why somebody was writing to me and calling me Dudley. It turned out that the BBC was mistakenly forwarding to me all these letters for Dudley from someone in Oxford who was besotted with him."

At the end of August, Dudley flew to London with Brogan to film his television autobiography. He had been reluctant at first, feeling it to be rather premature, but was persuaded by British television director Patricia ("Paddy") Foy, who had made the outstanding series *The Magic of Dance* with Margot Fonteyn.

Paddy Foy took him back to his Dagenham roots, to Oxford University, and to Peter Cook. He enjoyed this excursion into his past; it fitted into the sense of nostalgia he was feeling these days about his earlier life, and it brought him together with many old friends he had not seen for years.

The only time he balked at a confrontation was when Paddy wanted to enter the old house on Baron Road. "We drove around Dagenham and then sat in the car looking at the house," she recalls, "and I said we must go in. I needed to know if we could film there. But he didn't want to go inside. He really didn't. And it took a lot of persuasion on my part."

It was now that Dudley renewed his old friendship with Teifion Griffiths, the Welsh teenager who had lived up the road from him. "Although we stayed in touch, we hadn't seen each other for more than fifteen years," Teifion remembers, "but after the first ten minutes, it was as if we'd never been away. He's got that particular warmth."

When Paddy Foy filmed Dudley with Peter Cook, she felt none of the tension between them that she had expected. "Dudley was sure Peter wouldn't turn up. But he did, and I found him to be one of the most charming people I ever met in my life. They were so funny together, and warm, and it led to a delightful sequence in the program."

At his former church in Dagenham, Dudley crept in the side door and showed Paddy where he used to hang up his surplice when he was a choirboy. A lot of children were milling around at the time, and when they saw Dudley, they shouted excitedly to each other, "Patch is here!" They may not have known who Dudley was, but they certainly recognized the elf from *Santa Claus—The Movie.*

Patricia Foy enjoyed the weeks she spent filming with Dudley. She was a woman who was never intense about her work: "Unless I can laugh while I'm working," she considers, "I don't want to do it. And Dudley made me laugh all the time. That was his most endearing quality." Yet she also glimpsed a great sadness in him. Deep inside, she believed, he was not a happy man.

Following the unprecedented success of *Orchestra!*, Jonathan Hewes asked Dudley to host *Concerto!*, a six-part series for Channel 4. Sir Georg Solti, however, was unavailable, so Hewes brought in Michael Tilson Thomas. As Hewes points out, it was an interesting combination, for, whereas Dudley and Sir Georg had shared similar musical views, "Dudley and Michael disagreed with each other all the time. But that created a nice tension, in the sense that they were both very passionate about their subject."

Concerto! analyzed and performed six different concertos, one each week, but this time the piano expertise was left to Barry Douglas and Alicia de la Rocha.

Even away from the piano, Dudley clearly had fun. Victor Lewis-Smith, the *Evening Standard*'s TV critic who had followed Dudley's musical career closely, would later note that he evinced "more enthusiasm and understanding than the average academic and his scatological tendencies precisely mirror Mozart's own penchant for obscenity."

In Toronto in September, Dudley performed in two cabaret shows at the elegant Sutton Place Hotel. Coinciding with the opening of Toronto's annual Film Festival, his appearance became the talk of the town, enhanced by John Dankworth and Cleo Laine who joined him on stage. It was, the critics were quick to assess, "a rare treat for the denizens of Toronto," and many turned down the opportunity to attend a welcoming dinner for Robert Redford in favor of hearing Dudley.

"Something happens when he plays," says columnist George Christy, who saw lines around the hotel for each of Dudley's performances. "A room comes to life and it's almost like a psychic magic in the air."

But Dudley seemed incapable of really feeling all the appreciation for himself. "I don't understand," he remarked to Marsha Berger, a fan with whom he had struck up a friendship, "how I can be so popular as you say I am when I haven't had a hit film in ten years." Marsha laughed, "Not that I'm comparing," she told him, "but Jimmy Stewart hasn't had one in forty years."

A true devotee, Marsha had recruited a sizable part of the population of Denver to an unofficial fan club, and when he visited the city to address a class of music students, Dudley was astonished to discover that many of them were wearing T-shirts that sported his face on the front.

That month, September 1992, Dudley noted gloomily in his diary, "Got divorced!"

"We should never have been married," reflects Brogan sadly. "Somehow Dudley feels out of control with marriage. He fights it and becomes angry about it. Marriage is something the woman wants so she can feel she has something real, because a lot of the time it doesn't seem tangible. It's like one minute he's there and one minute he's not, and it just gives us that little more stability."

They had been together for more than seven years and had shared something special. In spite of the divorce, both were reluctant to relinquish their relationship. "He was like the love of my life," says Brogan wistfully. "You don't throw that away because you get divorced."

Dudley felt intensely guilty whenever a marriage or romance broke up. He never expected a collapse but it always seemed to happen, and then he was almost as hurt as the woman. He was deeply sensitive and was troubled to think he had been the cause of any pain. He was appalled at Brogan's anguish, and felt responsible. He had made a lifetime's commitment and been unable to fulfill it. At the very least he would remain in Brogan's life and ease her pain about their breakup.

Divorce did not come cheaply. For Dudley it was now the third time around. Between his three wives, it had cost him three houses, cars, a fortune in jewelry, and millions of dollars. And a son.

"Why do the Dudleys of the world marry?" asks Ben Shaktman. "Dudley's advice always was, 'Look for someone, find her, be with her and love her, but don't ever marry her.' When he and Brogan were breaking up, Dudley told me, 'Ben, if I ever, ever say the "M" word again, I want you to put me in a straitjacket and tie me up and send me away. Never, never again.'"

Ben should have told him *never* say never again.

CHAPTER 26

THE MELANCHOLY CLOWN

1992-1993

"His happiness doesn't last, because of the starvation within him. The search for perfection keeps Dudley from being able to enjoy the journey. In the sense that most of us know happiness, he will never be happy."

—DR. EVELYN SILVERS

The Brogan years had been gregarious ones, but toward the end Dudley had retreated more and more into his cocoon of isolation.

Throughout his life he had been dogged by a sense of melancholy that at times would subside but at others would engulf him to the point where he would stay in his bedroom for days at a time.

It had settled around him now.

Dudley had always worn the face of a clown and, like all clowns, he wore laughter as his mantle and kept the tears inside. The melancholia had never been overt except to those who knew him intimately, but in one area alone, it had always been apparent. Kenny G, who never saw or shared anything but laughter and humor with Dudley, nevertheless sensed it in his music, "which seemed very melancholic to me. But he never talked about where it came from."

Jazz singer Barbara Moore had always been touched by "an appalling sadness seeping through the notes," and, however jolly the music appeared, she always caught the sound of anguish emerging from somewhere deep in the chord structures. "You feel there's the little clown laughing at the world, but inside it's the *Pagliacci* thing. Deep down Dudley has never liked the thought of being the little man, because inside himself he's such a big chap."

As Leslie Bricusse had long ago observed, Dudley seemed to share a darkness with three other British comics. "Peter Sellers, Tony Newley, Ron Moody, and Dudley were all wildly funny people, but all were very complex, with a lot of pain. They're four of a kind, in that they're enormously talented but you just feel the dark side when you're around them.

"I think Dudley's angst has been with him all the time. I always had the impression those complexities were there long before he had any success. I once saw Newley and Dudley together on a television interview show, and they were like two brothers. It was amazing. Their mannerisms, their style, even the way they spoke were so similar, and I felt this strange, dark streak that ran through them related them perfectly. They were both basically pessimists and brilliant clowns who went through morose times."

Dudley's inability to feel peace within himself stemmed not only from his childhood but also from an eternal dissatisfaction with his work—a feeling that plagues many people with excessive talent, says Dr. Evelyn Silvers. "It causes enormous suffering, because, no matter how hard they work at accomplishing a goal, it's never good enough for them. It's wonderful because it's a motivating factor to be even more creative. But it's terrible because of the dissatisfaction and the inability to enjoy the achievement. There are moments, but the dissatisfaction overshadows it.

It was this dissatisfaction, coupled with a general ambivalence about life, that had led him into a dark arena.

Ever since his convincing portrayal of Arthur, Dudley had heard the rumors that he was an alcoholic. He wasn't and never had been. But his sporadic depression had led to an occasional drug indulgence.

He had discovered two drugs that gave him different kinds of a boost. One was ecstasy, an aphrodisiac that fueled his sexual fire. The other was speed, an amphetamine that accelerated the heart rate, giving a surge of tremendous energy. It had the same effect as the purple hearts he had taken back in the sixties when he was racing the clock to complete the score for one of Gillian Lynne's ballets. There were no hallucinations, no other effects, and no desires to try anything stronger, but when he took speed, he was elevated out of his depression for a while. Drugs had become his escape route. For a man who had always been driven by a need to feel in control, he came close to relinquishing it now.

Dudley was not addicted, and claimed to refuse any of the hard drugs like cocaine that occasionally he'd been offered at Hollywood parties and to which he was vehemently opposed. But friends warned him of the dangers to his health, and he became concerned himself when he felt his heart racing one day. "Your heart is in excellent condition," his doctor reassured him after an examination, but the momentary panic had been enough to cause him an intense anxiety and he stopped taking the drugs. For a while at least.

He became acutely health-conscious. He filled his refrigerator with vitamins and became more careful about what he ate, sticking mostly to fish and steamed vegetables, which he'd always preferred. His only weaknesses were for dessert—he had a sweet tooth, and could not imagine a meal that did not culminate in jelly or crème caramel—and chocolate, a craving he struggled with enormous willpower not to overindulge, even though, like a certain credit card, he never left home without it.

In early autumn Dudley began work on a small role in *Fatal Instinct*, a film for director Carl Reiner, starring Armand Assante and Kate Nelligan. Assante had never forgotten how, during the filming of *Unfaithfully Yours*, Dudley, who was always larking around, had dressed up in drag pretending to be his mother. Assante suggested to Reiner that Dudley re-create such a performance now, as mother of the film's baddie. It was not a part that had been written, but Reiner liked the idea. Dudley began wardrobe fittings, but at the end of the first day of rehearsal, Reiner had to tell him it was not going to work. The role simply didn't fit into the picture. They were both disappointed—especially Reiner, who had wanted for so long to work with Dudley.

By now Nicole had become so firmly entrenched in Dudley's life, even though they seldom ventured out together, that he had moved her into a twenty-two-hundred-dollar-a-month apartment close to his home, had given her a twenty-thousand-dollar sports car, and had instructed his business manager to pay her a monthly allowance. He was also helping her family and her ex-husband, Charles Cleveland.

Nicole's life was in a perpetual tangle, and Dudley was constantly helping her out of financial scrapes inflicted by her disorganization and irresponsibility. She had been known to tuck bills away into a drawer, and if she did not see them, they did not get paid. More than once, the utilities had been cut off. One evening Dudley returned home to find her latest message. She needed five thousand dollars. "How much!?" He jotted it down, startled. The expenses were endless, and she was always leaving messages on his answering machine, asking for more money. Hopeless at budgeting, with no sense of finance, money disappeared as quickly as she received it. "She doesn't understand where a dot or a comma goes," shrugs Dudley. The commas could have been useful! As one of her friends attests, "I've seen Nicky drop ten thousand dollars in two hours, no problem."

In spite of Dudley's affair with Nicole, a new woman was about to enter his life.

Jolie Jones was the daughter of jazz composer Quincy Jones, and they were introduced by Else Blangsted, Quincy's friend for more than thirty years. Else, unaware of Nicole's existence and knowing only that Dudley and Brogan were no longer together, thought a little matchmaking would not come amiss. Knowing them both so well, she was sure that Jolie and Dudley would make an ideal couple. "I pushed them towards each other and kept telling each of them how wonderful the other was."

They hit it off instantly. Jolie ("That's French for pretty," Dudley told a friend) was an attractive, kind, intelligent woman in her early forties, divorced with two children. Dudley thought she was beautiful, with the most gorgeous eyes, and he kept a photograph of her on top of the television in his study. When they weren't together, they exchanged long faxes. Else was delighted that her matchmaking had paid off.

Jolie had a sense of calm about her that was beneficial to Dudley. She was the complete antithesis of Nicole, and he savored her quietness. Jolie was touched by the sadness in Dudley. She saw his darkness and wanted to lighten it. Happiness, she told him, was a choice. She had already chosen happiness for herself, and she urged him to do the same. She didn't know about Nicole. Dudley hadn't told her.

He had to fly to London, and he told Jolie he was taking Brogan with him. She thought it was not a good idea—that he was holding on to his ex-wife, refusing to let go. This was true. He had made a decision to stay close to Brogan, and he would not change that, but it disturbed him that Jolie, who could be overwhelmingly independent, interpreted his actions as a lack of assertion and independence.

Dudley performed a royal charity concert at Buckingham Palace, presided over by Prince Edward. At the banquet beforehand, Brogan, who was sitting next to Edward, asked him, "When are you going to show me around this place?" He smiled reservedly. "There are rather a lot of rooms here," he replied. "That's all right," Brogan smiled encouragingly. "We can start with just one."

Afterward Dudley played cabaret in the music room adjacent to the banqueting hall. He was surprised to encounter a less-than-perfect piano, but did not let it spoil his performance. As Prince Edward later wrote to him, "I have had nothing but enthusiastic feedback from those present about how much they enjoyed the evening and this is due in no small part to your marvellous entertainment. I hope you enjoyed the event as much as we all did."

Dudley did, but was rather dismayed at the lack of available souvenirs. Checking out the men's room, hoping to spirit away a roll of toilet paper with "Buckingham Palace" printed all over it, he was disappointed to find the usual toilet tissue used by common folk. Nor were there any ashtrays bearing the royal insignia. "Brogan and I searched everywhere but we couldn't find a single thing to pilfer." Maybe the palace had experienced too many people stealing its household necessities. At least there was the menu from the evening, which Brogan ran back to retrieve as they were leaving.

Dudley increasingly felt drawn to his roots, and when Jim Johnson, his friend during his teenage years in Dagenham, asked him to perform a concert at Kingsley Hall while he was in England, he was happy to oblige. His sister, Barbara, now recovering well from her stroke, joined him. "She was so proud of him," recalls Jim Johnson. "We got her a seat at the front, and Dudley made a lot of his remarks from the stage directly to Barbara."

Afterward Dudley sat on the stage with Jim, who moderated questions from the audience. "How has it affected you in your life to be vertically challenged?" he was asked by a social worker. Dudley looked at Jim Johnson, himself a fairly short man, then asked him, "How's it affected you?" Jim grinned and replied, "Only at football matches." They both laughed, and the audience joined in, but Jim Johnson knew that Dudley had skipped the question.

"I'm only a couple of inches taller than him," observes Johnson, "but it's that couple of inches that has kept me from being melancholy about certain things. When you're that short it has a tremendous effect on you, and I think he's always been intimidated by that, although his genius at the piano has helped him get past it. But other people adoring him doesn't make him any taller. When you look in the mirror you don't see what they see."

Later in November, Dudley flew to Bordeaux with Brogan to film a new commercial for Tesco. It would be the last one, and finally he located the elusive chickens. He found thousands of them at a French farmhouse and filled his car with them; but, driving home, he was overcome by compassion and released them all.

Dudley had spent nearly three years in his search for the elusive chickens—a quest that had begun in the summer of 1989 and taken him halfway across the world. He had waded through rivers, careened over a cliff, swum in a vat of wine, and trudged through the outback (actually, Malibu Creek). Along the way he had found cheese in France, salmon in Scotland, grapes in Italy, wine in Chile, and pizza in America, but not a single, squawking chicken—until now. With these final commercials due to debut on Christmas Day, the British papers were full of stories about his Tesco adventures.

Back in Los Angeles, Brogan threw a black-tie Christmas party at Toluca Lake. A group of carol singers clustered to serenade the guests, and tiny candles lit up the pathway to the dining marquee in the backyard. "It threw me," recalls Paul Reiser, who was a guest with his wife, Paula, "because I knew they were divorced, and yet it was so loving and they were so fond of each other you'd never have thought it."

Brogan was a bubbly personality, and glittery with it, but at her core she was an earthy woman with a big heart. She gave everyone a little gift, and Paul Reiser still has the charming picture with its spiritual poem that she gave him that night. Before the night ended, Paul and Dudley ended up at the piano together, with a couple of brandies, and played some loose jazz.

Reiser has always remembered that evening, because "it was the first time I'd been to a party where everybody was given little disposable cameras to take photos. I think you were supposed to give the cameras back, but we kept ours and I've got a great picture on my piano that my wife took from that night."

A few days after the party, Dudley was with Jolie at a Beethoven concert, and then he flew to Aspen with Brogan and her girlfriend for a brief vacation. Although he had enjoyed skiing for a few years, the novelty had long since worn off. Aspen was beautiful and he loved being there, but now he preferred to remain indoors and play the piano while Brogan took to the slopes. "Skiing doesn't seem to be my cup of tea," Dudley wrote to Patrick. "My bum leg doesn't seem to hold me up too well when I turn to the right!"

As 1992 drew to a close, it was clear that music had dominated Dudley's year, and Lou Pitt had already scheduled concerts across America and Canada to take him well into the following year.

By the spring of 1993 Dudley still had not told Jolie about Nicole. Not even Brogan was aware of her existence in his life. Meanwhile, to confuse the whole issue, Dudley was growing closer to Jolie. ("J...I love you," he scribbled in his diary.) He had vague intentions of leaving Nicole, but whenever he tried to break it off, he was overcome by the thought of being without her and in the end he did nothing. But how much longer could the situation go on like this?

Juggling Jolie and Nicky was costing Dudley a great deal of anxiety and energy. Sometimes he'd spend a night or weekend at the Hotel Bel-Air with Jolie, and when he returned to his house, Nicole would join him there. Miraculously, though one seemed to leave as the other arrived, neither found out about the other. It was reminiscent of his movie *Micki and Maude*, where he had committed bigamy and kept both pregnant wives secret from the other. But whereas that had been farcical, the reality was proving downright exhausting—especially for a man who was only a few years away from turning sixty.

The American network CBS had not given up on trying to cast Dudley in a series, despite its disappointment in the earlier pilot. Now it came up with a new concept, if not title, and *Dudley* was reborn. This time Dudley played a pianist/composer whose ex-wife (Joanna Cassidy) turns up out of the blue and dumps on him their rebellious teenage son, believing he will benefit from some paternal influence—a view not shared by either of the males. After the first show, *TV Guide* noted, "Moore is cute and perfectly suited for sitcom silliness."

Dudley liked the immediacy of television and having to come up with a show every week. He had always thrived on pressure. But this time he was stretched to the limit, working five days a week, sometimes eighteen hours a day.

As it happened, Paul Reiser had also begun a new series, *Mad About You*, and he asked Dudley to join it, suggesting he play the eccentric prime minister of a tiny country seeking publicity for tourism. Dudley liked the idea, but Paul's show being on NBC and his on an opposing network presented a conflict, besides which it might also dilute the impact of his own show if he were seen simultaneously guesting on another. He would have done better to have accepted Reiser's offer. After just a few episodes *Dudley* was ingloriously canceled. And *Mad About You* shot to the top of the ratings, to become one of America's best-loved sitcoms.

Dudley was offered another show, this time in Britain. *Dudley Moore and Jazz with Friends* would have been a late-night light-entertainment program, mixing comedy with songs, jazz, and interviews with celebrities, but Dudley turned it down.

He also rejected an offer from Los Angeles Opera director Peter Hemmings to do a new Gilbert and Sullivan opera with Linda Ronstadt. Dudley liked the singer, with whom he'd once performed at a charity benefit, but the idea did not appeal to him. The only reason he had done Hemmings's earlier *Mikado* was to work with Jonathan Miller.

In April, Dudley took Jolie and her son Donovan to London for a charity concert at the Royal Festival Hall with the London Schools Symphony Orchestra. Suzy Kendall had invited them all to stay at Bentham House, but Jolie felt uncomfortable with that arrangement and they stayed instead at the St. James's Club.

It was Barbara and Bernard's ruby wedding anniversary, and Dudley surprised them by turning up unexpectedly, taking Jolie with him to the party in Upminster. Afterward, they drove to the Cotswolds and stayed at Le Manoir aux Quat' Saisons, where he had previously stayed with Brogan. But Dudley sensed that their affair was almost over.

They flew to Geneva to visit Else Blangsted for a few days. Else was delighted to see them, but sad, too, because she could tell that the romance was no longer ablaze. For Dudley the passion of the beginning of the affair had now died, dwindling into affection. Jolie's feelings, however, had grown even stronger. "I love you," she told him. But Dudley, who had now retreated into his long silences, replied, "I can't feel it."

Else blamed herself. "I pushed them towards each other and it wasn't good. It didn't take, and I think it was all my fault."

Meanwhile, Nicole had finally found out about Jolie. She was very angry, and after their return from Europe, she called Jolie and told her she was Dudley's lover. Jolie was shocked but didn't believe her, especially when Dudley denied it after she confronted him.

But everything was about to reach a climax.

Telling Jolie he would be away for the weekend, Dudley secluded himself at home for a few days of intimacy with Nicole. Jolie, however, drove past the house and saw in the garage the red Toyota convertible that Dudley had given Nicole. "Tell her I bought it for you," Dudley urged Tom Leahy, having denied the presence of any visitor when Jolie called to say she had been by. But Jolie never asked. She didn't need to.

Nicole had called her again, and this time Jolie had believed her, especially when Nicole played back intimate, revealing messages that Dudley had left on her answering machine. Jolie was appalled and devastated at the duplicity of the man she had thought she knew so well. Hurt and betrayed, she walked out of Dudley's life—one of the few women ever to have left him. She packed two suitcases with the many gifts and love letters Dudley had showered on her and returned them to him.

Dudley felt bad that he had lied to Jolie and, worse, that he'd been caught in that lie. He had never been honest with her, had never told her of Nicole's existence. He had led her to believe he was unattached, because he had expected to end his affair with Nicole. But their romance had moved too quickly, and as the weeks progressed, he had found it more impossible to tell Jolie the truth or to break off with Nicole.

He tried many times to write, to explain and apologize, but the words never came and in the end he did nothing. He felt a deep guilt, because he had never meant to hurt Jolie, but the bottom line was that he'd never really believed in monogamy. As he told one friend, he had an insatiable sexual demand and loved being with women. He did not understand Jolie's hurt over his having another girlfriend and thought it perfectly natural for a man to be with more than one woman.

"Why would you risk it?" his friends asked. "What's wrong with just one woman?" But he kept saying, "I love women—I just love women," and he couldn't understand why women seemed incapable of accepting that some men needed love from more than one direction at a time. After all, he knew from experience that women also sometimes needed love from more than one man. From his first adult love, Celia Hammond (who at the time was dating Terence Donovan), his conscience had not been deterred by the existence of another man in a woman's life. He had enjoyed affairs with several married women, including the wives of some of his close friends, among them the first wife of Peter Cook. Cook presumably forgave him, since he never confronted Dudley with the revelation, yet he also never forgot it, and discussed it in later years with another of his wives. As for Dudley, though he suspected he'd been found out, he never knew for sure whether Peter had discovered the affair. No, to be sure, Dudley did not see why he was expected to be monogamous, and he had always voiced a belief that fidelity did not matter in a relationship.

Dudley didn't understand the female sex. He never had. The only thing he was sure of was that it was women, and not men, who ruled the roost. "Men are ruled by women and by their penis," he once observed. He had never looked for specific qualities in a woman; his only real consideration was that she have a sense of humor. The most important factor for him was sexual compatibility—given that, he believed, everything else would fall into place. But it never did. It had never, in the end, been enough.

"With all of the women," says Else Blangsted, "he is the one who knows more and feels more, and it's almost as if their lack of knowledge becomes payment for his accumulation of it. And then he wakes up and yells at them for not knowing, or he becomes silent."

Ironically, it was now that the *Daily Mail* asked him to do an interview about his success with women. It was a request he greeted with a row of exclamation points on his message pad and, not surprisingly, emphatically declined.

A few years earlier, when the *Los Angeles Times* had run an article about celebrities' greatest-wish lists, comedian Phyllis Diller, an accomplished pianist herself, revealed that her idea of heaven would be to hear Dudley Moore play jazz at her house. "He read it and dropped me a note, telling me 'Any time,'" she recalls. "But it took about three years, because he was so busy. Finally we picked a date, and I asked if he'd mind if I shared it with a few close friends."

Her invitations gave away her excitement. "Come share my fondest dream come true," she wrote. "Dudley Moore is going to play jazz!" Thirty people showed up at her Brentwood home, a few doors away from O. J. Simpson's house, including her closest friends, Bob Hope and his wife, Dolores.

To her amazement, Dudley arrived with a bunch of sound equipment and a bass player. "He treated it like an actual performance, as if he'd been hired to play a concert," recalls Diller, "which I felt kind of bad about—especially since he was very shy and wouldn't mingle with everyone. But he was magnificent. I remember Bob sat on the floor and was completely enthralled by him. It was one of those wonderful evenings where you died and went to heaven."

It really wasn't so very different from Dudley's latter days at Oxford, when everyone invited him to their tea parties in the hope of having him entertain them. But his jazz-playing days were coming to an end.

He had already told Carol Doumani that he had no intention of ever playing again at 72 Market St. "He said he'd never want to play anymore with a group of people eating," recalls Carol. "I understood that it

might be distracting and insulting, and yet I was surprised, because that's
the way he'd always preferred it." Once he had been at his happiest when
playing impromptu, now he only wanted to play at concerts or by himself.

Dennis Koch, who looked after Dudley's dogs, always heard Dudley
playing when he arrived at the house. But the moment he walked inside,
Dudley stopped. Aware of this, Dennis, after walking the dogs, would return
to the house and sit outside the front door for a while. "The dogs loved his
music, and I told them their daddy was playing and to be very quiet, and the
three of us would just sit there and listen to him play. It was pure magic. I
had all these free concerts. But I never told him I did that, because I knew
it would embarrass him."

In May, Dudley flew to Toronto to play with the Toronto Symphony,
and then to Texas for another concert. He was now earning between thirty-
five thousand and fifty thousand dollars per concert, and with some bookings spread over a couple of nights, it was no mean achievement for a man
who had never believed he could sustain himself through playing classical
music.

With the sole exception of his visit to Phyllis Diller, Dudley had not
played jazz now for a long time—partly because the kind of jazz he played
required being part of a trio and he had now become quite isolated from
people, and, more significantly, because he felt he had lost the ability to
create. "It's a great pity," says Oscar Peterson, "because in my opinion he
had a lot to say creatively and compositionally, and I was hoping he would
always continue in the field."

Dudley's former drummer, Chris Karan, who had played with him
since the early sixties, felt particularly sad. "We had something so special,"
he reflects wistfully, "especially in the old days when we had Pete McGurk
with us. I miss them so much, and it's sad those times are gone."

His friends also missed his jazz, just as they were now missing Dudley
himself. "I used to love seeing him play jazz at the restaurant," recalls
Francis Megahy. "But then he just stopped, and I saw very little of him after
that, although I'd seen a great deal of him before."

What Dudley really wanted more than anything was to create and play
his own music, but he wasn't convinced he could make a living at it and he
lacked the impetus to push it. While people paid him to perform other
composers' works, this seemed the appropriate route to follow. It had
become almost a routine. In a sense he was biding time—as usual, allowing
things to happen instead of making them happen for himself.

In August, Dudley went to London, this time alone, to publicize
Concerto! While he was in London, he also helped launch Polygram's dis-
tribution of *Derek and Clive Get the Horn*, the video of the third album with
Peter Cook that had previously been only fleetingly available to the public.

Time had not diminished their public's appreciation, and the launch was a huge success.

Whenever he went to Britain, Dudley hired a car and drove through Dagenham ("Daggers" as he called it—rather appropriately, considering the pain he had suffered in his youth), past his old home on Baron Road, or the one on Monmouth Road from which his family had been evacuated during the war, when a bomb had hit it. Once, many years earlier, Jim Johnson had followed him and watched him stand wistfully staring at a house on Monmouth Road that looked like all the others. When Dudley later told Barbara he had been there, she laughed, "You silly sod, you got the wrong house!"

While he was in London, Dudley told reporters he had given up forever on marriage. It was altogether too painful when it unraveled, and he said he would die if he were to meet someone else and go through another breakup. "I used to fall in love all the time," he said, "but not any more. I don't think men and women can get on together. They're too different. Women for me are what life is about, so I'm basically saying no more life. I'm not sure loneliness is better than marriage, but no doubt I'll find out. At the moment I don't mind being by myself."

Yet he was not by himself at all. Nicole was ensconced in a nearby apartment, but clearly Dudley was not yet prepared to reveal her existence to the world.

Although Dudley had a need to be alone, it was only when the mood took him. Solitude as a permanent state did not rest well with him. He wanted companionship but he also needed the freedom sometimes to be on his own, and that was something women found hard to accept.

"Isn't it awful," he wrote in his diary, "that to love a woman seems to mean death to (me!) a man—his self. The alternative is NOTHING—never to see her again! The other alternative is not 'not to love'—but for the WOMAN to not let the focus on the man become a form of strangulation."

In August, *Concerto!* was transmitted in Britain to mostly exceptional reviews. "As he showed in *Orchestra!*" wrote the *Daily Telegraph*, "a bit of clowning does wonders for making classical composers more accessible." Victor Lewis-Smith noted in the *Evening Standard* that "his remarkable skills as an orchestrator and all-round musicologist are seldom acknowledged ... Moore is disarmingly irreverent but without sabotaging the discussion." But some critics were less kind, with the *Sunday Times* asserting that "once again he gives a virtuoso performance as the class buffoon, with a special talent for bad jokes and silly voices."

Dudley had decided to buy a house for Nicole, and she had found one on Hurricane Street, just a few yards away from his own place. Its cost was almost a half a million dollars. Dudley instructed his business manager to bid, but noted it was contingent on the sale of Noel Place, the Beverly Hills house he had bought with Susan Anton and which she still owned. In the event, he bought the new property and left Noel Place in Susan's hands. He also bought Nicole's house for one hundred thousand dollars, so that she would have liquid assets of her own. Nicole, however, neglected to sign over the title deeds to Dudley, and so the house effectively remained hers.

He was now fully supporting Nicole and her children, and also helping her four sisters, her mother, her ex-husband Charles, and Charles's mother, for whom he had bought an apartment in Las Vegas. Dudley believed it was morally imperative that a parent be allowed to remain accessible to his children, and he went out of his way to ensure that Charles could remain near to his offspring. Often that meant Charles stayed with them.

Life with Nicole was never predictable. Walking into the Marina house one day, Dudley and Dennis Koch, who'd just arrived to walk the dogs, found themselves slipping in a flood of water. Nicky had run a bath but forgotten about it, and it had overflowed and was pouring down the staircase. Both pianos were soaking wet, and so were the couches and rugs. The vision of Dudley scampering back and forth for more towels was Chaplinesque, recalls Koch, and they laughed heartily afterward.

Dudley had a series of concerts across the country and arranged for Nicole and her girlfriend, Casey Robinson, to join him. When he was performing, he had little time to devote to anything but the work on hand, so, aware that Nicole did not like being alone, he brought Casey along for company. Sometimes Charles also joined them.

In September he began a film for HBO. *Parallel Lives*, directed by Linda Yellen, reunited him with Liza Minnelli and featured appearances by Gena Rowlands, Ben Gazzara, Paul Sorvino, Treat Williams, JoBeth Williams, and Robert Wagner. It was a loose story, entirely improvised, about a high school reunion.

Liza Minnelli found it all rather strange "because not only were the lines improvised but also what happened to the characters, so we became the makers of our own destiny and never knew what the other person was going to say. Improvisation is a very frightening thing to do when you have no outline or idea of what a scene is about."

However, she was exuberant at being around Dudley again. "He's like a shot of adrenaline, and he always had me in fits of laughter." Especially when he told her about the coloratura singer to whom he used to mastur-bate whenever she hit the high Cs. "I found that story so funny," she recalls, "that I wrote it into my computer later. It made me laugh so hard that I felt as if I'd done four hundred sit-ups. My stomach ached for days."

Parallel Lives was an interesting experiment in improvisation, but the film lacked any real sense of story and made no dent in the ratings.

Dudley's overwhelming disappointment about the direction of his film career was coupled with confusion over his life with Nicole. Sometimes it was as if she had a dual personality, and at such moments her loving nature would be replaced by an unleashed and furious violence. There were perpetual fights between them, and friends who overheard them at the Marina house grew used to the sound of the thick pine doors almost being smashed in. Sometimes Nicole would walk out on Dudley; other times Dudley would make her leave, but she always came back. If she could not get in by climbing over the wall or by persuading the private security force that she had left her key inside, she would stand outside the house and scream obscenities about Dudley that would shock their genteel neighbors, until he finally let her back in. They were equally capable of deliberately antagonizing each other, and they lived on the rim of a bubbling volcano that was constantly threatening to erupt.

Their latest fight had taken place in a Salt Lake City hotel while on location for *Parallel Lives,* and a startled maid watched in astonishment as a screaming Nicole flew down the corridor dragging Dudley, who was grabbing on to one of her ankles, behind her.

Theirs had always been a tempestuous relationship. According to Nicole's former mother-in-law in an interview with a London tabloid, she was physically and verbally abusive and had been known to smash furniture and pull her hair out in clumps. Fights with Dudley often culminated with Nicole calling a girlfriend in the middle of the night to come and extricate her, but invariably when the friend turned up Nicole had calmed down and refused to leave.

Somehow, Dudley always ended up laughing.

Ever since she had first known him, Liza Minnelli had been struck by Dudley's ability to cover his pain with humor. "The British don't like to talk about money or pain, and Dudley would talk about his turmoil and it would get funnier and funnier and suddenly it was all right for him. His perspective on life is hilarious. He goes through what every single person in this world goes through, but he's got this wacky perspective on how to pull himself out of it. That's his strength and his power and his savior. He has an incredible ability to step back and be a third person when he's talking, and to see himself either whinging or whining, and suddenly he turns it into a whole comic routine."

Else Blangsted also appreciated his propensity for humor when he most needed it. "There is immense sadness in him, but we make each other laugh, not cry, because we know there is no end to it except for suicide. As M. Camus said, 'This is the only solution.' So you have to make yourself laugh—and, in his case, the world laugh, too."

Dudley had spent his life covering his sadness with laughter. But the laughs were becoming fewer and further between.

CHAPTER 27

N O W H E R E
T O   H I D E

1993-1994

*"You can understand his turmoil, because we've all been through it.
But you know he has the capability to pull himself out of it,
and I trust that instinct in him with my life."*

—LIZA MINNELLI

In late October 1993 Dudley's image was blasted sky high by an interview in the British press with Nicole's husband, Charles Cleveland, who was staying with a girlfriend in Paris. Claiming he and Nicole were still married to each other, he accused Dudley of having conducted a secret nine-year affair with his wife that had begun at the end of 1983 and continued throughout most of their marriage and through Dudley's own marriage to Brogan.

He talked of marathon five-day sex sessions between Dudley and Nicole in which they became so wild that Nicole had once knocked a twenty-eight-thousand-dollar Tiffany lamp off the bedside table and smashed it. Referring to her as Dudley's secret mistress, Charles told of thousands of dollars that Dudley had spent on Nicole for two breast-enlargement operations, two expensive cars, rent, bank accounts, clothes, and jewelry. He said that soon after he had uncovered the affair in 1989, Nicole had moved out and they obtained a divorce in Mexico. Later they had learned the divorce was not legal elsewhere and that they were therefore still married. Afraid of being cut out of his children's lives, Charles said he had taken on the role of nanny to their two children, for which he claimed Dudley paid him fifty dollars a day—or double if Nicole stayed out all night.

All this was true, but it was an extraordinary breach of confidence considering how generously Dudley had helped Charles, who after all, for some years had not only accepted their relationship but also derived considerable financial benefit from it.

But there was a bizarre twist to this tale. When Charles's story hit the London tabloids, a thirty-two-year-old Englishman, Daniel Parsons, came forward to claim that he, too, was married to Nicole. As it happens, this also was true.

Nicole had married Parsons, a former school friend who had been living in California, in August 1989, soon after obtaining her Mexican divorce, without realizing the divorce had not been valid and that she was therefore still legally married to Charles. For the last two years her lawyers had been trying to obtain Parson's consent to an annulment of this bigamous marriage, but he had vanished into British thin air.

There was one other element in this bizarre drama. Although Charles had said he and Nicole were still married, in fact their legal divorce had become final a few days before he gave the interview.

A self-confessed drug addict who was also HIV positive, Charles was unsuccessfully battling his addiction at the time that he had spoken so candidly to the press. Later he wrote to Dudley and begged forgiveness for everything he had said about the man who had always shown him the greatest generosity and kindness. "I have been clean and sober for 3 months," he wrote, "and it hurts my heart to know what I've done to a wonderful and loving person. If you can find it in your heart to forgive me, I would feel blessed. Drugs are the worst thing in the world, it will make you do and say anything. Thank you for taking care of my family."

Dudley did forgive him. He had always said that nothing surprised him about human nature, and he understood that Charles had spoken out in desperation for money. Dudley rather liked Charles. He found him amusing, and wanted to help him get back on his feet. Dr. Evelyn Silvers had once observed that Dudley's innate understanding of human beings would have made him an excellent psychotherapist, and he exemplified her words in his attitude toward Charles.

Throughout his life, Dudley had always felt a responsibility toward the family and friends surrounding the woman in his life at the time. It emanated from his caring nature, and reflected his need to help and protect. He had done the same for all his wives, and for Susan Anton and other girlfriends, and he had continued to help not only them but also Tuesday Weld's mother, who was in her eighties and living on social security. He was an exceptionally generous man, and there was no difference when it came to Nicole, only she had a rather large family—two children, four sisters, and a mother, as well as an ex-husband and his mother. Dudley was helping them all.

Apart from Nicole's own expenses, he had bought a car for her sister Danielle, to whom he was paying two thousand dollars a month to act as baby-sitter to Nicole and Charles's children, Lauren and Christopher. He had also bought a car for Charles and paid for his airline tickets to visit a girlfriend in Europe, and was in touch with rental agencies to find an apartment for him that he would finance. In the meantime he had rented one nearby for Charles's mother, Earline, a friendly woman with a calming effect on her son. Dudley saw nothing unusual about all this largesse. He had always been lavish with his gifts and probably always would be. It was part of the obligation he felt when he was committed to a woman.

In November, Dudley went to Kansas to open the Kansas City Symphony's winter season, and at last, after several years, he caught up with Ruth Forman, his former secretary, who had moved there to be near her parents. He arranged for them all to attend the performance as his guests, and after the concert, while Ruth and her parents were still in the theater preparing to leave, Dudley walked past the hundreds of fans gathered outside his dressing room and went into the auditorium to wish Ruth's parents a happy anniversary. "That music hall was enormous," says Ruth, "but nowhere near as big as the heart of that small and beautiful man."

Over lunch the next day, Dudley told Ruth of his deep feelings for Nicole. She was, he confided, an integral part of his life and his heart. Ruth remembered Nicole's name—she had first heard it during the Susan Anton years in the early eighties.

It was clear to Ruth that Nicole was profoundly important to Dudley— perhaps as important as his career. "I'd always felt his work was his love, that he was most fulfilled by his composing, and that his fulfillment with women was secondary. Yet now there was this woman who needed him and who he needed, and it seemed to me that she was not only comforting to Dudley but necessary."

In the meantime, Dudley's relationship with his son was growing more distant than ever, and about the only thing they shared in common now was a love of music. Dudley had always thrilled to hear Patrick pounding the piano in his studio at the top of the house, even if it was to a less delicate strain than classical music, which Patrick had never liked. In the past they had often played together or recorded insane Derek and Clive–like dialogues for their own amusement, but not for a long time now.

At seventeen, Patrick was having difficulty making the transition into a young man, and seemed unable to get on well with either of his parents. His mother was always reprimanding him, and her wavering affections confused him. When she drank too much, she had a tendency to become angry with him; later, when sober, she would say she hadn't meant the hurtful things she had said. Patrick was left bewildered, just as Dudley had been with his own mother.

Both his parents suffered from periods of depression. Tuesday, who was known to sleep sometimes until mid-afternoon, had a room painted entirely black, where she would go when she was depressed. Patrick found it intensely disturbing whenever he went in there. It was little different when he visited his father. Dudley, too, seemed to be depressed much of the time, and would wander around the house sighing occasionally to his son, "Well, Patrick, life sucks and then you die."

Patrick had never got on with his stepfather, Pinchas Zukerman, and had often begged his father to let him live with him. But Dudley had always prevaricated. "I remember times in New York," says Patrick, "when I really wanted to go to California to be with my dad. But he always sort of backed off. He'd tell me he knew how hard everything was for me and what I was going through, and I'd wait for him to say more, but it always ended up going nowhere."

His son yearned to hear his father tell him how much he loved him, but Dudley was uncomfortable at expressing such emotion. And so history repeated itself and, like Dudley before him, Patrick was growing up with the feeling that he was not deeply loved by either of his parents. One was too harsh and controlling, the other withdrawn and passive—just as Dudley's own parents had been.

Friends called to ask Dudley if he'd be going skiing in Aspen this Christmas. No, he told them—not this year. He probably never would again.

In January 1994 producer Jonathan Hewes arrived from London to attend, with Dudley, the Cable TV Ace Awards, for which *Concerto!* had received two nominations. Though they did not win, the same night they heard they had won an award at the New York Film and TV Festival. Later they would also win an Emmy Award. The next morning Hewes breakfasted with Dudley, then flew home.

His timing was fortuitous. It may have seemed that Dudley had been overly concerned about living in earthquake territory, but the day following Jonathan's departure his fears were realized.

At four o'clock that morning, a major earthquake hit Los Angeles, devastating freeways and apartment buildings and flattening homes and shopping malls throughout the county. Santa Monica sustained severe damage, and block upon block of apartments and shops were decimated.

Dudley was amazingly lucky. Though he lived barely a mile away from Santa Monica, his house escaped any structural damage, and even the severe aftershocks did not loosen the foundations. The worst casualties were some broken vases.

Dudley had not made a feature film now since *Blame It on the Bellboy*, in

1991. Nothing had particularly excited him, with the exception of *Parallel Lives*, the television movie. Now a project emerged that captured his interest, and he agreed to star in *The Guv'nor*, an independent £4 million British film to shoot in England under the direction of David Green.

A former BBC documentary director, Green had persuaded Dudley to take the role of the legendary boxing promoter Lennie McClain, and was in the process of lining up a top cast around him. Essentially a serious part, it tapped into all of Dudley's best qualities, and Green was convinced the part would firmly reestablish his film viability. "It had all the humor and pathos that Dudley was wonderful at projecting. Fight movies have had a good track record internationally, and I thought this would really bring him back into the mainstream."

While Dudley waited for the film's financing to be confirmed, he performed two concerts in Louisiana and Georgia and then found his longtime friend, choreographer Gillian Lynne, briefly in Los Angeles with her husband, Peter Land. Dudley lunched with them beside the pool of the Hotel Bel-Air, and as Gillian walked him to his car afterward, he told her he was contemplating getting married again. "What do you think?" he asked her curiously, clearly unsure about his own feelings.

"I told him I'd never heard anybody who sounded less ready to get married," she recalls, "but the more he said he wasn't going to do it and didn't see the necessity of it—that they were great friends without it—the more I was sure he was going to do it."

It was true that for some time Dudley had been considering marrying Nicole. She would soon be thirty, and for a long time she had been begging him to marry her. They had been together, off and on, for over ten years, and he had a nagging fear that if he didn't make the ultimate commitment, she might leave him—and he could not imagine life without her. Yet the thought of another marriage filled him with apprehension. As he had observed earlier, he functioned better on his own. "Anyone hidden like me is difficult to live with. That's my contribution to the mismanagement in any relationship."

His relationship with Nicole was indubitably the most volatile he had ever known. Somehow they always managed to provoke each other, and there was a great deal of yelling and fighting, although they always made up. Addicted to each other, each fed an equally gnawing need in the other. Riddled with massive insecurities, only together did they feel safe. It didn't sound an ideal recipe for a man who considered marriage to be anathema and who was also moody and melancholy.

Dudley had been thinking a lot about death lately, and was constantly changing his will. Committed to Nicole in every way except marriage, he felt entirely responsible for her. He wanted to be certain she would be protected if he weren't around, and he had already ensured that the new house on Hurricane Street would be legally hers in the event of his death.

His reflections about his own mortality had been fueled by the news that his former friend and flatmate George Hastings, ex-husband of Lysie Kihl, had committed suicide by shooting himself. "Are you angry about that?' Marsha Berger asked him when he told her. Dudley wasn't angry. He thought it was a courageous act. "If I were to lose all my health and money," he responded, "I would do the same thing."

In spite of his loving feelings for Nicole, at times she seemed so completely irrational that he thought he couldn't stand her any longer. He felt driven to desperation, but it didn't occur to him to ask her to leave—only that he could leave her, and then by only one means. "I want to die! There's no other way out," he told her girlfriend Casey Robinson one day in a distraught airplane phone call as he flew home from a concert.

Depressed over Nicole's latest behavior, Dudley was haunted by something his mother had told him when he was very young. Whenever he played up, she had always threatened him with the same unfinished phrase: "If you don't pull yourself together, I'll..." Dudley never knew for sure what it was she would do, but he had assumed she meant she would kill herself. Now he understood those chilling words.

"I couldn't see any other way out of life except death," he reflects. "If I'm preoccupied with a woman, that's the way I think about it. Not cutting her out, but that it's better if I die."

His morbid gloom transmitted itself when he talked with his ex-wife Suzy Kendall. "How can you think you could pass away and not break my heart?" she wrote to him afterward. "There are so many people who care about you and I'm just one of many. You are my past, my growing up, my middle years, and, God help me, my old age. You are a very giving, sensitive, sweet person and just to know you are there means a lot."

Nicole had now moved into the new house on Hurricane Street, and Dudley was helping to organize his chaotic second household. He was more involved with domestic chores than ever before in his life, often taking Lauren and Christopher to school or supervising the four dogs, who were being threatened with a visit to the local pound if they got loose again.

Nicole liked to feel open—it was the way she had been brought up—and she had a habit of not closing doors or windows. Dudley, who was fastidious about security, was always reminding her to close everything. It was this behavior, Nicole's irrationality and constant forgetfulness, that provoked so many of their fights. Nicole simply couldn't conceive that someone might walk in on her or that the animals would escape. She didn't think in those terms. It was the opposite for Dudley, whose thought process was strictly structured and logical. Nicole was also half Dudley's age, and he, though young in many respects, was exceedingly set in his ways.

Late in March, Dudley found himself blasted onto the front pages of many international newspapers by an outrageously public revelation of a private domestic dispute.

Nicole had discovered a message on his answering machine from another woman. It sounded innocuous—just someone saying she was thinking of him and was worried about him—but it had angered Nicole. Convinced he was cheating, she took off the ring he had given her and told him she was leaving.

"I thought when Nicole drove off the first time that it was all over between them," recalls Patrick, who was in the house at the time. He had always liked Nicole, who was, after all, only twelve years older than him. "I thought she was cool, and I always got along with her. She had a good heart and was a bit motherly, always trying to get to know me better."

A few hours later a rather drunken Nicole returned and almost took out half the side of the house with her car. Dudley told her to leave, but she refused, and their argument became louder and more heated until each began grabbing at the other. She ripped off his shirt, and finally Dudley called the police. A few minutes later, so did Nicole.

When they arrived, Dudley said they'd simply had a domestic tiff. But when the police caught up with Nicole, who'd already left and was walking down the alley to the other house, she claimed he had tried to strangle her in a drunken rage. Seeing marks on her neck, the police had no choice, under departmental policy (for which they later apologized), but to arrest him on suspicion of cohabitation abuse.

"We're going to have to take your dad to the police station," they told Patrick gently, "but we're not going to put any cuffs on him." Patrick wasn't distressed. It meant he would finally get some peace and quiet in the house. He found the episode rather amusing, although he had never seen his father quite so angry before. "I thought it was funny. He was screaming at her to get out, and she wouldn't. It sounded like a scene from *Arthur*. It was hilarious. But my dad was really ticked off and he looked so depressed, like he couldn't stand it any more."

Arrested long enough for charges to be brought against him, Dudley was released two hours later on fifty thousand dollars bail.

The newspapers—especially the British tabloids—went to town. Overnight, Dudley's gentle, caring demeanor was transformed by them into a portrait of a man whose violent dispute with his girlfriend had led to an attempt to strangle her. What had happened to the figure the world knew as gentle and kind? Had he, they asked, turned into someone capable of harming women? They managed to obtain his police mug shot, and splashed it across their pages. It was sordid and embarrassing.

Dudley was more hurt and angry than humiliated. He found the tone of the stories and the publication of his police photo utterly nauseating. Didn't most couples have domestic squabbles and fights? Weren't even the most tranquil of relationships punctuated now and then by fits of screaming and yelling? He couldn't understand what was so extraordinary about his fight with Nicole to turn it into such a huge story.

What made it so immense was that his image had been shattered.

Paul Bloch, Dudley's publicist, had witnessed much scandalous publicity over the years, representing as he did some of the biggest stars in Hollywood—among them Sylvester Stallone, Bruce Willis, and Nick Nolte, who had all taken massive print beatings in the past. But even he was shocked at the extent to which the tabloids magnified this story. "We were all surprised that they took such a big shot at him," he recalls. "They'd never done anything like that to him before. The media can turn on you pretty quickly. One day you're in phenomenal shape, and the next they turn on you and put you down. It's the way news is conducted. If it sells and people buy it, they'll go on writing about it."

The news traveled fast. Dudley's friends immediately rallied to his side, offering support and places of refuge, concerned less with the facts of the incident than with whether their friend was all right.

"I've had goodwill faxes from all over the world," Dudley wrote to Suzy, "as well as calls piling up here. We've had very little to say. I think the way to keep it going is to argue in the press about it publicly. You always lose, whatever happens!"

Not everyone agreed with his approach. Anxious to put the record straight as she saw it, Charles's mother, Earline, told the papers of Nicole's extreme temper and how in the past she had seen Nicole hit Charles and become violently abusive, sometimes even to herself. She spoke out in defense of Dudley, but it only served to perpetuate the incident in the media.

Peter Bellwood was shocked and horrified to hear about the episode, "but it made me laugh when he called me up a couple of days later and said, 'It's the Dagenham Mauler here.' I asked him if he had any advice to give me after all that. He laughed and said, 'Yes, don't ever call 911, whatever you do!'"

Within a day—predictably—Dudley and Nicole had made up and she was posing playfully on the bedroom balcony for photographers, pulling down her shirt collar to reveal her neck where Dudley had allegedly grabbed her. She dropped the charges against him—although the City Attorney's office had yet to decide whether he would be prosecuted—and retracted her earlier claims. She said she had been drunk and acting stupidly, and the whole thing had been a gross misunderstanding. The marks on her neck, she said, were scars from a thyroid cancer operation.

Privately, however, she admitted that Dudley had grabbed her neck and was choking her, although he certainly had never meant to hurt her.

In the midst of being the focus of such ignominious worldwide attention, Dudley began work on the pilot for a new television series. Though his previous series had been unsuccessful, CBS continued to believe that it would have a major hit on its hands, if it could find the right vehicle for Dudley. Now perhaps it had it. In *Daddy's Girls*, for which he was paid $250,000 for the pilot episode, he played the owner of a clothing business. When his wife runs off with his business partner, Dudley is left alone to bring up three very modern daughters with the usually unhelpful advice of Harvey Feinstein.

Dudley's work was about his only respite from the devastating attention with which he now found himself surrounded. He plunged into long hours of rehearsals and rewrites, but at the end of the day he was reminded of reality when he drove home and found the tabloid reporters still camping on his doorstep. He was thankful briefly to escape to a couple of concerts booked in Jacksonville and Oregon.

Just as interest seemed to be dying down, it suddenly flared up again with Charles telling the tabloids he had a sex video that Dudley had shot and he was offering it for sale for $1 million. The tape, he alleged, contained footage of Dudley taking drugs and having sex with famous women. But by now Charles's credibility was wearing rather thin and he found no buyers.

Dudley had long ago given up on refuting the various salacious stories that appeared in the tabloids. He shrugged them off, and once again forgave Charles for his extraordinary attempts to extract huge sums from the tabloids at the expense of Dudley's reputation and, possibly, livelihood.

Meanwhile Nicole's lawyer had obtained a court date for the annulment of her marriage to Daniel Parsons. With that in hand, Dudley saw his way ahead to marry Nicole, and he set a date for their wedding. He called Patrick to tell him that he was getting married for the fourth time, and then arranged for his restaurant to cater the affair. He ordered flowers and a minister, and instructed Sam, his secretary, to book several suites in the nearby Ritz-Carlton to accommodate various members of Nicole's family.

When news of his impending nuptials leaked out, the British tabloids had ample new fodder to feed their voracious appetite for Dudley-bashing. "Cuddly Dudley" was embarking on his fourth marriage, and this time to a childlike woman half his age with an ex-husband who seemed intent on destroying him—and just two weeks after his arrest for attacking her! Unflattering psychological assessments poured forth from the British agony columnists.

In mid-April Nicole's marriage to Daniel Parsons was formally annulled. Two days later she married Dudley.

Tom Leahy knew nothing about the wedding until a few days beforehand, when Nicole came downstairs in a wedding dress. She seemed to him almost nonchalant about the forthcoming event, and left many necessities untended. Tom hastily organized some flower arrangements and took her dress, which didn't fit properly, to the tailor for a quick alteration.

Of the dozens who crammed into the Marina beach house, only a handful of Dudley's own friends was present. Lou Pitt was there; so were Tom Leahy and Hugh Robertson, Dudley's legal adviser and business manager. The Doumanis from next door, who had generously lent the use of their vast parking area for the occasion, were also in attendance. The rest were Rothschild friends and family. A couple of security guards kept the hovering press at bay.

The ceremony should have begun at 2 P.M. but was delayed for more than an hour over some confusion taking place upstairs. Peter Rothschild, Nicole's stepfather, had read the prenuptial agreement listing Dudley's net worth at over $10 million but had balked at the wording and insisted it be changed before going ahead with the wedding. "I'm pissed off," Nicole told the disgruntled guests. "He's taking all the romance out of it with this contract."

There was an abundance of exotic food, but Nicole, who had low blood sugar and occasionally had to be treated for hypoglycemia if she was not careful what she ate, wandered around nibbling on a muffin and a bag of potato chips. As for Dudley, to one guest he appeared rather bewildered by the occasion.

After the ceremony—which was described by Nicole as short and funny ("Like me," added Dudley)—they played with the children on the beach, to the delight of the press on the doorstep. Dudley quipped that he'd invited the cops to the wedding, and then posed on their bedroom balcony with Nicole, who looked gorgeous in her silk bridal gown.

The news spread quickly. "Dearest Dud," faxed Peter Cook. "Good luck mate. Lots of love." Others wrote or cabled. Or didn't. "We just couldn't congratulate him," says Cleo Laine. "He knew we thought he was a mug to get married again."

In late April criminal charges against Dudley were formally dropped by the City Attorney's office after he and Nicole agreed to the condition to visit a marriage-guidance counselor. It was a rather bizarre ruling for a couple who had only been married a few days. "I'm sorry, honey," Nicole told him as they left the court. "It was all my fault. I was drunk as a skunk. Now it's over."

Lou Pitt had scheduled a new concert tour for Dudley that took him to Edmonton, Peoria, Dallas, and Vancouver. He was averaging two concerts a month now—an impressive record for a musician who, as he liked to put it, had come from behind. At this rate, as long as he sustained his piano-playing agility, he was guaranteed a long and highly lucrative career.

It was now that he learned to his dismay that *The Guv'nor* had been canceled. The money had collapsed. It was difficult to amass the finance to make a movie, Dudley wrote to Suzy Kendall, "unless you are as 'hot' as a piece of steaming shit."

Now, too, he was told of the cancellation of a concert series with Vladimir Ashkenazy that had been set for July in Britain. Indeed, work in Britain suddenly seemed to be crumbling around his ears. Even hopes for Jonathan Hewes to film his next concert at Carnegie Hall for BBC-2 were dashed when the BBC was unable to furnish sufficient money. Whether all this was due to the economic recession in Britain (it was) or to recent publicity about him he could only speculate. "Frankly I don't really care," he wrote to Peter Cork. "If people wish to read this stuff in the tabloids and believe it, then that's their problem."

At least there was *Daddy's Girls*, his new television show. He had just heard that CBS had given the green light to the pilot. Now he began taping the series.

He saw little of the old friends whom he'd known for so long—some for more than thirty years—and whenever they did see him they were saddened by the air of resignation that had crept over him.

"Nobody has endless success without setbacks," reflects Leslie Bricusse, "and Dudley's had so much success in so many areas and he still hasn't faded from view. He's a brilliant talent, and his musical brain is phenomenal, but I think the melancholic thing that's in him probably makes him feel unfulfilled, even though it's not justified."

Though outwardly Dudley professed to be satisfied with his music, he missed the acclaim that had accompanied his earlier work as an actor and the roles that had gone with it. He had never been prepared to relinquish his acting, just as he had never been able to stop playing some form of his music while at the height of his film stardom. One without the other had never been enough for him.

In her insightful bestseller *The Successful Self*, psychologist Dorothy Rowe offers an assessment that could be applied to Dudley: "The success that many of us desire is fame. Famous, we are significant, noticed, approved of and desired. Famous, we become more real than real. Fame, for both extroverts and introverts, is a way of proving you exist."

Dudley had often observed that his smallness led people to look at him with contempt until they realized who he was, "and I remember that's why I wanted to be famous in the first place—to obviate that awkwardness I always felt."

Dudley's self-image had always been in conflict with the outside perception. "He's one of the greatest physical comedians the world has ever seen," says Peter Bellwood, "and, as chairman of his supporters club, I'd always try to turn him back into that direction. But he's a very obstinate man, and what counts is his perception of things. If his perception is that he has presided over a film career that has rolled over and gone toes up, then I'm very sad, because I don't think it's true. I think those days are there for him again."

Dudley could not share that optimism.

His days were not happy now. Nor were they unhappy. But they were marked with a singular lack of optimism. Hope had dissipated, and with it any excitement about what each new dawn might bring. "There must be a point," he told me some years ago, "where you feel you have no curiosity left, and I think if one ever wants to die, it's because their curiosity has died."

Or perhaps their hope.

A religious documentary on public television caught Dudley's eye as he was channel-surfing one day. Normally he would not have lingered—religion did not interest him, nor did he believe in it—but he caught the words "man must live by three things alone" and he was curious to discover what were those three secrets to happiness. The first, he heard, was the love of a good woman. "OK, I've got that," he told the television set. The second was work. "That's good—I've got that too," he thought. The third was hope. "Well," he grimaced, "I haven't got that!" He said it not with any sadness, but with passive acceptance.

"I don't think he's particularly happy all the time,' says his sister, Barbara, "but it's very difficult to prise out of him what he's really feeling about things. He's had everything in the way of fame and money, but whether he's always happy about life ... I don't suppose he is."

Dudley felt himself drifting now, passing through time, simply existing. "I'm waiting to die," he told me many times in the course of my writing this book, though not in a morbid sense.

Given the comparative longevity of his parents (his father died aged seventy-one and his mother lived to be eighty-one), he estimated he had at least another twenty years ahead. Yet he saw them as years without hope, years that would unfold grayly without passion, years in which he would merely exist until time simply ran out. Nothing to expect, nothing to look forward to, nothing to hope for. The grayness that had pervaded his earlier years had never been so dark as now, and he accepted that it would remain with him always.

"I suppose I haven't made the dent in life that I hoped to," he reflects wistfully. "I think I've missed the boat a bit. Maybe I should have tried harder. I haven't become a full-out comedian or musician or composer. You could say I'm a Jack of all trades, master of none. If I'd been a physically different person, I might have concentrated more. I guess the incentive isn't there, and I feel it's too late to do anything. So now I'm really waiting to die."

He had never been sure what he truly wanted to do in life. "He's got gallons and gallons of talent," remarks Chris Karan, "but how do you channel all that and know what to do with it? With Dudley it's overflowing, and maybe it's too overwhelming for him."

Dudley had never really settled long enough to find the fulfillment that comes from a long-term involvement. He was one of the most talented people alive, but he was not a driven man and he lacked the perseverance that could have made him a great classical or jazz pianist or a greater actor. "Everything he does," Robert Mann has observed of Dudley's work, "he could have done a lot more."

Years earlier at Oxford University, a fellow student had remarked that Dudley's tombstone would probably read, "He had it all but what did he do with it? Nothing." Dudley believed that might be true. He had always hoped he would die at the pinnacle of his career. The worst scenario would be simply to fade away. Now he feared he was doing just that.

"I feel desperately sorry for him," says Peter Cork. "He's never found the serenity he'd have liked, but that creative demon which gets into people makes it impossible for them to have a personally happy life. I think his music means more to him than anything else. Music sets up standards of perfection that don't exist in people, and I think his unhappiness and insecurity is because he had a passion for music that he couldn't find in any other sphere."

Late in September 1994, *Daddy's Girls* debuted on television. The reviews were not only unanimously bad, but downright unkind. "How do you spell aggravation?" asked the *Los Angeles Times*. "Dudley Moore. The question is how the comedically gifted Moore got himself into such a series whose opening is pretty much a witless mess." *Entertainment Weekly* asked snidely, "Will you be needing a passport to get back into England, Mr. Moore?"

Dudley was vastly disappointed. He had liked the show and hoped it would work. "I don't know if my persona is something the great American public really wants to see," he mused to me wistfully. It was, but audiences wanted to see him in something that made the best use of his humor. *Daddy's Girls* did not go far enough. Certainly he was funny, but the show gave him no opportunity to express the physical comedy that his fans found so endearing.

"I felt badly for him," recalls Paul Reiser, whose own show, *Mad About*

You, was still a huge hit, "because he seemed to be awfully constrained in a vehicle that didn't make the full use of his talents. He's universally liked and wears so well, and it's a great idea to put him on TV. But American TV often tries to jam any component into a formula, and that doesn't work."

Reiser wanted to see the racier, Derek and Clive side of Dudley. "It's a great combination—this classy, educated, articulate guy for whom nothing could make him laugh more than a good blow-job joke. I'd love to see him hook up with someone who has a less conventional take on TV and can pull off the challenge."

Robin Williams also enjoyed Dudley's more ribald features. "Nobody's ever written anything that Dudley and I could do together," he reflects, "but I think we would be a wonderful combination for a film. My choice would be to make *Derek and Clive: The Movie* with him. I think we'd be fabulous!"

In September, Dudley played Mozart and Gershwin, his year's choice, in Syracuse, Oklahoma City, and Ohio. Then, accompanied by Nicole, he flew to New York for a challenging return to Carnegie Hall in a benefit for Music For All Seasons. For a long time he had been considering expanding his repertoire; he was particularly keen to play the Grieg piano concerto, but lacked the confidence to try. Now, spurred on and tutored by Rena Fruchter, he spent weeks solidly learning the work. "He really didn't think he could do it," recalls Fruchter, "because it's a tough one. It's intensely frenetic, and taking the decision to try it was a big hurdle for him to overcome. But he worked hard, and he played it extremely well." He performed it with success, and EMI was at Carnegie Hall to record it for a CD release the following year.

Dudley had now formed a production company with Rena to record future concerts for video and television transmission. They planned a solo concert for the following year—a retrospective in which he would both play and discuss his career. They also launched a short-story competition for young writers, with Dudley agreeing to set the winning entry to music, which he would play at another concert at Carnegie Hall set for April 1996.

In mid-October, after just three episodes, CBS pulled *Daddy's Girls* off the air, but ordered the remaining episodes to continue being taped for transmission at a later date. Dudley was disappointed but not surprised. Nothing much surprised him when it came to the unpredictability of what the public wanted to see on television or in films.

In the meantime he made a brief appearance in *The Disappearance of Kevin Johnson*, a film directed by his longtime friend Francis Megahy. It was a tense drama about a British television documentary crew investigating a wealthy British entrepreneur who had come to Hollywood to break into the movie business but had since vanished. The ensuing search uncovers a modern tale of power, money, and sex in the film world. Dudley appeared as one of Kevin Johnson's friends, along with James Coburn and Pierce Brosnan. Although his part was a brief one, Dudley was intrigued by the concept and enjoyed the fact that he had entirely to improvise the role. "He was very charming to do the film," says Megahy, "and he agreed without hesitation. But he's always been that way—immensely generous. He's a kind person, and he likes helping people."

For a long time Nicole had been begging to have a baby with Dudley, and he had at last agreed, despite having insisted on an earlier abortion. They decided to try artificial insemination. One embarrassing morning Dudley found himself masturbating into a plastic cup.

It worked. Nicole, simultaneously taking fertility pills, became pregnant.

By Christmas, Dudley was still uncertain about the future of *Daddy's Girls*. CBS was contemplating transmitting in the spring, but Dudley rather hoped the series would not get picked up again. It had been a tough grind and about the hardest work he had ever done in his life, and he was keeping his fingers crossed that the show would quietly be dropped.

It was.

CHAPTER 28

GOODBYEEE PETER COOK

1995

"It's almost impossible to define what Peter and Dudley shared together; it defies any simple explanation. Only the two of them could understand how intricate their relationship was. They were part of each other's family, and there was a deep affection between the two of them."

—LIN COOK

In January 1995 Peter Cook was taken to the hospital with a critical liver condition. When Lin Cook phoned Dudley to tell him the doctors would have to operate, he was left with an awful feeling of dread, and over the next few days he persistently called the London hospital for updates.

In the early hours of January 9, Lin woke Dudley with the news he had feared. Peter Cook had died. At the age of fifty-seven, a light had been switched out in the corridors of British comedy.

Dudley felt disorientated. He could not imagine Peter not being there any more. Overcome by a need to hear his voice, he telephoned Cook's answering machine, but he felt even stranger when he heard it. A disconnected voice on the other end was still in this world, yet the soul of the man who had put it there was no more.

Peter's death was the end of an era, and for Dudley the cutting of a thread that had bound them together for more than thirty years.

First brought together in *Beyond the Fringe* in 1960, their ludicrous comedy in three series of *Not Only ... But Also* had made them cult idols to millions of British viewers. Together they had made five films and a stage show that was seen on three continents, and they had given birth to Derek and Clive, two of the most obscene characters the world had ever heard.

Peter had been one of the great comic creators of his time, with an uncanny ability to improvise on any subject with outrageous and often tasteless absurdity. He could spin off into a world of verbal fantasy with a wit that was second to none, and his surreal brilliance never failed to astound Dudley.

His happiest years, Peter had often said, were the ones spent along-side Dudley. With him he found a home in which he could unleash his insane humor with unfettered abandon and have it returned with equal lunacy. Such a unity was bound to breed resentment and bitterness when it ended. "I think watching Dudley's success was probably very difficult for Peter," considers Peter Bellwood, a longtime friend to both. "When you have a partnership like that and one person goes off and does what appears to be better than the other, it's difficult because it's very confronting."

It was often said that Peter's ambitions had not been fulfilled, and that he felt frustration and rage that Dudley had achieved where he had not, but the reality in later years was actually rather different. The intense ambition of Peter's earlier youth had dissipated—"I lost it when I was twenty-four," he was fond of saying—and he was happy to potter around the golf course, read the newspapers, or saunter through the offices of *Private Eye*, in which he owned a majority share. Relative indolence appealed to him.

Though his life had appeared to be drowning in alcohol, he had begun to get that under control, too, feeling settled and loved by Lin and able for the first time to express his own love in return. He had mellowed greatly, and his acid tongue and acerbic wit had become less scathing in recent years and more sensitive to other people's feelings—something to which he had been inured for most of his life. Only the death of his beloved mother in June 1994 had turned him back to the bottle.

Peter was not dogged by unfulfilled ambition, as widespread belief had it, but he did have a need to find expression for the magnitude of his talent and be appreciated for it. It often seemed that there was no real outlet for his gifts, and if he appeared at times resentful or bitter about Dudley's achievements, it was not for what they had brought his friend but rather that the ensuing fame had allowed Dudley to find a niche for his own talent.

Humorist Martin Lewis once asked Peter, "Be honest—aren't you just a bit envious of all that fame Dudley has?" Peter looked at him for a second, then replied, "Martin, there's two kinds of fame. There's fame like Charles Manson and there's fame like Dudley. There has to be something between the two."

In spite of the British newspapers' constant claims of jealousy and resentment, the truth was that Peter had felt an intense pride in Dudley and a genuine pleasure in his achievements. He had a great love for his former partner, a love that never abated, and it was the very intensity of that feeling that had made him so resentful in the earlier days when they had split up. He had not been jealous of Dudley's success but upset that their working relationship, which had meant so very much to him, had come to an end.

The symbiosis between the former partners was eternal, but Peter had never truly recognized the depth of Dudley's sensitivity, and Dudley had been so greatly hurt by Peter's caustic references about him that, to the end, he remained slightly wary in his presence. Theirs had been a marriage of sorts: two people loving each other but unable to live together, yet each willing to cross the world to help the other if asked. The irony was that, although they appeared to be so very different, their equal inability to express their deepest intimate emotions prevented them from recognizing how similar they really were.

John Bassett, who had brought the *Beyond the Fringe* team together all those years before, happened to be in Los Angeles and had arranged to have lunch with Dudley on the very day Peter's death was announced. While TV cameras camped on the doorstep of 72 Market St., Dudley sat inside with his old friend, refusing to cancel their engagement. He looked, to Bassett, quite unlike his old self, as Francis Megahy also observed when they met a week later for a symbolic celebration to mourn Peter's passing. "We had a lot of laughs," says Megahy, "but he was very withdrawn and subdued and I was very worried about him. He wasn't the same as he used to be."

"The last time I saw Peter was a few years earlier," reflects Cook's longtime friend, Brenda Vaccaro. "He was very sad, and he broke down and cried. He said his whole life was alcoholic and there wasn't anything he could do about it. He just sat there crying, and there was nothing I could do. He said the people he loved the most would probably never see him again. I think he meant Dudley, but he didn't say so. I think he had a vision of himself going down.

"After Peter died, I phoned Dudley and we reminisced for the longest time, and he made me laugh and he made me cry. Peter was a powerful, incandescent light, and I think Dudley was terribly affected and deeply saddened by his death."

Lin Cook had always been touched by the depth of emotion that bonded the two men. That was why Dudley had been the first person she called when Peter died. "Dudley was the person Peter loved the most, but I think in the earlier years Dudley didn't realize how much Peter felt for him. Both of them had difficulty in expressing their love, and it was only in later years that Peter felt more able to express his emotions.

"He always felt sad for Dudley if he thought he was going through a bad patch or was unhappy because a relationship was breaking up. Sometimes he just sensed it, maybe because of something he'd read in the newspapers, and then he'd phone Dudley to cheer him up.

"I know Dudley was devastated by Peter's death. They were kindred spirits, and it would be impossible for anyone ever to take Peter's place. We'd both lost someone very special."

Dudley didn't know what he felt. In a sense, he wasn't feeling at all. His bond with Peter had been so great that he was quite numb. Now and then a deep sadness permeated that numbness and he was gripped by fierce panic attacks that would wake him suddenly in the middle of the night. Sitting up in the darkness, he was weighed down by the thought that he would never be able to see or talk to Peter again.

At least there was work to distract him. Ian Younghusband, who had been Jonathan Hewes's associate producer on *Orchestra!* and *Concerto!*, was making *Oscar's Orchestra*, a futuristic animated series about the orchestra, for the BBC. Introducing the great classical themes in a form accessible to children, the series provided an inspiring introduction to musical education, and Dudley narrated the voice of Oscar the piano.

Dudley's household on Hurricane Street (his second, for he still had his main house down the road to which he would occasionally retreat) now consisted of Nicole; her children Christopher and Lauren; her ex-husband Charles; and three dogs: Emil, a miniature Shetland collie, Patricia, a Pomeranian, and Garth, a dachshund that Dudley had named after the cartoon character in the *Daily Mirror*. There had been a fourth dog, Harry, a gentle Lhasa apso, but Dudley had moved him into the other house to join his own two dogs, Minka the samoyed and Chelsea the keeshond. For a brief time there had also been a cockatoo, but sometimes Nicole forgot to close the windows and doors, and when she came home one day, the cockatoo had apparently flown the coop. Later, however, they heard that Charles might have sold the bird for some ready cash.

Dudley seemed always to be running around after the Hurricane Street dogs, and feeding them, too, since Nicole often simply forgot—and finally he decided he'd had enough of picking up all the dog shit. Reluctantly he found new homes for all but Emil the sheltie.

At least he had someone to help sort out the chaos. And that was Charles. Dudley had had an extension room built on to the house and now Charles could be near Nicole and the children, and Charles was helping out in just about every possible manner, including chauffeur, family cook, and baby-sitter. Dudley bought him a secondhand Jeep so that he could more easily assist in various household errands, and his presence was invaluable when Nicole had cravings for carob cookies in the middle of the night.

It was decidedly unusual for a man to have his wife's ex-husband living with them, especially one who, according to the newspapers, was now suffering from fully blown AIDS (although he seemed quite healthy), and inevitably it led to speculation. Friends believed Dudley was being black-mailed, but he emphatically denied the suggestion—as he had when the police had put that same question to him. Still, it was costing him a fortune to have Charles around, particularly with all the medical bills he was paying.

His concern for Charles was completely in character. He had a hugely generous heart and had always felt compassion for those less well-off, had never easily tolerated seeing people on worse terms than himself. "I find it extraordinary," he reasons, "that some people who are more talented than others are rewarded accordingly. I don't like that. You're given a set of cards when you're born, but there are those who don't have such good hands."

"We like to keep the familiar around us," explains Casey Robinson, Nicole's best friend, "and Charles represented everything that was familiar to Nicky. He's a really nice man, and one cannot help but like him. Dudley didn't want to upset that, and he's tried to help Charles in so many ways. It's certainly not been his obligation, but he's done it anyway, because that's the kind of giving man he is."

Dudley now spent most of his time with Nicole at the new house. Sometimes he wandered back up the alley to his own house to check the mail or play the piano in the company of his adoring dogs Minka, Chelsea, and little Harry, but in the evening he always returned to Hurricane Street. He used to say how similar he was to Peter Cook in this regard—living in a separate home from his wife—but in fact Peter and Lin had spent every night together, either in his home or in hers up the road.

Despite Nicole's glorious naïveté, one thing he believed she instinctively understood was the difference between men and women. She had always told him he could go off and do and be with whom he wanted, as long as he told her about it, and he had only once let her down in this regard—over his affair with Jolie. Dudley had always yearned for such understanding, which he believed the entire male race deserved. Nicole's understanding, however, would fluctuate with her moods.

He once had written, "If only a woman could grant a man the respect of him being a separate being. All a man wants to hear is 'You are a free man and you can do whatever you like.' A man would no doubt stay forever if he was granted such respect. Similarly, a woman should be granted the same privileges."

As Nicole's pregnancy progressed, Dudley felt little of the trepidation that had preceded Patrick's birth nineteen years earlier. Then, terrified when Tuesday Weld told him she was pregnant, he had been afraid of passing on his own deformity and was plagued with memories of his unhappy, painful childhood. With Nicole if was different. The warmth and love in which she enveloped her children alleviated Dudley's anxiety, though not entirely.

"I wonder if you're really prepared for this,' Nicole kept telling him. He wondered, too. He feared the involvement, and was afraid he might not feel an emotional attachment. Yet there were moments when he became quite excited, especially when he put his hands on Nicole's stomach and could feel the baby bouncing around.

He felt calmer at the prospect of becoming a father this time. At forty he had worried that it would be fraught with danger. Now he did not. He felt better equipped to be a good parent. But the new baby often caused him to reflect on his relationship with Patrick. He was unhappy that they had grown so distant. "He can safely say that I sort of abandoned him," he frets.

In many ways he blamed his own upbringing. His father had been a passive man who had done little with his son, but Dudley had loved him anyway and never thought it particularly unusual that they did nothing together. He believed he was repeating that pattern with Patrick, and could only hope that his son would love him anyway.

On that front he should have had no doubts. Patrick worshipped his father and wanted nothing more than for them to be together. "Sometimes when I'm with my dad," says Patrick wistfully, "I get the feeling he expects me to dislike him or reject him, and I never understood that. The longer I was around him, the more confused he would get. I suppose that came from feeling rejected himself so many times in his life. I'm sure my dad loves me, but I think he's very uncomfortable with saying it—just like I am."

ICM's New York office, which arranged all his musical engagements, had organized a new concert tour, and Dudley set off across the nation, throwing himself into Mozart and Gershwin in the symphony halls of Tennessee, Alabama, Ohio, Michigan, and Canada. In the midst of this, however, he was facing a time of considerable change.

Nicole had decided she wanted to move out of Los Angeles and further down the coast, where she had grown up. Fixated on her, Dudley agreed. But he was apprehensive at the thought of living permanently in the same house with Nicole and the family. Although he was in fact with her most of the time, at least whenever he needed solitude, all he had to do was walk a few yards up the road to his own house. After the move, that safe retreat would be much further away.

Still, wanting to please her, he put down seventy-two thousand dollars for a year's rent on a seven-room home that Nicole liked in Corona del Mar, a quaint seaside community an hour south of Los Angeles. Organizing the hefty move from both homes in the Marina was no simple task, but Dudley took little from his own home, preferring to leave it intact for whenever he would be in Los Angeles. He did not intend selling either house, and Nicole's sister Danielle, who lived opposite the Hurricane Street home, would keep an eye on both properties.

It left him with one painful task. He had already told Sam, his secretary, that he was closing down the office and would no longer need him. Now he had to tell Tom Leahy, his loyal and devoted majordomo of the last nine years, that they were parting. He had thought briefly of asking him to make the move south, but it was an impractical idea.

Dudley felt guilty about Tom. It had always been difficult for him to break off any relationship, and this one he found quite impossible to sever. After Tom had prepared his breakfast one morning, he left the house and went over to Hurricane Street and asked Nicole to break the news.

Tom had no idea they were even planning to move, so when she telephoned to say Dudley would have to let him go, he was stunned. "When Dudley got back in the afternoon he was nervous and awkward," he recalls. "He told me he was sorry but he had to do this. He was moving on and changing his life."

He was indeed. He had begun to cut himself off from his past, wiping it out as if it had never existed.

There were few people now whom Dudley kept near him. He had divested himself of so many, yet Lou Pitt remained constant. They were like brothers. "I can't imagine anything that would hold me back from jumping in front of a train and stopping it if he were endangered," admits Pitt. "And that's not a professional thing. He simply is just the most extraordinary human being I've ever met."

Almost a year since his marriage, not a single one of his friends, except for Pitt and Rena Fruchter had met Nicole. She was almost as much of an enigma now as she had been during the years that she had been Dudley's mistress. With the exception of his sister, Pitt, Fruchter, Suzy Kendall, and his lawyer, Dudley told no one his new phone number, or indeed that he was moving when he did. When Patrick telephoned him a few weeks later, having obtained the number from Pitt, his father asked how he had got it.

Messages from old friends were not returned, and the people around him were worried. "Just leave a message while I'm out to tell me you're OK," Francis Megahy told Dudley's answering machine at the Marina house, but it was months before he heard from his friend of more than thirty years.

"I'm worried about him. What's happening?" his friends asked each other. Was he all right? Why had he moved? Why was he so withdrawn and isolated? Why wouldn't he see anybody? Had he lost all desire for his friends and his former life?

In a sense he had. He often had said he was unable to reciprocate friendship, and he knew he was bad at keeping up old relationships. But the woman in his life had now become his focus and his best friend. "I've really just followed where Nicky wanted to go," he explains. "She's a terrifically optimistic sort of person, and I like that about her."

For Dudley, who had lived in the same house for nearly twenty years, it was like starting a new life. He was now effectively cut off from all his previous friends and relationships. To his surprise, he liked Corona del Mar. It was a picturesque beachside village with a serenity he had not anticipated, very different from the crime-ridden streets of Los Angeles. Their house stood on a promontory overlooking the ocean, and it gave Nicole tremendous pleasure to gaze out at the view. "All you can see is water as far as the eye can stretch," she exulted. "I grew up around here, so it feels like I'm home again."

In April 1995 Dudley and Nicole celebrated their first wedding anniversary. Reflecting on their long romance, she told me then, "I feel my life couldn't get any better. I'm loving just being with him.

"He's so nice that you can't be anything but nice in return. And that's the perfect relationship. I hope it always stays like this. He's not been a real happy person, and I've always thought that was very sad. Behind all that funniness was a real serious, deeply hurt little person."

The following day Dudley turned sixty.

The birthday brought, oddly, a sense of relief. He was tired of being fifty-nine. He looked a good ten years younger than his age and still resembled the cute leprechaun of the sixties, when he was performing in Britain with Peter Cook. There were a few flecks of silver in his hair, which studios tended to cover, and the odd crease in his face, but otherwise time had been especially kind to Dudley. Fear of aging had plagued him on earlier birthdays, but this one was remarkably free of trauma.

It helped to have a wife half his age who giggled with him and talked in funny, squeaky voices. They were constantly laughing and having fun together, and that kept him in touch with his childlike side.

"One thing I've noticed," reflected Nicole, "is that he couldn't say 'I love you.' It was very hard for him to get into any kind of emotional conversation for long. Maybe he could say it in passing, but that was all. But the last year or two he's not been afraid to say it.

"I've always tried to tell him that I just want the best for him, I want him to be happy—whatever that is—and I love him and think he's the best thing that ever walked. I tell him that every day, at least a couple of times. And I really think he believes me now."

But their marriage was not as idyllic as she made it sound. There was something different about Dudley. He had changed over the last year, become more somber and less attentive, almost as if his signing of the wedding certificate had eradicated the need for any extra effort. They used to have so much fun together, she wailed to a girlfriend. Now it had gone, and Dudley seemed to be in a space of his own that she didn't understand. They weren't even making love anymore, she said. And yet they were soul mates, and considerably intertwined.

Dudley may have been repeating a past pattern, one common to many men. He had resisted marriage every time, only to succumb finally to the familiar refrain, "If you really loved me, you'd marry me ..." and once he was married, he felt as if he were caught in a trap. Though nothing ever really changed, inwardly he felt it had.

For many men, love flourishes when it can be enjoyed amid unfettered freedom. Once it is compressed within a commitment such as marriage, it becomes confining, perhaps to the point of suffocation, and then such a man might see himself as being caught in an imaginary net. Dudley had tried to explain this to Nicole in earlier days, when she had pleaded with him to marry her. But she, like so many women when they are in love, had believed this time it would be different.

At the end of April, Dudley flew to Michigan and Chicago for two concerts before continuing to London to attend Peter Cook's memorial service. It was the first time he'd been away from Nicole for more than a couple of days since their marriage, and she was so distraught that when the limousine arrived to pick him up, she shut herself in their bedroom long before he even left the house.

At the Chicago Symphony, formerly the home of Sir Georg Solti, Dudley played Mozart's Piano Concerto No. 21 and Gershwin's *Rhapsody in Blue*, capping off the evening with a few of his parodies. He was a resounding success with one of the world's most knowledgeable audiences.

So much of Dudley's time was spent on the road, but he never used these opportunities as an excuse for living it up. In planes, he slept, read, or telephoned his answering machine to check for messages; in hotels, he kept to himself.

Whichever city he was in, if it was to play a concert, he rarely left his hotel room except to go to the concert hall for rehearsals and performances. Hotels fed and served his compulsion for seclusion. They were an extension of the Marina beach house, an opportunity for isolation, and he would shut himself in his room and practice the piano—there was always one installed in his room wherever he stayed—or watch television, talk to Nicole on the phone, and sleep. He ate all his meals in his room and never ventured into the public restaurants unless it was to meet someone from the local symphony, a local reporter, or Rena Fruchter and Lou Pitt, who often flew in to attend his concerts.

Whenever he did emerge—usually to walk to the concert hall—he found himself approached at every turn. In Chicago, strangers were constantly stopping him. "It's him, it's Arthur!" they gasped, and tapped Dudley on the shoulder. He smiled self-consciously. There was the dichotomy again—the celebrity who was almost embarrassed to be treated in that way.

At Peter Cook's memorial service in May, most of Britain's comedic showbiz community turned out to pay tribute to Cook's extraordinary comic genius. Dudley, who was with Suzy Kendall, told a few lighthearted anecdotes and recalled the time when Peter came up with the notion of reading Braille on television—"I'm sorry I'll feel that again." At the end of the service, he played their longtime signature tune "Goodbyeee," accompanied by the choir from Peter's old school.

It was now that he learned just how much he had meant to his former partner and friend. Dudley had been mentioned in Peter's will, but Lin had not wanted to tell him that on the telephone and had waited to share with him this private expression of Peter's great affection for Dudley.

In the early sixties, while performing *Beyond the Fringe* in New York, Peter had bought an exquisite Tiffany lamp. It was one of the first items of any value that he had ever owned, and he always treasured it. It was this, his most prized possession, that he left to Dudley. "If Dudley ever doubted Peter loved or cared for him," says Lin, "all his doubts evaporated when he learned this. He was immensely moved, and in a mild state of shock."

Lin expected Dudley to take the lamp back with him to Los Angeles, but a few days later he told her he wanted her to have it. "In my mind," she says softly, "that was his way of showing how much he cared about Peter. Dudley realized how much Peter and I meant to each other, and it was his way of comforting me.

"There's a wonderful, special continuity about it. The fact that Peter left this most treasured item to Dudley was beautiful. The fact that Dudley gave it back to Peter, through me, was doubly beautiful."

For Lin, it was impossible to believe Peter was gone. Even months later, her life felt totally unreal. "I have this strange feeling that I'm still waiting for Peter to come home," she told me. "And in some ways I think Dudley feels the same. I think he's wondering, 'When's he going to ring me?' After all, Peter had been around in Dudley's life a lot longer than he was in mine. I only knew him for thirteen years; Dudley knew him for thirty-five. And, if I can miss him so terribly much, can you imagine the impact on Dudley?"

There was a huge hole in his universe, and it would be a long time before he could even begin to consider how he felt. For now, nearly six months after Peter's death, he had absolutely no idea. Aside from the obvious and the banal, he couldn't find any words to express his emotions. He could only reflect on the times they had shared and the work they had done, and wonder at the extraordinary scale and nerve of it all.

When he returned from London, life suddenly gathered speed. He had signed to appear in a new film for cable television. *Weekend in the Country* was an ensemble piece with intertwining stories in which Dudley costarred with Jack Lemmon, Christine Lahti, Richard Lewis, and Rita Rudner, wife of the film's director, Martin Bregman. Dudley played a vineyard owner romantically involved with Rita Rudner. It was not the first time he'd had an on-screen affair with a director's wife: in *10*, his girlfriend had been played by Julie Andrews, who was married to Blake Edwards; in *The Wrong Box* he had been smitten by Nanette Newman, who was the wife of Bryan Forbes.

He was also committed to a couple of concerts in Canada and America, and in between the weeks of filming, he found himself flying back and forth, while a now heavily pregnant Nicole fretted in Corona.

She was always afraid when Dudley left, and found it hard to function alone, relying as she did on his sense of control and organization. Years before they had even met, Dudley had explained his ideal woman as being "very much a child, because I enjoy the energy and creativity that comes with that. On the other hand, I want her to be independent of me, so that her neediness doesn't become suffocating."

Nicole could have traveled with Dudley as he had first planned, but she had changed her mind as she always did. Nicole lived in the "now." If something sounded good to her, then at that moment she wanted it, but with the dawn of a new day or some other distraction, she had either forgotten her earlier intention altogether, or she had changed her mind. She wavered back and forth with every decision, and Dudley was continually having to ask airlines to refund her unused tickets.

He made it back from his last concert with just a few days to spare. On June 28, 1995, Nicholas Anthony Moore was born after a long night of labor. While Charles watched through the delivery-room doors, Dudley stood at the head of the bed filming the delivery—too squeamish to stand at the other end and record the actual birth. He was so awed by the experience that he cried.

For some weeks Dudley had difficulty in knowing how to refer to his child. "They say 'the son' looks like me," he told me immediately after the birth, adding his surprise a few days later that "it" wasn't crying very much (a situation that changed with remarkable alacrity). Eventually Nicholas became "the baby," but it was a while before Dudley could bring himself to say "my son."

Dudley rarely went into Los Angeles now, and usually only for meetings and to check his mail at the Marina house. Sometimes he and Nicole would drive up and spend the weekend there, but, despite the apprehension he had felt before moving south, he was feeling fairly settled in Corona, even though he was entirely removed from everything familiar.

He felt greatly loved by Nicole, who was so caring and solicitous of his happiness. She was totally devoted to him and her children in a way that he had never felt before, and he felt little need to withdraw to his Marina house. When he needed solitude, he closed himself in his bedroom and Nicole seemed to understand that need.

Casey Robinson had always been touched to see the extent of Nicole's love for Dudley. "Nicky would sacrifice her life for Dudley," she observed. "There's so much giving and loving in her, and a lot of enmeshment between them."

In many ways Nicole was like a schoolgirl, with a laugh that reverberated through the house and was so contagious that Dudley was in constant convulsions even when he was in another room. Peals of laughter seemed to follow him everywhere.

Still, it was a boisterous and chaotic household with two hyperactive children. Nicole herself was energetic and spontaneous. He could never be sure where she would be at a given moment, which made it impossible to plan her participation in anything.

The children adored him. Lauren, eight, called him "Dudley"; Christopher, six, called him "Dad." He was fascinated by their vibrancy and how loved they were by Nicole. He had never seen a mother like her before.

Everything Dudley did now was in consideration of Nicole. He was offered various engagements, but was loath to accept anything that would take him far away from her. She was acutely averse to meeting new people or going anywhere far from her home, in part because of her tremendous lack of self-esteem. The only thing she cared about or even understood was her love for Dudley, her children, and her home life. And Dudley, whose life revolved around them now, was guided by what would be best for Nicky.

The one thing he could not do for her was retire. Nicole wanted him to give up acting and playing concerts—anything that would take him away from home. But the performer in Dudley could not submit to such an absolute withdrawal. He needed to perform.

As Nicole did not enjoy going out or meeting people, their days and nights were centered on the household. Often they were joined by members of Nicole's family: mother Gloria, stepfather Peter Rothschild, her father Richard, and her sisters. Nobody ever seemed to telephone first to say they were coming—they just turned up out of the blue, ignoring

Dudley's repeated requests that they phone beforehand. Dudley occasion-ally found the noise that accompanied all this pandemonium too much, and it was then that he would disappear to the quiet of his bedroom and curl up in front of the television.

Charles's presence made such escape easier. Playing the role of companion, maintenance man, cook, and nanny, he was a cheerful and optimistic person, and Dudley liked having him around.

He had to admit that sharing his life with Nicole with her ex-husband was not the tidiest arrangement, but Dudley knew no other way to handle it. He was solicitous of Charles's need to maintain a relationship with Lauren and Christopher and that he had nowhere else to go. Even the children's doctor remarked one day that it was the strangest ménage he'd ever encountered. Dudley had to agree, but Charles was part of Nicole's family and Dudley felt committed to helping them all, as he always had with his own family and any of his friends who had asked him for help through the years.

On the surface, it seemed as if they were all one happy family. But every so often there would be an explosive and violent fight between Dudley and Nicole, which usually resulted in one of them storming out and driving to the Marina house.

In August, the London tabloids claimed Dudley and Nicole had sep-arated. In fact, the story had been triggered by Nicole herself. After a tiff with Dudley she had called the newspapers to say they were breaking up. Nicole lived in the moment, and her actions were governed by whatever emotion she was feeling at that second. Just then she was angry, and this was a bid for attention. By the following day she had forgotten all about it. But the instability was growing.

Nicole was always urging Dudley to believe in God as she did. "Supposing I get to heaven and you're not there?" she often wailed to him. "You won't go to heaven if you don't believe." But Dudley could not, despite the early years of religion to which he'd been exposed in his parents' home. "I find it ridiculous that someone only 'goes to heaven' if they believe," he muses. "So I'm a bit dismissive of Nicole over this."

Dudley's kindness, whether to friends, strangers, or mere acquain-tances, had always been extreme, as British radio producer David Longman now discovered. He had written to Dudley to ask for an interview, and reminded him that he had been Dudley's first interviewer a few decades earlier, for an Oxford University newspaper. "My wife was over the moon," recalls Longman, "when Dudley suddenly telephoned me in London in response to my letter and agreed to do the interview. I was astonished. Stars don't do that. But Dudley does."

In October 1995 Dudley flew to London, where EMI was launching his first classical CD, of his Grieg piano concerto performance at Carnegie Hall. His arrival coincided with a new tabloid story about his marriage. After another argument between them, unknown to Dudley, Nicole had again called the British tabloids, offering to sell an interview about the couple's imminent breakup. By the following day she had simmered down, and each assured the newspapers that their marriage was in fine health. Times were far from harmonious, however, and it was bewildering for Dudley to hear Nicole threaten divorce every time they argued, or later to discover she had been calling the London newsrooms.

The uncertainty generated by her erratic behavior created among Dudley's circle of friends a sense of foreboding that one day the stories would be true and this seemingly codependent couple would push their love/hate relationship over the edge, with possibly devastating consequences for either or both of them.

Publicly, however, Dudley claimed to have no doubts about his feelings for Nicole, or that their marriage would endure. "She's nicer to me than any woman I've ever known," he said. As for Nicholas, his four-month-old son, he was bonding with him more and more.

After years of being pursued by advertisers Dudley made his first American commercials for National Car Rental. It was a series concept that tapped in to his comedic talent, just as the British Tesco ads had done. If audiences were bemoaning the fact that they hadn't seen much of Dudley in recent years, that would change when the ads began running on national television.

Meanwhile, film scripts continued to arrive on Lou Pitt's desk. Dudley was still in demand, and major directors continued to pursue him. One of them was Barbra Streisand.

Pitt was confident Dudley could recapture the success he had once known. He had often been criticized for not pushing Dudley's career more strongly in recent years, but in truth he had never ceased. The films Dudley had chosen to make had also been liked by Pitt, but somewhere in the translation to celluloid the scripts' potential had not been realized.

Barbra Streisand was offering Dudley a small role in what would undoubtedly be a significant film, *The Mirror Has Two Faces*. Streisand was not only directing the film but also starring in it, backed by a large cast that included many big names.

Dudley was ambivalent about the part, but Lou Pitt urged him to do it. Pitt could be bullish when he chose, and this time when his agent spoke, Dudley listened. He would make the film, and maybe it would revive his dormant acting career.

In November 1995 Dudley began work on the Streisand film.

But it was not to be.

CHAPTER 29

INTO THE
DARKNESS

1995-1996

*"He's one of the funniest people I know, and audiences out there still love him.
He's the greatest physical comedian who ever came down the pike, probably since
Chaplin or Keaton, and at his optimum he's as brilliant as those guys."*

—PETER BELLWOOD

The past month had been a busy one for Dudley. He had played a
couple of concerts, filmed the first commercials in his near million-
dollar deal with National Car Rental, and had hosted a two-day American
memorial tribute in Los Angeles to Peter Cook.

While he was busy on the work front, his home life was chaotic. The
week before flying to New York, Nicole decided she wanted to move to
Colorado, even though it had barely been six months since she had
persuaded Dudley to move out of his Marina home of twenty years down
the Southern California coast to Corona del Mar. Always anxious to please
her, Dudley took her for a weekend to Telluride, a town nestled in the
Colorado Rockies, and, after looking at countless homes, they made an
offer on a house overlooking the mountains that they both liked. A few
days later he flew to New York to start the new movie, his first feature film
in almost five years.

His role in Barbra Streisand's *The Mirror Has Two Faces* was not a large
one, but it was likely to be hugely significant, not least because for a long
time he had been accused of appearing in second-rate works that had not
made enough of his considerable talents.

The romantic comedy marked Streisand's first return to directing since 1991's *The Prince of Tides,* and boasted a stellar cast that teamed her with Jeff Bridges, supported by Pierce Brosnan, Lauren Bacall, Dudley, Brenda Vaccaro, and Mimi Rogers. Dudley had been reluctant to do the film, because the part was small, but he had eventually agreed to play one of the several elite cameos as Jeff Bridges's best friend. Streisand, whom he had known for several years, was playing a dowdy college professor who transforms herself to bring some passion into her platonic marriage.

The day before shooting began, the cast assembled for a full script reading. Streisand was ebullient that day. She had long wanted to make this film, and her enthusiasm filled the room. Many of the actors were meeting for the first time, and Streisand hosted the gathering like another hen, introducing everyone to each other and making sure there was plenty of food and refreshments on hand.

Though she must have been exhausted from months of preproduction work, she looked fresh even without makeup. Her shoulder-length hair bobbed from side to side as she chatted with everybody grouped around an oval table. The reading went well. Dudley was particularly funny, and earned approving words from his peers. Barbra was full of anticipation for the start of filming the following morning.

But back in his hotel room that night Dudley was beginning to fret. Nicole, who found it hard to shoulder much responsibility, had called several times to tell him she wanted to move immediately to Telluride without waiting for their house offer to be accepted. She would drive up and rent a place, she told him. Dudley implored her to wait until his return; he would only be in New York for about a week.

Worried and distracted, he found it hard to concentrate on work. He had yet to learn his lines fully for the movie, and he also needed to practice the piano for a concert two nights later in Montreal. He was incapable of doing either. His entire focus was on Nicole and the domestic machinations taking place three thousand miles away.

Early the following morning, while a limousine waited outside the hotel to take him to the film set, Dudley was still on the phone with Nicole, who was adamant about making the move overnight. She told him she would arrange for the furniture to be driven up and for her mother to drive his car out of his Los Angeles house where he had left it. "No, don't drive the car to Telluride," Dudley tried to dissuade her. "It'll take three days to get it there." It would also leave him without a car when he returned to L.A. "I don't want to keep saying no," he told her. Finally he stopped saying it and gave in. "Look, do what you want," he sighed. "It's OK with me, whatever you want to do."

With his mind full of the chaos taking place in California and the sheer logistics involved in moving his household to another state, Dudley tried to clear his head and concentrate on the job at hand.

On location in the grounds of New York's Columbia University, he ran through the lines with Streisand. He had two scenes that day: one with her, another in the afternoon with Jeff Bridges. Streisand, dressed for the role in a long white caftan, hat, and glasses, rehearsed a couple of times then decided to film the first scene. She was an exacting director who paid enormous attention to every detail, and though intensely focused on what she was doing at each moment, she was simultaneously aware of everything else taking place around her on the set.

Normally Dudley learned his lines loosely and then performed his own interpretation of them, which sometimes deviated slightly from the script. Such a method did not sit well with Streisand. She was punctilious about the written words, and Dudley was now finding it hard to remember his lines precisely. As the hours wore on, Streisand became increasingly exasperated. "I know you've got problems at home," she finally burst out, frustrated at the direction in which this was going, "but we've got to do something about remembering the lines!" Dudley looked at her. "I know" was all he replied quietly.

Streisand had their lines written on giant cue cards, but still Dudley could not get them right. He didn't like looking at the cue cards. They shot and reshot, and the more irritated and dissatisfied she became, the harder Dudley found it to focus at all. He had completely lost his stride. By the time they broke for lunch, the scene that should have taken a few hours to complete had only been partially shot. Dudley was not in a good mood now. He skipped lunch and remained in his trailer, collecting his thoughts and nibbling half-heartedly on two teaspoons of mashed potato.

The afternoon went no better. Streisand rehearsed Dudley's scene with Jeff Bridges, but with the light fading she had to abandon any hope of filming it and returned instead to securing close-ups for the earlier scene.

A limousine stood by to whisk Dudley to the airport for his flight to Montreal. He was exhausted, having barely eaten all day, and was still greatly distracted. His rehearsal the next morning with the Montreal Symphony lacked his usual verve and fluency, surprising and annoying conductor Charles Dutoit, who had worked with him previously and enjoyed his playing immensely. Mozart and Gershwin, for once, could not command Dudley's full concentration. Although he was marginally better equipped for his performance that evening, he was far from his usual form—a fact that did not escape the ears of local critics, nor those of Rena Fruchter, who had joined him in Montreal. As his musical partner, she was disappointed in his playing; as his friend, she was acutely concerned about his state of mind, which seemed to be in a perpetual state of anxiety.

It was no wonder that Dudley was having such a hard time. Nicole had now rented a house in Telluride and was in touch via cellular phone. The furniture had arrived, she told him, but they had not been able to fit it through the front door. Proudly she said she had resolved that problem by immediately renting another house with a larger front door. Dudley worried greatly about her having to handle such enormous responsibilities without him.

In New York the next day he met privately with Streisand, who was now seriously considering replacing him with another actor. But she was also genuinely worried about him. Was he OK? she asked. Was this an aberration?

In truth, Dudley would have been vastly relieved to be released from the film—he had not enjoyed the brief experience on set—but he felt it would be unprofessional to tell that to Streisand, since he had already committed himself to the work. He told her he was fine and would have his lines memorized by the time he returned to film more scenes the following week. Reasonably assured that she would have his total focus from now on, Streisand, who in only her third day of filming was now half a day behind schedule, decided to sleep on the matter.

Earlier in the year Dudley had narrated the voice of planet Earth in a National Geographic series, *Really Wild Animals*. It had proven a huge success, and while in New York, he recorded narration for a new series. His concentration was so unfocused—even though he was simply reading from scripts—that the voice-overs would later have to be redone.

In the midst of all this, the press was now reporting that Charles had skipped bail for his latest demeanor, an earlier charge for possession of drugs, for which Dudley as usual had posted bail. Not only that, they claimed, but he had also left the country. The implications could have been financially severe for Dudley, who had been the one to guarantee his presence for sentencing—but the report proved to be erroneous.

By now, hardly surprisingly, yet a new worry had surfaced. Dudley was frightened by a pounding in his heart and visited a heart doctor who put him through a variety of tests and then pronounced him fine. But the stress was clearly affecting him.

In the meantime, he had even more on his mind. He now could not reach Nicole at all. None of their cellular phones raised a response and, because she had given the wrong address to the phone company, the engineers had been unable to install phones at the new house. As he packed to fly back to Los Angeles, Dudley frantically tried to contact somebody in Telluride. He had arranged for Charles to collect his and Nicole's two children and baby Nicholas from the sister who was looking after them in Los Angeles, and to fly them from there to Telluride, where they would all be living together. But now he could not reach Charles, Nicole, or her sister.

Worried sick, he spent much of the flight back from New York trying to reach Nicole on the phone, his anxiety aggravated by the fact that it had now been over twenty-four hours since they had last spoken. At Los Angeles airport, instead of collecting his baggage, he headed straight for the telephone to try once again to reach her, without success. When he finally left the airport, having rented a car, he was so distracted that he brushed into another car as he merged into heavy traffic. Not until later that night did he learn that Charles and the children had safely reached Nicole.

The following day he joined them all in what was to be their new home. Nicole had now changed her mind about the first house they had found, which Dudley had liked so much. She preferred this new house they were renting instead, and asked him to make an offer on it. Dudley wanted her to be happy and he agreed—as he usually did. But he was tired now. He had seldom put his foot down where Nicole was concerned, but this, he told her, was it. There would be no more moves. If she didn't like it here, he would leave. He could not move again. He was far too tired.

Dudley was indeed exhausted, from the endless arrangements necessitated by moving homes, bidding on houses, and organizing everyone else. He was also tired from all the people who ended up around them, even though Nicole had initially told him she wanted them to live quietly in Colorado with only Charles and the children. Now she was persuading her sisters and her mother to move there, too. Dudley was surrounded by people when what he wanted more than anything else was peace and quiet. He craved it, and needed it.

Then, to compound his despair, he received a phone call from his agent with the news that every performer dreads. It was the first time Dudley had ever heard the words in his thirty-five-year-long career. That night he learned that Barbra Streisand had fired him from her film.

Ironically, the actor she turned to as his replacement was George Segal, the very man whom Dudley himself had replaced seventeen years earlier in *10*, the movie that had launched his film career in Hollywood. It seemed the compass had swung full circle.

Dudley was ambivalent when he heard the news of his ignominious release. He had not wanted to make the film in the first place, and was relieved not to have to face complicated flights back and forth to New York from the mountain town of Telluride. Still, he was uncomfortable that he had not performed to the best of his professional acuity.

The news leaked fast, and was exacerbated by Nicole's insistence that Dudley talk to the tabloids. When he did, they angled the story around yet another fight between the couple. Dudley, they wrote, had been incapable of remembering his lines because he was angry at Nicole's intention of having Charles, whom they described as her drug-addicted, AIDS-infected ex-husband, live with them in Colorado. Dudley insisted this was untrue, and said he had no objection to Charles being around.

For the next month Dudley remained in Telluride with Nicole, the children, two of her sisters who had moved into the apartment over the garage, and Charles. They spent a quiet Thanksgiving, during which Nicole ensconced herself in the kitchen cooking for half a day, with Dudley under orders not to show himself until she had finished. It was a lovely dinner, though Dudley felt guilty that she'd spent five hours preparing something that took only fifteen minutes to consume.

Nicole's priority in life was to please Dudley, and she was trying very hard indeed to do things the way he wanted. She struggled to remember and correct what it was that irritated him—like forgetting to turn off lights after leaving a room, or not turning up for appointments because she didn't remember having made them. She was even trying to lower the children's decibel level. He was impressed by her efforts and applauded her for them. Yet she always seemed to be walking on eggshells. "I've watched Nicky bust her ass to try and please him," reflects one of their friends, "only to have him walk in and find the one thing that's not right."

Most of the time Dudley filled his days just wondering what to do with himself. He had notions of composing something new, but found it hard to concentrate on work. Although he rarely ventured far, residents often saw him shopping in the local supermarket or taking the children to and from school, and when Nicole and Charles went out together, as they did on occasion, Dudley was left alone with the baby for several hours.

Chaos still prevailed. Charles was arrested for stealing a car from a hotel car park and for driving with a suspended license. Dudley himself was pulled over by police on suspicion of driving under the influence when they saw his car weaving all over the road. He wasn't drunk, but his distraction about unfolding events had allowed him to lose his focus even behind a wheel. It was not the first time that he had lost control of a car because of his lack of concentration. He was becoming like a cat with nine lives.

He was not happy about what was happening in his life and yearned for some tranquillity. He loved Nicole, and she often treated him with a love that he felt he had never had before from a woman. Much of the time everything between them was good, but every now and then she would transform into another person and fly into a violent and abusive rage that would last all day. It was these episodes that were making life intolerable and ridden with anxiety. Even when everything was going well and Nicole was being her loving self, he was apprehensive—worrying about when the next inevitable outburst would occur. He felt himself drowning in the confusion of his existence. For a man who needed to be in control, and who indeed spent most of his time organizing his erratic and forgetful wife, too often he found himself quite incapable of controlling her.

Tom Leahy, his former houseman, had always opined that Dudley, who was always thinking of other people, had to start thinking more about himself. "He's very fair and generous. I've never met a person so fair and so correct. But he needs to take care of himself and do the things that he wants to do, not what everybody else wants him to do. He has to learn to say no."

The most solid influence in Dudley's life these days was Rena Fruchter. They talked almost daily on the phone, and their closeness was not based solely on their musical partnership. Although she was thirteen years younger, Rena exercised an almost maternal understanding of Dudley, which to a large extent he relied on and found comforting.

Paralyzed by the life he was living in Colorado, he had abandoned his daily piano practice, and a couple of times Rena, her gentle nature exasperated, left her own family in New Jersey to fly to Telluride to encourage Dudley back to the keyboard. After all, they had work to do for Music For All Seasons, and there were concerts to perform together in the months ahead. Rena's husband, Brian Dallow, noticed the subtle influence she was having on Dudley. "Dudley is very much a collaborative person, and I think he works very well when he's got Rena to work with. He's come to depend on her, and I sense in him a feeling of security and comfort when he works with her."

With Rena's encouragement, Dudley finally settled down to composing for the first time in fifteen years. Their Carnegie Hall concert for MFAS was only a few months away, and he began applying himself to scoring the poem that had won their production company's young writers' award.

In mid-January 1996 Dudley and Nicole went down to the Marina to spend some time alone together, leaving the children and the baby behind with her sisters and Charles. Although one of the things that Dudley always said he most liked about Nicole was that she was a wonderful mother, ever since Nicholas had been just a few weeks old, she had appeared to have no qualms about leaving him with other people—sometimes for more than a week. Even when they were together as a family, the few visitors that came to the house would invariably see Charles holding the baby while wandering around in his dressing gown. The previous October, during Dudley's absence in London and with Nicholas only a few months old, a friend had walked into the main bedroom of the Marina house to find Nicole and Charles fast asleep together in bed, the baby snuggled in Charles's arms.

The Los Angeles sojourn developed into a couple of weeks, by which time Dudley was committed to concert engagements with Rena across the country. Leaving Nicole in the Marina, he returned briefly to Telluride to collect his concert clothes. Thinking they would be gone only a few days, rather than weeks, he had left his car at the airport and, guessing the battery now to be dead, he arranged for a tow truck to meet him there. It was a fortunate move as it turned out.

A powerful snowstorm had descended during the night and, after getting the car started, Dudley slowly followed the lights of the tow truck along the road to his mountain home. The snow was now falling again, and it was becoming hard for him to make out the truck's taillights as he wound his way along a cliff edge. And then suddenly the road was gone and he felt himself falling and turning over. He closed his eyes, and when he opened them again, he was lying still. The car had slid off the road and plunged 150 feet down the cliff.

Dudley did not believe in God, though once he had; but God clearly believed in him. For he was not only alive but virtually unhurt. The Lexus, however, was almost a total wreck, with damage later estimated at over ten thousand dollars. All its windows had been smashed out, and the entire left side of the car—the driver's side—was crushed.

Gingerly, Dudley managed to slither out of one of the windows. He tried to climb up the hill, but with every step he found himself sinking into a three-foot-deep snowdrift. As luck would have it, the truck driver had noticed in his rearview mirror that Dudley's headlights were no longer visible and he decided to turn back. Had he not, Dudley could have remained at the bottom of that cliff for the rest of the night in the midst of a heavy snowstorm.

His recuperative powers were extraordinary, and the next day, with only a few cuts and bruises to show for his near-fatal accident in the Lexus, which still remained at the bottom of the ravine, he flew to Washington to join Rena in playing Saint-Saens' *Carnival of the Animals* for two pianos with the National Symphony Orchestra. They were, an impressed *Washington Post* informed its readers the next day, "a formidable duo." But, in spite of his apparent recovery, it was obvious to Rena that Dudley was still in shock. "He kept visualizing the crash, all day and all night," she recalls, "going over and over it. He was exhausted."

Nicole was petrified when Dudley told her of the accident. Afraid that if they remained in Telluride, it could happen again, she insisted they move back to Los Angeles, then—as usual—kept changing her mind. First they would and then they wouldn't. But Dudley had been scared to the limit by his close brush with death, and finally Nicole said yes, they would leave. And so, barely two months after moving to Colorado, they moved again, into the Hurricane Street house down the road from Dudley's Marina home.

Over the next several weeks Dudley became more isolated than ever, surrounded only by the children, Nicole, and Charles. His only respite was a couple of concerts with Rena. Otherwise he was enmeshed in a life with Nicole and Charles that was tearing him apart.

Now Patrick had been unwittingly introduced into the situation. Nicole, who was deeply fond of her stepson, had persuaded Dudley to let him move into the Marina house. The twenty-year-old was exultant to be so close to his father, whom he idolized. But, as he later told Brogan, he was horrified to walk into the house one night and find Charles doing crack cocaine with a girlfriend, while baby-sitting nine-month-old Nicholas at the same time. Charles invited Patrick to join in—an offer he declined. Fearing the incident might reflect on Nicole, for whom he had a great affection, Patrick relayed none of the events to his father, who was already asleep.

Yet there had been many long drug sessions in that house—usually involving Charles and his girlfriend and one or two other friends. Often they took place after Dudley had gone to bed. During one such session, where crack was the main drug of use, a friend had to leave the room because she was afraid of getting a contact high from the smoke in the air. "If Dudley knew what was going on down here," remarked one of the participants laughingly, "there would be spilled blood!"

Lucky for them, then, that he never did find out.

Nicole herself had already had a near-fatal encounter with drugs. A stroke in 1992 had been thought to be drug-related, traced to a bad batch of ecstasy, although this was never proven conclusively since none of the drug had remained on which to perform tests. Dudley had been left with a strong sense of guilt, for it was he who had given her the ecstasy.

Although Dudley himself was now using drugs with increased regularity, often a few times a week when he was home, he was always wary of how they might affect him, and his intake was limited to the barest taste—just enough to give him a brief high. He knew that Nicole's desire for drugs was greater than his own, but not the extent to which she was practicing the habit outside of his presence. Only her subsequent explosive behavior gave her away.

Nicole's increasing indulgence had led to an earlier overdose, according to Nicole's close friend, Casey Robinson, and later corroborated by Nicole in a subsequent phone conversation. On that occasion, which took place before Dudley and Nicole were married, Dudley called Casey and asked her to take Nicole away to a local hotel after yet another argument between the sparring couple. "He was very adamant that he didn't want to have anything to do with her," recalls Casey, "didn't want to see her and didn't want to speak to her. I believed it was just another tiff but I think she thought it was final."

Casey settled the distraught Nicole into a hotel room, then slipped out briefly to bring back some dinner. When she returned, Nicole told her she had swallowed a dozen of Casey's potent tranquilizers and prescription pills because she wanted to kill herself. Aware that the combination could prove lethal, Casey called the paramedics who immediately transported Nicole to a hospital in the Marina where doctors treated her. Casey called Dudley and told him what had happened. "But he didn't come to the hospital. I think it was a bid for attention on Nicky's part. Maybe that's what he thought, too."

At Nicole's pleading, Casey, "against my better judgment," convinced an emergency social worker that the overdose had been an accident, not a suicide attempt, which would have resulted in hospitalization and the risk of Nicole having her children taken away. But although Casey finally satisfied the authorities, she remained deeply concerned about her friend. "At that time I was very into crusading to save Nicky, trying to get her clean and sober. In the hotel room the next day, I urged Nicole's mother and sister to persuade her to seek professional treatment, but they wouldn't stand together and get her committed. No one can ever tell Nicky to do something that she doesn't want to do. She said she just needed to spend a month in Palm Springs lying by a pool and that's what she did. It was her answer to everything."

Dudley's intimate life was, and should have remained, a private affair. Except for one thing. Nicole herself. When they fought, Nicole would invariably threaten to go to the newspapers with lurid details about his sex life. The few friends who knew what those details were felt convinced that she was holding this threat over Dudley's head as a form of emotional blackmail. They agonized over how to help him out of the situation in which they perceived his weakness had trapped him and from which he seemed incapable of extricating himself, despite his insistence that he loved Nicole. Should they keep silent and hope the problem would go away? Or would it not ultimately be more beneficial if one of them went to the papers, thus forcing the issue to be faced and then forgotten, before Nicole did it herself in what was certain to be an explosive and dramatic fashion?

The last time she had made this threat she had called three British newspapers and asked for one hundred thousand pounds in return for her story. She claimed she had no money of her own and that her prenuptial agreement would leave her with nothing after a divorce—a statement denied by Dudley, who insists she is well taken care of but that she has never properly read the agreement. The offer was refused and, anyway, by the next day she had changed her mind, their fight resolved.

It seemed fairly certain that the story—whatever it was—would be told at some time. The only question was when. In the meantime, it appeared to this handful of friends that Dudley was living with the constant night-mare of exposure, and they feared the stress would destroy him. Already his career had been all but abandoned, and he had sunk to a level of hopeless-ness about his life that they had never seen before.

True, Dudley was living as if tied to a bundle of dynamite that threat-ened at any moment to explode. But it was not fear of exposure that was pushing him to the outer limits of anxiety, for he wasn't particularly concerned about the details of his private life being made public: In his view he was doing nothing wrong and had nothing to hide. No, his despair was the result of Nicole's seemingly dual personality, for he believed he really loved her and wanted to stay with her forever. She had shown him more love than anyone else in his life at times, and such unreserved devotion meant the world to him. But when the other side of her nature emerged—as it did with increasing frequency—life became unbearable for him.

Yet he could not leave. He and Nicole shared a deep need for each other. When he was away from her, although there was a relief at being able to focus on his work without the chaotic confusion of home life, there was also an anxiety that obviated that relief. Was she OK? What was she doing? Where was she? He worried and thought about her constantly. "I know I only have two choices," he fretted to me, "to stay or to go. If I stay, it will probably kill me. But it will kill me if I leave." His entire life was so focused on Nicole—looking after her and taking care of her—that for the first time in any of his four marriages he had no interest in having an affair with another woman.

At the end of March, Dudley was in Palm Springs with Rena to perform three concerts—a prelude to their upcoming Carnegie Hall gala benefit for Music For All Seasons. Dudley was relieved when Nicole said she would remain in Los Angeles. It meant he would be able to concentrate purely on work, without the distractions that always ensued when she joined him—usually in the company of Charles, her children, the baby, and whomever else she might bring along for company.

On the Friday night, after his first concert, an angry Nicole suddenly descended on Dudley's Palm Springs hotel suite, accompanied by her sis-ter Danielle, Charles, their two children, baby Nicholas, and a dog she had picked up en route. She was incensed that a certain female journalist was arriving the next day and would stay overnight to work with him. Despite Nicole's suspicion that they were having an affair, Dudley saw no reason why the writer—whom he had known for sixteen years—should not be present, and the ensuing argument was not resolved.

Late the following afternoon, while Nicole, Charles, Danielle, the children, and the puppy were in one of the other rooms of the vast suite,

Rena and Dudley were practicing on two pianos in the spacious living room and conversing with the writer, who had now joined them. There was an easy camaraderie between the two pianists, and in the middle of rehearsing "The Swan," the most serious and beautiful movement of Saint-Saens' *Carnival of the Animals*, the pedal of Dudley's piano began to develop a loud squeak that sounded like a duck quacking. Its musical incongruity became increasingly funny, until the two of them could barely play, they were so doubled up with laughter.

Suddenly Nicole stormed into the living room. "Where are my cigarettes, you fucking little midget!" she screamed, then marched into the bedroom and began throwing hefty objects at the walls and onto the floor, yelling as she hurled everything in sight. An alarmed Dudley went to find out what was going on, followed rapidly by Charles—clad only in a towel—and by Rena, who found the door promptly slammed in her face by Nicole.

It seemed that Nicole's inherent insecurity had developed into a paranoia that had her convinced that Dudley was having an affair with the journalist—a belief that had no substance in fact but that she refused to relinquish despite Dudley's denials. Threatening to throw the visitor over the outside balcony, she refused to calm down, and only when her sister Danielle intervened did she allow herself to be steered out of the suite. As she left, she grabbed a three-foot ceramic urn off the table base to which it had been cemented and started to heave it at Dudley, until her sister wrestled it from her grasp.

Rena, who had never witnessed such an episode in her life, was shocked and bewildered. So was Dudley. In less than two hours he would have to walk onstage and perform to a high level of classical skill. But this was nothing new. He had so often been subjected to Nicole's abuse that he had almost inured himself to it by now.

That night, in the McCallum Theater, he performed *Carnival of the Animals* and Gershwin's *Rhapsody in Blue* to a standard that surprised and satisfied even Rena, his sternest critic.

After the concert Dudley returned to his suite, accompanied by Rena and the writer who had unwittingly provoked the earlier scene. Nicole was waiting. And simmering. Overwhelmed by her false suspicions, she now unleashed her anger with an unmitigated violence. She seemed like a madwoman possessed, screaming obscenities at the astonished woman and, with a strength rarely seen in a person except when under the influence of drugs, violently assaulted her. She slammed her head against a brick wall several times, forced her over to the door, and pushed her outside onto the balcony corridor. The journalist was completely defenseless against Nicole's relentless battering. There was absolutely nothing she could do to protect herself. Hotel management and guests, drawn to the scene by

Nicole's incessant screaming, came running in consternation. Nicole was oblivious. She flung her victim to the ground, then menacingly flew at Dudley, who was standing outside his suite with Rena, shocked and stunned. The yelling continued while they tried to maneuver Nicole inside, and, afraid that Dudley might now be physically attacked, the shocked journalist picked herself up and followed them.

But she was still the target, and Nicole threw herself at her again—this time dragging her across the suite by her long hair until it seemed the roots would all be pulled out of her head. Later she removed a fingernail that Nicole had broken off in her hair, so violent had been her hold. Rena kept shouting at Nicole to desist, but Dudley just stood by, immobilized in shock. True, he had seen Nicole's violence often enough in the past, but never aimed at somebody else. He was frozen in fear. He was incapable even of opening his mouth to implore his wife to stop. "I was scared," he later admitted. "I couldn't believe what was happening. I kept thinking it would stop." But it didn't stop—not until four security guards rushed into the room. It took two of the burly men to pull the crazed woman off her victim.

Anyone else would have been taken to jail, but Dudley urged the shaken woman not to press charges. Reluctantly, she acquiesced to his wish. In hindsight it was perhaps a foolish decision—after all, as a horrified Dudley later relayed events to a friend, "Nicky nearly killed her!" Jail might have led to treatment, which Nicole certainly appeared to need, and that might have prevented any future such violence. But hindsight is a luxury not afforded to us in the present, and so Nicole's actions went virtually ignored, although the sheriff's department was called to the scene and later filed a report.

None of this is journalistic hyperbole. I was there. I was the writer.

Before her last violent attack, it had seemed for a while that Nicole's onslaught would be confined to verbal abuse. She yelled obscenities even at Rena, and screamed at Dudley that she was going to drive back to Los Angeles and blow up his house. He believed her. And, she screamed, she would call the newspapers. She would tell them about the drugs. And the hookers.

This was the threat that Dudley's friends had erroneously believed was causing his despair. Now, finally, it was all out in the open. And it was all true.

There had been a number of shared sexual indiscretions taking place in Dudley's home for the last few years, but they had been confined to himself, Nicole, and a few of their friends. Sometimes Nicole, who for a while had enjoyed a lesbian relationship with one girlfriend, made love to other women while Dudley watched. Charles was excluded from these sessions, banished with his girlfriend to another room.

Years earlier Dudley had described himself as "a true hedonist." And so it seemed.

Though not from any choice of Nicole's, ever since their marriage, Dudley had ceased making love to her. Odd though it may sound, in her continuing efforts to please him, Nicole had offered to arrange for prostitutes to come to the Marina house, and Dudley had accepted her suggestion. They were young and attractive and, at five hundred dollars a session with a generous few hundred dollars' tip on top of that, they were happy to satisfy Dudley's chief desire that they dance for him in scant outfits.

Sometimes Nicole would open the door a crack and peek into the bedroom. To her, the girls—usually the same three—seemed so cute and so pretty. But Dudley refused to allow her to watch the activities, and ultimately she would retreat to another room and watch television, while in the bedroom her husband was indulging his sexual tastes. The next day she always regretted having instigated this behavior and hated herself for allowing it to take place. It tore her up inside, but she believed it brought him pleasure. And in her naïveté she thought it could only bring them closer as a couple.

Dudley had often publicly stated that sex was the most important part of anybody's life, and time apparently had not changed that belief. He was becoming slightly incautious, however, and he had written checks for the girls if he had not enough cash on hand. He saw nothing wrong with the idea of employing hookers—in his view, it was a simple question of demand and supply. He claimed he had nothing to hide and that it wouldn't bother him if people knew.

This was perhaps just as well, since some of his inner circle were already knowledgeable about these divertissements and, during the Moores' brief sojourn in the small town of Telluride, where the world's oldest profession was practiced by only a few, some of the local residents had also become aware of Nicole's summoning hookers to Dudley's address.

Yet in Hollywood—which not so long ago had been astounded by Hugh Grant's arrest for oral prostitution on Sunset Boulevard and, judging from his subsequent popularity, had fast ignored the revelation—such behavior seemed almost commonplace. Certainly it was swiftly forgotten. But Nicole always used the prostitutes as a threat when they fought, and Dudley—as usual—would try to placate her and cover up the gross abnormality in their marriage with nonchalance.

Something changed after Palm Springs, though. Dudley had been badly shaken by the events that had occurred, though Nicole herself had promptly forgotten them. He took a rare hard stand and insisted to Nicole that there would be no more drugs and that if she started using again, he would definitely leave her. And he insisted, too, that Charles had to go. It was time for them to try to start living a normal marriage where there was only one husband in the family. He had said all this before and seldom got his way, but somehow he hoped it might be different now. Certainly for the next few weeks Charles was less conspicuous but his absence didn't last. It never did. Still, for a while, a vague semblance of normality descended upon the Hurricane Street household.

Less than a month after the Palm Springs incident, the gala benefit for Music For All Seasons took place in Carnegie Hall—the third time Dudley had performed in that venerable auditorium. The evening, which happened to fall on Rena Fruchter's birthday, was a major achievement and triumph for MFAS—assisted in no small measure by Dudley, who had been involved from the start with Rena and her husband in planning the program, entitled "Great Narrations."

Accompanied by the New Jersey Symphony Orchestra under British conductor Christopher Seaman, Dudley and Lynn Redgrave narrated Sir William Walton's *Facade*, in which Dame Edith Sitwell's zany poetry is spoken against a series of musical settings. "Moore was funny," wrote the *New Jersey Star-Ledger*, "and Redgrave was enchanting." And so they were. Dudley was in top musical form.

His new orchestral composition received particular commendation. *Fantasy on a Gypsy Breeze* was the score for a children's poetic saga composed by nineteen-year-old J. Erin Sweeney. Its full title was *The Story of What Happened in a Small Town Following a Wonderful Breeze That Whirled Through and Filled Everybody with a Springtime Urge to Soar among the Clouds*, and Lynn delivered its verses with panache while Dudley's melodic score with its jazzy, syncopated rhythms captured every sense of the spirit communicated by the title. It was, said the *Star-Ledger*, "a real honey."

It was the first piece of orchestral music Dudley had composed since the *Six Weeks* score, fifteen years earlier, and he was secretly rather excited with it, although outwardly he would only admit to its being "OK." He seemed to Rena reluctant to acknowledge his pleasure. "Maybe if he admitted how good it was and how much he'd enjoyed doing it," she reflects, "he might then have had to answer the question, Why aren't you doing *more* of this?"

The evening ended with Dudley and Rena playing *Carnival of the Animals*, but Rena was surprised when Dudley insisted she remain on stage after they had taken their bows. Unknown to her, he had already plotted with Christopher Seaman and the orchestra to acknowledge her birthday. As Seaman lifted his baton, on cue the entire New Jersey Symphony Orchestra began playing "Happy Birthday to You." "It was very moving," said Rena. "Dudley had all of Carnegie Hall singing to me with full orchestral accompaniment. I was astonished and deeply touched."

The evening was a huge success for MFAS and for Dudley in particular with the debut of his latest composition. Many of his friends on the East Coast attended and were thrilled by his performance, but they were shocked at his appearance.

"He was profoundly depressed," said one friend, who had not seen him for two years. "Worse than that—hopeless. It freaked me out a bit. It seemed like he'd given up. He looked physically fine but psychically awful. He had the appearance of being ravaged by his life, and my impression was that he didn't want to be on this planet. When I asked him if there was joy in his life he said, 'No, not any more. Nothing.'"

How could a man who seemingly had so much in his life feel now that he had nothing? True, his life had slipped into chaos through an increasingly bizarre sequence of events, and his acting career had all but disintegrated, but both were restorable. He was still in demand for concerts and was booked for an East Coast tour in July with Liza Minnelli and an Australian tour with Rena Fruchter in November. Yet despair engulfed him. How much longer could he live like this?

When he returned to Los Angeles, the rows with Nicole increased. Once again Dudley found himself thinking about divorce. What alternative could there be to this crazy existence? How else was he to salvage his sanity and his life? Divorce thoughts weren't new. They had first entered Dudley's mind just three weeks after their marriage. Since then the word had perpetually been dangled as a threat, either by him or by Nicole.

Along with her drug use and volatility, Nicole's wild spending had been out of control for far too long; it was now a constant source of their arguments. Dudley urged her to exercise more prudence with money, but Nicky simply had no concept of limits. The spending continued and at such an alarming rate that Dudley's business manager was forced to step in with a warning. Already in the last year Nicole had gone through something in the region of half a million dollars, and now she had taken out a whopping loan of a similar figure, for which Dudley was responsible, since she had no income of her own. Nicky herself tried to take control. "I've cut up all the credit cards except one," she told me tearfully. "I wish he hadn't given them to me. I don't mean to spend his money but it just happens. I can't help it."

In May the arguments over money escalated into another bitter fight. "I want one hundred thousand dollars a year," Nicole told reporters, omitting that she was insisting it be for life. Dudley had refused to commit himself to that.

Although the tabloids were fond of reporting that Dudley was always arguing with his wife and attacking her, in fact the reverse was true. For a long time he had been an abused husband. He had always been very passive, and his usual reaction when Nicole flew off the handle was either to stand there and not respond, or else to walk away. It was one of Nicole's complaints about him. His silence only made her angrier and drove her to violence.

As it did now. Tired of Nicole's screaming, Dudley walked out of the bedroom, but Nicole pursued him through the house until her volatility erupted into violence. Despite being only five foot five, less than three inches taller than him, Nicole was an exceptionally strong girl, and she grabbed Dudley and dug her nails into his face, ripping his skin and punching him in the eye. She pushed him to the ground and then jumped on him, kicking him as he curled up, trying futilely to protect himself from this woman who once again was out of control.

It was an extraordinary act of violence for a woman who was always professing to love Dudley. Later Nicole told him she had only attacked him because she was afraid he would hurt her. Yet he never had laid a hand on her except in self-defense, to try to ward off her attacks. He was always the one to bear the physical scars after her brutal onslaughts. By the next day, as usual, she had completely forgotten her rage of the day before. Until she saw Dudley's face, covered in bruises and lacerations.

"Everything's fine," Dudley told the tabloid press who hovered around his house, although he looked far from happy.

But everything was not fine. It was far from it. Their union was now being called Hollywood's most dangerous marriage. And not only by the tabloid press. Friends told him they wanted to kidnap him, to get him away from the frightening situation from which he seemed unable to extricate himself. Dudley smiled wearily. In truth, he would not have been averse to such an action, yet the greater part of him wanted to stay.

In spite of her onslaughts, Dudley always felt the need to protect Nicole. "I don't like it when I hear that she's been maliciously attacked for what she's said or done," he told me. "She can't seem to help it. She just has a very quixotic mind which leads from one thing to another, and it's very difficult to know from one day to the next what is happening."

Still, when their fights became public it was always Nicole's version that was printed. Dudley would neither talk to the press nor refute the reports. Consequently, he was being portrayed as being as violent as his wife. It was not true. Only out of a need to protect her was he keeping silent.

"I don't always understand Nicky," Dudley admits, "but apart from being the most unusual person I've ever known, she is also capable of being the most wonderful person. She has a place very deep in my heart, and I care very much about her and what happens to her. She is an amazing girl, relentlessly full of stamina and energy and love. And she has this very gentle side of her that wants absolutely no trouble at all. Yet there's this other side to her which is very perplexing. These events that happen are all very strange."

Nicole was always remorseful after each incident where she had lost control and become violent toward Dudley. "I know I freak out sometimes," she cried to me, "but I don't mean to. I love Dudley so much. I keep asking myself where I go wrong. I really embarrass myself, and I act like a maniac!"

Nicole truly did love Dudley, but she was incapable of controlling her behavior, and she took it out on him.

Dudley had become a battered husband.

He was forced to contemplate divorce with a greater intensity than before. It seemed the only way to save himself from a wife who was increasingly violent. His facial scars reminded him of that every time he looked in the mirror. He loved Nicole, but there seemed no other answer. With a heavy heart he instructed his lawyer to file a divorce petition.

Soon after that, Nicole went berserk again. This time she attacked some of Dudley's most treasured possessions. She smashed his beloved grandfather clock, hurled to the ground dozens of his cherished glass animals on top of the pianos, and destroyed the miniature globe that Brogan had made for him, containing symbols of his life. Nothing was sacred.

She smashed the glass doors of the kitchen china cabinet—along with much of the china and magnums of wine that had been stored there for years. Glass flew in all directions along with obscenities, screams, and blows. Dudley's Marina house looked like a bomb had exploded on the ground floor.

Dudley insisted she move into the Hurricane Street house, and he would remain in his own. But she had no concept of rules and did not recognize them when they were imposed. She was back and forth between the two homes. In desperation, he left her in his house and moved into the other, but still she was back and forth. He gave up, returned to his house and arranged to change the locks: It was the only way to protect his property.

The volatile lifestyle was destroying a gentle man who wanted nothing more than peace and tranquillity in his life.

Even before their marriage Dudley had told a friend that this was the most destructive relationship he had ever had. Now it was downright dangerous. And yet he could not remove himself. Dudley was suffering from addiction. And addiction to a human being is every bit as deadly and devastating as addiction to a substance.

As with his marriage to Tuesday Weld, Dudley had kept hoping he could change Nicole into the person he knew she was capable of being, the person who emerged every now and then. But she refused to accept the help she needed, and refused medical intervention.

Dudley had become Nicole's caretaker and in the process he had become addicted. He had never learned how to care without caretaking.

The renowned Hazelden Foundation describes caretaking as an "obsessive controlling," and when one is obsessed with controlling another's behavior, says the clinic, one often tries to control or cure that person's addiction, and to manage their life while trying to rescue them by removing the consequences of their actions.

Like most caretakers, Dudley suffered from low self-esteem, a desire for control, fear of abandonment, guilt and fear of facing his own problems and responsibilities. While he was obsessed with Nicole's problems, he was able to avoid having to resolve his own. And like most caretakers, Dudley was attracted to people who seemed weak, needy, or helpless; it fed his self-worth and made him indispensable to someone unable to face her own responsibilities. Dudley always said that *Nicole* needed him. This was true. But true, too, was the fact that *he* needed to be needed.

In spite of their recent fight, Dudley withdrew his divorce motion. Then Nicky took out her own. It was a roundabout without end. Since their marriage, he had stopped making love to Nicole, and she tormented herself over what might be the reasons. Their earlier life together had been based on a vigorous sex life; since their marriage that had ceased to exist between them. The marriage had been doomed from the start, but Dudley was sure he loved Nicole, and he would hang in there for as long as he could, not only for himself and Nicky, but also for baby Nicholas with whom he was bonding more and more. Such was the nature of this melancholy man whose life had been governed by a search for love and who at times had found it with this woman.

Racked with anguish, Dudley left for New York to embark on a concert tour with Liza Minnelli.

It was far from a happy time for the boy from Dagenham who had overcome enormous odds, including a crippled leg, to rise to the heights of international stardom as an actor and musician, who had romanced some of the most beautiful women of his time and yet who had spent his life struggling for acceptance and pleasing people.

Dudley once wrote, "The ending of fear and sorrow is the beginning of wisdom. We have no choice but to accept ourselves, otherwise we are doomed to a fruitless struggle that is fixed by fear and sorrow and frustration."

Dudley never had accepted himself but, at sixty-one, he needed to end that fruitless struggle—a struggle that had been perpetuated by his belief that he would never be free of the childhood angst and suffering that had so patterned his adult behavior.

He had brought infinite happiness to millions of people over the years. Now he deserved to start taking some of it back for himself.

He had always lived with the past haunting his present. It was time now to leave it behind and go forward into the future. Time to lay aside the hopelessness. Time to shed the despair. Time to start living again—before it was too late.

In July 1996, Dudley Moore and Liza Minnelli were reunited for a concert tour in a fifteenth anniversary tribute to *Arthur*.

It had been eight years since they made *Arthur 2: On the Rocks*, and Liza had been trying ever since to persuade Dudley to do a concert tour with her. This reunion would take them to five main cities on the East Coast of the United States.

Liza was ecstatic to see Dudley when he arrived backstage for their first rehearsal. Dressed in a pink chenille dressing gown, her urchin haircut dripping wet from a shower, she threw her arms around him and hugged him tightly, to the disapproving jealousy of her cairns terrier, Miss Lilly, who lapped at Dudley's ankles. "I've missed you so much," Liza told him in the cockney voice she often adopted around Dudley.

Dudley had the first half of the show and in it he displayed his immense versatility at the piano and as a composer. He even powerfully conducted the orchestra in the second movement of Mozart's Concerto No. 21. Liza followed him for the second half and then the two joined together on stage for some hilarity—Dudley at the piano, dressed as Arthur, and Liza singing with him.

But in each of the first four cities Dudley had to face predominantly Liza audiences. He sensed their disinterest and, although at the piano he was little short of excellent, his jokes fell flat, punctuated with long pauses while he tried to conjure up some witty repartee that would pull the audience over to his side. Only at the end of these shows, when he came back on stage in the guise of Arthur to join Liza, was he feted and warmly applauded.

Meanwhile, back in Los Angeles his fourth wife, Nicole Rothschild, was wavering back and forth on their divorce issue. A few days before his tour Dudley had withdrawn the divorce motion he had filed two weeks earlier. Now Nicole had filed. She told him she had rented a trailer to take her and the children north to look for a new place to live near one of her sisters in northern California. The following day, after loading up the truck, she changed her mind.

Distracted by the daily shuffling of events back in Los Angeles, Dudley found it hard to concentrate on work. No matter how early he went to bed, Nicole was on the phone, sometimes till midnight; some mornings she would wake him early when he had planned to sleep late. Her calls interrupted his piano practice sessions. And so it went on.

He was drained. Confused thoughts whirled around in his head, affecting him to the point where he could barely function. And now Nicole had changed her mind again and wanted them to stay together. "I never know which Nicole I'm going to find," he pondered wearily. "It's the uncertainty that's killing me."

At an age when he should have been slowing down and enjoying a more tranquil lifestyle, his days were filled with more turbulence and chaos than he had ever known, and were veiled with a heavy, dark depression. The strain was beginning to show. The boyish features that had changed so little over the years were now altering visibly. Though he still did not look his age, he looked closer to it than ever before. He bore a slightly haggard look, as if a lifetime of pain had taken him over at last and was now etched deep into his face.

For a long time his friends had been worried about the change that had come over him. Where, they asked, had his humor gone? His sense of fun? His ribald playfulness that had been so prevalent in years gone by? He was constantly vague and distracted and intensely forgetful. Could he be ill? Or did he simply want, as it seemed, to retreat into seclusion?

Dudley was not a happy man. The life he was living with Nicole was destroying him. And yet he still cared about her. "The terrible thing about all this is that we love each other," he told me. "I find that very difficult to walk away from. At times I've never felt so loved by anyone in my life before. She's been so devoted to me and so sweet. There are things in our life together that are extraordinary and lovely. I don't know how we got to this point."

Saddened, he sat at the piano in his hotel suite and mused aloud. "I can't bear the thought that Nicky and I might break up. She's been so sweet and devoted to me. I love that side of her. She's an integral part of my life and my heart. She needs me and I find I need her."

Marriage had never been easy for Dudley. His last two marriages—to Tuesday Weld and Brogan Lane—had also been tempestuous roller-coaster rides. Both those marriages went through divorce motions that were constantly being filed and withdrawn over a couple of years before the final splits took place.

And yet, for all his turmoil, he was gaining more direction during the tour. Distance from his warring wife was giving him a slightly more solid perspective, though it was still clouded. His biographer traveled with him and noted that, although he liked to retreat into solitude, at times he also liked to come out from that isolation and seek companionship. Away from the turmoil of home, he played and practiced at the piano more in those days than he had in a long time.

His classical music partner, pianist Rena Fruchter, joined him in one city and together they practiced Gershwin's *An American in Paris* for their upcoming November concert tour of Australia. With Rena, Dudley was more focused and alert than he had been for a long time. Astute and studious, he pounced on mistakes in the score and corrected them to his satisfaction. He was in absolute command, confident and self-assured and, when they played the entire piece all the way through for the first time, he was excited and thrilled. Not yet perfect; nevertheless it sounded quite wonderful.

The first four concerts had not been good ones for Dudley. But in Boston, the last city on their tour, Dudley found his own audience waiting.

The concert had been postponed in the face of a vengeful torrent from Hurricane Bertha that hit the East Coast. Liza remained in New York, while producer Ed Kasses watched the weather anxiously.

The following afternoon was remarkably bright and clear after the previous two days' storm damage. Dudley was driven to the outdoor performing arena. There was a feeling of optimism in the air. From a distance, the outdoor shell, flanked by Boston Harbor, resembled the Sydney Opera House. Dudley had gazed at it from his hotel window for the past two days while the storm raged and was reminded of Sydney, which he had always loved so much. Maybe that, too, was in his mind when he went out there.

He was stopped everywhere. In the hotel, in the street. Fans had learned where he was staying and grouped outside the hotel to catch a glimpse as he exited. Everybody wanted to greet him. For once, the windows of the limousine were not opaque and passersby waved as they peered inside and saw Dudley as the car maneuvered through the heavy traffic. It was all there still. The applause, the adulation, the love.

When Dudley stepped on stage at the Boston Harbor Arts Center, there was a palpable excitement. The audience were thrilled to see him. With every joke they roared and with every piece he played on the piano they applauded wildly. Dudley reacted, as he always had, to the audience. His jokes became funnier and funnier and he took them further than scripted. He bantered with the audience and they loved it. Producer Ed Kasses was beaming. "That's the man I've always loved and found so funny!" he exclaimed. "He's back! Where's he been?"

Where had he been indeed? He had been sucked into melancholia over his turbulent marriage and crumbling career for such a long time. Yet the audience's immense response had erased that, at least for now. There had been some who perceived Dudley Moore's career as over and there were others who insisted it was not. That afternoon in Boston, Dudley proved the latter group to be right.

He had become resigned to the belief that he had no real place in entertainment anymore. He had lost confidence in himself and felt ready to go where fate would take him now. By fate he meant death. And by death he meant an eternal state of sleep, of nothingness. "I'm waiting to die," he had told me so often lately. "I know it's sad because I have so much to give, but I've tried to come back and people don't like what I do. I'm resigned to that."

The resignation was destroying him.

Yet the world loves the comeback kid and his longtime friend, Peter Bellwood, is not alone when he says wistfully, "It would be great to think there are some projects that could put Dudley back on top of the heap. I wish that he would have the energy and desire to come back."

Dudley knew now that he had recaptured it. He needed to perform to feel alive. Knew too that he could. All his focus and concentration had been on his fourth wife, and if one thing was able to rise above that it was public acclamation. In front of the audience he could truly feel loved and wanted, if only for that moment when he was in front of them. The feeling was so powerful that it briefly eradicated his self doubts and inner torment.

Dudley was back. The audience knew it. Dudley knew it. That afternoon he was the man he had always been, the consummate performer they had always loved.

His fans clamored at the stage door for autographs. Security guards tried to send them away, but Dudley, ever appreciative of his public, insisted on greeting them. As his limo drove him away—after the chauffeur had locked himself out of the car with Dudley already inside it—crowds of people flanked the road to shout to him and wave and blow him kisses. He smiled back, drained and almost embarrassed.

And yet, despite his exhaustion, there was a new spiritual energy about him. The resignation that his career was over had forsaken him for the moment, replaced with a spark of hope that had been kindled by the overwhelming response that Boston audiences had shown him.

For far too long, Dudley's world had been wrapped up with taking care of Nicole. It was time to let go. Time to take care of himself and recover all that he held dear: his work—the longest love affair of his life.

Two weeks later, Dudley left his fourth wife.

The anguish he felt was immense, but to protect his sanity and recover his life and career, this normally passive man had finally found the strength to take control of his own life. He prayed that strength would remain and that the split would be permanent. For too long he had sat at the crossroads, unable to take the necessary step toward the right path.

In time, the pain of being without Nicole would diminish, and ahead of him lay a new future, a rebirth of sorts. His agent had secured a deal for a new film in Europe. Concerts had been scheduled for the spring of the following year. And there was an upcoming Australian concert tour in November.

His heart was in his work. He remembered that now. There was a new vitality about him, a subtle rejuvenation. He felt more alive than he had in months. The desire had returned, along with the urgency, the passion to perform. He could see a light now, a light far ahead at the end of the long dark tunnel in which he had lost himself for so long.

Dudley Moore was on his way back.

CHAPTER 30

TRAGIC REVELATION

1996-1999

*"While Dudley seems to view his achievements as though they were
created by somebody outside himself, he nevertheless derives great comfort
and pride from the knowledge of what he has given the world."*

—BRIAN DALLOW

Throughout the fall of 1996, Dudley concentrated hard on the upcoming Australian tour with Rena Fruchter. They were to play in four main cities, with additional concerts set for Hawaii, New Zealand, and Hong Kong, and he hoped it would prove a resurgence of his ailing career.

But something was amiss with his playing. Sometimes he sounded good, other times it was as if his fingers simply refused to play the notes he instructed them to play. He pushed himself harder to practice three or four hours a day. No matter how tired Rena got, he would urge her on. It was, they believed, a product of his emotional unhappiness, as was his increasing incoherence.

Sentences begun would sometimes trail into rambling nonsense; too often he found himself losing his train of thought. "Are you all right?" I would ask when he seemed not to be making sense. "No I'm NOT," he would shout in frustration without knowing why. Concerned about his increased mental confusion, he saw his doctor but was told everything was fine and was sent away with another inevitable batch of Ativan pills to control his anxiety.

Meanwhile, Nicole had tracked him down in London, where he had been staying with Suzy Kendall and her family, and begged him to come home. Against the advice of his friends, he had given in, believing in Nicole's optimistic promises that everything would be different. But the fights continued. They were usually about money, drugs, or sex.

Over the last year Dudley had been doing drugs with Nicole more frequently than ever, sometimes three times a week. Methamphetamines ("speed") had long been proven to be lethal; for a man of Dudley's age, he was playing with very dangerous fire indeed. "I'm only taking enough for an effect," he kept saying, insisting he took minimal amounts. Finally his fear at the potential damage and his deep concern for Nicole's own safety made him stop. For a long while he had focused on getting her help. Briefly he persuaded her to go into a drug rehabilitation center. At the end of the first day, she came home and wailed, "I'm not going back there, it's full of drug addicts!"

The day before leaving for the 1996 *Arthur* tour, Dudley had arranged an intervention, at last succeeding where Nicole's friend, Casey Robinson, had failed. After weeks of planning he persuaded her family to back him up with the support that was needed. They had arrived as one, to urge her into medical treatment and counseling. It was a stormy, traumatic afternoon and ultimately ineffective. Nicole refused the treatment. Dudley was in despair. He could not do anything more without her cooperation. "I'm very anxious because I'm very much in love with her but I can't go on this way," he told me. "I think she's beyond help."

The domestic scene was growing increasingly unhealthy. The fights continued. He wanted her to stop drugs, she wanted more money. And then came the big explosion. Months earlier, Nicole had taken a new lesbian girlfriend and this latest intimate relationship stabbed Dudley to the heart. She flaunted her girlfriend in front of him and would sneak off to her house when Dudley was asleep. "She shows me more affection and makes me feel good," Nicole told me later.

Dudley could stand it no longer. Another physical onslaught by Nicole had left him battered and bruised. He packed his bags and checked into a local hotel for a night before joining Rena for a performance in Phoenix. She was alarmed at his appearance and state; finally Dudley admitted to her that Nicole had beaten him up the previous day. Amid Rena's worry for her friend, the concert went well and they departed immediately for Melbourne and the start of their heavily hyped Australian tour.

By then, events had preceded them. An earlier television interview Dudley had given in Boston had alarmed the tour's organizers. Viewers were left wondering what he was on. He had come across as rambling and incoherent, as he did increasingly when under immense emotional strain.

The strain was about to get worse.

For several months, the Moores had been under close scrutiny by the world's tabloids whose reporters had taken to staking out the couple's homes. Stories proliferated, most without foundation. The tabloids dangled five-figure amounts in front of me to reveal the truth about what was happening in the marriage and, aware of the interest and the offers, the British publishers of this book agreed to a lucrative British tabloid serialization for October 1996. It was an extraordinary departure from normal practice, given that the book's publication was not due for another five months. My vociferous protests went unheeded. Curtly I was reminded that the author had no say in such a deal. My only involvement was to make any necessary corrections to the tabloid "abridgment" that would be faxed to me with a few hours' notice. Despite promises by the publishers that they would strictly monitor the percentage of space given to the Moore marriage, more than two-thirds of the serialization turned out to be an "abridged" revelation of their marital habits.

About the time Dudley was landing in Melbourne, two British tabloid reporters stole the faxed draft newspaper serialization of this book from my apartment. By the following day the unapproved contents had been relayed to Nicole.

Dudley had always believed that she was resigned to her inevitable inclusion in his biography; she was, after all, his wife and such omission would be unthinkable. And she had hardly maintained a low profile in their volatile life together. But he had misjudged her. Reaching the weary Dudley halfway across the world, Nicole went ballistic. Denouncing all references to her as flagrant untruths and an invasion of her privacy, her anger was unrestrained. She threatened to burn down his house for having allowed the mentions of her and it took all of Rena's diplomatic and soothing efforts to dissuade her entirely.

She was not placated. Phone calls continued at all hours. They became so disturbing that eventually Dudley had the hotel operators block his calls and he adopted a pseudonym in the hotels. In the meantime, although he had changed the locks, Nicole got into his house and began methodically emptying its contents, carting away files to her own home, particularly those with information about his finances. Dudley's precious mementos were destroyed, smashed, or discarded. Others were burned. The fire department, alerted to smoke by alarmed neighbors, arrived to find her burning his favorite videos. "You could see the smoke over in the next town," said one neighbor. "She didn't realize you can't burn videotape."

Casey Robinson recalled her friend's wrath. "She told me she wanted to destroy everything that meant anything to Dudley. She felt betrayed and wanted to hurt him."

On the other side of the world, Dudley was plagued by emotional distress. When he wasn't performing, he retreated to his suite and slept.

Rena found him increasingly unable to function normally and became convinced his strong medication was to blame. At her urging, he cut back the Ativan and he became a little more responsive. Nevertheless, his prowess at the piano, which in earlier tours had provided such memorable highlights for Australian audiences, was now noticeably lacking. There seemed no explanation for this loss of musical acuity and the papers were largely scathing about a talent apparently fast souring.

The Australian tour fell just short of being a total disaster. It had begun well. The opening concert was nationally televised and for a while it seemed that Dudley was able to push aside his woes and perform to a pleasurable level. But gradually the decline set in. By the end of the tour he had barely hung on to his musical reputation.

Not so his marriage that was now in tatters. Flying back to Los Angeles, Dudley holed up in a hotel at the airport without going to his home ten minutes away. The next day he was on a plane to London and the safety of Suzy Kendall, her husband Sandy, and their daughter Elodie. Once there, he entered a clinic and was treated for what had become an addiction to Ativan.

His divorce was still on the court calendar in Los Angeles. In a public demonstration of vitriol, Nicole had her lawyer file a massive declaration in which she made dozens of lurid allegations. Dudley Moore, she denounced to the world, was an unconscionable reprobate. She described him as a sexual pervert and drug addict who, during and before their marriage, had paid tens of thousands of dollars to support her and members of her family, including her ex-husband. The money had been spent on everything from cars to plastic surgery to drugs and prostitutes. The very accusations she had threatened to reveal to the tabloids at the time of her assault on myself in Palm Springs would now become public knowledge in far greater and more scandalous detail.

The court document became front-page news in Britain. "Dudley's shopping list of shame," said one headline.

None of this lured Dudley out of his London sanctuary. Nicole gave a Los Angeles television interview and a double-page spread to a British tabloid claiming that Dudley had disappeared and had left her destitute without money to put food on the table to feed her children. The media had another field day. Dudley, they said, was a cad and a wife abuser. In fact Dudley had put all such arrangements in the hands of his business and investment manager, Hugh Robertson, who for many years had been taking care of his financial interests. Dudley himself rarely had much knowledge of such matters or how they were being conducted. He left it to Robertson, to whom he gave power of attorney, to carry out his instructions, although increasing lack of confidence would eventually lead to Dudley firing him.

Throughout the spring of 1997, Dudley held out. He was unhappy, pining and yearning for Nicole, but determined this time not to go back. In April he returned to America and performed at the annual benefit concert at Carnegie Hall for Music For All Seasons. The gala coincided with his birthday and his narration of *Peter and the Wolf*, which was a resounding success.

But it was obvious now that something was seriously wrong with him. The day before, he had appeared on Rosie O'Donnell's talk show. Brogan called me immediately afterward. "Oh my God, has Dudley had a stroke? He has, hasn't he?" His speech was discordant and his balance was now very unsteady; at any given moment he would trip while walking or climbing stairs. He had developed an odd tendency to fall backward. His eyesight had become more impaired. He was having trouble focusing and was suffering double vision.

But it was all still a mystery. Almost every obvious brain disorder had been eliminated. His erratic behavior, obvious confusion, and memory losses had all pointed to Alzheimer's but the tests had been negative. A brain tumor had also been dismissed. Dudley himself believed he'd had a stroke but even this was indeterminate. He told me that doctors in Britain had determined he'd had a series of small strokes. According to Suzy Kendall, no doctor ever told him that and his doctors in New York agreed, saying he hadn't had a stroke.

His erratic disposition led to disturbing rumors. He was, it was said, an alcoholic. Arthur had been no act. Drugs and alcohol had destroyed his mind and motor functions. He could scarcely stand up straight, it was reported. Often he stumbled or fell over his own feet. On occasion his speech became incomprehensible and he would splutter or spiral into peculiar ramblings. The British papers were particularly unkind. It was, they said with smug belief, no less than could have been expected. What a waste to see him go the way of his former partner, Peter Cook. Dudley, through it all, kept silent. What was there to say, after all? Even he didn't know what was wrong.

Despite his intentions to remain apart, when Nicole located him in his New York hotel, he was overjoyed. She, now contrite and missing him, begged him to come home and try again. She was sorry for her past behavior and again promised everything would be different. He warned her he was feeble but she said she'd be happy to push him down the street in a wheelchair. All she wanted, she told him, was for him to grow old with her and she bought him a walking stick to celebrate their reunion.

It lasted less than a week. There was another fight and another separation. And another reunion. And on and on careened the rollercoaster. Until, in June 1997, during another attempt at domestic harmony, Nicole slapped Dudley (and myself) with a $10 million lawsuit that accused him of emotional and physical abuse and defamation. Challenging the facts in this biography, she claimed she had never taken drugs before meeting Dudley and that he had cajoled her into taking them. She talked of being forced to dance for him in scantily cut outfits for twenty-four hours at a time. She claimed she had never laid a hand on him but that he had often hit her. The list was long, the dozens of allegations sordid.

Dudley was less upset by the accusations than he was concerned about Nicole's state of mind. "She thinks she's behaving rationally. She has vilified me unbelievably and to keep doing this is out of this world. It's strange. But I don't want her to be victimized for it."

In spite of the lawsuit there were more attempts to reconcile the marriage. Dudley believed he still loved Nicole; loved the side of her, at least, that on occasion he had seen. The fun-loving, caring girl who all too often receded behind the darker image. And yet whenever he was near her or left his house unattended, he felt the need to have permanent protection in the form of security personnel. (He refused to call them bodyguards.) It was an extraordinary way to live. Suspicion and fear surrounded him.

In August 1997, they gave it a last shot. Retract certain references to her in the book, Nicole told Dudley, and she'd drop the lawsuit. He refused. Then drop the divorce, she begged. He agreed. He dismissed the divorce but Nicole did not drop the civil suit. The next day Dudley told her he was refiling the divorce. The ensuing argument was loud and demonstrative. But this time, Dudley was protected by Bill, a former policeman. When Nicole lunged at Dudley, the "bodyguard" pulled her off him. A restraining order was sought and once it had been instigated, Dudley made preparations to leave for New Jersey to begin working with Rena on a Gershwin album.

The album was never completed. Two days after starting work on the intricate piano pieces, it became clear that something was terribly wrong. No matter how hard he practiced, his fingers would not obey the messages being sent from his brain. He phoned me in Los Angeles early one morning in some distress. "My fingers won't go where I tell them to go; they don't play the right notes," he mourned. "I don't know what's happening." The next day he entered the world-famous Mayo clinic in Minnesota for tests.

At the Mayo clinic, the week of neurological tests had to be interrupted when doctors found a hiatal hernia. They put him on medication through a catheter, which led to the discovery of a hole in his heart. Then, even as he was being prepared for surgery to repair the hole, a blocked artery was detected.

Although neither was life threatening, both heart problems required an operation that lasted over three hours and kept Dudley in pain for several days.

When Nicole learned of the heart surgery, she tried to reach him but the hospital had been instructed to refuse any calls from his wife.

Neurological testing resumed soon after surgery. The Mayo clinic referred him to JFK Medical Center's movement disorder clinic in Edison, New Jersey. It also was the home of Dr. Martin Gizzi, a specialist in the rare disease, progressive supranuclear palsy (PSP). It was there in February 1998 that Dr. Gizzi became convinced that Dudley was suffering from PSP, a cousin of Parkinson's.

PSP is activated by clumps of "tau" proteins that attach themselves to cells in an area of the mid-brain and render them ineffective. Early symptoms are indicated by backward falls, an apparent loss of concentration and clarity of thought, and altered focus of vision as a result of lesions in the brain that prevent the eyes from moving properly and lead to a paralysis that halts downward movement. It progresses gradually, affecting breathing, articulation of thoughts, and, most seriously, impeding the ability to swallow.

In itself PSP is not fatal, but as the disease worsens, the difficulty in swallowing often leads to patients dying from choking on food or contracting pneumonia when liquids get into the lungs. In advanced stages some people are unable to eat solid foods and may need tube feeding into the stomach.

The earliest signs of PSP are often subtle and, while taking several years to evolve, it is often misdiagnosed as Parkinson's, Alzheimer's, motor neuron disease, strokes, or alcohol intoxication. Its origin is unknown and there is no cure. Only a few of the Parkinson's drugs are effective and even then only for alleviating the symptoms.

Dr. Gizzi recalls the day in February 1998 when he gave Dudley his diagnosis. "He didn't accept it. He kept saying if this is what it was, why had no other doctors picked up on this? He was in denial."

But the other doctors on Dudley's medical team challenged the diagnosis. It would need further corroboration. And so the testing continued. Dudley remained in New Jersey, under the caring attention of Rena and her family. He attended daily physical rehabilitation at the nearby Kessler Institute where Christopher Reeve had been treated after the riding accident that had left him paralyzed. And he underwent counseling for his addiction—an addiction not to drugs, but to Nicole. Over the many weeks he came to understand the behavior that had taken place. Not only hers, but his. He was taught with charts that depicted the destructive progress of addiction. One doctor explained to him that what he was dealing with was akin to a Vietnam verteran who was suffering from battle fatigue. And he was told that under no circumstances could he ever again be in the same room with Nicole.

Meanwhile, rumors about his health continued to swirl in every direction: He'd had a series of strokes, they wrote, he was an alcoholic, always falling down drunk and slurring his words, he had been mentally affected by a drug addiction. The few people who knew of the unfolding tragedy were sworn to secrecy and they respected Dudley's need for silence. But now inaccurate and misplaced statements made by his long-time lawyer, Allan Siegel, whom Dudley eventually fired, fueled stories that took on a far more sinister tone.

Siegel announced that Dudley was "gravely ill." Nicole's lawyers said Siegel told them that Dudley had Alzheimer's disease. Faced with these comments and the obvious implications, it was inevitable that searing headlines would follow. Tabloids declared Dudley to be on the verge of death, even while he was still undergoing tests and had yet to receive a firm diagnosis.

He refused to deny the rumors of strokes or that he was dying. "I wanted to wait until I knew without doubt what was wrong," he shrugged. "It seemed kind of nuts to say anything until then." But the stories were hurtful and Nicole's interviews with the tabloids kept the feeding frenzy alive.

In the summer of 1997, Nicole began calling me, begging to be put in touch with Dudley. She didn't believe he was really ill, she said, but if she dropped the lawsuit then they could be together again. Couldn't they?

Two weeks later she dropped her $10 million action. Dudley still refused all contact and in November 1997 their divorce was finalized. His shaky signature on the divorce agreement was almost the sad finale to the most painful chapter of his life.

He continued to undergo therapy and more testing. There was still no conclusive diagnosis. But he had already come to believe what Dr. Gizzi had told him in February. At Christmas, with a member of Rena's family by his side, he returned to Los Angeles and for the first time in over a year, saw his beloved seafront home again. He promised his doctors and friends that he would not speak to Nicole. But the moment he was back on mutual soil he could not resist.

Despite a mutual restraining order, he visited her at the Hurricane Street house, which she had retained in the divorce, and for the first time in fifteen months he saw his son Nicholas, a smiling, chubby three-year-old. It could almost have been the perfect family reunion. There were excursions to the cinema, shopping trips, and a visit to Dudley's local doctor. Nicole's boyfriend (who she told Dudley was merely a friend) ferried Dudley back and forth by car to his house up the alley when he chose to go home, just as her ex-husband Charles had done before him.

Christmas had always been a special time for Dudley. But not this year. There was finally the inevitable fight over money. Dudley left her house, never to return. He went back to his own home, packed his suitcase, and on Christmas Eve flew back to New Jersey. He had spent less than a week in his home.

In April 1999, on Dudley's sixty-fourth birthday, nearly three hundred people from the world of entertainment sent me letters to assemble in a monumental collection that I bound in two huge albums. Among them were a David Hockney original in the form of a birthday card, Paul McCartney's parody on the Beatles' hit "When I'm 64," Leslie Bricusse's minimusical on rolled parchment, Paul Anka's dedication of his "My Way" song sheet, Phil Collins's three-page fan letter, Quincy Jones's entire spiritual collection of jazz, letters from Dudley's heroes—surviving Goons Harry Secombe, Eric Sykes, and Spike Milligan, a Rolling Stones caricature of Dudley with their ribald comments scribbled around the face, loving epistles from Kenny G, Elton John, Bette Midler, Whoopi Goldberg, Neil Simon, Milton Berle, Jack Lemmon, Mel Brooks, and hundreds more. They offered inspiration and messages of love to a man who had given them happiness through his music and his humor. And they reminded him how much they held him dear and in his thoughts.

Dudley was overwhelmed. Accompanied by Rena, he flew to Los Angeles the following month and came to see me. He looked frail but oddly less tense than I'd seen him in years. He shuffled into my apartment with the aid of a cane and Rena's supporting arm. Leaning back on a couch, one of my birds perched on his hand, it almost felt like old times. He was deeply touched that so many of his colleagues had written him such loving and expressive letters.

"It gave me some encouragement to think a bit more or pleasantly about myself, to think more positively about myself," he reflected.

The next night, Nicole discovered Dudley was in L.A. and went to his house with her boyfriend. As she had done in the past, she stood outside shouting, banging on the gate. Dudley not only could hear her, he could see her on the security video. He was terrified. Even Rena was afraid. Nicole and her boyfriend tried climbing over the wall to get in. To Dudley, it was all too familiar a scene. "I felt like a prisoner in my own home," he said the next day. Neighbors called the police and Nicole was arrested for violating a restraining order.

Dudley knew it was all over then. Knew he probably could never return to his home. That night he packed various cartons for shipment of what was left of his most prized mementos. The next morning, he and Rena flew back to New Jersey. He was severing his final connection with Los Angeles. The move was complete.

Barely weeks later, Dudley finally was given the news he'd been dreading for the last fifteen months since Dr. Gizzi had diagnosed him with progressive supranuclear palsy. Now at last it was confirmed by JFK's Dr.

Lawrence Golbe, who recognized the ultimate clue of Dudley's slowed vertical eye movement. That was the conclusive information that Dudley had been dreading for over a year. He was neither shocked nor surprised. He had come to believe that Dr. Gizzi was right and that PSP was the most likely explanation. He had already accepted that he was living with a degenerative condition. One that afflicted less than three people in two hundred thousand.

Having walked around with what he perceived as a potential ticking bomb, it was almost a relief at last to put a name on his illness. "I was just relieved in the sense that I could go around and say I'm PSP, what do you think?"

In typical fashion he managed to inject some humor into the brief statement that he put out in September. There were, he announced, one hundred thousand members in the Screen Actors Guild and he hoped they would appreciate that he had taken on PSP so as to spare the remaining members from this rare disease.

But privately, although he'd been anticipating the terrible diagnosis, the final confirmation was devastating. At sixty-four, Dudley was now marked with a limited life expectancy.

A few weeks later I joined him in New Jersey. At last the full tragic story would be revealed to the world.

CHAPTER 31

FACING THE CHALLENGE

1999

"Dudley believes that what has happened to him has happened for a reason. Tragic though it is to be left without the ability to play the piano and ever accepting of his 'fate worse than death' (as he quips), he now feels that he has been chosen to bring attention and trigger a cure for a rare disease. That is his mission now, and he is comfortable with it."

—RENA FRUCHTER

Dudley's health had already been the focus of endless discussions between us for a couple of years. Since early 1995 there had been clear signs of neurological disorder. He had begun to appear unsteady and forget simple things. Time only made balance and speech increasingly elusive. By the end of that year, early aberrations symptomatic of Alzheimer's led me to urge him to have neurological tests. Other voices added persuasion, but the tests had proved negative. Further tests over the next year also dismissed Parkinson's, brain tumors, and strokes, all common misdiagnoses. PSP is so rare that it is easily missed. In hindsight, the signs had been everywhere but they always ended up being attributed to the emotional turbulence and confusion he was concurrently suffering as a result of his tumultuous lifestyle with Nicole.

Back then, Dudley was depressed and miserable. He believed that his drug taking had played a fatal role. "I'm afraid the damage is done," he told me in 1997. "I fear they have affected my brain and that it's not reversible."

Whether his problems at that time were the result of drug use or not, his doctor, Martin Gizzi, told me there is no evidence to support a theory that drugs play a role in PSP. As for Dudley's intensive memory failings at that time, Dr. Gizzi said he believed it to have been the result of severe depression that he was experiencing.

Dudley felt only mild relief that his illness had not been his fault. "At least I don't have to deal with the guilt that I may have made it happen. It's unbelievable to me that the effect of drugs doesn't enter into the acquisition of this disease. I didn't take them to excess but I regret it now. It was an awful time."

Progressive supranuclear palsy is so rare that it is believed that as many as fifteen thousand Americans may be walking around with it, undiagnosed. After nearly two years of therapy at three hospitals, Dudley had yet to meet another PSP sufferer.

He felt no animosity toward the earlier doctors who failed to recognize the symptoms. "I think they were just protecting themselves from coming to a decision that was possibly too early in my diagnosis."

In his own way, Dudley has been fighting back. His natural preference would be to remain in bed most of the day. Instead, he was getting up in the morning, preparing his own breakfast—sometimes taking it back to bed, other times eating standing up at the kitchen counter.

He was fighting back in another way, too. In a move that could only be described as incredibly gutsy, he agreed to take part in a charity performance for Rena's organization, Music For All Seasons, where he and Julie Andrews narrated Ogden Nash's verses to Saint-Saens' *The Carnival of the Animals*, one of his all-time favorites.

It was his first public performance in nearly two years, and he narrated alternate verses of *Carnival* with Julie. He had practiced this for months with speech therapists but still it was an arduous task, alleviated by Julie's presence and conarration and Rena and Brian on piano. But it was also deeply pleasing to him to be facing an audience once more. It was not the way he could ever have foreseen what history may later record as one of his last public performances as an entertainer, but the standing ovation he was given, in acclaim for his past achievements and recognition of his present struggle, was immeasurably warming. His public, like the piano, had always been an enduring love of his life.

Already, his plight has begun to raise international awareness of his rare and deadly disease. Dudley had been president of the MFAS advisory board for nine years and at a benefit, Richard Branson pledged a donation to MFAS on behalf of the Virgin Healthcare Foundation to establish the Dudley Moore Research Fund, which would be administered through the PSP Society.

With profound regret Dudley conceded that his acting career was definitely over. But he hoped to do more narration and in that way at least hang on to a remnant from his past life as a performer. The spontaneity of acting now defeated him but his memory was still intact and he felt more confident about learning lines for narration where he would not have to rely on body movements.

But he did miss acting. Looking back at his career, his face lit up when we reminisced about special moments—landmark comedy he had provided with Peter Cook in *Not Only ... But Also* and early films he made with Cook—*The Wrong Box* and *Bedazzled*. And then there was *Arthur*. Gleefully he quoted specific lines that he still remembered with particular fondness.

Sometimes I glimpsed the rascally twinkle of his Arthur and then it was gone, replaced just as quickly by a vivid shudder as he remembered all that he had had and would never have again.

Life was starkly different now. Once glamorous women had hung on his arm but now, when he most needed to derive solace from companionship, he faced the future without wife or girlfriend. "I don't think about being with another woman," he told me. "I feel that part of my life is over because of my illness." There was a time, I reminded him, when the most important things in his life were sex and Chinese food. "I still like Chinese food," he deadpanned. But sex was no longer important? "No. I don't mind. I'm fairly au fait with the situation." Another pendulum swing—later he claimed to miss sex dreadfully.

His life had been strewn with broken relationships and then came the dreadful last act of a depraved marriage to Nicole Rothschild—"a union created in hell" as one friend described it. After two years of endless reunions and bitter wranglings, their divorce became final at the end of 1998. It had been more than a year since Dudley had seen their four-year-old son Nicholas, but "although I think about him, I don't think it will be much good to make him accept me as a father because I'm only going to deteriorate in front of him. And anyway there's not a great deal of feeling between us."

Nor had he any interest in seeing his son Patrick, twenty-three, who had remained strangely silent for months after the announcement of Dudley's illness. "I don't really have a desire to see Patrick," he shrugged, "and I think that's pissed him off."

Support from the ex's had been mixed. First wife Suzy Kendall, with whom he remained close friends, continued to be a staunch supporter. Third wife Brogan Lane had called and left tender messages of concern, and Susan Anton, with whom he once shared a long relationship, had expressed her deep sorrow for Dudley's illness. As for Tuesday Weld, who had remained as silent as their son, Patrick, "...pft! that's another story. I don't believe she is very supportive of me. She hasn't expressed her concern. Not at all. But why should she put herself out?"

His illness promised to take everything from him and he was facing the fact that he might live for less than another decade. The head of his team of doctors, Lawrence Golbe, put the average life expectancy at eight years from time of diagnosis, although other authorities ranged between three to fifteen years. Death had always been an intangible abstract for Dudley. Now it had become a reality. Yet it was not the thought of death that frightened him. What he dreaded was being bedridden and unable to participate in normal physical tasks. But his greatest fear was of dementia. "I'll obviously have to face it at some point. I find that very frightening and I do think about it often."

When one part of his brain began to fail, it took with it at least one negative emotion. Gone was the anxiety that had plagued him from youth, a learned behavior he inherited from his mother. There seemed to be no bitterness, no anger. Even his earlier dismay at Nicole for her volatile treatment had been supplanted by regret and compassion, mingled with a little sadness.

"I don't have any harsh feelings about everything that happened. I realize she couldn't help herself. I still think about her. But I recognized it was an addiction and it's one reason I left California and came here."

Only after undergoing intensive therapy with a counselor who specialized in addiction to people did he now understand the bizarre intricacies of that relationship.

Suicide had not been far from his thoughts in those days while he was still battling with Nicole. Yet he had prevailed. "It seems to take more strength and courage to decide to live than to decide to die," he sighed wearily.

His decision to release a statement about his medical condition was courageous ("it doesn't seem to be") and was made in the hope that it would evoke some understanding. "I felt it was necessary," he said. "So many stories that were circulating were misplaced and a lot of them were downright untrue. So it was a relief to me to have the truth out because there's nothing like the truth to dispel the untruth. There were stories put around that I was drunk, which was not true and never had been. I was disappointed that it was the way people understood it." There was a long pause while he struggled to locate the words to continue. Finally he gave up. "I do want to add something to that," he sighed, "but I can't."

It was the stories that he was a raging alcoholic that were perhaps the most hurtful when he was actually suffering from symptoms beyond his control. The image had grown out of his most acclaimed performance as Arthur, the lovable millionaire drunk. Even some friends bought into the belief. "Yes it's been hard for me because of Arthur," Dudley conceded. "But he happens to be the one character that I love. It was an outrageous performance but I think it wouldn't have worked if it hadn't been outrageous and it wouldn't have set in the mind of so many people that I was alcoholic myself.

"I really would have liked to have been like him. Less drunk. He was a very attractive man, very, very humorous and I liked that part of him. Not so much the intoxication but the wit, the wit! That was what was so attractive about him—that wonderful wit."

In a sense, his movie career declined because of *Arthur*. The public wanted more of him in that persona. In their perception Dudley and Arthur were intertwined. Anything else became less than embraceable.

"We were actually grateful to learn what was wrong," reflects Brian Dallow of the painful period leading to the diagnosis. "The cruelty of public speculation and that belief that he was an alcoholic was so deeply hurtful to Dudley. It only added to his natural propensity to withdraw."

The cause of PSP is mysterious, linked possibly to an outbreak in Guam, but doctors have not ruled out a possible genetic connection. Its progression is highly individualized and not even the doctors could predict to Dudley the point of further deterioration. A lot may depend on his therapy to strengthen his legs and speech. Sardonically, Dudley remarked that much of his therapy appeared to be "mainly my doctor telling me to enjoy myself!" Like what?, I asked. "Doing whatever I do to enjoy myself." And what is that?, I pressed. A flash of his irrepressible humor jumped to the foreground. "What do I do to enjoy myself? Have as many orgasms as I can—which I do!"

There was something immensely reassuring—indeed, hopeful—about these moments where his old humor jumped in, reminders that Dudley, though physically impaired, was the same man inside.

But he admitted he found it hard to be humorous as in the past. "Stuff takes so long to get out so it can't be economically witty. I don't join in the conversations at Rena's family gatherings as much as I would like to because I can't get my thoughts out quickly enough. I'm still in touch with my sense of humor, but it isn't as readily available as it was. It's a combination of things, emotionally you don't feel like being funny and psychologically it's difficult. But one's reaction to things is very emotional. One finds oneself crying at things that one shouldn't cry at or wouldn't cry at, while things that are funny you find yourself not batting an eyelid."

Until Christmas 1998, Dudley had every intention of returning to Britain, but such a move became financially prohibitive once he learned his British health insurance had expired. At least in America he was covered for his hefty medical bills.

He had never expected anyone to take care of him. That Rena and Brian had taken him in and given him such support was an endless source of bemusement mingled with eternal gratitude. "They've adapted their life entirely to fit me into it and I've come to rely on them greatly. Their generosity is astonishing and they absolutely refuse to take any money from me to pay for my upkeep. They are remarkable. I feel comfortable here. Life is very quiet and nice and extremely supportive. It's an extraordinary thing that Rena and Brian have done these last few years and I'm very grateful for it. They're like the family I've never had."

His interest in the outside world was now limited. He no longer read the newspapers or magazines and scarcely watched television news, preferring entertainment that required him not to think. He had become a devotee of MTV and an adept surfer, landing on any program that appeared to be amusing.

Nor did he read for pleasure any more. His restricted downward vision meant that in order to see something clearly, he had to focus on a point above it. And, too, with his concentration often fragmented, reading was an arduous undertaking. A friend had recently given him a catalogue of audio books, but he seemed disinclined to select any.

His hair, streaked with gray, was as unruly as ever. But when he got around to brushing it, usually by lunch time, he looked like the old Dudley. He was less reclusive, often accompanying Rena and Brian to concerts and luncheons. "He's part of real life," Rena told me. "He's not spending every day in bed sleeping."

For all of that, he retained an independence borne out of his proclivity for isolation. When he wanted to retreat into his bedroom and be alone, they left him to it. It was a need that he had never shaken off from the early years when he was forced into long periods of isolation in hospitals undergoing one of many operations on his deformed leg. Sometimes his parents would leave him for as long as two weeks, and the young boy grew to accept isolation as a familiar friend. Throughout his life he would retreat into it. He bought homes for his girlfriends and wives so that he would always have his own place to go when he needed to return to that familiar isolation.

I had received dozens of calls from friends wanting to get in touch with Dudley, to see him, or just to talk to him. He rarely wanted to answer them, partly out of embarrassment. "I'd be appalled for them to see me like this...and then again I suppose I'm a bit indecisive about that question."

Around the household, he was surrounded by three cats and a dog. An animal lover who had always owned pets, he had become deeply attached to them all. Walking unexpectedly into the living room, I almost fell over him lying on the floor where he was slowly stroking and playing with Jasmine, a sable and chestnut calico cat. The animals adored him, greeting him and waiting for the attention they knew he would give them.

Lunch had become the high point of his day. It was more than a meal, it was an event. Where to go was one of the two main topics of midmorning phone conversations (the other was which film to see that evening). Dudley still enjoyed eating well and there was no shortage of good restaurants in the town. This social gathering of the day usually brought together Dudley, Rena, Brian, and one or more of their daughters who live nearby. But eating was a laborious task interrupted constantly with coughing bouts, which could prove fatal.

Though participating little in the conversation, nothing escaped him. Every now and then he injected a comment, but on the whole he found it easier to be less a contributor than an observer. "I want to say things, but by the time I get them out, the conversation has already moved on elsewhere," he fretted. It's especially tough for the man whose comedy timing was considered to be one of his greatest talents. "Dudley used to retreat if he could not contribute to the conversation in time," said Rena. "We've told him we don't care if you say anything or just smile and sit there, it doesn't bother us so long as you can get something out of just being there and part of the group. That's enough for us. And I think that's made a difference." Dudley agreed: "I don't feel the pressure of having ever to be on."

Along with his speech impediment, another frustration was his inability to transfer food to his mouth without dropping some en route. A pile of food on the floor lay testimony to his failed attempts, the result of his damaged vision coupled with the lack of coordination in his right hand.

"We make a lot of fun of things," said Brian Dallow. "Sometimes it's the only way to deal with it, to make a joke out of it. When he starts falling backwards, we tell him 'forwards Dudley, that's the way we go.' You have to make it humorous because it's so frustrating."

At lunch, a new young waiter came over. Covering up his shyness, he blithely blurted out: "You're Dudley Moore!" "Oh ye...es!" replied Dudley, as if the fact has just dawned on him. The young waiter lurched on. "So what's it like having such a successful career?" he asked, blushing. "It helps," replied Dudley dryly, without skipping a beat, his timing for once happily immaculate. Whereas Peter Cook would have delivered that line with the full weight of his acerbic strength, Dudley managed to be both terse and approachable at the same time.

Driving home from the restaurant, he began to play his own *Songs Without Words* CD. The music swelled to a haunting crescendo. It was his own evocative score from *Six Weeks*, probably his most outstanding composition. Dudley's eyes filled with tears as he listened to the poignant music. Rena, who was driving, instinctively felt Dudley's anguish. She reached out and put a maternal arm around him. His sadness was palpable.

He spent a great deal of time these days listening to a lot of his own music. It was as if no longer able physically to play the music, this had become his substitute. His ears had replaced his fingers. He no longer visualized himself at the piano at concerts and was not obsessed by mental images of that nature.

"I don't find that I'm missing the beat of a concert. You get used to the idea of saying 'good-bye, good-bye practical world.' I was there for a while and I don't feel the need to remember some moments concertizing. But there are regrets. It's very hurtful not to be able to produce that irresistible beat and to realize that one can't function in the same way ever again. So I just listen to my old records and feel it's something unachievable by today's standards, but it was achievable in the past."

There was an irony in that because for most of his career he was never quite satisfied with what he was doing. He always felt there was more he could have done.

After lunch, Dudley retreated to his bed with the inevitable glass of ginger ale. Mental and physical exertions had taken a massive toll. He tired easily and a couple of naps throughout the day were not unusual. Yet if he said he wanted a two-hour nap, that's all he would take. Somewhere in his head was buried a ticking alarm clock. He never bothered to set the one by his bed but always managed to be up on the dot of any prearranged time. It was almost uncanny that the man who had now been forced by sickness to relinquish so much control over his life could remain so firmly structured in matters of time, even down to checking his watch several times an hour.

He had become an avid film fan, going to the cinema two or three times a week. Other evenings were spent watching videos—"We've seen about everything ever released in the last few years," said Dallow.

Dudley reveled in watching his old friend Blake Edwards's *Shot in the Dark* ("I sit there and marvel at some of the stuff that Peter Sellers did"). But he seldom laughed out loud any more when watching comedy. "It is fairly hard to make me laugh," he conceded. In fact his tendency is to cry, a symptom of PSP. "I cry often. Which is surprising to me but it is part of the disease it seems and it's wearing. You feel sad on occasions and you feel touched by things emotionally that previously I would not have been touched by. I'm still in touch with my sense of humor but it's less readily available these days."

Another day, leaving the restaurant, he leaned on Maurice, his faithful hare-headed cane, and took my arm. Rena brought up the rear, in the event of one of Dudley's backward falls. "What's that?" I asked of a red gash on his forearm. He gave a nonchalant shrug, "That's from falling over the other day and catching my arm on the cabinet door." The falls have been many; only a few have warranted medical attention. "I've got a place on my thigh which is black and blue," he muttered. "I mean, it isn't black and blue but it should be because I took a really big fall and it's very painful."

But more than any pain was the acute embarrassment he suffered from these tumbles. Sometimes, he admitted, it seemed altogether easier for him just to sit and stay put rather than run the risk of falling and embarrassing himself. It was one reason he had shied away from old friends.

It is a sad truism that when prominent people contract incurable diseases previously unknown, they focus attention on the plight of other sufferers and to the need for research funding. David Niven brought attention to motor neuron disease, Rock Hudson to AIDS, Richard Pryor to multiple sclerosis, Muhammad Ali and Michael J. Fox to Parkinson's. Now through his tragic illness, Dudley Moore is bringing awareness of progressive supranuclear palsy to the world.

Dudley harbors no hope for a cure to be found for this deadly disease. But he continues to fight the battle. And hold on to a shred of strength. A strength given to him by his few closest friends and a devoted medical team who believe that a cure is possible. And as long as they believe, he will not give in entirely.

The battle is being fought, even as I write. It may never be won. But there is strength in the effort. And for Dudley Moore, whose final career curtain looked like a tainted descent into ignominy, his courage brings victory.

EPILOGUE

The Californian pink chateau (actually terra-cotta), as the British tabloids insisted on dubbing Dudley's house in the Los Angeles suburb of Marina del Rey, had lain virtually empty for almost a year. It was there that his American odyssey had begun—marriage to Tuesday Weld, his stardom in 10—and where it had ended with his disastrous fourth marriage and the decline of his health and career. For twenty years his sentimental home, it had fallen victim now to his dwindling fortunes and was on the selling block.

His once multimillion-dollar empire had been cut down to a mere memory. He was living on borrowed money, a loan from the bank. Selling his Marina house had been less a choice than a need for survival. "I would have liked to have kept the house," he said ruefully. "But I need the money now, so I have to sell it." For the same reason, Susan Anton had agreed to sell her Beverly Hills house in which Dudley had a half share, having bought it with her back in the early '80s when they were dating.

At one time he had been one of the highest paid actors in Hollywood. There should have been millions. So where had all the money gone? "I don't know," he answered wearily. "I just don't know. I believed I had a lot more money than I apparently have. I only recently saw a list from my agent of how much money has been paid to me and I don't know where it's all gone. I thought there were investments everywhere but now it seems there aren't."

At least he believed he would have enough money to live on. "I think it'll be all right as long as I'm retired and get my pension from the Screen Actors Guild. But it's strange and sad, after all these years of affluence, now to be worrying about money or thinking about anything I spend."

This is a tragic last chapter to a richly decorated career of achievements. It has been sad to witness and sad to write. And especially sad to see that Dudley had lost so much motivation to his life. Too often he seemed to be focusing on the end of his life, terrified at ending up bedridden, with no control over his functions. This was the perpetual nightmare that he kept visualizing. "He's self destructive," one of his doctors reflected. "He seems to be stuck in this role and that's it."

It is a strange and horrible fate that Dudley's life seems destined to end the way it began—with a dreadful plague of medical handicaps. The physical deformities of a withered, twisted leg and two clubfeet that accompanied his birth and led to years of operations instilled in him an emotional deprivation that was never erased. In many ways, emotionally he was now revisiting the old traumas, mentally preparing for another round.

Before leaving New Jersey, I asked Dudley again if he would play for me. In the old days, it took little persuasion to get him to the piano. Now it was different. He was becoming used to giving in to his demons, afraid of what he would hear where once there had been real music. But demons are able to be forced occasionally into the background.

Finally, he was cajoled into attempting something from his exquisite *Six Weeks* score. No, it didn't sound the same. But the sound was there. The ability from his left hand ensured that, and transported by the possibility, he kept on playing. And just as occasionally as in his conversation, a flash now of the old Dudley materialized in the music. When he couldn't sustain the classical sound, he suddenly transformed it into a moment of improvised jazz, as he used to do with his irreverent Bach parodies.

It is particularly cruel that such a debilitating disease should hit a man who brought so much joy as an entertainer to so many people. It had seemed that his humor and his music would be part of our lives forever. In one sense it will be, through the numerous recordings that still exist. Now Dudley has become one of us, a viewer and listener. For the first time in his life, he had become able to sit back and regard his work with some genuine appreciation.

While his future appeared bleak, there was nevertheless a marked difference in him. Throughout the years of my writing his biography and beyond, he had repeatedly told me he was "waiting to die." Back then, he was submerged in a marriage that had plunged him deep into an abyss of depression from which people close to him feared he would be unable to emerge. Suicide was in his thoughts a lot. "I thought I'd make a fairly undramatic farewell, a fairly loose, ordinary farewell," he confided. "A bunch of pills and going to sleep and not waking up kind of thing."

But after his divorce, a certain equilibrium had been restored to his psychological makeup. Despite the horrors of his illness and the nightmare thoughts of what might lie ahead, Dudley was in a better place emotionally than he had been for years.

So was he still, I asked gently, waiting to die? "No," he answered without hesitation. "I'm not waiting to die. I know what I say about all this is very depressing and I don't really have any hope...but at the same time I suppose I do grab onto the hope of the people around me that a cure may be found in my lifetime. That possibility prevents me from wanting to do anything silly."

Dudley smiled gamely. And there was a flicker of determination in his eyes that had been absent earlier. "I'm not going to give up," he said. "I owe it to other PSP people to go on. And maybe that's meant to be my purpose in life now."

After three days in New Jersey, it was time for me to return to Los Angeles. I left the same way as I had arrived. With a long, tight hug from Dudley and his face puckered into that boyish pixie smile. Ever the caretaker, he stood at the door, leaning on his faithful Maurice, waiting as I slid into the car he had arranged to take me to the airport. As I was sped away down that glorious tree-lined avenue, I looked back through the window.

Dudley still stood by the front door, watching and waving to me, his face wistful. And the words of his earlier unanswerable cry echoed now in my ears. "Why me? Why someone who has so much still to offer the world with his music? Oh Gawd, why me?"

AFTERWORD

"Dudley doesn't take responsibility for his life, he takes responsibility for everyone else's. He's a caretaker. And the problem with caretakers is they constantly take care of other people, but never take care of themselves."

—THOMAS LEAHY

It is the tragedy of Dudley Moore that, despite all the happiness he has brought to others, he has never truly been able to find it for himself. The inheritance that was his at birth was a traumatic one, and he has never been able to shake loose of it.

He never came to terms with his mother's failure to demonstrate love toward him, and all the fame in the world could not make up for that. Indeed, the outpouring of affection from strangers, such a torrent of public approbation, served only to highlight what he had never received from her. His life has been an endless pursuit of that maternal love—a love he futilely tried to find in other women.

What keeps us excluded from the spontaneity, joy, and hope that allow us to live life to the full, wrote psychologist Dorothy Rowe, is that we keep on fighting old battles instead of recognizing that we are engaged in new ones. Today's arguments are rarely about the here and now: they are usually action replays of a child's unresolved battles with his parents.

Dudley never resolved those battles. He submerged himself within them and carried forward the angst they produced until it became a part of him. There has always been a conflict in him. He was never able to accept the massive disparity between the imperfect child unworthy of love—short, with a clubfoot and a deformed leg—and the world-famous celebrity adored by many. When officially "on," he was always happy to be the clown; privately, he would find himself trapped by the need to be "the star" and by others' expectations that he would be. He craves acclamation and embraces appreciation, yet shrinks from walking outside in public.

There have been times, to be sure. When he felt deserving of the applause, he could respond warmly, but when he didn't feel that approval inside him, it became an intrusion on the man he believed himself to be—a man far different from the celebrity the world knew.

He always yearned for fame but too often has felt safer in anonymity. There is an ineffable irony in that, for the respect and gratitude he harbors toward his public has been the longest and most loving association of his life. His own perception of himself as inferior always governed his self-esteem; how, then, he wonders, can he possibly deserve the acclamation that continues to come his way?

Although he grew to shun religion and God, he has lived his life with the same precepts that provide the foundation for all religion. He is a man without pretensions, whose immense kindness and generosity to others—be they friends, family, or strangers—have known few boundaries. He has a huge, giving heart, yet it is one that could never give to himself.

Like Lord Byron, who was born with similar afflictions—a clubfoot and short stature—Dudley always carried with him a brooding air and a reputation for his sexual exploits. Almost in defiance of what he considered his deformities, he notched up an extraordinary number of sexual conquests. Yet he never sustained happiness with any of the women he loved. He found it with them for a while, but ultimately it never survived, because the most important relationship—his own with himself—has not been happy. Inevitably, that always obviated the brief satisfaction he felt with others.

There was always an uncanny resemblance to Peter Sellers, another highly gifted performer who left a brilliant career in Britain for sporadic fame in Hollywood, some wealth but little personal fulfillment. It is no coincidence that Dudley twice stepped into roles originally intended for Sellers and refused another that would have seen him as Sellers's replacement as Inspector Clouseau in Blake Edwards's *Pink Panther* films. Like Sellers, Dudley possessed an extraordinary propensity for physical comedy, the likes of which have seldom been seen since the heyday of Hollywood's great clowns.

Dudley's years in America and in therapy have broken through much of his English inhibitions and repression and opened him up far beyond his expectations. Yet he remains intrinsically a hidden man. For all his frankness and the endless vocal soul-searching, he is an enigma to his friends, revealing only as much as he feels comfortable in showing and withholding a considerable amount.

Different friends know different facets of him; not one of them knows the entirety of this man. He admits there are elements of his character that have never been revealed to anybody—not to friends or wives; not even to psychotherapists. They may never be. He has told me he will go to his grave without revealing certain secrets about himself and that is very probably true.

"It's the damnedest thing with this guy," rues Peter Bellwood, an intimate friend for over thirty years, "because I feel so very close to him and yet to some extent I feel I don't really know him. I think there's a great deal of the unknowable in him."

"What ever happened to everyone's favorite clown?" Dudley's character asked in *Best Defense*. "The one who laughed away twenty years." We might well ask the same question of Dudley.

He has always lived with melancholia. It has been the one constant partner of his life. Now and then he and his shadow have separated and gone off in different directions, but never for long. They always returned to each other, as if belonging together, as Dudley surely believed they did— a perception echoed by those who have known him the most intimately.

"Dudley's happiness doesn't last," explained his former psychotherapist Dr. Evelyn Silvers in 1995, "because of the starvation he has within himself to make everything—his work, his life, other people—more beautiful. He never rests; there's nothing that allows him to have any peace. He is exhausted and his mind and emotions are worn out from the inner turmoil. The search for perfection keeps him from being able to enjoy the journey. In the sense that you and I know happiness, he will never be happy. But if he could take the totality of himself and say, without judging, 'This is who I am,' then and only then will he find peace."

Dudley Moore is a brilliant, cerebral man, who has been plagued with a multitude of questions about himself. For all his intelligence, he should have had and surely deserved a more placid life. And yet, as Phyllis Diller shrewdly observes, "It's the irritation that makes the greatness. An oyster doesn't produce a pearl without an irritation, and that's what makes a person interesting and fabulous."

If hope has abandoned Dudley, his legacy has not. His amazing facility to switch between jazz, classic music, acting, and comedy that made him one of the most versatile and multifaceted performers of our time, is captured for posterity on records, CDs, tapes, and film. In none of those arenas did he perform with mere adequacy—rather, he was outstandingly brilliant. He was one of the world's most gifted and adored performers. We know it. The sadness is that he does not.

As a close friend wrote to him a few years ago, "There is too much left in you to be wasted on self-doubt and emotional confusion. What you have done is in itself a celebration of life. You've so far left a legacy of superb wit, smiles and laughter, and some gorgeous music."

Dudley's music has charmed presidents, queens, princes, and

princesses, and his movies have enchanted audiences across the world. Yet he never felt any real accomplishment. "You would think somebody *that* successful would be able to sit back and feel good about it," says his first wife Suzy Kendall, "but he never has."

The bitter irony is that perhaps only now, when he has been robbed of the ability to perform because of a tragic incurable illness, can he at last look at his work with some of the appreciation that was always afforded to him through others.

It has been Dudley's burden in life that he never knew in which direction to travel, save that he never really wanted to follow only one path, and it was the resulting fragmentation of his talents that instilled in him a sense of unfulfillment. If he had pursued classical music alone, he could have become one of the world's great pianists, yet we would have missed out on his extraordinary comic gifts. How could we imagine Pete without Dud or Clive without Derek? Inconceivable. And a cinema without his Arthur? What we would have missed! So he followed it all—and lucky for us that he did—and in the end he accomplished more than most of us can hope to achieve in a lifetime on any one of those many paths on which he has traveled.

How could one man, with so many talents, ever have hoped to fulfill his desires along each of those highroads? Dudley's failing, such as it was, was to not push himself further. Passive like his father, he allowed things to happen to him, rather than seek them of his own volition and push the boundaries of his talent to their limit.

It is possible for success, even great success, to be achieved without active pursuit, but boundaries cannot be pushed back without it. Dudley was an extraordinary composer, but he always lacked the impetus to push himself in that direction. That is our loss, but it also is his, for in this lies perhaps his greatest sense of incompleteness.

He has touched people's hearts, both young and old. He has been embraced by the world in a way that is rare for any performer today. He is not just loved, he is beloved.

Except by the one person who alone has the power to make him believe it. Himself.

> Barbra Paskin
> Los Angeles
> January 2000

CREDITS

Stage

Beyond the Fringe (1960–64) Opened Lyceum, Edinburgh, 1960. Transferred to Fortune Theatre, London 1961–62. Moved to John Golden Theater, Broadway, 1962–64.

Play It Again, Sam (1970) Globe Theatre, London. 1970. Directed by Joseph Hardy.

Behind the Fridge (1971–75) Opened Australia 1971 with Peter Cook. Transferred to Cambridge Theatre, London, 1972. Directed by Joseph McGrath. Moved to Plymouth Theater, New York, 1973, retitled *Good Evening*, then toured the USA. Directed by Jerry Adler.

The Mikado (1988) Directed by Jonathan Miller for Los Angeles Opera.

Lay of the Land (1992) Directed by Lee Grant for Los Angeles Theater Complex.

Television

Strictly for the Birds (Southern TV, 1961).

Beyond the Fringe (BBC, 1964).

Not Only ... But Also (BBC, 1965) Producer: Joe McGrath.

Not Only ... But Also (BBC, 1966) Producer: Dick Clement.

Goodbye Again (ATV, 1968).

Not Only ... But Also (BBC, 1970) Producer: Jimmy Gilbert.

Not Only ... Dudley Moore But Also ... Peter Cook (ABC-TV, Australia. 1972).

Not Only Lulu But Also Dudley Moore (BBC, 1972).

To Russia ... With Elton (ITC, 1979) Producer: Dick Clement.

Orchestra! (Channel 4, 1990) With Sir Georg Solti. Producer: Jonathan Hewes.

Dudley (CBS, 1993).

Concerto! (Channel 4, 1993) with Michael Tilson Thomas. Producer: Jonathan Hewes.

Daddy's Girls (CBS, 1994).

National Geographic's Really Wild Animals (CBS, 1994, 1995, 1996) Producer: Joan F. Wood.

Oscar's Orchestra (BBC, 1995, 1996) Producer: Jan Younghusband.

Films

The Wrong Box (Columbia Pictures, 1965) Produced and directed by Bryan Forbes; screenplay by Larry Gelbart; photography by Gerry Turpin; music by Clifford Bevan. Cast: Ralph Richardson, John Mills, Michael Caine, Peter Cook, Dudley Moore, Nanette Newman, Peter Sellers, Tony Hancock, Wilfrid Lawson, Thorley Walters, Cicely Courtneidge, Irene Handl, Gerald Sim, John Le Mesurier.

Bedazzled (Twentieth Century Fox, 1967) Produced and directed by Stanley Donen; screenplay by Peter Cook, based on an idea by Peter Cook and Dudley Moore; photography by Austin Dempster; music and songs by Dudley Moore. Cast: Dudley Moore, Peter Cook, Eleanor Bron, Barry Humphries, Raquel Welch, Daniele Noel, Parnell McGarry, Robin Hawdon, Michael Trubshawe, Michael Bates, Alba.

30 Is a Dangerous Age, Cynthia (Columbia, 1967) Directed by Joseph McGrath; produced by Walter Shenson; screenplay by Dudley Moore, Joseph McGrath, John Wells; photography by Billy Williams; music by Dudley Moore. Cast: Dudley Moore, Eddie Foy Jr., Suzy Kendall, John Bird, Duncan Macrae, John Wells, Patricia Routledge, Peter Bayliss, Frank Thornton, Derek Farr, Nicky Henson, Clive Dunn, The Dudley Moore Trio.

Those Daring Young Men in Their Jaunty Jalopies (UK title: *Monte Carlo or Bust*,
    Paramount, 1969) Produced and directed by Ken Annakin; screenplay
    by Jack Davies, Ken Annakin; photography by Gabor Pogany; music
    by Ron Goodwin. Cast: Tony Curtis, Susan Hampshire, Dudley
    Moore, Peter Cook, Terry-Thomas, Eric Sykes, Marie Dubois, Jack
    Hawkins, Hattie Jacques, Derren Nesbitt, William Rushton, Gert
    Frobe, Walter Chiari, Bourvil, Mireille Darc.

The Bed-Sitting Room (United Artists, 1969) Produced and directed by
    Richard Lester; screenplay by John Antrobus and Charles Wood,
    based on the play by Spike Milligan and John Antrobus; photography
    by David Watkin; music by Ken Thorne. Cast: Rita Tushingham,
    Dudley Moore, Peter Cook, Dandy Nichols, Spike Milligan, Michael
    Hordern, Richard Warwick, Roy Kinnear, Arthur Lowe, Mona
    Washbourne, Frank Thornton, Ronald Fraser, Harry Secombe, Ron
    Moody, Jimmy Edwards, Marty Feldman.

Alice's Adventures in Wonderland (Fox-Rank, 1972) Produced by Josef Shaftel,
    Derek Horne; directed and written by William Sterling; photography
    by Geoffrey Unsworth; music by John Barry; lyrics by Don Black.
    Cast: Fiona Fullerton, Michael Crawford, Spike Milligan, Hywel
    Bennett, Dudley Moore, Robert Helpmann, Michael Hordern,
    Michael Jayston, Ralph Richardson, Dennis Price, Flora Robson,
    Peter Sellers, Rodney Bewes, Ray Brooks, Peter Bull, Roy Kinnear,
    Dennis Waterman, Richard Warwick.

Foul Play (Paramount, 1978) Produced by Thomas L. Miller, Edward K.
    Milkis; directed and written by Colin Higgins; photography by David
    M. Walsh; music by Charles Fox. Cast: Goldie Hawn, Chevy Chase,
    Dudley Moore, Burgess Meredith, Rachel Roberts, Eugene Roche,
    Billy Barty, Pat Ast, Chuck McCann, Don Calfa, Brian Dennehy.

The Hound of the Baskervilles (Hemdale, 1977) Produced by John Goldstone,
    directed by Paul Morrissey; screenplay by Peter Cook, Dudley Moore,
    Paul Morrissey; photography by Dick Bush, John Wilcox; music by
    Dudley Moore. Cast: Dudley Moore, Peter Cook, Irene Handl,
    Denholm Elliott, Joan Greenwood, Terry-Thomas, Max Wall,
    Kenneth Williams, Hugh Griffith, Dana Gillespie, Roy Kinear,
    Prunella Scales, Penelope Keith, Spike Milligan, Jessie Matthews.

10 (Orion/Warner Bros., 1979) Produced by Blake Edwards, Tony
  Adams; directed and written by Blake Edwards; photography by Frank
  Stanley; music by Henry Mancini. Cast: Dudley Moore, Julie
  Andrews, Bo Derek, Robert Webber, Dee Wallace, Sam Jones, Brian
  Dennehy, Rad Daly, Don Calfa.

Wholly Moses (Columbia-EMI-Warner, 1980) Produced by Freddie Fields,
  David Begelman; directed by Gary Weis; screenplay by Guy Thomas;
  photography by Frank Stanley; music by Patrick Williams.
  Cast: Dudley Moore, Laraine Newman, James Coco, Jack Gilford,
  Paul Sand, Dom DeLuise, Richard Pryor, John Ritter, Madeline
  Kahn, John Houseman.

Arthur (Orion/Warner Bros., 1980) Produced by Robert Greenhut;
  directed and written by Steve Gordon; photography by Fred Schuler;
  music by Burt Bacharach. Cast: Dudley Moore, Liza Minnelli, John
  Gielgud, Geraldine Fitzgerald, Jill Eikenberry, Stephen Elliott, Ted
  Ross, Barney Martin, Anne DeSalvo.

Six Weeks (Polygram/Rank, 1982) Produced by Peter Guber, Jon Peters;
  directed by Tony Bill; screenplay by David Seltzer, based on the novel
  by Fred Mustard Stewart; photography by Michael D. Margulies;
  music by Dudley Moore. Cast: Dudley Moore, Mary Tyler Moore,
  Katherine Healy, Shannon Wilcox, Bill Calvert, Joe Regalbuto, Ann
  Ditchburn, Clement St. George.

Lovesick (Columbia-EMI-Warner, 1983) Produced by Charles Okun;
  directed and written by Marshall Brickman; photographed by Gerry
  Fisher; music by Philippe Sarde. Cast: Dudley Moore, Elizabeth
  McGovern, Alec Guiness, John Huston, Gene Saks, Renee Taylor,
  Christine Baranski, Kent Broadhurst, Lester Rawlins, Wallace Shawn,
  Anne Kerry, Ann Gilespie, Ron Silver.

Romantic Comedy (MGM-UA/UIP, 1983) Produced by Walter Mirisch,
  Morton Gottlieb, directed by Arthur Hiller; screenplay by Bernard
  Slade, based on his original stage play; photography by David M.
  Walsh; music by Marvin Hamlisch. Cast: Dudley Moore, Mary
  Steenburgen, Frances Sternhagen, Janet Eilber, Robyn Douglass, Ron
  Leibman.

Unfaithfully Yours (Twentieth Century Fox, 1983) Produced by Marvin
Worth, Joe Wizan; directed by Howard Zieff; screenplay by Valerie
Curtin, Barry Levinson, Robert Klane, based on a 1948 script by
Preston Sturges; photography by David M. Walsh; music by Bill Conti.
Cast: Dudley Moore, Natassja Kinski, Armand Assante, Albert
Brooks, Cassie Yates, Richard Libertini.

Best Defense (Paramount, 1983) Produced by Gloria Katz; directed by
Willard Huyck; screenplay by Gloria Katz and Willard Huyck, based
on the novel *Easy and Hard Ways Out* by Robert Grossbach; photography
by Don Peterman; music by Patrick Williams. Cast: Dudley Moore,
Eddie Murphy, Kate Capshaw, George Dzundza, Helen Shaver, Mark
Arnott, Peter Michael Goetz, Tom Noonan, David Rasche.

Micki and Maude (Columbia-EMI-Warner, 1984) Produced by Tony Adams;
directed by Blake Edwards; screenplay by Jonathan Reynolds;
photography by Harry Stradling; music by Lee Holdridge.
Cast: Dudley Moore, Amy Irving, Ann Reinking, Richard Mulligan,
George Gaynes, Wallace Shawn, Emma Walton.

Santa Claus—The Movie (Rank, 1985) Produced by Ilya and Alexander
Salkind, Pierre Spengler; directed by Jeannot Szwarc; screenplay by
David Newman; photography by Arthur Ibbetson; music by Henry
Mancini. Cast: Dudley Moore, John Lithgow, David Huddleston,
Burgess Meredith, Judy Cornwell, Jeffrey Kramer.

Like Father, Like Son (Tri-Star/Columbia, 1987) Produced by Brian Grazer,
David Valdes; directed by Rod Daniel; screenplay by Lorne Cameron,
Steven L. Bloom; photography by Jack N. Green; music by Miles
Goodman. Cast: Dudley Moore, Kirk Cameron, Margaret Colin,
Catherine Hicks, Patrick O'Neal, Sean Astin, Micah Grant, Bill
Morrison.

Arthur 2: On the Rocks (Warner Bros., 1988) Produced by Robert Shapiro;
directed by Bud Yorkin; screenplay by Andy Breckman; photography
by Steve Burum; music by Burt Bacharach, Carole Bayer Sager.
Cast: Dudley Moore, Liza Minnelli, John Gielgud, Cynthia Sykes,
Stephen Elliott, Geraldine Fitzgerald, Ted Ross, Barney Martin.

The Adventures of Milo and Otis (Columbia, 1988) Produced by Masaru Kakutani, Satoru Ogata; directed by Masanori Hata, from his original story; screenplay by Mark Saltzman; music by Michael Boddicker. Narration by Dudley Moore.

Crazy People (UIP, 1989) Produced by Thomas Barad; directed by Tony Bill; screenplay by Mitch Markowitz; photography by Victor J. Kemper; music by Cliff Eidelman. Cast: Dudley Moore, Daryl Hannah, Paul Reiser, J. T. Walsh, Bill Smitrovich, Alan North, David Paymer.

Blame It on the Bellboy (Warner Bros., 1992) Produced by Jennie Howarth, Steve Abbott; directed and written by Mark Herman; photography by Andrew Dunn; music by Trevor Jones. Cast: Dudley Moore, Bronson Pinchot, Bryan Brown, Richard Griffiths, Andreas Katsulas, Patsy Kensit, Alison Steadman, Penelope Wilton, Lindsay Anderson.

Parallel Lives (HBO, 1992) Produced and directed by Linda Yellen; screen play by Gisela Bernice, based on a story by Linda Yellen; photography by Paul A. Cameron; music by Patrick Seymour. Cast: Liza Minnelli, Dudley Moore, Robert Wagner, Gena Rowlands, Paul Sorvino, Ben Gazzara, Mira Sorvino, Jack Kiugman, Ally Sheedy, James Brolin, LeVar Burton, Lindsay Crouse, James Belushi, Helen Slater, JoBeth Williams.

The Disappearance of Kevin Johnson (Wobblyscope, 1995) Produced by Scott Wolf; written and directed by Francis Megahy; photography by John Newby; music by John Coda. Cast: Pierce Brosnan, Dudley Moore, James Coburn, Michael Brandon, Richard Beymer, Carrie Wuhrer.

Weekend in the Country (Rysher Entertainment, 1995) Produced and written by Rita Rudner, Martin Bregman; directed by Martin Bregman. Cast: Jack Lemmon, Christine Lahti, Rita Rudner, Dudley Moore, Richard Lewis, Jennifer Cox.

Recordings

Strictly for the Birds (1959) Produced by George Martin. Composed by Dudley Moore.

Private Eye's Blue Record (Transatlantic, 1964) With Peter Cook, William Rushton, Barry Humphries, John Glashan, John Wells, Richard Ingrams.

Beyond the Fringe (Parlophone, 1961) Extracts from stage show recorded at Fortune Theatre with Alan Bennett, Jonathan Miller, Peter Cook.

Theme from Beyond the Fringe & All That Jazz (Atlantic, 1962) With Peter McGurk, bass; Chris Karan, drums. Includes *Fringe* theme composed by Dudley Moore.

Beyond the Fringe—Original Broadway Cast (Capitol, 1962) Extracts from the stage show in New York with Alan Bennett, Jonathan Miller, Peter Cook.

Goodbyeee (Decca, 1965) With Peter Cook.

Not Only Peter Cook ... But Also Dudley Moore (Decca, 1965) With Peter Cook, excerpts from BBC television series.

The Other Side of the Dudley Moore Trio (Decca, 1965) With Peter McGurk, bass; Chris Karan, drums. Includes music composed by Dudley Moore. Later reissued on Decca under the title *The World of Dudley Moore.*

Once Moore with Peter Cook (Decca, 1966) With Peter Cook. Excerpts from BBC television series.

Genuine Dud (Decca, 1966) With Peter McGurk, bass; Chris Karan, drums. Includes music composed by Dudley Moore.

L. S. Bumble Bee (Decca, 1967) With Peter Cook.

Goodbye Again (Decca, 1968) With Peter Cook. Excerpts from ATV television series.

Bedazzled (Decca, 1968) With Peter McGurk, bass; Chris Karan, drums. Soundtrack of film score composed by Dudley Moore.

The Dudley Moore Trio (Decca, 1969) With Jeff Clyne, bass; Chris Karan, drums. Music composed by Dudley Moore.

30 Is a Dangerous Age, Cynthia (London, 1968. Issued in UK on Decca, 1969, under the title *The Music of Dudley Moore*) With Peter McGurk, bass;

Chris Karan, drums; Barbara Moore, vocals. Soundtrack of film score composed by Dudley Moore.

Peter Cook & Dudley Moore "Not Only ... But Also ..." (Decca, 1971) With Peter Cook, excerpts from BBC television series.

Today—with the Dudley Moore Trio (Atlantic, 1971) Recorded in Australia with Peter Morgan, bass; Chris Karan, drums. Includes music composed by Dudley Moore. Also issued on WEA, 1971, under the title *The Dudley Moore Trio—Song for Suzy*.

Behind the Fridge (Atlantic, 1973) With Peter Cook from London stage show.

Good Evening (Island, 1974) With Peter Cook. Recorded in New York from Broadway stage show.

Dudley Moore at the Wavendon Festival (Black Lion, 1976) With Peter Morgan, bass; Chris Karan, drums. Includes music composed by Dudley Moore.

Derek and Clive (Live) (Island, 1976) With Peter Cook. Recorded in New York.

Derek and Clive Come Again (Virgin, 1977) With Peter Cook.

Derek and Clive ad Nauseam (Virgin, 1978) With Peter Cook. Also released on video as *Derek and Clive Get the Horn*.

The Dudley Moore Trio (WEA, 1978) With Peter Morgan, bass; Chris Karan, drums. Recorded live at Sydney Town Hall. Includes music composed by Dudley Moore. Also issued on Cube Records under the title *Dudley Down Under*.

The Clean Tapes: The Very Best of Peter Cook & Dudley Moore (Cube/Pye, 1978) With Peter Cook. Excerpts from BBC television series *Not Only ... But Also*.

Smilin' Through (Finesse, 1982) With Cleo Laine, John Dankworth. Recorded in Los Angeles.

Orchestra! (Decca, 1991) From Channel 4 television series with Sir Georg Solti and the Schleswig-Holstein Festival Orchestra.

Songs Without Words (GRP, 1991) With Kenny G on saxophone. Music composed by Dudley Moore.

Concerto! (RCA Victor, 1992) From Channel 4 television series with Michael Tilson Thomas and the London Symphony Orchestra.

The Best of What's Left of Not Only ... But Also (BBC video, 1992) With Peter Cook.

An Evening with Peter Cook, Dudley Moore & E. L. Wisty (Polygram, 1994) With Peter Cook.

Grieg Piano Concerto in A Minor (EMI, 1995) Also includes parodies composed by Dudley Moore.

Composer: Film and Stage Scores

Royal Shakespeare Company (1958–62). Incidental music for productions at Aldwych Theatre.

Royal Court Theatre as above.

English Stage Company (1959–60). Incidental music for productions at Royal Court Theatre.

The Owl and the Pussycat (Western Theatre Ballet, 1962) Ballet score composed by Dudley Moore.

England Our England (RSC, 1962) Prince's Theatre, London. Stage score by Dudley Moore.

Just One More Time (New Realm, 1962) Produced, written, and directed by Francis Megahy. Music composed by Dudley Moore.

Symbol, Collages, Soccer (Gillian Lynne Dance Company, 1963) Ballet scores composed by Dudley Moore.

The Hat (1964) Music composed by Dudley Moore and Dizzy Gillespie.

Bedazzled (Twentieth Century Fox, 1966) Directed by Stanley Donen. Music composed by Dudley Moore.

30 Is a Dangerous Age, Cynthia (Columbia, 1967) Directed by Joseph
    McGrath. Music composed by Dudley Moore.

Inadmissible Evidence (Paramount, 1968) Directed by Anthony Page. Music
    composed by Dudley Moore.

Staircase (Twentieth Century Fox, 1969) Directed by Stanley Donen.
    Music composed by Dudley Moore.

The Hound of the Baskervilles (Hemdale, 1977) Directed by Andy Morrissey.
    Music composed by Dudley Moore.

Six Weeks (Universal, 1981) Directed by Tony Bill. Music composed by
    Dudley Moore.

Fantasy on a Gypsy Breeze (MFAS, 1996) Poem written by J. Erin Sweeney.
    Music composed by Dudley Moore.

INDEX

Acapulco, 194

Adams, Tony, 176, 188, 205, 252

Adler, Jerry, 134, 139

Adventures of Milo and Otis, The, 298–99

"African Waltz," 61

Albery, Donald, 56

Alexandra of Kent, Princess, 316

Alice's Adventures in Wonderland, 127

Allen, Dave, 126

Allen, Steve, 50

Allen, Woody, 118–19, 137, 185, 229

Alley, Kirstie, 244, 275

Altman, Robert, 172

American Humane Society, 299

Amnesty International charity shows, 89, 147, 305

Anderson, Lindsay, 47, 51, 66

Andrews, Eamonn, 279

Andrews, Julie, 171–76, 181, 183, 205, 250, 277

Anka, Paul, 408

Annakin, Ken, 113

Ansen, David, 161

Antony and Cleopatra, 38

Anton, Susan. Acting career, 213, 216; birthday party, 237, 212–14; on Dudley Moore, 221–22, 227; motor accident, 246; other men, 233–34; relationship with Dudley Moore, 291–95, 200–8, 211, 218, 224–25, 233–34, 237, 245, 281, 345, 412, 419; split-up, 250–51, 258

"Anxiety," 20, 278

Arthur. Anniversary tribute, 395–99; awards for, 228, 233; filming, 185–86, 194–203; financing, 264; gross takings, 216, 217, 295; musical version, 276; private screening, 213; release, 215; reviews, 215–17, 232–33

Arthur 2: On the Rocks, 288–89, 295, 395

Ashkenazy, Vladimir, 357

Aspen Music Festival, 246

Assante, Armand, 242

Atkinson, Rowan, 272

Atlantic Records, 49

Austin, Michael, 24

Australia. Concert tour, 396, 398, 400–3; Jazz Festival, 323; jazz trio tour of, 162; stage show in, 124–25; television appearances in, 121, 122–23

awards. Academy (Oscars), 228, 233, 243–44, 308; Cable TV Ace, 350; Golden Apple, 169; Golden Globe, 163, 190, 228, 239, 258; Grammy, 138; Male Star of the Year, 237; Tony, 81, 132, 138

BBC, 95–96, 99–100, 115, 127, 270, 257, 365

Bacall, Lauren, 377

Bacharach, Burt, 109, 228

Baker, Joan, 15

Baltimore Symphony Orchestra, 329

Barnes, Clive, 132

Barry, John, 127

Baryshnikov, Mikhail, 194

Bassett, John, 39, 42, 49, 53, 54–56, 57, 60, 66, 71, 73–74, 76, 150, 250, 364

Bassett Hounds, The, 39–40, 42

Bassey, Shirley, 222

Beard, Brian, 294

Beatty, Warren, 228, 233

Bed-Sitting Room, The, 111, 118

Bedazzled, 103–105, 110, 161, 165

Beethoven, Ludwig van (Triple Concerto), 244–46, 281

Begelman, David, 187

Behind the Fridge. In London, 122, 124–25, 129–132; in U.S. (as *Good Evening*), 133–34, 139–40, 142

Bellwood, Peter, 51, 59, 73, 79–81, 90, 110, 139, 167, 170, 184, 208, 244, 261, 267, 269, 275, 321, 354, 398, 424

Bellwood, Sarah, 261, 275

Bennett, Alan. In *Beyond the Fringe,* 54–55, 57–60, 70–74, 147, 277; on Dudley Moore, 62, 90, 184, 270; on Peter Cook, 99; playwright, 315

Bentham House, Hampstead, 101–2, 109–10, 114–15, 116, 120, 140, 150, 339

Berger, Marsha, 332–33, 352

Berle, Milton, 408

Bernheimer, Martin, 291

Best Defense, 247–48, 419

Best of What's Left of Not Only . . . But Also, The, 305, 309, 316–17

Beyond the Fringe. In Brighton, 57; Dudley Moore's book on, 277; in Edinburgh, 54–56; at Fortune Theatre, London, 56–78; in New York, 67–68, 70–74, 122; reunion (failed), 320; television show for BBC, 82, 85; Tony Award, 81, 132. *See also* One-Legged Tarzan

Bill, Tony, 223–24, 227, 253, 279, 303

Bird, John, 63, 147

Birds, The, 53

Bisset, Jacqueline, 248

Blame It on the Bellboy, 319, 323, 328

Blangsted, Else, 236, 246, 261, 287–88, 292, 327, 336, 340, 342, 346

Bloch, Paul, 180, 190, 215, 238, 263, 354

Blue Angel Club, 53, 72

Bogdanovich, Peter, 244

Bond, Rosemary and Patsy, 62

Bora Bora, Tahiti, 214–15, 294, 321

Borge, Victor, 59

Boyd, Hugo, 46, 51, 61, 64, 113

Breckman, Andy, 288
Bregman, Martin, 372
Brickman, Marshall, 229–232, 244, 278
Bricusse, Evie, 162, 174, 248
Bricusse, Leslie, 125, 136, 162, 174, 198, 215, 233, 244, 248, 250, 270, 274, 290, 335, 403
Bridges, Jeff, 377, 378
Brighton, Sussex, 57
British Board of Film Censors, 207
Britten, Benjamin, 59
"Brogan," 302
Bron, Eleanor, 63, 103, 147
Brooke-Taylor, Tim, 147
Brooks, Albert, 242
Brooks, Mel, 403
Brosnan, Pierce, 377
Brown, Bryan, 319
Brown, Ray, 212, 216, 237, 264, 279, 281, 302
Brown, Tina, 114
Buckingham Palace, 337
Burke's Club, 153
Burton, Richard, 115
Burton, Sybil, 73
Bush, George, 244

Café des Artistes, London, 47
Cahn, Sammy, 279, 318
Caine, Michael, 95, 181, 233, 248, 250, 256, 293, 316
Caine, Shakira, 181
Caldwell, Zoe, 51
Cambridge Arts Festival, 159
Cameron, Kirk, 280, 284
camping, 275
Cannon, Dyan, 172
Carnival of the Animals, The, 411
Capshaw, Kate, 247–48
Carnegie Hall, New York, 244–45, 357, 360, 382
Caron, Leslie, 189
Carson, Johnny, 278, 285
Cassidy, Cindy, 73, 74, 78–79
Caucasian Chalk Circle, 52–53
Ceroli, Nick, 212, 216, 237
Changeling, The, 38–39
Charles, Prince of Wales, 269
Chase, Chevy, 159–161, 165, 279, 284
Chausson, Ernest, 201
Chiari, Walter, 113
Chicago Tribune, 188
Chong, Lin. See Cook, Lin
Christy, George, 232
classical music. See musical career
Cleese, John, 88
Clement, Dick, 98, 99, 115
Cleveland, Charles, 336, 347–48, 355, 365–66, 374, 379–82, 384, 386–88, 390
Cleveland, Earline, 354

Coco, James, 186, 188
Coe, Peter, 287
Cohen, Alexander, 60, 71–72, 132, 133–34, 142, 167–68
Collages, 75–78
Collins, Jackie, 248, 272, 279, 307
Collins, Oscar, 272
Coltart family, 8, 19
Comfort, Alex, 168
comic entertainer. Acting ability, 95, 234, 242, 280–81, 291; acting style, 229–30; barrier to deflect hostility, 93; as a boy, 22, 29; comedy expressing emotions, 228, 231–32; Dudley Moore playing himself, 258; expressing hostility, 40; funny voices, 29, 107, 129; guest star, 127; obscene language, 126, 134–35, 147, 149; at Oxford, 34; with Peter Cook, see Cook, Peter; popularity poll of actors, 240; professionalism, 108; style, 95. See also films; stage performances; television appearances
"Comic Relief," 272, 285
Complete Beyond the Fringe, The, 277
Concerto!, 332, 343–44, 350
Conti, Tom, 222
Cook, Judy, 136, 144
Cook, Lin, 271, 297, 306, 362–65
Cook, Peter
    alcoholism, 125–26, 129–32, 134, 139–40, 141, 175, 315, 362, 363–64
    in America, 108
    in Beyond the Fringe, 54, 56–60, 67–68, 70–74, 147
    charitableness, 318
    comic character, 89
    death, 362–65, 371–72
    and Establishment Club, 63, 86
    marriage, 306, 341
    partnership with Dudley Moore: Australian tour, 124–25, 127; Behind the Fridge, 124–26, 129–32; "Comic Relief," 285; Derek and Clive, see Derek and Clive tapes and albums; Dudley Moore Show, The, 87; filming, 95–96, 102–5, 110–14, 115–16, 149–55; improvisations, 86; Not Only . . . But Also, 87–90, 119–21, 305; Pete and Dud sketches, 88, 99–100; records, 86; Secret Policeman's 10th Anniversary Ball, The, 305; television autobiography, 331; television shows, 115, 155
    relationship with Dudley Moore: friendship strained, 102, 114, 130–32, 137–38, 139–40, 167–68, 175, 309; gulf in life styles, 285; jealousy, 56, 120, 226, 236–37, 255, 270–71, 296–97, 315; reunions, 208, 209, 270; revival of friendship, 271, 285, 317, 329
    solo career, 131, 226
    and Tuesday Weld, 136–37, 139–40
    unprofessionalism, 134

Cooke, Alistair, 70, 322
Cool Elephant Club, London, 53, 92, 93
Cork, Peter, 25, 27, 32, 34, 43, 150, 189, 211, 312–13, 316
Courtney, Tom, 55
Crawford, Michael, 127
Crazy People, 302–4, 316
Crisp, Quentin, 297
Cuany, Jennifer, 55
Curtis, Tony, 113

Daddy's Girls, 355, 357, 359
Dagenham, Essex. Becontree Estate, 3–4; County High School, 18–22, 25, 32; Dudley Moore's return visits, 62, 94, 115, 123, 151, 153, 344; Ford plant, 4, 8; Kingsley Hall, 27–28, 63, 306, 338
Daily Mail, 316, 342
Daily News, 284
Daily Telegraph, 344
Dallow, Brian, xiii, 330, 382, 406, 414–16
Daniel, Rod, 280–81, 292, 302
Dankworth, John, 43, 47, 50–51, 58–59, 61, 92, 169, 212, 250, 279, 332
Darlinda, 236
Davis, Ivor, 297
de la Rocha, Alicia, 332
DeLuise, Dom, 186
de Paul, Lynsey, 127–28
Delfont, Bernard, 127
Derek, Bo, 173–74, 176–77, 182, 184, 279, 308
Derek, John, 176
Derek and Clive tapes and albums, 134–35, 147, 149, 159, 166, 175, 180, 248, 301, 343; censorship problems, 207–8
Devine, George, 47–51
Diener, Joan, 71
Diller, Barry, 163
Diller, Phyllis, 342, 419
Disappearance of Kevin Johnson, The, 360–61
Disney, Anthea, 118
Dobie, Alan, 51
Dog Soldiers, 152
Donaldson, William, 56–57
Donen, Stanley, 102–5, 115, 286
Donner, Clive, 109
Donovan, Terence, 68, 73, 75, 76
Doonican, Val, 127
Douglas, Barry, 332
Douglas, Michael, 283
Douglas-Home, Sir Alec, 86
Doumani, Carol, 278, 272, 310, 342
Drucker, Stanley, 226
"Duddley Dell," 53
Dudley, 329, 339
Dudley Moore Research Fund, 413
Dudley Moore Show, The, 87

Dullea, Keir, 287, 329
Dullea, Susie, 287, 328, 329
Duplex Club, New York, 49–50
Durbin, Deanna, 316
Dutoit, Charles, 378
Dylan, Bob, 272

Earl Jones, James, 82
East, Roy, 48
Eastwood, Clint, 240
Eatwell, Brian, 108
Edinburgh Festival, 54–55
Edinburgh Festival Ballet, 56
Edward, Prince, 337
Edwards, Blake, 164, 168, 169–82, 204–5, 251–52, 257, 263, 277
Eikenberry, Jill, 197
Eisner, Michael, 163, 168
Elizabeth II, Queen, 58
Emperor Jones, 81–82
England Our England, 66
Entertainment Weekly, 359
Epstein–Barr Syndrome, 277
Ertegun, Ahmet, 49
Esquire, 60, 110
Establishment Club. London, 63, 65, 66, 68, 73, 86, 315; New York, 73
Evening Standard, 161, 332, 344
Experimental Theatre Club (ETC), 38

Facade, 390
Fantasy on a Gypsy Breeze, 390
Fatal Instinct, 336
Faye, Alice, 189
Feather, Leonard, 212, 264, 302
Ferman, James, 207
Ferret, The, 165, 181
Field, Shirley Anne, 91
Fields, Freddie, 189
Fiji, 123
film-making. With Cleo Laine, 61; Dudley Moore as sex symbol, 176, 182, 240; Dudley Moore's choice of roles, 263, 272; failures ridiculed in British press, 297; financing, 264; giggling, 235; letter-writing, 232; piano-playing, 225, 231; practical jokes, 107, 224–25, 230, 235, 243, 252
film scores. The Hat, 81; Inadmissible Evidence, 109; *Just One More Time*, 52; public performances of, 281; *Six Weeks*, 227, 231, 236, 237, 307; *Staircase*, 115; *30 Is a Dangerous Age, Cynthia*, 108–9
films. *Adventures of Milo and Otis, The*, 298–99; *Alice in Wonderland*, 127; *Arthur, see Arthur*; *Arthur 2: On the Rocks*, 288, 295; *Bed-Sitting Room, The*, 111, 118; *Bedazzled*, 103–5, 110, 161, 165; *Best Defense*, 248; *Blame It on the Bellboy*, 319, 323, 328; *Crazy People*, 302–4, 316; *Disappearance of Kevin Johnson, The*, 360; documentary on Erroll Garner, 48; *Fatal Instinct*,

336; *Ferret, The*, 165, 179; *Foul Play*, 159–63, 178, 181; *Guv'nor, The*, 351, 357; *Hound of the Baskervilles, The*, 149, 153–56; *Joy of Sex, The*, 151, 168, 170, 261; *Like Father, Like Son*, 301, 284; *Micki and Maude*, 251–52; *Mirror Has Two Faces, The*, 375–80; *Monte Carlo or Bust!*, 113, 118; *Parallel Lives*, 345; *Poke in the Eye, A*, 147; *Really Wild Animals*, 379; *Romantic Comedy*, 234–36, 247; *Santa Claus—The Movie*, 253–54, 264, 269, 332; *Six Weeks, see Six Weeks; Sketch Life*, 301–2; *30 Is a Dangerous Age, Cynthia*, 106–9, 116–17; *Unfaithfully Yours, see Unfaithfully Yours; Weekend in the Country*, 372; *Wholly Moses*, 186–88, 206, 263; *Wind in the Willows, The*, 323; *Wrong Box, The*, 95–7

Finney, Albert, 51
Fire Raisers, The, 66
Fleischman, Ernest, 212–14
Fonda, Henry, 228, 233
Fonda, Jane, 244
Footlights Club, Cambridge University, 38, 51, 54, 73
Forbes, Bryan, 85, 95–96, 108, 138, 161, 198
Ford, Betty, 330
Ford, Glenn and Cynthia, 244
Forman, Ruth, 181–82, 187, 195, 204, 213, 225, 349
Fortune Theatre, London, 56, 58
Foul Play, 159–61, 178
Foy, Patricia ("Paddy"), 331–32
Freud, Sigmund, 112
Frobe, Gert, 124
Frost, David, 51, 67, 278
Frost Report, The, 89
Fruchter, Rena, xii, xvi, 311, 330, 360, 378, 382–83, 390, 400, 401–2, 403, 408, 410–11, 414–17
Fuller, Frederick, 287
Fullerton, Fiona, 127

G, Kenny, 317, 321, 329, 403
Garbo, Greta, 273
Garland, Patrick, 33, 40–41, 45, 146
Garner, Erroll, 30, 45, 47–48, 50, 212, 299, 302
Gaskill, Bill, 52–53
Genuine Dud, 95
George, Susan, 244
Gero, Mark, 202
Gershwin, George, 212, 215–16, 396
Gielgud, Sir John, 67, 74, 195, 197–203, 215, 228, 233, 288–89
Gilbert, Jeanne, 49
Gilbert and Sullivan operas, 273, 290, 340
Gillespie, Dizzy, 81
Gizzi, Dr. Martin, 406–9, 410–11
Golbe, Dr. Lawrence, 408–9, 413
Goldberg, Whoopi, 408
Good Evening. See Behind the Fridge
Goodbye Again, 115

"Goodbyeee," 90, 371
Gordon, Steve, 198–99, 201, 213, 263, 288, 289
Gospel Truth, 125
Gowers, Patrick, 93
Grant, Cary, 189, 252, 258, 274–75
Grant, Lee, 323
Green, David, 351
"Green Green Grass of Delilah," 212
Grenada, 102
Griffiths, Richard, 319
Griffiths, Teifion, 18, 25–29, 32, 35, 36, 39–40, 46, 153, 154, 331
Griffiths family, 25–26, 28–29
Guber, Peter, 223
Guildhall School of Music, 22–23, 86
Guiness, Sir Alec, 230
Guv'nor, The, 351, 357

Hall, Peter, 53
Halliwell, Leslie, 116
Hamilton, George, 174
Hamilton, Jeff, 281
Hammond, Celia, 68–69, 73–79, 91, 107, 341
Hampshire, Susan, 113
Hancock, Sheila, 127
Hancock, Tony, 95
HandiGas, 224–25, 230, 243, 252
Hannah, Daryl, 302
Harmer, Herbert, 8, 19
Harper, Sandy, 208
Harrell, Lynn, 211
Harrison, Rex, 56, 72, 115
Harvey, Laurence, 198
Harz, Claude, 136, 144, 189
Hastings, George, 61, 66, 68, 74–76, 86, 90–92, 101, 116, 144, 189, 352
Hastings, Lysie. *See* Kihl, Alys
Hauser, Gayelord, 273
Hawkins, Jack, 124
Hawn, Goldie, 160–61, 237
Hazard, Richard, 236
Healy, Katherine, 223, 224
Helpmann, Robert, 127
Hemmings, Peter, 391, 340
Hepburn, Audrey, 223
Hewes, Jonathan, 312, 332, 350
Higgins, Colin, 160, 163, 234
Hiller, Arthur, 234–35
Hobbs, Lyndall (Lindy), 122–24, 127, 189
Hockney, David, 181, 244, 408
Hogg, Derek, 55, 61, 66
Hoggard, Irene, 16
Hollywood. Decision of Dudley Moore to be success, 152; Hollywood Bowl performances, 216, 281; Hollywood Raj, 233; Hollywoodization of Dudley Moore, 297; Tramp's Club, 272; Walk of Fame, 285; Women's Press Club, 169. *See also*

film-making; films; Los Angeles
Hollywood Reporter, 188, 216, 281, 291
Hope, Bob, 279, 281
Hordern, Michael, 127
Hound of the Baskervilles, The, 149, 153–56
Houseman, John, 186
Huddleston, David, 254
Hudson, Eddie, 219–20
Hughes, William Owen, 7
Humphries, Barry, 147
Hussey, Marmaduke, 309
Huston, Angelica, 218
Huston, John, 229–30, 244
Huxtable, Judy. *See* Cook, Judy

ITV, 115, 222
Illustrated London News, 297
Inadmissible Evidence, 109
Ingrams, Richard, 86
Irving, Amy, 251–52
Islington, London, 140, 150, 306

Jack of Clubs, London, 61
Jade Princess, The, 51
Japan, 217
Jayston, Michael, 127
jazz. *See* musical career
JFK Medical Center, 406, 408
Joffe, Charles, 185–86
John, Elton, 403
Johnson, Dr. Samuel, 269
Johnson, Jim, 27–28, 35, 63, 338
Johnstone, Iain, 252
Jones, Jolie, 336–37, 339–41
Jones, Quincy, 403
Jones, Terry, 89, 147, 328
Jones, Tom, 250
Joy of Sex, The, 151, 168, 170, 261
Juilliard String Quartet, 56, 115, 150–51
Just One More Time, 52

Kahn, Madeline, 186
Karan, Chris, 66, 68, 85, 94, 121, 149, 162, 190,
  214, 329, 343
Kasses, Ed, 397
Kaye, Danny, 135
Keller, Marthe, 189
Kelly, Gene, 189
Kendall, Suzy
  on Dudley Moore, 122, 314
  as Dudley Moore's girlfriend, 92–94, 98, 101–3
  film actress, 107, 110
  marriage to Dudley Moore, 112–16. Divorce,
    129, 140; marital problems, 119–20, 122–26;
    post-divorce friendship, 137, 190, 196, 208,
    340, 400, 403
Kennedy, Jacqueline, 111

Kennedy, John F., 71
Kenny, Sean, 63
Kensit, Patsy, 319
Kessler Institute, *xvi*
Kidder, Margot, 218
Kihl (Hastings), Alys (Lysie). Affair with Dudley
  Moore, 128–29, 132–33, 189; friendship with
  Dudley Moore, 86, 90–91, 101, 110, 116, 120,
  140, 155, 189, 298, 327
King, Larry, 278
Kingsley Hall. *See* Dagenham, Essex
Kinski, Nastassja, 242–43
Koch, Dennis, 296, 345
Koch, Howard, 243
Krosnick, Joel, 226

La Cage aux Folles, 276
Lady Chatterly's Lover, 94
Lahti, Christine, 372
Laine, Cleo, 43, 58, 61, 169, 208, 212, 250, 279,
  332
Laing, R. D., 112
Lambert, Tony, 26
Lancaster, Burt, 228, 233
Lane, Brogan, 228
  actress, 274, 281, 301
  appearance, 266
  character, 267, 269, 274, 276
  on Dudley Moore, 266, 318, 324
  emotional problems, 304
  encouraging Dudley Moore's friendships, 269
  influence over Dudley Moore, 286–87
  makeup artist, 281, 286
  marriage to Dudley Moore, 289, 292, 296.
    Marriage problems and divorce, 304, 314, 323,
    326–29, 333; post-divorce friendship, 337,
    399, 412; premarriage relationship, 275–76
  naïveté, 316
  nostalgic feelings, 292
  outdoor interests, 275, 296–97
  relationship with Patrick, 304
  Sunday lunches, 286
Langan, Peter, 255
Lange, Jessica, 194
Langham, Chris, 293
Late Night Line-Up, 85
Lawson, Wilfrid, 95
Lazar, Swifty, 246
Leahy, Thomas, 273, 296, 298, 307, 326, 382
Lemmon, Jack, 174, 292, 372, 408
Lennon, John, 87
Leroy, Anna, 62
Lester, Richard, 111–12
Levin, Bernard, 58
Levine, Ruth, 29
Lewis, Martin, 146, 293, 363
Lewis, Richard, 372

Lewis, Vic, 47–48, 53, 93, 198, 302
Lewis-Smith, Victor, 314, 332
Like Father, Like Son, 280, 284
Lithgow, John, 254–55, 257
Lloyd-Jones, David, 35
Lobb, Jill, 45
Long-Distance Runner, The, 34
Longman, David, 374
Los Angeles. Chamber music society, 211; Chamber
    Orchestra, 245; earthquakes, 307, 350; *Good
    Evening* run, 142; isolation in, 310; Jonathan
    Miller on, 298; Philharmonic Orchestra, 212,
    216; Theater Complex, 322; Venice Family
    Clinic, 317. *See also* Moore, Dudley, homes;
    Hollywood
Los Angeles Herald Examiner, 216, 291
Los Angeles Times, 110, 181, 212, 291, 302, 342
Love Story, 94
Lovesick. Filming, 228–31; magic trick by Dudley
    Moore, 231; reviews, 239
Lowe, Arthur, 111
Luard, Nick, 86
Lulu, 127, 222
Lyceum Theatre, Edinburgh, 55
Lynne, Gillian, 65–66, 75–76, 113, 327, 351
"Lysie Does It," 86

Ma, Yo-Yo, 282
McCartney, Paul, 403
McClennan, Colin, 122, 323
McDermott, Louise, 107
McDowell, Malcolm, 233, 235, 292
McGarry, Parnell, 107
McGovern, Elizabeth, 229–31, 239
McGrath, Joseph, 86–87, 89, 106–8, 113, 116, 127,
    129, 132
McGurk, Pete, 64, 66, 68, 85, 113
MacLaurin, Sir Ian, 314
Magdalen College, Oxford. Commemorative May
    Ball, 43; organ scholarship, 31; picture carpet of,
    292; return visits, 206, 311. *See also* Oxford
    University
Malkovich, John, 303
Mancini, Henry, 172, 177, 279
Mann, Robert, 56, 115, 116, 120, 136–37, 139, 151,
    201, 204, 210, 226, 279, 286
Marceau, Marcel, 85
Marchant, Leonard, 26
Margaret, Princess, 198
Marie-José, 29–30, 36
Markowitz, Mitch, 302
Marquee Club, London, 61
Martin, George, 53
Masterpiece Theatre, 322
Matthau, Walter, 244
Maxwell Davies, Peter, 52
Mayo clinic, 400

Medavoy, Mike, 176, 185–86
Megahy, Francis, 51–52, 114, 118, 152, 185, 190,
    215, 244, 272, 301, 317, 343, 364
Melbourne Herald, 124
Melbourne Sun, 124
Melly, George, 130
Menotti, Gian Carlo, 330
Merrick, David, 49
Michaels, Lorne, 278
Micki and Maude, 251–53, 257–58
Middler, Bette, 408
Mikado, The, 273, 290–91
Miles, Christopher, 92
Miller, Jonathan. In *Beyond the Fringe,* 54–55, 58–61,
    70–72, 147, 277; directing *The Mikado,* 274,
    290–91; on Dudley Moore, 59–60, 63, 90, 149,
    270; on Los Angeles, 291; opera and film pro-
    ducer, 178, 274, 280, 290–91, 315
Milligan, Spike, 111, 127, 408
Mills, John, 95–96
Minnelli, Liza, 195, 197–203, 213, 215, 228, 244,
    253, 288, 295, 330, 345, 394, 395, 397
Mirror Has Two Faces, The, 375, 380
Monitor, 52, 87
Monte Carlo or Bust!, 113, 118
Monty Python, 69, 88, 89, 147, 186, 208, 328
Moody, Ron, 335
Moore, Ada Francis
    caution with money, 196, 217
    character, 6, 13, 15, 28
    death and funeral, 220–22
    music teacher, 11
    relationship with Dudley Moore: attitude to
        physical defect, 3; concern for welfare, 14, 15,
        17, 18, 38, 94, 107; correspondence, 137,
        138–39, 141, 175, 178, 195, 208, 217; Dudley
        Moore's emotional inheritance, 222, 287, 305;
        lack of love, 6, 13–14, 16–17, 94, 175, 179, 422;
        pride in achievements, 57, 59, 89, 94, 164;
        strictness, 12, 26
    relationship with Susan Anton, 206
    relationship with Suzy Kendall, 94, 115, 126
    relationship with Tuesday Weld, 144
Moore, Barbara (sister). *See* Stevens, Barbara
Moore, Barbara (singer), 46–47, 55, 64–65, 77,
    105, 253
Moore, Dudley
    business interests: production company, 360;
        restaurant, 253
    car accident, 246
    career. *See* comic entertainer; film scores; films;
        music student; musical career; records; stage
        appearances; stardom
    drink and drugs allegations, 355, 399, 407
    drug use, 335, 401
    early years: birth, 3; bombing, 10; cinema visits,
        11, 16, 24; dancing, 24; evacuation, 8; excused

national service, 32; family outings and holidays, 7, 20, 31; old piano in Hollywood home, 292–93; sports, 21, 24; teenage friends, 24–28

education: academic ability, 14, 22, 40; bullying, 19; Dagenham County High School, 18–22, 25, 32; Fanshawe Infants School, 9; Guildhall School of Music, 22–24; music studies, *see* music student; Oxford University, 33–44; university aspirations, 25, 31. *See also* Oxford University

family: aunts and uncles, 6; escaping from, 46; finances, 7, 20, 25, 36; financial help for, 77, 89, 196; grandparents, 4, 6; lack of motherly love, 6, 13–14, 17, 94, 175, 179, 422

films. *See* film-making; film scores; films

finances: at home with parents, 7–8, 20, 25, 36; investments, 271, 279; lifestyle, 175, 296; New York, 78; at Oxford, 36, 38; percentage from films, 190; tax exile, 150; wealth, 98, 141, 183, 186, 240, 263, 285; West End, 57, 68

friendships, 269

health: aging worries, 258, 261; car accident, 383; heart problems, 379; low white blood-cell count, 277; overwork, 67; progressive supranuclear palsy, xiv, xvii, 406, 408–9, 411, 414–18; records found by journalist, 219–20; vitiligo, 268; weight problems, 150, 172, 319, 322, 336. *See also* psychotherapy

homes: Bentham House, Hampstead, 101–2; Cheyne Walk, Chelsea, 150; Corona del Mar, 367–69; Hurricane Street, Los Angeles, 365–66, 368, 383, 393, 407; Islington, 140, 150, 306; Marina del Rey, 154–55, 180, 267, 272, 278, 281, 286, 296–99, 309, 321, 323, 368, 393; permanent residence in U.S., 155, 180; Telluride, Colorado, 376–82; Toluca Lake, 281, 287, 304, 307, 309, 321, 338

marriage: divorce settlements, 218, 333; fear of loss of freedom, 143, 148, 154, 218, 247, 283, 310; on love and marriage, 247, 250–51, 256, 396. *See also* Kendall, Suzy; Lane, Brogan; Rothschild, Nicole; Weld, Tuesday; women and sex

musical career. *See* musical career

personal characteristics: anger expressed in comedy, 231–32; class consciousness, 33, 35–36, 39, 59; depression at aging, 391; despair, 248–49; emotional escape in music, 14, 129, 145; fear of failure, 258; generosity, 286, 248–49, 365–66; intellectual capacity, 14, 22, 315; lack of self esteem, 91, 394; laughter hiding emotion, 222, 228; likeability, 33; love of cats, 110; melancholia, 34, 101, 117–18, 164, 202, 231, 236, 281, 298, 327–28, 334–36, 352, 358–59, 424; nostalgia, 315–16; outdoor interests, 275, 339, 349; palate, 203, 271–72,

278, 286, 309; passivity, 205; reclusiveness, 310; repression, 205; sense of humor, 224–25; shyness, 68–69, 248; silly giggle, 243; social conscience, 306, 317–18, 329; speaking voice and accent, 36, 50, 59; untidiness, 52, 62, 65, 69

physical disablity: bullying at school, 19; childhood problems, 417–18; lack of height, 19, 20, 59, 171, 172–73, 192, 205, 338; operations in childhood, 5, 12–15, 17, 262; physiotherapy, 9; sensitiveness over, 69, 76, 172–73, 261–62, 283, 322; special shoes, 15, 21, 24, 31, 35, 262

religion: abandonment of beliefs, 374, 383, 418; church attendance, 11; thoughts of, 358;

sex. *See* women and sex

women. *See* women and sex

writing, 277, 299

Moore, John (Jock). Character, 5, 7, 9, 16–17, 28; illegitimacy, 9; pride in Dudley Moore's achievements, 294–95; relationship with Dudley Moore, 9, 287; death, 123–24;

Moore, Mary Tyler, 223–24

Moore, Nicholas Anthony, 372, 375, 382, 394, 407, 412

Moore, Patrick Havlin. Character, 189–90; difficulties with, 282–83; on Dudley Moore, 325; Dudley Moore's love for, 227, 163; Dudley Moore's role as parent, 227, 268, 278, 321; early years, 145–46, 149–51, 153, 163, 164, 175, 179, 181, 189–90, 196; relationship with Brogan, 304; relationship with Dudley Moore, 349–50, 367, 412; on set with Dudley Moore, 231, 234; staying with Dudley Moore, 246, 321, 324

Moore, Roger, 219, 296, 276, 293, 331

Morgan, Peter, 113, 121, 149, 162, 190, 214, 329

Morley, Sheridan, 119, 131

Morrissey, Paul, 154

Mozart, Wolfgang Amadeus, 395

Muggeridge, Malcolm, 127

Muir, Frank, 99

Mull, Martin, 185, 189

Mulligan, Gerry, 72

Murphy, Eddie, 248

Music For All Seasons, 330, 360, 382, 386, 390, 399, 411

music student. In childhood, 9–11, 15–16, 25; chorister, 16, 30; early compositions, 20, 23–24; emotional refuge in, 14; extemporizing, 26, 40; family influence, 7; improvisations, 40, 52; jazz, 30, 39; organist, 24, 30, 34, 35, 40, 43, 44; at Oxford, 34, 35, 37, 39–40, 41–44; pianist, 9–11, 16, 23, 28, 43, 116; sight-reading ability, 25, 303; versatility, 420; violinist, 22–23, 27, 35

Musical Bumps, 277

musical career

Amnesty International concerts, 89, 147, 305

beginner, 52, 53

classical concerts: Carnegie Hall, 244–45, 382; Hollywood Bowl, 216; Metropolitan Museum, 226; New Jersey, 281–82; tours, 327, 329, 339, 342, 343, 349, 353, 356–57, 360, 367, 370, 383

classical music, 25–26. Conductor, 56, 109, 236, 242, 313; failure to practice, 92, 93, 116; incidental music, 47, 51–53; modesty about, 313; own compositions, 47, 51, 92, 302, 306–7, 381, 382, 390

early engagements, 45–48

humor in music, 60, 312

jazz: ability of Dudley Moore, 284; after classical concerts, 291; compositions, 86; John Dankworth's Orchestra, 50. *See also* Dankworth, John; liner notes for Garner recordings, 299; in London clubs, 46–48, 53, 61, 85–86, 91, 153; performances ended, 342–43; pianist, 45–51, 61, 66, 212, 233, 302; records and albums, *see* records; in restaurant, 284; trio, 61, 64–66, 72–73, 86, 92–95, 118, 121, 149, 153, 162, 237, 329; Vic Lewis Orchestra, 47–49

jingles for commercials, 51–52

performing in movies, 242. Practicing, 267, 286, 313; reaction to criticism, 238; scores, 51, 56, 65–66, 75–78. *See also* film scores

records. *See* records

satirical music, 99

television appearances. *See* television

See also film scores; records

Nash, Ogden, 411

National Association of Theater Owners, 191, 208, 237

National Car Rental commercials, 375

Negrin, Daniel, 82

New Jersey Star-Ledger, 390

New York. *Beyond the Fringe* on Broadway, 70–74; Duplex Club, 49; jazz clubs, 49, 72, 134, 137; Metropolitan Museum of Art concert, 204; Michael's Pub, 137. *See also* Carnegie Hall

New York Daily News, 244, 300

New York Post, 245, 282, 284

New York Times, 131, 182, 216, 226, 238, 239, 245, 284, 295, 318

New Yorker, 118, 215

New Zealand tours, 162

Newley, Anthony, 250, 335

Newman, Laraine, 286–88

Newman, Paul, 228, 233

Newman (Forbes), Nanette, 95, 138, 149–50, 198

Newsweek, 161, 182

Newton-John, Olivia, 217

Niven, David, 298

Nolte, Nick, 163, 223

Norman, Barry, 272

Not Only . . . But Also, 87–90, 92, 95, 99, 102, 114, 115, 119, 121, 175, 207, 305, 309

Not Only Lulu But Also Dudley Moore, 127

obscene language, 126, 134–35, 147

Oddie, Bill, 147

One-Legged Tarzan, 89–90, 103, 124, 285, 305

One Way Pendulum, 47

O'Neal, Ryan, 168

O'Neill, Carlotta, 82

O'Neill, Eugene, 81

Orchestra!, 311–13

Orion Company, 176, 182, 185–86

Osborne, John, 109

Oscar's Orchestra, 365

Other Side of Dudley Moore, 94

Oxford University
    Dudley Moore as undergraduate: acting, 38–39, 41; class consciousness, 33, 37, 39; comic in demand, 40–41; degree work, 35; frugal existence, 36, 38; musical ability, 35, 37, 43
    dramatic societies, 38
    Dramatic Society (OUDS), 38
    graduation, 311
    Orchestra, 37
    organ scholarship at Magdalen College, 31
    Queen's College, 43–44
    revisiting, 206, 269, 331

Paar, Jack, 49

Pacino, Al, 127, 189

Page, Anthony, 34, 38, 39, 47, 109, 148, 315

Palladium Theatre, London, 169

Palmer, Lilli, 67, 74

Papa's Got a Brand New Bag, 99

Parallel Lives, 345

Paramount Studios, 163, 168, 185, 247

Parkinson's disease, xiv, 401

Parks, Hildy, 329

Parsons, Daniel, 348

Pasetta, Marty, 244

Pears, Peter, 59

Peck, Gregory, 276

Percival, Lance, 92

Perkins, Anthony, 135

Perlman, Itzhak, 262, 279, 282, 317

Pete and Dud sketches, 88–89, 99. Gospel Truth, 124; One-Legged Tarzan, 89, 103, 124, 285, 305

Peters, Jon, 223

Peters, Roberta, 330

Peterson, Oscar, 233, 302

Phipps, Diana, 98

Pinchot, Bronson, 319

Pinewood Studios, 253

Pitt, Berta, 261, 275

Pitt, Lou, 152, 159, 176, 182, 186, 194, 197, 216, 227, 237, 245, 258, 261, 275, 292, 293, 300, 368; Dudley Moore's indebtedness to, 225

Platanov, 56
Play It Again, Sam, 118—19
Playboy interview, 238—39
Plumstead, Norfolk, 8
Poke in the Eye, A, 147
Polanski, Roman, 94
Ponsonby, Robert, 54, 55
Powell, Jonathan, 150
practical jokes, 107—8, 224—25, 230, 235, 237, 243, 252
Presley, Elvis, 135
Previn, André, 233
Priest, Jean, 36, 37
Princess Grace Foundation, Los Angeles, 268
Private Eye, 86, 363
progressive supranuclear palsy (PSP), *xiii—xvii*, 410—11, 413—14. Cause of, 414; diagnosis, 406; life expectancy with, 409; raising awareness of, 411; symptoms, 406, 417; treatment, *xiv*
Pryor, Richard, 186
PSP. *See* progressive supranuclear palsy
PSP Society, 411
Psychotherapy. Dudley Moore's complex over mother, 222, 287—88, 305; emotion causing physical ailments, 287; group, 162, 164, 172; and marriage problems, 305; overcoming need for, 218—19; sensitivity about, 232; therapy sessions, 80, 100—1, 112, 137—38, 151, 209, 262, 283
Puck, Wolfgang, 292
Punch, 131
Puttnam, David, 273, 298

Queen's College, Oxford, 43—44
Question of Guilt, A, 155

Ray, Robin, 67
Really Wild Animals, 379
records. *All That Jazz*, 68; "Duddley Dell," 53; *Dudley Moore Trio*, 118; *Dudley Moore Trio Live*, 162; *Genuine Dud*, 65; "Goodbyeee," 90, 371; Grieg concerto at Carnegie Hall, 360, 375; *Other Side of Dudley Moore*, 94; *Private Eye Sings*, 86; *Private Eye's Blue Record*, 86; "singing" album, 318; *Smilin' Through*, 212; *Songs Without Words*, 307; "Strictly for the Birds," 53, 212; *Theme From Beyond The Fringe*, 68; *Today*, 121
Redgrave, Lynn, 390
Redgrave, Vanessa, 162
Reeve, Christopher, *xvi*, 234, 406
Reinking, Ann, 251
Reiser, Paul, 303, 318, 338—39, 359—60
Reynolds, Burt, 168, 240
Rhapsody in Blue, 215—16
Richardson, Sir Ralph, 55, 95—96, 111, 127
Richardson, Tony, 34, 51
Rigg, Diana, 127
Rivers, Joan, 270—71, 272, 279, 290
Roberts, Glenys, 296

Roberts, Rachel, 56
Robertson, Hugh, 398
Robin, Mado, 37
Robinson, Casey, 366, 373, 396—97, 401, 402
Robson, Flora, 127
Rogers, Mimi, 377
Rogers, Wayne, 244
Rolling Stones, 408
Romance of the Pink Panther, 204
Romantic Comedy. Filming, 234—36; release, 247; storyline, 234
Ronnie Scott's Jazz Club, 46
Rose, Dr. Bernard, 43—44, 150, 206—7, 311
Rosen, Nathaniel, 244
Ross, Ted, 279
Rothschild, Nicole
affair with Dudley Moore, 249, 290, 326, 336, 344—46 Dudley Moore's arrest for assault, 353—54, 356; fights, 351, 380—81, 391—93; husband's interview on, 347—48; press disclosures, 353—55
background, 325
character, 326, 352—53
divorce and bigamous marriage, 347—48, 355—56
drug addiction, 384—85, 391, 401
health, 356
house purchase, 344
illness, 328
and Jolie, 339, 340—41
marriage to Dudley Moore, 351, 356. Children of first marriage, 373—74; divorce, 400—1, 403, 407; isolation following, 368—69
pregnancy and birth of son, 361, 366—67
reaction to biography, 397—400
sexual perversions, 388—89
talk of separation, 374—75, 394, 404
Rowe, Dorothy, 297, 357, 417
Royal Albert Hall, 42, 329
Royal College of Music, 150
Royal Command Performance, 99
Royal Court Theatre, 42, 66. Dudley Moore as resident composer, 47, 51
Royal Festival Hall, 51
Royal Shakespeare Company, 52
Rudner, Rita, 372
Ruehl, Mercedes, 303
Rushton, William, 86
Russell, Sidney, 27—28, 36, 306

"Sad One for George," 86
St. Barthélemy, 282
St. Peter's Church, Dagenham, 16, 221
St. Thomas's Church, Dagenham, 16, 26
Salkind, Ilya and Alex, 253—54
Santa Claus—The Movie, 253—54, 257, 264, 269, 332
Santa Monica, and 1994 earthquake, 350
satirical revues, 54—55, 58, 69, 178, 270

Saturday Night Live, 159, 161, 186, 278
Scales, Prunella, 42
Schickel, Richard, 250
Schlatter, George, 275, 284
Schwarzenegger, Arnold, 292, 300
Screen Actors Guild, 409, 419
Seaman, Christopher, 390
Sebag-Montefiore, Dr. Stephen, 101, 120
Secombe, Harry, 305
Secret Policeman's 10th Anniversary Ball, The, 336
Segal, George, 168, 170
Selig, Richard, 38
Sellers, Peter, 85, 88, 95, 127, 164, 170, 171, 199, 204, 229, 241, 258, 335, 423
Seltzer, David, 224
72 Market St., 253, 261, 316, 342, 364
sex symbol. *See* women and sex
Seymour, Jane, 181, 233
Shaktman, Ben, 45, 51, 80, 82, 153, 269, 328
Shanks, Dr. Jean, 220
Shapiro, Mel, 322
Shaver, Helen, 248
Shenson, Walter, 106, 108
Sheridan, Nicollette, 321
Shosatkovich, Maxim, 330
Shot in the Dark, 412
Shulman, Milton, 161
Siegel, Allan, 407
Silvers, Dr. Evelyn, 162, 179, 208, 261, 267, 284, 334, 348, 424
Silvers, Phil, 162
Simon, Neil, 408
Sinatra, Frank, 276, 284, 331
Sinatra, Tina, 244–53
Siskel, Gene, 188
Six Weeks, 219. Filming, 223–25; release, 237–38; reviews, 238, 244, 248; score, 227–28, 231, 236, 237; storyline, 223
Sketch Life, 301–2
skiing, 275, 339, 350
Slade, Bernard, 234
Sloane, Tom, 87, 89
Smith, Maggie, 55
Soccer, 75
Solti, Sir Georg, 312, 330, 370
Song in the Theatre, 51
Songs Without Words, 307, 411
Speight, Johnny, 88
Spielberg, Steven, 237, 248, 252
stage performances. In Australia, 124; in childhood, 11, 20; *Lay of the Land,* 322–23; *Mikado, The,* 290–91; at Oxford, 38, 40–41; *Play It Again, Sam,* 118. *See also Behind the Fridge; Beyond the Fringe;* obscene language
Staircase, 115
Stallone, Sylvester, 192, 195, 223
Stamford Theater Works, 329

stardom. British denigration of, 178, 315, 353–54; Cook's envy of, 270; effect on women, 190–91; in Hollywood elite, 182–92, 217–18; public acclaim, 182; reasons for seeking fame, 357–59. *See also* Cook, Peter; women and sex
Steenburgen, Mary, 234–36, 244, 292
Steinberg, David, 262
Stepford Wives, The, 138
STEPS, 322
Sterling, Will, 127
Stern, Isaac, 56
Stevens, Barbara
    concern for Dudley Moore, 16, 30–31, 37, 39, 144, 221
    on Dudley Moore: babyhood, 4, 11; and father's death, 123–24; schooldays, 24; untidiness, 52
    friendship with Dudley Moore, 317, 319, 340
    illness, 322
Stevens, Bernard, 221, 322, 340
Stevenson, Parker, 244, 275
Stewart, Rod, 248
Streisand, Barbra, 375–80
"Strictly for the Birds," 53, 212
Successful Self, The, 357
Sullivan, Ed, 49
Sunday Mirror, 178
Sydney, Australia, 122–25, 162
Sykes, Eric, 113, 403
Symbol, 75, 77

talipes, 4–5
Tatler, 119
Taylor, John Russell, 116
Taylor, Leslie, 23
television appearances. American, 159; *An Audience with Dudley Moore,* 222; Australian, 121; autobiography, 331; *The Best of What's Left of Not Only . . . But Also,* 305, 309, 317; *The Body in Question,* 178; commercials, 308, 314, 317, 318, 338, 375, 376; *Concerto!,* 332, 344, 387; *Daddy's Girls,* 355, 357, 359–61; *Dudley Moore Show,* 87; *Dudley,* 329, 339; *Goodbye Again,* 115; *Lady Chatterly's Lover,* 94; *Late Night Line-Up,* 51, 85; *Love Story,* 94; *Offbeat,* 94; *Orchestra!,* 311–13; *Oscar's Orchestra,* 365; *Pete and Dud Down Under,* 121; roles turned down, 340; *Strictly for the Birds,* 63; talk shows, 94, 277, 317; *Tempo,* 85
Telluride, 376–83
Tempo, 85
10, 151, 168, 169–83, 184, 190
Tesco commercials, 308–9, 314, 317, 318, 338
That Was The Week That Was, 69
30 Is a Dangerous Age, Cynthia, 106–9, 110–11, 116–17, 227, 242
This Is Your Life, 264, 279
Thomas, Terry, 113
Thorndike, Dame Sybil, 27
Those Daring Young Men in Their Jaunty Jalopies, 113

Tilson Thomas, Michael, 216, 232
Time, 110, 182, 238, 239, 245, 250, 295
Times, 51, 59, 116, 118, 131, 252, 305
"To the Queen! A Salute to Elizabeth II," 155
Toronto Film Festival, 332
Tracy, Spencer, 230
Tushingham, Rita, 111–12
Twentieth Century Fox, 241
Tynan, Kenneth, 58, 63

Unfaithfully Yours. Fee for, 240; filming, 241–43;
   release, 250
United States of America. Dudley Moore and
   American women, 193; permanent residence,
   154, 180; touring with Vic Lewis Orchestra,
   48–49. *See also* Hollywood; Los Angeles; New
   York
USA Today, 295
Ustinov, Peter, 94, 170

Vaccaro, Brenda, 208, 218, 265, 364, 377
Van Dyke, Dick, 289
Vanity Fair, 297
Vare, Kenny, 20
Vare, Shirley, 24
Variety, 118, 156, 186, 188, 284, 291
Veta, Sam, 226, 237, 296
Victor/Victoria, 277
Vilanch, Bruce, 308
Village Voice, 215
Virgin Healthcare Foundation, 411
vitiligo, 268
Voight, Jon, 172

Walker, James, 211
Wallman, Jan, 50
Wardle, Irving, 118
Warner Bros. Studios, 168, 295
Washbourne, Mona, 111–12
Washington Post, 227
Watson, John, 9
Watts, Andre, 330
Weekend in the Country, 372
Weis, Gary, 186–87
Welch, Raquel, 103–5
Weld, Jo, 135, 141–42, 144–45, 148, 155, 165, 189
Weld, Natasha, 136, 140, 143–46, 165, 175
Weld, Tuesday
   acting career, 135, 138, 148, 152, 155, 162, 185
   character, 135–56, 139, 146, 151–53
   and Dudley Moore: marriage, 143–44, 149–50;
      marriage problems and divorce, 147–48, 163,
      179, 181, 184, 189, 195, 218, 183; relationship,
      135–48, 294
   ill health, 165–66
   other men, 155

and Patrick, 349–50
   pregnancies and childbirth, 141–43, 145–46
   remarriage, 245
Wells, John, 86, 106
West, Elizabeth, 65
Western Theatre Ballet, 65
Wexler, Dr. Milton, 146, 151, 162, 209
White, Jo Mullin, 75
White, Michael, 127
White, Sir Gordon, 250
white-water rafting, 275
Wholly Moses, 186–87, 206, 263
Williams, Robin, 279, 302, 360
Williamson, Nicol, 109
Wind in the Willows, The, 323
wines, 271–72
Winifred House, Barnet, 320
Wogan, Terry, 278
women and sex. Addiction to sex, 283; American
   women, 73, 193, 205, 233; attractiveness of
   Dudley Moore, 62, 65–66, 264; early girlfriends,
   23, 29–30, 36, 68, 73–78; first sex, 42–43;
   Hollywood sex symbol, 176, 182, 240, 351;
   inflatable doll, 177; keeping in touch with old
   flames, 208, 214; meaningful one-night stands,
   190–91; monogamy, aversion to, 265; obsession
   with, 239, 283, 341, 344; philandering, 145–46,
   150, 182, 190–91, 217–18, 245, 249, 304,
   341–42; *Playboy* interview, 238–39; prostitutes,
   389; sexual prowess, 276, 418; unrequited love,
   257. *See also* Hastings, Alys; Kendall, Suzy; Moore,
   Dudley, marriage
World War II, 8–10
Wrong Box, The, 95–97

Yarmouth, Norfolk, 8
Yellen, Linda, 345
York, Andrew and Sarah, Duke and Duchess of,
   293
York, Michael, 181, 228, 233, 244
Yorkin, Bud, 181, 244, 289
Younghusband, Ian, 365

Zieff, Howard, 241–43
Zukerman, Pinchas, 244–45, 268, 282, 321, 350